MODERN

BRITISH

ELOQUENCE

CHOICE   JAN. '70

Speech, Theater & Dance

STROTHER, David B., ed.   Modern British Eloquence.   Funk & Wagnalls, 1969.   492p il bibl 78-79249.   12.50
The emphasis on the spoken word today is responsible for the growth of interest in men and their speeches in the past and present. Strother (University of Washington) in this text shows how public opinion was shaped by important speeches in England from 1766 to the present. The full text of one of each speaker's greatest addresses (two from Churchill) is included. A splendid portrait attractively illustrates each treatment. A well documented essay describes the contribution of each speaker to the principles of self-government developed by the mother of Western democracies. Unlike *An Historical Anthology of Select British Speeches* (CHOICE, June 1968) by Bryant, et al, which begins with 597, this text focuses on the modern era. And Bower Aly's *Speeches in English* (1968) contains but two British speeches. An extended bibliography makes Strother's book valuable to classes in British oratory.

270

DAVID BOYD STROTHER is Associate Professor of Speech at Washington State University. He received his Ph.D. from the University of Illinois, and holds other degrees from Georgetown College and Northwestern University. He has written a number of articles for professional journals.

Modern British Eloquence

EDITED BY

DAVID B. STROTHER

FUNK & WAGNALLS   *New York*

". . . this country and Empire, saved by its
sons from the worst perils which have confronted it
during its long history, remains still able to guide,
to encourage, and in a larger measure to inspire
the peoples of the world." —WINSTON CHURCHILL

Preface

•

This book is about twenty-four men whose eloquence served both to produce and to chronicle moments of creative stress—climactic hours in British history when judgments were altered, soon or late, leading to new directions in policy. While not always immediate, as was often the case with the "radical" speakers prior to the Reform Act of 1832, the impress of their ideas, nevertheless, lived to ripen and to be consumed ultimately by a nation with a long tradition of tolerance for the innovator, the instigator, the agitator.

Each spokesman is represented in the following manner: (1) by a portrait as he must have looked at about the time he presented the speech included in this volume; (2) by a documented character sketch containing testimony of historians on (a) the significance of the individual to British political development, (b) the specific political acts for which this person was a prime moving force, (c) the significance of his oratory, (d) a specific speech which by its nature was climactic, and (e) the immediate or ultimate impact of that speech; and (3) by the text of the speech itself. I have judiciously sought texts of speeches which, by all apparent indications, are complete. Wherever possible I have warily avoided edited texts, preferring other sources instead. I believe that transcription at the moment of utterance is likely to be more accurate than copies of the speeches subsequently released in a volume. Where I resort to collections of speeches, I have done so only after careful collation with other texts. All but two speeches are printed in their entirety. Because of their length and the complex nature of their subjects only the introduction and conclusion appear in the speeches of Lord Brougham and Ernest Bevin.

I am most appreciative for the assistance of Ruth M. Kirk and her staff of the Interlibrary Loan office of the University of Washington and to Hanna Krueger and her staff at Washington State University for securing scores of books necessary to complete this project from sources throughout the United States and Canada; to Retha Chapman, Betty

Welling, and members of the secretarial staff of the Department of Speech of the University of Washington, and to Van Cassatt and the secretarial staff of the Department of Speech of Washington State University for their patient and efficient assistance in the preparation of this manuscript; to Bonnie Johnson for her editorial assistance; and to colleagues near and far whose encouragement was a great source of inspiration. Finally, I wish to dedicate this volume to the twenty-four statesmen who, their labors done, died in their beds. The British people are assured that as sound and fertile projectors of public measures these men have preserved for Great Britain its rightful heritage as the Mother of Western Democracies.

DAVID B. STROTHER

Pullman, Washington
May 15, 1968

Contents

•

ix

Portraits

•

MODERN
BRITISH
ELOQUENCE

Introduction

•

Eloquence is the ability to move men to action. It possesses not a style of its own, but is clothed in the style of the man who responds to the cries of the abused, the powerless, the inarticulate. In all parliamentary nations, it is inextricably linked with events in which eloquence itself becomes a moment in history expressing, achieving, and chronicling political and social change. Great Britain, in particular, echoes statesmen who boldly pricked the conscience, eloquently advocated democratic reforms, and restlessly viewed their achievements.

To catalogue these achievements into distinctive chronological groupings is a superficial undertaking, at best. The noted historian, Asa Briggs, calls it arbitrary and unconvincing.[1] But even Briggs acknowledges its necessity, for the study of history must have a beginning and an end, and it must possess an internal structure which will lend unity to the entire work. I have chosen, therefore, to present the political speakers who may be considered the chief architects of change in modern British political history.

The first phase may be called the *formative* stage. The Industrial Revolution had begun, but its impact had not yet affected the social, economic, or political life of the common man. George III ruled the empire by manipulating the majority of the lawmakers in Parliament. It was a period in time which began with colonial restlessness and ended with an independent United States of America eager to combat the mother country whenever its sovereign rights appeared to be abused; with the masses in Great Britain accepting life as it existed, and ending with threats of open rebellion unless enfranchisement were broadened to include a more representative House of Commons; with parliamentarians whose oratory reflected the noblest traditions of family and education, with the grand style as the common style regaled in a splendor fit for a king, or a king's

---

[1] Asa Briggs, *The Making of Modern England: 1783–1867* (New York: Harper and Row, 1959), p. 1.

3

friend, and ending in much the same way. Small wonder that the sentiments of "radical" opposition members like Wilkes, Chatham, Burke, and Fox went virtually unheeded for more than a generation.

The return of Wellington's victorious troops from Waterloo in 1815 signaled a transition which promised to shake the British Constitution to its very foundation. Farm workers, filled with illusions of a better life, bloated the cities. During the first thirty years of the nineteenth century, for example, Birmingham and Sheffield doubled in size, while Liverpool, Leeds, Manchester, and Glasgow more than doubled. London by 1820 had a population, of 1,274,000.[2] The inability of the cities to absorb these people produced conditions of blight and depravity. As a result, idleness and discontent produced crime waves requiring drastic measures to suppress. No fewer than 220 offenses were punishable by death, and the situation grew so intolerable that Parliament suspended habeas corpus to further deter lawlessness bred from squalor.

An antiquated Constitution vested political control to the rural aristocracy whose main sympathies were with the producer of corn, not with the producer of finished manufactured products from the city. Not only did the aristocracy control the House of Lords by virtue of peerage, but it controlled the House of Commons, as well. Even the admission to Commons of one hundred Irish members in 1801 did little to democratize that body. In 1816, of 658 members, 487 were returned by the nomination of the government or of private patrons.[3] Representation in the early nineteenth century was about the same as in 1766 when Lord Mansfield jostled the American colonists for complaining of "taxation without representation."

In the insulation of a chamber 33 feet broad and 47 feet long, with benches sufficient to accommodate only 366 members at one sitting, these lawmakers addressed the Crown and each other. In their attempts to safeguard their freedom of expression, no official transcripts of the debates were kept, and it was not until the first decade of the nineteenth century that newspaper reporters were permitted to occupy the back row of the Strangers Gallery. Even with publication of *Cobbett's Parliamentary Debates,* which first appeared in 1803 and provided the first connected record of Parliamentary proceedings in British history,[4] the vast majority of the people, who were not enfranchised anyway, were ill-informed about political happenings.

Passage of the Reform Bill of 1832 ushered in the *innovative* stage of

---

[2] David Thomson, *England in the Nineteenth Century* (Baltimore: Penguin Books, 1962), p. 9.

[3] Theodore F. T. Plucknett, *Taswell-Langmead's English Constitutional History* (Boston: Houghton Mifflin Co., 1960), p. 564.

[4] For an enlightening history of Parliamentary reporting, see Michael MacDonagh, *The Reporter's Gallery* (London: Hodder and Stoughton, 1921).

modern British political history. There were now members in Parliament representing the business world, and a few even to represent the masses. William Cobbett, Daniel O'Connell, and Charles Stewart Parnell stood in the front ranks of those who championed the rights of the common man, while Richard Cobden, John Bright, Benjamin Disraeli, and William Ewart Gladstone, among others, took a practical view of British political life, advocating measures for the benefit of many, not a privileged few.

Eloquence, too, assumed a new and different form. Its vitalizing influence upon the growth of the British Constitution took on an importance unprecedented in history—it expressed more often the feelings of the ordinary man, clothed in a style more readily understood. No longer were issues confined to the debates at Westminster; politicians sought popular support by journeying into the hustings, taking their cases to the people. Oratory became, in the words of T. M. Kettle, "at once the expression and the chronicle of that creative stress which has shaped the course of political development in every parliamentary country." [5]

The third stage, which could well have its origin with Lloyd George's Limehouse speech, is *modulatory* in nature. It exists now. Its spokesmen respond to the needs of the people with a still greater degree of sensitivity. In wars, the people called for statesmen with determination, inspiring qualities, and unsurpassed eloquence—David Lloyd George and Winston Churchill answered the call. In peace, they asked for statesmen to speak for their rightful claims in a society committed to providing them—Ernest Bevin and Aneurin Bevan responded. They did not ask for the grand flights of oratory characteristic of earlier generations. They received, instead, extrapolations carefully woven into transcripts. Can this, then, be a great age of eloquence? Any age whose spokesmen succeed in achieving a greater measure of individual freedom is a great age.

---

[5] *Irish Orators and Oratory,* with an Introduction by T. M. Kettle (Dublin: The Talbot Press, Ltd.), p. x.

William Pitt

·

FIRST EARL OF CHATHAM

William Pitt, first Earl of Chatham

[Born NOVEMBER 15, 1708—*Died* MAY 11, 1778]

. . . he looked the part which he had selected for himself to play. His fine Roman nose, his high forehead, his noble and distinguished manner, his commanding presence, his graceful figure, all combined to impress any listener who was not blind.—E. KEBLE CHATTERTON

Gifted with the qualities of popular leadership . . . [and] an instinctive sympathy with national feeling," [1] William Pitt attained the position which raised England from "Despair to exaltation" in international affairs.[2] Frederic Harrison refers to him as "founder of the Empire," and one of only four creative statesmen Great Britain has known in eight centuries:

William the Conqueror made all England an organic nation. Edward the First conceived and founded Great Britain. Cromwell made the United Kingdom and founded our Sea Power. Chatham made the Colonial System and was the founder of the Empire.[3]

Although Pitt's imperial ideals became the keynote for the development of Great Britain for the next century and a half,[4] his domestic achievements have to be viewed not in tangible acts, but in the "vaguer region of sentiment and opinion." [5] He was a great man living in a time of great men whose efforts in domestic reform were to serve as a foundation for use by men of later generations.

Pitt was a creative statesmen whose oratory achieved great political stature on the issue of transatlantic dominion.[6] Green calls him the greatest antagonist in debate the British Parliament has known.[7] With his facile mind, ready tongue, a voice so excellently trained that it could be heard in every portion of the House, he was a "born actor," writes E. Keble Chatterton, "knowing how to register with eyes and facial expression the biting scorn, the superior indignation which his words were suggesting." [8] Green believes that Pitt's oratory possessed an invective "unequalled among the moderns. . . ." [9] As a manic depressive, he gave a "divine frenzy" to his oratory, according to J. H.

---

1 Walford Davis Green, *William Pitt: Earl of Chatham* (New York: G. P. Putnam's Sons, 1906), p. 380.

2 *Ibid.,* p. 377.

3 Frederic Harrison, *Chatham* (New York: The Macmillan Co., 1905), p. 1.

4 *Ibid.,* p. 2.

5 Green, *op. cit.*

6 Harrison, *op. cit.,* p. 25.

7 Green, *op. cit.,* p. 381.

8 E. Keble Chatterton, *England's Greatest Statesman: A Life of William Pitt* (Indianapolis: The Bobbs-Merrill Co., 1930), p. 67.

9 Green, *op. cit.,* p. 380.

9

Plumb, causing all who listened to believe that he was a "mouth-piece of destiny." [10]

Basil Williams records 170 speeches delivered by Pitt in Parliament between the years 1736 and 1778,[11] and there can be little doubt that his greatest flights of eloquence concerned his attempts to spare England from a long and costly struggle with her colonies in America. The first of those great efforts occurred on January 14, 1766, and contained many of his noblest utterances.[12] It is the only speech of which there are exact accounts, largely through the efforts of Sir R. Dean, assisted by Lord Charlemont.[13]

It had long been the practice for Pitt to remain in seclusion for long periods of time, and to emerge only on momentous occasions. Having spent this year in silence, the suspense surrounding his appearance in Parliament to speak on the right of taxing America was on this day very great. Macaulay writes, "Never was the magic of his name so powerful, never was he regarded by his country with such superstitious veneration, as during this year of silence and seclusion." [14]

Following his plea, on February 26 a bill to repeal the Stamp Act, an odious form of taxation, was introduced and received Royal assent on March 18. This action undoubtedly delayed revolution, though failing to prevent it. Pitt presented four great speeches on the American question in 1777, but his pleas were expressed in vain for all but subsequent generations. For them he expounded the great principles on which all States can successfully be governed: "[on] the principles of justice and true wisdom, of fore-thought and of healthy national pride, a pride which dares on occasion yield." [15]

---

10 J. H. Plumb, *Chatham* (London: Collins, 1953), p. 15.

11 Basil Williams, *The Life of William Pitt: Earl of Chatham*, II (London: Longmans, Green, and Co., 1913), pp. 338–351. Williams includes in this summary the date of the speech, the subject, the reference in his two volumes, and sources for the text.

12 Harrison, *op. cit.*, p. 159.

13 Williams, *op. cit.*, p. 336.

14 Thomas Babington Macaulay, *Second Essay on the Earl of Chatham* (Boston: Leach, Shewell, and Sanborn, 1891), p. 70.

15 Williams, *op. cit.*, p. 320.

On the Right
of Taxing America[1]

•

HOUSE OF COMMONS   *January 14, 1766*

Mr. Speaker: I came to town but to-day. I was a stranger to the tenor of His Majesty's speech, and the proposed address, till I heard them read in this House. Unconnected and unconsulted, I have not the means of information. I am fearful of offending through mistake, and therefore beg to be indulged with a second reading of the proposed address. [*The address being read, Mr. Pitt went on:*] I commend the King's speech, and approve of the address in answer, as it decides nothing, every gentleman being left at perfect liberty to take such a part concerning America as he may afterward see fit. One word only I cannot approve of: an 'early,' is a word that does not belong to the notice the ministry have given to Parliament of the troubles in America. In a matter of such importance, the communication ought to have been *immediate!*

I speak not now with respect to parties. I stand up in this place single and independent. As to the late ministry [*turning himself to Mr. Grenville, who sat within one of him*], every capital measure they have taken has been entirely wrong! As to the present gentlemen, to those at least whom I have in my eye [*looking at the bench where General Conway sat with the Lords of the Treasury*], I have no objection. I have never been made a sacrifice by any of them. Their characters are fair; and I am always glad when men of fair character engage in His Majesty's service. Some of them did me the honour to ask my opinion before they would

---

1 Charles Kendall Adams, *Representative British Orations* (New York: G. P. Putnam's Sons, 1892), pp. 98–119. This is the speech reported by Sir Robert Dean, assisted by Lord Charlemont. According to Adams, though it was "evidently much abridged in the process of reproduction," it is supposed to be more nearly as the speech was spoken than is contained in any other report of the same speech. See p. 98.

engage. These will now do me the justice to own, I advised them to do it—but, notwithstanding for I love to be explicit, *I cannot give them my confidence*. Pardon me, gentlemen [*bowing to the ministry*], confidence is a plant of slow growth in an aged bosom. Youth is the season of credulity. By comparing events with each other, reasoning from effects to causes, methinks I plainly discover the traces of an *overruling* influence.

There is a clause in the Act of Settlement obliging every minister to sign his name to the advice which he gives to his sovereign. Would it were observed! I have had the honour to serve the Crown, and if I could have submitted to *influence,* I might have still continued to serve: but I would not be responsible for others. I have no local attachments. It is indifferent to me whether a man was rocked in his cradle on this side or that side of the Tweed. I sought for merit wherever it was to be found. It is my boast, that I was the first minister who looked for it, and found it, in the mountains of the North. I called it forth, and drew into your service a hardy and intrepid race of men—men, who, when left by your jealousy, became a prey to the artifices of your enemies, and had gone nigh to have overturned the state in the war before the last. These men, in the last war, were brought to combat on your side. They served with fidelity, as they fought with valour, and conquered for you in every part of the world. Detested be the national reflections against them! They are unjust, groundless, illiberal, unmanly! When I ceased to serve his Majesty as a minister, it was not the *country* of the man by which I was moved—but the *man* of that country wanted wisdom, and held principles incompatible with freedom.

It is a long time, Mr. Speaker, since I have attended in Parliament. When the resolution was taken in this House to tax America, I was ill in bed. If I could have endured to be carried in my bed—so great was the agitation of my mind for the consequences—I would have solicited some kind hand to have laid me down on this floor, to have borne my testimony against it! It is now an act that has passed. I would speak with decency of every act of this House; but I must beg the indulgence of the House to speak of it with freedom.

I hope a day may soon be appointed to consider the state of the nation with respect to America. I hope gentlemen will come to this debate with all the temper and impartiality that his Majesty recommends, and the importance of the subject requires; a subject of greater importance than ever engaged the attention of this House, that subject only excepted, when, near a century ago, it was the question whether you yourselves were to be bond or free. In the meantime, as I cannot depend upon my health for any future day (such is the nature of my infirmities), I will beg to say a few words at present, leaving the justice, the equity, the policy, the expediency of the act to another time.

I will only speak to one point—a point which seems not to have been generally understood[.] I mean to the *right*. Some gentlemen [*alluding to Mr. Nugent*] seem to have considered it as a point of honour. If gentlemen consider it in that light, they leave all measures of right and wrong, to follow a delusion that may lead to destruction. It is my opinion, that this kingdom has no right to lay a tax upon the colonies. At the same time, I assert the authority of this kingdom over the colonies to be sovereign and supreme, in every circumstance of government and legislation whatsoever. They are the subjects of this kingdom; equally entitled with yourselves to all the natural rights of mankind and the peculiar privileges of Englishmen; equally bound by its laws, and equally participating in the constitution of this free country. The Americans are the sons, not the bastards of England! Taxation is no part of the governing or legislative power. The taxes are a voluntary *gift* and *grant* of the Commons alone. In legislation the three estates of the realm are alike concerned; but the concurrence of the peers and the Crown to a tax is only necessary to clothe it with the form of a law. The gift and grant is of the Commons alone. In ancient days, the Crown, the barons, and the clergy possessed the lands. In those days, the barons and the clergy gave and granted to the Crown. They gave and granted what was their own! At present, since the discovery of America, and other circumstances permitting, the Commons are become the proprietors of the land. The Church (God bless it!) has but a pittance. The property of the Lords, compared with that of the Commons, is as a drop of water in the ocean; and this House represents those Commons, the proprietors of the lands; and those proprietors virtually represent the rest of the inhabitants. When, therefore, in this House, we give and grant, we give and grant what is our own. But in an American tax, what do we do? 'We, your Majesty's Commons for Great Britain, give and grant to your Majesty'—what? Our own property! No! 'We give and grant to your Majesty' the property of your Majesty's Commons of America! It is an absurdity in terms.

The distinction between legislation and taxation is essentially necessary to liberty. The Crown and the peers are equally legislative powers with the Commons. If taxation be a part of simple legislation, the Crown and the peers have rights in taxation as well as yourselves; rights which they will claim, which they will exercise, whenever the principle can be supported by power.

There is an idea in some that the colonies are *virtually* represented in the House. I would fain know by whom an American is represented here. Is he represented by any knight of the shire, in any county in this kingdom? Would to God that respectable representation was augmented to a greater number! Or will you tell him that he is represented by any representative of a borough? A borough which, perhaps, its own representatives never saw! This is what is called the rotten part of the Constitution. It cannot continue a century. If it does not drop, it must be amputated. The idea of a virtual representation of America in this House is the most contemptible idea that ever entered into the head of a man. It does not deserve a serious refutation.

The Commons of America represented in their several assemblies, have ever been in possession of the exercise of this, their constitutional right, of giving and granting their own money. They would have been slaves if they had not enjoyed it! At the same time, this kingdom, as the supreme governing and legislative power, has always bound the colonies by her laws, by her regulations, and restrictions in trade, in navigation, in manufactures, in every thing, except that of taking their money out of their pockets without their consent.

Here I would draw the line:

Quam ultra citraque neque consistere rectum

[*When Lord Chatham had concluded, Mr. George Grenville secured the floor and entered into a general denunciation of the tumults and riots which had taken place in the colonies, and declared that they bordered on rebellion. He condemned the language and sentiments which he had heard as encouraging a* revolution. *A portion of his speech is here inserted, as it is necessary for a complete understanding of the reply of Lord Chatham.*]

Mr. Grenville: I cannot understand the difference between external and internal taxes. They are the same in effect, and differ only in name. That this kingdom has the sovereign, the supreme legislative power over America, is granted; it cannot be denied; and taxation is a part of that sovereign power. It is one branch of the legislation. It is, it has been, exercised over those who are not, who were never represented. It is exercised over the India Company, the merchants of London, the proprietors of the stocks, and over many great manufacturing towns. It was exercised over the county palatine of Chester, and the bishopric of Durham, before they sent any representatives to Parliament. I appeal for proof to the preambles of the acts which gave them representatives to Parliament. I appeal for proof to the preambles of the acts which gave them representatives; one in the reign of Henry VIII., the other in that of Charles II. [*Mr. Grenville then quoted the acts, and desired that they might be read; which being done, he said*]: When I proposed to tax America, I asked the House if any gentleman would object to the right; I repeatedly asked it, and no man would attempt to deny it. Protection and obedience are reciprocal. Great Britain protects America; America is bound to yield obedience. If not, tell me when the Americans were emancipated? When they want the protection of this kingdom, they are always very ready to ask it. That protection has always been afforded them in the most full and ample manner. The nation has run herself into an immense debt to give them their protection; and now, when they are called upon to contribute a small share toward the public expense—an expense arising from themselves—they renounce your authority, insult your officers, and break out, I might almost say, into open rebellion. The seditious spirit of the colonies owes its birth to the factions in this House. Gentlemen are careless of the consequences of what they say, provided it answers the purposes of opposition. We were told we trod on tender ground. We were bid to expect disobedience. What is this but telling the Americans to stand out against the law, to encourage their obstinacy with the expectation of support from hence? 'Let us only hold out a little,' they would say, 'our friends will soon be in power.' Ungrateful people of America! Bounties have been extended to them. When I had the honour of serving the Crown, while you yourselves were loaded with an enormous debt, you gave bounties on their lumber, on their iron, their hemp, and many other articles. You have relaxed in their favor the Act of Navigation, that palladium of the British commerce; and yet I have been abused in all the public papers as an enemy to the trade of America. I have been particularly charged with giving orders and instructions to prevent the Spanish trade, and thereby stopping the channel by which alone North America used to be supplied with cash for remittances to this country. I defy any man to produce any such orders or instructions. I discouraged no trade but what was illicit, what was prohibited by an act of Parliament. I desire a West India merchant [Mr. Long], well known in the city, a gentleman of character, may be examined. He will tell you that I offered to do every thing in my power to advance the trade of America. I was above giving an answer to anonymous calumnies; but in this place it becomes one to wipe off the aspersion.

[*Here Mr. Grenville ceased. Several members got up to speak, but Mr. Pitt seeming to rise, the House was so clamorous for Mr.* Pitt! *Mr.* Pitt! *that the speaker was obliged to call to order.*]

Mr. Pitt said: I do not apprehend I am speaking twice. I did expressly reserve a part of my subject, in order to save the time of this House; but I am compelled to proceed in it. I do not speak twice; I only finish what I designedly left imperfect. But if the House is of a different opinion, far be it from me to indulge a wish of transgression against order. I am content, if it be your pleasure, to be silent. [*Here he paused. The House resounding with Go on! go on! He proceeded:*]

Gentlemen, sir, have been charged with giving birth to *sedition* in America. They have spoken their sentiments with freedom against this unhappy act, and that freedom has become their crime. Sorry I am to hear the liberty of speech in this House imputed as a crime. But the imputation shall not discourage me. It is a liberty I mean to exercise. No gentleman ought to be afraid to exercise it. It is a liberty by which the gentleman who calumniates it might have profited. He ought to have desisted from his project. The gentleman tells us, America is obstinate; America is almost in open rebellion. I rejoice that America has resisted. Three millions of people, so dead to all the feelings of liberty as voluntarily to submit to be slaves, would have been fit instruments to make slaves of the rest. I come not here armed at all points, with law cases and acts of Parliament, with the statute book doubled down in dog's ears, to defend the cause of liberty. If I had, I myself would have cited the two cases of Chester and Durham. I would have cited them to show that, even under former arbitrary reigns, Parliaments were ashamed of taxing a people without their consent, and allowed them representatives. Why did the gentleman confine himself to Chester and Durham? He might have taken a higher example in Wales—Wales, that never was taxed by Parliament till it was incorporated. I would not debate a particular point of law with the gentleman. I know his abilities. I have been obliged to his diligent researches. But, for the defence of liberty, upon a general principle, upon a constitutional principle, it is a ground on which I stand firm—on which I dare meet any man. The gentleman tells us of many who are taxed, and are not represented—the India company, merchants, stockholders, manufacturers. Surely many of these are represented in other capacities, as owners of land, or as freemen of boroughs. It is a misfortune that more are not equally represented. But they are all inhabitants, and as such, are they not virtually represented? Many have it in their option to be actually represented. They have connections with those that elect, and they have influence over them. The gentleman mentioned the stockholders. I hope he does not reckon the debts of the nation as a part of the national estate.

Since the accession of King William, many ministers, some of great, others of more moderate abilities have taken the lead of government. [*Here Mr. Pitt went through the list of them, bringing it down till he came to himself, giving a short sketch of the characters of each, and then proceeded:*] None of these thought, or even dreamed, of robbing the colonies of their constitutional rights. That was reserved to mark the era of the late administration. Not that there were wanting some, when I had the honour to serve His Majesty, to propose to me to burn my fingers with an American stamp act. With the enemy at their back, with our bayonets at their breasts, in the day of their distress, perhaps the Americans would have submitted to the imposition; but it would have been taking an ungenerous, an unjust advantage. The gentleman boasts of his bounties to America! Are not these bounties intended finally for the benefit of this kingdom? If they are not, he has misapplied the national treasures!

I am no courtier of America. I stand up for this kingdom. I maintain that the Parliament has a right to bind, to restrain America. Our legislative power over the colonies is sovereign and supreme. When it ceases to be sovereign and supreme, I would advise every gentleman to sell his lands, if he can, and embark for that country. When two countries are connected together like England and her colonies, without being incorporated, the one must necessarily govern. The greater must rule the less. But she must so rule it as *not to contradict the fundamental principles that are common to both.*

If the gentleman does not understand the difference between external and internal taxes, I cannot help it. There is a plain distinction between taxes levied for the purposes of raising a revenue, and duties imposed for the regulation of trade, for the accommodation of the subject; although, in the consequences, some revenue may incidentally arise from the latter.

The gentleman asks, when were the colonies emancipated? I desire to know, when were they made slaves? But I dwell not upon words. When I had the honour of serving His Majesty, I availed myself of the means of information which I derived from my office. I speak, therefore, from knowledge. My materials were good, I was at pains to collect, to digest, to consider them; and I will be bold to affirm, that the profits to Great Britain from the trade of the colonies through all its branches, is two millions a year. This is the fund that carried you triumphantly through the last war. The estates that were rented at two thousand pounds a year, three-score years ago, are at three thousand at present. Those estates sold then from fifteen to eighteen years purchase; the same may now be sold for thirty. You owe this to America. This is the price America pays you for her protection. And shall a miserable financier come with a boast, that he can bring 'a pepper-corn' into the exchequer by the loss of millions to the nation? I dare not say how much higher these profits may be augmented. Omitting, i.e., not taking into account the immense increase of people, by natural population, in the northern colonies, and the emigration from every part of Europe, I am convinced on other grounds that the commercial system of America may be altered to advantage. You have prohibited where you ought to have encouraged. You have encouraged where you ought to have prohibited. Improper restraints have been laid on the continent in favor of the islands. You have but two nations to trade with in America. Would you had twenty! Let acts of Parliament in consequence of treaties remain; but let not an English minister become a custom-house officer for Spain, or for any foreign power. Much is wrong! Much may be amended for the general good of the whole!

Does the gentleman complain he has been misrepresented in the public prints? It is a common misfortune. In the Spanish affair of the last war, I was abused in all the newspapers for having advised His Majesty to violate the laws of nations with regard to Spain. The abuse was industriously circulated even in hand-bills. If administration did not propagate the abuse, administration never contradicted it. I will not say what advice I did give the King. My advice is in writing, signed by myself, in the possession of the Crown. But I will say what advice I did not give the King. I did *not* advise him to violate any of the laws of nations.

As to the report of the gentleman's preventing in some way the trade for bullion with the Spaniards, it was spoken of so confidently that I own I am one of those who did believe it to be true.

The gentleman must not wonder he was not contradicted when, as minister, he asserted the right of Parliament to tax America. I know not how it is, but there is a modesty in this House which does not choose to contradict a minister. Even your chair, sir, looks too often toward St. James'. I wish gentlemen would get the better of this modesty. If they do not, perhaps the collective body may begin to abate of its respect for the representative. Lord Bacon has told me, that a great question would not fail of being agitated at one time or another. I was willing to agitate such a question at the proper season, viz., that of the German war—*my* German war, they called it! Every session I called out, Has any body any objection to the German war? Nobody would object to it, one gentleman only excepted, since removed to the Upper House by succession to an ancient barony [Lord Le Despencer, formerly Sir Francis Dashwood]. He told me he did not like a German war. I honoured the man for it, and was sorry when he was turned out of his post.

A great deal has been said without doors of the power, of the strength of America. It is a topic that ought to be cautiously meddled with. In a good cause, on a sound bottom, the force of this country can crush America to atoms. I know the valour of your troops. I know the skill of your officers. There is not a company on foot that has served in America, out of which you may not pick a man of sufficient knowledge and experience to make a governor of a colony there. But on this ground, on the Stamp Act, which so many here will think a crying injustice, I am one who will lift up my hands against it.

In such a cause, your success would be hazardous. America, if she fell, would fall like the strong man; she would embrace the pillars of the State, and pull down the Constitution along with her. Is this your boasted peace —not to sheathe the sword in its scabbard, but to sheathe it in the bowels of your countrymen? Will you quarrel with yourselves, now the whole house of Bourbon is united against you; while France disturbs your fisheries in Newfoundland, embarrasses your slave trade to Africa, and withholds from your subjects in Canada their property stipulated by treaty; while the ransom for the Manillas is denied by Spain, and its gallant conqueror basely traduced into a mean plunderer; a gentleman [Colonel Draper] whose noble and generous spirit would do honour to the proudest grandee of the country? The Americans have not acted in all things with prudence and temper: they have been wronged: they have been driven to madness by injustice. Will you punish them for the madness you have occasioned? Rather let prudence and temper come first from this side. I will undertake for America that she will follow the example. There are two lines in a ballad of Prior's, of a man's behaviour to his wife, so applicable to you and your colonies, that I can not help repeating them:

> Be to her faults a little blind;
> Be to her virtues very kind.

Upon the whole, I will beg leave to tell the House what is my opinion. It is, that the Stamp Act be repealed absolutely, totally, and immediately. That the reason for the repeal be assigned, viz., because it was founded on an erroneous principle. At the same time, let the sovereign authority of this country over the colonies be asserted in as strong terms as can be devised, and be made to extend to every point of legislation whatsoever; that we may bind their trade, confine their manufactures, and exercise every power whatsoever, except that of taking their money out of their pockets without their consent.

John Wilkes

John Wilkes

[*Born* OCTOBER 17, 1727—*Died* DECEMBER 26, 1797]

Wilkes was rather above the middle height. His features were irregular to the point of ugliness, and a squint lent them a sinister expression. . . .—J. M. RIGG

N.

athaniel Wraxall calls John
Wilkes, "The most interesting individual of the age in which he
lived." [1] So popular was he with the House of Commons that he was
denied his rightful seat for eleven years, even though he was repeatedly elected by the voters of Middlesex. For his ridicule of the policies
of the Government of King George III, he was imprisoned for libel
and later forced to flee Great Britain for a time. Seldom, if ever,
has a fugitive earned the right to be called, in the words of Charles
Chenevix Trench, one of the half dozen most significant men of his
century.[2]

It is perhaps fair to say that the only real friends Wilkes possessed
were the people of England, and with their support he evolved a tech-
nique of opposition, never violent, but "turbulent, forcible, unscrupulous, and damnably effective." [3] The fruit of such turbulence was
to arrest Parliamentary encroachments upon a member duly elected
by the people, to strike the first blow for the freedom of the press, and
to do battle on behalf of those wishing to report the proceedings of
Parliament.

Although Wilkes was considered ugly in features, unscrupulous
in character, and insincere in expression, he nevertheless was considered by Horace Bleackley to be a prominent Parliamentarian possessing the ear of the House whenever he chose to appeal to it.[4] He
lacked the natural endowments of Chatham, Burke, and Fox, but "his
ability as an actor, combined with the wit, gaiety, and the animal
spirits of the man, more than compensated for the defects of his elocution." [5] His speeches were carefully written out, memorized, and presented in a manner which "attained the high literary standard that

---

[1] Sir Nathaniel William Wraxall, *Memoirs*, II (London: Bickers and Son, 1884),
p. 49.

[2] Charles Chenevix Trench, *Portrait of a Patriot* (Edinburgh: William Blackwood
and Sons Ltd., 1962), p. 370.

[3] *Ibid.*, p. 372. See also R. W. Postgate, *That Devil Wilkes* (New York: The Vanguard Press, 1929), p. 160. According to Postgate, the public meeting was one such
method of opposing government policies used by Wilkes's supporters: "To organize a
political campaign at all was an innovation, and the method chosen was another new
thing. This was the revival, or introduction, of public meetings, and from this historians
of every school date the beginning of the popular control of the government."

[4] Horace Bleackley, *Life of John Wilkes* (London: The Bodley Head, 1917), p. 299.

[5] *Ibid.*, p. 301.

satisfied the expectations of the elect." [6] Wilkes is often reported to
have said of his ugliness, that he could talk away his face, and be only
a "quarter behind the handsomest man." [7] According to Wraxall, if
it is pleasing to observe a speaker who squinted, lisped, and who had
lost his teeth, Wilkes might be so esteemed.[8]

His biographers point to a number of speeches delivered by Wilkes
to the House of Commons as his greatest contributions.[9] Among them
was his speech against the war with America on February 6, 1775,[10]
his motion for the reform of Parliament on March 21, 1776,[11] and his
speech against the impeachment of Warren Hastings on May 9, 1787.[12]
Included in this volume, however, is a speech delivered on February
22, 1775, when he moved to rescind all the resolutions of Commons
regarding the Middlesex election.[13] This speech was presented on the
first personal occasion Wilkes had to speak in the House after having
finally been seated. The motion aroused much interest, and the House
was full when he arose to speak. Bleackley calls this speech a "fluent
and well-ordered oration, full of common-sense, logical and intelligent, occasionally gleaming with a flash of eloquence," [14] though possessing the destructible character of insincerity. Following an eight-
hour debate, his motion was defeated. Unperturbed by the setback,
Wilkes annually introduced the motion until, on May 3rd, 1782, he
made the appeal for the last time, certain of victory, and forevermore
blocking the right of Commons to declare a duly elected member in-
eligible to take his seat. Such an exertion as this earned for John
Wilkes the epitaph, "A Friend of Liberty."

---

6 *Ibid.*, p. 299.

7 Percy Fitzgerald, *The Life and Times of John Wilkes*, II (London: Ward and
Downey, 1888), p. 221.

8 Wraxall, *op. cit.*

9 See Bleackley, *op. cit.*, p. 301. "Wilkes made a dozen set speeches in the House between 1775 and 1776. During the next two years he spoke sixteen times. In 1779 and
1780 he was reported at more or less full length on fourteen occasions."

10 *Ibid.*, p. 303. "In 1775 on three occasions he spoke against government policies in
America," and "Not unfrequently they had the true ring of eloquence."

11 See Postgate, *op. cit.*, p. 210. Postgate considers this speech to be Wilkes's most
important and creditable.

12 See Bleackley, *op. cit.*, p. 378. "It was acclaimed a superlative speech, the best he
had ever delivered. . . ."

13 Wilkes's motion was that the Resolution of the 17th of February, 1769, which expelled him from the House, should be expunged from the Journals.

14 Bleackley, *op. cit.*, p. 287.

Motion for Redress[1]

•

A *motion was made, and the question put,* "That the Resolution of this House, of the 17th day of February 1769, that John Wilkes, Esquire, having been in this session of Parliament expelled this House, was, and is, incapable of being elected a Member to serve in this present Parliament, be expunged from the Journals of this House, as being subversive of the rights of the whole body of electors of this kingdom;"

The Lord Mayor, Mr. Wilkes, said,

Mr. Speaker,

The motion, which I shall have the honour of submitting to the House, affects, in my opinion, the very vitals of this constitution, the great primary sources of the power of the people, whom we represent, and by whose authority only, delegated to us for a time, we are a part of the legislative body of this kingdom. The proceedings of the last Parliament, in the business of the Middlesex elections, gave a just alarm to almost every elector in the nation. The fatal precedent then attempted to be established was considered as a direct attack on the inalieniable [*sic*] rights of the people. Many of the most respectable bodies in this kingdom expressed their abhorrence of those arbitrary measures. They proceeded so far as to petition the Crown for the dissolution of that Parliament, as having been guilty of a flagrant abuse of their trust. Above 60,000 of our fellow-subjects, freeholders of the realm, carried their complaints to the foot of the throne; a number surely deserving of the highest regard from

---

1 *Speeches of Mr. Wilkes in the House of Commons* (1786), pp. 19–39. The editor of this volume has collected these speeches from newspapers and oral tradition. "I think no apology necessary either to the public, or to that gentleman (Wilkes), for the freedom which I have used in the notes with some characters of high rank and dignity. Truth ought to be preferred to every motive and consideration."

every Minister, whose whole attention was not engrossed by the 6000 borough electors, who return a majority for him to this House. The people, sir, were in a ferment, which has not yet subsided. They made my cause their own; for they saw all the powers of government exerted against the constitution, which was wounded through my sides, and the envenomed shafts of a wicked administration pointed at our laws and liberties no less than at a hated individual. The plan was carried on for some years with a spirit of malevolence and rancour, which would have disgraced the very worst, but with a perseverance which would have done honour to the best, cause. I do not mean, sir, to go through in irksome detail of the various persecutions and injuries which that person suffered, I hope with a becoming fortitude. I have forgiven them. All the great powers of the state were at one time combined to pour their accumulated vengeance on me. The two Houses of Parliament chose me as the most acceptable victim, which could be sacrificed at the shrine of their court idolatry; and even imperial *Jove* pointed his thunder-bolts, *red with uncommon wrath* at my devoted head. I was scorched, but not consumed. The broad shield of the law protected me. A generous public, and my noble friends, the freeholders of Middlesex, the ever steady friends of liberty and their country, poured balm into my wounds. They are healed so that scarcely a scar remains. But, sir, I feel, I deeply feel the wounds given to the constitution. They are still bleeding, and this House only can heal them, as well as restore the constitution to its former state of purity, health, and vigour. May I be permitted to point out the mode of cure, and the salutary methods, which I think you ought to apply? Before I proceed to the remedy, I shall beg the indulgence of the House to state the case with precision and accuracy. I hope they will forgive a dry, but candid and short, narrative of the principal facts, because I mean to argue from them. I will give them as brief as possible, and with all the impartiality of a bye-stander.

Mr. Wilkes was first elected for the county of Middlesex, on the 28th of March 1768. He was expelled the 3d of February 1769, and the second time chosen, without opposition, the 16th day of the same month. On the day following the election was vacated, and he was declared by a majority of the House *incapable* of being elected into that Parliament. Notwithstanding this resolution of the House, he was a third time, on the 16th of March, elected without opposition; for I suppose the ridiculous attempt of a Mr. Dingley, who had not a single freeholder to propose, or vote for him, can hardly be called an opposition. *That* election however was declared void the next day. On the 13th of April Mr. Wilkes was a fourth time elected, by a majority of 1143 votes against Mr. Luttrell, who had only 296. The same day this House voted, "that Mr. Luttrell ought to have been returned." On the 29th of April, a *Petition* was presented to the House from the freeholders of Middlesex by a worthy Baronet, who is not only an honour to this House, but to human nature; notwithstanding which, the House on the 8th of May resolved, "the Henry Lawes Luttrell, Esquire, is duly elected a Knight of the Shire to serve in this present Parliament for the county of Middlesex."

These, sir, are the great outlines, the leading facts. I will not trouble the Clerk to read all the resolutions, to which I have alluded. They are fresh, I am persuaded, in the memories of gentlemen. I only call for that of Feb. 17, 1769, respecting *incapacity* as the certain consequence of *expulsion.*

[*The Clerk read the Resolution*]

Now, Sir, I think it fair to state to the House the whole of what I intend to move in consequence of the facts stated, and the resolution just read. The first motion I intend is, "that the Resolution of this House of the 17th of February, 1769, '*That John Wilkes, Esquire, having been, in this Session of Parliament, expelled this House, was, and is, incapable of being elected a member to serve in this present Parliament,*' be expunged from the Journals of this House, as being subversive of the rights of the whole body of electors of this kingdom." This I hold of necessity to restore the constitution, which that Resolution tears up by the roots. I shall then, if I succeed, if justice and a reverence for the constitution prevail in this Parliament, proceed to the other Motion, "That all the declarations, orders, and resolutions of this House, respecting the election of John Wilkes, Esquire, for the County of Middlesex, as a void election, the due and legal election of Henry Lawes Luttrell, Esquire, into the last Parliament, for the County of Middlesex, and the incapacity of John Wilkes, Esquire, to be elected a Member to serve in the said Parliament, be expunged from the Journals of this House, as being subversive of the rights of the whole body of electors of this kingdom."

The words of the Resolution of the 17th of February 1769, which I mean more particularly to combat, are, "*was* and *is* incapable," and the explanation of them the same day in the order for a new writ, "in the room of John Wilkes, Esquire, who is adjudged incapable of being elected a Member to serve in this present Parliament." In the first formation of this government, in the original settlement of our constitution, the people expressly reserved to themselves a very considerable part of the legislative power, which they consented to share jointly with a King and House of Lords. From the great population of our island this right could not be claimed and exercised personally, and therefore the *many* were compelled to delegate that power to a *few,* who thus were chosen their deputies and agents only, their representatives. It follows, from the very idea of a choice, that such choice must be free and uncontrouled, admitting of no restrictions, but the law of the land, to which the King and the Lords are equally subject, and what must arise from the nature of the trust. A Peer of Parliament, for instance, cannot be elected a Member of the House of Commons, because he already forms a part of another branch of the same legislative body. A lunatic has a natural incapacity. Other instances might be mentioned, but these two are sufficient. The freedom of election is then the common right of the people of England, their fair and just share of power; and I hold it to be the most glorious inheritance of every subject of this realm, the noblest, and I trust, the most solid part of that beautiful fabric, the English constitution. Here I might lean, sir, on the most respectable authorities which can be cited, the supreme judicature of this kingdom, and the venerable judges of former ages as well as of our own times. *I met them accidentally this morning in the course of my reading,* as an old friend of *Wilkes and Liberty,* now alas! lost to every sense of duty to his country, frequently tells another great assembly, that he *accidentally meets* in this manner all his tiresome quotations. The House of Peers, sir, in the case of Ashby and White in 1704, determined, "a man has a right to his freehold by the common law; and the law having annexed his right of voting to his freehold, it is of the nature of his freehold, and must depend upon it." On the same occasion likewise they declared, "it is absurd to say, the electors' right of chusing is founded upon the law and custom of parliament. It is an *original right, part of the constitution of the kingdom, as much as a parliament is,* and from whence the persons elected to serve in parliament do derive their authority, and can have no other but that which is given to them by those that have the original right to chuse them." The greatest law authorities, both ancient and modern, agree in the opinion, that every subject of the realm, not disqualified by law, is eligible of common right. Lord Coke, Lord Chief Justice Holt, and Mr. Blackstone, are the only authorities which I shall cite. I regard not, sir, the slavish, *courtly* doctrines propagated by lawyers in either house of Parliament, as to the rights of the subject, no more than I do as to what they pronounce high treason and *rebellion.* Such doctrines are delivered here only to be *reported* elsewhere. These men *have their reward.* But the venal tongue of a prostitute advocate or judge is best answered by the wise and sober pen of the same man, when in a former cool moment, unheated by party rage or faction, after the fullest deliberation, he gave to the nation, to the present age, and to posterity, a fair and impartial detail of their undoubted rights, and when he laid down in clear and express terms the plain law of the land. Lord Coke says, "He which is eligible of common right, cannot be disabled by the said ordinance in Parliament, unless it had been by act of Parliament." Lord Chief Justice Holt declares, "the election of knights belongs to the freeholders of counties; and it is an original right, vested in and inseparable from the freehold, and can no more be severed from their freehold, than their freehold itself can be taken away." Mr. Justice Blackstone, in the first book of his *Commentaries on the laws of England,* has the following words, "sub- ject to these restrictions and disqualifications, *every* subject of the realm is eligible of *common right."* This *common right* of the subject, sir, was violated by the majority of the last house of Commons; and I affirm, that they, and in particular, if I am rightly informed, the noble Lord with the blue ribband, committed by that act *high treason against Magna Charta.* This house only, without the interference of the other parts of the legisla- ture, took upon them to make the law. They adjudged me *incapable* of being elected a member to serve in that Parliament, although I was quali- fied by the law of the land, and the noble Lord declared in this house, "if any other candidate had only six votes, he would seat him for Middlesex." I repeat it, sir, this violence was a direct infringement of Magna Charta, *high treason* against the sacred charter of our liberties. The words, to which I allude, ought always to be written in letters of gold: "No freeman shall be disseized of his freehold, or liberties, or free customs, unless by the lawful judgment of his peers, or by the law of the land." By the con- duct of that majority, and of the noble Lord, they assumed to themselves the power of making the law, and at the same moment invaded the rights of the People, the King, and the Lords. The two last tamely acquiesced in the exercise of a power, which had been in a great instance fatal to their predecessors, had put an end to their very existence; but the people, sir, and in particular the spirited freeholders of this county, whose ruling passion is the love of liberty, have not yet forgiven the attack on *their* rights. So dangerous a *precedent,* of usurped power, which may in future times be cited and adopted in practice by a despotic minister of the crown, ought to be expunged from the Journals of this House.

I have heard and read much of *precedents* to justify the proceedings of the last House of Commons. I own, sir, I value very little the doctrine of precedents. There is scarcely any new villainy under the sun. A precedent can never justify any action in itself wicked, a robbery for instance on the heaths of Hounslow or Bagshot, of which there are innumerable prece- dents. The basest actions may be justified by precedents drawn from bad times and bad men. The sole question is, Whether this power is not a direct usurpation on the rights of the people? If *that* is proved, I care not how long the usurpation has continued, how often been practised. It is high time to put an end to it. It was the case of *General Warrants.* One precedent however, the most insisted upon, I must take notice of, because it is said fully to come up to the point, but, in my opinion, in almost every part it proves the contrary of what it has been brought to support. I mean the remarkable case of Mr. Walpole in 1711, a period, in which the rank- est *Tory* principles were countenanced more than in any other of our history prior to 1760. The case, sir, has been so partially quoted, even by a person whose sole merit here was an assumed accuracy, which he never possessed, that I shall desire it may be read to the House from the Journals.

[*The Clerk Read,*]

"Resolved, that Robert Walpole, Esquire, having been, this session of Parliament, committed a prisoner to the Tower of London, and expelled this House, *for an high breach of trust in the execution of his office, and notorious corruption, when Secretary at War,* was and is incapable of being elected a Member to serve in the present Parliament."

Now, sir, I must observe, that even *that* House of Commons, at an aera so hostile to the liberties not only of England but of Europe, did not venture to adjudge Mr. Walpole incapable of being elected a member to serve in that Parliament *only* because he was expelled; but in the body of the Resolution itself they added another reason, which would be trifling, if the former was sufficient and adequate to the point, *the high breach of trust in the execution of his office, and notorious corruption, when Secretary at War.* As trustees for the nation, they assigned a public cause, which must interest every member of the community. In the case of Mr. Wilkes, the last House of Commons declared, "that John Wilkes, Esquire, having been, in this Session of Parliament, expelled this House, *was* and *is* incapable of being elected a Member to serve in this present Parliament." The *having been expelled,* whether justly or unjustly, is the *only* reason, which they gave to the world. I shall not yet, sir, dismiss the case of Mr. Walpole. It will prove another proposition maintained by me: it will shew the injustice of the late House of Commons in seating Mr. Luttrell, as Representative for the County of Middlesex. The fact was, that the House in Queen Anne's time, having expelled Mr. Walpole, ordered immediately the issuing of a new writ. At the subsequent election Mr. Walpole was again returned. A Mr. Taylor, who had a minority of votes, petitioned; but the election was vacated. Had the doctrine propagated by the late majority, and by the noble Lord with the blue ribband, been just and founded, Mr. Taylor ought to have been the fitting member, the House should have resolved that he *ought* to have been returned, and that the grossest injustice had actually been committed against him. But even that Parliament, whose memory the nation execrates, stopped short in their career of iniquity, and did not proceed to such enormous wickedness. It was reserved for the present aera, when shame has lost its blush. Mr. Luttrell was for some years permitted to sit here as representing the County of Middlesex, although a great majority of the freeholders abhorred and reprobated the idea of *his* representing them, on every public occasion declared it, and in their *Petition* to this House gave the record of it under their hands to all posterity.

Sir, when the strong, unanswerable reasons, on which any doctrine is founded, bear me out, I care little about precedents. I recollect however another instance in more auspicious times, when a glorious monarch defended the constitution, which he had restored. It directly meets the objection so much relied upon; "that *expulsion* necessarily implies *incapacity.*" It is the last, which I shall desire the Clerk to read. I wish him to turn to the Journals of Feb. 20, 1698.

[*The Clerk read,*]

"Resolved, that Richard Woolaston, Esquire, being a Member of this House of Commons, and having since been concerned, and acted, as a receiver of the duties upon houses, as also upon births, marriages, and burials, contrary to the Act, made in the fifth and sixth years of His Majesty's reign, for granting several duties upon salt, beer, ale, and other liquors, *be expelled this House.*"

Now, sir, I defy all the subtlety of the most expert court lawyer among us, all the sophistry of the bar, to reconcile Mr. Woolaston's case with the favourite court tenet, "that *expulsion* necessarily implies *incapacity.*" The fact is ascertained, and indeed admitted, that a new writ did issue for the borough of Whitchurch in Hampshire, and that Mr. Woolaston was re-elected, and sat in the same Parliament. *Incapacity* therefore in the same Parliament does not necessarily follow *expulsion.*

I am ready to admit, that, where a clear *legal* incapacity exists, all votes given to a person incapacitated are thrown away, if they are knowingly given to him. But, sir, I beg leave to assert, that this was not the case in the Middlesex business. Mr. Wilkes was qualified by the law of the land; and the freeholders, who perfectly understood the clear point of law, as well as their own rights, expressly declared in the Petition presented on the 29th of April 1769 to the House, "Your Petitioners beg leave to represent to this honourable House, that the said Henry Lawes Luttrell had not the majority of legal votes at the said election, nor did the majority of the freeholders, when they voted for John Wilkes, Esquire, mean thereby to throw away their votes, or to waive their right of representation; nor would they, by any means, have chosen to be represented by the said Henry Lawes Luttrell, Esquire. Your Petitioners therefore apprehend he cannot sit as the representative of the said County of Parliament, without a manifest infringement of the rights and privileges of the freeholders thereof."

This House, sir, is created by the people, as the other is by the King. What right can the majority have to say to any county, city, or borough, you shall not have a particular person to be your representative, only because he is obnoxious to us, when he is qualified by the law? Every county, city, or borough, has an equal right with all other counties, cities, and boroughs, to its own choice, to its own distinct deputy in the great council of the nation. Each is free and independent, invested with precisely the same powers.

I do not mean, sir, now to enter into the argument, whether it may not be fit to give this House the power of expulsion in the first instance, for very flagrant and infamous crimes, either committed, or of which the member may be convicted, subsequent to his election. The sending the member back to his constituents on such ground might be considered as an appeal to the people. If however his constituents should differ in opinion from the majority of this House, if they should think him fit to be re-elected, he ought to be admitted, because he claims his seat under the same authority by which every member holds the privilege of sitting and voting here, a delegation from the people, their free choice. The first appeal to the constituents might in many cases appear just and reasonable. The appeal certainly lies to them, for they are the fountain of this power. We exercise their right. By their representation only we are a House of Parliament. They have the right of chusing for themselves, not a Majority here for them.

Sir, I will venture to assert, that the law of the land, by which all courts of judicature are equally bound, is overturned by the power lately exercised by a Majority of a House of Commons. The right of election by law is vested in the freehold. It is not placed in you, but in other hands, in those of the freeholders, or the constituents. Your predecessors not only robbed a particular county of its noblest privileges, but they changed the constitution of a House of Commons. The freeholders of this county and the nation abhorred the proceeding, and poured their execrations on the treacherous authors. From us not only they, but the law and constitution, now expect a full reparation of the injury, by rescinding the Resolution.

This usurpation, if acquiesced under, would be attended with the most alarming consequences. If you can reject those disagreeable to a majority, and expel whom you please, the House of Commons will be *self-created and self-existing*. You may expel till you approve, and thus in effect you nominate. The original idea of this House being the representative of the commons of the realm will be lost. The consequences of such a principle are dangerous in the extreme. A more forcible engine of despotism cannot be put into the hands of a Minister. I wish gentlemen would attend to the plain consequences of such proceedings, and consider how they may be brought home to themselves. A member hated, or dreaded, by the Minister, is accused of a crime; for instance, of being the author of what he thinks a libel. I select this case, as being the crime the least likely to be committed by any one gentleman of the present majority of this House. No proof whatever is given on oath before you, because you cannot administer an oath, except in the cases provided for by act of Parliament. You determine the *fact* however, and thus the Minister begins with invading the rights of *juries*. Before any trial, he gets the paper voted a libel, and the member he wishes expelled is voted to be the author, which is a *fact* this House is not competent to try and determine. *Expulsion* means always, as it is pretended, *incapacity*. The member is accordingly adjudged *incapable*. He cannot in consequence be re-elected, and thus is totally excluded from Parliament. By such manœuvres a Minister may garble a House of Commons till not a single enemy of his own, or a friend of his country, is left here, and the representation of the people in a great degree annihilated. Corruption had not lent despotism wings to fly so high in the reign of Charles I, or the minister of that day would have been contented with expelling *Hampden,* and the *four* other heroes, because they had immediately been adjudged *incapable,* and thereby incapacitated from thwarting in Parliament the arbitrary measures of a wicked court. My expulsion was an easy victory over liberty and the constitution. It went with wonderful expedition through all the forms of this House, for it was known to be a measure previously adopted in the cabinet, whose members have through the present reign frequently dared to deliberate on the invasion of the dearest rights of their country.

Upon all these considerations, sir, in order to quiet the minds of the people, to restore our violated constitution to its original purity, to vindicate the injured rights of this county in particular, and of all the electors of this kingdom, and that not the least trace of the violence and injustice of the last Parliament in this important cause may disgrace our records, I humbly move, "that the resolution of this House of the 17th of February 1769, *that John Wilkes, Esquire, having been, in this session of Parliament, expelled this House, WAS and IS, incapable of being elected a Member to serve in the present Parliament,* be expunged from the Journals of this House, as being subversive of the rights of the whole body of electors of this kingdom."

Edmund Burke

Edmund Burke

[*Born* JANUARY 12, 1729—*Died* JULY 9, 1797]

The marks about the jaw, the firmness of the lines about the mouth, the stern glance of the eye, and the furrows on the expansive forehead, were all the sad ravages left by the difficulties and sorrows of genius, and by the iron which had entered the soul.—THOMAS MACKNIGHT

. A .

ny student wishing to master
the study of politics, writes Sir Phillip Magnus, acquires a knowledge
of Burke who is the beginning of wisdom,[1] and whose impress is borne
on the average Englishman for all time.[2] Burke was an instinctive em-
piricist who believed in no abstract rules or general political laws. It
mattered little about which of the five great crises he debated in his
career, whether it be on America, Ireland, Constitutional Reform,
France, or India, he stoutly maintained that laws and constitutions
must be based upon the nature of man, and as man changes in character and circumstance, so also must his political environment. Such
beliefs led Magnus to call Burke "a crusader . . . on behalf of ordered liberty. . . ."[3]

Combined with his wisdom was an eloquence which "approached
the ancient standard of perfection."[4] There is no evidence to suggest
that Burke ever spoke from a prepared manuscript, relying instead
upon a "tenacious memory"[5] which reflected the fruit of immense
research and the most elaborate preparation.[6] His convictions were
communicated in a manner which left them stamped indelibly on the
minds of the listeners:

His voice was of great compass, and, expressing the depth of his convictions, gave much energy to the communication of his ideas. He never
hesitated for want of words. His utterance was rapid and vehement; but
quick as it was, his thoughts flowed forth with still greater freedom, and
threatened to overcome the power of speech.[7]

Despite his genius, Burke often spoke to excessive lengths. It was
not uncommon for him to speak three hours on a question, leaving
little or nothing for his allies to say. There is evidence to suggest that
he was not insensitive to the occasional dread meted out to him by
the audience when he rose to speak. Sir Samuel Romilly records one

---

1 Sir Phillip Magnus, *Edmund Burke* (London: John Murray, 1939), p. 302.
2 *Ibid.*, p. 300.
3 *Ibid.*, p. 302.
4 Sir James Prior, *A Life of Edmund Burke* (London: George Bell and Sons, 1891),
p. 493.
5 *Ibid.*, p. 103.
6 Magnus, *op. cit.*, p. 86.
7 Thomas Macknight, *History of the Life and Times of Edmund Burke,* I (London:
Chapman and Hall, 1858), p. 230.

37

such instance when Burke sought to speak on Pitt's motion for more
equal representation:

Burke rose to speak; but it was late, and a great many members, dreading
the length of his oration, quitted the house at the very same moment,
which so much offended him that he sat down without speaking: this has
happened to him more than once.[8]

Bertram Newman considers his chief literary and philosophical
works to be the concluding portion of the *Thoughts on the present
discontents,* portions of the speech on the *East India Bill,* the middle
part of *Reflections on the French Revolution,* and his speech on *Conciliation with America.*[9] Of these, Robert Murray believes the speech
on *Conciliation with America* was Burke's great effort, and "in some
ways his very greatest." [10] Others deserving mention are the addresses
to the Bristol electors in 1774, described by Murray as "perfect little
gems," [11] and his letter to the sheriffs of Bristol in 1777.

As background to the speech on *Conciliation with America,* revolution appeared imminent, and in one last great effort, on March 22,
1775, Edmund Burke stood in the House of Commons to advocate a
Whig proposal to revert to the situation as it was before passage of the
Stamp Act. Prior to the speech, strangers were rigidly excluded from
the gallery, and there were few members present to hear him either,
the majority comprising a hostile ministerial audience. When the
vote was taken, only seventy-eight supported the measures while two
hundred and seventy opposed them. The effect Burke failed to achieve
by the temporal test of votes was later achieved by an American military triumph. John Morley calls this War of Independence virtually
a second English civil war, and the ruin of the American cause would
have also been the ruin of the constitutional cause in England.[12]

Ironically, Burke died believing he had failed to influence belief,
but the ultimate effect of his oratory "attained the furthest summit of
political wisdom, and as literature his prose remains imperishable and
unsurpassed." [13]

---

8 Sir Samuel Romilly, *Memoirs* (3rd ed.: London, John Murray, 1842), p. 208.

9 Bertram Newman, *Edmund Burke* (London: G. Bell and Sons, Ltd., 1927), p. 338.

10 Robert H. Murray, *Edmund Burke* (London: Oxford University Press, 1931),
p. 406.

11 *Ibid.,* p. 237.

12 John Morley, *Burke* (London: Macmillan and Co., 1888), p. 87.

13 Magnus, *op. cit.,* p. 87.

On Conciliation with America[1]

•

HOUSE OF COMMONS *March 22, 1775*

I hope, Sir, that notwithstanding the austerity of the Chair, your good nature will incline you to some degree of indulgence towards human frailty. You will not think it unnatural that those who have an object depending which strongly engages their hopes and fears should be somewhat inclined to superstition. As I came into the House, full of anxiety about the event of my motion, I found, to my infinite surprise, that the grand penal bill by which we had passed sentence on the trade and sustenance of America is to be returned to us from the other House. I do confess, I could not help looking on this event as a fortunate omen. I look upon it as a sort of providential favor by which we are put once more in possession of our deliberative capacity, upon a business so very questionable in its nature, so very uncertain in its issue. By the return of this bill, which seemed to have taken its flight forever, we are at this very instant nearly as free to choose a plan for our American government as we were on the first day of the session. If, Sir, we incline to the side of conciliation, we are not at all embarrassed (unless we please to make ourselves so) by any incongruous mixture of coercion and restraint. We are therefore called upon, as it were by a superior warning voice, again to attend to America; to attend to the whole of it together; and to review the subject with an unusual degree of care and calmness.

Surely it is an awful subject, or there is none so on this side of the grave. When I first had the honour of a seat in this House, the affairs of that continent pressed themselves upon us as the most important and most delicate object of parliamentary attention. My little share in this great deliberation oppressed me. I found myself a partaker in a very high trust; and having no sort of reason to rely on the strength of my natural

[1] *Speech of Edmund Burke, Esq., on Moving his Resolutions for Conciliation with the Colonies* (2nd ed.; London, Printed for J. Dodsley, 1775).

abilities for the proper execution of that trust, I was obliged to take more than common pains to instruct myself in everything which relates to our colonies. I was not less under the necessity of forming some fixed ideas concerning the general policy of the British Empire. Something of this sort seemed to be indispensable, in order, amidst so vast a fluctuation of passions and opinions, to concentre my thoughts, to ballast my conduct, to preserve me from being blown about by every wind of fashionable doctrine. I really did not think it safe or manly to have fresh principles to seek upon every fresh mail which should arrive from America.

At that period I had the fortune to find myself in perfect concurrence with a large majority in this House. Bowing under that high authority, and penetrated with the sharpness and strength of that early impression, I have continued ever since, without the least deviation, in my original sentiments. Whether this be owing to an obstinate perseverance in error, or to a religious adherence to what appears to me truth and reason, it is in your equity to judge.

Sir, Parliament, having an enlarged view of objects, made, during this interval, more frequent changes in their sentiments and their conduct than could be justified in a particular person upon the contracted scale of private information. But though I do not hazard anything approaching to a censure on the motives of former Parliaments to all those alterations, one fact is undoubted,—that under them the state of America has been kept in continual agitation. Everything administered as remedy to the public complaint, if it did not produce, was at least followed by, an heightening of the distemper; until by a variety of experiments that important country has been brought into her present situation—a situation which I will not miscall, which I dare not name, which I scarcely know how to comprehend in the terms of any description.

In this posture, Sir, things stood at the beginning of the session. About that time a worthy member of great parliamentary experience, who in the year 1766 filled the Chair of the American Committee with much ability, took me aside and, lamenting the present aspect of our politics, told me things were come to such a pass that our former methods of proceeding in the House would be no longer tolerated; that the public tribunal (never too indulgent to a long and unsuccessful opposition) would now scrutinize our conduct with unusual severity; that the very vicissitudes and shiftings of ministerial measures, instead of convicting their authors of inconstancy and want of system, would be taken as an occasion of charging us with a predetermined discontent which nothing could satisfy, whilst we accused every measure of vigour as cruel, and every proposal of lenity as weak and irresolute. The public, he said, would not have patience to see us play the game out with our adversaries; we must produce our hand: it would be expected that those who for many years had been

active in such affairs should show that they had formed some clear and
decided idea of the principle of colony government, and were capable of
drawing out something like a platform of the ground which might be laid
for future and permanent tranquillity.

I felt the truth of what my honourable friend represented; but I felt
my situation too. His application might have been made with far greater
propriety to many other gentlemen. No man was, indeed, ever better disposed or worse qualified for such an undertaking than myself. Though I
gave so far into his opinion that I immediately threw my thoughts into a
sort of parliamentary form, I was by no means equally ready to produce
them. It generally argues some degree of natural impotence of mind, or
some want of knowledge of the world, to hazard plans of government
except from a seat of authority. Propositions are made, not only ineffec-
tually, but somewhat disreputably, when the minds of men are not properly disposed for their reception; and for my part, I am not ambitious of
ridicule, not absolutely a candidate for disgrace.

Besides, Sir, to speak the plain truth, I have in general no very exalted
opinion of the virtue of paper government, nor of any politics in which
the plan is to be wholly separated from the execution. But when I saw
that anger and violence prevailed every day more and more, and that
things were hastening towards an incurable alienation of our colonies, I
confess my caution gave way. I felt this as one of those few moments in
which decorum yields to a higher duty. Public calamity is a mighty level-
ler; and there are occasions when any, even the slightest, chance of doing
good must be laid hold on even by the most inconsiderable person.

To restore order and repose to an empire so great and so distracted as
ours, is, merely in the attempt, an undertaking that would ennoble the
flights of the highest genius and obtain pardon for the efforts of the meanest understanding. Struggling a good while with these thoughts, by degrees I felt myself more firm. I derived, at length, some confidence from
what in other circumstances usually produces timidity. I grew less anxious, even from the idea of my own insignificance. For judging of what
you are by what you ought to be, I persuaded myself that you would not
reject a reasonable proposition, because it had nothing but its reason to
recommend it. On the other hand, being totally destitute of all shadow of
influence, natural or adventitious, I was very sure that if my proposition
were futile or dangerous, if it were weakly conceived or improperly timed,
there was nothing exterior to it, of power to awe, dazzle or delude you.
You will see it just as it is, and you will treat it just as it deserves.

The proposition is peace. Not peace through the medium of war; not
peace to be hunted through the labyrinth of intricate and endless negotiations; not peace to arise out of universal discord fomented from principle in all parts of the empire; not peace to depend on the juridical

determination of perplexing questions, or the precise marking the shadowy boundaries of a complex government. It is simple peace, sought in its natural course and in its ordinary haunts. It is peace sought in the spirit of peace, and laid in principles purely pacific. I propose, by removing the ground of the difference, and by restoring the former unsuspecting confidence of the colonies in the mother country, to give permanent satisfaction to your people; and (far from a scheme of ruling by discord) to reconcile them to each other in the same act and by the bond of the very same interest which reconciles them to British government.

My idea is nothing more. Refined policy ever has been the parent of confusion, and ever will be so long as the world endures. Plain good intention, which is as easily discovered at the first view as fraud is surely detected at last, is, let me say, of no mean force in the government of mankind. Genuine simplicity of heart is an healing and cementing principle. My plan, therefore, being formed upon the most simple grounds imaginable, may disappoint some people when they hear it. It has nothing to recommend it to the pruriency of curious ears. There is nothing at all new and captivating in it. It has nothing of the splendour of the project which has been lately laid upon your table by the noble lord in the blue ribbon. It does not propose to fill your lobby with squabbling colony agents, who will require the interposition of your mace at every instant to keep the peace amongst them. It does not institute a magnificent auction of finance, where captivated provinces come to general ransom by bidding against each other, until you knock down the hammer, and determine a proportion of payments beyond all the powers of algebra to equalize and settle.

The plan which I shall presume to suggest derives, however, one great advantage from the proposition and registry of that noble lord's project. The idea of conciliation is admissible. First, the House, in accepting the resolution moved by the noble lord, has admitted, notwithstanding the menacing front of our address, notwithstanding our heavy bill of pains and penalties, that we do not think ourselves precluded from all ideas of free grace and bounty.

The House has gone farther; it has declared conciliation admissible, *previous* to any submission on the part of America. It has even shot a good deal beyond that mark, and has admitted that the complaints of our former mode of exerting the right of taxation were not wholly unfounded. That right thus exerted is allowed to have something reprehensible in it, something unwise or something grievous; since, in the midst of our heat and resentment, we of ourselves have proposed a capital alteration; and, in order to get rid of what seemed so very exceptionable, have instituted a mode that is altogether new,—one that is, indeed, wholly alien from all the ancient methods and forms of Parliament.

The *principle* of this proceeding is large enough for my purpose. The means proposed by the noble lord for carrying his ideas into execution, I think, indeed, are very indifferently suited to the end; and this I shall endeavour to show you before I sit down. But, for the present, I take my ground on the admitted principle. I mean to give peace. Peace implies reconciliation; and where there has been a material dispute, reconciliation does in a manner always imply concession on the one part or on the other. In this state of things I make no difficulty in affirming that the proposal ought to originate from us. Great and acknowledged force is not impaired, either in effect or in opinion, by an unwillingness to exert itself. The superior power may offer peace with honour and with safety. Such an offer from such a power will be attributed to magnanimity. But the concessions of the weak are the concessions of fear. When such a one is disarmed, he is wholly at the mercy of his superior; and he loses forever that time and those chances which, as they happen to all men, are the strength and resources of all inferior power.

The capital leading questions on which you must this day decide are these two: first, whether you ought to concede; and secondly, what your concession ought to be. On the first of these questions we have gained (as I have just taken the liberty of observing to you) some ground. But I am sensible that a good deal more is still to be done. Indeed, Sir, to enable us to determine both on the one and the other of these great questions with a firm and precise judgment, I think it may be necessary to consider distinctly the true nature and the peculiar circumstances of the object which we have before us: because after all our struggle, whether we will or not, we must govern America according to that nature and to those circumstances, and not according to our own imaginations, not according to abstract ideas of right; by no means according to mere general theories of government, the resort to which appears to me in our present situation no better than arrant trifling. I shall therefore endeavour, with your leave, to lay before you some of the most material of these circumstances in as full and as clear a manner as I am able to state them.

The first thing that we have to consider with regard to the nature of the object is the number of people in the colonies. I have taken for some years a good deal of pains on that point. I can by no calculation justify myself in placing the number below two millions of inhabitants of our own European blood and colour, besides at least 500,000 others who form no inconsiderable part of the strength and opulence of the whole. This, Sir, is, I believe, about the true number. There is no occasion to exaggerate where plain truth is of so much weight and importance. But whether I put the present numbers too high or too low is a matter of little moment. Such is the strength with which population shoots in that part of the world, that, state the numbers as high as we will, whilst the dispute con-

tinues, the exaggeration ends. Whilst we are discussing any given magnitude, they are grown to it. Whilst we spend our time in deliberating on
the mode of governing two millions, we shall find we have millions more
to manage. Your children do not grow faster from infancy to manhood,
than they spread from families to communities, and from villages to nations.

I put this consideration of the present and the growing numbers in the
front of our deliberation, because, Sir, this consideration will make it
evident to a blunter discernment than yours, that no partial, narrow, contracted, pinched, occasional system will be at all suitable to such an object. It will show you that it is not to be considered as one of those *minima*
which are out of the eye and consideration of the law; not a paltry excrescence of the state; not a mean dependent, who may be neglected with
little damage and provoked with little danger. It will prove that some
degree of care and caution is required in the handling such an object; it
will show that you ought not, in reason, to trifle with so large a mass of
the interests and feelings of the human race. You could at no time do so
without guilt; and be assured you will not be able to do it long with
impunity.

But the population of this country, the great and growing population,
though a very important consideration, will lose much of its weight, if not
combined with other circumstances. The commerce of your colonies is out
of all proportion beyond the numbers of the people. This ground of their
commerce, indeed, has been trod some days ago, and with great ability, by
a distinguished person at your bar. This gentleman, after thirty-five years,
—it is so long since he first appeared at the same place to plead for the
commerce of Great Britain,—has come again before you to plead the same
cause, without any other effect of time than that to the fire of imagination
and extent of erudition which even then marked him as one of the first
literary characters of his age, he has added a consummate knowledge in
the commercial interest of his country, formed by a long course of enlightened and discriminating experience.

Sir, I should be inexcusable in coming after such a person with any
detail, if a great part of the members who now fill the House had not the
misfortune to be absent when he appeared at your bar. Besides, Sir, I
propose to take the matter at periods of time somewhat different from his.
There is, if I mistake not, a point of view from whence, if you will look at
this subject, it is impossible that it should not make an impression upon
you.

I have in my hand two accounts: one a comparative state of the export
trade of England to its colonies, as it stood in the year 1704, and as it
stood in the year 1772; the other a state of the export trade of this country
to its colonies alone, as it stood in 1772, compared with the whole trade of

England to all parts of the world (the colonies included) in the year 1704. They are from good vouchers: the latter period from the accounts on your table, the earlier from an original manuscript of Davenant, who first established the Inspector-General's office, which has been ever since his time so abundant a source of parliamentary information.

The export trade to the colonies consists of three great branches: the African, which, terminating almost wholly in the colonies, must be put to the account of their commerce; the West Indian; and the North American. All these are so interwoven that the attempt to separate them would tear to pieces the contexture of the whole; and, if not entirely destroy, would very much depreciate the value of all the parts. I therefore consider these three denominations to be, what in effect they are, one trade.

The trade to the colonies, taken on the export side, at the beginning of this century, that is, in the year 1704, stood thus:

Exports to North America and the West Indies	£483,265
To Africa	86,665
	£569,930

In the year 1772, which I take as a middle year between the highest and lowest of those lately laid on your table, the account was as follows:

To North America and the West Indies	£4,791,734
To Africa	866,398
To which if you add the export trade from Scotland, which had in 1704 no existence	364,000
	£6,022,132

From five hundred and odd thousand it has grown to six millions. It has increased no less than twelvefold. This is the state of the colony trade, as compared with itself at these two periods within this century; and this is matter for meditation. But this is not all. Examine my second account. See how the export trade to the colonies alone in 1772 stood in the other point of view, that is, as compared to the whole trade of England in 1704:

The whole export trade of England, including that to the colonies, in 1704	£6,509,000
Export to the colonies alone in 1772	6,024,000
Difference	£485,000

The trade with America alone is now within less than £500,000 of being equal to what this great commercial nation, England, carried on at the beginning of this century with the whole world! If I had taken the largest year of those on your table, it would rather have exceeded. But, it will be said, is not this American trade an unnatural protuberance that has drawn the juices from the rest of the body? The reverse. It is the very food that has nourished every other part into its present magnitude. Our general trade has been greatly augmented, and augmented more or less in almost every part to which it ever extended, but with this material difference, that of the six millions which in the beginning of the century constituted the whole mass of our export commerce, the colony trade was but one-twelfth part; it is now (as a part of sixteen millions) considerably more than a third of the whole. This is the relative proportion of the importance of the colonies at these two periods: and all reasoning concerning our mode of treating them must have this proportion as its basis; or it is a reasoning weak, rotten and sophistical.

Mr. Speaker, I cannot prevail on myself to hurry over this great consideration. It is good for us to be here. We stand where we have an immense view of what is, and what is past. Clouds, indeed, and darkness rest upon the future. Let us, however, before we descend from this noble eminence, reflect that this growth of our national prosperity has happened within the short period of the life of man. It has happened within sixty-eight years. There are those alive whose memory might touch the two extremities. For instance, my Lord Bathurst might remember all the stages of the progress. He was in 1704 of an age at least to be made to comprehend such things. He was then old enough *acta parentum jam legere, et quae sit poterit cognoscere virtus*. Suppose, Sir, that the angel of this auspicious youth, foreseeing the many virtues which made him one of the most amiable, as he is one of the most fortunate, men of his age, had opened to him in vision, that when in the fourth generation the third prince of the House of Brunswick had sat twelve years on the throne of that nation which (by the happy issue of moderate and healing counsels) was to be made Great Britain, he should see his son, Lord Chancellor of England, turn back the current of hereditary dignity to its fountain, and raise him to a higher rank of peerage, whilst he enriched the family with a new one;—if, amidst these bright and happy scenes of domestic honour and prosperity, that angel should have drawn up the curtain and unfolded the rising glories of his country, and, whilst he was gazing with admiration on the then commercial grandeur of England, the genius should point out to him a little speck, scarcely visible in the mass of the national interest, a small seminal principle rather than a formed body, and should tell him,—"Young man, there is America, which at this day serves for little more than to amuse you with stories of savage men and uncouth manners; yet shall, before you taste of death, show itself equal to the whole of that commerce which now attracts the envy of the world. Whatever England has been growing to by a progressive increase of improvement, brought in by varieties of people, by succession of civilizing conquests and civilizing settlements in a series of seventeen hundred years, you shall see as much added to her by America in the course of a single life!" If this state of his country had been foretold to him, would it not require all the sanguine credulity of youth and all the fervid glow of enthusiasm to make him believe it? Fortunate man, he has lived to see it! Fortunate indeed, if he lives to see nothing that shall vary the prospect and cloud the setting of his day!

Excuse me, Sir, if, turning from such thoughts, I resume this comparative view once more. You have seen it on a large scale; look at it on a small one. I will point out to your attention a particular instance of it in the single province of Pennsylvania. In the year 1704 that province called for £11,459 in value of your commodities, native and foreign. This was the whole. What did it demand in 1772? Why, nearly fifty times as much; for in that year the export to Pennsylvania was £507,909, nearly equal to the export to all the colonies together in the first period.

I choose, Sir, to enter into these minute and particular details, because generalities, which in all other cases are apt to heighten and raise the subject, have here a tendency to sink it. When we speak of the commerce with our colonies, fiction lags after truth, invention is unfruitful, and imagination cold and barren.

So far, Sir, as to the importance of the object in the view of its commerce, as concerned in the exports from England. If I were to detail the imports, I could show how many enjoyments they procure which invigourate the springs of national industry, and extend and animate every part of our foreign and domestic commerce. This would be a curious subject indeed,—but I must prescribe bounds to myself in a matter so vast and various.

I pass, therefore, to the colonies in another point of view,—their agriculture. This they have prosecuted with such a spirit that, besides feeding plentifully their own growing multitude, their annual export of grain, comprehending rice, has some years ago exceeded a million in value. Of their last harvest, I am persuaded, they will export much more. At the beginning of the century some of these colonies imported corn from the mother country. For some time past the Old World has been fed from the New. The scarcity which you have felt would have been a desolating famine if this child of your old age, with a true filial piety, with a Roman charity, had not put the full breast of its youthful exuberance to the mouth of its exhausted parent.

As to the wealth which the colonies have drawn from the sea by their fisheries, you had all that matter fully opened at your bar. You surely thought those acquisitions of value, for they seemed even to excite your envy; and yet the spirit by which that enterprising employment has been exercised ought rather, in my opinion, to have raised your esteem and admiration. And pray, Sir, what in the world is equal to it? Pass by the other parts, and look at the manner in which the people of New England have of late carried on the whale fishery. Whilst we follow them among the tumbling mountains of ice, and behold them penetrating into the deepest frozen recesses of Hudson Bay and Davis Strait, whilst we are looking for them beneath the Arctic Circle, we hear that they have pierced into the opposite region of polar cold, that they are at the antipodes and engaged under the frozen Serpent of the south. Falkland Island, which seemed too remote and romantic an object for the grasp of national ambition, is but a stage and resting-place in the progress of their victorious industry. Nor is the equinoctial heat more discouraging to them than the accumulated winter of both the poles. We know that whilst some of them draw the line and strike the harpoon on the coast of Africa, others run the longitude and pursue their gigantic game along the coast of Brazil. No sea but what is vexed by their fisheries. No climate that is not witness to their toils. Neither the perseverance of Holland nor the activity of France nor the dexterous and firm sagacity of English enterprise ever carried this most perilous mode of hardy industry to the extent to which it has been pushed by this recent people—a people who are still, as it were, but in the gristle, and not yet hardened into the bone of manhood. When I contemplate these things; when I know that the colonies in general owe little or nothing to any care of ours, and that they are not squeezed into this happy form by the constraints of watchful and suspicious government, but that through a wise and salutary neglect a generous nature has been suffered to take her own way to perfection;—when I reflect upon these effects, when I see how profitable they have been to us, I feel all the pride of power sink, and all presumption in the wisdom of human contrivances melt and die away within me. My rigour relents. I pardon something to the spirit of liberty.

I am sensible, Sir, that all which I have asserted in my detail is admitted in the gross, but that quite a different conclusion is drawn from it. America, gentlemen say, is a noble object; it is an object well worth fighting for. Certainly it is, if fighting a people be the best way of gaining them. Gentlemen in this respect will be led to their choice of means by their complexions and their habits. Those who understand the military art will of course have some predilection for it. Those who wield the thunder of the state may have more confidence in the efficacy of arms. But I confess, possibly for want of this knowledge, my opinion is much more in favour of prudent management than of force,—considering force not as an odious, but a feeble, instrument for preserving a people so numerous, so active, so growing, so spirited as this, in a profitable and subordinate connection with us.

First, Sir, permit me to observe that the use of force alone is but *temporary*. It may subdue for a moment, but it does not remove the necessity of subduing again; and a nation is not governed which is perpetually to be conquered.

My next objection is its *uncertainty*. Terror is not always the effect of force, and an armament is not a victory. If you do not succeed, you are without resource: for conciliation failing, force remains; but force failing, no further hope of reconciliation is left. Power and authority are sometimes bought by kindness, but they can never be begged as arms by an impoverished and defeated violence.

A further objection to force is that you *impair the object* by your very endeavours to preserve it. The thing you fought for is not the thing which you recover, but depreciated, sunk, wasted and consumed in the contest. Nothing less will content me than *whole America*. I do not choose to consume its strength along with our own; because in all parts it is the British strength that I consume. I do not choose to be caught by a foreign enemy at the end of this exhausting conflict, and still less in the midst of it. I may escape, but I can make no insurance against such an event. Let me add that I do not choose wholly to break the American spirit; because it is the spirit that has made the country.

Lastly, we have no sort of *experience* in favour of force as an instrument in the rule of our colonies. Their growth and their utility have been owing to methods altogether different. Our ancient indulgence has been said to be pursued to a fault. It may be so; but we know, if feeling is evidence, that our fault was more tolerable than our attempt to mend it, and our sin far more salutary than our penitence.

These, Sir, are my reasons for not entertaining that high opinion of untried force, by which many gentlemen, for whose sentiments in other particulars I have great respect, seem to be so greatly captivated. But there is still behind a third consideration concerning this object, which serves to determine my opinion on the sort of policy which ought to be pursued in the management of America, even more than its population and its commerce: I mean its *temper* and *character*.

In this character of the Americans a love of freedom is the predominating feature which marks and distinguishes the whole: and as an ardent is always a jealous affection, your colonies become suspicious, restive and untractable, whenever they see the least attempt to wrest from them by force or shuffle from them by chicane what they think the only advantage worth living for. This fierce spirit of liberty is stronger in the English colonies, probably, than in any other people of the earth; and this from a great variety of powerful causes, which, to understand the true temper of their minds and the direction which this spirit takes, it will not be amiss to lay open somewhat more largely.

First, the people of the colonies are descendants of Englishmen. England, Sir, is a nation which still, I hope, respects, and formerly adored, her

freedom. The colonists emigrated from you when this part of your character was most predominant; and they took this bias and direction the moment they parted from your hands. They are therefore not only devoted
to liberty, but to liberty according to English ideas and on English principles. Abstract liberty, like other mere abstractions, is not to be found.
Liberty inheres in some sensible object; and every nation has formed to
itself some favourite point, which by way of eminence becomes the criterion of their happiness. It happened, you know, Sir, that the great contests for freedom in this country were from the earliest times chiefly upon
the question of taxing. Most of the contests in the ancient commonwealths turned primarily on the right of election of magistrates or on the
balance among the several orders of the state. The question of money was
not with them so immediate. But in England it was otherwise. On this
point of taxes the ablest pens and most eloquent tongues have been exercised, the greatest spirits have acted and suffered. In order to give the
fullest satisfaction concerning the importance of this point, it was not
only necessary for those who in argument defended the excellence of the
English Constitution to insist on this privilege of granting money as a dry
point of fact, and to prove that the right had been acknowledged in ancient parchments and blind usages to reside in a certain body called a
House of Commons. They went much farther: they attempted to prove,
and they succeeded, that in theory it ought to be so, from the particular
nature of the House of Commons as an immediate representative of the
people, whether the old records had delivered this oracle or not. They
took infinite pains to inculcate, as a fundamental principle, that in all
monarchies the people must in effect themselves, mediately or immediately, possess the power of granting their own money, or no shadow of
liberty could subsist. The colonies draw from you, as with their life-blood,
these ideas and principles. Their love of liberty, as with you, fixed and
attached on this specific point of taxing. Liberty might be safe or might be
endangered in twenty other particulars without their being much pleased
or alarmed. Here they felt its pulse; and as they found that beat, they
thought themselves sick or sound. I do not say whether they were right or
wrong in applying your general arguments to their own case. It is not
easy, indeed, to make a monopoly of theorems and corollaries. The fact is
that they did thus apply those general arguments; and your mode of governing them, whether through lenity or indolence, through wisdom or
mistake, confirmed them in the imagination that they, as well as you, had
an interest in these common principles.

They were further confirmed in this pleasing error by the form of their
provincial legislative assemblies. Their governments are popular in an
high degree: some are merely popular; in all the popular representative is
the most weighty; and this share of the people in their ordinary govern-

ment never fails to inspire them with lofty sentiments and with a strong aversion from whatever tends to deprive them of their chief importance.

If anything were wanting to this necessary operation of the form of government, religion would have given it a complete effect. Religion, always a principle of energy, in this new people is no way worn out or impaired; and their mode of professing it is also one main cause of this free spirit. The people are Protestants, and of that kind which is the most adverse to all implicit submission of mind and opinion. This is a persuasion not only favourable to liberty, but built upon it. I do not think, Sir, that the reason of this averseness in the dissenting churches from all that looks like absolute government is so much to be sought in their religious tenets as in their history. Every one knows that the Roman Catholic religion is at least coeval with most of the governments where it prevails; that it has generally gone hand in hand with them, and received great favour and every kind of support from authority. The Church of England too was formed from her cradle under the nursing care of regular government. But the dissenting interests have sprung up in direct opposition to all the ordinary powers of the world, and could justify that opposition only on a strong claim to natural liberty. Their very existence depended on the powerful and unremitted assertion of that claim. All Protestantism, even the most cold and passive, is a sort of dissent. But the religion most prevalent in our northern colonies is a refinement on the principle of resistance: it is the dissidence of dissent and the Protestantism of the Protestant religion. This religion, under a variety of denominations agreeing in nothing but in the communion of the spirit of liberty, is predominant in most of the northern provinces, where the Church of England, notwithstanding its legal rights, is in reality no more than a sort of private sect, not composing most probably the tenth of the people. The colonists left England when this spirit was high, and in the emigrants was the highest of all; and even that stream of foreigners which has been constantly flowing into these colonies has, for the greatest part, been composed of dissenters from the establishments of their several countries, and have brought with them a temper and character far from alien to that of the people with whom they mixed.

Sir, I can perceive by their manner that some gentlemen object to the latitude of this description, because in the southern colonies the Church of England forms a large body and has a regular establishment. It is certainly true. There is, however, a circumstance attending these colonies which, in my opinion, fully counterbalances this difference and makes the spirit of liberty still more high and haughty than in those to the northward. It is, that in Virginia and the Carolinas they have a vast multitude of slaves. Where this is the case in any part of the world, those who are free are by far the most proud and jealous of their freedom. Freedom is to

them not only an enjoyment, but a kind of rank and privilege. Not seeing
there that freedom, as in countries where it is a common blessing and as
broad and general as the air, may be united with much abject toil, with
great misery, with all the exterior of servitude, liberty looks, amongst
them, like something that is more noble and liberal. I do not mean, Sir, to
commend the superior morality of this sentiment, which has at least as
much pride as virtue in it; but I cannot alter the nature of man. The fact
is so; and these people of the southern colonies are much more strongly
and with a higher and more stubborn spirit attached to liberty than those
to the northward. Such were all the ancient commonwealths; such were
our Gothic ancestors; such in our days were the Poles; and such will be all
masters of slaves, who are not slaves themselves. In such a people the
haughtiness of domination combines with the spirit of freedom, fortifies
it, and renders it invincible.

Permit me, Sir, to add another circumstance in our colonies, which
contributes no mean part towards the growth and effect of this untractable spirit: I mean their education. In no country perhaps in the world is
the law so general a study. The profession itself is numerous and powerful, and in most provinces it takes the lead. The greater number of the
deputies sent to the Congress were lawyers. But all who read (and most
do read) endeavour to obtain some smattering in that science. I have been
told by an eminent bookseller that in no branch of his business, after
tracts of popular devotion, were so many books as those on the law exported to the plantations. The colonists have now fallen into the way of
printing them for their own use. I hear that they have sold nearly as many
of Blackstone's *Commentaries* in America as in England. General Gage
marks out this disposition very particularly in a letter on your table. He
states that all the people in his government are lawyers or smatterers in
law, and that in Boston they have been enabled by successful chicane
wholly to evade many parts of one of your capital penal constitutions.
The smartness of debate will say that this knowledge ought to teach them
more clearly the rights of legislature, their obligations to obedience and
the penalties of rebellion. All this is mighty well. But my honourable and
learned friend on the floor, who condescends to mark what I say for ani-
madversion, will disdain that ground. He has heard, as well as I, that
when great honours and great emoluments do not win over this knowledge to the service of the state, it is a formidable adversary to government.
If the spirit be not tamed and broken by these happy methods, it is stubborn and litigious. *Abeunt studia in mores.* This study renders men
acute, inquisitive, dexterous, prompt in attack, ready in defence, full of
resources. In other countries the people, more simple and of a less mercu-
rial cast, judge of an ill principle in government only by an actual grievance; here they anticipate the evil and judge of the pressure of the griev-

ance by the badness of the principle. They augur misgovernment at a distance and snuff the approach of tyranny in every tainted breeze.

The last cause of this disobedient spirit in the colonies is hardly less powerful than the rest, as it is not merely moral, but laid deep in the natural constitution of things. Three thousand miles of ocean lie between you and them. No contrivance can prevent the effect of this distance in weakening government. Seas roll and months pass between the order and the execution; and the want of a speedy explanation of a single point is enough to defeat a whole system. You have, indeed, winged ministers of vengeance, who carry your bolts in their pounces to the remotest verge of the sea. But there a power steps in that limits the arrogance of raging passions and furious elements, and says, "So far shalt thou go, and no farther." Who are you, that you should fret and rage, and bite the chains of Nature? Nothing worse happens to you than does to all nations who have extensive empire; and it happens in all the forms into which empire can be thrown. In large bodies the circulation of power must be less vigorous at the extremities. Nature has said it. The Turk cannot govern Egypt and Arabia and Kurdistan as he governs Thrace; nor has he the same dominion in Crimea and Algiers which he has at Brusa and Smyrna. Despotism itself is obliged to truck and huckster. The sultan gets such obedience as he can. He governs with a loose rein, that he may govern at all; and the whole of the force and vigour of his authority in his centre is derived from a prudent relaxation in all his borders. Spain in her provinces is perhaps not so well obeyed as you are in yours. She complies, too; she submits; she watches times. This is the immutable condition, the eternal law, of extensive and detached empire.

Then, Sir, from these six capital sources: of descent, of form of government, of religion in the northern provinces, of manners in the southern, of education, of the remoteness of situation from the first mover of government—from all these causes a fierce spirit of liberty has grown up. It has grown with the growth of the people in your colonies, and increased with the increase of their wealth: a spirit that unhappily meeting with an exercise of power in England, which, however lawful, is not reconcilable to any ideas of liberty, much less with theirs, has kindled this flame that is ready to consume us.

I do not mean to commend either the spirit in this excess or the moral causes which produce it. Perhaps a more smooth and accommodating spirit of freedom in them would be more acceptable to us. Perhaps ideas of liberty might be desired more reconcilable with an arbitrary and boundless authority. Perhaps we might wish the colonists to be persuaded that their liberty is more secure when held in trust for them by us, as their guardians during a perpetual minority, than with any part of it in their own hands. The question is not whether their spirit deserves praise or blame, but what, in the name of God, shall we do with it? You have before you the object, such as it is, with all its glories, with all its imperfections on its head. You see the magnitude, the importance, the temper, the habits, the disorders. By all these considerations we are strongly urged to determine something concerning it. We are called upon to fix some rule and line for our future conduct, which may give a little stability to our politics and prevent the return of such unhappy deliberations as the present. Every such return will bring the matter before us in a still more untractable form. For what astonishing and incredible things have we not seen already! What monsters have not been generated from this unnatural contention! Whilst every principle of authority and resistance has been pushed, upon both sides, as far as it would go, there is nothing so solid and certain, either in reasoning or in practice, that has not been shaken. Until very lately all authority in America seemed to be nothing but an emanation from yours. Even the popular part of the colony constitution derived all its activity, and its first vital movement, from the pleasure of the crown. We thought, Sir, that the utmost which the discontented colonists could do was to disturb authority; we never dreamt they could of themselves supply it, knowing in general what an operose business it is to establish a government absolutely new. But having for our purposes in this contention resolved that none but an obedient assembly should sit, the humours of the people there, finding all passage through the legal channel stopped, with great violence broke out another way. Some provinces have tried their experiment, as we have tried ours; and theirs has succeeded. They have formed a government sufficient for its purposes, without the bustle of a revolution or the troublesome formality of an election. Evident necessity and tacit consent have done the business in an instant. So well they have done it that Lord Dunmore (the account is among the fragments on your table) tells you that the new institution is infinitely better obeyed than the ancient government ever was in its most fortunate periods. Obedience is what makes government, and not the names by which it is called: not the name of governor, as formerly, or committee, as at present. This new government has originated directly from the people, and was not transmitted through any of the ordinary artificial media of a positive constitution. It was not a manufacture ready formed, and transmitted to them in that condition from England. The evil arising from hence is this: that the colonists having once found the possibility of enjoying the advantages of order in the midst of a struggle for liberty, such struggles will not henceforward seem so terrible to the settled and sober part of mankind as they had appeared before the trial.

Pursuing the same plan of punishing, by the denial of the exercise of government, to still greater lengths, we wholly abrogated the ancient government of Massachusetts. We were confident that the first feeling, if not the very prospect, of anarchy, would instantly enforce a complete submission. The experiment was tried. A new, strange, unexpected face of things appeared. Anarchy is found tolerable. A vast province has now subsisted, and subsisted in a considerable degree of health and vigour, for near a twelvemonth, without governor, without public council, without judges, without executive magistrates. How long it will continue in this state, or what may arise out of this unheard-of situation, how can the wisest of us conjecture? Our late experience has taught us that many of those fundamental principles formerly believed infallible are either not of the importance they were imagined to be, or that we have not at all adverted to some other far more important and far more powerful principles, which entirely overrule those we had considered as omnipotent. I am much against any further experiments which tend to put to the proof any more of these allowed opinions which contribute so much to the public tranquillity. In effect, we suffer as much at home by this loosening of all ties and this concussion of all established opinions, as we do abroad. For, in order to prove that the Americans have no right to their liberties, we are every day endeavouring to subvert the maxims which preserve the whole spirit of our own. To prove that Americans ought not to be free, we are obliged to depreciate the value of freedom itself; and we never seem to gain a paltry advantage over them in debate, without attacking some of those principles, or deriding some of those feelings, for which our ancestors have shed their blood.

But, Sir, in wishing to put an end to pernicious experiments, I do not mean to preclude the fullest inquiry. Far from it. Far from deciding on a sudden or partial view, I would patiently go round and round the subject, and survey it minutely in every possible aspect. Sir, if I were capable of engaging you to an equal attention, I would state that, as far as I am capable of discerning, there are but three ways of proceeding relative to this stubborn spirit which prevails in your colonies and disturbs your government. These are: to change that spirit, as inconvenient, by removing the causes; to prosecute it as criminal; or to comply with it as necessary. I would not be guilty of an imperfect enumeration; I can think of but these three. Another has indeed been started, that of giving up the colonies; but it met so slight a reception that I do not think myself obliged to dwell a great while upon it. It is nothing but a little sally of anger, like the forwardness of peevish children, who, when they cannot get all they would have, are resolved to take nothing.

The first of these plans, to change the spirit, as inconvenient, by removing the causes, I think is the most like a systematic proceeding. It is radical in its principle; but it is attended with great difficulties, some of them little short, as I conceive, of impossibilities. This will appear by examining into the plans which have been proposed.

As the growing population in the colonies is evidently one cause of their resistance, it was last session mentioned in both Houses by men of weight, and received not without applause, that in order to check this evil, it would be proper for the crown to make no further grants of land. But to this scheme there are two objections. The first, that there is already so much unsettled land in private hands as to afford room for an immense future population, although the crown not only withheld its grants, but annihilated its soil. If this be the case, then the only effect of this avarice of desolation, this hoarding of a royal wilderness, would be to raise the value of the possessions in the hands of the great private monopolists, without any adequate check to the growing and alarming mischief of population.

But if you stopped your grants, what would be the consequence? The people would occupy without grants. They have already so occupied in many places. You cannot station garrisons in every part of these deserts. If you drive the people from one place, they will carry on their annual tillage and remove with their flocks and herds to another. Many of the people in the back settlements are already little attached to particular situations. Already they have topped the Appalachian Mountains. From thence they behold before them an immense plain, one vast, rich, level meadow, a square of five hundred miles. Over this they would wander without a possibility of restraint; they would change their manners with the habits of their life; would soon forget a government by which they were disowned; would become hordes of English Tartars, and pouring down upon your unfortified frontiers a fierce and irresistible cavalry, become masters of your governors and your counsellors, your collectors and comptrollers, and of all the slaves that adhered to them. Such would, and in no long time must, be the effect of attempting to forbid as a crime, and to suppress as an evil, the command and blessing of Providence, "Increase and multiply." Such would be the happy result of an endeavour to keep as a lair of wild beasts that earth which God, by an express charter, has given to the children of men. Far different and surely much wiser has been our policy hitherto. Hitherto we have invited our people, by every kind of bounty, to fixed establishments. We have invited the husbandman to look to authority for his title. We have taught him piously to believe in the mysterious virtue of wax and parchment. We have thrown each tract of land, as it was peopled, into districts, that the ruling power should never be wholly out of sight. We have settled as we could, and we have carefully attended every settlement with government.

Adhering, Sir, as I do, to this policy, as well as for the reasons I have just given, I think this new project of hedging-in population to be neither prudent nor practicable.

To impoverish the colonies in general, and in particular to arrest the noble course of their marine enterprises, would be a more easy task. I freely confess it. We have shown a disposition to a system of this kind,—a disposition even to continue the restraint after the offence, looking on ourselves as rivals to our colonies, and persuaded that of course we must gain all that they shall lose. Much mischief we may certainly do. The power inadequate to all other things is often more than sufficient for this. I do not look on the direct and immediate power of the colonies to resist our violence as very formidable. In this, however, I may be mistaken. But when I consider that we have colonies for no purpose but to be serviceable to us, it seems to my poor understanding a little preposterous to make them unserviceable in order to keep them obedient. It is, in truth, nothing more than the old and, as I thought, exploded problem of tyranny, which proposes to beggar its subjects into submission. But remember, when you have completed your system of impoverishment, that Nature still proceeds in her ordinary course; that discontent will increase with misery; and that there are critical moments in the fortune of all states, when they who are too weak to contribute to your prosperity may be strong enough to complete your ruin. *Spoliatis arma supersunt.*

The temper and character which prevail in our colonies are, I am afraid, unalterable by any human art. We cannot, I fear, falsify the pedigree of this fierce people and persuade them that they are not sprung from a nation in whose veins the blood of freedom circulates. The language in which they would hear you tell them this tale would detect the imposition; your speech would betray you. An Englishman is the unfittest person on earth to argue another Englishman into slavery.

I think it is nearly as little in our power to change their republican religion as their free descent, or to substitute the Roman Catholic as a penalty, or the Church of England as an improvement. The mode of inquisition and dragooning is going out of fashion in the Old World, and I should not confide much to their efficacy in the New. The education of the Americans is also on the same unalterable bottom with their religion. You cannot persuade them to burn their books of curious science, to banish their lawyers from their courts of laws, or to quench the lights of their assemblies by refusing to choose those persons who are best read in their privileges. It would be no less impracticable to think of wholly annihilating the popular assemblies in which these lawyers sit. The army, by which we must govern in their place, would be far more chargeable to us; not quite so effectual; and perhaps in the end full as difficult to be kept in obedience.

With regard to the high aristocratic spirit of Virginia and the southern colonies, it has been proposed, I know, to reduce it by declaring a general enfranchisement of their slaves. This project has had its advocates and panegyrists; yet I never could argue myself into any opinion of it.

Slaves are often much attached to their masters. A general wild offer of liberty would not always be accepted. History furnishes few instances of it. It is sometimes as hard to persuade slaves to be free as it is to compel freemen to be slaves; and in this auspicious scheme we should have both these pleasing tasks on our hands at once. But when we talk of enfranchisement, do we not perceive that the American master may enfranchise too, and arm servile hands in defence of freedom?—a measure to which other people have had recourse more than once, and not without success, in a desperate situation of their affairs.

Slaves as these unfortunate black people are, and dull as all men are from slavery, must they not a little suspect the offer of freedom from that very nation which has sold them to their present masters? from that nation, one of whose causes of quarrel with those masters is their refusal to deal any more in that inhuman traffic? An offer of freedom from England would come rather oddly, shipped to them in an African vessel, which is refused an entry into the ports of Virginia or Carolina, with a cargo of three hundred Angola negroes. It would be curious to see the Guinea captain attempting at the same instant to publish his proclamation of liberty and to advertise his sale of slaves.

But let us suppose all these moral difficulties got over. The ocean remains. You cannot pump this dry; and as long as it continues in its present bed, so long all the causes which weaken authority by distance will continue.

> Ye gods, annihilate but space and time,
> And make two lovers happy!

was a pious and passionate prayer, but just as reasonable as many of the serious wishes of very grave and solemn politicians.

If then, Sir, it seems almost desperate to think of any alterative course for changing the moral causes (and not quite easy to remove the natural) which produce prejudices irreconcilable to the late exercise of our authority, but that the spirit infallibly will continue; and continuing, will produce such effects as now embarrass us,—the second mode under consideration is to prosecute that spirit in its overt acts as *criminal*.

At this proposition I must pause a moment. The thing seems a great deal too big for my ideas of jurisprudence. It should seem, to my way of conceiving such matters, that there is a very wide difference in reason and policy between the mode of proceeding on the irregular conduct of scattered individuals, or even of bands of men, who disturb order within the state, and the civil dissensions which may, from time to time, on great questions, agitate the several communities which compose a great empire. It looks to me to be narrow and pedantic to apply the ordinary ideas of criminal justice to this great public contest. I do not know the method of drawing up an indictment against a whole people. I cannot insult and ridicule the feelings of millions of my fellow-creatures, as Sir Edward Coke insulted one excellent individual (Sir Walter Raleigh) at the bar. I am not ripe to pass sentence on the gravest public bodies, entrusted with magistracies of great authority and dignity, and charged with the safety of their fellow-citizens, upon the very same title that I am. I really think that for wise men this is not judicious; for sober men, not decent; for minds tinctured with humanity, not mild and merciful.

Perhaps, Sir, I am mistaken in my idea of an empire as distinguished from a single state or kingdom. But my idea of it is this: that an empire is the aggregate of many states under one common head, whether this head be a monarch or a presiding republic. It does in such constitutions frequently happen (and nothing but the dismal, cold, dead uniformity of servitude can prevent its happening) that the subordinate parts have many local privileges and immunities. Between these privileges and the supreme common authority the line may be extremely nice. Of course disputes—often, too, very bitter disputes—and much ill blood will arise. But though every privilege is an exemption (in the case) from the ordinary exercise of the supreme authority, it is no denial of it. The claim of a privilege seems rather, *ex vi termini,* to imply a superior power; for to talk of the privileges of a state or of a person who has no superior is hardly any better than speaking nonsense. Now in such unfortunate quarrels among the component parts of a great political union of communities, I can scarcely conceive anything more completely imprudent than for the head of the empire to insist that, if any privilege is pleaded against his will or his acts, [that] his whole authority is denied; instantly to proclaim rebellion, to beat to arms, and to put the offending provinces under the ban. Will not this, Sir, very soon teach the provinces to make no distinction on their part? Will it not teach them that the government against which a claim of liberty is tantamount to high treason is a government to which submission is equivalent to slavery? It may not always be quite convenient to impress dependent communities with such an idea.

We are, indeed, in all disputes with the colonies, by the necessity of things, the judge. It is true, Sir. But I confess that the character of judge in my own cause is a thing that frightens me. Instead of filling me with pride, I am exceedingly humbled by it. I cannot proceed with a stern, assured, judicial confidence, until I find myself in something more like a judicial character. I must have these hesitations as long as I am compelled to recollect that, in my little reading upon such contests as these, the sense of mankind has at least as often decided against the superior as the subordinate power. Sir, let me add, too, that the opinion of my having some abstract right in my favour would not put me much at my ease in passing sentence, unless I could be sure that there were no rights which, in their exercise under certain circumstances, were not the most odious of all wrongs and the most vexatious of all injustice. Sir, these considerations have great weight with me, when I find things so circumstanced that I see the same party at once a civil litigant against me in point of right and a culprit before me, while I sit as a criminal judge on acts of his, whose moral quality is to be decided upon the merits of that very litigation. Men are every now and then put, by the complexity of human affairs, into strange situations; but justice is the same, let the judge be in what situation he will.

There is, Sir, also a circumstance which convinces me that this mode of criminal proceeding is not (at least in the present stage of our contest) altogether expedient; which is nothing less than the conduct of those very persons who have seemed to adopt that mode, by lately declaring a rebellion in Massachusetts Bay, as they had formerly addressed to have traitors brought hither, under an act of Henry the Eighth, for trial. For though rebellion is declared, it is not proceeded against as such; nor have any steps been taken towards the apprehension or conviction of any individual offender, either on our late or our former address; but modes of public coercion have been adopted, and such as have much more resemblance to a sort of qualified hostility towards an independent power than the punishment of rebellious subjects. All this seems rather inconsistent; but it shows how difficult it is to apply these juridical ideas to our present case.

In this situation, let us seriously and coolly ponder. What is it we have got by all our menaces, which have been many and ferocious? What advantage have we derived from the penal laws we have passed, and which, for the time, have been severe and numerous? What advances have we made towards our object, by the sending of a force which, by land and sea, is no contemptible strength? Has the disorder abated? Nothing less. When I see things in this situation, after such confident hopes, bold promises and active exertions, I cannot for my life avoid a suspicion that the plan itself is not correctly right.

If, then, the removal of the causes of this spirit of American liberty be for the greater part, or rather entirely, impracticable; if the ideas of criminal process be inapplicable, or, if applicable, are in the highest degree inexpedient; what way yet remains? No way is open but the third and last—to comply with the American spirit as necessary; or, if you please, to submit to it as a necessary evil.

If we adopt this mode, if we mean to conciliate and concede, let us see of what nature the concession ought to be. To ascertain the nature of our concession, we must look at their complaint. The colonies complain that they have not the characteristic mark and seal of British freedom. They complain that they are taxed in a Parliament in which they are not represented. If you mean to satisfy them at all, you must satisfy them with regard to this complaint. If you mean to please any people, you must give them the boon which they ask—not what you may think better for them, but of a kind totally different. Such an act may be a wise regulation, but it is no concession; whereas our present theme is the mode of giving satisfaction.

Sir, I think you must perceive that I am resolved this day to have nothing at all to do with the question of the right of taxation. Some gentlemen startle, but it is true; I put it totally out of the question. It is less than nothing in my consideration. I do not indeed wonder, nor will you, Sir, that gentlemen of profound learning are fond of displaying it on this profound subject. But my consideration is narrow, confined, and wholly limited to the policy of the question. I do not examine whether the giving away a man's money be a power excepted and reserved out of the general trust of government, and how far all mankind, in all forms of polity, are entitled to an exercise of that right by the charter of Nature; or whether, on the contrary, a right of taxation is necessarily involved in the general principle of legislation and inseparable from the ordinary supreme power. These are deep questions, where great names militate against each other, where reason is perplexed, and an appeal to authorities only thickens the confusion: for high and reverend authorities lift up their heads on both sides, and there is no sure footing in the middle. This point is the great

> Serbonian bog,
> Betwixt Damiata and Mount Casius old,
> Where armies whole have sunk.

I do not intend to be overwhelmed in that bog, though in such respectable company. The question with me is, not whether you have a right to render your people miserable, but whether it is not your interest to make them happy. It is not what a lawyer tells me I *may* do, but what humanity, reason and justice tell me I *ought* to do. Is a politic act the worse for being a generous one? Is no concession proper but that which is made from your want of right to keep what you grant? Or does it lessen the grace or dignity of relaxing in the exercise of an odious claim, because you have your evidence-room full of titles and your magazines stuffed with arms to enforce them? What signify all those titles and all those arms? Of what avail are they, when the reason of the thing tells me that the assertion of my title is the loss of my suit, and that I could do nothing but wound myself by the use of my own weapons?

Such is steadfastly my opinion of the absolute necessity of keeping up the concord of this empire by a unity of spirit, though in a diversity of operations, that if I were sure the colonists had at their leaving this country sealed a regular compact of servitude, that they had solemnly abjured all the rights of citizens, that they had made a vow to renounce all ideas of liberty for them and their posterity to all generations: yet I should hold myself obliged to conform to the temper I found universally prevalent in my own day, and to govern two million of men, impatient of servitude, on the principles of freedom. I am not determining a point of law: I am restoring tranquillity; and the general character and situation of a people must determine what sort of government is fitted for them. That point nothing else can or ought to determine.

My idea, therefore, without considering whether we yield as matter of right or grant as matter of favor, is *to admit the people of our colonies into an interest in the Constitution;* and by recording that admission in the journals of Parliament, to give them as strong an assurance as the nature of the thing will admit, that we mean forever to adhere to that solemn declaration of systematic indulgence.

Some years ago, the repeal of a revenue act, upon its understood principle, might have served to show that we intended an unconditional abatement of the exercise of a taxing power. Such a measure was then sufficient to remove all suspicion and to give perfect content. But unfortunate events since that time may make something further necessary; and not more necessary for the satisfaction of the colonies than for the dignity and consistency of our own future proceedings.

I have taken a very incorrect measure of the disposition of the House, if this proposal in itself would be received with dislike. I think, Sir, we have few American financiers. But our misfortune is, we are too acute; we are too exquisite in our conjectures of the future, for men oppressed with such great and present evils. The more moderate among the opposers of parliamentary concession freely confess that they hope no good from taxation; but they apprehend the colonists have further views, and if this point were conceded, they would instantly attack the trade laws. These gentlemen are convinced that this was the intention from the beginning, and the quarrel of the Americans with taxation was no more than a cloak and cover to this design. Such has been the language, even of a gentleman of real moderation and of a natural temper well adjusted to fair and equal government. I am, however, Sir, not a little surprised at this kind of discourse whenever I hear it; and I am the more surprised on account of the arguments which I constantly find in company with it, and which are often urged from the same mouths and on the same day.

For instance, when we allege that it is against reason to tax a people under so many restraints in trade as the Americans, the noble lord in the blue ribbon shall tell you that the restraints on trade are futile and useless, of no advantage to us, and of no burden to those on whom they are imposed; that the trade to America is not secured by the Acts of Navigation, but by the natural and irresistible advantage of a commercial preference.

Such is the merit of the trade laws in this posture of the debate. But when strong internal circumstances are urged against the taxes; when the scheme is dissected; when experience and the nature of things are brought to prove, and do prove, the utter impossibility of obtaining an effective revenue from the colonies;—when these things are pressed, or rather press themselves, so as to drive the advocates of colony taxes to a clear admission of the futility of the scheme; then, Sir, the sleeping trade laws revive from their trance, and this useless taxation is to be kept sacred, not for its own sake, but as a counterguard and security of the laws of trade.

Then, Sir, you keep up revenue laws which are mischievous in order to preserve trade laws that are useless. Such is the wisdom of our plan in both its members. They are separately given up as of no value; and yet one is always to be defended for the sake of the other. But I cannot agree with the noble lord, nor with the pamphlet from whence he seems to have borrowed these ideas, concerning the inutility of the trade laws; for without idolizing them, I am sure they are still in many ways of great use to us, and in former times they have been of the greatest. They do confine, and they do greatly narrow, the market for the Americans. But my perfect conviction of this does not help me in the least to discern how the revenue laws form any security whatsoever to the commercial regulations; or that these commercial regulations are the true ground of the quarrel; or that the giving way in any one instance of authority is to lose all that may remain unconceded.

One fact is clear and indisputable: the public and avowed origin of this quarrel was on taxation. This quarrel has indeed brought on new disputes on new questions; but certainly the least bitter and the fewest of all on the trade laws. To judge which of the two be the real, radical cause of quarrel, we have to see whether the commercial dispute did, in order of time, precede the dispute on taxation. There is not a shadow of evidence for it. Next, to enable us to judge whether at this moment a dislike to the trade laws be the real cause of quarrel, it is absolutely necessary to put the taxes out of the question by a repeal. See how the Americans act in this position, and then you will be able to discern correctly what is the true object of the controversy, or whether any controversy at all will remain. Unless you consent to remove this cause of difference, it is impossible with decency to assert that the dispute is not upon what it is avowed to be. And I would, Sir, recommend to your serious consideration, whether it be prudent to form a rule for punishing people, not on their own acts, but on your conjectures. Surely it is preposterous at the very best. It is not justifying your anger by their misconduct, but it is converting your ill-will into their delinquency.

But the colonies will go further. Alas! alas! when will this speculating against fact and reason end? What will quiet these panic fears which we entertain of the hostile effect of a conciliatory conduct? It is true that no case can exist in which it is proper for the sovereign to accede to the desires of his discontented subjects? Is there anything peculiar in this case to make a rule for itself? Is all authority of course lost, when it is not pushed to the extreme? Is it a certain maxim that the fewer causes of dissatisfaction are left by government, the more the subject will be inclined to resist and rebel?

All these objections being in fact no more than suspicions, conjectures, divinations, formed in defiance of fact and experience, they did not, Sir, discourage me from entertaining the idea of a conciliatory concession, founded on the principles which I have just stated.

In forming a plan for this purpose, I endeavoured to put myself in that frame of mind which was the most natural and the most reasonable, and which was certainly the most probable means of securing me from all error. I set out with a perfect distrust of my own abilities, a total renunciation of every speculation of my own, and with a profound reverence for the wisdom of our ancestors, who have left us the inheritance of so happy a constitution and so flourishing an empire, and, what is a thousand times more valuable, the treasury of the maxims and principles which formed the one and obtained the other.

During the reigns of the kings of Spain of the Austrian family, whenever they were at a loss in the Spanish councils, it was common for their statesmen to say that they ought to consult the genius of Philip the Second. The genius of Philip the Second might mislead them; and the issue of their affairs showed that they had not chosen the most perfect standard. But, Sir, I am sure that I shall not be misled when, in a case of constitutional difficulty, I consult the genius of the English Constitution. Consulting at that oracle (it was with all due humility and piety), I found four capital examples in a similar case before me: those of Ireland, Wales, Chester and Durham.

Ireland, before the English conquest, though never governed by a despotic power, had no Parliament. How far the English Parliament itself was at that time modelled according to the present form is disputed among antiquarians. But we have all the reason in the world to be assured that a form of Parliament such as England then enjoyed she instantly communicated to Ireland; and we are equally sure that almost every successive improvement in constitutional liberty, as fast as it was made here, was transmitted thither. The feudal baronage and the feudal knighthood, the roots of our primitive constitution, were early transplanted into that soil, and grew and flourished there. Magna Charta, if it did not give us originally a House of Commons, gave us at least a House of Commons of weight and consequence. But your ancestors did not churlishly sit down alone to the feast of Magna Charta. Ireland was made immediately a partaker. This benefit of English laws and liberties, I confess, was not at first extended to *all* Ireland. Mark the consequence. English authority and English liberties had exactly the same boundaries. Your standard could never be advanced an inch before your privileges. Sir John Davies shows beyond a doubt that the refusal of a general communication of these rights was the true cause why Ireland was five hundred years in subduing; and after the vain projects of a military government, attempted in the reign of Queen Elizabeth, it was soon discovered that nothing could make that country English, in civility and allegiance, but your laws and your forms of legislature. It was not English arms, but the English Constitution, that conquered Ireland. From that time Ireland has ever had a general Parliament, as she had before a partial Parliament. You changed the people, you altered the religion, but you never touched the form or the vital substance of free government in that kingdom. You deposed kings; you restored them; you altered the succession to theirs as well as to your own crown; but you never altered their constitution, the principle of which was respected by usurpation, restored with the restoration of monarchy, and established, I trust, forever by the glorious Revolution. This has made Ireland the great and flourishing kingdom that it is: and from a disgrace and a burden intolerable to this nation, has rendered her a principal part of her strength and ornament. This country cannot be said to have ever formally taxed her. The irregular things done in the confusion of mighty troubles and on the hinge of great revolutions, even if all were done that is said to have been done, form no example. If they have any effect in argument, they make an exception to prove the rule. None of your own liberties could stand a moment if the casual deviations from them at such times were suffered to be used as proofs of their nullity. By the lucrative amount of such casual breaches in the Constitution, judge what the stated and fixed rule of supply has been in that kingdom. Your Irish pensioners would starve if they had no other fund to live on than taxes granted by English authority. Turn your eyes to those popular grants from whence all our great supplies are come, and learn to respect that only source of public wealth in the British Empire.

My next example is Wales. This country was said to be reduced by Henry the Third. It was said more truly to be so by Edward the First. But though then conquered, it was not looked upon as any part of the realm of England. Its old constitution, whatever that might have been, was destroyed, and no good one was substituted in its place. The care of that tract was put into the hands of Lords Marchers—a form of government of a very singular kind, a strange, heterogeneous monster, something between hostility and government: perhaps it has a sort of resemblance, according to the modes of those times, to that of commander-in-chief at present, to whom all civil power is granted as secondary. The manners of the Welsh nation followed the genius of the government: the people were ferocious, restive, savage, and uncultivated, sometimes composed, never pacified. Wales, within itself, was in perpetual disorder, and it kept the frontier of England in perpetual alarm. Benefits from it to the state there were none. Wales was only known to England by incursion and invasion.

Sir, during that state of things Parliament was not idle. They attempted to subdue the fierce spirit of the Welsh by all sorts of rigourous laws. They prohibited by statute the sending all sorts of arms into Wales, as you prohibit by proclamation (with something more of doubt on the legality) the sending arms to America. They disarmed the Welsh by statute, as you attempted (but still with more question on the legality) to disarm New England by an instruction. They made an act to drag offenders from Wales into England for trial, as you have done (but with more hardship) with regard to America. By another act, where one of the parties was an Englishman, they prevented the Welsh from the use of fairs and markets, as you do the Americans from fisheries and foreign ports. In short, when the statute-book was not quite so much swelled as it is now, you find no less than fifteen acts of penal regulation on the subject of Wales.

Here we rub our hands—A fine body of precedents for the authority of Parliament and the use of it!—I admit it fully; and pray add likewise to these precedents, that all the while Wales rid this kingdom like an *incubus;* that it was an unprofitable and oppressive burden; and that an Englishman travelling in that country could not go six yards from the high-road without being murdered.

The march of the human mind is slow. Sir, it was not until after two hundred years discovered that by an eternal law Providence had decreed vexation to violence, and poverty to rapine. Your ancestors did, however, at length open their eyes to the ill-husbandry of injustice. They found that the tyranny of a free people could of all tyrannies the least be endured, and that laws made against an whole nation were not the most effectual methods for securing its obedience. Accordingly, in the twenty-seventh year of Henry the Eighth, the course was entirely altered. With a preamble stating the entire and perfect rights of the crown of England, it gave to the Welsh all the rights and privileges of English subjects. A political order was established; the military power gave way to the civil; the marches were turned into counties. But that a nation should have a right to English liberties, and yet no share at all in the fundamental security of these liberties,—the grant of their own property,—seemed a thing so incongruous that eight years after—this is, in the thirty-fifth of that reign—a complete and not ill-proportioned representation by counties and boroughs was bestowed upon Wales by act of Parliament. From that moment, as by a charm, the tumults subsided; obedience was restored; peace, order and civilisation followed in the train of liberty. When the day-star of the English Constitution had arisen in their hearts, all was harmony within and without:—

> —Simul alba nautis
> Stella refulsit,
> Defluit saxis agitatus humor;
> Concidunt venti, fugiuntque nubes,
> Et minax (quod sic voluere) ponto
> Unda recumbit.

The very same year the County Palatine of Chester received the same relief from its oppressions and the same remedy to its disorders. Before this time Chester was little less distempered than Wales. The inhabitants, without rights themselves, were the fittest to destroy the rights of others; and from thence Richard the Second drew the standing army of archers with which for a time he oppressed England. The people of Chester applied to Parliament in a petition penned as I shall read to you:—

To the King our Sovereign Lord, in most humble wise shewen unto your most excellent Majesty the inhabitants of your Grace's County Palatine of Chester: (1) That where the said County Palatine of Chester is and hath been always hitherto exempt, excluded and separated out and from your high court of Parliament, to have any knights and burgesses within the said court; by reason whereof the said inhabitants have hitherto sustained manifold disherisons, losses and damages, as well in their lands, goods and bodies, as in the good, civil and politic governancy and maintenance of the commonwealth of their said country. (2) And forasmuch as the said inhabitants have always hitherto been bound by the acts and statutes made and ordained by your said Highness and your most noble progenitors, by authority of the said court, as far forth as other counties, cities and boroughs have been, that have had their knights and burgesses within your said court of Parliament, and yet have had neither knight ne burgess there for the said County Palatine; the said inhabitants, for lack therof, have been oftentimes touched and grieved with acts and statutes made within the said court, as well derogatory unto the most ancient jurisdictions, liberties and privileges of your said County Palatine, as prejudicial unto the commonwealth, quietness, rest and peace of your Grace's most bounden subjects inhabiting within the same.

What did Parliament with this audacious address? Reject it as a libel? Treat it as an affront to government? Spurn it as a derogation from the rights of legislature? Did they toss it over the table? Did they burn it by the hands of the common hangman? They took the petition of grievance, all rugged as it was, without softening or temperament, unpurged of the original bitterness and indignation of complaint; they made it the very preamble to their act of redress, and consecrated its principle to all ages in the sanctuary of legislation.

Here is my third example. It was attended with the success of the two former. Chester, civilised as well as Wales, has demonstrated that freedom, and not servitude, is the cure for anarchy; as religion, and not atheism, is the true remedy for superstition. Sir, this pattern of Chester was followed in the reign of Charles the Second with regard to the County Palatine of Durham, which is my fourth example. This county had long lain out of the pale of free legislation. So scrupulously was the example of Chester followed, that the style of the preamble is nearly the same with that of the Chester act; and without affecting the abstract extent of the authority of Parliament, it recognises the equity of not suffering any considerable district in which the British subjects may act as a body, to be taxed without their own voice in the grant.

Now if the doctrines of policy contained in these preambles and the force of these examples in the acts of Parliaments avail anything, what can be said against applying them with regard to America? Are not the people of America as much Englishmen as the Welsh? The preamble of the act of Henry the Eighth says the Welsh speak a language no way resembling that of His Majesty's English subjects. Are the Americans not as numerous? If we may trust the learned and accurate Judge Barrington's account of North Wales, and take that as a standard to measure the rest, there is no comparison. The people cannot amount to above 200,000, —not a tenth part of the number in the colonies. Is America in rebellion? Wales was hardly ever free from it. Have you attempted to govern America by penal statutes? You made fifteen for Wales. But your legislative authority is perfect with regard to America. Was it less perfect in Wales, Chester, and Durham? But America is virtually represented. What! does the electric force of virtual representation more easily pass over the Atlantic than pervade Wales, which lies in your neighborhood? or than Chester and Durham, surrounded by abundance of representation that is actual and palpable? But, Sir, your ancestors thought this sort of virtual representation, however ample, to be totally insufficient for the freedom of the inhabitants of territories that are so near and comparatively so inconsiderable. How then can I think it sufficient for those which are infinitely greater and infinitely more remote?

You will now, Sir, perhaps imagine that I am on the point of proposing to you a scheme for a representation of the colonies in Parliament. Perhaps I might be inclined to entertain some such thought; but a great flood stops me in my course. *Opposuit natura*—I cannot remove the eternal barriers of the creation. The thing, in that mode, I do not know to be possible. As I meddle with no theory, I do not absolutely assert the practicability of such a representation: but I do not see my way to it; and those who have been more confident have not been more successful. However, the arm of public benevolence is not shortened, and there are often several means to the same end. What Nature has disjoined in one way Wisdom may unite in another. When we cannot give the benefit as we would wish, let us not refuse it altogether. If we cannot give the principal, let us find a substitute. But how? Where? What substitute?

Fortunately I am not obliged for the ways and means of this substitute to tax my own unproductive invention. I am not even obliged to go to the rich treasury of the fertile framers of imaginary commonwealths; not to the *Republic* of Plato, not to the *Utopia* of More, not to the *Oceana* of Harrington. It is before me; it is at my feet,—

> And the rude swain
> Treads daily on it with his clouted shoon.

I only wish you to recognise, for the theory, the ancient constitutional policy of this kingdom with regard to representation, as that policy has been declared in acts of Parliament; and as to the practice, to return to that mode which a uniform experience has marked out to you as best, and in which you walked with security, advantage and honour until the year 1763.

My resolutions, therefore, mean to establish the equity and justice of a taxation of America by *grant,* and not by *imposition;* to mark the *legal competency* of the colony assemblies for the support of their government in peace and for public aids in time of war; to acknowledge that this legal competency has had *a dutiful and beneficial exercise,* and that experience has shown the *benefit of their grants* and the *futility of parliamentary taxation as a method of supply*.

These solid truths compose six fundamental propositions. There are three more resolutions corollary to these. If you admit the first set, you can hardly reject the others. But if you admit the first, I shall be far from solicitous whether you accept or refuse the last. I think these six massive pillars will be of strength sufficient to support the temple of British concord. I have no more doubt than I entertain of my existence that, if you admitted these, you would command an immediate peace, and, with but tolerable future management, a lasting obedience in America. I am not arrogant in this confident assurance. The propositions are all mere matters of fact; and if they are such facts as draw irresistible conclusions even in the stating, this is the power of truth, and not any management of mine.

Sir, I shall open the whole plan to you, together with such observations on the motions as may tend to illustrate them where they may want explanation. The first is a resolution,—

That the colonies and plantations of Great Britain in North America, consisting of fourteen separate governments, and containing two millions and upwards of free inhabitants, have not had the liberty and privilege of electing and sending any knights and burgesses, or others, to represent them in the high court of Parliament.

This is a plain matter of fact, necessary to be laid down, and (excepting the description) it is laid down in the language of the constitution; it is taken nearly *verbatim* from acts of Parliament.

The second is like unto the first,—

That the said colonies and plantations have been liable to, and bounden by, several subsidies, payments, rates and taxes, given and granted by Parliament, though the said colonies and plantations have not their knights and burgesses in the said high court of Parliament, of their own election, to represent the condition of their country; by lack whereof they have been oftentimes touched and grieved by subsidies given, granted and assented to, in the said court, in a manner prejudicial to the commonwealth, quietness, rest and peace of the subjects inhabiting within the same.

Is this description too hot or too cold, too strong or too weak? Does it arrogate too much to the supreme legislature? Does it lean too much to the claims of the people? If it runs into any of these errors, the fault is not mine. It is the language of your own ancient acts of Parliament:—

> Non meus hic sermo, sed quae praecepit Ofellaeus,
> Rusticus, abnormis sapiens.

It is the genuine produce of the ancient, rustic, manly, home-bred sense of this country,—I did not dare to rub off a particle of the venerable rust that rather adorns and preserves, than destroys, the metal. It would be a profanation to touch with a tool the stones which construct the sacred altar of peace. I would not violate with modern polish the ingenuous and noble roughness of these truly constitutional materials. Above all things, I was resolved not to be guilty of tampering,—the odious vice of restless and unstable minds. I put my foot in the tracks of our forefathers, where I can neither wander nor stumble. Determining to fix articles of peace, I was resolved not to be wise beyond what was written; I was resolved to use nothing else than the form of sound words, to let others abound in their own sense, and carefully to abstain from all expressions of my own. What the law has said, I say. In all things else I am silent. I have no organ but for her words. This, if it be not ingenious, I am sure is safe.

There are indeed words expressive of grievance in this second resolution, which those who are resolved always to be in the right will deny to contain matter of fact, as applied to the present case, although Parliament thought them true with regard to the counties of Chester and Durham. They will deny that the Americans were ever "touched and grieved" with the taxes. If they consider nothing in taxes but their weight as pecuniary impositions, there might be some pretence for this denial. But men may be sorely touched and deeply grieved in their privileges as well as in their purses. Men may lose little in property by the act which takes away all their freedom. When a man is robbed of a trifle on the highway, it is not the twopence lost that constitutes the capital outrage. This is not confined to privileges. Even ancient indulgences withdrawn, without offence on the part of those who enjoyed such favors, operate as grievances. But were the Americans then not touched and grieved by the taxes, in some measure, merely as taxes? If so, why were they almost all either wholly repealed or exceedingly reduced? Were they not touched and grieved even by the regulating duties of the sixth of George the Second? Else why were the duties first reduced to one-third in 1764, and afterwards to a third of that third in the year 1766? Were they not touched and grieved by the Stamp Act? I shall say they were, until that tax is revived. Were they not touched and grieved by the duties of 1767, which were likewise repealed, and which Lord Hillsborough tells you (for the ministry) were laid contrary to the true principle of commerce? Is not the assurance given by that noble person to the colonies of a resolution to lay no more taxes on them, an admission that taxes would touch and grieve them? Is not the resolution of the noble lord in the blue ribbon, now standing on your journals, the strongest of all proofs that parliamentary subsidies really touched and grieved them? Else why all these changes, modifications, repeals, assurances and resolutions?

The next proposition is,—

That, from the distance of the said colonies and from other circumstances, no method hath hitherto been devised for procuring a representation in Parliament for the said colonies.

This is an assertion of a fact. I go no further on the paper, though in my private judgment a useful representation is impossible. I am sure it is not desired by them; nor ought it, perhaps, by us: but I abstain from opinions.

The fourth resolution is,—

That each of the said colonies hath within itself a body, chosen in part or in the whole by the freemen, freeholders or other free inhabitants thereof, commonly called the general assembly, or general court, with powers legally to raise, levy and assess, according to the several usages of such colonies, duties and taxes towards defraying all sorts of public services.

This competence in the colony assemblies is certain. It is proved by the whole tenor of their acts of supply in all the assemblies, in which the constant style of granting is, "An aid to His Majesty"; and acts granting to the crown have regularly for near a century passed the public offices without dispute. Those who have been pleased paradoxically to deny this right, holding that none but the British Parliament can grant to the crown, are wished to look to what is done, not only in the colonies, but in Ireland, in one uniform, unbroken tenor every session. Sir, I am surprised that this doctrine should come from some of the law servants of the crown. I say that if the crown could be responsible, His Majesty—but certainly the ministers, and even these law officers themselves through whose hands the acts past, biennially in Ireland or annually in the colonies, are in an habitual course of committing impeachable offences. What habitual offenders have been all presidents of the council, all secretaries of state, all first lords of trade, all attorneys and all solicitors-general! However, they are safe, as no one impeaches them; and there is no ground of charge against them, except in their own unfounded theories.

The fifth resolution is also a resolution of fact,—

That the said general assemblies, general courts, or other bodies legally qualified as aforesaid, have at sundry times freely granted several large subsidies and public aids for His Majesty's service, according to their abilities, when required thereto by letter from one of His Majesty's principal secretaries of state; and that their right to grant the same and their cheerfulness and sufficiency in the said grants have been at sundry times acknowledged by Parliament.

To say nothing of their great expenses in the Indian wars, and not to take their exertion in foreign ones so high as the supplies in the year 1695, not to go back to their public contributions in the year 1710, I shall begin to travel only where the journals give me light,—resolving to deal in nothing but fact authenticated by parliamentary record, and to build myself wholly on that solid basis.

On the 4th of April, 1748, a committee of this House came to the following resolution:

Resolved, That it is the opinion of this committee *that it is just and reasonable* that the several provinces and colonies of Massachusetts Bay, New Hampshire, Connecticut and Rhode Island, be reimbursed the expenses they have been at in taking and securing to the crown of Great Britain the island of Cape Breton and its dependencies.

These expenses were immense for such colonies. They were above £200,000 sterling: money first raised and advanced on their public credit.

On the 28th of January, 1756, a message from the king came to us to this effect:

His Majesty, being sensible of the zeal and vigour with which his faithful subjects of certain colonies in North America have exerted themselves in defence of His Majesty's just rights and possessions, recommends it to this House to take the same into their consideration, and to enable His Majesty to give them such assistance as may be a *proper reward and encouragement.*

On the 3d of February, 1756, the House came to a suitable resolution, expressed in words nearly the same as those of the message, but with the further addition that the money then voted was as an *encouragement* to the colonies to exert themselves with vigour. It will not be necessary to go through all the testimonies which your own records have given to the truth of my resolutions. I will only refer you to the places in the journals:

VOL. XXVII. 16th and 19th May, 1757.

VOL. XXVIII. June 1st, 1758; April 26th and 30th, 1759; March 26th and 31st, and April 28th, 1760; January 9th and 20th, 1761.

VOL. XXIX. January 22d and 26th, 1762; March 14th and 17th, 1763.

Sir, here is the repeated acknowledgment of Parliament that the colonies not only gave, but gave to satiety. This nation has formally acknowledged two things: first, that the colonies had gone beyond their abilities, Parliament having thought it necessary to reimburse them; secondly, that they had acted legally and laudably in their grants of money and their maintenance of troops, since the compensation is expressly given as reward and encouragement. Reward is not bestowed for acts that are unlawful; and encouragement is not held out to things that deserve reprehension. My resolution therefore does nothing more than collect into one proposition what is scattered through your journals. I give you nothing but your own; and you cannot refuse in the gross what you have so often acknowledged in detail. The admission of this, which will be so honourable to them and to you, will indeed be mortal to all the miserable stories by which the passions of the misguided people have been engaged in an unhappy system. The people heard, indeed, from the beginning of these disputes, one thing continually dinned in their ears,—that reason and justice demanded that the Americans, who paid no taxes, should be compelled to contribute. How did that fact of their paying nothing stand when the taxing system began? When Mr. Grenville began to form his system of American revenue, he stated in this House that the colonies were then in debt two million six hundred thousand pounds sterling money, and was of opinion they would discharge that debt in four years. On this state, those untaxed people were actually subject to the payment of taxes to the amount of six hundred and fifty thousand a year. In fact, however, Mr. Grenville was mistaken. The funds given for sinking the debt did not prove quite so ample as both the colonies and he expected. The calculation was too sanguine; the reduction was not completed till some years after, and at different times in different colonies. However, the taxes after the war continued too great to bear any addition with prudence or propriety; and when the burdens imposed in consequence of former requisitions were discharged, our tone became too high to resort again to requisition. No colony since that time ever has had any requisition whatsoever made to it.

We see the sense of the crown and the sense of Parliament on the productive nature of a *revenue by grant*. Now search the same journals for the produce of the *revenue by imposition*. Where is it? Let us know the volume and the page. What is the gross, what is the net produce? To what service is it applied? How have you appropriated its surplus? What, can none of the many skilful index-makers that we are now employing find any trace of it?. Well, let them and that rest together. But are the journals, which say nothing of the revenue, as silent on the discontent? Oh, no! a child may find it. It is the melancholy burden and blot of every page.

I think, then, I am, from those journals, justified in the sixth and last resolution, which is,—

That it hath been found by experience that the manner of granting the said supplies and aids by the said general assemblies hath been more agreeable to the said colonies, and more beneficial and conducive to the public service, than the mode of giving and granting aids in Parliament, to be raised and paid in the said colonies.

This makes the whole of the fundamental part of the plan. The conclusion is irresistible. You cannot say that you were driven by any necessity to an exercise of the utmost rights of legislature. You cannot assert that you took on yourselves the task of imposing colony taxes, from the want of another legal body that is competent to the purpose of supplying the exigencies of the state without wounding the prejudices of the people. Neither is it true that the body so qualified and having that competence had neglected the duty.

The question now, on all this accumulated matter, is,—whether you will choose to abide by a profitable experience or a mischievous theory; whether you choose to build on imagination or fact; whether you prefer enjoyment or hope; satisfaction in your subjects or discontent?

If these propositions are accepted, everything which has been made to enforce a contrary system must, I take it for granted, fall along with it. On that ground I have drawn the following resolution, which, when it comes to be moved, will naturally be divided in a proper manner:—

That it may be proper to repeal an act made in the seventh year of the reign of His present Majesty, entitled, "An act for granting certain duties in the British colonies and plantations in America; for allowing a drawback of the duties of customs upon the exportation from this kingdom, of coffee and cocoanuts of the produce of the said colonies or plantations; for discontinuing the drawbacks payable on China earthenware exported to America; and for more effectually preventing the clandestine running of goods in the said colonies and plantations."—And that it may be proper to repeal an act made in the fourteenth year of the reign of His present Majesty, entitled, "An act to discontinue, in such manner and for such time as are therein mentioned, the landing and discharging, lading or shipping, of goods, wares and merchandise, at the town and within the harbour of Boston, in the province of Massachusetts Bay, in North America."—And that it may be proper to repeal an act made in the fourteenth year of the reign of His present Majesty, entitled, "An act for the impartial administration of justice in the cases of persons questioned for any acts done by them in the execution of the law, or for the suppression of riots and tumults, in the province of Massachusetts Bay, in New England."—And that it may be proper to repeal an act made in the fourteenth year of the reign of His present Majesty, entitled, "An act for the better regulating the government of the province of the Massachusetts Bay, in New England."—And also, that it may be proper to explain and amend an act made in the thirty-fifth year of the reign of King Henry the Eighth, entitled, "An act for the trial of treasons committed out of the king's dominions."

I wish, Sir, to repeal the Boston Port Bill, because (independently of the dangerous precedent of suspending the rights of the subject during the king's pleasure) it was passed, as I apprehend, with less regularity and on more partial principles than it ought. The corporation of Boston was not heard before it was condemned. Other towns, full as guilty as she was, have not had their ports blocked up. Even the Restraining Bill of the present session does not go to the length of the Boston Port Act. The same ideas of prudence which induced you not to extend equal punishment to equal guilt, even when you were punishing, induced me, who mean not to chastise but to reconcile, to be satisfied with the punishment already partially inflicted.

Ideas of prudence and accommodation to circumstances prevent you from taking away the charters of Connecticut and Rhode Island, as you have taken away that of Massachusetts Colony, though the crown has far less power in the two former provinces than it enjoyed in the latter, and though the abuses have been full as great and as flagrant in the exempted as in the punished. The same reasons of prudence and accommodation have weight with me in restoring the charter of Massachusetts Bay. Besides, Sir, the act which changes the charter of Massachusetts is in many particulars so exceptionable that, if I did not wish absolutely to repeal, I would by all means desire to alter it, as several of its provisions tend to the subversion of all public and private justice. Such, among others, is the power in the governor to change the sheriff at his pleasure, and to make a new returning officer for every special cause. It is shameful to behold such a regulation standing among English laws.

The act for bringing persons accused of committing murder under the orders of government to England for trial is but temporary. That act has calculated the probable duration of our quarrel with the colonies, and is accommodated to that supposed duration. I would hasten the happy moment of reconciliation; and therefore must, on my principle, get rid of that most justly obnoxious act.

The act of Henry the Eighth for the trial of treasons I do not mean to take away, but to confine it to its proper bounds and original intention; to make it expressly for trial of treasons (and the greatest treasons may be committed) in places where the jurisdiction of the crown does not extend.

Having guarded the privileges of local legislature, I would next secure to the colonies a fair and unbiased judicature; for which purpose, Sir, I propose the following resolution:—

That from the time when the general assembly, or general court, of any colony or plantation in North America shall have appointed, by act of assembly duly confirmed, a settled salary to the offices of the chief justice and other judges of the superior court, it may be proper that the said chief justice and other judges of the superior courts of such colony shall hold his and their office and offices during their good behaviour, and shall not be removed therefrom but when the said removal shall be adjudged by His Majesty in council, upon a hearing on complaint from the general assembly, or on a complaint from the governor or council or the house of representatives, severally, of the colony in which the said chief justice and other judges have exercised the said offices.

The next resolution relates to the courts of admiralty. It is this:—

That it may be proper to regulate the courts of admiralty or vice-admiralty authorized by the fifteenth chapter of the fourth of George the Third, in such a manner as to make the same more commodious to those who sue or who are sued in the said courts; and to provide for the more decent maintenance of the judges in the same.

These courts I do not wish to take away: they are in themselves proper establishments. This court is one of the capital securities of the Act of Navigation. The extent of its jurisdiction, indeed, has been increased; but this is altogether as proper, and is indeed on many accounts more eligible, where new powers were wanted, than a court absolutely new. But courts incommodiously situated in effect deny justice; and a court partaking in the fruits of its own condemnation is a robber. The Congress complain, and complain justly, of this grievance.

These are the three consequential propositions. I have thought of two or three more; but they come rather too near detail and to the province of executive government, which I wish Parliament always to superintend, never to assume. If the first six are granted, congruity will carry the latter three. If not, the things that remain unrepealed will be, I hope, rather unseemly incumbrances on the building than very materially detrimental to its strength and stability.

Here, Sir, I should close: but I plainly perceive some objections remain which I ought, if possible, to remove. The first will be that, in resorting to the doctrine of our ancestors as contained in the preamble to the Chester Act, I prove too much; that the grievance from a want of representation, stated in that preamble, goes to the whole of legislation as well as to taxation; and that the colonies, grounding themselves upon that doctrine, will apply it to all parts of legislative authority.

To this objection, with all possible deference and humility, and wishing as little as any man living to impair the smallest particle of our supreme authority, I answer that *the words are the words of Parliament, and not mine;* and that all false and inconclusive inferences drawn from them are not mine, for I heartily disclaim any such inference. I have chosen the words of an act of Parliament which Mr. Grenville, surely a tolerably zealous and very judicious advocate for the sovereignty of Parliament, formerly moved to have read at your table in confirmation of his tenets. It is true that Lord Chatham considered these preambles as declaring strongly in favor of his opinions. He was a no less powerful advocate for the privileges of the Americans. Ought I not from hence to presume that these preambles are as favourable as possible to both, when properly understood,—favourable both to the rights of Parliament and to the privilege of the dependencies of this crown? But, Sir, the object of grievance in my resolution I have not taken from the Chester, but from the Durham Act, which confines the hardship of want of representation to the case of subsidies, and which therefore falls in exactly with the case of the colonies. But whether the unrepresented counties were *de jure* or *de facto* bound, the preambles do not accurately distinguish; nor indeed was it necessary; for whether *de jure* or *de facto,* the legislature thought the exercise of the power of taxing, as of right or as of fact without right, equally a grievance and equally oppressive.

I do not know that the colonies have, in any general way or in any cool hour, gone much beyond the demand of immunity in relation to taxes. It is not fair to judge of the temper or disposition of any man or any set of men, when they are composed and at rest, from their conduct or their expressions in a state of disturbance and irritation. It is, besides, a very great mistake to imagine that mankind follow up practically any speculative principle, either of government or of freedom, as far as it will go in argument and logical illation. We Englishmen stop very short of the principles upon which we support any given part of our Constitution, or even the whole of it together. I could easily, if I had not already tired you, give you very striking and convincing instances of it. This is nothing but what is natural and proper. All government, indeed every human benefit and enjoyment, every virtue, and every prudent act, is founded on compromise and barter. We balance inconveniences; we give and take; we remit some rights that we may enjoy others; and we choose rather to be happy citizens than subtle disputants. As we must give away some natural liberty to enjoy civil advantages, so we must sacrifice some civil liberties for the advantages to be derived from the communion and fellowship of a great empire. But in all fair dealings the thing bought must bear some proportion to the purchase paid. None will barter away the immediate jewel of his soul. Though a great house is apt to make slaves haughty, yet it is purchasing a part of the artificial importance of a great empire too dear to pay for it all essential rights and all the intrinsic dignity of human nature. None of us who would not risk his life rather than fall under a government purely arbitrary. But although there are some amongst us who think our Constitution wants many improvements to make it a complete system of liberty, perhaps none who are of that opinion would think it right to aim at such improvement by disturbing his country and risking everything that is dear to him. In every arduous enterprise we consider what we are to lose as well as what we are to gain; and the more and better stake of liberty every people possess, the less they will hazard in a vain attempt to make it more. These are *the cords of man*. Man acts from adequate motives relative to his interest, and not on metaphysical speculations. Aristotle, the great master of reasoning, cautions us, and with great weight and propriety, against this species of delusive geometrical accuracy in moral arguments, as the most fallacious of all sophistry.

The Americans will have no interest contrary to the grandeur and glory of England, when they are not oppressed by the weight of it; and they will rather be inclined to respect the acts of a superintending legislature, when they see them the acts of that power which is itself the security, not the rival, of their secondary importance. In this assurance my mind most perfectly acquiesces; and I confess I feel not the least alarm from the discontents which are to arise from putting people at their ease; nor do I apprehend the destruction of this empire from giving, by an act of free grace and indulgence, to two millions of my fellow-citizens, some share of those rights upon which I have always been taught to value myself.

It is said, indeed, that this power of granting, vested in American assemblies, would dissolve the unity of the empire, which was preserved entire, although Wales and Chester and Durham were added to it. Truly, Mr. Speaker, I do not know what this unity means; nor has it ever been heard of, that I know, in the constitutional policy of this country. The very idea of subordination of parts excludes this notion of simple and undivided unity. England is the head, but she is not the head and the members too. Ireland has ever had from the beginning a separate, but not an independent, legislature, which, far from distracting, promoted the union of the whole. Everything was sweetly and harmoniously disposed through both islands for the conservation of English dominion and the communication of English liberties. I do not see that the same principles might not be carried into twenty islands, and with the same good effect. This is my model with regard to America, as far as the internal circumstances of the two countries are the same. I know no other unity of this empire than I can draw from its example during these periods when it seemed to my poor understanding more united than it is now, or than it is likely to be by the present methods.

But since I speak of these methods, I recollect, Mr. Speaker, almost too late, that I promised, before I finished, to say something of the proposition of the noble lord on the floor, which has been so lately received, and stands on your journals. I must be deeply concerned whenever it is my misfortune to continue a difference with the majority of this House. But as the reasons for that difference are my apology for thus troubling you, suffer me to state them in a very few words. I shall compress them into as small a body as I possibly can, having already debated that matter at large when the question was before the committee.

First, then, I cannot admit that proposition of a ransom by auction, because it is a mere project. It is a thing new, unheard of, supported by no experience, justified by no analogy, without example of our ancestors or root in the Constitution. It is neither regular parliamentary taxation nor colony grant. *Experimentum in corpore vili* is a good rule which will ever make me adverse to any trial of experiments on what is certainly the most valuable of all subjects,—the peace of this empire.

Secondly, it is an experiment which must be fatal in the end to our Constitution. For what is it but a scheme for taxing the colonies in the antechamber of the noble lord and his successors? To settle the quotas and proportions in this House is clearly impossible. You, Sir, may flatter yourself you shall sit a state auctioneer with your hammer in your hand, and knock down to each colony as it bids. But to settle (on the plan laid down by the noble lord) the true proportional payment for four or five and twenty governments, according to the absolute and the relative wealth of each, and according to the British proportion of wealth and

burden, is a wild and chimerical notion. This new taxation must therefore come in by the back door of the Constitution. Each quota must be
brought to this House ready formed. You can neither add nor alter. You
must register it. You can do nothing further. For on what grounds can
you deliberate either before or after the proposition? You cannot hear the
counsel for all these provinces, quarrelling each on its own quantity of
payment and its proportion to others. If you should attempt it, the committee of provincial ways and means, or by whatever other name it will
delight to be called, must swallow up all the time of Parliament.

Thirdly, it does not give satisfaction to the complaint of the colonies.
They complain that they are taxed without their consent; you answer
that you will fix the sum at which they shall be taxed. That is, you give
them the very grievance for the remedy. You tell them, indeed, that you
will leave the mode to themselves. I really beg pardon; it gives me pain to
mention it; but you must be sensible that you will not perform this part
of the compact. For suppose the colonies were to lay the duties which
furnished their contingent upon the importation of your manufactures,
you know you would never suffer such a tax to be laid. You know, too,
that you would not suffer any other modes of taxation. So that when you
come to explain yourself, it will be found that you will neither leave to
themselves the quantum nor the mode; nor indeed anything. The whole
is delusion from one end to the other.

Fourthly, this method of ransom by auction, unless it be *universally*
accepted, will plunge you into great and inextricable difficulties. In what
year of our Lord are the proportions of payments to be settled? To say
nothing of the impossibility that colony agents should have general
powers of taxing the colonies at their discretion, consider, I implore you,
that the communication by special messages and orders between these
agents and their constituents on each variation of the case, when the parties come to contend together and to dispute on their relative proportions,
will be a matter of delay, perplexity and confusion that never can have an
end.

If all the colonies do not appear at the outcry, what is the condition of
those assemblies who offer, by themselves or their agents, to tax themselves
up to your ideas of their proportion? The refractory colonies who refuse
all composition will remain taxed only to your old impositions, which,
however grievous in principle, are trifling as to production. The obedient
colonies in this scheme are heavily taxed; the refractory remain unbur-
dened. What will you do? Will you lay new and heavier taxes by Parliament on the disobedient? Pray consider in what way you can do it. You
are perfectly convinced that in the way of taxing you can do nothing but
at the ports. Now suppose it is Virginia that refuses to appear at your
auction, while Maryland and North Carolina bid handsomely for their

ransom, and are taxed to your quota: how will you put these colonies on a par? Will you tax the tobacco of Virginia? If you do, you give its death-wound to your English revenue at home and to one of the very greatest articles of your own foreign trade. If you tax the import of that rebellious colony, what do you tax but your own manufactures or the goods of some other obedient and already well-taxed colony? Who has said one word on this labyrinth of detail which bewilders you more and more as you enter into it? Who has presented, who can present you with a clue to lead you out of it? I think, Sir, it is impossible that you should not recollect that the colony bounds are so implicated in one another (you know it by your other experiments in the bill for prohibiting the New England fishery) that you can lay no possible restraints on almost any of them which may not be presently eluded, if you do not confound the innocent with the guilty, and burden those whom, upon every principle, you ought to exonerate. He must be grossly ignorant of America who thinks that, without falling into this confusion of all rules of equity and policy, you can restrain any single colony, especially Virginia and Maryland, the central and most important of them all.

Let it also be considered that either in the present confusion you settle a permanent contingent, which will and must be trifling, and then you have no effectual revenue; or you change the quota at every exigency, and then on every new repartition you will have a new quarrel.

Reflect besides, that when you have fixed a quota for every colony, you have not provided for prompt and punctual payment. Suppose one, two, five, ten years' arrears. You cannot issue a treasury extent against the failing colony. You must make new Boston Port Bills, new restraining laws, new acts for dragging men to England for trial. You must send out new fleets, new armies. All is to begin again. From this day forward the empire is never to know an hour's tranquillity. An intestine fire will be kept alive in the bowels of the colonies, which one time or other must consume this whole empire. I allow indeed that the empire of Germany raises her revenue and her troops by quotas and contingents; but the revenue of the empire and the army of the empire is the worst revenue and the worst army in the world.

Instead of standing revenue, you will therefore have a perpetual quarrel. Indeed, the noble lord who proposed this project of a ransom by auction seemed himself to be of that opinion. His project was rather designed for breaking the union of the colonies than for establishing a revenue. He confessed he apprehended that his proposal would not be to *their taste*. I say this scheme of disunion seems to be at the bottom of the project; for I will not suspect that the noble lord meant nothing but merely to delude the nation by an airy phantom which he never intended to realize. But whatever his views may be, as I propose the peace and union of the colonies as the very foundation of my plan, it cannot accord with one whose foundation is perpetual discord.

Compare the two. This I offer to give you is plain and simple; the other full of perplexed and intricate mazes. This is mild; that harsh. This is found by experience effectual for its purposes; the other is a new project. This is universal; the other calculated for certain colonies only. This is immediate in its conciliatory operation; the other remote, contingent, full of hazard. Mine is what becomes the dignity of a ruling people,—gratuitous, unconditional, and not held out as a matter of bargain and sale. I have done my duty in proposing it to you. I have indeed tired you by a long discourse; but this is the misfortune of those to whose influence nothing will be conceded, and who must win every inch of their ground by argument. You have heard me with goodness. May you decide with wisdom! For my part, I feel my mind greatly disburdened by what I have done to-day. I have been the less fearful of trying your patience, because on this subject I mean to spare it altogether in future. I have this comfort, that in every stage of the American affairs I have steadily opposed the measures that have produced the confusion, and may bring on the destruction, of this empire. I now go so far as to risk a proposal of my own. If I cannot give peace to my country, I give it to my conscience.

"But what," says the financier, "is peace to us without money? Your plan gives us no revenue." No! But it does; for it secures to the subject the power of REFUSAL, the first of all revenues. Experience is a cheat and fact a liar, if this power in the subject of proportioning his grant, or of not granting at all, has not been found the richest mine of revenue ever discovered by the skill or by the fortune of man. It does not indeed vote you £152,750 11 s. 2¾ths, nor any other paltry limited sum; but it gives the strong-box itself, the fund, the bank, from whence only revenues can arise amongst a people sensible of freedom. *Posita luditur arca.* Cannot you in England, cannot you at this time of day, cannot you, an House of Commons, trust to the principle which has raised so mighty a revenue and accumulated a debt of near 140 millions in this country? Is this principle to be true in England and false everywhere else? Is it not true in Ireland? Has it not hitherto been true in the colonies? Why should you presume that in any country a body duly constituted for any function will neglect to perform its duty and abdicate its trust? Such a presumption would go against all governments in all modes. But in truth this dread of penury of supply from a free assembly has no foundation in nature. For first observe, that besides the desire which all men have naturally of supporting the honour of their own government, that sense of dignity and that security to property which ever attends freedom has a tendency to increase the stock of the free community. Most may be taken where most is accumulated. And what is the soil or climate where experience has not uniformly proved that the voluntary flow of heaped-up plenty, bursting from the weight of its own rich luxuriance, has ever run with a more copious stream of revenue than could be squeezed from the dry husks of oppressed indigence by the straining of all the politic machinery in the world?

Next, we know that parties must ever exist in a free country. We know, too, that the emulations of such parties, their contradictions, their reciprocal necessities, their hopes and their fears, must send them all in their turns to him that holds the balance of the state. The parties are the gamesters; but government keeps the table, and is sure to be the winner in the end. When this game is played, I really think it is more to be feared that the people will be exhausted than that government will not be supplied. Whereas, whatever is got by acts of absolute power, ill obeyed because odious, or by contracts ill kept because constrained, will be narrow, feeble, uncertain and precarious.

> Ease would retract
> Vows made in pain, as violent and void.

I, for one, protest against compounding our demands. I declare against compounding for a poor limited sum the immense, ever-growing, eternal debt which is due to generous government from protected freedom. And so may I speed in the great object I propose to you, as I think it would not only be an act of injustice, but would be the worst economy in the world, to compel the colonies to a sum certain, either in the way of ransom or in the way of compulsory compact.

But to clear up my ideas on this subject: a revenue from America transmitted hither,—do not delude yourselves; you never can receive it,—no, not a shilling. We have experience that from remote countries it is not to be expected. If, when you attempted to extract revenue from Bengal, you were obliged to return in loan what you had taken in imposition, what can you expect from North America? For certainly, if ever there was a country qualified to produce wealth, it is India; or an institution for the transmission, it is the East India Company. America has none of these aptitudes. If America gives you taxable objects on which you lay your duties here, and gives you at the same time a surplus by a foreign sale of her commodities to pay the duties on these objects which you tax at home, she has performed her part to the British revenue. But with regard to her own internal establishments, she may,—I doubt not she will,—contribute in moderation. I say in moderation; for she ought not to be permitted to exhaust herself. She ought to be reserved to a war, the weight of which, with the enemies that we are most likely to have, must be considerable in her quarter of the globe. There she may serve you, and serve you essentially.

For that service, for all service, whether of revenue, trade or empire,

my trust is in her interest in the British Constitution. My hold of the
colonies is in the close affection which grows from common names, from
kindred blood, from similar privileges and equal protection. These are
ties which, though light as air, are as strong as links of iron. Let the colonies always keep the idea of their civil rights associated with your government,—they will cling and grapple to you, and no force under heaven will
be of power to tear them from their allegiance. But let it be once understood that your government may be one thing and their privileges another; that these two things may exist without any mutual relation, the
cement is gone, the cohesion is loosened and everything hastens to decay
and dissolution. As long as you have the wisdom to keep the sovereign
authority of this country as the sanctuary of liberty, the sacred temple
consecrated to our common faith, wherever the chosen race and sons of
England worship freedom, they will turn their faces towards you. The
more they multiply, the more friends you will have; the more ardently
they love liberty, the more perfect will be their obedience. Slavery they
can have anywhere. It is a weed that grows in every soil. They may have it
from Spain; they may have it from Prussia. But until you become lost to
all feeling of your true interest and your natural dignity, freedom they
can have from none but you. This is the commodity of price of which you
have the monopoly. This is the true Act of Navigation which binds to you
the commerce of the colonies, and through them secures to you the wealth
of the world. Deny them this participation of freedom, and you break that
sole bond which originally made and must still preserve the unity of the
empire. Do not entertain so weak an imagination as that your registers
and your bonds, your affidavits and your sufferances, your cockets and
your clearances, are what form the great securities of your commerce. Do
not dream that your letters of office and your instructions and your suspending clauses are the things that hold together the great contexture of
the mysterious whole. These things do not make your government. Dead
instruments, passive tools as they are, it is the spirit of the English communion that gives all their life and efficacy to them. It is the spirit of the
English Constitution, which, infused through the mighty mass, pervades,
feeds, unites, invigorates, vivifies every part of the empire, even down to
the minutest member.

Is it not the same virtue which does everything for us here in England?
Do you imagine, then, that it is the Land Tax Act which raises your
revenue? that it is the annual vote in the Committee of Supply which
gives you your army? or that it is the Mutiny Bill which inspires it with
bravery and discipline? No! surely no! It is the love of the people; it is
their attachment to their government, from the sense of the deep stake
they have in such a glorious institution, which gives you your army and
your navy, and infuses into both that liberal obedience without which

your army would be a base rabble, and your navy nothing but rotten timber.

All this, I know well enough, will sound wild and chimerical to the profane herd of those vulgar and mechanical politicians who have no place among us,—a sort of people who think that nothing exists but what is gross and material; and who, therefore, far from being qualified to be directors of the great movement of empire, are not fit to turn a wheel in the machine. But to men truly initiated and rightly taught, these ruling and master principles, which in the opinion of such men as I have mentioned have no substantial existence, are in truth everything and all in all. Magnanimity in politics is not seldom the truest wisdom; and a great empire and little minds go ill together. If we are conscious of our station, and glow with zeal to fill our places as becomes our situation and ourselves, we ought to auspicate all our public proceedings on America with the old warning of the church, *Sursum corda!* We ought to elevate our minds to the greatness of that trust to which the order of Providence has called us. By adverting to the dignity of this high calling, our ancestors have turned a savage wilderness into a glorious empire, and have made the most extensive, and the only honourable conquests, not by destroying, but by promoting the wealth, the number, the happiness of the human race. Let us get an American revenue as we have got an American empire. English privileges have made it all that it is; English privileges alone will make it all it can be.

In full confidence of this unalterable truth, I now (*quod felix faustunque sit!*) lay the first stone of the Temple of Peace; and I move you,—

That the colonies and plantations of Great Britain in North America, consisting of fourteen separate governments, and containing two millions and upwards of free inhabitants, have not had the liberty and privilege of electing and sending any knights and burgesses, or others, to represent them in the high court of Parliament.

Upon this resolution the previous question was put and carried: for the previous question, 270; against it, 78.

William Pitt

.

William Pitt
[*Born* MAY 28, 1759—*Died* JANUARY 23, 1806]

In his clean-shaven features, unconcealed by a beard, there was now only a reminiscence of the youth that had been. The adorable face . . . was now inclined to be puffy; the cheeks had filled out and the complexion was no longer as clear as the doctors desired. Late hours, deep potations, prolonged labour had engraved their inevitable record on his countenance.—P. W. WILSON

$\cdot$ W $\cdot$ illiam Pitt became Minister at
the age of twenty-four. At forty-seven he was dead, a broken man
whose "infallibility was fortified by failure." [1] Lord Rosebery places
Pitt's political life into two parts: the first, to 1793, was "entirely
praiseworthy," and the period which followed was entirely and "con-
spicuously blameworthy." [2] Pitt seemed best suited to guide the nation through a period of tranquil progress.[3] John Derry believes his
"enduring claim to fame" rests with his reform of the customs, the
pruning of wasteful expenditures, restoration of national self-respect,
and his "courageous defense of English and European liberties
"threatened by an absolutism more powerful than the old. . . ." [4]

Rosebery calls Pitt a "political mystic," sometimes sublime, sometimes impossible, and sometimes insane.[5] He was seldom seen by his
countrymen, and few could boast that they had ever read one of his
speeches, but Pitt possessed the ability to inspire which gave to his
eloquence a "piercing and terrible note which no other English eloquence has touched. . . ." [6] Pitt was, in fact, an oratorical statesman,
writes Walter Bagehot:

. . . he had the singular power, which not half a dozen men in his generation possess, of imparting to a large audience the exact copy of the
feelings, the exact impress of the determination, with which they are
themselves possessed.[7]

When he spoke in the House of Commons, Pitt rarely used notes
to produce a "ready and spontaneous flow" of speech. His voice was
rich and sonorous, although it appeared to lack variety and melody.
His actions were vehement and ungraceful, "sawing the air with wind-
mill arms, sometimes almost touching the ground." [8]

Earl Stanhope considers the three greatest speeches ever delivered

---

1 P. W. Wilson, *William Pitt, the Younger* (Garden City: Doubleday, Doran and
Co., 1930), p. 2.

2 Lord Rosebery, *Pitt* (London: Macmillan and Co., Ltd., 1904), p. 279.

3 Wilson, *op. cit.*

4 John W. Derry, *William Pitt* (New York: Arco Publishing Co., 1963), p. 152.

5 Rosebery, *op. cit.*, p. 284.

6 *Ibid.*

7 Mrs. Russell Barrington (ed.), *Works and Life of Walter Bagehot*, IV (London:
Longmans, Green, and Co., 1915), p. 34.

8 Rosebery, *op. cit.*, p. 269.

by Pitt to be his speech on the Fox-North Coalition in February of 1783, his speech on the Slave Trade on April 2, 1792, and the speech on renewal of the war with France in May, 1803.[9] Stanhope places his "luminous" expositions on national finance in a separate category. Of all Pitt's great speeches, Lord Brougham believes the one on Slave Trade to be the greatest effort of his genius:

. . . it combined . . . the most impassioned declamation, the deepest pathos, the most lively imagination, and the closest reasoning . . . and we have it from Mr. Windham that he walked home lost in amazement at the compass, to then unknown to him, of human eloquence.[10]

Before rising to speak on this occasion, Pitt was forced to take medicine to allay violent irritation of his stomach. During the speech, however, he showed no signs of disability, and his peroration reached an "imaginative flight" as he stood inspired before the rising sun, climaxing a night of intense debate.[11]

Pitt's immediate effort was an extraordinary display of eloquence —the greatest ever heard by Fox, Gray, or Windham.[12] He lost the vote for immediate and total abolition of slave trade to one favoring gradual abolition by 192 to 125, but slave trade was doomed to perish a short time later.

9 Earl Stanhope, *Life of the Right Honourable William Pitt,* IV (London: John Murray, 1862), p. 45.
10 Henry Lord Brougham, *Historical Sketches of Statesmen Who Flourished in the Time of George III,* I (2nd ed.; London, Charles Knight and Co., 1839), p. 205.
11 Rosebery, *op. cit.,* p. 98.
12 J. Holland Rose, *William Pitt and National Revival* (London: G. Bell and Sons, Ltd., 1911), p. 471.

Abolition of the Slave-trade[1]

•

HOUSE OF COMMONS *April 2, 1792*

The House, after receiving a number of petitions, praying for the Abolition of the Slave-trade, resolved itself into a committee of the whole House, to take the circumstances of the trade into considera- tion: —when Mr. Wilberforce moved the following resolution: "That it is the opinion of this committee, that the trade carried on by British subjects, for the purpose of obtaining slaves on the coast of Africa, ought to be abolished."

Mr. Pitt, at a late hour, rose and addressed the committee as follows:

At this hour of the morning I am afraid, Sir, I am too much exhausted to enter so fully into the subject before the committee as I could wish; but if my bodily strength is in any degree equal to the task, I feel so strongly the magnitude of this question, that I am extremely earnest to deliver my sentiments, which I rise to do with the more satisfaction; because I now

---

1 *The Speeches of the Right Honourable William Pitt in the House of Commons.* The third Edition. I (of three) London: Longman, Hurst, Rees, Orme, and Brown, 1817, pp. 363–397.

"From the journals of Debrett and Woodfall, and from other public reports of ad- mitted authenticity, the work has principally derived its materials. These, however, have not been the only channels, through which intelligence has been received. Other sources of more difficult access, but at the same time of more authoritative information, have been consulted, and have contributed very valuable assistance: and it has been by collating these various authorities, by detecting the misrepresentations of some through the avowed fidelity of others, by discarding errors where they could be ascertained, and supplying defects where the means of amendment were within reach, that a compilation has been formed, not inadequate, it is hoped, to the expectations of the public. Some few of the speeches that appear in this collection underwent the revision of Mr. Pitt himself; some were communicated by respectable members of the House of Commons from private notes in their own possession; and of the remainder, the greater part has been sanctioned by the testimony of those, whose frequent observation of the style and character of the speaker enabled them to determine the degree of accuracy with which the speeches were reported."

look forward to the issue of this business with considerable hopes of success.

The debate has this day taken a turn, which, though it has produced a variety of new suggestions, has, upon the whole, contracted this question into a much narrower point than it was ever brought into before.

I cannot say, that I quite agree with the right honourable gentleman over the way; I am far from deploring all that has been said by my two honourable friends. I rather rejoice that they have now brought this subject to a fair issue, that something, at least, is already gained, and that the question has taken altogether a new course this night. It is true, a difference of opinion has been stated, and has been urged with all the force of argument that could be given to it. But give me leave to say, that this difference has been urged upon principles very far removed from those which were maintained by the opponents of my honourable friend when he first brought forward his motion. There are very few of those who have spoken this night, who have not thought it their duty to declare their full and entire concurrence with my honourable friend in promoting the abolition of the slave-trade, as their ultimate object. However we may differ as to the time and manner of it, we are agreed in the abolition itself; and my honourable friends have expressed their agreement in this sentiment with that sensibility upon the subject, which humanity does most undoubtedly require. I do not, however, think they yet perceive what are the necessary consequences of their own concession, or follow up their own principles to their just conclusion.

The point now in dispute between us, is, a difference merely as to the period of time, at which the abolition of the slave-trade ought to take place. I therefore congratulate this House, the country, and the world, that this great point is gained; that we may now consider this trade as having received its condemnation; that its sentence is sealed; that this curse of mankind is seen by the House in its true light; and that the greatest stigma on our national character which ever yet existed, is about to be removed! And, Sir, (which is still more important,) that mankind, I trust, in general, are now likely to be delivered from the greatest practical evil that ever has afflicted the human race—from the severest and most extensive calamity recorded in the history of the world!

In proceeding to give my reasons for concurring with my honourable friend in his motion, I shall necessarily advert to those topics which my honourable friends near me have touched upon; and which they stated to be their motives for preferring a gradual, and, in some degree, a distant abolition of the slave-trade, to the more immediate and direct measure now proposed to you. Beginning as I do, with declaring that in this respect I differ completely from my right honourable friends near me, I do not, however, mean to say, that I differ as to one observation which has been pressed rather strongly by them. If they can show that their proposition of a gradual abolition is more likely than ours to secure the object which we have in view—that by proceeding gradually we shall arrive more speedily at our end, and attain it with more certainty, than by a direct vote immediately to abolish: —if they can shew to the satisfaction both of myself and the committee, that our proposition has more the appearance of a speedy abolition than the reality of it, undoubtedly they will in this case make a convert of me, and my honourable friend who moved the question; they will make a convert of every man among us, who looks to this, which I trust we all do, as a question not to be determined by theoretical principles or enthusiastic feelings, but considers the practicability of the measure—aiming simply to effect his object in the shortest time, and in the surest possible manner.

If, however, I shall be able to shew that our measure proceeds more directly to its object, and secures it with more certainty and within a less distant period; and that the slave-trade will on our plan be abolished sooner than on his; may I not then hope, that my right honourable friends will be as ready to adopt our proposition, as we should in the other case be willing to accede to theirs?

One of my right honourable friends has stated, that an act passed here for the abolition of the slave-trade would not secure its abolition. Now, Sir, I should be glad to know, why an act of the British legislature, enforced by all those sanctions which we have undoubtedly the power and the right to apply, is not to be effectual: at least, as to every material purpose? Will not the executive power have the same appointment of the officers and the courts of judicature, by which all the causes relating to this subject must be tried, that it has in other cases? Will there not be the same system of law by which we now maintain a monopoly of commerce? If the same law, Sir, be applied to the prohibition of the slave-trade, which is applied in the case of other contraband commerce, with all the same means of the country to back it, I am at a loss to know why the actual and total abolition is not likely to be effected in this way, as by any plan or project of my honourable friends, for bringing about a gradual termination of it. But my observation is extremely fortified by what fell from my honourable friend who spoke last: he has told you, Sir, that if you will have patience with it for a few years, the slave-trade must drop of itself, from the increasing dearness of the commodity imported, and the increasing progress, on the other hand, of internal population. Is it true, then, that the importations are so expensive and disadvantageous already, that the internal population is even now becoming a cheaper resource? I ask then, if you leave to the importer no means of importation but by smuggling, and if, besides all the present disadvantages, you load him with all the charges and hazards of the smuggler, by taking care that the laws against smuggling are in this case watchfully and rigorously enforced, is there any danger of any considerable supply of fresh slaves being poured into the islands through this channel? And is there any real ground of fear, because a few slaves may have been smuggled in or out of the islands, that a bill will be useless and ineffectual on any such ground? The question under these circumstances will not bear a dispute.

Perhaps, however, my honourable friends may take up another ground, and say, "It is true your measure would shut out further importations more immediately; but we do not mean to shut them out immediately. We think it right, on grounds of general expediency, that they should not be immediately shut out." Let us therefore now come to this question of the expediency of making the abolition distant and gradual, rather than immediate.

The argument of expediency, in my opinion, like every other argument in this disquisition, will not justify the continuance of the slave-trade for one unnecessary hour. Supposing it to be in our power (which I have shewn it is) to enforce the prohibition from this present time, the expediency of doing it is to me so clear, that if I went on this principle alone, I should not feel a moment's hesitation. What is the argument of expediency stated on the other side? It is doubted whether the deaths and births in the islands are as yet so nearly equal as to ensure the keeping up of a sufficient stock of labourers: in answer to this, I took the liberty of mentioning, in a former year, what appeared to me to be the state of population at that time. My observations were taken from documents which we have reason to judge authentic, and which carried on the face of them the conclusions I then stated; they were the clear, simple, and obvious result of a careful examination which I made into this subject, and any gentlemen who will take the same pains may arrive at the same degree of satisfaction.

These calculations, however, applied to a period of time that is now four or five years past. The births were then, in the general view of them, nearly equal to the deaths; and, as the state of population was shewn, by a considerable retrospect, to be regularly increasing, an excess of births must before this time have taken place.

Another observation has been made as to the disproportion of the sexes; this, however, is a disparity which existed in any material degree only in former years; it is a disparity of which the slave-trade has been itself the cause; which will gradually diminish as the slave-trade diminishes, and must entirely cease, if the trade shall be abolished; but which, nevertheless, is made the very plea for its continuance. I believe this disproportion of the sexes, taking the whole number in the islands, Creole as well as imported Africans, the latter of whom occasion all the disproportion, is not now by any means considerable.

But, Sir, I also shewed, that the great mortality which turned the balance so as to make the deaths appear more numerous than the births, arose too from the imported Africans, who die in extraordinary numbers in the seasoning. If, therefore, the importation of negroes should cease, every one of the causes of mortality which I have now stated, would cease also. Nor can I conceive any reason why the present number of labourers should not maintain itself in the West Indies, except it be from some artificial cause, some fault in the island; such as the impolicy of their governors, or the cruelty of the managers and officers whom they employ.

I will not reiterate all that I said at that time, or go through island by island. It is true, there is a difference in the ceded islands; and I state them possibly to be, in some respects, an excepted case. But, if we are to enter into the subject of the mortality in clearing new lands, this, Sir, is undoubtedly another question; the mortality here is tenfold; and this is to be considered, not as the carrying on of a trade, but as the setting on foot of a slave-trade for the purpose of peopling the colony; a measure which I think will not now be maintained. I therefore desire gentlemen to tell me fairly, whether the period they look to is not now arrived? Whether, at this hour, the West Indies may not be declared to have actually attained a state in which they can maintain their population? and upon the answer I must necessarily receive, I think I could safely rest the whole of the question.

One honourable gentleman has rather ingeniously observed that one or other of these two assertions of ours, must necessarily be false: that either the population must be decreasing, which we deny; or if the population is increasing, that the slaves must be perfectly well treated, (this being the cause of such population,) which we deny also. That the population is rather increasing than otherwise, and also that the general treatment is by no means so good as it ought to be, are both points which have been separately proved by different evidences; nor are these two points so entirely incompatible. The ill treatment must be very great indeed, in order to diminish materially the population of any race of people. That it is not so extremely great as to do this, I will admit. I will even admit, if you please, that this charge may possibly have been sometimes exaggerated; and I certainly think, that it applies less and less as we come nearer to the present times.

But, let us see how this contradiction of ours, as it is thought, really stands, and how the explanation of it will completely settle our minds on the point in question. Do the slaves diminish in numbers? It can be nothing but ill treatment that causes the diminution. This ill treatment the abolition must and will restrain. In this case, therefore, we ought to vote for the abolition. On the other hand, Do you choose to say that the slaves clearly increase in numbers? Then you want no importations, and, in this case also, you may safely vote for the abolition. Or, if you choose to say, as the third and only other case which can be put, and which perhaps is the nearest to the truth, that the population is nearly stationary, and the treatment neither so bad nor so good as it might be; then surely, Sir, it will not be denied, that this of all others is, on each of the two grounds, the proper period for stopping further supplies: for your population, which you own is already stationary, will thus be made undoubtedly to increase from the births; and the good treatment of your present slaves, which I am now supposing is but very moderate, will be necessarily improved also by the same measure of abolition. I say, therefore, that these propositions, contradictory as they may be represented, are in truth not at all inconsistent, but even come in aid of each other, and lead to a conclusion that is decisive. And let it be always remembered, that in this branch of my argument I have only in view the well-being of the West Indies, and do not now ground any thing on the African part of the question.

But, Sir, I may carry these observations respecting the islands much further. It is within the power of the colonists, (and is it not then their indispensable duty?) to apply themselves to the correction of those various abuses by which population is restrained. The most important consequences may be expected to attend colonial regulations for this purpose. With the improvement of internal population, the condition of every negro will improve also; his liberty will advance, or at least he will be approaching to a state of liberty. Nor can you increase the happiness, or extend to the freedom of the negro, without adding in an equal degree to the safety of the islands, and of all their inhabitants. Thus, Sir, in the place of *slaves,* who naturally have an interest directly opposite to that of their masters, and are therefore viewed by them with an eye of constant suspicion, you will create a body of valuable *citizens and subjects,* forming a part of the same community, having a common interest with their superiors, in the security and prosperity of the whole.

And here let me add, that in proportion as you increase the happiness of these unfortunate beings, you will undoubtedly increase in effect the quantity of their labour also. Gentlemen talk of the diminution of the labour of the islands! I will venture to assert, that, even if in consequence of the abolition there were to be some decrease in the number of bands, the quantity of work done, supposing the condition of the slaves to improve, would by no means diminish in the same proportion; perhaps would be far from diminishing at all. For if you restore to this degraded race the true feelings of men; if you take them out from among the order of brutes, and place them on a level with the rest of the human species; they will then work with that energy which is natural to men, and their labour will be productive, in a thousand ways, above what it has yet been;

as the labour of a man is always more productive than that of a mere brute.

It generally happens, that in every bad cause some information arises out of the evidence of its defenders themselves, which serves to expose in one part or other the weakness of their defence. It is the characteristic of such a cause, that if it be at all gone into, even by its own supporters, it is liable to be ruined by the contradictions in which those who maintain it are for ever involved.

The committee of the privy council of Great Britain sent over certain queries to the West-India islands, with a view of elucidating the present subject; and they particularly inquired, whether the negroes had any days or hours allotted to them, in which they might work for themselves. The assemblies, in their answers, with an air of great satisfaction state the labour of the slaves to be moderate, and the West-India system to be well calculated to promote the domestic happiness of the slaves: they add, "that proprietors are not compelled by law to allow their slaves any part of the six working days of the week for themselves, but that it is the general practice to allow them one afternoon in every week out of crop time, which, with such hours as they choose to work on Sundays, is time amply sufficient for their own purposes:" now, therefore, will the negroes, or I may rather say, do the negroes work for their own emolument? I beg the committee's attention to this point: the assembly of Grenada proceeds to state—I have their own words for it—"That though the negroes are allowed the afternoons of only one day in every week, they will do as much work in that afternoon, when employed for their own benefit, as in the whole day when employed in their masters' service."

Now, Sir, I will desire you to burn all my calculations; to disbelieve, if you please, every word I have said on the present state of population; nay, I will admit, for the sake of argument, that the numbers are decreasing, and the productive labour at present insufficient for the cultivation of those countries: and I will then ask, whether the increase in the quantity of labour which is reasonably to be expected from the improved condition of the slaves, is not, by the admission of the islands themselves, by their admission not merely of an argument but a fact, far more than sufficient to counterbalance any decrease which can be rationally apprehended from a defective state of their population. Why, Sir, a negro, if he works for himself, and not for a master, will do double work! This is their own account. If you will believe the planters, if you will believe the legislature of the islands, the productive labour of the colonies would, in case the negroes worked as free labourers instead of slaves, be literally doubled. Half the present labourers, on this supposition, would suffice for the whole cultivation of our islands on the present scale. I therefore confidently ask the House, whether, in considering the whole of this question, we may not fairly look forward to an improvement in the condition of these unhappy and degraded beings, not only as an event desirable on the ground of humanity and political prudence, but also as a means of increasing very considerably indeed, (even without any increasing population,) the productive industry of the islands?

When gentlemen are so nicely balancing the past and future means of cultivating the plantations, let me request them to put this argument into the scale; and the more they consider it, the more will they be satisfied, that both the solidity of the principle which I have stated, and the fact which I have just quoted in the very words of the colonial legislature, will bear me out in every inference I have drawn. I think they will perceive also, that it is the undeniable duty of this House, on the grounds of true policy, immediately to sanction and carry into effect that system which ensures these important advantages; in addition to all those other inestimable blessings which follow in their train.

If, therefore, the argument of expediency, as applying to the West-India islands, is the test by which this question is to be tried, I trust I have now established this proposition, namely, that whatever tends most speedily and effectually to meliorate the condition of the slaves, is undoubtedly on the ground of expediency, leaving justice out of the question, the main object to be pursued.

That the immediate abolition of the slave-trade will most eminently have this effect, and that it is the only measure from which this effect can in any considerable degree be expected, are points to which I shall presently come; but before I enter upon them, let me notice one or two further circumstances.

We are told (and by respectable and well-informed persons) that the purchase of new negroes has been injurious instead of profitable to the planters themselves; so large a proportion of these unhappy wretches being found to perish in the seasoning. Writers well versed in this subject have been advised that, in order to remove the temptation which the slave-trade offers to expend large sums in this injudicious way, the door of importation should be shut.—This very plan which we now propose, the mischief of which is represented to be so great as to outweigh so many other momentous considerations, has actually been recommended by some of the best authorities, as a plan highly requisite to be adopted on the very principle of advantage to the island; nay, not merely on that principle of general and political advantage on which I have already touched, but for the advantage of the very individuals who would otherwise be most forward in purchasing slaves. On the part of the West-Indians it is urged, "The planters are in debt; they are already distressed; if you stop the slave-trade, they will be ruined." Mr. Long, the celebrated historian of Jamaica, recommends the stopping of importations, as a receipt for enabling the plantations which are embarrassed to get out of debt. I will quote his words. Speaking of the usurious terms on which money is often borrowed for the purchase of fresh slaves, he advises "the laying of a duty equal to a prohibition on all negroes imported for the space of four or five years, except for re-exportation.—Such a law," he proceeds to say, "would be attended with the following good consequences. It would put an immediate stop to these extortions; it would enable the planter to retrieve his affairs by preventing him from running in debt, either by renting or purchasing negroes; it would render such recruits less necessary, by the redoubled care he would be obliged to take of his present stock, the preservation of their lives and health: and lastly, it would raise the value of negroes in the island.—A North-American province, by this prohibition alone for a few years, from being deeply plunged in debt, has become independent, rich, and flourishing."

On this authority of Mr. Long I rest the question, whether the prohibition of further importations is that rash, impolitic, and completely ruinous measure, which it is so confidently declared to be with respect to our West-Indian plantations.

I do not, however, mean, in thus treating this branch of the subject, absolutely to exclude the question of indemnification on the supposition of possible disadvantages affecting the West-Indies through the abolition of the slave-trade. But when gentlemen set up a claim of compensation merely on those general allegations, which are all that I have yet heard from them, I can only answer, let them produce their case in a distinct and specific form; and if upon any practicable or reasonable grounds it shall claim consideration, it will then be time enough for parliament to decide upon it.

I now come to another circumstance of great weight, connected with this part of the question. I mean the danger to which the islands are exposed from those negroes who are newly imported. This, Sir, like the observation which I lately made, is no mere speculation of ours; for here again I refer you to Mr. Long, the historian of Jamaica. He treats particularly of the dangers to be dreaded from the introduction of Coromantine negroes; an appellation under which are comprised several descriptions of negroes obtained on the Gold Coast, whose native country is not exactly known, and who are purchased in a variety of markets, having been brought from some distant island. With a view of preventing insurrections, he advises, that "by a laying a duty equal to a prohibition, no more of these Coromantines should be bought;" and after noticing one insurrection which happened through their means, he tells you of another in the following year, in which thirty-three Coromantines, most of whom had been newly imported, suddenly rose, and in the space of an hour murdered and wounded no less than nineteen white persons.

To the authority of Mr. Long, both in this and other parts of his work, I may add the recorded opinion of the committee of the house of assembly of Jamaica itself; who, in consequence of a rebellion among the slaves, were appointed to enquire into the best means of preventing future insurrections. The committee reported, "That the rebellion had originated (like most or all others) with the Coromantines; and they proposed that a bill should be brought in for laying a higher duty on the importation of these particular negroes," which was intended to operate as a prohibition.

But the danger is not confined to the importation of Coromantines. Mr. Long, carefully investigating as he does the causes of such frequent insurrections, particularly at Jamaica, accounts for them from the greatness of its general importations. "In two years and a half," says he, "27,000 negroes have been imported.—No wonder we have rebellions! Twenty-seven thousand in two years and a half!" Why, Sir, I believe that in some late years there have been as many imported into the same island within the same period! Surely, Sir, when gentlemen talk so vehemently of the safety of the islands, and charge us with being so indifferent to it; when they speak of the calamities of St. Domingo, and of similar dangers impending over their own heads at the present hour, it ill becomes *them* to be the persons who are crying out for further importations. It ill becomes *them* to charge upon *us* the crime of stirring up insurrections— upon us who are only adopting the very principles, which Mr. Long, which in part even the legislature of Jamaica itself, laid down in the time of danger, with an avowed view to the prevention of any such calamity.

The House, I am sure, will easily believe it is no small satisfaction to me, that among the many arguments for prohibiting the slave-trade which crowd upon my mind, the security of our West-India possessions against internal commotions, as well as foreign enemies, is among the most prominent and most forcible. And here let me apply to my two right honourable friends, and ask them, whether in this part of the argument they do not see reason for *immediate* abolition! Why should you any longer import into those countries that which is the very seed of insurrection and rebellion? Why should you persist in introducing those latent principles of conflagration, which, if they should once burst forth, may annihilate in a single day the industry of an hundred years? Why will you subject yourselves, with open eyes, to the evident and imminent risk of a calamity, which may throw you back a whole century in your profits, in your cultivation, in your progress to the emancipation of your slaves? and, disappointing at once every one of those golden expectations, may retard not only the accomplishment of that happy system which I have attempted to describe, but may cut off even your opportunity of taking any one introductory step? Let us begin from this time! Let us not commit these important interests to any further hazard! Let us prosecute this great object from this very hour! Let us vote that the abolition of the slave-trade shall be immediate, and not left to I know not what future time or contingency! Will my right honourable friends answer for the safety of the islands during any imaginable intervening period? Or do they think that any little advantages of the kind which they state, can have any weight in that scale of expediency in which this great question ought undoubtedly to be tried?

Thus stated, and thus alone, Sir, can it be truly stated, to what does the whole of my right honourable friend's arguments, on the head of expediency, amount? It amounts but to this:—the colonies on the one hand would have to struggle with some few difficulties and disadvantages at the first, for the sake of obtaining on the other hand immediate security to their leading interests; of ensuring, Sir, even their own political existence; and for the sake also of immediately commencing that system of progressive improvement in the condition of the slaves, which is necessary to raise them from the state of brutes to that of rational beings, but which never can begin until the introduction of these new disaffected and dangerous Africans into the same gangs, shall have been stopped.

If any argument can in the slightest degree justify the severity that is now so generally practised in the treatment of the slaves, it must be the introduction of these Africans. It is the introduction of these Africans that renders all idea of emancipation for the present so chimerical; and the very mention of it so dreadful. It is the introduction of these Africans that keeps down the condition of all plantation-negroes. Whatever system of treatment is deemed necessary by the planters to be adopted towards these new Africans extends itself to the other slaves also. Instead therefore of deferring the hour when you will finally put an end to importations, vainly purposing that the condition of your present slaves should previously be mended, you must, in the very first instance, stop your importations, if you hope to introduce any rational or practicable plan, either of gradual emancipation, or present general improvement.

Having now done with this question of expediency as affecting the islands, I come next to a proposition advanced by my right honourable friend, which appeared to intimate, that on account of some patrimonial rights of the West-Indians, the prohibition of the slave-trade might be considered as an invasion on their legal inheritance.

Now, in answer to this proposition, I must make two or three remarks, which I think my right honourable friend will find some considerable difficulty in answering.—First, I observe that his argument, if it be worth any thing, applies just as much to gradual as immediate abolition. I have no doubt, that at whatever period he should be disposed to say the abolition should actually take place, this defence will equally be set up; for it certainly is just as good an argument against an abolition seven, or seventy years hence, as against an abolition at this moment. It supposes, we have no right whatever to stop the importations; and even though the disadvantage to our plantations, which some gentlemen suppose to attend the measure of immediate abolition, should be admitted gradually to lessen by the lapse of a few years, yet in point of principle the absence of all right of interference would remain the same. My right honourable friend, therefore, I am sure will not press an argument not less hostile to his proposition than to ours. But let us investigate the foundation of this objection, and I will commence what I have to say, by putting a question to my right honourable friend. It is chiefly on the presumed ground of our being bound by a parliamentary sanction heretofore given to the African slave-trade, that this argument against the abolition is rested. Does then my right honourable friend, or does any man in this House think, that the slave-trade has received any such parliamentary sanction, as must place it more out of the jurisdiction of the legislature for ever after, than the other branches of our national commerce? I ask, is there any one regulation of any part of our commerce, which, if this argument be valid, may not equally be objected to, on the ground of its affecting some man's patrimony, some man's property, or some man's expectations? Let it never be forgotten, that the argument I am canvassing would be just as strong, if the possession affected were small, and the possessors humble; for on every principle of justice, the property of any single individual, or small number of individuals, is as sacred, as that of the great body of West-Indians. Justice ought to extend her protection with rigid impartiality to the rich and to the poor, to the powerful and to the humble. If this be the case, in what a situation does my right honourable friend's argument place the legislature of Britain? What room is left for their interference in the regulation of any part of our commerce? It is scarcely possible to lay a duty on any one article, which may not, when first imposed, be said in some way to affect the property of individuals, and even of some entire classes of the community. If the laws respecting the slave-trade imply a contract for its perpetual continuance, I will venture to say, there does not pass a year without some act, equally pledging the faith of parliament to the perpetuating of some other branch of commerce. In short, I repeat my observation, that no new tax can be imposed, much less can any prohibitory duty be ever laid on any branch of trade, that has before been regulated by parliament, if this principle be once admitted.

Before I refer to the acts of parliament by which the public faith is said to be pledged, let me remark also, that a contract for the continuance of the slave-trade must, on the principles which I shall presently insist on, have been void, even from the beginning; for if this trade is an outrage upon justice, and only another name for fraud, robbery, and murder,— will any man urge that the legislature could possibly by any pledge what- ever incur the obligation of being an accessory, or I may even say a prin- cipal, in the commission of such enormities, by sanctioning their counte- nance? As well might an individual think himself bound by a promise to commit an assassination. I am confident, gentlemen must see, that our proceedings on such grounds would infringe all the principles of law, and subvert the very foundation of morality.

Let us now see, how far the acts themselves shew that there is this sort of parliamentary pledge to continue the African slave-trade. The act of 23d Geo.II.c.31. is that by which we are supposed to be bound up by contract to sanction all those horrors now so incontrovertibly proved. How surprised then, Sir, must the House be to find, that by a clause of their very act, some of these outrages are expressly forbidden! It says,"No commander, or master of a ship, trading to Africa, shall by fraud, force, or violence, or by any indirect practice whatsoever, take on board or carry away from the coast of Africa, any negro, or native of the said country, or commit any violence on the natives, to the prejudice of the said trade, and that every person so offending shall for every such offence forfeit"—When it comes to the penalty, sorry am I to say, that we see too close a resem- blance to the West-India law, which inflicts the payment of 30 l. as the punishment for murdering a negro. The price of blood in Africa is 100 l.; but even this penalty is enough to prove that the act at least does not sanction, much less does it engage to perpetuate enormities; and the whole trade has now been demonstrated to be a mass, a system of enormi- ties; of enormities which incontrovertibly bid defiance not only to this clause but to every regulation which our ingenuity can devise, and our power carry into effect. Nothing can accomplish the object of this clause but an extinction of the trade itself.

But, Sir, let us see what was the motive for carrying on the trade at all? The preamble of the act states it,—"Whereas the trade to and from Africa is very advantageous to Great Britain, and necessary for the supplying the plantations and colonies thereunto belonging with a sufficient number of negroes at reasonable rates, and for that purpose the said trade should be carried on," & c.—Here then we see what the parliament had in view when it passed this act; and I have clearly shewn that not one of the occasions on which it grounded its proceedings now exists. I may then plead, I think, the very act itself as an argument for the abolition. If it is shewn, that instead of being "very advantageous" to Great Britain, this trade is the most destructive that can well be imagined to her interest; that it is the ruin of our seamen; that it stops the extension of our manu- facturers; if it is proved in the second place that it is not now necessary for the "supplying our plantations with negroes;" if it is further established that this traffick was from the very beginning contrary to the first principles of justice, and consequently that a pledge for its continuance, had one been attempted to have been given, must have been completely and absolutely void;—where then in this act of parliament is the contract to be found, by which Britain is bound, as she is said to be, never to listen to her own true interests, and to the cries of the natives of Africa? Is it not clear that all argument, founded on the supposed pledged faith of parliament, makes against those who employ it? I refer you to the principles which obtain in other cases. Every trade-act shews undoubtedly that the legislature is used to pay a tender regard to all classes of the community. But if for the sake of moral duty, or national honour, or even of great political advantage, it is thought right, by authority of parliament, to alter any long-established system, parliament is competent to do it. The legislature will undoubtedly be careful to subject individuals to as little inconvenience as possible; and if any peculiar hardship should arise, that can be distinctly stated, and fairly pleaded, there will ever, I am sure, be a liberal feeling towards them in the legislature of this country, which is the guardian of all who live under its protection. On the present occasion, the most powerful considerations call upon us to abolish the slave-trade; and if we refuse to attend to them on the alleged ground of pledged faith and contract, we shall depart as widely from the practice of parliament, as from the path of moral duty. If indeed there is any case of hardship, which comes within the proper cognizance of parliament, and calls for the exercise of its liberality,—well! But such a case must be reserved for calm consideration, as a matter distinct from the present question.

I beg pardon for dwelling so long on the argument of expediency, and on the manner in which it affects the West-Indies. I have been carried away by my own feelings on some of these points into a greater length than I intended, especially considering how fully the subject has been already argued. The result of all I have said is, that there exists no impediment, no obstacle, no shadow of reasonable objection on the ground of pledged faith, or even on that of national expediency, to the abolition of this trade. On the contrary, all the arguments drawn from those sources pleaded for it; and they plead much more loudly, and much more strongly in every part of the question, for an immediate than for a gradual abolition.

But now, Sir, I come to Africa. That is the ground on which I rest, and here it is that I say my right honourable friends do not carry their principles to their full extent. Why ought the slave-trade to be abolished? Because it is incurable injustice. How much stronger then is the argument for immediate than gradual abolition? By allowing it to continue even for one hour, do not my right honourable friends weaken—do not they desert, their own argument of its injustice? If on the ground of injustice it ought to be abolished at last, why ought it not now? Why is injustice to be suffered to remain for a single hour? From what I hear without doors, it is evident that there is a general conviction entertained of its being far from just; and from that very conviction of its injustice, some men have been led, I fear, to the supposition, that the slave-trade never could have been permitted to begin, but from some strong and irresistible necessity; a necessity, however, which, if it was fancied to exist at first, I have shewn cannot be thought by any man whatever to exist now. This plea of necessity, thus presumed, and presumed, as I suspect, from the circumstance of injustice itself, has caused a sort of acquiescence in the continuance of this evil. Men have been led to place it among the rank of those necessary evils, which were supposed to be the lot of human creatures, and to be permitted to fall upon some countries or individuals, rather than upon others, by that Being, whose ways are inscrutable to us, and whose dispensations, it is conceived, we ought not to look into. The origin of evil is indeed a subject beyond the reach of human understandings; and the permission of it by the Supreme Being, is a subject into which it belongs not to us to enquire. But where the evil in question is a moral evil which a man can scrutinise, and where that moral evil has its origin with ourselves, let us not imagine that we can clear our consciences by this general, not to say irreligious and impious way of laying aside the question. If we reflect at all on this subject, we must see that every necessary evil supposes that some other and greater evil would be incurred were it removed; I therefore desire to ask, what can be that greater evil, which can be stated to overbalance the one in question?—I know of no evil that ever has existed, nor can imagine any evil to exist, worse than the tearing of seventy or eighty thousand persons annually from their native land, by a combination of the most civilised nations, inhabiting the most enlightened part of the globe, but more especially under the sanction of the laws of that nation which calls herself the most free and the most happy of them all. Even if these miserable beings were proved guilty of every crime before you take them off, (of which however not a single proof is adduced,) ought we to take upon ourselves the office of executioners? And even if we condescend so far, still can we be justified in taking them, unless we have clear proof that they are criminals?

But if we go much farther,—if we ourselves tempt them to sell their fellow-creatures to us, we may rest assured, that they will take care to provide by every method, by kidnapping, by village-breaking, by unjust wars, by iniquitous condemnations, by rendering Africa a scene of bloodshed and misery, a supply of victims increasing in proportion to our demand. Can we then hesitate in deciding whether the wars in Africa are their wars or ours? It was our arms in the river Cameroon put into the hands of the trader, that furnished him with the means of pushing his trade; and I have no more doubt that they are British arms, put into the hands of Africans, which promote universal war and desolation, than I can doubt their having done so in that individual instance.

I have shewn how great is the enormity of this evil, even on the supposition that we take only convicts and prisoners of war. But take the subject in the other way; take it on the grounds stated by the right honourable gentlemen over the way; and how does it stand? Think of EIGHTY THOUSAND persons carried away out of their country by we know not what means! for crimes imputed! for light or inconsiderable faults! for debt perhaps! for the crime of witchcraft! or a thousand other weak and scandalous pretexts! besides all the fraud and kidnapping, the villainies and perfidy, by which the slave-trade is supplied. Reflect on these eighty thousand persons thus annually taken off! There is something in the horror of it, that surpasses all the bounds of imagination. Admitting that there exists in Africa something like to courts of justice; yet what an office of humiliation and meanness is it in us, to take upon ourselves to carry into execution the partial, the cruel, iniquitous sentences of such courts, as if we also were strangers to all religion, and to the first principles of justice! But that country, it is said, has been in some degree civilised, and civilised by us. It is said they have gained some knowledge of the principles of justice. What, Sir, have they gained principles of justice from us? Their civilisation brought about by us!! Yes, we give them enough of our intercourse to convey to them the means, and to initiate them in the study of mutual destruction. We give them just enough of the forms of justice to enable them to add the pretext of legal trials to their other modes of perpetrating the most atrocious iniquity. We give them just enough of European improvements, to enable them the more effectually to turn Africa into a ravaged wilderness. Some evidences say, that the Africans are addicted to the practice of gambling; that they even sell their wives and children, and ultimately themselves. Are these then the legitimate sources of slavery? Shall we pretend that we can thus acquire an honest right to exact the labour of these people? Can we pretend that we have a right to carry away to distant regions, men of whom we know nothing by authentic enquiry, and of whom there is every reasonable presumption to think, that those who sell them to us, have no right to do so? But the evil does not stop here. I feel that there is not time for me to make all the remarks which the subject deserves, and I refrain from attempting to enumerate half the dreadful consequences of this system. Do you think nothing of the ruin and the miseries in which so many other individuals, still remaining in Africa, are involved in consequence of carrying off so many myriads of people? Do you think nothing of their families which are left behind? of the connections which are broken? of the friendships, at-

tachments, and relationships that are burst asunder? Do you think nothing of the miseries in consequence, that are felt from generation to generation? of the privation of that happiness which might be communicated
to them by the introduction of civilisation, and of mental and moral improvement? A happiness which you withhold from them so long as you
permit the slave-trade to continue. What do you yet know of the internal
state of Africa? You have carried on a trade to that quarter of the globe
from this civilised and enlightened country; but such a trade, that, instead of diffusing either knowledge or wealth, it has been the check to
every laudable pursuit. Instead of any fair interchange of commodities;
instead of conveying to them, from this highly favoured land, any means
of improvement, you carry with you that noxious plant by which everything is withered and blasted; under whose shade nothing that is useful
or profitable to Africa will ever flourish or take root. Long as that continent has been known to navigators, the extreme line and boundaries of its
coasts is all with which Europe is yet become acquainted; while other
countries in the same parallel of latitude, through a happier system of
intercourse, have reaped the blessings of a mutually beneficial commerce.
But as to the whole interior of that continent you are, by your own principles of commerce, as yet entirely shut out: Africa is known to you only
in its skirts. Yet even there you are able to infuse a poison that spreads its
contagious effects from one end of it to the other, which penetrates to its
very centre, corrupting every part to which it reaches. You there subvert
the whole order of nature; you aggravate every natural barbarity, and
furnish to every man living on that continent, motives for committing,
under the name and pretext of commerce, acts of perpetual violence and
perfidy against his neighbor.

Thus, Sir, has the perversion of British commerce carried misery instead of happiness to one whole quarter of the globe. False to the very
principles of trade, misguided in our policy, and unmindful of our duty,
what astonishing—I had almost said, what *irreparable* mischief, have we
brought upon that continent? I would apply this thought to the present
question. How shall we ever repair this mischief? How shall we hope to
obtain, if it be possible, forgiveness from Heaven for those enormous evils
we have committed, if we refuse to make use of those means which the
mercy of Providence hath still reserved to us for wiping away the guilt
and shame with which we are now covered? If we refuse even this degree
of compensation, if, knowing the miseries we have caused, we refuse even
now to put a stop to them, how greatly aggravated will be the guilt of
Great Britain! and what a blot will the history of these transactions for
ever be in the history of this country! Shall we then DELAY to repair
these injuries, and to begin rendering this justice to Africa? Shall we not
count the days and hours that are suffered to intervene and to delay the

accomplishment of such a work? Reflect, what an immense object is before you—what an object for a nation to have in view, and to have a prospect, under the favour of Providence, of being now permitted to attain! I think the House will agree with me in cherishing the ardent wish to enter without delay upon the measures necessary for these great ends: and I am sure that the immediate abolition of the slave-trade is the first, the principal, the most indispensable act of policy, of duty, and of justice, that the legislature of this country has to take, if it is indeed their wish to secure those important objects to which I have alluded, and which we are bound to pursue by the most solemn obligations.

There is, however, one argument set up as an universal answer to every thing that can be urged on our side; whether we address ourselves to gentlemen's understandings, or to their hearts and consciences. It is necessary I should remove this formidable objection; for though not often stated in distinct terms, I fear it is one which has a very wide influence. The slave-trade system, it is supposed, has taken so deep root in Africa, that it is absurd to think of its being eradicated; and the abolition of that share of trade carried on by Great Britain (and especially if her example is not followed by other powers) is likely to be of very little service. Give me leave to say, in answer to so dangerous an argument, that we ought to be extremely sure indeed of the assumption on which it rests, before we venture to rely on its validity; before we decide that an evil which we ourselves contribute to inflict is incurable, and on that very plea refuse to desist from bearing our part in the system which produces it. You are not sure, it is said, that other nations will give up the trade, if you should renounce it. I answer, if this trade is as criminal as it is asserted to be, or if it has in it a thousandth part of the criminality, which I and others, after thorough investigation of the subject, charge upon it, God forbid that we should hesitate in determining to relinquish so iniquitous a traffic, even though it should be retained by other countries! God forbid, however, that we should fail to do our utmost towards inducing other countries to abandon a bloody commerce which they have probably been in great measure led by our example to pursue! God forbid, that we should be capable of wishing to arrogate to ourselves the glory of being singular in renouncing it!

I tremble at the thought of gentlemen's indulging themselves in this argument (an argument as pernicious as it is futile) which I am combating. "We are friends," say they, "to humanity. We are second to none of you in our zeal for the good of Africa,—but the French will not abolish,—the Dutch will not abolish. We wait, therefore, on prudential principles, till they join us, or set us an example."

How, Sir, is this enormous evil ever to be eradicated, if every nation is thus prudentially to wait till the concurrence of all the world shall have been obtained?—Let me remark too, that there is no nation in Europe that has, on the one hand, plunged so deeply into this guilt as Britain; or that is so likely, on the other, to be looked up to as an example, if she should have the manliness to be the first in decidedly renouncing it. But, Sir, does not this argument apply a thousand times more strongly in a contrary way? How much more justly may *other* nations point to *us,* and say, "Why should we abolish the slave-trade when Great Britain has not abolished? Britain, free as she is, just and honourable as she is, and deeply also involved as she is in this commerce above all nations, not only has not abolished, but has refused to abolish.—She has investigated it well, she has gained the completest insight into its nature and effects; she has collected volumes of evidence on every branch of the subject. Her senate has deliberated—has deliberated again and again—and what is the result? She has gravely and solemnly determined to sanction the slave-trade. She sanctions it at least for a while—her legislature, therefore, it is plain, sees no guilt in it, and has thus furnished us with the strongest evidence that she can furnish,—of the justice unquestionably,—and of the policy also, in a certain measure and in certain cases at least, of permitting this traffic to continue."

This, Sir, is the argument with which we furnish the other nations of Europe, if we again refuse to put an end to the slave-trade. Instead, therefore, of imagining, that by choosing to presume on their continuing it, we shall have exempted ourselves from guilt, and have transferred the whole criminality to them; let us rather reflect that on the very principle urged against us, we shall henceforth have to answer for their crimes, as well as our own. We have strong reasons to believe that it depends upon us, whether other countries will persist in this bloody trade or not. Already we have suffered one year to pass away, and now that the question is renewed, a proposition is made for gradual, with the view of preventing immediate abolition. I know the difficulty that exists in attempting to reform long-established abuses; and I know the danger arising from the argument in favour of delay, in the case of evils which nevertheless are thought too enormous to be borne, when considered as perpetual. But by proposing some other period than the present, by prescribing some condition, by waiting for some contingency, or by refusing to proceed till a thousand favourable circumstances unite together; perhaps until we obtain the general concurrence of Europe (a concurrence which I believe never yet took place at the commencement of any one improvement in policy or in morals); year after year escapes, and the most enormous evils go unredressed. We see this abundantly exemplified, not only in public, but in private life. Similar observations have been applied to the case of personal reformation. If you go into the streets, it is a chance but the first person who crosses you is one, *"Vivendi recte qui prorogat horam."* We may wait; we may delay to cross the stream before us, till it has run down; but we shall wait for ever, for the river will still flow on, without being exhausted. We shall be no nearer the object which we profess to have in view, so long as the step which alone can bring us to it is not taken. Until the actual, the only remedy is applied, we ought neither to flatter ourselves that we have as yet thoroughly laid to heart the evil we affect to deplore; nor that there is as yet any reasonable assurance of its being brought to an actual termination.

It has also been occasionally urged, that there is something in the disposition and nature of the Africans themselves, which renders all prospect of civilisation on that continent extremely unpromising. "It has been known," says Mr. Frazer in his evidence, "that a boy has been put to death, who was refused to be purchased as a slave." This single story was deemed by that gentleman a sufficient proof of the barbarity of the Africans, and of the inutility of abolishing the slave-trade. My honourable friend, however, has told you, that this boy had previously run away from his master there several times; that the master had to pay his value, according to the custom of his country, every time he was brought back; and that partly from anger at the boy for running away so frequently, and partly to prevent a still further repetition of the same expense, he determined to put him to death. Such was the explanation of the story given in the cross-examination. This, Sir, is the signal instance that has been dwelt upon of African barbarity.—This *African*, we admit, was *unenlightened*, and altogether barbarous: but let us now ask, what would a *civilised* and *enlightened West Indian*, or a body of West Indians, have done in any case of a parallel nature? I will quote you, Sir, a law passed in the West Indies, in the year 1722, which, in turning over the book, I happened just now to cast my eye upon; by which law, this very same crime of running away, is, by the legislature of the island,—by the grave and deliberate sentence of that enlightened legislature, punished with death; and this, not in the case only of the third offence, but even in the very first instance. It is enacted, "that if any negro, or other slave shall withdraw himself from his master, for the term of six months; or any slave that was absent, shall not return within that time, it shall be adjudged felony, and every such person shall suffer death." There is also another West Indian law, by which every negro's hand is armed against his fellow-negroes, by his being authorised to kill a runaway slave, and even having a reward held out to him for doing so. Let the House now contrast the two cases. Let them ask themselves which of the two exhibits the greater barbarity? Let them reflect, with a little candour and liberality, whether on the ground of any of those facts, and loose insinuations as to the sacrifices to be met with in the evidence, they can possibly reconcile to themselves the excluding of Africa from all means of civilisation? Whether they can possibly vote for the continuance of the slave-trade upon the principle, that the Africans have shewn themselves to be a race of *incorrigible barbarians?*

I hope, therefore, we shall hear no more of the moral impossibility of civilising the Africans, nor have our understandings and consciences again insulted, by being called upon to sanction the slave-trade, until other nations shall have set the example of abolishing it. While we have been deliberating upon the subject, one nation, not ordinarily taking the lead in politics, nor by any means remarkable for the boldness of its councils, has determined on a gradual abolition; a determination, indeed, which, since it permits for a time the existence of the slave-trade, would be an unfortunate pattern for our imitation. France, it is said, will take up the trade, if we relinquish it. What! is it supposed that in the present situation of St. Domingo, of an island which used to take three-fourths of all the slaves required by the colonies of France, she, of all countries, will think of taking it up? What countries remain? The Portuguese, the Dutch, and the Spaniards. Of those countries let me declare it is my opinion, that if they see us renounce the trade, after full deliberation, they will not be disposed, even on principles of policy, to rush further into it. But I say more: How are they to furnish the capital necessary for carrying it on? If there is any aggravation of our guilt, in this wretched business, greater than another, it is that we have stooped to be the carriers of these miserable beings from Africa to the West Indies for all the other powers of Europe. And now, Sir, if we retire from the trade altogether, I ask, where is that fund which is to be raised at once by other nations, equal to the purchase of 30 or 40,000 slaves? A fund, which if we rate them at 40 l. or 50 l. each, cannot make a capital of less than a million and a half, or two millions of money. From what branch of their commerce is it that these European nations will draw together a fund to feed this monster?— to keep alive this detestable commerce? And even if they should make the attempt, will not that immense chasm, which must instantly be created in the other parts of their trade, from which this vast capital must be withdrawn in order to supply the slave-trade, be filled up by yourselves?—Will not these branches of commerce which they must leave, and from which they must withdraw their industry and their capitals, in order to apply them to the slave-trade, be then taken up by British merchants?—Will you not even in this case find your capital flow into these deserted channels?—Will not your capital be turned from the slave-trade to that natural and innocent commerce from which they must withdraw their capitals, in proportion as they take up the traffic in the flesh and blood of their fellow-creatures?

The committee sees, I trust, how little ground of objection to our proposition there is in this part of our adversaries' argument.

Having now detained the House so long, all that I will further add, shall be on that important subject, the civilisation of Africa, which I have already shewn that I consider as the leading feature in this question. Grieved am I to think that there should be a single person in this country, much more that there should be a single member in the British parliament, who can look on the present dark, uncultivated, and uncivilised state of that continent, as a ground for continuing the slave-trade,—as a ground not only for refusing to attempt the improvement of Africa, but even for hindering and intercepting every ray of light which might otherwise break in upon her,—as a ground for refusing to her the common chance and the common means, with which other nations have been blessed, of emerging from their native barbarism.

Here, as in every other branch of this extensive question, the argument of our adversaries pleads against them; for, surely, Sir, the present deplorable state of Africa, especially when we reflect that her chief calamities are to be ascribed to us, calls for our generous aid, rather than justifies any despair on our part of her recovery, and still less any further repetition of our injuries.

I will not much longer fatigue the attention of the House; but this point has impressed itself so deeply on my mind, that I must trouble the committee with a few additional observations. Are we justified, I ask, on any one ground of theory, or by any one instance to be found in the history of the world, from its very beginning to this day, in forming the supposition which I am now combating? Are we justified in supposing that the particular practice which we encourage in Africa, of men's selling each other for slaves, is any symptom of a barbarism that is incurable? Are we justified in supposing that even the practise of offering up human sacrifices proves a total incapacity for civilisation? I believe it will be found, and perhaps much more generally than is supposed, that both the trade in slaves, and the still more savage custom of offering human sacrifices, obtained in former periods, throughout many of those nations which now, by the blessings of Providence, and by a long progression of improvements, are advanced the farthest in civilisation. I believe, Sir, that, if we will reflect an instant, we shall find that this observation comes directly home to our own selves; and that, on the same ground on which we are now disposed to proscribe Africa for ever from all possibility of improvement, we ourselves might, in like manner, have been proscribed and for ever shut out from all the blessings which we now enjoy.

There was a time, Sir, which it may be fit sometimes to revive in the remembrance of our countrymen, when even human sacrifices are said to have been offered in this island. But I would peculiarly observe on this day, for it is a case precisely in point, that the very practice of the slave-trade once prevailed among us. Slaves, as we may read in Henry's History of Great Britain, were formerly an established article of our exports.

"Great numbers," he says, "were exported like cattle, from the British coast, and were to be seen exposed for sale in the Roman market." It does not distinctly appear, by what means they were procured; but there was unquestionably no small resemblance, in the particular point, between the case of our ancestors and that of the present wretched natives of Africa —for the historian tells you that "adultery, witchcraft, and debt were probably some of the chief sources of supplying the Roman market with British slaves—that prisoners taken in war were added to the number— and that there might be among them some unfortunate gamesters who, after having lost all their goods, at length staked themselves, their wives, and their children." Every one of these sources of slavery has been stated, and almost precisely in the same terms, to be at this hour a source of slavery in Africa. And these circumstances, Sir, with a solitary instance or two of human sacrifices, furnish the alleged proofs, that Africa labours under a natural incapacity for civilisation; that it is enthusiasm and fanaticism to think that she can ever enjoy the knowledge and the morals of Europe; that Providence never intended her to rise above a state of barbarism; that Providence has irrevocably doomed her to be only a nursery for slaves for us free and civilised Europeans. Allow of this principle, as applied to Africa, and I should be glad to know why it might not also have been applied to ancient and uncivilised Britain. Why might not some Roman senator, reasoning on the principles of some honourable gentlemen, and pointing to *British barbarians,* have predicted with equal boldness, "*There* is a people that will never rise to civilisation—*there* is a people destined never to be free—a people without the understanding necessary for the attainment of useful arts; depressed by the hand of nature below the level of the human species; and created to form a supply of slaves for the rest of the world." Might not this have been said, according to the principles which we now hear stated, in all respects as fairly and as truly of Britain herself, at that period of her history, as it can now be said by us of the inhabitants of Africa?

We, Sir, have long since emerged from barbarism—we have almost forgotten that we were once barbarians—we are now raised to a situation which exhibits a striking contrast to every circumstance, by which a Roman might have characterised us, and by which we now characterise Africa. There is indeed one thing wanting to complete the contrast, and to clear us altogether from the imputation of acting even to this hour as barbarians; for we continue to this hour a barbarous traffic in slaves; we continue it even yet in spite of all our great and undeniable pretensions to civilisation. We were once as obscure among the nations of the earth, as savage in our manners, as debased in our morals, as degraded in our understandings, as these unhappy Africans are at present. But in the lapse of a long series of years, by a progression slow, and for a time almost imperceptible, we have become rich in a variety of acquirements, favoured above measure in the gifts of Providence, unrivalled in commerce, pre-eminent in arts, foremost in the pursuits of philosophy and science, and established in all the blessings of civil society; we are in the possession of peace, of happiness, and of liberty; we are under the guidance of a mild and beneficent religion; and we are protected by impartial laws, and the purest administration of justice: we are living under a system of government which our own happy experience leads us to pronounce the best and wisest which has ever yet been framed; a system which has become the admiration of the world. From all these blessings, we must for ever have been shut out, had there been any truth in those principles which some gentlemen have not hesitated to lay down as applicable to the case of Africa. Had those principles been true, we ourselves had languished to this hour in that miserable state of ignorance, brutality, and degradation, in which history proves our ancestors to have been immersed. Had other nations adopted these principles in their conduct towards us; had other nations applied to Great Britain the reasoning which some of the senators of this very island now apply to Africa, ages might have passed without our emerging from barbarism; and we, who are enjoying the blessings of British civilisation, of British laws, and British liberty, might at this hour have been little superior either in morals, in knowledge, or refinement, to the rude inhabitants of the coast of Guinea.

If then we feel that this perpetual confinement in the fetters of brutal ignorance, would have been the greatest calamity which could have be-fallen us; if we view with gratitude and exultation the contrast between the peculiar blessings we enjoy, and the wretchedness of the ancient in-habitants of Britain; if we shudder to think of the misery which would still have overwhelmed us, had Great Britain continued to the present times to be the mart for slaves to the more civilised nations of the world, through some cruel policy of theirs, God forbid that we should any longer subject Africa to the same dreadful scourge, and preclude the light of knowledge, which has reached every other quarter of the globe, from hav-ing access to her coasts!

I trust we shall no longer continue this commerce, to the destruction of every improvement on that wide continent; and shall not consider our-selves as conferring too great a boon, in restoring its inhabitants to the rank of human beings. I trust we shall not think ourselves too liberal, if, by abolishing the slave-trade, we give them the same common chance of civilisation with other parts of the world, and that we shall not allow to Africa the opportunity—the hope—the prospect of attaining to the same blessings which we ourselves, through the favourable dispensations of Di-vine Providence, have been permitted, at a much more early period, to enjoy. If we listen to the voice of reason and duty, and pursue this night the line of conduct which they prescribe, some of us may live to see a reverse of that picture, from which we now turn our eyes with shame and regret. We may live to behold the natives of Africa engaged in the calm occupations of industry, in the pursuit of a just and legitimate commerce. We may behold the beams of science and philosophy breaking in upon their land, which, at some happy period in still later times, may blaze with full lustre; and joining their influence to that of pure religion, may illuminate and invigorate the most distant extremities of that immense continent. Then may we hope that even Africa, though last of all the quarters of the globe, shall enjoy at length, in the evening of her days, those blessings which have descended so plentifully upon us in a much earlier period of the world. Then also will Europe, participating in her improvement and prosperity, receive an ample recompense for the tardy kindness (if kindness it can be called) of no longer hindering that continent from extricating herself out of the darkness which, in other more fortunate regions, has been so much more speedily dispelled.

> . . . Nos primus equis oriens afflavit anhelis;
> Illic sera rubens accendit lumina Vesper.

Then, Sir, may be applied to Africa, those words, originally used indeed with a different view:

> His demum exactis . . .
> Devenere locos laetos, et amaena vireta
> Fortunatorum nemorum, sedesque beatas:
> Largior hic campos Æther, et limine vestit
> Purpureo.

It is in this view, Sir,—it is as an atonement for our long and cruel injustice towards Africa, that the measure proposed by my honourable friend most forcibly recommends itself to my mind. The great and happy change to be expected in the state of her inhabitants, is, of all the various and important benefits of the abolition, in my estimation, incomparably the most extensive and important.

I shall vote, Sir, against the adjournment; and I shall also oppose to the utmost every proposition, which in any way may tend either to prevent, or even to postpone for an hour, the total abolition of the slave-trade: a measure which, on all the various grounds which I have stated, we are bound, by the most pressing and indispensable duty, to adopt.

The House divided on an amendment moved by Mr. Dundas, for inserting in the motion the word "gradually,"

Ayes	*195*
Noes	*125*

and the question thus amended was then put, and, after a second division, carried.

Ayes	230
Noes	85

Charles James Fox

Charles James Fox

[*Born* JANUARY 24, 1749—*Died* SEPTEMBER 13, 1806]

He was a good fellow; he rolled into the House, fat, good-humoured, and popular.—WALTER BAGEHOT

· U ·

upon Rockingham's death in 1782, Charles James Fox became the "undisputed" leader of the Whig party for the next twenty years,[1] achieving the distinction of being called "perhaps" the greatest figure in the history of parliamentary opposition in England.[2] Edward Lascelles contends that without the presence of Fox in Parliament during certain critical moments, the claims of democracy might well have been drawn from constitutional into revolutionary methods.[3] Fox's contributions to British constitutional history were "solid and substantial":

He helped to create sentiment against the American war; he defeated Pitt's petty attack upon him through the Westminster Scrutiny; he succeeded in amending Pitt's Irish commercial treaty considerably, and lent his prestige to aid its defeat in the Irish Parliament. He prevented an ill-considered war with Russia in 1791, contributed greatly to freedom of the press by passage of his Libel Act, and won the high respect of historians for his diplomatic ability during his several short terms as Secretary of State for Foreign Affairs. At the same time, he held together a vigorous Whig minority during the dark and reactionary days of the French Revolution, when English liberties reached their lowest ebb since the days of the Stuarts. He prepared the way for the abolition of the slave trade. Finally . . . he originated the great Liberal Party, which renovated and reformed English politics during the nineteenth century.[4]

Fox was first and foremost a debater whose skill was unsurpassed. Brougham considers him to have been the most accomplished debater who ever appeared in the theatre of public affairs in any age of the world.[5] A speech by Fox was an outstanding event of any day. To the King's Bench, he was a powerful adversary; to his followers, he was a man who had given them a purpose and a "cause worth many sacri-

---

[1] Robert T. Oliver, *Four Who Spoke Out* (Syracuse: Syracuse University Press, 1946), p. 80.

[2] John Drinkwater, *Charles James Fox* (New York: Cosmopolitan Book Corp., 1928), p. 371.

[3] Edward Lascelles, *The Life of Charles James Fox* (London: Oxford University Press, 1936), p. 159.

[4] Oliver, *op. cit.*

[5] Brougham, *op. cit.*, p. 178. For complete reference, see *fn* 10 in discussion of William Pitt.

fices"; [6] and to observers, he was a wit who possessed the facility to expose to ridicule the absurdity or inconsistency of an adverse argument.[7] Fox was always at his best in reply. He required no formal preparation beyond the mental review of materials relating to the question[8] before pouring forth his arguments in an "impetuous torrent of urgency" with his harsh, "thrilling voice" and rapid delivery.[9] While never failing to go direct to the heart of any argument in his lengthy discourses, he enjoyed parrying with the opposition by "Circling round and about the point . . . composing at the moment, and, as he laughingly confessed, forgetting every line of every speech . . . he ever uttered. . . ." [10]

There is much disagreement among historians and biographers concerning which of Fox's speeches was the most outstanding. Walpole believes the address delivered on November 18, 1783, in support of his "famous" bill for the government of India is one Fox himself never surpassed.[11] Others believe his defense in the Westminster Scrutiny of 1784–85 to be among the most brilliant of his speeches.[12] The address selected for this volume, however, was delivered on December 13, 1792, protesting the call-up of the militia. Lascelles believes it is one of Fox's most eloquent utterances, and, unlike many of his great speeches, is well reported.[13] As was often the fate of the eloquent, but out-numbered, Whig opposition, the will of the King prevailed, and the original motion carried 290 to 50.

---

[6] Lascelles, op. cit., p. 158.

[7] Brougham, op. cit., p. 185.

[8] Robert H. Murray, Edmund Burke (London: Oxford University Press, 1931), p. 176.

[9] Lascelles, op. cit., p. 162.

[10] George Otto Trevelyan, The Early History of Charles James Fox (New York: Harper and Brothers, 1904), p. 429.

[11] B. C. Walpole, Charles James Fox (London: The Grolier Society, 1806?), p. 98.

[12] See Earl Stanhope, Life of the Right Honourable William Pitt, II (London: John Murray, 1861), p. 142. Stanhope thinks the three "highest efforts" were Fox's speech upon Russian armament on March 1, 1792, the Westminster Scrutiny, and that on French armament in 1803. Brougham, op. cit., p. 186, omits the Westminster Scrutiny, and includes a speech in 1791 on Russian armament, and one on Parliamentary Reform in 1797.

[13] Lascelles, op. cit., p. 246.

Address on the King's Speech[1]

•

HOUSE OF COMMONS *December 13, 1792*

The session was this day opened by His Majesty, with the following speech to both Houses:

My lords, and gentlemen; having judged it necessary to embody a part of the militia of this kingdom, I have, in pursuance of the provisions of the law, called you together within the time limited for that purpose, and it is on every account a great satisfaction to me to meet you in parliament at this conjuncture. I should have been happy if I could have announced to you the secure and undisturbed continuance of all the blessings which my subjects have derived from a state of tranquillity; but events have recently occurred which require our united vigilance and exertion, in order to preserve the advantages which we have hitherto enjoyed. The seditious practices which had been in a great measure checked by your firm and explicit declaration in the last session, and by the general concurrence of my people in the same sentiments, have of late been more openly renewed, and with increased activity. A spirit of tumult and disorder (the natural consequence of such practices) has shewn itself in acts of riot and insurrection, which required the interposition of a military force in support of the civil magistrate. The industry employed to excite discontent on various pretexts, and in different parts of the kingdom, has appeared to proceed from a design to attempt the destruction of our happy constitution, and the subversion of all order and government; and this design has evidently been pursued in connection and concert with persons in foreign countries. I have carefully observed a strict neutrality in the present war on the continent, and have uniformly abstained from any interference with respect to the internal affairs of France; but it is

1 *Speeches of the Right Honourable Charles James Fox in the House of Commons,* Vol. IV. Edited by J. Wright (London: Longman, Hurst, Rees, Orme, and Brown, 1815), pp. 442-463.

impossible for me to see, without the most serious uneasiness, the strong and increasing indications which have appeared there of an intention to excite disturbances in other countries, to disregard the rights of neutral nations, and to pursue views of conquest and aggrandisement, as well as to adopt towards my allies the States General (who have observed the same neutrality with myself), measures which are neither conformable to the law of nations, nor to the positive stipulations of existing treaties. Under all these circumstances, I have felt it my indispensable duty to have recourse to those means of prevention and internal defence with which I am entrusted by law; and I have also thought it right to take steps for making some augmentation of my naval and military force, being persuaded that these exertions are necessary in the present state of affairs, and are best calculated both to maintain internal tranquillity, and to render a firm and temperate conduct effectual for preserving the blessings of peace. Nothing will be neglected on my part that can contribute to that important object consistently with the security of my kingdoms, and with the faithful performance of engagements which we are bound equally by interest and honour to fulfil. . . .

Mr. Fox rose and said: Although, Sir, what has fallen from the noble earl behind me contains the substance of almost all that I have to offer, and although it must have produced the effects which good sense, truth, and solid argument never fail to produce on a great body, the tacit acknowledgment of all who heard him, insomuch, that no one seemed ready to venture to rise up in answer to the noble earl, yet I cannot avoid offering my opinion on the present most critical and most alarming occasion. I am not so little acquainted with the nature of man, as not to know, that in public speaking, in order to engage the attention of the hearers, besides the efficacy of fair and candid reasoning, a man ought always to be in temper and unison with his audience. He ought to shew, that however they may differ upon points, they are still pursuing in reality the same object, namely, the love of truth. With this object in view, I shall, Sir, state explicitly what are my sentiments on the subjects now presented to our notice by the speech from the throne. And first, I state it to be my conviction, that we are assembled at the most critical and momentous crisis, not only that I have ever known, but that I have ever read of in the history of this country—a crisis not merely interesting to ourselves but to all nations; and that on the conduct of parliament at this crisis depends not only the fate of the British constitution, but the future happiness of mankind.

His Majesty's speech, Sir, is full of a variety of assertions, or perhaps I should not make use of the word assertions, without adding, that it has also a variety of insinutations conveyed in the shape of assertions, which must impress every man with the most imminent apprehensions for the safety of every thing that is justly dear to Englishmen. It is our first duty to inquire into the truth of these assertions and insinuations so conveyed to us from the throne. I am sure I need not recur to the old parliamentary usage of declaring, that when I speak of the King's speech, I mean to be considered as speaking of the speech of the minister, since no one, I trust, will impute to me a want of due and sincere respect for His Majesty. It is the speech which His Majesty has been advised, by his confidential servants, to deliver from the throne. They are responsible for every letter of it, and to them and them only, every observation is addressed. I state it, therefore, to be my firm opinion, that there is not one fact asserted in His Majesty's speech which is not false—not one assertion or insinuation which is not unfounded. Nay, I cannot be so uncandid as to believe, that even the ministers themselves think them true. This charge upon His Majesty's ministers is of so serious a kind, that I do not pronounce it lightly; and I desire that gentlemen will go fairly into the consideration of the subject, and manifest the proper spirit of the representatives of the people in such a moment. What the noble earl said is most strictly true. The great, prominent feature of the speech is, that it is an intolerable calumny on the people of Great Britain; an insinuation of so gross and so black a nature, that it demands the strictest inquiry, and the most severe punishment.

The next assertion is, that there exists at this moment an insurrection in this kingdom. An insurrection! Where is it? Where has it reared its head? Good God! an insurrection in Great Britain! No wonder that the militia were called out, and parliament assembled in the extraordinary way in which they have been. But where is it? Two gentlemen have delivered sentiments in commendation and illustration of the speech; and yet, though this insurrection has existed for fourteen days, they have given us no light whatever, no clue, no information where to find it. The right honourable magistrate tells us, that, in his high municipal situation, he has received certain information which he does not think proper to communicate to us. This is really carrying the doctrine of confidence to a length indeed. Not content with ministers leading the House of Commons into the most extravagant and embarrassing situations, under the blind cover of confidence, we are now told that a municipal magistrate has information of an insurrection, which he does not chuse to lay before the Commons of England, but which he assures us is sufficient to justify the alarm that has spread over the whole country! The honourable gentleman who seconded the motion tells us, that the "insurrections are too notorious to be described." Such is the information which we receive from the right honourable magistrate, and the honourable gentleman, who have been selected to move and second the address. I will take upon me to say, Sir, that it is not the notoriety of the insurrections which prevents those gentlemen from communicating to us the particulars, but their non-existence.

The speech goes on in the same strain of calumny and falsehood, and says, "the industry employed to excite discontent on various pretexts, and in different parts of the kingdom, has appeared to proceed from a design to attempt the destruction of our happy constitution, and the subversion of all order and government." I beseech gentlemen to consider the import of these words, and I demand of their honour and truth, if they believe this assertion to be founded in fact. There have been, as I understand, and as every one must have heard, some slight riots in different parts of the country, but I ask them, were not the various pretexts of these different tumults false, and used only to cover an attempt to destroy our happy constitution? I have heard of a tumult at Shields, of another at Leith, of some riot at Yarmouth, and of something of the same nature at Perth and Dundee. I ask gentlemen if they believe that in each of these places the avowed object of the complaint of the people, was not the real one—that the sailors at Shields, Yarmouth, &c. did not really want some increase of their wages, but were actuated by a design of overthrowing the constitution? Is there a man in England who believes this insinuation to be true? And in like manner of every other meeting, to which, in the present spirit, men may give the name of tumultuous assembling. I desire to know if there has been discovered any motive other than their open and avowed one. And yet, with this conviction in our minds, we are called upon to declare directly our belief and persuasion that these things are so. We are called upon to join in the libel upon our constituents. The answer to the speech says, that we know of the tumult and disorder, but as to the actual insurrection, it more modestly makes us say, "that we are sorry to hear there is an insurrection." Of the tumults and disorders, then, we have personal knowledge; but the insurrection we learn from His Majesty's speech!

I do not wish to enter at length into the affairs of France, which form the next prominent passage in His Majesty's speech; but though I do not desire to enter at length into this part, I cannot conceal my sentiments on certain doctrines which I have heard this night. The honourable gentleman who seconded the motion thought proper to say, as a proof that there existed a dangerous spirit in this country, that it was manifested "by the drooping and dejected aspect of many persons, when the tidings of Dumourier's surrender arrived in England." What, Sir, is this to be considered as a sign of discontent, and of a preference to republican doctrines? That men should droop and be dejected in their spirits, when they heard that the armies of despotism had triumphed over an army fighting for liberty; if such dejection be a proof that men are discontented with the constitution of England, and leagued with foreigners in an attempt to destroy it, I give myself up to my country as a guilty man, for I freely confess, that when I heard of the surrender or retreat of Dumourier, and that there was a probability of the triumph of the armies of Austria and Prussia over the liberties of France, my spirits drooped, and I was dejected. What, Sir, could any man who loves the constitution of England, who feels its principles in his heart, wish success to the Duke of Brunswick, after reading a manifesto which violated every doctrine that Englishmen hold sacred, which trampled under foot every principle of justice and humanity and freedom and true government; and upon which the combined armies entered the kingdom of France, with which they had nothing to do; and when he heard, or thought that he saw a probability of their success, could any man possessing true British feelings be other than dejected? I honestly confess, Sir, that I never felt more sincere gloom and dejection in my life; for I saw in the triumph of that conspiracy, not merely the ruin of liberty in France, but the ruin of liberty in England; the ruin of the liberty of man. But, am I to be told that my sorrow was an evident proof of my being connected with the French nation, or with any persons in that nation, for the purpose of aiding them in creating discontents in England, or in making any attempt to destroy the British constitution? If such a conclusion were to be drawn from the dejection of those who are hostile to the maxims of tyranny, upon which the invasion of France was founded, what must we say of those men who acknowledge that they are sorry the invasion did not prosper? Am I to believe that the honourable gentleman, and all others, who confess their sorrow at the failure of Prussia and Austria, were connected with the courts in concert, and that a considerable body of persons in this country were actually in the horrid league formed against human liberty? Are we taught to bring this heavy charge against all those, whose spirits drooped on the reverse of the news, and when it turned out that it was not Dumourier, but the Duke of Brunswick who had retreated? No; he would not charge them with being confederates with the invaders of France; nor did they believe, nor could they believe, that the really constitutional men of England, who rejoiced at the overthrow of that horrid and profligate scheme, wished to draw therefrom any thing hostile to the established government of England.

But what, Sir, are the doctrines that they desire to set up by this insinuation of gloom and dejection? That Englishmen are not to dare to have any genuine feelings of their own; that they must not rejoice but by rule; that they must not think but by order; that no man shall dare to exercise his faculties in contemplating the objects that surround him, nor give way to the indulgence of his joy or grief in the emotions that they excite, but according to the instructions that he shall receive. That, in observing the events that happen to surrounding and neutral nations, he shall not dare to think whether they are favourable to the principles that contribute to the happiness of man, or the contrary; and that he must take, not merely his opinions, but his sensations from His Majesty's ministers and their satellites for the time being! Sir, whenever the time shall come that the character and spirits of Englishmen are so subdued; when they shall consent to believe that every thing which happens around is indifferent both to their understandings and their hearts; and when they shall be brought to rejoice and grieve, just as it shall suit the taste, the caprice, or the ends of ministers, then I pronounce the constitution of this country to be extinct. We have read, Sir, of religious persecutions, of the implacable oppressions of the Roman see, of the horrors of the inquisition of Spain; but so obdurate, so hard, so intolerable a scheme of cruelty, was never engendered in the mind of, much less practised by, any tyrant, spiritual or temporal. For see to what lengths they carry this system of intellectual oppression! "On various pretexts there have been tumults and disorder, but the true design was the destruction of our happy constitution." So says the speech; and mark the illustration of the right honourable magistrate: "There have been various societies established in the city of London, instituted for the plausible purpose of merely discussing constitutional questions, but which were really designed to propagate seditious doctrines." So, then, by this new scheme of tyranny, we are not to judge of the conduct of men by their overt acts, but are to arrogate to ourselves at once the province and the power of the Deity: we are to arraign a man for his secret thoughts, and to punish him, because we chuse to believe him guilty! "You tell me, indeed," says one of these municipal inquisitors, "that you meet for an honest purpose, but I know better: your plausible pretext shall not impose upon me: I know your seditious design: I will brand you for a traitor by my own proper authority." What innocence can be safe against such a power? What inquisitor of Spain, of ancient or of modern tyranny, can hold so lofty a tone? Well and nobly and seasonably, has the noble earl said—and I would not weaken the sentiment by repeating it in terms less forcible than his own, but that eternal truth cannot suffer by the feebleness of the terms in which it is conveyed—"There are speculative people in this country, who disapprove of the system of our government, and there must be such men as long as the land is free; for it is of the very essence of freedom for men to differ upon speculative points." Is it possible to conceive, that it should enter into the imaginations of freedom to doubt this truth? The instant that the general sense of the people shall question this truth, and that opinion shall be held dependant on the will of ministers and magistrates, from that moment I date the extinction of our liberties as a people. Our constitution was not made, thank God! in a day. It is the result of gradual and progressive wisdom. Never has the protecting genius of England been either asleep or satisfied.

> . . . "O but man, proud man!
> Drest in a little brief authority,
> Plays such fantastic tricks before high heaven,
> As make the angels weep."

Now, it seems, the constitution is complete—now we are to stand still. We are to deride the practice and the wisdom of our forefathers: we are to elevate ourselves with the constitution in our hands, and to hold it forth to a wondering world as a model of human perfection. Away with all further improvement, for it is impossible! Away with all further amelioration of the state of man in society, for it is needless! Let no man touch this work of man; it is like the work of heaven, perfect in all its parts, and, unlike every other work of man, it is neither capable of perversion nor subject to decay! Such is the presumptuous language that we hear; and, not content with this haughty tone, they imitate the celebrated anathema of brother Peter, in the Tale of a Tub, and exclaim, "G—d confound you both eternally if you offer to believe otherwise."

Now this, Sir, is the crisis, which I think so truly alarming. We are come to the moment, when the question is, whether we shall give to the King, that is, to the executive government, complete power over our thoughts: whether we are to resign the exercise of our natural faculties to the ministers for the time being, or whether we shall maintain, that in England no man is criminal, but by the commission of overt acts forbidden by the law. This I call a crisis more imminent and tremendous than any that the history of this country ever exhibited. I am not so ignorant of the present state of men's minds, and of the ferment artfully created, as not to know that I am now advancing an opinion likely to be unpopular. It is not the first time that I have incurred the same hazard. But I am as ready to meet the current of popular opinion now running in favour of those high lay doctrines, as in the year 1783 I was to meet the opposite torrent, when it was said, that I wished to sacrifice the people to the crown. I will do now as I did then. I will act against the cry of the moment, in the confidence, that the good sense and reflection of the people will bear me out. I know well that there are societies who have published opinions, and circulated pamphlets, containing doctrines tending, if you please, to subvert our establishments. I say that they have done nothing unlawful in this; for these pamphlets have not been suppressed by law. Shew me the law that orders these books to be burnt, and I will acknowledge the illegality of their proceedings: but if there be no such law, you violate the law in acting without authority. You have taken upon you to do that for which you have no warrant; you have voted them to be guilty. What is the course prescribed by law? If any doctrines are published tending to subvert the constitution in church and state, you may take cognizance of the fact in a court of law. What have you done? Taken upon you by your own authority to suppress them—to erect every man, not merely into an inquisitor, but into a judge, a spy, an informer— to set father against father, brother against brother, and neighbour against neighbour, and in this way you expect to maintain the peace and tranquillity of the country! You have gone upon the principles of slavery in all your proceedings: you neglect in your conduct the foundation of all legitimate government, the rights of the people: and, setting up this bug-bear, you spread a panic for the very purpose of sanctifying this infringe-ment, while, again, the very infringement engenders the evil which you dread. One extreme naturally leads to another. Those who dread republi-canism, fly for shelter to the crown. Those who desire reform and are calumniated, are driven by despair to republicanism. And this is the evil that I dread!

These are the extremes into which these violent agitations hurry the people, to the gradual decrease of that middle order of men who shudder as much at republicanism on the one hand, as they do at despotism on the other. That middle order of men, who have hitherto preserved to this country all that is dear in life, I am sorry to say it, is daily lessening; but permit me to add, that while my feeble voice continues, it shall not be totally extinct; there shall at least be one man who will, in this ferment of extremes, preserve the centre point. I may be abused by one side, I may be libelled by the other; I may be branded at one and the same time with the terms of firebrand and lukewarm politician; but though I love popular-ity, and own that there is no external reward so dear to me as the good opinion and confidence of my fellow citizens, yet no temptation whatever shall ever induce me to join any association that has for its object a change in the basis of our constitution, or an extension of that basis be-yond the just proportion. I will stand in the gap, and oppose myself to all the wild projects of a new-fangled theory, as much as against the mon-strous iniquity of exploded doctrines. I conceive the latter to be more our present danger than the former. I see, not merely in the panic of the timorous, but in the acts of the designing, cause for alarm against the most abhorrent doctrines. The new associations have acted with little dis-guise. One of them, the association for preserving liberty and property against republicans and levellers, I must applaud for the sincerity of its practise. Mr. Chairman Reeves says, that they will not only *prosecute,* but they will *convince* men, and they recommend, among other publica-tions, a hand-bill, entitled, "One Pennyworth of Truth from Thomas Bull to his brother John," in which, among other odd things, it is said, "Have you not read the Bible? Do you not know that it is there written,

that kings are the Lord's anointed? But whoever heard of an anointed republic?" Such is the manner in which these associations are to "convince"
the minds of men! In the course of the present century, their recommendation would have been prosecuted as high treason. In the years 1715 and
1745, the person who dared to say that kings derived their power from
divine right, would have been prosecuted for treason; and I ask if, even
now, this is the way to inculcate the principles of genuine loyalty? No, Sir,
thank God, the people of this country have a better ground of loyalty to
the house of Brunswick than that of Divine right, namely, that they are
the sovereigns of their own election; that their right is not derived from
superstition, but from the choice of the people themselves; that it originated in the only genuine fountain of all royal power, the will of the
many; and that it has been strengthened and confirmed by the experience
of the blessings they have enjoyed, because the house of Brunswick has
remembered the principles upon which they received the crown. It is
rather extraordinary, Sir, that such language should be held at this precise moment: that it should be thought right to abuse republics, at the
very moment that we are called upon to protect the republic of Holland.
To spread the doctrine that kings only govern by divine right, may indis-
pose your allies to receive your proposed succour. They may not choose to
receive into their country your admirals and generals, who being appointed by this king, in divine right, must partake of the same anger, and
be supposed sworn enemies to all forms of government not so sanctified.
Surely, independent of the falsehood and the danger of preaching up such
doctrines at home, it is the height of impolicy at this time to hold them in
regard even to our neighbours. It may be asked, would I prosecute such
papers? To this I answer very candidly, I would not. I never yet saw the
seditious paper that I would have thought it necessary to prosecute; but
this by no means implies that emergencies may not make it proper; but
surely there is nothing so essential to the true check of sedition, as impartiality in prosecution. If a government wishes to be respected, they must
act with the strictest impartiality, and shew that they are as determined to
prevent the propagations of doctrines injurious to the rights of the people,
as of those which are hostile to the rights of the crown. If men are to be
encouraged to rally round the one standard, you must not, you ought not
to prevent volunteers from rallying round the other; unless you desire to
stifle in the breasts of men the surest and most active principle of obedience, a belief in your impartiality.

When I first heard, Sir, that the militia were called out, I felt more
anxiety and consternation than ever possessed my mind. I thought that
information had certainly been received of some actual insurrection, or
impending invasion. But when I heard that they were not called out to
enable ministers to send the troops to any distant part, to Ireland, or to

Scotland, (where they might know of disturbances, though I did not), but that troops were assembling round London, I firmly believed the whole to be a fraud; for I have friends in and about London, as intelligent, as vigilant, as much interested in the tranquillity of the metropolis, as the right honourable magistrate; and I was confident, that an insurrection could not actually exist in London without being known. I pronounced it in my own mind to be a fraud, and I here again pronounce it to be so. I am not given to make light assertions in this House, nor do I desire to receive implicit belief. I deprecate confidence on my bare assertion. On the contrary, I state, that I believe this pretext to be a fraud, and I intreat you to inquire, that you may ascertain the truth. I know that there are societies who have indulged themselves, as I think, in silly and frantic speculations, and who have published toasts, &c. that are objectionable; but that there is any insurrection, or that any attempt was making to overthrow the constitution, I deny. Now, if this assertion of ministers is a falsehood, is it an innocent falsehood? Are the people of this country playthings in the hands of ministers that they may frighten them and disturb them at pleasure? Are they to treat them as some weak, jealous-pated, and capricious men treat their wives and mistresses—alarm them with false stories, that they may cruelly feast on the torture of their apprehensions, and delight in the susceptibility that drowns them in tears! Have they no better enjoyment than to put forth false alarms, that they know may draw from the people the soothing expressions of agitated loyalty? Or do they think that these expressions, generously, readily made, in favour of the King, whom the people rationally love, may extend in its influence to all the persons that are near his throne? Indulging in this passion, they may keep us incessantly in the tumult of apprehension, until at last they so habituate the mind to dread the evil in this quarter, as to look for it in no other, or to stun it by repeated shocks of fiction into an insensibility of real attack.

His Majesty, in the next passage of the speech, brings us to the apprehension of a war. I shall refrain at this time from saying all that occurs to me on this subject, because I wish to keep precisely to the immediate subject: but never, surely, had this country so much reason to wish for peace; never was a period so little favourable to a rupture with France, or with any other power. I am not ready to subscribe exactly to the idea of the noble lord, or the propriety of a resolution never to go to war, unless we are attacked; but I wish that a motion was proposed by some one, to express our disapprobation of entering upon any war, if we can by any honourable means avoid it. Let no man be deterred by the dread of being in a minority. A minority saved this country from a war against Russia. And surely it is our duty, as it is our true policy, to exert every means to avert that greatest of national calamities. In the year 1789 we all must remember that Spain provoked this country by an insult, which is a real aggression: we were all agreed on the necessity of the case, but did we go headlong to war? No; we determined with becoming fortitude on an armed negociation. We did negociate, and we avoided a war. But now we disdain to negociate. Why? Because we have no minister at Paris. Why have we no minister there? Because France is a republic! And thus we are to pay with the blood and treasure of the people, for a punctilio! If there are discontents in the kingdom, Sir, this is the way to inflame them. It is of no consequence to any people what is the form of the government with which they may have to treat. It is with the governors, whatever may be the form, that in common sense and policy they can have to do. Having no legitimate concern with the internal state of any independent people, the road of common sense is simple and direct. That of pride and punc-tilio is as entangled as it is crooked. Is the pretext the opening of the Scheldt? I cannot believe that such an object can be the real cause. I doubt even if a war on this pretext would be undertaken with the appro-bation of the Dutch. What was the conduct of the French themselves under their depraved old system, when the good of the people never en-tered into the contemplation of the cabinet? The Emperor threatened to open the Scheldt in 1786. Did the French go to war with him instantly to prevent it? No. They opened a negociation, and prevented it by interfer-ing with their good offices. Why have we not so interfered? Because, for-sooth, France is an unanointed republic! Oh miserable, infatuated Frenchmen! Oh lame and inconsiderate politicians! Why, instead of breaking the holy vial of Rheims, why did you not pour some of the sa-cred oil on the heads of your executive council, that the pride of states might not be forced to plunge themselves and you into the horrors of war, rather than be contaminated by your acquaintance! How short-sighted were you to believe, that the prejudices of infants had departed with the gloom of ignorance, and that states were grown up to a state of manhood and reason!

This naturally brings us back again to the business of this day, namely, whether any address should be agreed to or not. I desire, then, to put it seriously to the conscience and honour of gentlemen to say, whether they will not be aiding the object of republicans and levellers, if they should agree to plunge this country headlong into a war, or give any pledge whatever to the crown, until they inquire and ascertain whether there is an insurrection in this country or not? Shall we declare war with-out inquiring whether we are also to have commotions at home? Shall we pledge our constituents to submission, to compliance, without first prov-ing to them that the strong measure of government has been authorised by truth? If you would have the laws respected by the people, I say again, you must begin by showing that they are respected from above. If you do not prove to the people that there is an actual insurrection, (for I leave out impending invasion and rebellion, as these are not even pretended), you cannot withhold from them the knowledge that you have acted illegally. And how can you expect rational obedience to the laws when you yourselves counteract them? When you set up the *ratio suasoria* as the *ratio justifica,* the people will clearly discern the futility and falsehood of your logic, and translate at once your terms into their true English of real causes and false pretexts. *"Ut ameris amabilis esto,"* is as true in government and legislation as it is in manners and private life, and is as well established by experience. The people will not be cheated. They will look round, and demand where this danger is to be seen. Is it in England? They see it overflowing in expressions of loyalty, and yet they libel it with imputations of insurrection. In Ireland, you know there is danger, and dare not own it. There you have prorogued the parliament to the 17th instant, but not to meet till the end of January for the dispatch of business, though you know that there a most respectable and formidable convention—I call it formidable, because I know nothing so formidable as reason, truth, and justice—will oblige you by the most cogent reasons to give way to demands, which the magnanimity of the nation ought to have anticipated. There you have thus prorogued the parliament, and deprived yourselves of the means of doing that gracefully which you must do, and which you ought to have done long ago, to subjects as attached to their King, and as abundantly endowed with every manly virtue as any part of the United Kingdom. And while the claims of generous and ill-treated millions are thus protracted, and, in addition to the hardship of their condition, they are insulted with the imprudent assertion of the tyrannical ascendancy, there is a miserable mockery held out of alarms in England which have no existence, but which are made the pretext of assembling the parliament in an extraordinary way, in order, in reality, to engage you in a foreign contest. What must be the fatal consequence when a well-judging people shall decide—what I sincerely believe—that the whole of this business is a ministerial manœuvre? Will the ministers own the real truth, and say that they wanted a pretext to assemble parliament to make up for their want of vigilance? They must take their choice, and submit to incur the indignation of their country, or feel themselves in a state of contempt. There are men who in this very act give them the praise of vigilance. They did all this, to be sure, with a little harmless fraud, to prevent evils! Let us examine their claim to vigilance.

This vigilant ministry saw, nay (if we may take their character from their associates) hoped, that France was on the brink of falling a sacrifice to the united force of Austria and Prussia, the two powers, of all others, whose union would be the most dreadful to England; but they saw no danger in this conquest to England, though thereby these great military

powers were to become maritime. They saw no danger in the union con-
certed between them, nay, when they had given away Poland in the mean
time, because, I suppose, they thought that when Oczakow was gone, the
balance of Europe went with it, and they retreated out of the field with
disgrace. They gave away Poland with as little compunction as honour,
and with the unenviable certainty, that their blustering was laughed at
and despised in every court in Europe. I know that some of them have
inordinate self-complacency; yet I will not be so uncandid as to conceal
my honest opinion, that there is not among them a single man, whose
talents for great and commanding policy have either attracted or secured
the confidence of any quarter of Europe. Do they boast of their vigilance?
The dexterous surrender of Oczakow, as they now know, might have
saved the fall and ruin of Poland. Do they boast of their vigilance? And
had they no apprehension of the union between Austria and Prussia? Had
they such perfect reliance on the moderation of Prussia, on his intimate
friendship with, his gratitude to, his confidence in, our faithful cabinet?
Do they boast of their vigilance, and yet saw nothing of their present
dread for Holland and Brabant, on the 30th of September, when to the
joy of every man whose heart is warmed with the love of freedom, the
Duke of Brunswick retreated before the armies of France? Were they vigilant, not to foresee the consequences of that retreat; or did they flatter
themselves with the weak, the false hope, that still the steadiness of men
bred up in the trammels of tactics and discipline, would be an overmatch
for the impetuosity of men, animated by the glorious flame of liberty? If
so, the battle of Jemappe ought, I should think, to have shewn these vigilant men their error. That battle happened on the 6th of November. On
the same day the government of the Netherlands took to flight, and the
news arrived in England on the 10th or 12th. Now, what did these vigilant
ministers? On the 17th they prorogued the parliament to the 3d of January, without even saying that it was then to meet for the dispatch of business! And yet on these vigilant men we are to repose, although in the eyes
of Europe, and in the hearts of Englishmen, an armament in their hands is
a proof and earnest of their future humiliation!

They call for subsidiary aid from the loyalty of the people, and to
procure this they have recourse to history, and search out for the lucky
frauds of former times: they find one of the most lucky frauds was the
popish plot in the reign of Charles the Second. The same cry in the present moment they knew was impossible; but a similar one was feasible in
the enmity against a republic. The protestant dissenters then, as now,
were made the object of terror, and every art was used to provoke the
rage of ignorance and barbarity. The fraud was too successful. Many of
my friends, from the best motives, were deluded into the snare, and that
most calamitous of all measures, the proclamation, unfortunately for Eng-

land, met with their countenance. I cannot better describe this calamity than by reading a passage from an eminent historian, Ralph, on the fatal consequences of the delusion of the popish plot. By comparing my friends on the present occasion to the celebrated Lord Russell at that time, I think that I cannot pay a better compliment to them, or at the same time a more just and deserved tribute to the memory of that excellent person. Both, in consequence of their high integrity and attachment to the country, have become the dupes of deception. The passage is as follows: "But there were persons, it seems, ready to adopt his (Oates's) intelligence, imperfect, chimerical, or fictitious as it was, and to make use of it as a firebrand to light up such a flame of dissention as had like to have laid waste the kingdom; and of these, according to the distinction already made, some were weak and some were wicked. The weak were those who thought popery the greatest mischief that comprehended all others, who mistook prejudice for conviction, credulity for candour, and rigour for righteousness. These, however, meant well, though they acted ill; and while doing the drudgery of a party, persuaded themselves they were saving the nation. The wicked were the master politicians of the times, who considered kings not as they were, good or ill in themselves, but as they were ill or good with respect to their own immediate views: now the plot, whether true or false, was formed of the happiest ingredients imaginable to advance their interest."

Now, Sir, let me address one word to my valued friends. I entreat them to reflect on the consequences of their recent delusion—not dissimilar to the above. The measure of the proclamation is now stated to be over—it has failed: let them avoid all farther snares of the same kind. They will reflect on the necessity of union from the experience of the advantages which have flowed from it. They cannot feel more sensibly than I do the benefits of the cordial co-operation of that body of men who have, through the whole of the present reign, had to struggle with prejudice as well as enmity. Let them recollect the manner in which the present ministers came into power: let them recollect the insidious attempts that have been made to disjoin them; and now that the fatal measure of the proclamation is over, let them avoid, I say, all farther snares of the same kind. Of the declarations, which it is now the fashion to sign, I certainly cannot in general approve. Of all that I have seen, that of the Merchants of London appears best calculated to conciliate the approbation of constitutional men; but I see and hear on every side such violent doctrines, and such afflicting measures, as no man who is actuated by the wish of preserving peace in this country can subscribe to. A noble lord, (Fielding), for whom I have a high respect, says he will move for a suspension of the habeas corpus act. I hope not. I have a high respect for the noble lord; but no motive of personal respect shall make me inattentive to my duty.

Come from whom it may, I will with my most determined powers, oppose so dreadful a measure.

But, it may be asked, what would I propose to do in times of agitation like the present? I will answer openly. If there is a tendency in the dissenters to discontent, because they conceive themselves to be unjustly suspected and cruelly calumniated, what would I do? I would instantly repeal the test and corporation acts, and take from them, by such a step, all cause of complaint. If there were any persons tinctured with a republican spirit, because they thought that the representative government was more perfect in a republic, I would endeavour to amend the representation of the Commons, and to shew that the House of Commons, though not chosen by all, should have no other interest than to prove itself the representative of all. If there were men dissatisfied in Scotland or Ireland, or elsewhere, on account of disabilities and exemptions, of unjust prejudices, and of cruel restrictions, I would repeal the penal statutes, which are a disgrace to our law books. If there were other complaints of grievances, I would redress them where they were really proved; but above all, I would constantly, cheerfully, patiently listen. I would make it known, that if any man felt, or thought he felt, a grievance, he might come freely to the bar of this House and bring his proofs: and it should be made manifest to all the world, that where they did exist, they would be redressed; where they did not, that it should be made evident. If I were to issue a proclamation, this would be my proclamation:—"If any man has a grievance, let him bring it to the bar of the Commons' House of Parliament with the firm persuasion of having it honestly investigated." These are the subsidies that I would grant to government. What, instead of this, is done? Suppress the complaint—check the circulation of knowledge—command that no man shall read; or, that as no man under a £100 a year can kill a partridge, so no man under £20 or £30 a year, shall dare to read or to think!

I see in Westminster the most extraordinary resolutions of parochial meetings. In that city, with which I am intimately connected, and to which I owe high obligations, there have been resolutions and associations which militate against every idea that I was ever taught to entertain both of law and of the constitution. In the parish of St. Anne, Soho, at the head of which parochial meeting I see a much respected friend of mine, Sir Joseph Bankes, they have demanded a register of all the strangers living in the parish. In St. Clement's and elsewhere, publicans are threatened with the loss of their licenses if they shall suffer any newspapers to be read in their houses that they shall think seditious. Good God! where did justices find this law? I have always thought that there was no one thing of which the law was more justly jealous, than the exercise of the discretionary power given to justices with regard to li-

censes, and that above all things it was not permitted them to suffer political motives to interfere in the giving or withholding them. And publicans, too, are to be made judges of libel! No newspaper or pamphlet is to
be read, but such as they shall determine to be free from sedition! No
conversation is to be suffered but what they shall judge to be loyal! And
yet in this very House, not more than a twelvemonth ago, when I brought
in a bill with regard to libels, we all heard it asserted, that the knowledge
of what was a libel could not be safely left to the determination of twelve
jurymen—it could be judged of only by sages in the law. How can these
publicans be conceived capable of judging, or by what rule are they to
act? Are they to take their opinions from these associations? They recommend to them that loyal paper called "One Pennyworth of Advice," in
which, among other things, it is pretty plainly insinuated, that it would
have been well if Petion, the late mayor of Paris, had been assassinated
when in England, and that it would be an excess of virtue to exterminate
the dissenters! Are they to be told, that such writings as these are perfectly
harmless and praiseworthy, but that discussions on the constitution, debating societies, (although, by the bye, I never knew London without
debating societies, and I cannot see by what law any magistrate can inter-
rupt their peaceable discussions,) and all papers and conversations, where
there are free opinions on the nature of government, are libellous? What,
Sir, must be the consequence of all this, but that these publicans must
decide, that that is libellous which is disapproved of by ministers for the
time being, and by these associations, and that all freedom of opinion,
and all the fair and impartial freedom of the press is utterly destroyed!

Sir, I love the constitution as it is established. It has grown up with me
as a prejudice and a habit, as well as from conviction. I know that it is
calculated for the happiness of man, and that its constituent branches of
King, Lords, and Commons, could not be altered or impaired, without
entailing on this country the most dreadful miseries. It is the best adapted
to England, because, as the noble earl truly said, the people of England
think it the best; and the safest course is to consult the judgment and
gratify the predilections of a country. Heartily convinced, however, as I
am, that, to secure the peace, strength, and happiness of the country, we
must maintain the constitution against all innovation; yet I do not think
so superstitiously of any human institution, as to imagine, that it is incapable of being perverted: on the contrary, I believe that it requires an
increasing vigilance, on the part of the people, to prevent the decay and
dilapidations to which every edifice is subject. I think, also, that we may
be led asleep to our real danger by these perpetual alarms to loyalty,
which, in my opinion, are daily sapping the constitution. Under the pretext of guarding it from the assaults of republicans and levellers, we run
the hazard of leaving it open on the other and more feeble side. We are

led insensibly to the opposite danger; that of increasing the power of the crown, and of degrading the influence of the Commons' House of Parliament. It is in such moments as the present, that the most dangerous, because unsuspected, attacks may be made on our dearest rights; for let us only look back to the whole course of the present administration, and we shall see, that from their outset to the present day, it has been their invariable object to degrade the House of Commons in the eyes of the people, and to diminish its power and influence in every possible way.

It was not merely in the outset of their career, when they stood up against the declared voice of the House of Commons, that this spirit was manifested, but uniformly and progressively throughout their whole ministry the same disposition has been shewn, until at last it came to its full, undisguised demonstration on the question of the Russian war, when the House of Commons was degraded to the lowest state of insignificance and contempt, in being made to retract its own words, and to acknowledge that it was of no consequence or avail what were its sentiments on any one measure. The minister has regularly acted upon this sort of principle:—"I do not care what the House of Commons may think, or what may be thought of them. It is not their verdict that is to acquit me in any moment of difficulty or any hour of trial. I will agitate the people without: I will see whether they will bear me up in my measures; and as for the House of Commons, if, in the height of their confidence in me, they shall be made to say one thing to-day, I will make them, with equal ease, and without regard to their character, say another to-morrow." Such is the true English of the principle of the right honourable gentleman's conduct, and this principle he has constantly acted upon, to the vilification of the popular branch of the constitution. And what is this, Sir, but to make it appear that the House of Commons is in reality what Thomas Paine, and writers like him, say it is, namely, that it is not the true representative and organ of the people? In the same way, and by the same language, might Thomas Paine bring a slander upon our courts of law, and upon the trial by jury. In the same tone, he might assert: "Do not tell me what a jury of twelve men may say of my book: do not tell me what these associations say: I reject all tribunals, either constituted by legal authority, or self-erected: give me the people for my judges, and I will prove that my doctrines are agreeable to them." Such language would square completely with that of ministers, and constantly have they resorted to the dangerous innovation of supporting themselves, without regard to the opinion of the House of Commons, by appeals one day to the crown, the next to the Lords, and the third to the people, uniformly striving to exhibit parliament in the disgraceful and pitiful light of complete incapacity. Is it not wonderful, Sir, that all the true constitutional watchfulness of England should be dead to the only real danger that the present day exhibits, and that they should be alone roused by the idiotic clamour of republican phrenzy and of popular insurrection, which do not exist?

Sir, I have done my duty. I have, with the certainty of opposing myself to the furor of the day, delivered my opinion at more length than I intended, and perhaps I have intruded too long on the indulgence of the House. [*A general cry of "Hear him!" bespoke the perfect attention of the House.*] I have endeavoured to persuade you against the indecent haste of committing yourselves to these assertions of an existing insurrection, until you shall have made a rigorous inquiry where it is to be found. To avoid involving the people in the calamity of a war, without at least ascertaining the internal state of the kingdom, and to prevent us from falling into the disgrace of being, as heretofore, obliged perhaps in a week to retract every syllable that we are now called upon to say: to carry this into effect, I shall move, that after the first sentence of the proposed motion, "That an humble address be presented to His Majesty, humbly to thank His Majesty for his most gracious speech from the throne," the following words be substituted in the room of all that follow in the original motion:

"To express to His Majesty our most zealous attachment to the excellent constitution of this free country, our sense of the invaluable blessings which we derive from it, and our unshaken determination to maintain and preserve it.

"To assure His Majesty that, uniting with all His Majesty's faithful subjects in these sentiments of loyalty to the throne, and attachment to the constitution, we feel in common with them the deepest anxiety and concern, when we see those measures adopted by the executive government, which the law authorises only in cases of insurrection within this realm.

"That His Majesty's faithful Commons, assembled in a manner new and alarming to the country, think it their first duty, and will make it their first business, to inform themselves of the causes of this measure, being equally zealous to enforce a due obedience to the laws on the one hand, and a faithful execution of them on the other."

The House then divided on the address moved by the Lord Mayor: Yeas 290; Noes 50.

Sir Samuel Romilly

·

Sir Samuel Romilly

[*Born* MARCH 1, 1757—*Died* NOVEMBER 2, 1818]

. . . his easy and impressive elocution was enhanced by a tall and graceful figure, a melodious voice, and features of classical regularity.—J. M. RIGG

$\cdot$ I $\cdot$

f poverty and discontent were the bitter fruit of the Industrial Revolution, civil disorder was the acrid residue which threatened infestation throughout Great Britain. The government reacted by rigorously upholding capital punishment for menial crimes, relegating human life to the caprices of the ruling class in Parliament.

Few voices were raised in opposition to such willful actions, and criminal reforms were treated lightly save by one person whose parliamentary career was dedicated to the principle that rendering justice to the oppressed should be the first object of all Governments.[1] That man was Sir Samuel Romilly, son of a jeweller, grandson of a Huguenot refugee, barrister, and member of the House of Commons. C. G. Oakes calls Romilly "perhaps the greatest, and certainly the most pertinacious, law reformer who sat in the House of Commons in the nineteenth century." [2] His name, writes William Heath Bennet, "like the spell of the enchanter, awakens every feeling that responds to all that is good and noble and elevated in human nature." [3] To those who knew Romilly, it was difficult to speak of him in "merely ordinary or measured terms of love and veneration." [4]

While his personality and character endeared him to his friends, Romilly's zeal, intellect, and eloquence were admired by his adversaries at the Bar and in the House of Commons. According to Lord Brougham, the eloquence of Romilly "united all the more severe graces of oratory, both in manner and substance." [5] Bennet, who observed Romilly on many occasions, was impressed by his vocal animation, his erect stance, and his energy.[6] His ideas were presented without embellishment, and were "entirely free from sophism" while his arguments were those of a man who "has mastered his subject

---

1 Sir Samuel Romilly, *Memoirs*, II (London: John Murray, 1842), p. 331.

2 C. G. Oakes, *Sir Samuel Romilly* (London: George Allen and Unwin Ltd., 1935), p. xi.

3 William Heath Bennet, *Select Biographical Sketches from the Note-Books of a Law Reporter* (London: George Routledge and Sons, 1867), p. 19.

4 Coleman Phillipson, *Three Criminal Law Reformers: Beccaria, Bentham, Romilly* (London: J. M. Dent and Sons Ltd., 1923), p. 237.

5 Henry Lord Brougham, *Historical Sketches of Statesmen Who Flourished in the Time of George III,* I (2nd ed., London: Charles Knight and Co., 1839), p. 293.

6 Bennet, *op. cit.*, p. 35.

thoroughly, marshalled his arguments with care, and presented . . . with a precision which defied convincing replies." [7]

Romilly acquired his eloquence, not from the popular debating societies of his time, but from a "very useful expedient" suggested by Quintilian:

. . . that of expressing to myself in the best language I could, whatever I had been reading; of using the arguments I had met with in Tacitus or Livy, and making with them speeches of my own, not uttered, but composed and existing only in thought. Occasionally, too, I attended the two Houses of Parliament; and used myself to recite in thought, or to answer the speeches I had heard there. That I might lose no time, I generally reserved these exercises for the time of my walking or riding; and, before long, I had so well acquired the habit of it, that I could think these compositions as I was passing through the most crowded streets.[8]

This early training provided him with a faculty he possessed above all competition. When repeatedly called upon to speak without prior preparation, "he never wasted time by unnecessary or frivolous remarks, or dwelt long upon matters of minor importance; but kept the question in hand as the landmark of his address." [9]

Few of the criminal code reforms were enacted during Romilly's lifetime. His overt successes were limited to the repeal of the death penalty for picking pockets in 1808, the repeal of the death penalty for thefts from bleaching grounds in 1811, and the removal of capital punishment in the cases of soldiers and sailors convicted of vagrancy or begging without a pass in 1812.[10]

According to Gary Hawkins, Romilly believed his speech opposing suspension of Habeas Corpus to be the most significant of his ten years in the House of Commons. This speech was one of his last, and was "probably one of his best parliamentary addresses." [11] Although his pleas were in vain, his ideas were recorded, preserved, and acted upon by men of vision who were to follow.

---

7 Oakes, *op. cit.,* p. 328.

8 *Memoirs,* I, p. 34.

9 Bennet, *op. cit.,* p. 34.

10 Oakes, *op. cit.,* p. 298.

11 Gary J. Hawkins, "The Speech Education of Sir Samuel Romilly," unpublished M.A. thesis (Ohio University), 1960, p. 23.

Habeas Corpus Suspension Bill[1]

•

HOUSE OF COMMONS   *February 26, 1817*

L ord Castlereagh moved the Order of the Day for the first reading of the Habeas Corpus Suspension Bill. The Motion was opposed by Mr. Bennett, Mr. J. H. Smyth, Lord Althorpe, &c. and supported by Mr. F. Lewis, the Lord Advocate of Scotland, Mr. C. Wynn &c.

Sir, however unwilling to occupy the attention of the House, I cannot consent to give a silent vote on the most important question which has been ever discussed since I had a seat in Parliament. In whatever view we may contemplate the proposed measure, whether in relation to its immediate effects on the liberties of the people, or as a precedent for the conduct of future Ministers and future Parliaments, it is a subject which deserves the maturest deliberation. On the inestimable value of that part of the constitution which it tends to annul, there can be but one sentiment. It will be for the House to inquire, whether there exists any thing in the present state of the country,—whether the causes of alarm are so serious, and so imminent, as to demand nothing less than this fatal sacrifice. That evils exist,—that poverty and discontent have been followed by partial outrages and disorder, few will be disposed to deny. But does the Statute Book afford no remedy,—or, supposing some extraordinary measure to be necessary, is the remedy now proposed, adapted to the nature of the disease?

Sir, to justify the present application, it is incumbent on those who make it, to show that the ordinary means have been duly tried, and that those means have failed of success. The noble Lord, indeed, has spoken of the extraordinary vigilance of Government, but where is the evidence of it? In what does this boasted vigilance consist,—to what does it amount? —It amounts, in truth, to nothing! The noble Lord's own statement suffi-

---

1 *The Speeches of Sir Samuel Romilly.* (London: Printed for James Ridgway and Sons, Piccadilly, 1820), pp. 155–166.

ciently disproves the claim, which has been made on the part of himself and colleagues on this occasion. He has told us that traitorous designs had been long proceeding,—that for a considerable time before the aid of Parliament was required, the most insidious attempts had been made upon the loyalty, the morals, and the religion of the people, by the industrious circulation of seditious and blasphemous publications, and yet (though Ministers so boldly assert these facts,—though they even profess to have been long apprised of their existence), up to the present moment not a single prosecution has been instituted against their authors! How then can it be said, in the language of the Report, that 'the utmost vigilance of Government, under the existing laws, has been found inadequate to the danger?' Far be it from me to condemn lealty on the part of those invested with power; far be it from me to urge extreme rigour in the execution of laws; though I do contend that the existing laws should at least have been tried, before the Legislature was called upon to enact new.

But the excuse of the Attorney General for this procrastination is the most extraordinary. He says, that the libels which have been laid before him were so numerous, that he really could not see where the prosecutions were to end! Where they were to end, Sir, I do not pretend to decide; though it could not surely have been so difficult to determine, where they ought to have begun. The libels may have been numerous, though certainly nothing was publicly known of them until very lately. The more numerous, however, the more urgent the necessity of proceeding against some of their authors, as a terror and an example to the rest. Sir, the present case has been assimilated to that of 1794. But what were the circumstances attending the suspension of the Habeas Corpus Act at that time? What was the conduct of Government on that occasion? The Ministers of that day, whatever else may be imputed to them, were at least guiltless of bearing the sword in vain. They resorted not to Parliament for new powers until they had enforced the old. Prosecutions for sedition had been instituted at the different Assizes and Quarter Sessions in every corner of the kingdom. Not that I would be supposed to hold up this conduct on the part of Government to the imitation of their successors. The error was then on the side of rigour. The laws were too severely enforced. Though examples might in some cases have been necessary, the indiscriminate and sweeping punishments awarded against every petty offender can be vindicated on no principles of justice or sound policy. I am surprised to observe the smile of contempt on the face of the Hon. and learned Gentlemen (the Attorney General), intended as it is to deride the censure of conduct so opposite to that which he has thought fit to pursue. He is, however, mistaken, if he imagines that I have contrasted the different proceedings of His Majesty's Law Officers at the two periods, for the purpose of passing judgment either on the one or the other. My object has been rather to show the extreme variance between them, and that Ministers (even if we admit their representations, as to the disordered and alarming state of the country, to be substantially correct) are not justified by the precedent to which they so triumphantly appeal, in imposing new restraints upon the liberty of the subject, until they have proved the inefficacy of those already in existence.

Sir, the learned Lord Advocate of Scotland, to the surprise and dismay of his surrounding friends, has produced an oath, said to have been taken by some deluded persons at Glasgow. But were not Ministers long ago acquainted with the circumstance? Or did they imagine that the Legislature had overlooked the offence?—Is it possible that they were ignorant of the penalty attached to it? That it is felony without the benefit of clergy, unless the individual, taking the oath, within fourteen days afterwards, abandons his associates and betrays their purposes? What more does the learned Lord require than the severest punishment which is known to the laws of this kingdom?

As to the question, whether or not the proposed remedy is adapted to the nature of the evil, there is no one who pretends that it is so, except the honourable Member who spoke last (Mr. C. Wynn). He has, indeed, contended, that as sufficient evidence cannot be procured to convict, it is, therefore, proper to give Ministers unlimited power to imprison! As the delinquent cannot be brought to trial, he is to be punished without it! On the contrary, Sir, I contend, that this measure is in no way calculated to meet the evil. Who are the fomenters of these troubles? Who are the redoubted chiefs in these scenes of mischief, whose arrest is at once to check the progress of disaffection and defeat the operations of the minor agents? Are they persons of leading influence or talent? No; they are all alike insignificant,—objects rather of pity and contempt, than of public jealousy and alarm. According to the account of Ministers, the real evil exists in the extent to which the infection has spread and is spreading,— in the intricate ramifications through which the poison is conveyed to the public mind. Will the imprisonment therefore of ten or twenty poor wretches prevent its diffusion? If, indeed, two or three were publicly tried, regularly convicted, and exemplarily punished, something probably might be gained; others might be deterred, for the fact would be known; but the mere un-heard-of confinement of a few mechanics will effect nothing in a case of active mischief like that which has been described.

Sir, on every former occasion when this Act has been suspended, the state of things was widely different from the present. There existed at least enough to warrant the apprehensions, even in the opinions of those who thought it their duty to oppose the measures of Ministers. The country was in a state of actual war, or actual rebellion, or both. Such was the case in 1794, in 1798, and in 1801. External danger was aggravated by internal co-operation. The fears of an invasion from France were heightened by the rage of disaffection in England and of open rebellion in Ireland. Whatever difference of opinion might prevail in Parliament, as to the remedy, no one denied either the existence or the extent of the evil. No petitions were then presented, humbly praying that Parliament would reform itself. The avowed object of the disaffected was not to reform, but to supersede Parliament, and to substitute in its stead a National Assembly like that of France, which boasted of its active correspondence with this country. Such, Sir, was the state of the country at the periods to which I have been alluding,—periods in which some Gentlemen have affected to discern so striking a similitude to the present.

Sir, much as I must reprobate the adoption of such a measure, at the present moment, I am not one of those who think that the Habeas Corpus Act ought never to be suspended. Under certain circumstances it may be just and necessary. Such were the circumstances which more than once occurred within the first sixty years after the Revolution, when there was a Pretender to the Throne; when persons of the highest rank and authority were in active league and correspondence with the enemy, and were endeavouring to expose their country to the united horrors of foreign invasion and civil war. The arrest of the leaders was, in such cases, necessary, as it paralysed the traitorous designs of all their dependents. But is there any such necessity at the present moment? Where can Ministers find one man of influence or consequence among the disaffected of our day? Where can they find even a man of the middle rank of life among the ignorant and deluded wretches against whom Ministers are about to launch their vengeance? How then can this Suspension be useful; unless, indeed, our Government shall follow the example of one which it has recently supported against the avowed wishes of the people, where not merely obnoxious individuals, but the inhabitants of whole villages and towns, have been thrown into dungeons?—Is not this, I confidently demand, a powerful reason for refusing what is now required? Will the House intrust Ministers with a power by which persons of low rank and obscure occupations will be placed, in shoals, at the mercy of every truckling Informer?—Sir, the noble Lord (Castlereagh) on a former evening thought proper to advert to the names of individuals in higher stations, who have been placed by these infatuated Reformers upon what they term the Committee of Safety or Conservative Body. But because misguided and illiterate men have had the audacity, without the slightest authority, to place upon this list persons of undoubted loyalty and elevated rank, does it afford such a presumption of guilt as to justify the bold declaration of the noble Lord, that in the eyes of God and man they are answerable for all the consequences of rebellion? Undoubtedly the names of those most respectable persons are found there on account of the general sentiments they are known to entertain on public affairs. But is this an argument (as it has been advanced by the noble Lord and the Right Hon. Gentleman who spoke after him), is this an argument against the support of popular doctrines? Is every one who presumes to argue in favour of Parliamentary Reform, the liberty of the Press, or any other topic displeasing to those in power, to be included in the dreadful denunciation of the noble Lord? Sir, I am not fond at any time of making personal allusions, and I am the more unwilling to make them now on account of the unusual soreness which has been shown by the noble Lord on certain topics this night; but I cannot help observing, that there was a period, even in his life, when he might have had the misfortune to fall under his own denunciation, and to be included in the list of a Committee of Safety! The liberality of the noble Lord's former opinions, and the pledges of championship in the cause of Parliamentary Reform, given by him at an early period of his political life, before he entered into office, or was transplanted into any of the hotbeds or nurseries for young Statesmen[2], might have rendered even him responsible in the eyes of God and man for the consequences of disaffection and rebellion[3]!

Sir, reverting once more to the question more immediately before us, I implore the House not to withdraw from the lower classes a protection to which they are as much entitled as the most exalted individuals in the State. It is impossible to calculate on the abuses to which a measure like this may be subject; it is impossible to foresee the misery and ruin which it may be the means of occasioning, even to the most innocent individuals; and yet, AT THE EXPIRATION OF THE PROPOSED ACT, MINISTERS WILL ONLY HAVE TO COME DOWN TO THE HOUSE WITH A BILL OF INDEMNITY, AND THEIR RESPONSIBILITY WILL BE AT AN END!—Sir, our ancestors never consented to the Suspension of the Habeas Corpus Act but in cases of extreme danger. The proposal therefore of such a measure now is the more alarming on account of the precedent which it will establish. It is now for the *first* time laid down, that under any circumstances of alarm the Rights of Englishmen are to be dispensed with! In the years 1767 and 1768, when, according to the Letters of Dr. Franklin, great distress, unusual scarcity, and alarming riots prevailed, no person ever dreamt of suspending the Habeas Corpus Act. Now, however, in time of profound peace, it is contended, that the race of Englishmen have become so degenerate as to be incapable

---

2 See Mr. Canning's Speech in the Debate on Sir M. W. Ridley's Motion, for reducing the number of the Lords of the Admiralty.

3 At the commencement of the election for the county of Down, in June 1790, Lord Castlereagh (then the Hon. Robert Stewart) subscribed a TEST, pledging himself, amongst other things, to be governed by the instructions of his Constituents, and to promote, with all his abilities and influence, both in and out of Parliament, the success of a Bill for amending the representation of the people.

of their own protection; now, their weakness and pusillanimity are such, that they are willing to make a voluntary sacrifice of their liberties, and to surrender their dearest rights into the hands of Ministers! True it is, that dangers threaten the country; but, IS THERE NO DANGER IN EM- POWERING A FEW INDIVIDUALS TO IMPRISON ALL THE REST OF THEIR FELLOW-CITIZENS, AND THAT TOO, WITHOUT THE SLIGHTEST RESPONSIBILITY? Is there no danger in this Sus- pension at a period like the present, when the standing army is so over- grown, and when the Government already possesses a more extended and uncontrolled influence than has been ever before enjoyed in any former age? Is there no danger even to general liberty, when foreign States, al- ready sufficiently disposed to check its growth, shall see this once free coun- try placed under the absolute dominion of its Ministers, on account of the absurd schemes of a few miserable Spenceans? Is there no danger in pub- lic opinion, and that even to Ministers themselves? Are they well assured that, this measure will have, in truth, the effect of strengthening their weak hands? Will not the people see through the artifice of those, who, under the pretence of public security, are only endeavouring to aggran- dise or to secure themselves? Sir, in every point of view I consider this measure objectionable. The dangers may be great, but the existing laws have not yet been tried; and if tried, they will be found sufficient for every purpose of national protection.

The House divided:

Ayes	*273*
Noes	*98*
Majority	*175*

The Bill was then read for the first time. In a subsequent stage of the Bill, on the Motion of Sir Samuel Romilly an amendment was made, limit- ing its operation, in Scotland as well as in England, to persons committed to prison for Treason or suspicion of Treason upon a warrant signed by six Privy Counsellors, or one of the principal Secretaries of State. As the Bill stood originally, it extended to all persons in the former country com- mitted by any subordinate Magistrate.

Henry Peter Brougham and Vaux[1]

[1] Brougham claimed kinship with the French House of Vaux. Many, however, are skeptical that such a relationship ever existed.

Henry Peter Brougham and Vaux, first Baron
[*Born* SEPTEMBER 19, 1778—*Died* MAY 7, 1868]

Tall and slenderly built, his figure was awkward and ungainly in the extreme. His face was thin and pale, his cheek bones prominent, his hair dark. . . . But his most prominent feature was not his piercing, aquiline eyes, but his long, turned-up nose, whose twitching betrayed his highly-strung state.—ARTHUR ASPINALL

·G·

. T. Garratt calls Brougham a reformer and a controversialist "who did more than anyone to free his countrymen's minds from the lumber of eighteenth-century ideas and inhibitions." [2] Though Brougham held office for only four years of a half-century in politics, he successfully advocated abolition of slavery, parliamentary reform, popular education, and law reform—remarkable feats for one who possessed neither a personal following nor attached himself to a group of any kind.[3]

According to Arthur Aspinall, Brougham, "by universal consent," made himself the most powerful orator of the day.[4] During his parliamentary life, he made hundreds of speeches. Walter Bagehot, in fact, calls him a "hundred-subject agitator" [5] who can make motions, addresses, orations, and move amendments like a machine "when you wish and on what you wish." [6] Brougham's speeches are characterized by their versatility and detail, capable of battering anything at any moment. Most of Brougham's addresses were "fighting" speeches which tended to crush adversaries by their overwhelming force. With Demosthenes as his model, the force and vigor of his presentations contained sarcasm and irony which have rarely been surpassed.[7] His voice was loud, sometimes deafening, and his gestures, "wild and absurd . . . excited ridicule when they ceased to intimidate." His language was often "recklessly extravagant," due largely to his fluency and readiness of speech.[8]

Three of Brougham's speeches are considered his most outstanding. Aspinall likes, particularly, his address opening the defense of Queen Caroline on a charge of adultery, and the speech in support of the Reform Bill delivered in the House of Lords on October 7, 1831.[9] A third speech, "sometimes considered as his greatest oratorical ef-

---

2 G. T. Garratt, *Lord Brougham* (London: Macmillan and Co., Ltd., 1935), p. 2.
3 *Ibid.*
4 Arthur Aspinall, *Lord Brougham and the Whig Party* (Manchester: University Press, 1927), p. 244.
5 Mrs. Russell Barrington (ed.), *Works and Life of Walter Bagehot,* II (London: Longmans, Green, and Co., 1915), p. 306.
6 *Ibid.*, p. 302.
7 Aspinall, *op. cit.*, p. 245.
8 *Ibid.*
9 *Ibid.*

fort," [10] was delivered to the House of Commons on February 7, 1828, on the subject of Law Reform. For six hours and three minutes, Brougham moved from point to point "detailing, illustrating, suggesting remedies." [11] He had a good House throughout, listening captivated to seemingly endless detail of abuses perpetrated under the existing legal framework. As Brougham spoke, he would intermittently suck on oranges supplied him by the caterer to the House, occasionally cursing him when he came across a bad orange.[12] Garratt claims that Brougham presented a case so overwhelming there was little reply except for promises to remedy certain abuses.[13]

The ultimate effect of the speech was, indeed, "prodigious." [14] Approximately three-fourths of Brougham's proposed reforms were adopted in the next ten years, and virtually everything he advocated has since been carried out.[15]

---

10 Garratt, *op. cit.*, p. 207.

11 Frances Hawes, *Henry Brougham* (London: Jonathan Cape, 1957), p. 201.

12 Chester W. New, *The Life of Henry Brougham to 1830* (Oxford: Clarendon Press, 1961), p. 392.

13 Garratt, *op. cit.*

14 Bagehot, *op. cit.*, p. 298.

15 New, *op. cit.*, p. 400.

Present State of the Law [1]

•

In rising to address the House upon one of the most important subjects that can possibly be submitted to the Legislature, I feel at the same time deeply impressed with the conviction, that it is also one of the most difficult, and certainly the largest, that could engage its attention. I am aware that I stand engaged to bring before you the whole state of the Common Law of this country, (the Common Law, I call it, in contradistinction to Equity), with the view of pointing out those defects which may have existed in its original construction, or which time may have engendered, as well as of considering the remedies appropriate to correct them. Nothing, I do assure you, at all strengthens and bears me up under the pressure of this vast and overwhelming burthen, but a conviction of the paramount importance, nay, the absolute necessity, of no longer delaying the inquiry, or postponing the needful amendments; and the intimate persuasion I feel, that I shall be able so to deal with the subject, (such is my deep veneration for all that is good in our judicial system, and my habitual respect for those in whose hands the administration of it is placed), as neither to offend the prejudices of one class, nor vex the personal feelings of another. But I feel a confidence, also, which is unspeakable, resting on another ground. I come not here to raise cavils before men

---

1 *Present State of the Law* (London: Henry Colburn, 1828), pp. 1–120. In the Advertisement, the editors have made the following statement: "The Speech of Mr. Brougham, on the Present State of the Law, embracing an almost unlimited number of technical details, and presenting a solid foundation for one of the most important inquiries ever instituted, has appeared to demand a more careful revision than is usually bestowed upon general political questions. The present Edition has, therefore, been accurately prepared, not only from a comparison of the published Reports of the Speech with the Notes of the Editors, who were present at the debate, but with the great advantage of the corrections of Mr. Brougham himself, which that gentleman has given as fully as was compatible with his numerous and important avocations."

ignorant of the details and niceties of the profession I belong to, and who, in that unavoidable ignorance, would be unfit judges of their merits; I am determined to avail myself in no respect of their situation, or of the absence of the learned Body of the Profession, for the sake of a futile and pitiful triumph over what is most valuable in our jurisprudence. I am comforted and confirmed in my resolution, by the accidental circumstances that have joined me, in some sort, to the administration of the law in which I have had so considerable an experience. I have seen so much of its practical details, that it is, in my view, no speculative matter whether for blame or praise. I pledge myself, through the whole course of my statements, as long as the House may honour me with its attention, in no one instance to make any observation, to bring forward any grievance, or mark any defect, of which I am not myself competent to speak from personal knowledge. I do not merely say, from observation as a bystander; I limit myself still further, and confine myself to causes in which I have been council for one party or the other. By these considerations, emboldened on the one hand, and on the other impressed with a becoming sense of the arduous duty I have undertaken in this weighty matter, I will without further preface go on, in the first place, to state the points which I intend to avoid.

I shall omit Equity in every branch, unless where I may be compelled to mention it incidentally, from its interference with the course of the common law; not that I think nothing should be done as to Equity, but because in some sort it has been already taken up by Parliament. A Commission sat, and inquired into the subject, and produced a Report, received, though not yet acted upon. The Noble and Learned Lord, who presides in the other House, has announced his intention of proposing a Bill, founded on that Report. I may also add, that the subject has, to his own great honour, and to the lasting benefit of the country, been for many years in the hands of my Honourable and Learned Friend, the Member of Durham (Mr. M. A. Taylor): it is still with him, and I trust his care of it will not cease.

For reasons of a like kind, I pass over the great head of Criminal Law. That inquiry, happily for the country, since the time when first Sir Samuel Romilly (a name never to be pronounced by any without veneration, nor ever by me without sorrow) devoted his talents and experience to it, has been carried forward by my Honourable and Learned Friend, the Member of Knaresborough (Sir James Mackintosh) with various success, until at length he reaped the fruit of his labours, and prevailed upon this House, by a narrow majority, to bend its attention towards so great a subject. On a smaller scale, on one indeed of a very limited nature, these inquiries have been since followed up by the Right Honourable Gentleman who is now again Secretary of State for the Home Department. It is not so much for any thing he has actually done, that I feel disposed to thank him, as for the countenance he has given to the subject. He has power, from his situation, to effect reforms which others hardly dare propose. His connections in the Church and State render his services in this department almost invaluable. They have tended to silence the clamours that would otherwise have been raised against the reform of the law, and might possibly have proved fatal to it. If (which I do not believe) he intended to limit his efforts to what he has already accomplished; if he were disposed to say, "Thus far have I gone, and no further can I go with you," the gratitude of his country would still be due to him in an eminent degree, for having abashed the worst enemies of improvement by his countenance and support. But I trust he will again direct the energies of his mind to the great work of reformation, and bestow his exertions over a wider space.

Another reason for avoiding this part of the subject altogether, is to be found in the nature and objects of the Criminal Law. I do not think it right to unsettle the minds of those numerous and ignorant classes, on whom its sanctions are principally intended to operate. It might produce no good effects if they were all at once to learn, that the Criminal Law in the mass, as it were, had been sentenced to undergo a revision—that the whole Penal Code was unsettled and about to be remodelled.

I intend also to leave out of my view the Commercial Law. It lies within a narrow compass, and it is far purer and freer from defects than any other part of the system. This arises from its later origin. It has grown up within two centuries, or little more, and been formed by degrees, as the exigency of mercantile affairs required. It is accepted, too, in many of its main branches, by other States, forming a code common to all trading nations, and which cannot easily be changed without their general consent. Accordingly, the provisions of the French Civil Code, unsparing as they were of the old municipal law, excepted the law merchant, generally speaking, from the changes which they introduced.

Lastly, Sir, the law of Real Property forms no immediate subject of my present consideration; not that I shall not have much to propose intimately connected with it, and many illustrations to derive from it; but I am flattered with the hope that the Secretary for the Home Department intends himself, on this subject, to bring forward certain measures, by which the present system will eventually undergo salutary alterations: And I cannot help here saying, that whatever the Criminal Law owes to the persevering and enlightened exertions of the late Sir Samuel Romilly, and of his successor, the Member for Knaresborough (Sir J. Mackintosh), I am sure an almost equal debt of gratitude has been incurred on the part of the law of Real Property, to the honest, patient, and luminous discussion which it has received from one of the first conveyancers and lawyers this country could ever boast of. My Honourable and Learned Friend (the Solicitor-General) opposite, and those Members of the House who are conversant with our profession, will easily understand that I can only allude to Mr. Humphreys.

With these exceptions, which I have now stated as shortly as I was able, and for which I shall offer no apology, because it was absolutely necessary that I should begin by making the scope of my present purpose understood, I intend to bring all the Law as administered in our Courts of Justice under the review of the House; and to this ample task I at once proceed. But I shall not enlarge, after the manner of some, on the infinite importance and high interest which belongs to the question, and the attention which it, of right, claims from us, whether we be considered as a branch of the Government, or as the Representatives of the people, or as a part of the people ourselves. It would be wholly superfluous; for every one must at once admit, that if we view the whole establishments of the country—the Government by the King, and the other Estates of the Realm,—the entire system of Administration, whether civil or military,—the vast establishments of land and of naval force by which the State is defended,—our foreign negotiations, intended to preserve peace with the world,—our domestic arrangements, necessary to make the Government respected by the people,—or our fiscal regulations, by which the expense of the whole is to be supported,—all shrink into nothing, when compared with the pure, and prompt, and cheap Administration of Justice throughout the community. I will indeed make no such comparison; I will not put in contrast things so inseparably connected; for all the establishments formed by our ancestors, and supported by their descendants, were invented and are chiefly maintained, in order that justice may be duly administered between man and man. And, in my mind, he was guilty of no error,—he was chargeable with no exaggeration,—he was betrayed by his fancy into no metaphor, who once said, that all we see about us, King, Lords, and Commons, the whole machinery of the State, all the apparatus of the system, and its varied workings, end in simply bringing twelve good men into a box. Such—the administration of justice—is the cause of the establishment of Government—such is the use of Government: it is this purpose which can alone justify restraints on natural liberty—it is this only which can excuse constant interference with the rights and the property of men. I invite you, then, Sir, to enter upon an unsparing examination of this mighty subject: I invite the House to proceed with me, first of all, into the different Courts—to mark what failures, in practice, are to be found in the system, as it was originally framed, as well as what errors time has engendered by occasioning a departure from that system; and afterward to consider whether we may not, safely and usefully, apply to those defects remedies of a seasonable and temperate nature, restoring what is decayed, if it be good—lopping off what experience has proved to be pernicious.

I. CONSTITUTION OF OUR COURTS OF JUSTICE
    i. Superior Courts of Westminster Hall
        Conflict of King's Bench and Common Pleas
        Competition of the three Courts not real
        Monopoly of Advocates in Common Pleas
        ———— of Attornies in Exchequer
        King's Bench overloaded with business
        Ineffectual attempts to relieve it
        Evils of the Three Judge Court
        Bail and Chamber business
        Necessity of more Judges
        Real innovation of adhering to old practices
        Two proposals for lightening and equalizing the business of the
            Courts
        Expediency of paying Judges in a small proportion by fees
        Evils of party considerations influencing the choice of Judges
    ii. Administration of Justice in Wales
        Evils of the system
        Remedy proposed
        Digression concerning Moveable Terms and Circuits
    iii. Civil Law Courts
        Bad mode of paying the Judges
        Bad mode of appointing them
        Bad Constitution of the Court of Delegates
    iv. Courts of Appeal in the Privy Council
        Vast extent of Colonial Jurisdiction
        Needless aggravations of the necessary evils of ignorance and
            distance
        Composition, sittings, and business of the Court
        Case of Ramnad
        Jury Trial recommended for East Indian settlements
        Political and Legal advantages
    v. Justices of the Peace
        Defects of the system as to Appointment and Removal
        Clerical Magistrates
        Licensing

Game Laws
No responsibility and no revision
Court of Quarter Sessions supreme
Service not wholly gratuitous

II. STATE OF THE LAW
　　Introductory Matter
　　　　Different Laws in different places
　　　　Different Laws for different persons
　　　　Inequality to Crown and Subject where Equality is pretended
　　　　Instance of its operation
　　　　Inequalities avowed—under five heads
　　　　Instances of their operation
　i. Means of Preventing Needless Litigation
　　Principles
　　Practice
　　Fines and Recoveries
　　Cases of Bankrupt
　　————— Tenant in tail
　　————— Feme Covert
　　Absurd fiction of recompense in value
　　Strict Settlement
　　Statute of Uses
　　Equitable Interest
　　Equitable and Legal Jurisdiction
　　Ejectment
　ii. Means of Preventing Litigation being Needlessly Prolonged
　　Principles
　　Practice
　　Remedies
　iii. Commencement of Suits
　　Principles
　　Practice
　　Arrest on Mesne Process
　　Outlawry to compel appearance
　iv. Pleading
　　Praises of it by Lords Coke and Mansfield
　　Superiority of Ancient Pleading
　　Principles
　　Practice
　　1. Generality—Count—examples in Assumpsit and Trover

Sir, in casting an eye over the wide field which we have been survey-ing, I trust the House will perceive that, although I have, for the most part, arranged my observations under the different stages through which causes are carried in our superior courts, I have yet been enabled to dis-cuss the greater and by much the more important parts of our municipal jurisprudence. Indeed, with the exception of Commercial law, I am not aware of having left any branch untouched that seemed to require amendment. I stated, in the outset, the reason why that formed no immed-iate part of my plan. A great portion of it is common to all trading coun-tries, the Law-merchant, and is extremely well adapted to its purpose, being of comparatively modern growth, and framed according to the exi-gencies of commerce. Some other parts, however, are exceedingly defec-tive. It would be difficult to point out greater uncertainty or more caprice in any branch of the system than are to be found in the law of Partner-ship. A man can hardly tell whether he is a partner or not: being a part-ner, the extent of his liability is scarcely less difficult to ascertain; and he will often find it in vain to consult his lawyer on these important matters. The distribution of estates under the Bankrupt law is likewise capable of very great improvement. After all that was lately done in arranging and simplifying this code, it remains full of contradictions, and the source of innumerable frauds and endless litigation. But into these things I abstain from entering. I must, however, once more press upon the attention of the House, the necessity of taking a general view of the whole system in what-ever inquiries may be instituted. Partial legislation on such a subject is pregnant with mischief. Timid men, but still more blind than they are timid, recommend taking a single branch at a time, and imagine that they are consulting the safety of the mass. It is the very reverse of safe. In the body of the law all the members are closely connected; you cannot touch one without affecting the rest; and if your eye is confined to the one you deal with, you cannot tell what others may be injured, and how. Even a manifest imperfection may not be removed without great risk, when it is not in some wholly insulated part; for it oftentimes happens that, by long use, a defect has given rise to some new arrangement extending far be-yond itself, and not to be disturbed with impunity. The topical reformer,

who confines his care to one flaw, may thus do as much injury as a surgeon
who should set himself about violently reducing a luxation of long standing, where nature had partially remedied the evil by forming a false joint,
or should cut away some visceral excrescence in which a new system of
circulation and other action was going on. Depend upon it, the general
reformation of such a mechanism as our law is not only the most effectual,
but the only safe course. This, in truth, alone deserves the name of either
a rational or a temperate reform.

Then, what ground can there be for taking alarm at the course I recommend of amendment, and proceeding by careful, but general inquiry?
It is, indeed, nothing new, even of late years, in this country. We appointed
a Commission to investigate the whole administration of justice in Scotland; and it ended in altering the constitution of the Courts, and introducing a new mode of trying causes. Yet Scotland, to say nothing of the
treaty of Union, so often set up as a bulwark against all change, might
urge some very powerful reasons for upholding her ancient system, which
we in England should vainly seek to parallel. She might hold up her statute book in three small pocket volumes, the whole fruit of as many centuries of legislation, while your table bends beneath the laws of a single
reign—and of your whole jurisprudence, it may be said as of the Roman
before Justinian, that it would overload many camels. But I do not
merely cite, against alarms or scruples, that bold and wise and safe measure of Lord Grenville; older authorities, and in the Courts of Westminster, are with me. I will rely on Lord Hale, whose celebrated Treatise *Of
the Amendment of the Law,* (far less studied, I fear, by our Jurisconsults,
than that of Fortescue*) well exposes the folly of such fears, with their
origin. "By long use and custom (says he) men especially that are aged,
and have been long educated to the profession and practice of the law,
contract a kind of superstitious veneration of it beyond what is just and
reasonable. They tenaciously and rigorously maintain these very forms
and proceedings and practices, which, though possibly at first they were
seasonable and useful, yet by the very change of matters they become not
only useless and impertinent, but burthensome and inconvenient, and
prejudicial to the common justice and the common good of mankind; not
considering the forms and prescripts of laws were not introduced for their
own sakes, but for the use of public justice; and therefore, when they
become insipid, useless, impertinent, and possibly derogatory to the end,
they may and must be removed." Such is the language of Sir M. Hale.
After Lord Coke and Littleton himself, there is no higher authority in the
law than Shepherd, the author of the *Touchstone,* who, in another of his
works, called "England's Balm, or Proposals by way of Grievance and

---

* De Laudibus Legum Angliae.

Remedy, &c., towards the Regulation of the Law and better Administration of Justice," reminds his legal brethren, that "taking away the abuse of the law will establish the use of the law—*stabilit usum qui tollit abusum*—and that rooting up the tares will not destroy the wheat*." If the House require further authorities upon this point, I can refer them to one of the ablest and most instructive books published of late years, that of Mr. Parkes, a respectable Solicitor in Warwickshire, who, in giving the history of the Court of Chancery, has collected most of the authorities upon the subject of Legal Reform.

But our predecessors, members of this House in the seventeenth century, an age fruitful of great improvements, most of which were retained in more quiet times, undertook the amendment of the Law systematically, and with a spirit and a wisdom every way worthy of so great a work. In 1654, a Commission was formed partly of the House, partly of learned strangers. At the head of the former, I find my Honourable Friend the Solicitor General's less learned and more martial predecessor, called in the Journals "Lord General Cromwell." But in front of the latter stands "Mr. Mathew Hale," afterwards the great Chief Justice, whose name is ever cited amongst the most venerable supporters of our Civil and our Religious Establishment. With them were joined all the great Jurisconsults and Statesmen of that illustrious age. They sat for five years, and proposed a number of the most important and general reforms. I will read the titles of a few Acts, the draughts of which the Commissioners prepared.

1. For taking away Fines upon Bills, Declarations, and Original Writs.
2. For taking away Common Recoveries, and the unnecessary Charges of Fines, and to pass and charge Lands entailed as Lands in Fee-simple.
3. For ascertaining of Arbitrary Fines upon Descent and Alienation of Copyholds of Inheritance.
4. For the more speedy recovery of Rents.
5. For the better regulating of Pleaders and their Fees.
6. For the more speedy and easy recovery of Debts and Damages not exceeding the sum of Four Pounds.
7. For the further declaration and prevention of Fraudulent Contracts and Conveyances.
8. Against the Sale of Offices.
9. For the recovery of Debts owing by Corporations.

---

* There is certainly a notion of Mr. Justice Doddridge being the author of this excellent book, or at least standing in the same relation to it that C. B. Gilbert does to Bacon's Ab.; for the dates of some works cited in it make it impossible he should have written it all.

10. To make Debts assignable.

11. To prevent solicitation of Judges, Bribery, Extortion, Charge of Motions, and for restriction of Pleaders.

12. An Act for all County Registers, Will, and Administrators; and for preventing Inconvenience, Delay, Charge, and Irregularity, in Chancery and Common Law (as well in common pleas as criminal Causes).

13. Acts for settling County Judicatures, Guardians of Orphans, Courts of Appeal, County Treasurers, and Workhouses, with Tables of Fees and Short Forms of Declaration.

14. An Act to allow Witnesses to be sworn for prisoners.

The House is aware that till much later in our history, by the great wisdom, justice, and humanity of our ancestors, it was provided that the witnesses for a defendant should not deliver their testimony upon oath; until the time of Queen Anne, the prosecutor only was allowed to prove his case, by sworn evidence; and the communication of the same right to the defendant, may be looked upon by some as a rude invasion of the ancient system, and a cruel departure from the perfections of the olden time.

This is not the only measure prepared by that celebrated Commission which has been since adopted, as the House will see by the enumeration I have given*. But steps were taken immediately after the restoration, for prosecuting its plans more systematically. A Committee was appointed by this House to examine the state of the Law and its practice; Sergeant Maynard and other eminent lawyers were members of it. From their numbers, fifty-one, I presume they subdivided themselves for the convenience of inquiring separately into different branches of the subject. Upon their reports several Bills were brought in for the general reform of the Law; but in tracing their progress through the House, the prorogation appears to have come before any of them was passed. After a long interval of various fortune, and filled with vast events, but marked from age to age by a steady course of improvement, we are again called to the grand labour of surveying and amending our Laws. For this task, it well becomes us to begird ourselves, as the honest representatives of the people. Dispatch and vigour are imperiously demanded; but that deliberation, too, must not be lost sight of, which so mighty an enterprise requires. When we shall have done the work, we may fairly challenge the utmost approval of our constituents, for in none other have they so deep a stake.

In pursuing the course which I now invite you to enter upon, I avow that I look for the co-operation of the King's Government; and on what

---

* Sir S. Romilly's valuable MSS. contain the exposition and discussion of many reforms in the law, written thirty years ago. More than one-half of the measures there propounded, have, of late years, and most of them since his lamented decease, been adopted by the legislature; a strong presumption in favour of his plans generally.

are my hopes founded? Men gather not grapes from thorns, nor figs from thistles. But that the vine should no longer yield its wonted fruit—that the fig tree should refuse its natural increase required a miracle to strike it with barrenness. There are those in the present Ministry, whose known liberal opinions have lately been proclaimed anew to the world, and pledges have been avouched for their influence upon the policy of the State. With them, others may not, upon all subjects, agree; upon this, I would fain hope there will be found little differences. But, be that as it may, whether I have the support of the Ministers or no—to the House I look with confident expectation, that it will control them, and assist me; if I go too far, checking my progress—if too fast, abating my speed—but heartily and honestly helping me in the best and greatest work, which the hands of the lawgiver can undertake. The course is clear before us; the race is glorious to run. You have the power of sending your name down through all times, illustrated by deeds of higher fame, and more useful import, than ever were done within these walls. You saw the greatest warrior of the age—conqueror of Italy—humbler of Germany—terror of the North—saw him account all his matchless victories poor, compared with the triumph you are now in a condition to win—saw him contemn the fickleness of Fortune, while, in despite of her, he could pronounce his memorable boast, "I shall go down to posterity with the Code in my hand!" You have vanquished him in the field; strive now to rival him in the sacred arts of peace! Outstrip him as a lawgiver, whom in arms you overcame! The lustre of the Regency will be eclipsed by the more solid and enduring splendour of the Reign. The praise which false courtiers feigned for our Edwards and Harrys, the Justinians of their day, will be the just tribute of the wise and good to that Monarch under whose sway so mighty an undertaking shall be accomplished. Of a truth, sceptres are most chiefly to be envied for that they bestow the power of thus conquering and ruling thus. It was the boast of Augustus—it formed part of the glare in which the perfidies of his earlier years were lost—that he found Rome of brick, and left it of marble; a praise not unworthy a great prince, and to which the present reign has its claims also. But how much nobler will be our Sovereign's boast, when he shall have it to say, that he found law dear, and left it cheap; found it a sealed book—left it a living letter; found it the patrimony of the rich—left it the inheritance of the poor; found it the two-edged sword of craft and oppression—left it the staff of honesty and the shield of innocence! To me, much reflecting on these things, it has always seemed a worthier honour to be the instrument of making you bestir yourselves in this high matter, than to enjoy all that office can bestow—office, of which the patronage would be an irksome incumbrance, the emoluments superfluous to one content with the rest of his industrious fellow-citizens, that his own hands minister to his wants:

And as for the power supposed to follow it—I have lived near half a century, and I have learned that power and place may be severed. But one power I do prize: that of being the advocate of my countrymen here, and their fellow-labourer elsewhere, in those things which concern the best interests of mankind. That power, I know full well, no government can give—no change take away!

I move you, Sir, "That an humble Address be presented to His Majesty, praying that he will be graciously pleased to issue a Commission for inquiring into the defects occasioned by time and otherwise in the Laws of this realm, and into the measures necessary for removing the same."

Sir Arthur Wellesley

·

FIRST DUKE OF WELLINGTON

Sir Arthur Wellesley, first Duke of Wellington

[Born APRIL 29, 1769—*Died* SEPTEMBER 14, 1852]

. . . his features, with the wavy black hair, fine blue eyes rather deeply sunk, aquiline nose, immensely strong jaw and pointed chin, indicated above all things, character.—SIR JOHN FORTESCUE

.T.

he Duke of Wellington is prob-
ably the greatest military hero Great Britain has ever produced. His
triumph over Napoleon at Waterloo in 1815 not only preserved the
British Constitution from being ravaged by foreign encroachment,
but it also set the stage for a long period of relative tranquillity during
which time Britain enjoyed unprecedented prosperity. While Wellington's military feats are revered, his political contributions are
fairly ignored in deference. The opinion of Sir Charles Petrie is,
perhaps, a reflection of the sentiments of other historians when he
states that "Few men in middle age have entered politics who were
less fitted for it than was Wellington." [1]

As one whose parliamentary life spanned more than forty-five
years, and whose cabinet experience covered nearly thirty years,[2] it
would seem that Wellington's political career was as much a part of
his character as was his life as a soldier. With a nation inundated
in social ferment, and a regency bent on controlling Parliament, it
is to Wellington's credit that the Government was preserved.

The Duke's regard for the Constitution was both his strength and
his weakness. More than any other spokesman of his day, he represented the last stronghold of the aristocracy's hold on the Government. Wellington adamantly maintained that aristocratic rule over
Britain had to prevail, for they only possessed the necessary training
and acumen to manage properly the affairs of state. So strongly did
he sense this conviction that in face of a ground-swell of popular
sentiment to oust the landed gentry from Commons, who were
blamed for the agricultural distress plaguing the nation, Wellington
became the leading spokesman in the House of Lords opposing
reform.

He had become so unpopular that his heroic feats on the battle-
field were forgotten, and he had become an enemy of the people. On
the 27th of April, 1831, his home, Apsley House, was stoned by a
mob which dispersed only after it had been informed that the Duke
was in mourning for his wife who had died two days earlier and whose
remains were still in the house.[3]

---

1 *Wellington* (London: James Barrie, 1956), p. 215.
2 Charles Stewart, "The Duke of Wellington," in *British Prime Ministers* (New
York: Roy Publishers), p. 68.
3 Herbert Maxwell, *The Life of Wellington* (London: Sampson Law, Marston and

The climax of orderly popular agitation for reform occurred on October 3, 1831, with the proposal in Lords for the second reading, having already passed the House of Commons. "Never," writes G. R. Gleig, ". . . has eloquence more brilliant been displayed in an assembly of free men, than that which from either side of the Woolsack, electrified the House of Lords on that memorable occasion." [4] On October 4 the Duke arose to speak in opposition to the measure, and its effect both in parliament and throughout the country, was "prodigious." [5] After several days of debate, Lords rejected the measure by a majority of forty-one, and the entire nation "fell into a state of anarchy." [6] Later, it was the same Wellington who successfully urged Lords to accept the bill rather than plunge the nation into rebellion.

As a speaker Wellington was "far from brilliant." [7] Joseph Hendershot Park calls his articulation indistinct and his dictation bleak,[8] and in his latter years he was prone to repeat himself, occasionally employing terms which amounted to exaggeration.[9] There appears little doubt, however, about his ability to persuade. Because of his directness and good sense, he was "invariably listened to, both in the House of Lords and elsewhere, with deference and respect." [10]

Co., Ltd., 1907), p. 270. Beginning with this page, Maxwell describes several events depicting mob vengeance against Wellington which put him into the "depth of odium."

[4] G. R. Gleig, *History of the Life of Arthur, Duke of Wellington,* IV (London: Longman, Green, Longman, and Roberts, 1860), p. 413.

[5] *Ibid.*

[6] *Ibid.,* p. 416.

[7] Joseph Hendershot Park, *British Prime Ministers of the Nineteenth Century* (New York: New York University Press, 1950), p. 54.

[8] *Ibid.*

[9] Gleig, *op. cit.,* p. 235.

[10] *Ibid.*

Against Parliamentary Reform [1]

•

HOUSE OF LORDS *October 4, 1831*

I concur, my Lords, entirely with the Noble Lord who spoke last [Viscount Melbourne], in the opinion that this measure is a most extensive one. It goes to overturn the whole system of our representation: it affects the counties, towns, and boroughs; it destroys or disturbs every existing interest; and, as the Noble Lord said, it will require further changes. It alters all the relations of representation, and even the proportions of the representatives of the different parts of the monarchy. It is the most considerable alteration and change ever proposed. The Noble Lord says it would not be sufficient unless it went to a great extent; and he tells your Lordships it ought to go to a Committee; and that we should not reject the measure now, but proceed to consider its details in a Committee. Notwithstanding all the changes it is to effect, it will be followed by other changes, in order to render it fit for working, and to adapt it practically to our Constitution. Ought we not to know what those changes are before we are called upon to consider this Bill in a Committee?

Before I go any further, I wish to observe on a statement made by the Noble Earl, when he introduced the measure. He did me the honour to notice my conduct. The Noble Earl, when he opened the measure to your Lordships, made some observations on me. He seems to prefer that course to explaining or defending his own measures. The Noble Earl seemed to forget that there was any necessity to defend his own measure or explain it to the House, and chose rather to criticise me and my language, and the language of my Right Honourable Friend, and our conduct and language in Parliament during the last Session. The Noble Earl thought

---

1 John Henry Barrow (ed.), *Mirror of Parliament*, III (London: Published by the Proprietors, 1831), pp. 2679–2684. See also, 7 H.L. Deb. 3s., cols. 1186–1205. This text is reprinted from a corrected report, published by Murray. Interestingly, the two texts, allegedly from different sources, are identical in content and phrasing.

proper to find fault with my language relating to the constitution of Parliament, and attributed to me, and to what I said in Parliament, the spirit of reform in the country, and the breaking up of the late Government. The Noble Earl found fault with my opinion of Parliament; but what had the Parliament done up to the moment when I was speaking to make it undeserving of our approbation? My Noble Friend, who has spoken with great ability, regretted that I should have made the statement I did make to your Lordships of the character and conduct of Parliament. My Lords, I beg my Noble Friend and the Noble Earl to recollect, that when I spoke of the Parliament, I spoke as the King's Minister, and that it is the duty of the King's Minister to support the institutions of the country: it had never, when I was in office, been the practice for the King's Ministers to give up the institutions of the country, and abandon them the moment they were attacked.

But, my Lords, if I wanted an example of the opinions of the value of the House of Commons, I should find it in the opinion of the Noble Earl the last time, I believe, that he spoke of the House of Commons. In the month of February, 1817, the Noble Lord said—

Constituted as it now was, he in his conscience believed that the House of Commons was, of all other institutions, in all the other countries of the world, the institution best calculated for the general protection of the subject. Supported by the people in temperate and firm claims for redress, it was not only able, but certain to remedy every wrong. It was capable to act as the most efficient control upon the executive, by diminishing the means of corruption, and reducing the pressure of a severe and grinding taxation.

That was the opinion of the Noble Earl himself in 1817; and what, I would ask, had the Parliament done subsequently to deserve the disapprobation of the Noble Earl—what had it done between 1817 and the moment when I pronounced that approbation of Parliament of which my Noble Friend and the Noble Earl have expressed so much disapprobation? When the Noble Earl quotes what I said not quite a twelvemonth ago, he might, I think, quote it correctly. What I said was, that Parliament had done its duty by the country, and enjoyed its confidence. I said that if I had to create a constitution of Parliament, I could not create that which existed, because I did not believe that the wit of man could invent such a system; but I said that I would do my endeavour to establish one like it, in which property, and particularly property in land, should be preponderant. That was what I said; and I afterwards had the satisfaction to hear the Noble Marquess (Lansdowne) deliver a similar opinion. He stated, that in any system of representation which he could support, property and learning must be preponderant. I said that I should consider it my duty to resist the adoption of any plan of reform that should be brought forward: I spoke as a Minister of the Crown, and as a Minister of the Crown I meant to resist reform.

The Noble Lords say that this statement of mine caused great enmity to me, and created that spirit of reform which has since pervaded the whole country. I beg the Noble Earl's pardon; but the spirit of reform in this country was the consequence of the French revolution. It is true, that ever since the American war a desire for Parliamentary Reform has been manifested in this country,—it has been manifested particularly when any disturbance or insurrection has occurred in any of the neighbouring foreign countries—above all, since the French revolution; and when there has been any extraordinary distress or difficulty in the country. At the same time, I believe, that, from year to year, the manifestations of such a desire have been less frequent. I have, indeed, the authority of those most friendly to reform for saying, that the manifestations of the desire for reform were less frequent till the period of the revolution of July, 1830, than they had formerly been for a number of years. It happened, unfortunately, that a few days before the ordinances were issued in Paris, his Majesty had dissolved the Parliament. At the elections, my Lords, a strong spirit of Parliamentary Reform was exhibited. In several contests, candidates for seats in Parliament were called upon to pledge themselves upon the subject of Parliamentary Reform. In many contested elections, the contest was decided in favour of the candidate who declared himself a reformer.

The Noble Earl has likewise referred to what I said on the 2d of November in this House, as to the cause of the disturbed state of the city of London and its neighbourhood, and the circumstances which occasioned the letter from the Secretary of State to the Lord Mayor, communicating to him, that his Majesty would not visit the city on the 9th of November. This letter was written on the 7th of November. The circumstances which rendered it necessary to write it were known to the King's servants on the 5th and 6th. The Noble Lords have the papers in their own hands. I beg to know whether, in their opinion, the information we had received was not sufficient to warrant the advice which we considered it our duty to give our Sovereign, and to obtain his commands, on the 7th of November. The Noble Lords have not themselves thought proper to advise his Majesty as yet to pay a visit to the city. I may fairly presume, therefore, that our advice was judicious on the 7th of November. But it is said, that the circumstances which rendered this advice necessary were occasioned by what I said in Parliament; that is to say, that having spoken in Parliament on the 2d, the effect produced in the city, and in the neighbourhood, was such, by the 5th, that the King's servants were obliged to advise the King on the 7th not to visit the city. Is this possible, my Lords? I call upon Noble Lords to say whether we were not justified in giving the advice which we did give. My Lords, the state of the public feeling and opinion in London, as well as in the north of England, and elsewhere in the country, had been influenced by the state of affairs in France, in Belgium, and in other parts of Europe. It was the state of affairs that occasioned those circumstances which induced us to advise the King not to visit the city; and not any opinion of mine on Parliamentary Reform, delivered in this House on the night of the 2d of November, and which could not have been known at all till the 3d, and could not therefore have occasioned, by the 5th, the circumstances to which I have referred. Then the Noble Lord has, notwithstanding my repeated contradictions and explanations, asserted that my opinions upon Parliamentary Reform, as delivered upon the 2d of November, occasioned the resignation of the King's late Ministers, my colleagues and myself.

My Lords, we retired from the King's service on Tuesday the 16th of November, because we found, that on Monday the 15th, on an important question, we no longer possessed the confidence of the House of Commons. We decided, in consequence, to resign, and we actually requested his Majesty to accept our resignation Tuesday, the day following. If we had delayed to carry our design into execution, the great question of Parliamentary Reform, in which I cannot but think that the interests of the monarchy are involved, would have been discussed in the House of Commons on Tuesday, and those interests defended by a Ministry no longer possessing the confidence of the House, and which must therefore have gone out of office. If the question, on Monday the 15th of November, had been that of Parliamentary Reform, it is not clear to me that we should have been in a minority. My reason for being of that opinion is, that it appears on the division, on the second reading of the Noble Lord's Bill in March last, that many Members voted against it who had been in the majority on the 15th of November. Whatever might be the degree in which the Members of the late Parliament were pledged to reform, I think myself justified in the statement, that my opinion upon Parliamentary Reform did not occasion our resignation; and that most probably it was not the cause of the loss of the confidence of the House of Commons. The Noble Earl assumed his office on the 22d of November, and on that day he stated to your Lordships on what principles he intended to conduct the Government of the country. Among other intentions he stated that of proposing a plan of Parliamentary Reform. He stated that he had obtained the King's consent to enable him to bring forward this proposition, as the Minister, and with the power and influence of Government. The Noble Lord's words upon that occasion were very remarkable, and deserving of your Lordships' attention. Your Lordships will observe, that the Noble Lord told you that he intended to found his plan of reform "on the basis of the institutions of the country;" and, as he explained, "a reform, limited by a desire to stand, as far as prudence will permit, by the ancient landmarks, and to prevent the sudden disturbance of our settled institutions by too large and extensive changes." He now tells you that he has brought in a measure which will effect a great change in them; and the Noble Secretary of State adds, that these changes must be followed by others. They must be so followed, or the Government of the country will be impracticable.

A Bill was introduced into the other House of Parliament, according to the Noble Lord's plan, which, after long discussion, was read a second time by the decision of a small majority. This measure altered everything, —it changed or destroyed every interest in the country. Instead of proceeding upon the basis of the established institutions, it destroyed them all; and, among other things, altered the relative numbers of the representatives in Parliament from the different kingdoms of the united empire. It was proposed in the House of Commons, that the proportion of representatives for England should not be diminished, to which proposition, after long debate, the House of Commons agreed by a majority of seven. The principle of the Noble Lord's Bill had been agreed to. Why did not the Noble Lords persevere and carry through their Bill, making such alterations as might render it palatable to the House of Commons, and consistent with the established practice of the Constitution? This did not suit their purpose. They dissolved the Parliament, and advised their Sovereign to appeal to his people. I attribute all our misfortunes to that event. The Noble Lords advised their Sovereign upon that occasion to come to Parliament, and to make this speech:—

I have come to meet you for the purpose of proroguing this Parliament, with a view to its immediate dissolution. I have been induced to resort to this measure for the purpose of ascertaining the sense of my people, in the way in which it may be most constitutionally and authentically expressed, on the expediency of making such changes in the representation as circumstances may seem to require; and which, founded upon the acknowledged principles of the Constitution, may tend at once to uphold the just rights and prerogatives of the Crown, and to give security to the liberties of my people.

The dissolution then made, and the speech delivered by His Majesty, were both upon a principle entirely different from that of the precedents according to which the measure was adopted. In 1784, the King, George III, differed from his Ministers upon a great question. They retired from his service, and His Majesty appointed other Ministers. Those Ministers did not enjoy the confidence of the House of Commons, and the King dissolved his Parliament, and put an end to the Session, in the words which I am about to read to your Lordships:—

On a full consideration of the present situation of affairs, and of the extraordinary circumstances which have produced it, I am induced to put an end to this Session of Parliament. I feel it a duty I owe to the Constitution and to the country, in such a situation, to recur as speedily as possible to the sense of my people by calling a new Parliament.

I trust that this measure will tend to obviate the mischiefs arising from the unhappy divisions and distractions which have lately subsisted; and that the various important objects which well require consideration may be afterwards proceeded upon with less interruption and happier effect. I can have no other object but to preserve the true principles of our free and happy Constitution; and to employ the powers entrusted to me by law for the only end for which they were given—the good of my people.

I will not give your Lordships the trouble of listening to the case of 1807, which stands precisely upon the same principles as that of 1784. In both, the King differed in opinion with his Ministers and with the Parliament upon measures upon which His Majesty had decided; and he appealed to the sense of his people, and called upon them to elect a Parliament which should give their confidence to the Ministers of his choice, in carrying on the measures which he approved. The transaction was brought to a close before the appeal was made to the people. The people were not called upon to deliberate upon any measure; but the appeal to them was rather, it may be said, in favour of the men whom His Majesty had named as his Ministers. In the case of 1831, however, the Noble Lords advised their Sovereign to refer for discussion to the people—not whether the King was to be supported in naming his Ministers—not whether Parliament was to be reformed, because, upon the principle of reform, there was a majority in the late House of Commons,—but upon a particular plan of reform, which was accordingly discussed throughout the country.

It is on the ground of the dissolution, and of this Speech from the Throne, that I charge the Noble Lords with having excited the spirit which existed in the country at the period of the last general election; and with having been the cause of the unconstitutional practice, hitherto unknown, of electing delegates for a particular purpose of Parliament,—delegates to obey the daily instructions of their constituents, and to be cashiered if they should disobey them, whatever may be their own opinion; instead of being, as they have been hitherto, independent Members of Parliament to deliberate with their Colleagues upon matters of common concern, and to decide according to the best of their judgment, after such deliberation and debate. This is an evil of which the country will long feel the consequences, whatever may be the result of these discussions. My Lords, this measure, thus debated by the people, and thus brought forward by the Government in Parliament, for the decision of

Members thus delegated to give it the force of a law, alters everything; and requires, as the Noble Secretary of State says, still further alterations in the State, in order to render it practicable to carry on the Government at all.

I will not, at this late hour of the night, enter much into the details of the system proposed, which have been well considered and exposed by my Noble Friends, the Noble Earl (Lord Harrowby), and the Noble Baron (Lord Wharncliffe) behind me. One of my objections to the system proposed for the formation of the constituency of the boroughs and towns is its uniformity, and which objection was, by-the-bye, mentioned by one of my Noble Friends. The electors are all the householders, payers of a rent of 10 l. and upwards; these householders in towns in the south of England —I mean the counties of Kent, Sussex, Surrey, Hants., Berkshire, and Oxford—will consist of the occupiers of every house in such towns as will not require a supplement under to the Bill to be allotted by the Commissioners; these will be generally the shopkeepers—a class of persons of all others the most likely to combine in political views,—and to be acted upon by political clubs and societies of the description of that formed some months ago in the Strand, with a view to assist these newly-formed corporations in selecting their representatives in Parliament.

It is true that this society dissolved itself as soon as its existence was observed upon here or in the other House of Parliament. But political combination among these voters in boroughs or towns will, hereafter, be much more probable than it has been heretofore among the various interests of which the borough constituency has been formed. These combinations, or the influence of such an association as I have described and has existed, would be very injurious to the public interests. I beg your Lordships, besides, to observe that, in nearly every town not requiring a supplement, every householder will have a vote, including daily labourers, every description of menial servant, waiters, hostlers, postilions at inns, and such like.

With respect to counties, it appears that sixty-two Members are to be added to this branch of the representation; of which fifty to counties to be divided, two to Yorkshire, and ten to counties which are to have three Members each. An addition is to be made to the county constituency, by enabling 10 l. copyholders to vote as well as freeholders, and leaseholders holding tenements of 50 l. yearly rent, and even occupiers of land paying that sum. I cannot consider that this system will place the landed interest in the same relation towards the commercial or manufacturing interest, as that in which it stands at present. I doubt the county representation, as it stands at present, being capable of protecting the landed interest of the country without the assistance of the Members for the close boroughs. These are the true protectors of the landed interest of the country. The increase of riches in all towns, owing to the vast increase of manufactures and commerce, has given great influence to the inhabitants of towns in all county elections. This influence will be increased by giving votes to copyholders and holders of 50 l. leases: these are generally inhabitants of towns and shopkeepers. Throughout the whole of some counties in England there is not a single acre of land, not in a town, held by a lease.

Towns placed in Schedules A and B, deprived of their Members, will continue to influence the elections of Members for the counties in which they are situated—which elections will be further influenced by other arrangements of the Bill; giving votes to the freeholders of certain counties of towns in the elections of neighbouring counties. The Members for counties will, therefore, be nearly as much under the control of the constituency residing in towns, as the Members for the towns themselves will. But, my Lords, the question for us to consider, in the formation of this new system, is, not only what is the system which will best maintain the balance between the county interest and the town interest, but what will best form for the country a government. That is the most important point for our consideration, and for the people. We must take care that after all this shall be done, there will be a government in the country. We must consider not only the representation of England, but likewise that of Scotland and Ireland. With respect to Scotland and its representation, I do not know enough of either to pronounce whether the representation ought or ought not to be reformed; but I must repeat the words of a Noble Lord, whose loss I shall never cease to lament, respecting that country (I mean the late Earl of Liverpool), "that Scotland was the best-conditioned country in Europe." I believe I may say that it is one of the best-governed countries in the world; and I am sure that for the last sixty or seventy years it has been the most prosperous. We are bound to look at what is about to be done in respect of the representation of Scotland. In counties in Scotland, freeholders, leaseholders, copyholders (allowing for the difference of tenure), and occupiers of land paying a rent of 50 l. a year, are to have votes the same as in the counties in England. The inhabitants of towns will have the same influence over the elections for counties as in England; but this influence will be more powerful in Scotland than in England, because there are more large towns in Scotland, which, under the system, will not send representatives of their own, than there will be in England. The county Members from Scotland can no longer be reckoned upon as supporters of the landed interest. The franchises of the borough towns in Scotland will be given to 10 l. householders, as in England; and these will, of course, be in what is called the commercial or manufacturing interest.

With respect to Ireland, the change is the same as in England and Scotland. In Ireland, there are few holders of land except upon lease. But every tenant upon every estate will have a vote for a county. In the towns, 10 l. householders are to vote. These towns may be divided into two classes—close corporations and counties of towns. The first were formed by King James I., for the purpose of supporting in Parliament the establishment of the Church of England in Ireland, upon which I will say a word or two presently. The returns for these corporations are now to be made by the 10 l. householders of these same towns. In counties of towns the voters are to be the resident freemen of the corporation, and 40 s. freeholders, as at present, and resident 10 l. householders. All these arrangements depart from those of the Acts of 1828. Those Acts left the right of election in corporations and in counties of towns, as they had been settled and left at the Union. They deprived 40 s. freeholders of their right of voting for Members of counties, because it was supposed that the exercise of that right gave an undue preponderating influence to persons professing the Roman Catholic religion. The 50 l. leaseholders will, under the new arrangement, take the place of the 40 s. freeholders, and all will equally be the tool of the priest. For the close corporations established by King James, 10 l. householders are to vote. These are all Roman Catholics. In counties of towns we refused to deprive 40 s. freeholders of their franchise. The freemen of these corporations are generally, if not always, Protestants, and they can be increased without limitation. The freeholders are generally Roman Catholics. We did not think proper to alter the balance between the two, by leaving to the corporations the unlimited power of increasing its freemen, while the 40 s. freehold right should have been extinguished. But the Noble Lords have gone to work in another way, and, having first deprived non-resident freemen of these counties of towns, who are Protestants, of their votes, they have left untouched the Roman Catholic 40 s. freeholders, and have besides added to the constituency of those counties of towns all the 10 l. householders. These are likewise Roman Catholics. The Noble Lords have thus had the merit of establishing a Roman Catholic predominant interest in every county of a town in Ireland, in every close corporation formed for the protection of the Church of England, and in every county.

I will refer presently to the consequences of these arrangements upon the interests of the Church of England in Ireland. In the mean time, I beg your Lordships to observe, that the Irish representation in the Imperial Parliament cannot be considered as in the interest of the land. The due balance between the landed interest and the commercial and manufacturing interests in Parliament must be considered a matter of small importance, in comparison with the more important object of considering what will be the sort of House of Commons which such a constituency, so formed, will give us. Throughout the whole of the empire, persons in the lowest condition of life, liable to, and even existing under, the most pernicious influences, are to have votes, or, in other words, are to exercise political power. Persons in those stations of life do exercise political power already; but in few places in large masses preponderating over the influence of other classes of society. What must we expect when these lower classes will preponderate everywhere? We know what sort of representatives are returned by the places I have described. What are we to expect when the whole representation, or nearly the whole, will be of the same description?

We hear sometimes of radical reform; and we know that the term applies to universal suffrage, vote by ballot, annual Parliaments, and their consequences. But I declare, that looking at these changes pervading every part of the representation, root and branch, destroying or changing everything that has existed, even to the relative numbers of the representatives from the three kingdoms fixed by treaty, I should call this a radical reform, rather than reform of any other description. Is there no danger that, bad as what is proposed is, it will go further than would appear to be contemplated by the Noble Lords? A Noble Friend of mine has stated the danger which will result from this measure in consequence of the principle on which it stands. It stands, with respect to large towns, on the principle of population. Certain towns are selected to send two Members, because they have above 20,000 inhabitants; certain others to send one Member because they have above 9000 or 10,000 inhabitants.

There is in reserve a number of about thirty or forty Members not yet allotted to any constituency. Will it be possible to refuse to extend the right of sending Members to Parliament to any town or parish, which may prove that its numbers exceed 10,000 or 20,000 inhabitants? But we are told that this is not a question of numbers. How does it happen that there are four or five most beautiful, rich, and flourishing county towns in England placed in Schedule B? These county towns are not only rich in themselves, and by the settlements of gentry residing in their neighbourhood, but they are more populous than is required, in order to continue in the enjoyment of their accustomed number of representatives. It happens, however, that a part of the population of each inhabit a part of the existing town, not in, but contiguous to the corporation as fixed by its ancient charters; such limits not containing 4000 souls, the numbers required. We are then told that numbers have nothing to do with the various settlements of the representation under this Bill.

Taking the whole view of this system of representation to be established in England, Scotland, and Ireland, I cannot but consider that the House of Commons returned by it, will be a democratical assembly of the worst description; that radical reform, vote by ballot, and all the evil consequences to be expected from the deliberations of such an assembly, must follow from its establishment. I entreat your Lordships to pause before you agree to establish such a system in your country. But we are told that the people wish for this measure; and when we express our sense of the danger which attends it on account of the democratical power which it tends to establish, an endeavour is made to calm our apprehensions by the assurance that the people are attached to the government of King, Lords, and Commons. If we are to rely upon that feeling of the people,— if we are to adopt this measure because it is the pleasure of the people, and because they are attached to the government of King, Lords, and Commons, why do not we at once adopt the measure which we know that the people prefer,—I mean radical reform; that is to say, universal suffrage, vote by ballot, and annual Parliaments? If we are to make a change, there can be no reason for not going the full length that the people wish, if we can be sure that the measure will not injure the government—that to which they are attached—of King, Lords, and Commons.

But before we go further, it is desirable that we should examine what is the government of King, Lords, and Commons, as established in this kingdom. In this government, the King is at the head of everything. All the power is in his hands. He is the head of the Church, the head of the law. Justice is administered in his name. He is the protector of the peace of the country, the head of its political negotiations, and of its armed force,—not a shilling of public money can be expended without his order and signature. But, notwithstanding these immense powers, the King can do nothing that is contrary to the law, or to the engagements of himself or his predecessors. The King calls Parliament to assist him with its counsels *de arduis regni,* and those are responsible for his acts who carry them into execution. His Ministers are responsible not only for the legality, but for the prudence and fitness of his acts. To whom are they responsible? To this and the other House of Parliament,—to the latter principally, on account of the greater activity of its inquisitorial power, on account of its possessing exclusively the power of the purse, and for other reasons. Every act of the Government, or of the King, is liable to be brought under discussion in, and is, in fact, controlled by the House of Commons; and for this reason alone, it is important that we should consider of what description of men the House of Commons is likely to be composed, when we are discussing a question of Parliamentary Reform, in order that we may be quite certain that they will exercise their high functions with wisdom and discretion.

It was on these grounds that I some time ago called upon the Noble Earl to state by what influence he intended to carry on the King's Government in Parliament, according to the principles fixed at the period of the Revolution, and in practice from that period to this, when this Reform Bill should be passed. The Noble Lord answered immediately not by means of corruption. I am aware of that, my Lords. I am convinced that the Noble Lord is incapable of resorting to such means, as I hope he believes that I am incapable of resorting to them. I did not consider this any answer to my question, which I repeated in a subsequent discussion, on a motion by my Noble Friend the Noble Baron behind me. The Noble Earl said that the Government had nothing to do with such questions; that Parliament was to decide for itself; and that there was no necessity for the interference of Government. I beg your Lordships to consider what are the questions which, in every week, and on every day, are brought under the discussion of the House of Commons,—questions affecting the honour, the interests, the rights, the property of every individual in the country, which the King is bound by his oath to protect, and in the protection of which all are equally interested. They are questions regarding the proceedings of courts of justice, regarding the use of the public force, and hundreds of others, which daily occur, in which every individual is interested. I put legislation out of the question: but can the King, from that throne, give to his subjects the necessary protection for their rights and property? No, my Lords. It is only by the influence of property over the elections of Members of the House of Commons, and by the influence of the Crown and of this House, and of the property of the country upon its proceedings, that the great powers of such a body as the House of Commons can be exercised with discretion and safety. The King could not perform the duties of his high station, nor the House of Lords, if the House of Commons were formed on the principle and plan proposed by this Bill.

There is one institution which would become peculiarly liable to attack in such a House of Commons, to which I wish to draw the attention of the Right Reverend Bench, and that is, the establishment of the Church of England in Ireland. This Church is the object of a fundamental article of the treaty of Union between the two countries, and is secured by Acts of both Parliaments, and the King is besides sworn to maintain its right and possessions. Can any man believe that, when the representatives for Ireland come to be elected in the manner proposed by the Bill, the Church of England in Ireland can be maintained?

I have already shewn that these representatives must be elected under the influence of the Roman Catholic hierarchy. Who are those that now shew the greatest hostility to the Church, its rights and possessions?—the Members for populous places. The reason is, that the deprivation of the Church of their property is one of the popular objects of the day. The object of the Bill is, and its effects will be, to increase the number of this description of Members in Parliament, and to render the influence of this party predominant and irresistible.

I believe the Noble Earl has already found the Members returned by Ireland, under this influence, very inconvenient to himself, upon more than one occasion; and it appears, that the Right Honourable Gentleman who conducts the affairs of Ireland in the House of Commons was under the necessity, very lately, of giving up a measure which he thought important for the benefit and peace of Ireland, because the Members from Ireland, of this party, were opposed to it. How can the Noble Lord suppose, that the Church of England can be protected, or even the Union itself preserved in a reformed Parliament? There is no man, who considers what the Government of King, Lords, and Commons is, and the details of the manner in which it is carried on, who must not see that Government will become impracticable when the three branches shall be separate; each independent of the other, and uncontrolled in its action by any of the existing influences.

A Noble Earl, who has spoken on this side of the House, has made an observation to your Lordships which well deserves your attention. The Noble Earl has told you, that if you increase but a little the democratic power in the State, the step can never be withdrawn. Your Lordships must continue in the same course till you have passed through the miseries of a revolution, and hence to a military despotism, and the evils which attend that system of government. It is not denied, that this Bill must increase beyond measure the democratic power of the State—that it must constitute in the House of Commons a fierce democracy:—What must be the consequences, your Lordships will judge.

I will not detain your Lordships by adverting to the merits of the system of government which has existed up to the present moment, upon which my opinion is by no means altered. No man denies that we have enjoyed great advantages; that we have enjoyed a larger share of happiness, comfort, and prosperity, for a long course of years, then were ever enjoyed by any nation; that we have more riches, the largest fortunes, personal as well as real, more manufactures and commerce, than all the nations of Europe taken together; the richest, most extensive, most peopled, and most prosperous foreign colonies and possessions, than any nation ever possessed. There is not an important position in the world, whether for the purpose of navigation, commerce, or military defence, that does not belong to us.

If this democratic assembly should once be established in England, does any man believe that we should continue to enjoy these vast advantages? A democracy has never been established in any part of the world, that it has not immediately declared war against property,—against all payment of the public debt,—and against all the principles of conservation, which are secured by, and are, in fact, the principal objects of the British Constitution, as it now exists. Property and its possessors will become the common enemy. I do not urge this argument as one in which your Lordships are peculiarly interested: it is not you alone, nor even other proprietors, who are interested in the protection of property; the whole people, middling classes as well as the lower orders, are interested in this subject. Look at the anxiety prevailing in every part of London, in respect to the great revolution to be made by this Bill.

My Noble Friend, the Noble Baron behind me, has been ridiculed for adverting to the opinions of tradesmen in Bond-street and St. James's-street. Those in Bond-street consist of more than two hundred respectable persons, who are well able to form an opinion of the effect of this Bill upon the resources of themselves, the middling classes, and the poor, as they supply the luxuries of persons in easier circumstances residing in that quarter of the town. Anything which can affect the resources of their customers must be interesting to them; and they do feel that this Bill must affect property, private expenditure, and the resources of themselves, and of those whom they employ.

The Noble Lord on the other side, who adverted to this topic, greatly underrated the wealth of these tradesmen. I know of one, residing in Bond-street, who employs at all times from two thousand to four thousand workmen, whose trade depends, as well as the employment of this body of people, upon the expenditure of his customers: is he not interested in upholding the public faith and the system of property now established in England? Are not the people of all classes and descriptions, down to the lowest, interested in the maintenance of our extensive manufactures and commerce, in the conservation of our enormous dominions abroad, and the continued respect of all nations?

If I am right in thinking that this fierce democracy will be established in the House of Commons, does any man believe that that harmony can continue between the King and his Government, and the House of Commons, so necessary to insure to both general respect, and to the King's Government the strength which is necessary to enable His Majesty to protect and keep in order his foreign dominions, and to ensure the obedience of their inhabitants? We shall lose these colonies and foreign possessions, and with them our authority and influence abroad. There is no instance of any country having maintained its strength or its influence in its foreign possessions, or the respect of foreign nations, during the existence of internal troubles and disturbance; and there is no instance of the existence, without such troubles, of a Government consisting of King, Lords, and Commons, independent of each other, and the Members of the latter depending solely upon the popular choice, and being delegates of the people. We have had an example in England of a House of Commons which was independent of the influence of the Crown, and of this House, and of the property of the country. After banishing or imprisoning the most respectable Members of this House, turning the Spiritual Lords out of it, and murdering their Sovereign, they voted the House of Lords useless. I will read your Lordships the account given by a man who was knowing in his time (Oliver Cromwell), of what this House became.

The Parliament which had so vigorously withstood the encroachments of the royal power, became themselves too desirous of absolute authority; and not only engrossed the legislative, but usurped the executive power. All causes, civil and criminal, all questions of property, were determined by Committees, who, being themselves the Legislature, were accountable to no law, and for that reason their decrees were arbitrary, and their proceedings violent. Oppression was without redress, unjust sentence without appeal; there was no prospect of case or inter-mission. The Parliament had determined never to dissolve themselves. At length the army interfered. They soon perceived that, unless they made one regulation more, and crushed this many-headed monster, they had hitherto ventured their lives to little purpose, and had, instead of assuring their own and their country's liberty, only changed one kind of slavery for another.

This is the account of the state of a House of Commons acting independently of all influence, and of the condition to which it brought the country. My Lords, I have stated to you what will be the probable action of the system established by the Bill on the government of the country— that is the real question—what is the nature of our government, and what the share of the House of Commons in its details; in what manner it controls them all; and how important the composition of that House is to the very existence of Government. I have shewn you in what manner the protection of property by Government is necessary, and the dependence of all the sources of our national prosperity upon the continuance of a good understanding between the King and his Parliament. I have stated my reasons for thinking that all these will be destroyed by the Bill. I have likewise stated to your Lordships my opinion that the King's Ministers, by the speech which they recommended the King to deliver from the Throne, on the 22d of April, on the dissolution of Parliament, excited the spirit which pervaded the late election of Members to serve in Parliament, and occasioned the election of delegates for a particular purpose, instead of Members of Parliament.

My Lords, the King's speech, upon the occasion to which I have referred, has materially altered the state of this question. The people have been called upon by the King to deliberate upon it, and have been led to expect that a change would be made. In recommending your Lordships to vote against this Bill, I earnestly entreat you to avoid pledging yourselves, whether in public or private, against any other measure that may be brought forward. I recommend you to keep yourselves free to adopt any measure upon this subject which shall secure to this country the blessings of a good Government. By so doing, you will perform your duty by your country, and will deserve its thanks, and the gratitude of posterity.

William Cobbett

William Cobbett

[*Born* MARCH 9, 1763—*Died* JUNE 16, 1835]

His figure is tall and portly: he has a good sensible face, rather full, with little grey eyes, a hard, square forehead, a ruddy complexion, with hair grey or powdered. . . .—WILLIAM HAZLITT

T.

he Reform Act of 1832 was the first great victory of the rising middle class in its struggle against an aging aristocratic rule. Brougham, Russell, and Grey drafted the measure, to be sure, but the chief provoker who rallied popular support was William Cobbett, journalist, agitator, and, in the waning years of his life, member of the House of Commons.[1] William Hazlitt calls Cobbett "unquestionably" the most powerful political writer of his day and one of the best writers in the language.[2] G. D. H. Cole notes that nearly 200 titles of Cobbett's works are known, published in at least treble that number of separate editions and issues.[3] Throughout his life, Cobbett wrote and spoke on behalf of the "inarticulate, unrepresented, often illiterate peasant," [4] exploited in an agricultural economy and later in a capitalistic society. In a magnificent biography, Cole calls the history of Cobbett the spiritual history of the common people of his day:

. . . of their uprooting from the land of their fathers, of their un-ease and maladjustment under the new conditions, thrust upon them by the torrential flow of economic revolution. It is a history not of ideas, but of facts and feelings.[5]

To Cole, Cobbett was the last great tribune of the agrarians, and by force of circumstance was also the first great tribune of the industrial

---

1 J. L. and Barbara Hammond, *Lord Shaftsbury* (London: Constable and Co., 1925), p. 52. "In the late twenties Cobbett had urged that all the discontents of the time should be melted down in a common agitation for the Reform of Parliament, and it was to the success of this policy that the passing of the Reform Bill was due."

2 William Hazlitt, *The Spirit of the Age* (4th ed., London: George Bell and Sons, 1906), p. 285.

3 M. L. Pearl, *William Cobbett,* with a Foreword by G. D. H. Cole (London: Oxford University Press, 1953), p. 2. "His *Political Register,* begun in 1800, had run to eighty-eight volumes when he died in 1835, and during his active period as a writer at least fourteen different periodicals of one sort or another were started by him." Cobbett was also instrumental in organizing labors for the *French and English Dictionary* and the *Parliamentary Debates.* See also John W. Osborne, *William Cobbett* (New Brunswick, N.J.: Rutgers University Press, 1966), p. 257. "The best parts of the Register have been selected to form books such as *Rural Rides* [the best known of all his writings]; the rest is seldom read."

4 Marjorie Bowen, *Peter Porcupine* (London: Longmans, Green and Co., 1935), p. 293.

5 G. D. H. Cole, *The Life of William Cobbett* (New York: Harcourt, Brace and Co., 1924), p. 434.

proletariat who helped to speed the acquisition of the rising middle class to its share of political power.[6]

Cobbett's agitation was not confined to his writings. Since the turn of the nineteenth century, he had spoken on numerous occasions to the class he wished to guide. The high point of his political involvement, however, was between the years 1830 and 1835 when his adjutation was centered at Westminster. To his adversaries, in particular, Cobbett was "easily the most quarrelsome man in England." [7] In the House of Commons, he was considered a "general nuisance." [8] With a speaking style closely resembling that in which he wrote, no one could stand against him. "With his brandished club," writes Hazlitt, ". . . he knocks out their brains: and not only no individual, but no corrupt system, could hold out against his powerful and repeated attacks." [9] Reasoning was never a strong point of Cobbett's oratory, and he preferred, instead, to present the "whole solid mass, refuse and all." [10] Nevertheless, he envisioned the oratorical value of good humor, and with his sense for apt nicknames which stuck he was able to make his presence known.[11]

As a leading spokesman for factory reform, a question which occupied the first reformed Parliament, Cobbett spoke on July 19, 1833, in the House of Commons, on behalf of a bill introduced by Lord Ashley who sought to reduce the working hours of child laborers. The speech was short, the more effective for its brevity, writes Cole, for brevity was not usually among Cobbett's virtues.[12] The bill was defeated, and another of Cobbett's vain attempts to elevate the common man is recorded for posterity.

---

6 *Ibid.*

7 Hammonds, *op. cit.*, p. 19.

8 Osborne, *op. cit.*, p. 249.

9 Hazlitt, *op. cit.*, p. 290.

10 *Ibid.*, p. 295.

11 Hammonds, *op. cit.*, p. 67. When referring to Brougham, for example, Cobbett coined the expression "feelosopher."

12 Cole, *op. cit.*, p. 401.

The Factory Bill[1]

•

HOUSE OF COMMONS   *July 19, 1833*

At about one o'clock this morning, the House of Commons divided on the Factory Bill of Lord Ashley, and defeated his bill, in fact, by 238 votes against 93. The Mill-Owners, as they call them in Yorkshire and Lancashire, thus carried their point so far. I shall give a more full account of the matter another time. It is now six o'clock, and I did not get to bed till half-after two; and this must be printed and published this afternoon. I think it right, to prevent misrepresentation, to report what I said upon the subject, especially as it was so very little. I attempted to speak four or five times during the evening; but did not get an opportunity. The debate was closing at half-after twelve; and the main argument of the opponents of Lord Ashley was, that if two hours labour from these children, under eighteen years of age, were taken off, the consequences, on a *national scale,* might be 'truly dreadful'! It might, and would, destroy manufacturing capital; prevent us from carrying on competition with foreign manufacturers; reduce mills to a small part of their present value; and break up, as it were, the wealth and power of the country; render it comparatively feeble; and expose it to be an easy prey to foreign nations. What I said, was that which here follows, as near as I can recollect, word for word.

'Sir, I will make but one single observation upon this subject; and that is this: that this *"reformed"* House has, this night, made a *discovery* greater than all the discoveries that all former Houses of Commons have ever made, even if all their discoveries could have been put into one. Heretofore, we have sometimes been told that our ships, our mercantile traffic with foreign nations by the means of those ships, together with our body of rich merchants; we have sometimes been told that these form the

---

[1] *Political Register,* July 20, 1833, cols. 180–182. Cobbett's report of the circumstances leading to the speech are included with the speech, itself.

source of our wealth, power, and security. At other times, the land has stepped forward, and bid us look to it, and its yeomanry, as the sure and solid foundation of our greatness and our safety. At other times, the Bank has pushed forward with her claims, and has told us, that great as the others were, they were nothing without "PUBLIC CREDIT," upon which, not only the prosperity and happiness, but the very independence of the country depended. But, Sir, we have this night discovered, that the shipping, the land, and the Bank and its credit, are all nothing worth compared with the labour of three hundred thousand little girls in Lancashire! Aye, when compared with only an eighth part of the labour of those three hundred thousand little girls, from whose labour, if we only deduct two hours a day, away goes the wealth, away goes the capital, away go the resources, the power, and the glory of England! With what pride and what pleasure, sir, will the right hon. Gentleman opposite (Mr. P. Thomson), and the honourable Member for MANCHESTER behind me, go northward with the news of this discovery, and communicate it to that large portion of the little girls whom they have the honour and the happiness to represent!'

Strange to say, our Chancellor of the Exchequer really appeared to be *angry* with me for this! For, having complimented the mill-owners on the '*strong minds,*' of which they had given proof, he was '*free to confess,* that in the speech of the *honourable Member for Oldham* he found a very *striking contrast*' with the effusions of those strong minds!

Daniel O'Connell

Daniel O'Connell

[Born AUGUST 6, 1775—*Died* MAY 15, 1847]

Slightly under six feet, he was broad in proportion. His complexion was good, and his features, with the exception of his nose, which was short, were regular, but it was his mouth, which was finely chiselled, that gave to his face its chief charm.—ROBERT DUNLOP

T

he centuries-old struggle of Irish-
men against religious persecution was largely passive until Daniel
O'Connell appeared on the scene. According to T. M. Kettle, O'Connell was "the pioneer in all Western countries of the open-air meeting, as he is of the democratic agitation in general." [1] His is the first
instance of forcing legislative action by the instrument of political
agitation. Seán O'Faoláin calls him, "the greatest of all Irish realists,
who knew that if he could but once define, he would thereby create.
. . . He left his successors nothing to do but to follow him." [2]

To Claude G. Bowers, O'Connell's oratory was "one of the most
marvelous the world has known." [3] Although a formidable adversary
in Parliament,[4] his greatest gift was his "personal magnetism and
commanding appearance" coupled with his knowledge of human
nature incarcerated in his audiences of "unlettered millions." [5] As
a force possessing greater moral than political characteristics, he
thrilled crowds by his oratory:

. . . with its power of appeal that no previous leader had ever possessed,
in its variety of range, from passionate eloquence to the broadest farce.
But they loved him for his own gift of human sympathy—for his gaiety,
his infectious humour, his transparent sincerity, his cordial, affectionate
generosity, his hatred of injustice and oppression, and, above all, his challenging courage in an age when few Catholics dared to assert their self-
respect.[6]

O'Connell had a voice which was "seductively musical," and of
great compass, capable of expressing every imaginable emotion. His
gestures were free and bold, and his eyes reflected the sentiments he
expressed.[7]

---

1 *Irish Orators and Oratory*, with an Introduction by T. M. Kettle (Dublin: The
Tabot Press Ltd.), p. xii.
2 Seán O'Faoláin, *King of the Beggars* (New York: The Viking Press, 1938), p. 330.
3 Claude G. Bowers, *The Irish Orators* (Indianapolis: The Bobbs-Merrill Co., 1916),
p. 320.
4 See Michael Tierney, *Daniel O'Connell* (Dublin: Browne and Nolan Ltd., 1949),
p. 162. Tierney believes O'Connell reached his greatest heights as a parliamentary debater while opposing the Coercion Act of 1833.
5 Bowers, *op. cit.*, p. 322.
6 Denis Gwynn, *Daniel O'Connell* (Oxford: Cork University Press, 1947), p. 10.
7 Bowers, *op. cit.*, p. 323.

Some of the finest examples of O'Connell's platform speeches occur between 1840 and 1843 when he campaigned vigorously throughout the countryside of Ireland for Catholic Emancipation. These speeches were calculated to appeal to the patriotic pride of the Irish people.[8] The largest of these "monster meetings" took place at Tara, seat of the ancient kings. Several historians have referred to the London *Times'* estimate of one million people in attendance. O'Faoláin describes the assembling of the crowd in this manner:

All night long the crowds poured across the plains, camped on the hillsides, slept under the hedges; and when dawn lit the countryside there was not a road for miles around but was blackened by trudging men. In the morning, forty-two bands were playing to the people in the fields about. Not a vehicle of any sort was left in the city of Dublin.[9]

O'Connell did not have to be heard by the throngs, and there is doubt that he was. O'Faoláin observes that those far beyond the radius of his voice would "sit or lie on the trampled grass . . . playing with their children as if this were some popular festival, or some sportive occasion. . . ."[10] Bowers indicates that in those areas where O'Connell could scarcely be heard "his gestures were understood, and the people . . . stood still in perfect silence—awed by the mere sight of the speaker."[11] Kettle, in relating a story told him by an "old-timer" who claims to have heard the speech, suggests that everyone was able to hear every word:

Everybody heard Dan. For Dan raised his hand and told all about the platform to repeat his words. He said 'Silence,' and silence came out to us as the wind upon the barley. Then each man spoke after Dan, and every other man said the words, and out to us all on the edge of the crowd came the speech of Dan O'Connell.[12]

As an agitator, O'Connell was often careless with the truth of historical detail. He seemed content to be right "in the gross and was little troubled at being wrong by retail."[13] Before the multitudes, writes O'Faoláin, he "almost killed truth, and he warped honour. . . ."[14] But the Ireland of today is simply a refinement of the recipe left by Daniel O'Connell:

8 *Ibid.,* p. 301.
9 O'Faoláin, *op. cit.,* p. 305.
10 *Ibid.*
11 Bowers, *op. cit.,* p. 308.
12 Kettle, *op. cit.,* p. xiii.
13 *Ibid.,* p. xii.
14 O'Faoláin, *op. cit.,* p. 329.

The content of Irish life is the content of the Irish character, the dregs and the lees and the pure wine of this one man's recipe—to be purified indeed, to grow more rich in the wood with time, but never to lose the flavour of his reality, and the composition of his mind.[15]

---

15 *Ibid.*, p. 330.

Speech at Tara [1]

•

August 15, 1843

I t would be the extreme of affectation in me to suggest that I have not
some claims to be the leader of this majestic meeting. It would be
worse than affectation—it would be drivelling folly, if I were not to
feel the awful responsibility of the part I have taken in this majestic
movement imposed upon me (*hear, hear*). I feel responsibility to my
country—responsibility to my Creator. Yes, I feel the tremulous nature of
that responsibility—Ireland is aroused, is aroused from one end to another. Her multitudinous population have but one expression, and one
wish, and that is the extinction of the Union, the restoration of her nationality.

A Voice—There is no compromise.

Mr. O'Connell—Who is that that talks of compromise? I am not here
for the purpose of making anything like a schoolboy's attempt at declam-
atory eloquence; I am not here to revive in your recollection any of those
poetic imaginings respecting the spot on which we stand, and which have
really become as familiar as household words; I am not here to exaggerate
the historical importance of the spot on which we are congregated—but it
is impossible to deny that Tara has historical recollections that give to it
an importance, relatively, to other portions of the land, and deserves to be
so considered by every person who comes to it for political purposes, and
gives it an elevation and point of impression in the public mind that no
other part of Ireland can possibly have. History may have tarnished by
exaggeration, but the fact is undoubted that we are at Tara of the Kings.
We are on the spot where the monarchs of Ireland were elected, and
where the chieftains of Ireland bound themselves by the sacred pledge of
honour and the tie of religion to stand by their native land against the

1 *Irish Orators and Oratory, op. cit.,* pp. 303–321.

Danes or any other stranger (*cheers*). This is emphatically the spot from which emanated the social power—the legal authority—the right to dominion over the furthest extremes of the island, and the power of concentrating the force of the entire nation for the purpose of national defence. On this important spot I have an important duty to perform—I here protest in the face of my country, in the face of my Creator—in the face of Ireland and her God, I protest against the continuance of the unfounded and unjust Union. My proposition to Ireland is that the Union is not binding upon us; it is not binding, I mean, upon conscience—it is void in principle—it is void as matter of right—and it is void in constitutional law. I protest everything that is sacred, without being profane, to the truth of my assertion, there is really no union between the two countries. My proposition is that there was no authority vested in any person to pass the Act of Union. I deny the authority of the act—I deny the competency of the two legislatures to pass that act. The English legislature had no such competency—that must be admitted by every person. The Irish legislature had no such competency; and I arraign the Union, therefore, on the ground of the incompetency of the bodies that passed it. No authority could render it binding but the authority of the Irish people consulted individually through the counties, cities, towns, and villages; and if the people of Ireland called for the Union, then it was binding on them, but there was no other authority that could make it binding. The Irish Parliament had no such authority; they were elected to make laws and not legislatures, and it had no right to the authority which alone belonged to the people of Ireland. The trustee might as well usurp the right of the person who trusts him; the servant might as well usurp the power of the master; the Irish Parliament were elected as our trustees—we were their masters—they were but our servants, and they had no right to transfer us to any other power on the face of the earth. This doctrine is manifest, and would be admitted by every person; if it were applied to England, would any person venture to assert that the Parliament of England should have the power to transfer its privileges to make laws from England to the legislative chamber of France. Would any person be so insane as to admit it, and that insanity would not be mitigated even if they were allowed to send over their representatives to France. Yes, every person would admit in that case that the Union was void. I have no higher affection for England than France—they both are foreign authorities to me. The highest legal authority in England has declared us aliens in blood, aliens in religion, and aliens in language from the English. Let no person groan him— I thank him for the honesty of the expression. I never heard of any other act of honesty on his part, and the fact of his having committed one act of honesty ought to recommend him to your good graces. I can refer you to the principle of constitutional law, and to Locke on government, to show that the Irish Parliament had no power or authority to convey itself away. I will only detain you on that point by citing the words of Lord Chancellor Plunket. He declared in the Irish House of Commons that they had no right to transfer the power of legislation from the country. He called upon them to have his words taken down, and he defied the power of Lord Castlereagh to have him censured for the expression, limiting the authority of Parliament. He said to them that they could not transfer their authority—that the maniacal suicide might as well imagine that the blow by which he destroyed his miserable body could annihilate his immortal soul, as they to imagine they could annihilate the soul of Ireland, her constitutional right. The illustration is a happy one. I am here the representative of the Irish nation, and in the name of that great, that virtuous, that moral, temperate, brave, and religious nation, I proclaim the Union a nullity for it is a nullity in point of right. Never was any measure carried by such iniquitous means as the Union was carried. The first thing that taints it in its origin, and makes it, even if it were a compact, utterly void, is the fraud committed in fomenting discord in the country, and encouraging the rebellion until it broke out, and in making that rebellion and the necessity for crushing it the means of taking from Ireland her constitution and her liberties. There was this second fraud committed on her, that at the time of the passing of the Act of Union Ireland had no legal protection; the habeas corpus was suspended, martial law was proclaimed, trial by jury was at an end, and the lives and liberties of all the King's subjects in Ireland were at the mercy of the courts martial. Those among you who were old enough at the time remember when the shriek from the triangle was heard from every village and town, and when the troops would march out from Trim and lay desolate the country for nine or ten miles around. The military law was established in all its horrors throughout every district of the country and the people were trampled in the dust under the feet of the yeomanry, army, and fencibles. The next fraudulent device to which England has recourse in order to carry this infamous measure, and to promote her own prosperity on the ruins of the Irish nationality, was to take the most effective means in order to prevent the Irish people from meeting to remonstrate against the insult and the injury which was about to be inflicted upon them. The Union was void no less from the utter incompetency of the contracting parties to enter into any such contract than by reason of the fact, that it was carried into operation by measures most iniquitous, atrocious and illegal; the habeas corpus act was suspended, torture, flogging, pitch caps, and imprisonment were the congenial agencies whereby England endeavoured to carry her infamous designs, and executions upon the gallows for no other crime than that of being suspected to be suspicious, were of daily occurrence in every part of the kingdom. Thus it was that they endeavoured to crush the expression of the people's feelings, whom they resolved to plunder and degrade. The people were not permitted to assemble together for the purpose of remonstrating against the Union. Meetings—convened by the officers of justice—by the high sheriffs of counties, were dispersed at the point of the bayonet. The people were not permitted to meet together for remonstrance, but they got up petitions in every direction, to testify their feelings upon the subject, and although no less than seven hundred and seven thousand signatures were signed to petitions against the Union, despite of all the corrupt influence of the Government, more than three thousand wretches could not be found to sign a petition in favour of the measure. The next impeachment which I bring against the Union is that it was brought about not only by physical force, but by bribery the most unblushing and corruption the most profligate. One million two hundred and seventy-five thousand pounds were expended upon the purchase of rotten boroughs alone, and no less a sum than two millions of money were lavished upon peculation unparalleled, and bribery the most enormous and most palpable that ever yet disgraced the annals of humanity. There was not an office, civil, military, or ecclesiastical in the country, which was not flung open to the Unionist as the price and wages of his political depravity. Six or seven judges bought their seats upon the bench by giving in their adhesion to the Union; and having no claim to wear the ermine other than that which was to be derived from the fact of their being recreants to their country, they continued in right of this during their lives to inflict the effects of their iniquity upon the people whom they betrayed. Twelve bishops obtained their sees by voting for the Union, for the spirit of corruption spared nothing. Men were made prelates, generals, admirals, commissioners, for supporting the ministry in this infamous design, and every office in the revenue and customs was placed at the disposal of those who were base enough to sell their country for a mess of porridge. In fact, corruption was never known to have been carried before or since to such excess in any country of the world, and if such a contract, if contract it could be called, was to be binding on the Irish nation, there was no longer any use for honesty or justice in the world. But strong as was the influence of corruption on the human mind, the victory which the English ministry achieved was slow, and by no means easy of accomplishment, for the intimidation to the death upon the one hand, and bribery on the other, were impotent to procure a majority for them in the Irish House of Commons in the first session, when the bill was introduced. On the contrary, when the first attempt was made to frustrate our liberties, there was a majority of eleven against the Union bill. But the despoiler was not easy to be foiled, nor was he apt to be disheartened by a single failure. The work of corruption was set on foot with redoubled energy, and the wretches who were not so utterly abandoned as to suffer themselves to be bribed for the direct and positive purpose of giving their vote for the Union accepted bribes on the condition of withdrawing from the House altogether, and accordingly they vacated their seats, and in their place stepped in Englishmen and Scotchmen who knew nothing of Ireland, and who were not impeded by any conscientious scruples whatever from giving their unqualified sanction to any plot of the English, how infamous soever, to oppress and plunder the country. By these accumulated means the Union was carried and the fate of Ireland sealed. But the monster evil of the Union is the financial robbery which by its means was practised upon Ireland. A scandalous injustice thus inflicted would be in itself sufficient even in the absence of other arguments (even if other arguments were wanting) to render the Union void and of no effect. At the passing of that fatal act (badge of our ruin and disgrace) Ireland owed only twenty millions, England owed four hundred and forty six millions, and the equitable terms on which the contract was based, whereby both countries were to be allied and identified—identified indeed!—were these, that England was generously to undertake the liability of one-half of her national debt, on condition that we would undertake the responsibility of one-half of hers. This is not a befitting time nor season to enter into minute details relative to the particulars of this financial swindle, but I may be permitted to direct your attention to this very obvious fact, that whereas England has only doubled her debt since the passing of the Union, the increase of the national debt of Ireland during the same period cannot with justice be estimated on a different ratio, and that consequently Ireland, at the very highest calculation, cannot in reality, and as of her own account, owe a larger sum than forty millions; and I will tell you, my friends, that never will we consent to pay one shilling more of a national debt than that. I say it in the name and on behalf of the Irish nation. But I will tell you this as a secret, and you may rely upon it as a truth, that in point of fact we do not owe one farthing more than thirty millions; and in proof of the truth of this assertion I beg leave to refer you to a work published by a very near and dear relative of mine—my third son, the member of Kilkenny—who, by the most accurate statistical calculations, and by a process of argument intelligible to the humblest intellect, has made the fact apparent to the world, that according to the terms of honest and equitable dealing, as between both countries, Ireland's proportion of the national debt cannot be set down at a larger sum than I state—thirty millions. I am proud that there is a son of mine who, after the Repeal shall have been carried, will be able to meet the cleverest English financier of them all, foot to foot and hand to hand, and prove by arguments most incontestible how grievous and intolerable is the injustice which was inflicted upon our country in this respect of the Union. The project of robbing Ireland by joining her legislatively with England was no new scheme which entered the minds of the English for the first time about the year 1800. It was a project which was a favourite theme of dissertation with all the English essayists for years previous to the period when it was carried into practical effect, and the policy towards Ireland, which their literary men were continually urging upon the English people for their adoption, was similar to that of the avaricious housewife who killed the goose who laid her golden eggs. Yes, such was the course they pursued towards Ireland, and you will deserve the reputation of being the lineal descendants of that goose if you be such ganders as not to declare in a voice of thunder that no longer shall this system of plunder be permitted to continue. My next impeachment of the Union is founded upon the disastrous effects which have resulted therefrom to our commercial and manufacturing interests, as well as to our general national interests. Previous to the Union, the county Meath was filled with the seats of noblemen and gentlemen. What a contrast does its present state present! I on Monday read at the Association a list of the deserted mansions which are now to be found ruined and desolate in your country. Even the spot where the Duke of Wellington (famed the world over for his detestation of his country) drew his first breath, instead of bearing a noble castle, or splendid mansion, presented the aspect of ruin and desolation, and briars and nettles adequately marked the place that produced him. The county of Meath was at one time studded thickly with manufactories in every direction, and an enormous sum was expended yearly in wages, but here, as in every other district of the country, the eye was continually shocked with sights which evidenced with too great eloquence the lamentable decay which has been entailed upon our country by the Union. The linen trade at one period kept all Ulster in a state of affluence and prosperity. Kilkenny was for ages celebrated for its extensive blanket manufactures—and Cork also—and Carrick-on-Suir, and in a thousand other localities too numerous to mention, thousands were kept in constant and lucrative employment, at various branches of national industry, from year's end to year's end, before the passing of the Union. But this is no longer the case, and one man is not now kept in employment for a thousand who were employed before the Union. The report of the English commissioners themselves has declared this appalling fact to the world—that one-third of our population are in a state of actual destitution; and yet, in the face of all this, men may be found who, claiming to themselves the character of political honesty, stand up and declare themselves in favour of the continuance of the Union. It is no bargain—it was a base swindle. Had it, indeed, been a fair bargain, the Irish would have continued faithful to it to the last, regardless of the injuries which it might have entailed upon them—for the Irish people have been invariably faithful to their contracts; whereas England never yet made a promise which she did not violate, nor ever entered into a contract which she did not shamelessly and scandalously outrage. Even the Union itself, beneficial as it is to England, is but a living lie to Ireland. Everybody now admits the mischief that the Union has produced to Ireland. The very fact of its not being a compact is alone sufficient to nullify the Union, and on that ground I here proclaim, in the name of the Irish nation, that it is null and void. It is a union of legislators, but not a union of nations. Are you and I one bit more of Englishmen now than we were twenty or forty years ago? If we had a Union would not Ireland have the same parliamentary franchise that is enjoyed by England? But calling it a Union, could anything be more unjust on the part of England than to give her own people a higher and more extensive grade of franchise, and to the Irish people a more limited and an extinguishing and perishing franchise? She has given to her people an extended municipal reform, and to Ireland a wretched and a miserable municipal reform. Even within the last week a plan was brought forward by Lord Elliot and the sneaking Attorney-General Smith, that will have the effect of depriving one-third of those who now enjoy the franchise of its possession. No, the Union is void, but it is more peremptorily void on the ground of the ecclesiastical revenues of the country being left to support a church of a small portion of the people. In England the ecclesiastical revenues of the country are given to the clergy that the majority of the people believe to teach the truth. In Scotland the ecclesiastical revenues are, or at least were up to a late period, paid to the clergy of the majority of the people; but the Irish people are compelled to pay the clergy of a small minority, not amounting to more than the one-tenth of the people of the entire island. The Union was effected against all constitutional principle—by the most atrocious fraud—by the most violent and most iniquitous exercise of force—by the most abominable corruption and bribery—by the shifting of Irish members out of their seats, and the putting of Englishmen and Scotchmen into their places; and that was followed by the destruction of our commerce, by the annihilation of our manufactures, by the depreciation of our farmers—and you know I speak the truth when I talk of the depression of the farming interests—by financial robbery, on an extensive scale to be sure, but a robbery on that very account, only the more iniquitous, fiendish and harsh. I contend, therefore, that the Union is a nullity; but do I, on that account, advise you to turn out against it? No such thing. I advise you to act quietly and peaceably and in no other way.

A Voice—Any way you like.

Mr. O'Connell—Remember that my doctrine is that "the man who commits a crime gives strength to the enemy," and you should not act in any manner that would strengthen the enemies of your country. You should act peaceably and quietly, but firmly and determinedly. You may be certain that your cheers here to-day will be conveyed to England. (*The vast assemblage here commenced cheering for several minutes in the most deafening and enthusiastic manner, and the distant lines of human beings that on the walls and hedges marked the limits of the immense assemblage might be seen waving their hats and handkerchiefs in response, though, of course, without knowing the sentiment that called forth the burst of enthusiasm.*) Yes, the overwhelming majesty of your multitude will be taken to England, and will have its effect there. The Duke of Wellington began by threatening us. He talked of civil war, but he does not say a single word of that now. He is now getting eyelet holes made in the old barracks, and only think of an old general doing such a thing, just as if we were going to break our heads against stone walls. I am glad to find that a great quantity of brandy and biscuits has been latterly imported, and I hope the poor soldiers get some of them. But the Duke of Wellington is not now talking of attacking us, and I am glad of it; but I tell him this—I mean no disrespect to the brave, the gallant, and the good conducted soldiers that compose the Queen's army; and all of them that we have in this country are exceedingly well conducted. There is not one of you that has a single complaint to make against any of them. They are the bravest army in the world, and therefore I do not mean to disparage them at all, but I feel it to be a fact, that Ireland roused as she is at the present moment, would, if they made war upon us, furnish women to beat the entire of the Queen's forces. At the last fight for Ireland, when she was betrayed by having confided in England's honour—but oh! English honour will never again betray our land, for the man will deserve to be betrayed who would confide again in England. I would as soon think of confiding in the cousin-german of a certain personage having two horns and a hoof. At that last battle, the Irish soldiers, after three days' fighting, being attacked by fresh troops, faltered and gave way, and 1,500 of the British army entered the breach. The Irish soldiers were fainting and retiring when the women of Limerick threw themselves between the contending forces, and actually stayed the progress of the advancing enemy. I am stating matter of history to you, and the words I use are not mine, but those of Parson Story, the chaplain of King William, who describes the siege, and who admits that the Limerick women drove back the English soldiers from fifteen to thirty paces. Several of the women were killed, when a shriek of horror resounded from the ranks of the Irish. They cried out, "Let us rather die to the last man than our women should be injured," and then they threw themselves forward, and, made doubly valiant by the bravery of the women, they scattered the Saxon and the Dane before them. Yes, I have women enough in Ireland to beat them if necessary; but, my friends, it is idle to imagine that any statesman ever existed who could resist the cry that Ireland makes for justice.

Having cautioned the meeting against Ribbonism, and alluded in terms of effusive loyalty to Queen Victoria, Mr. O'Connell continued:

We will break no law. See how we have accumulated the people of Ireland for this Repeal Year. When, on the 2nd of January, I ventured to call it the Repeal Year, every person laughed at me. Are they laughing now? It is our turn to laugh at present. Before twelve months more the Parliament will be in College Green. I said the Union did not take away from the people of Ireland their legal rights. I told you that the Union did not deprive the people of that right, or take away the authority to have self-legislation. It has not lessened the prerogatives of the crown, or taken away the rights of the Sovereign, and amongst them is the right to call her Parliament wherever the people are entitled to it, and the people of Ireland are entitled to have it in Ireland. And the Queen has only tomorrow to issue her writs and get the Chancellor to seal them, and if Sir Edward Sugden does not sign them she will soon get an Irishman that will, to revive the Irish Parliament. The towns which sold their birthright have no right to be reckoned amongst the towns sending members to Parliament. King James the First, in one day, created forty boroughs in Ireland, and the Queen has the same right as her predecessor to do so. We have a list of the towns to return members according to their population, and the Queen has only to order writs to issue, and to have honest ministers to advise her to issue those writs, and the Irish Parliament is revived by its own energy, and the force of the Sovereign's prerogative. I will only require the Queen to exercise her prerogative, and the Irish people will obtain their nationality again. If, at the present moment, the Irish Parliament was in existence, even as it was in 1800, is there a coward amongst you—is there a wretch amongst you so despicable that would not die rather than allow the Union to pass?

A Voice—Yes, to the last man (*cheers*).

Mr. O'Connell—Let every man who, if we had an Irish Parliament, would rather die than allow the Union to pass lift up his hands. (*The immense multitude lifted up their hands.*) Yes, the Queen will call that Parliament; you may say it is the act of her ministry, if you please. To be sure it would be the act of her ministry, and the people of Ireland are entitled to have their friends appointed to the ministry. The Irish Parliament will then assemble, and I defy all the generals, old and young, and all the old women in pantaloons. Nay, I defy all the chivalry of the earth to take away that Parliament from us again. Well, my friends, may I ask you to obey me in the course of conduct I point out to you, when I dismiss you to-day; when you have heard the resolutions put, I am sure you will go home with the same tranquillity with which you came here, every man of you; and if I wanted you again, would you not come again to Tara Hill for me? Remember me, I lead you into no peril. If danger existed, it

would arise from some person who would attack us, for we will attack
nobody; and if that danger exists you will not find me in the rear rank.
The Queen will be able to restore our Parliament to us. The absentee
drains, which caused the impoverishment of the country, will be at an
end—the wholesale ejectment of tenants and turning them out on the
highway—the murdering of tenants by the landlords shall be at an end.
The rights of the landlords will be respected, but their duties shall be
enforced—an equitable tenure will take the place of the cruel tyranny of
the present code of laws, and the protection of the occupying tenants of
Ireland be inscribed on the banner of Repeal. Carry home with you my
advice—let there be peace and quiet, law and order, and let every one of
you enroll yourselves Repealers—men, women, and children. Give me
three millions of Repealers, and I will soon have them. The next step is
being taken, and I announce to you from this spot, that all the magistrates that have been deprived of the commisssion of the peace shall be
appointed by the association to settle all the disputes and differences in
their neighbourhood. Keep out of the petty sessions court, and go them on
next Monday. We will submit a plan to choose persons to be arbitrators to
settle the differences of the people without expense, and I call upon every
man that wishes to be thought the friend of Ireland, to have his disputes
settled by the arbitrators, and not again to go to the petty sessions. We
shall shortly have the preservative society to arrange the means of procuring from Her Majesty the exercise of her prerogative, and I believe I am
able to announce to you that twelve months cannot possibly elapse without having a hurra for our Parliament in College Green. Remember, I
pronounce the Union to be null—to be obeyed, as an injustice must be
obeyed, when it is supported by law until we have the royal authority to
set the matter right, and substitute our own Parliament. I delight at having this day presided over such an assemblage on Tara Hill. Those shouts
that burst from you were enough to recall to life the Kings and Chiefs of
Ireland. I almost fancy that the spirits of the mighty dead are hovering
over us—that the ancient Kings and Chiefs of Ireland are from yonder
clouds listening to us. Oh, what a joyous and cheering sound is conveyed
in the chirrup for Old Ireland! It is the most beautiful—the most fertile—
the most abundant—the most productive country on the face of the earth.
It is a lovely land, indented with noble harbours—intersected with transcendent, translucent streams—divided by mighty estuaries. Its harbours
are open at every hour for every tide, and are sheltered from every storm
that can blow from any quarter of Heaven. Oh, yes, it is a lovely land,
and where is the coward that would not dare to fight for it! Yes, our
country exhibits the extreme of civilization, and your majestic movement
is already the admiration of the civilized world. No other country could
produce such an amount of physical force, coupled with so much decorum

and propriety of conduct. Many thousands of persons assembled together, and, though they have force sufficient to carry any battle that ever was fought, they separate with the tranquillity of schoolboys breaking up in the afternoon. I wish you could read my heart, to see how deeply the love of Ireland is engraven upon it, and let the people of Ireland, who stood by me so long, stand by me a little longer, and Ireland shall be a nation again.

Sir Robert Peel

Sir Robert Peel

[*Born* FEBRUARY 5, 1788—*Died* JULY 2, 1850]

Sir Robert Peel had a tall commanding figure, and a frame so strong as to endure the labours of prime minister sixteen hours a day.—HON. GEORGE PEEL

• G •reat Britain, battered by the Napoleonic wars, looked inward to find itself submerged in deep social, economic, and political turmoil. It sought and found a leader who, according to Tresham Lever, "laid the firm foundation of that great period of prosperity that characterized and glorified the Victorian era."[1] Sir Robert Peel was that man, and during the period from the Reform Bill to Corn Law Repeal in 1846, he exercised over the Conservative party a predominance which has never been equaled.[2] W. Cooke Taylor calls Peel's public life "the history of his age," during which time all the great principles of the nineteenth century evolved.[3]

Peel was an outstanding parliamentarian who could boast that he never proposed a measure which failed to pass.[4] He was an adroit practitioner, not a theorist or a political philosopher. He saw merit in ideas advanced by Romilly, Mackintosh, Horner, Cobden, and Bright, and he persuaded Parliament to implement them. He sought, above all, real solutions to real problems. He was not above jeopardizing his own political stature within his party when he detected the untenability of his position on an issue. In the first of two noteworthy instances of this, Peel reversed his opposition to Catholic emancipation, and, he helped carry the measure in Parliament. In the second instance, he was swept into office because of his opposition to free trade, but five years later reversed his position, and successfully repealed the Corn Laws at the cost of losing the leadership of the Conservative party.

As a speaker, Peel chose to adapt his style to a Parliament which was becoming more and more an assembly of businessmen who demanded an eloquence of "business-precision and practicality. . . ."[5] In deference, Peel chose "facts to phrases,"[6] developing the facility to compose tight, logical argumentation, "very able and very com-

---

1 Tresham Lever, *The Life and Times of Sir Robert Peel* (London: George Allen and Unwin Ltd., 1942), p. 310.

2 *Ibid.*, p. 307.

3 W. Cooke Taylor, *Life and Times of Sir Robert Peel*, I (London: Peter Jackson, Late Fisher, Son, and Co.), Preface.

4 Lever, *op. cit.*

5 Justin McCarthy, *Sir Robert Peel* (New York: Harper and Bros., 1891), p. 11.

6 Norman Gash, *Mr. Secretary Peel* (Cambridge, Mass.: Harvard U. Press, 1961), p. 14.

petently produced." [7] Lord Rosebery describes his speeches as "grave, dignified, weighty, with the roll of phrase which veils so many defeats, and which in an argument acts as a permanent saving clause." [8] Lever claims that Peel possessed a voice which was one of the finest ever heard within the walls of Parliament.[9] In manner, he appeared to exercise the same deliberation as he did in composition:

. . . he would rise slowly, sumptuously dressed, and wearing a watch chain and bunch of seals of unusually large dimensions and great splendor. He would arrange his coat tails carefully. . . . At the beginning of an important speech he would rest his left hip, his right he would use to strike the box on the table in front of him . . . Sometimes he used to turn right around and speak to his party behind him when he thought to catch their applause.[10]

Among several of Peel's speeches still consulted by "experts" is one on Currency Reform, delivered to the House of Commons on May 6, 1844.[11] J. R. Thursfield describes it as "the most authoritative exposition of the true principles of the national currency." [12] Another of his memorable speeches was his Address in Answer to the Speech of the Queen on January 22, 1846,[13] at which time he completely reversed his opposition to Corn Law Repeal, setting the scene for one of the most bitter attacks ever leveled at a Prime Minister in the House of Commons (see Disraeli).

[7] George Kitson Clark, *Peel and the Conservative Party* (London: Frank Cass and Co., Ltd., 1964), p. 97.

[8] Lord Rosebery, *Miscellanies: Literary and Historical,* I (London: Hodder and Stoughton, Ltd., 1921), p. 217.

[9] Lever, *op. cit.*

[10] Clark, *op. cit.*

[11] Rosebery, *op. cit.*

[12] J. R. Thursfield, *Peel* (London: Macmillan and Co., Ltd., 1904), p. 194.

[13] See 83 H.C. Deb. 3 s., Cols. 67–95.

Bank Charter—The Currency [1]

•

HOUSE OF COMMONS *May 6, 1844*

O n the Motion of Sir Robert Peel the House resolved itself into a Committee on the Bank of England Charter Act. Sir R. Peel rose, and addressing Mr. Greene, who was in the Chair, said—

Sir, there are occasionally questions of such vast and manifest importance, and which prefer such a claim, I should rather say such a demand, on the attention of the House, that all rhetorical prefaces, dilating on their magnitude or enjoining the duty of patient consideration, are superfluous and impertinent. I shall, therefore, proceed at once to call the attention of this Committee to a matter which enters into every transaction of which money forms a part. There is no contract, public or private, —no engagement, national or individual, which is unaffected by it. The enterprises of commerce, the profits of trade, the arrangements made in all the domestic relations of society, the wages of labour, pecuniary transactions of the highest amount and of the lowest, the payment of the national debt, the provision for the national expenditure, the command which the coin of the smallest denomination has over the necessaries of life, are all affected by the decision to which we may come on that great question which I am about to submit to the consideration of the Committee. The circumstances under which the duty imposed on me arises are shortly these:—In the year 1833, an Act of Parliament passed which continued to the Bank of England certain privileges until the year 1855, and after the year 1855 until Parliament should determine to give one year's notice to the Bank of its determination to revise the charter. Before, however, the expiration of the full period of twenty-one years, before the arrival of that term of 1855, there was reserved to Parliament the power, after the lapse of ten years, by notice to be given to the Bank, of revising

[1] 74 H.C. Deb. 3 s., Cols. 720–754.

the charter and reconsidering this whole subject. That period will arrive in August next. After August next it will be competent to this House, by notice given through the Speaker, to intimate to the Bank that within six months next following this House will reconsider the charter of the Bank of England. If that opportunity be let pass, the charter of the Bank and all the privileges it confers will endure until the year 1855. In the present state of this country—in the present state of the currency—after the inquiries which have been instituted, after the degree to which public attention has been called to this subject, Her Majesty's Government feel it to be their duty to avail themselves of the opportunity thus given to them by law, and to consider the revision of the charter of the Bank. They are of opinion, that inquiry has been exhausted—that all the information which is essential to the formation of a satisfactory judgment has been collected, and that it is incumbent on the Ministers of the Crown to submit to the decision of Parliament the measures which in their opinion it may be fitting to adopt. Sir, I am perfectly satisfied that the Members of this House, rising superior to all party considerations, and to all private interests, will consider it their duty to apply their deliberate and impartial consideration to this great subject. I have that confidence in the House of Commons, from past experience of their superiority to mere party views and personal interests where matters of such paramount importance come under review, that I feel assured such will be the course they will pursue on this occasion. I would even deprecate the expression of opinion. I ask you to listen to the proposals I shall make—to hear the evidence and arguments by which they shall be supported—to read and consider the resolutions which I shall move, *pro forma;* and, after having deliberated maturely on the subject, hereafter to pronounce a cool and impartial judgment upon it. Sir, I am not shaken in the confidence I repose in the House by publications I have seen, inviting the attendance of Members on this occasion. I hold in my hand the resolutions adopted at a meeting of the General Committee of Private Country Bankers on the 17th April last. They are to this effect: "That the refusal of Government to give information on the subject of their measure concerning Banks and issue, naturally leads to the conclusion that it is their intention to propose some measure affecting country banks generally, and this meeting considers it most probably that it relates to the local circulation of the country." "That under these circumstances it is most desirable that the banks of issue, whether private or joint-stock banks, should unite to oppose any alteration in the local circulation of the country, or in the conditions on which it is now allowed by law; and that the several joint-stock banks and banks of issue throughout the United Kingdom be invited to co-operate with the private bankers in such opposition." The third Resolution is, "That all bankers be requested, as far as possible, to bring the question fully under the consideration of all Members of Parliament with whom they may be acquainted or connected, and endeavour to induce them to oppose any such alterations in the local circulation of the country." Sir, I complain not of these resolutions. I complain not, at least, that the Bankers have invited Members of Parliament to attend in their place and consider this subject; but I do hope that Members of Parliament will resist the subsequent appeal, and that they will not come here determined beforehand to oppose any alteration in the existing law which may be proposed for their consideration. Are you so satisfied with the existing state of things,—are you so convinced that it is utterly impossible in any particular to suggest alteration, that you will come prepared, before hearing the discussion on the subject, to offer, after previous concert and understanding, an insuperable obstacle to any amendment of the existing law? I know that to be impossible. I hold in my hand the proof of evils flowing from the present state of the law, which should make it impossible that any such previous compact and understanding, if entered into, could be fulfilled. My immediate proposition relates to Banking Concerns, and to the issue of Promissory Notes; but, considering that ten years have now elapsed since this subject was brought under consideration, I hope I shall be excused if I take a wider range than the immediate questions for decision might seem to justify, and if I advert at the outset to the great principles which govern, or ought to govern, the Measure of Value, and the Medium of Exchange. They lie, in truth, at the very foundation of our discussion. We cannot hope to agree on the Measure to be adopted with regard to Paper Currency, unless we are agreed on the principles which determine the value of that of which Paper is the representative, and on the nature of the obligation which is imposed upon the issuer of Promissory Notes. Now I fear there is not a general agreement on those fundamental principles—that there is still a very material difference of opinion as to the real nature and character of the Measure of Value in this country. My first question, therefore, is, what constitutes this Measure of Value? What is the signification of that word "a Pound," with which we are all familiar? What is the engagement to pay a "Pound?" Unless we are agreed on the answer to these questions, it is in vain we attempt to legislate on the subject. If a "Pound" is a mere visionary abstraction, a something which does not exist either in law or in practice, in that case one class of measures relating to Paper Currency may be adopted; but if the word "Pound," the common denomination of value, signifies something more than a mere fiction—if a "Pound" means a quantity of the precious metals of certain weight and certain fineness—if that be the definition of a "Pound," in that case another class of measures relating to Paper Currency will be requisite. Now, the whole foundation of the proposal I am about to make rests upon the assumption that according to practice, according to law, according to the ancient monetary policy of this country, that which is implied by the word "Pound" is a certain definite quantity of gold with a mark upon it to determine its weight and fineness, and that the engagement to pay a Pound means nothing, and can mean nothing else, than the promise to pay to the holder, when he demands it, that definite quantity of gold. What is the meaning of the "Pound" according to the ancient monetary policy of this country? The origin of the term was this:—In the reign of William the Conqueror a pound weight of silver was also the pound of account. The "Pound" represented both the weight of metal and the denomination of money. By subsequent debasements of the currency a great alteration was made, not in the name, but in the intrinsic value of the Pound sterling, and it was not until a late period of the reign of Queen Elizabeth that silver, being then the standard of value, received that determinate weight which it retained without variation, with constant refusals to debase the standard of silver, until the year 1816, when gold became the exclusive standard of value. The standard of silver was fixed about 1567; but in 1717, the value of the guinea was determined to be 21s., and for a certain period, both gold and silver constituted the mixed standard of value. In the year 1774, it being then enacted that no legal contract should be discharged in silver for any sum of more than 25s., gold became substantially the measure of value, and so it continued to be legally and practically until 1797, when that fatal measure for restricting cash payments by the Bank was passed, and the parties were enabled to issue at their discretion Paper Money not convertible into coin at the will of the bearer. From 1797 to 1810 public attention was not much directed to this important subject; but in 1810 men of sagacity observed that the exchanges had been for a considerable period unfavourable to this country—more unfavourable than could be accounted for by the balance of trade or the monetary transactions of the country. A Committee was appointed to inquire into the subject, and opinions, not really novel, but at that time very startling, were enounced, to the effect that the "Pound" meant, in fact, nothing else than a definite quantity of the precious metals, and that those who promised to pay a Pound ought to pay that quantity. That theory was very much contested at the time. The House of Commons was not convinced by the arguments used in favour of it. The public mind, confused by the practice that had prevailed since the issue of inconvertible paper, would not admit the doctrine of a metallic standard. Those who contested it were, however, called upon to give their definition of the Pound Sterling, and it must be admitted that they responded to the call. They did not evade the question, as is now the practice, by writing long and unintelligible pamphlets, but, confident in their own theories, gave, in brief and compendious forms, their definitions of the standard of value. One writer said, "that a Pound might be defined to be a sense of value in reference to currency as compared with commodities." Another writer was dissatisfied with that definition, thinking the public had a right to something more definite and tangible, and that the meaning of "a reference to currency as compared with commodities," was not very obvious to enlightened minds. This writer said, "There is a standard and there is an unit which is the measure of value, and that unit is the interest of 33 *l*. 6s. 8d. at 3 per cent., that being 1 1., and being paid in a Banknote as money of account." The last definition of the standard of value which I shall quote is this:—"The standard is neither gold nor silver, but it is something set up in the imagination, to be regulated by public opinion." Such were the absurdities into which ingenious men were betrayed, in the attempt to set up some other standard of value, more consistent with inconvertible paper than a metallic standard. It was supposed at that time that the doctrines propounded by the Bullion Committee were the visionary speculations of theorists, and were unknown in the former monetary history of this country. But that is not the case. Refer to every writer of eminence—to Mr. Locke, to Sir W. Petty, to any one who wrote before 1797, and who had not been familiar with inconvertible paper currency, and you will find they arrive at precisely the same conclusions with the Bullion Committee. Take the opinion of Mr. Harris, an officer of the Mint, and an eminent writer on the subject a century before the Bank Restriction Act:—

"In all countries (says Mr. Harris) there is established a certain standard both as to weight and fineness of the several species of those coins.

"In England, the silver monies are to contain 111 parts of fine silver, and 6 parts of alloy. That is, the pound troy with us contains 11 oz. 2 pennyweights of fine silver, and 18 pennyweights of alloy; and of a pound troy of this standard silver, our money pound contains 20/62 parts, that is to say a pound of this silver is coined into 62s. This standard has continued invariable ever since the 43rd Elizabeth.

"By the standard of money is always meant the quantity of pure or fine metal contained in a given sum. In England accounts are kept by the pound sterling, which is a certain quantity of fine silver appointed by law for a standard." (He was writing at a time when silver was the standard in England.) "All payments abroad are regulated by the course of exchange, and that is founded upon the intrinsic value, and not on the mere names of coins.

"We may break the public faith here, and curtail the long-established measure of property, but foreigners will make ample allowance for what we may do, and however we may rob and cheat one another, will secure themselves, and make an advantage of our discredit, by bringing the exchange against us beyond the part."

These are the true doctrines as to the measure of value, doctrines delivered one hundred years before the Report of the Bullion Committee was made, but in precise conformity with that Report. The truth of them is not, I fear, even now admitted. Publications daily issue from the press contesting it. Here is a volume published at Birmingham since the commencement of the present year, not the production, I presume, of a single author, for it professes to be written by Gemini. I have no wish to withhold justice from writers who give that proof of their sincerity, which is implied by the publication of an octavo volume. And I admit at once, that I do not believe this work could have proceeded from any other town in the Queen's dominions than Birmingham, and that the efforts of no single writer are equal to the production of so much nonsense. This volume collects and repeats all the old exploded fallacies on the subject of the standard of value and the currency. Its authors bewail the darkness of the age which adheres to a standard which was adopted in the reign of Queen Elizabeth, and which they consider wholly unsuitable as a measure of value now, considering the extent of our commerce, and the increase of all pecuniary transactions in number and amount. They might with equal justice complain, that since travelling has been increased by the completion of railways, the foot measure is still adhered to. There is no better reason for making the sovereign pass for twenty-five shillings instead of twenty, than for making the foot consist of sixteen inches instead of twelve. They consider it absurd, that with the progress we have made in wealth and knowledge, we should still coin the ounce of gold into a sum represented by $3l.$ 17s. $10\frac{1}{2}$d. "Coin the ounce of gold," say they, "into $5l.$, and we shall then have relief from our burthens, and encouragement to industry and trade." Now, let us consider what is meant by affixing to the ounce of gold a value, represented in coin by the sum of $3l.$ 17s. $10\frac{1}{2}$d.? According to the regulations of the Mint, before the alteration of the silver coin in 1816, a pound weight of standard gold was coined into $44\frac{1}{2}$ guineas; a pound weight of standard silver was coined into 62s; and a guinea was made current for 21s. We are thus enabled to calculate the relative value of gold and silver according to the Mint regulations. The sum of $44\frac{1}{2}$ guineas in gold, that is a pound of gold, was equivalent to 1,869 sixpences in silver, and the pound of silver being equal to 124 sixpences in coin, the value of gold was to that of silver, as 1,869 to 124, or as 15-9/124 to 1. The ounce of gold in coin was equivalent to the corresponding amount in silver, namely, the twelfth part of 1,869 sixpences, that is to say, to 155 sixpences and 9/12 of a shilling, or $3l.$ 17s. $10\frac{1}{2}$d. There was, indeed, a small difference in the amount of alloy in a pound of coined gold and a pound of coined silver, for which it is necessary to make allowance, and that allowance being made, the relative value of pure gold to pure silver in the coins of the two metals was as 15-2859/13460 to 1. Silver has ceased to be a standard of value, and the silver coin being now a mere token, the former relative value of gold coin to silver coin is not now preserved. The above calculations explain our meaning when we say that the ounce of gold is coined into the sum of 3*l*. 17s. 10½d. These terms express the relation of gold and silver coin, according to the Mint regulations at the time that silver coin was made of standard silver. You may now enact, no doubt, that the ounce of gold shall be coined into 5l. in money of account, that is to say, you may debase the standard to that extent. And what will be the effect of this? All debtors will no doubt gain by it. In the case of all unfulfilled contracts, he who has to receive payment will receive much less in point of real value than he stipulated for. The creditor will be defrauded—the debtor will have a corresponding advantage. But this will be the whole effect. No new transaction will be affected by your choosing to call an ounce of gold 5*l*. As Mr. Harris says, you may cheat each other at home, but foreign countries will adjust their dealings with you, not on account of the name to be given to your coin, but according to its real value. All new contracts at home will be regulated by the same principles. The real and not the nominal value of that which is made by law the medium of exchange, will regulate prices and all future contracts. Even the relative value of gold and silver will not be adjusted by your laws. You may insist on coining the ounce of gold into 5*l*. instead of 3*l*. 17s. 10½d., that is to say, into 200 sixpences instead of, as at present, into 155 sixpences and fourpence halfpenny, but silver will disobey your law, and will insist on finding its own value in the market on principles which you cannot control. The Mint regulations do not, it is true, correctly express the present relative value of gold and silver in the bullion market. Silver is not worth 5s. 2d. an ounce, not more, I believe, than 5s. an ounce, and there would be an apparent present advantage to the debtor in taking silver rather than gold as the standard, since the relative value of gold to silver when standard-silver is 5s. per ounce, is as 15.575 to 1, instead of 15–285/1346 to 1. But there is reason to doubt whether those who wish for a relaxation of the standard, and who, for the purpose of benefiting the debtor, recommend either a joint standard of silver and gold, or the substitution of silver for gold as the standard, would attain their object were either of those Measures adopted. There is reason to believe, adverting particularly to the rapid increase of the annual supply of gold from mines within the dominions of the Emperor of Russia, that the value of gold in the general markets of the world is on the decrease, and that the interest of the debtor would not be permanently advanced by the abandonment of gold for silver as the standard of value in the country. But to revert to the errors of those who are the advocates of some measure of value other than the precious metals. They object to the selection of gold as the standard of value, because gold is an article of commerce,—because there is a demand for it as bullion, affecting, therefore, its value as coin, and disqualifying it to be the measure of value. Now, no one contends that there is or can be an absolutely fixed and invariable standard of value. No one denies that the value of gold, with reference to all commodities, excepting gold itself, may be subject to slight variations. But what other substance is not more subject to variations in value than the precious metals? What other substance possessing intrinsic value will not also be in demand as an article of commerce? It is because gold is an article of commerce, because there are no restrictions upon its export or its import, that you can at all times depend upon such a supply of gold for the purposes of coin as may be sufficient for the wants of this country. The precious metals are distributed among the various countries of the world in proportion to their respective necessities, by laws of certain though not very obvious operation, which, without our interference, will allot to our share all that we require. Some entertain the apprehension that we may be drained of all our gold in consequence of a demand for gold from foreign countries, either for the payment of their armies in time of war, or in consequence of sudden and unforeseen demand for foreign corn for our own internal consumption. It is supposed that gold, being an article in universal demand, and having at all times and in all places an ascertained value, is more subject to exportation than anything else. But the export of gold, whether coin or bullion, is governed by precisely the same laws by which the export of any other article is governed. Gold will not leave this country unless gold be dearer in some other country than it is in this. It will not leave this country, merely because it is gold, nor while there is any article of our produce or manufacture which can be exported in exchange for foreign produce with a more profitable return. If gold coin be in any country the common medium of exchange; or if the promissory notes, which perform in part the functions of gold coin, are at all times and under all circumstances of equal value with gold, and are instantly convertible into gold; there are causes in operation which, without any interference on our part, will confine within known and just limits the extent to which gold can be exported. There may no doubt be temporary pressure from the export of gold, even when it is confined within those limits; but none for which you may not provide, none to which you would not be subject, in a higher degree probably, were any other standard of value adopted in preference to gold. I have thus stated the grounds which justify the conclusion, that, according to the ancient monetary policy of the country, according to the law, according to the practice that prevailed at all times, excepting during the period of inconvertible paper currency, a certain quantity of the precious metals, definite in point of weight and fineness, has constituted, and ought to constitute, the measure of value. The minds of men, habituated during the Bank Restriction to a departure from that measure of value, were loth to admit those great elementary truths which are at the foundation of the whole system of currency, paper credit, and foreign exchange. Ingenious writers have from time to time laboured to prove the unsoundness of these doctrines, to show that a metallic standard was neither practically nor theoretically the measure of value in this country, and have cited various facts apparently irreconcilable with the theory. But when all the circumstances attending each fact have been fully stated, they have been sufficient to account for the seeming contradiction. When Sir Isaac Newton had established the planetary system on the principle of gravitation and attraction, there were phenomena apparently at variance with the theory. But succeeding philosophers, starting from the point which in the progress of science had been reached by Sir Isaac Newton, applying his principles with improved means of investigating truth, solved the doubts which he had not been able to solve, and showed that the apparent contradictions, when all the disturbing influences were taken into account, became in fact new demonstrations of the soundness of the original theory. And the same result has followed, and will follow, in the case of objections which have been, and will continue to be, urged against the principle of the metallic standard. It must at the same time be admitted that it would be quite consistent with that principle to adopt some other measure of value than that which we have adopted. It would be consistent with that principle to select silver instead of gold as the standard,—to have a mixed standard of gold and silver, the relative values of the two metals being determined,—to dispense with gold coin altogether, and regulate the amount and value of paper currency by making it convertible only, according to the proposal of Mr. Ricardo, into gold bullion of a given minimum amount. I trust, however, this House will adhere to the present standard,—will resolve on the maintenance of a single standard, and of gold as that standard. All the great writers on this subject, Sir William Petty, Mr. Locke, Mr. Harris, and Lord Liverpool, have been decidedly in favour of a single, in preference to a double standard. Mr. Locke, indeed, was of opinion that silver ought to be the standard; but there appears good ground to doubt the soundness of that opinion; and there are, at any rate, the most cogent reasons, since gold has been for a long course of years the standard in this country, for the continued maintenance of it. They are well stated in the admirable Treatise on Coins, written by the first Lord Liverpool. In that treatise a system of coinage is recommended, which is in exact conformity, both in point of principle and detail, with the system which we have adopted. Lord Liverpool observes:—

After full consideration of this extensive, abstruse, and intricate subject, I humbly offer to Your Majesty, as the result of my opinion.

First, That the coins of this Realm which are to be the principal measure of property and instrument of commerce, should be made of one metal only.

Secondly, That in this Kingdom the gold coins only have been for many years past, and are now, in the practice and opinion of the people, the principal measure of property and instrument of commerce.

. . . .

It has been shown that, in a country like Great Britain, so distinguished for its affluence and for the extent of its commercial connections, the gold coins are best adapted to be the principal measure of property; in this Kingdom, therefore, the gold coin is now the principal measure of property and standard coin, or, as it were, the sovereign archetype by which the weight and value of all other coins should be regulated.

It is the measure of almost all contracts and bargains; and by it, as a measure, the price of all commodities bought and sold is adjusted and ascertained. For these reasons the gold coin should be made as perfect and kept as perfect as possible.

. . . .

Thirdly. It is evident, that where the function of the gold coins as a measure of property ceases, there that of the silver coins should begin; and that where the function of the silver coins, in this respect, ceases, there that of copper should begin: it is clear, therefore, that so far only these silver and copper coins should be made legal tender and no further, at least not in any great degree; and it follows that the coins, both of silver and copper, are subordinate, subservient, and merely representative coins; and must take their value with reference to the gold coins according to the rate which the sovereign sets upon each of them.

These are, in fact, the principles which regulate our present coinage. We have a single standard, and that standard gold,—the metal which was practically the standard for many years previously to the suspension of cash payment. The silver coin is a mere token, auxiliary and subordinate to the gold coin; the ounce of silver being now coined into 66s. instead of 62s., and silver coin not being a legal tender for any greater sum than 40s. By the abolition, in this part of the United Kingdom, of the promissory notes below 5l., you introduce the gold coin into general use for the purpose of effecting small payments; you enable the holder of the smallest note to demand payment in gold, and thus insure the maintenance of a very considerable quantity of gold as a part of the circulating medium. There is, no doubt, some expense in the maintenance of a metallic circulation, but none, in my opinion, sufficient to countervail the advantage of having gold coin generally distributed throughout the country, accessible to all, and the foundation of paper credit and currency. It is contended by some, that if you were to dispense with coin altogether, to adopt the principle of Mr. Ricardo's plan, and make bank notes not convertible into gold at the will of the holder, excepting when presented to the amount of a very considerable sum (300*l*. or 400*l*. for instance), and then convertible into bullion and not coin, you would provide a security against the effects of a panic connected with political causes, causing a sudden demand for gold. I very much doubt the policy of taking such precautions against such a contingency, and consider that the most effectual measure for promoting permanent confidence in the paper circulation of the country, is to require that the gold coin shall be in general use for small payments and that the promissory note shall be of equal value with the coin which it professes to represent. I shall here close my observations on the measure of value and the coinage, and proceed to the more immediate subject for consideration, namely, the state of the paper circulation of the country, and the principles which ought to regulate it. I must state, at the outset, that in using the word money, I mean to designate by that word the coin of the Realm, and promissory notes payable to bearer on demand. In using the words paper currency, I mean only such promissory notes. I do not include in those terms bills of exchange, or drafts on bankers, or other forms of paper credit. I will not weary the House with a discussion as to the precise nature of deposits, and whether they constitute a part of the currency of the country. There is a material distinction, in my opinion, between the character of a promissory note payable to bearer on demand, and other forms of paper credit, and between the effects which they respectively produce upon the prices of commodities and upon the exchanges. The one answers all the purposes of money, passes from hand to hand without endorsement, without examination, if there be no suspicion of forgery: and it is in fact, what its designations imply it to be, currency or circulating medium. I do not deny that other forms of paper credit have some effects in common with Bank notes, that they all have a tendency to economise the use of metallic money, and have a common influence on the value of gold to the extent to which they dispense with the use of it, and thus leave a larger quantity available for the general purposes of the world than there would otherwise be. But I think experience shows that the paper currency, that is, the promissory notes payable to bearer on demand, stands in a certain relation to the gold coin and the foreign exchange in which other forms of paper credit do not stand. There are striking examples of this adduced in the Report of the Bullion Committee of 1810, in the case both of the Bank of England, and of the Irish and Scotch Banks. In the case of the Bank of England, shortly after its establishment there was a material depreciation of paper in consequence of its excessive issue. The notes of the Bank of England were at a discount of 17 per cent. There was no doubt as to the solvency of the Bank, for bank stock, on which 60 per cent. had been paid, was selling at 110 per cent. After trying various expedients, it was at length determined to reduce the amount of bank notes outstanding. The consequence was an immediate increase in the value of those which remained in circulation, the restoration of them to par, and a corresponding improvement in the foreign exchanges. In the case of Ireland, in the year 1804 the exchange with England was very unfavourable. A Committee was appointed to consider the causes. It was denied by most of the witnesses from Ireland that they were at all connected with excessive issues of Irish notes. It was then stoutly maintained—and it was afterwards in 1810—that "notes issued only in proportion to the demand in exchange for good and convertible securities, payable at specific periods, could not tend to any excess in circulation, or to any depreciation." In the spring of 1804, the exchange of Ireland with England was so unfavourable that it required 118*l.* 10s. of the notes of the Bank of Ireland to purchase 100*l.* of the notes of the Bank of England. Between the year 1804 and the year 1806 the notes of the Bank of Ireland were reduced from 3,000,000*l.* to 2,410,000*l.*, and the effect of this, taken in conjunction with an increase of the English circulation, was to restore the relative value of Irish paper and the exchange with England to par. In the same manner, an unfavourable state of the exchange between Scotland and England has been more than once corrected by a contraction of the paper circulation of Scotland. In all these cases the action has been upon that part of the paper credit of the country which has consisted of promissory notes payable to the bearer on demand. There has been no interference with other forms of paper credit, nor was it contended then, as it is now contended by some, that promissory notes are identical in their nature with bills of exchange, and with checks on bankers, and with deposits, and that they cannot be dealt with on any separate principle. There is a passage in the work to which I have before referred, the treatise of Lord Liverpool, which draws the just distinction between paper credit and paper currency, and exposes the fallacy of those who deprecate any attempt to regulate by law the paper currency, on the ground that it is not distinguishable in its nature from paper credit. Lord Liverpool observes—

"It has been a common artifice, practised by those who have written on paper currency, to confound paper credit with paper currency; and even the higher sorts of paper currency with the inferior sorts, such as immediately interfere with the use of the coins of the realm. Paper credit is not only highly convenient and beneficial, but is even absolutely necessary in carrying on the trade of a great commercial kingdom.

"Paper currency is a very undefined term, as used by speculative writers. To find arguments in its support, at least to the extent to which it is at present carried, they have been obliged to connect it with paper credit; so that the principles on which the use of paper credit is truly founded, may be brought in support of a great emission of paper currency. Paper currency, strictly speaking, consists only of bills or notes payable or convertible into cash on demand by the person who issued the same at the will of the holder."

That appears to me to be the true definition of paper currency, as distinguished from paper credit. It is the substitute for, and the immediate representative of coin, and with coin it constitutes "money." And if you will adhere to the standard of value, and will adopt such measures as shall ensure the uniform equivalency of Bank notes to coin, you may safely, in my opinion, leave untouched other forms of paper credit, and entrust the regulation and control of them to individual caution and discretion. There are some, however, who admit the validity of this distinction, and yet contend that no new legislative interference is required in the case of promissory notes. In their opinion the true principles which should govern the issue of such notes are, freedom of competition, and immediate convertibility into coin at the will of the holder. The combination of these principles will, in their opinion, afford to the public a complete security against abuse of the privilege of issue. In support of that opinion they have, undoubtedly, the high authority of Adam Smith and of Ricardo. Both these eminent writers assume that immediate convertibility into coin is all that is requisite to prevent the excessive issue of paper. It is no impeachment of their sagacity, if, in the progress which this science, like all other sciences, is making, there be reason to doubt the soundness of any particular opinion which they may have delivered. And it is our duty to disregard their authority, and to act on the conclusions of our own judgment, if either reason or experience convinces us that they are safer guides. It appears to me that we have, from reasoning, from experience, from the admissions made by the issuers of paper money, abundant ground for the conclusion, that, under a system of unlimited competition, although it be controlled by convertibility into coin, there is not an adequate security against the excessive issue of promissory notes. We should infer, certainly from reasoning, that free competition in the supply of any given article will probably ensure us the most abundant supply of that article at the cheapest rate. But we do not want an abundant supply of cheap promissory paper. We want only a certain quantity of paper, not, indeed, fixed and definite in nominal amount, but just such a quantity of paper, and that only, as shall be equivalent in point of value to the coin which it represents. If the paper be cheaper than the coin, it is an evil and not an advantage. That system, therefore, which provides a constant supply of paper equal in value to coin, and so varying in amount as to insure at all times immediate convertibility into coin, together with perfect confidence in the solvency of the issuers of paper, is the system which ought to be preferred. Now, unless the issuers of paper conform to certain principles, unless they vigilantly observe the causes

which influence the influx or efflux of coin, and regulate their issues of
paper accordingly, there is danger that the value of the paper will not
correspond with the value of coin. The difference may not be immediately
perceived,—nay, the first effect of undue issue, by increasing prices, may
be to encourage further issues; and as each issuer, where there is unlimited competition, feels the inutility of individual efforts of contraction,
the evil proceeds, until the disparity between gold and paper becomes
manifest, confidence in the paper is shaken, and it becomes necessary to
restore its value by sudden and violent reductions in its amount, spreading ruin among the issuers of paper, and deranging the whole monetary
transactions of the country. If we admit the principle of a metallic standard, and admit that the paper currency ought to be regulated by immediate reference to the foreign exchanges,—that there ought to be early con-
tractions of paper on the efflux of gold,—we might, I think, infer from
reasoning, without the aid of experience, that an unlimited competition in
respect to issue will not afford a security for the proper regulation of the
paper currency. Let us now refer to the admissions made by those who are
the advocates for unlimited competition. Several country bankers were
examined by the Select Committee, and their evidence is important: it
demonstrates the absence of that controlling check upon issue which
ought to be applied, if the principles for which I contend are just. Mr.
Hobhouse a banker, in the south-west of England, (a brother of the right
hon. Baronet the Member for Nottingham,) who spoke with some authority from his having been Chairman of the Committee of Private Bankers,
and their selected organ, was examined before the Committee. What account did he give of the issues of private bankers? He was asked—

"With a rise of prices, would there be an increased paper issue by
country bankers?"

He answered—

"Yes, there will be an increase in the local circulation when prices rise.
Gold is a commodity, of which there may be a glut as well as a scarcity;
and I could never see any reason to be frightened at an export or drain of
gold."

He was then asked—

"Ought not there to be a contraction of the circulation under such
circumstances?"

He answers—

"Whether there ought or ought not, I cannot tell; but I am sure, that,
in fact, there could not be. I am perfectly satisfied that it is quite impossible for these local currencies to be influenced by the price of gold or the
foreign exchanges."

He is then asked—

"Does it not often happen that your circulation is increased in the beginning of a drain of gold?"

He answers—

"Yes; we do not pretend that our circulation is at all governed by it. It is governed by what I have stated already."

Another witness examined was Mr. Stuckey. He was asked this question—

"Supposing it should be ultimately thought that it is desirable that the country circulation should have a general conformity to the state of the foreign exchanges; do you conceive that this could, in any way, be effected by the country bankers?"

He answers—

"I do not at present see how it could be accomplished; and I may take the liberty of going further in answer to that question, and saying that it appears to me that the country issues, as conducted in the West of England, have very little or nothing to do with foreign exchanges."

Now, the effect of this evidence is, to prove that country banks do not and cannot control their issues according to the state of the foreign exchanges. The amount of their issues is governed by prices, rather than by a reference to the exchange. When speculation is active, and prices rise, that is to say, at the very time at which a check may most probably be required on the increased issues of the country banks, their activity is stimulated. Just at the period when that warning is given, so far from the warning being attended to, there is increased action in the opposite direction. Prices are rising. The country bankers have no control over their currency. The increase of price compels increase of issue, and thus there is going on at the same time the reciprocal action of increased speculation, and an additional stimulus given to that speculation by increased issues. The first witness from whose evidence I quoted, when asked whether the circulation of country banks was governed, as that of the Bank of England was, by the state of the exchanges, fairly admitted that it was not. He was asked,

"Do you not mean that when a drain of gold was beginning, that was the time when frequently the circulation of the country banks was increased?"

The answer of Mr. Hobhouse, is—

"Yes; there is an increase at the beginning of a drain of gold, and the circulation is not governed by it."

The fact is, there is no sense of individual responsibility; each issuer says, and says naturally enough, "It is in vain for me, individually, to contract my issues, when others will not do the same. I shall suffer by doing so. My efforts will produce no effect on the aggregate, while some

competitor will take that share of the circulation which I may withdraw."
And thus, each refusing to make the individual sacrifice (which, indeed,
is useless where only made individually,) the crisis comes,—there is a demand for gold which cannot be satisfied, and the end of all is, much individual suffering and many fortunes ruined, from the necessity of a sudden
and violent effort to establish, by the contraction of issue, an equilibrium
between gold and paper. Thus it appears to me that the conclusions of
reason against unlimited competition of issue, are amply confirmed by the
admission of the advocates for it. Are the lessons of experience at variance
with the conclusions we are entitled to draw from reason and from evidence? What has been the result of unlimited competition in the United
States? In the United States the paper circulation was supplied, not by
private bankers, but by Joint-Stock Banks established on principles apparently the most satisfactory. There was every precaution taken against
insolvency; unlimited responsibility of partners—excellent regulations
for the publication and audit of accounts—immediate convertibility of
paper into gold. If the principle of unlimited competition, controlled by
such checks, be safe, why has it utterly failed in the United States? How
can it be shown that the experiment was not fairly made in that country?
Observe this fact. While there existed a central Bank (the United States
Bank), standing in some such relation to the other Banks of the United
States as the Bank of England stands to the Banks of the country, there
was some degree (imperfect it is true) of control over the general issues of
paper. But when the privileges of the Central Bank ceased, when the
principle of free competition was left unchecked, then came, notwithstanding professed convertibility, immoderate issues of paper, extravagant
speculation, and the natural consequences, suspension of cash payments
and complete insolvency. Hence I conclude that reason, evidence, and
experience combine to demonstrate the impolicy and danger of unlimited
competition in the issue of paper. I have now stated—with respect to the
measure of value, with respect to the coinage and currency—and with
respect to promissory notes payable on demand—the broad and general
principles which I think ought to regulate these three great elements of
our monetary system. I have done on this occasion what I have done on
others. I have stated, without the slightest compromise or concealment, the
leading principles to which, in my opinion, our legislation in those matters ought to conform. I have now to state the extent to which I propose to
carry out those principles. If I do not carry them out immediately to their
full and entire extent, I may be told, as I have been told before, that very
good principles have been laid down in the abstract, but that practically I
shrink from their application. Nevertheless, the opinion which I have formerly expressed I still entertain—that it is of great importance that public men should acknowledge the great principles by which important

measures should be regulated: and, in discussing a question of such magnitude as the present, I had rather it were said, "You fall short in the application of sound and admitted principles," than that "You have concealed or perverted those principles for the purpose of justifying your limited application of them." In addressing the House on this important subject, I have, in the first instance, stated principles which I deem to be correct, and which ought to be the rule and guide of our future legislation. I have now to consider, with the same unreservedness, how far the consideration due to special circumstances, to existing interest, to the usages and habits of the community, demands caution and limitation in the immediate application of these principles. All I can promise is, that I will propose no practical measure which is inconsistent with the principles which I have laid down, and which does not tend to their ultimate establishment. It is, however, most important that those who are responsible for the management of the affairs of a great country like this—seeing how easy it is, by unwise legislation, to create panic or introduce confusion into the monetary transactions of the country—it is most important that they should deal considerately with private interests: first, because justice requires it; and, secondly, because there is danger that the cause or progressive amendment and reform will be injured, if you cannot reconcile reform with a due regard to the welfare and happiness of individuals. In what mode then, admitting the principles I have announced to be correct, in what mode shall we best provide for the present application and ultimate establishment of them, with the least disturbance of existing interest? Some have contended, and I am not prepared to deny the position, that if we had a new state of society to deal with, the wisest plan would be, to claim for the State the exclusive privilege of the issue of promissory notes, as we have claimed for it the exclusive privilege of coinage. They consider that the state is entitled to the whole profits to be derived from that which is representative of coin, and that if the State had the exclusive power of issuing paper, there would be established a controlling power which would insure, as far as possible, an equilibrium in the currency. At the same time there have been men, whose judgment is also entitled to weight, who have expressed a different opinion on this subject. This question was under the consideration of the House when Lord Althorp brought forward the Bank Charter Bill, in 1833. It had also been the subject of consideration in the Select Committee of 1832; and Lord Althorp, in moving the extension of the Bank Charter, discussed the policy of a single bank of issue to be constituted by and responsible to the Government. Having mentioned the name of Lord Althorp, I must, though I differ from that noble Lord in respect to politics, bear testimony to his integrity, and to the soundness of his judgment in all financial matters. No man who ever filled the office which the noble Lord then held is entitled to stand higher in public estimation as respects those qualifications for a public trust. On the occasion to which I have just referred, Lord Althorp said:—

Another point for consideration is, whether the profits, which must necessarily be derived from the circulating medium of the country, should be possessed by Government, or should be allowed to remain in private hands? Now, Sir, the advantages, the only advantages, which I have been enabled to discover in a Government bank, as compared with a private company, are those which result from having responsible persons to manage the concern, the public deriving the benefit of it; but then, on the other hand, I think these advantages are much more than counterbalanced by the political evils which would inevitably result from placing this bank under the control of the Government. I think that the effect of the State having the complete control of the circulating medium in its own hands would be most mischievous. Under these circumstances, Sir, I certainly am prepared to propose the continuation of a single bank of issue in the metropolis, subject to the control of the publicity of their accounts. If we were now, for the first time, establishing a system of banking on which the country should proceed, I think this would be the most advisable mode of establishing a bank in the metropolis. But, Sir, this proposition has the additional advantage—and it is no mean one—that it will occasion the least change; because I certainly am of opinion that, unless some great advantages could be derived from a change in the monetary system of this country, nothing could be more ill-advised—nothing could be more useless, than to depart from it.

In the latter part of Lord Althorp's observations I entirely agree. The true policy in this country is to work, so far as it be possible, with the instruments you have ready for your hand—to avail yourselves of that advantage which they possess from having been in use, from being familiar from constituting a part of the habits and usages of society. They will probably work more smoothly than perfectly novel instruments of greater theoretical perfection. If we disturb that which is established, let us have some good practical reason for the change. It is now incumbent on me to detail and explain the practical measures which I propose for the regulation of the currency. I will state them consecutively, and without intermediate comment, in order that the House may be in full possession of the plan recommended by the Government. We think it of great importance to increase the controlling power of a single Bank of Issue. We think it the wisest course to select the Bank of England as that controlling and central body, rather than to appoint Commissioners acting under the authority of Parliament for the purpose of the issue of a Paper Currency. I therefore propose, with respect to the Bank of England, that it should continue in possession of its present privileges of Issue, but that there should be a complete separation of the business of banking from that of

Issue; that there should be a department of Issue separate from the department of Banking, with separate officers and separate accounts. I propose that to the Issue department should be transferred the whole amount of bullion now in the possession of the Bank, and that the Issue of Bank Notes should hereafter take place on two foundations, and two foundations only:—first, on a definite amount of public securities; secondly, exclusively upon bullion. The action of the public will regulate the amount of that portion of the note circulation which is issued upon bullion. With respect to the banking business of the Bank, I propose that it should be governed on precisely the same principles as would regulate any other Body dealing with Bank of England notes. The fixed amount of securities on which I propose that the Bank of England should issue notes, is 14,-000,000*l.*, the whole of the remainder of the circulation to be issued exclusively on the foundation of bullion. I propose that there should be a complete periodical publication of the accounts of the Bank of England, both of the Banking and Issue Department. Objections were urged in 1833, to frequent publications of these accounts; but, in my opinion, those objections are without foundation. I have the strongest impression that nothing will more conduce to the credit of the Bank itself, and to the prevention of needless alarm, than the complete and immediate disclosure of its transactions. I would, therefore, propose to enact by law that there should be returned to the Government a weekly account of the issue of notes by the Bank of England, of the amount of bullion, of the amount of deposits, of securities, in short, a general summary of every transaction both in the Issue department and the Banking department of the Bank of England; and that the Government should forthwith publish unreservedly, and weekly, the account which they receive from the Bank. It is desirable, in order to make the whole plan more clearly understood, that I should now state the regulations we propose to establish with respect to other banking establishments, and afterwards, that I should revert to the subject of the Bank of England, and state the terms which we have made with the Bank, subject to the ratification of Parliament. Our general rule is, to draw a distinction between the privilege of Issue and the conduct of the ordinary banking business. We think they stand on an entirely different footing. We think that the privilege of Issue is one which may be fairly and justly controlled by the State, and that the banking business, as distinguished from Issue, is a matter in respect to which there cannot be too unlimited and unrestricted a competition. The principle of competition, though unsafe in our opinion when applied to Issue, ought, we think, to govern the business of banking. After the issue of paper currency has once taken place, it is then important that the public should be enabled to obtain the use of that issue on as favourable terms as possible. With regard to banks in England and Wales other than the Bank of England, we propose, that

from this time, no new bank of issue should be constituted. I have stated
that our object is to effect the change we contemplate, with as little detriment as possible to individual interests. We, therefore, do not propose to
deprive existing banking establishments, which are now actually banks of
issue, of the privilege they possess. We do not wish to raise that alarm
which we fear would be excited if there should be any sudden extinction
of the power of issue now possessed by these banking establishments.
Leaving, therefore, to the existing banks, which are actually banks of
issue, their privilege of issue, we subject them to the condition that they
shall not exceed the existing amount of their Issue; this amount to be
determined by the average Issue of each Bank for a definite preceding
period, of two or three years, for instance. The Bank of England will thus
be acquainted with the extent of the Issue from all other establishments. I
know I am liable to be told that the Issues of these Banks may be much
larger, under particular circumstances and at particular periods, than at
others: but I have obtained Returns, of a confidential nature, from ten of
the best conducted banks in the country, six of them being in agricultural, and four in manufacturing districts; and the amount of their variation of Issue is much less than might be imagined. If, however, there
should at any time be a demand for an increased Issue, there would always be the ready means of supplying it; as the Banks may, by investing a
portion of their capital in public securities, command a given amount of
Bank of England Notes by the sale of such securities, and, with those
Notes, may supply any occasional demand for increased local issues.
While we thus restrain the issue of Promissory Notes, we intend to facilitate the Banking business. Many of the Joint-Stock Banking Companies
have not at present the privilege of suing and being sued. There are two
descriptions of Joint-Stock Banks; those constituted under the Act of
1826, and those established under the Act of 1833. The time has come
when you must determine whether you will permit and encourage the
system of Joint-Stock Banks, or extinguish it. If you determine to retain
the system, then you ought to give the Banks every facility for the transaction of their business. The Joint-Stock Banks ask for the privilege of suing
and being sued; but this privilege, if granted, is a privilege not only to
them, but to the public, who will have readier means of procuring redress
in case of wrong. Proceeding on the principles of facilitating Banking
operations, we propose to amend the existing operations, we propose to
amend the existing law in other particulars. The place whence legal notice may be issued by Joint-Stock Banks, or where it may be served, is at
present imperfectly defined. Again, the Joint-Stock Banks are bound by
the acts of an unauthorized partner, it being the principle of partnerships
that the acts of one bind the rest of the partners. But in the case of Joint-
Stock Banks with a very large proprietary, there are no means of control-

ling the admission of individual partners. The purchase of shares constitutes a partner. We propose, therefore, to exempt the Company from
liability on account of the unauthorized acts of a simple partner; still
making the Company responsible for the unauthorized acts of a Director of
the Bank. The appointment to be a Director implies choice, and the confidence of the elective body; and this distinction between liabilities for
the acts of a Director, and that for a simple partner is therefore a just one.
The chief complaint of the Joint-Stock Banks in London is, that they
cannot accept Bills for a less date than six months. Other private Banking
Establishments in London have an unlimited power of acceptance, but
Joint-Stock Banks labour under the prohibition I have mentioned. This
was insisted on by the Bank of England, when the last Charter was discussed, in order that the Joint-Stock Banks should not come into competition with that establishment and the London Private Banks, by being
allowed the power of acceptance for a less date than six months. We propose to place the Joint-Stock Banks in London on a perfect equality in
this respect, and to give them the power of accepting Bills of any amount
and for any period. It is thought by some that this privilege might be so
perverted as to give rise to a paper currency differing in form, but not in
principle, from Promissory Notes. The power has been held by Private
Banks from time immemorial, and it has not hitherto been accompanied
by any abuse; and why should it be anticipated that Joint-Stock Banks
would abuse a similar power, contrary to the intentions of the Legislature? But I give public notice, that, if the power should be abused,—if it
should be attempted to circulate small Bills so accepted, within the limits
reserved to the Bank,—I shall not hesitate to appeal to Parliament on the
instant, for the purpose of correcting that evil. These, then, are the facilities we propose to extend to the Joint Stock Banks. I will now mention the
conditions or restrictions we propose to apply to all existing Banks. In the
first place, we require of all such Banks, that there be a full and complete
periodical publication of the names of all Partners and Directors. This is
what the London and Westminster Bank voluntarily publishes. It is said,
that the public have a great security against loss, in the fact, that each partner is liable to the extent of his whole fortune for the debts of the Bank to
which he belongs. Very well. Let the public then know who the partners
are. Let us know the transfers of shares that take place; let us determine
how long the responsibility for the possession of shares will attach to a
party; as we have the comfort of unlimited responsibility, give us the names
of those who are our guarantees. There is another condition we have a right
to insist upon. We are to continue to existing Banks the privilege of Issue.
Let us know the amount of the Issues. We are going to demand from the
Bank of England a weekly account of Issues, and any Bank exercising the
privilege of Issue ought to make a similar publication. If a Bank objects to

the condition of publication, it can absolve itself from it by issuing only Bank of England paper. It is said, that the weekly publication of Issues will disclose secrets of which a rival may take advantage; that it will show "the weak point." Now I wish "the weak point" (if there be one) to be shown, and that the public may have the advantage of knowing it. It is said, erroneous inferences will be drawn from weekly publication; that the issues at one time will appear large, and at another comparatively small. But the frequency of publication will enlighten the public mind on these points, and will dispel the erroneous impressions to which ignorance or the attempt at concealment gives rise. Having required the publication of their Issues from all Banks to which the privilege of Issue is continued, I do not propose to carry further the demand for publicity. I do not wish to pry into the affairs of each Bank, and above all, I deprecate the taking of delusive securities against mismanagement and abuse. The public will hereafter know the names of the persons by whom Banking business is to be conducted, and the public must rely on their own caution and discretion as a security against being injured or defrauded. It has been frequently proposed to require from each bank a periodical publication of its liabilities, its assets, and the state of its transactions generally. But I have seen no form of account which would be at all satisfactory—no form of account which might not be rendered by a bank on the very verge of insolvency, if there were the intention to conceal a desperate state of affairs. The return for instance of "overdrawn accounts" might lead to very erroneous inferences as to the condition of a bank making such a return. A large amount of overdrawn accounts might in one case be indicative of gross mismanagement. It might in another case be perfectly compatible with the security of a bank, acting on the Scotch principle, and making advances at interest to customers in whom the bank had entire confidence. It has been proposed by some that the shares of Joint-Stock Banks should be prohibited below a certain minimum; that there should be no shares of amounts less than 100*l.* or 50*l.*, or some fixed amount. But as, under the encouragement of the Legislature, banks have been established with 20*l.* and 10*l.* shares, and now exist, and, I believe, in many cases, have conducted their business satisfactorily, it would be harsh to insist on a sudden alteration in the amount of shares in the case of existing banks. Then, again, as to calling on all existing banks to invest a portion of their capital in Government securities, I have considered this maturely: but I see great difficulty in the way of forcing upon existing banks any compulsory arrangement of this nature, little prospect of any additional security from loss. As to future companies we have a right to make what regulations we please, and to adopt as to them what we may deem a better principle for their establishment. We propose, then, that no new Joint-Stock Bank of deposit (of course it cannot be one of issue) shall be constituted except upon application to a department of the Government for this purpose; that there shall be a registration of the prospectus, a certain amount of paid-up capital, and a limitation as to the nominal amount of each share. We propose also to require that the deed of settlement should be drawn up according to a prescribed form. The deeds at present are drawn up according to no fixed form, and there is great difficulty in ascertaining, by a reference to the deeds of settlement, from their complexity and want of uniformity, what are the powers and liabilities of banks, and what are the regulations under which they act. We expect that new banks will be constituted, conforming to the principles we thus establish; issuing, if they are Banks of Issue, the paper of the Bank of England, and by their conformity to those principles, establishing claims upon the public confidence. They may, no doubt, interfere with the business and profits of existing banks; but we exclude no existing bank from the power of adapting the new regulations to its own concerns, and we consider that species of interference which arises, not from vexatious intermeddling with the affairs of an existing bank, but from a purification and improvement of the system of Banking, to be perfectly legitimate. Having thus stated the proposed regulations as to the other banks, I now revert to the position of the Bank of England, and the relation in which it is to stand to the Government. I interrupted my statement as to the Bank, because I can make our proposed relations to the Bank more intelligible by having first described the regulations applicable to other Banking Establishments. I have stated that the issues of the Bank are to be upon bullion and upon a fixed amount of securities. We propose that 14,000,000*l.* should be that amount of securities. Seeing no advantage in a change, we propose to continue upon the present terms the existing loan of 11,000,000*l.* made by the Bank to the Government, at 3 per cent. This debt of the Government to the Bank is to be assigned as part of the security on which the issues of the Bank are to take place. There will then remain 3,000,000*l.* of additional securities, Exchequer bills or other securities, over which the Bank are to have entire control. We propose that the Bank should have a right, in case of necessity, to limit its issues upon that portion of the securities, viz. 3,000,000. Circumstances might possibly arise in which the Bank might find it necessary to restrict its issues within the amount of 14,000,000*l.* In that case the Bank will have full power to diminish the 3,000,000*l.* of securities which are to be deposited in addition to the 11,000,000*l.* of debt assigned. I can hardly conceive a case in which it would be advisable to limit the issues to less than 11,000,000*l.* I have said that the Bank shall be restricted from issuing notes upon securities to any greater extent than 14,000,000*l.* This restriction applies, however, to ordinary circumstances and the present state of the affairs of the Bank. The case may occur in which it would be reasonable, and indeed might be necessary, that there should be an increase of the issues of the Bank upon securities. Suppose the country circulation to amount to 8,000,000*l*., and of this amount 2,000,000*l*. to be withdrawn, either in consequence of the failure of banks, or in consequence of agreements with the Bank of England to issue Bank of England paper—in that case, in order to supply the void, it may be necessary that the Bank should make an increased issue. A part of this issue may fairly be made upon securities. Our proposal is, that the profit to be derived from such an issue shall be placed to the account of the Government; and that no increased issue upon securities shall take place without a communication from the Bank to the Government, and without the express sanction of three Members of the Government: the First Lord of the Treasury, the Chancellor of the Exchequer, and the President of the Board of Trade. We do not contemplate, and do not intend to provide for, an increased issue upon securities in any other case than to that which I have referred, namely, the supply of a void caused by the withdrawal of some considerable portion of the existing country circulation. Let me here advert to an Enactment which passed when the Bank Charter was last continued, which passes by the name of the Legal Tender Clause. It enabled other banks than the Bank of England to pay their notes in notes of the Bank of England, and thus relieved them from the obligation of paying in coin. I opposed this Clause at the time, considering it to be at variance with the principle of immediate convertibility. I do not now propose to repeal it, seeing that it has been in operation for several years, and that it may facilitate the substitution of Bank of England notes for the notes of other banks. It may serve to increase the controlling influence of the Bank, and to habituate the public to the use of its notes. The consequences either of the continuance or of the repeal of the Clause are probably less than is generally supposed. I will now detail the pecuniary engagements made with the Bank upon the part of Government. The Bank is to retain the privilege of issuing notes on securities to the amount of 14,000,000*l*. On an interest of 3 per cent., the gross gains of the Bank upon this total issue would be 420,000*l*. In estimating the net profits, we must consider the deductions to be made. First, what is the cost of the issue? The Bank, for the sake of the public, conducts its issue on a liberal principle. It does not reissue notes; it provides the means of keeping every note issue within ten years; it gives therefore great facilities to the public in the detection of fraud or the tracing of transactions within that period. The total cost to the Bank, on an issue of 20,000,000*l*., has been estimated (by the Committee of 1833) at 117,000*l*., but I am inclined to estimate it at about 113,000*l*., which, taken from 420,000*l*., leaves 303,000*l*.? There is then to be deducted about 60,000*l*. composition with the Stamp Office, for the privilege of issuing notes. There is also about 24,000*l*. paid by the Bank to those bankers who undertake to issue Bank of England notes, receiving a commission of 1 per cent. The result is, after subtracting these items, that there would be a net profit of 220,000*l.* derived from the issuing of notes. What is the sum we are to claim from the Bank for continued privileges? The Bank thinks we ought to make a material deduction from the sum fixed when the Charter was last renewed and paid at present, namely, 120,000*l.* But though in some respects we affect the peculiar privileges of the Bank, we give to the Bank increased control over the paper currency, and increased stability to their banking business. We have, therefore, insisted on an equal payment in future. We have, of course, had negotiations on the subject; and I must, in justice to the Gentlemen who have conducted it on the part of the Bank (the Governor and Deputy Governor), declare that I never saw men influenced by more disinterested or more public-spirited motives than they have evinced throughout our communications with them. They have reconciled their duties as managers of a great institution, bound to consult the interests of the proprietors, with enlightened and comprehensive views of the public interests. I hope the House will feel that, in the Resolutions which I intend to propose, there is nothing to which the Bank and the country ought not to accede with readiness. Hitherto the Bank of England has been accustomed to pay to the Government a sum of 120,000*l.* I now propose that the Bank should, in addition to that sum, pay once for all 60,000*l.*, being the amount of fixed annual composition for the issue of its notes, which will bring the entire amount to a sum of 180,000*l.*, to be paid annually by the Bank. The net profit of the Bank, to be derived from the issue of notes, will probably not exceed the sum of 100,000*l.* The House will no doubt bear in mind that the public pay to the Bank an annual sum of 248,000*l.*, under the provisions of certain Acts of Parliament, on account of the management, by the Bank, of the Public Debt. From this payment of 248,000*l.* will hereafter be deducted 180,000*l.*, leaving the total payment of the public to the Bank, on the balance of the two accounts, a sum of 68,000*l.* As to the duration of the Charter, we propose that it should be renewed for a period of twenty-one years, with a power of revision by Parliament at the expiration of ten years. We propose, however, a departure from the arrangement made when the Charter was last renewed, in the following respects. Under the existing Charter, the power to revise accrues at the expiration of ten years; but, if the opportunity be not then taken advantage of, the Charter will endure without alteration for a further period of eleven years. We propose that at any time, after the lapse of ten years, there shall be the power of revision; that Parliament, for instance, may permit twelve or fifteen years to pass, and may then, should they think fit, revise the Charter of the Bank and its relation to the Government. Of Ireland and Scotland I have hitherto made no mention; I propose to reserve for separate legislation the state of the currency of each of those parts of the United Kingdom. The prohibition against the establishment of new Banks of Issue will extend to them. They, also, will be included in those enactments which will require the performance, for the future, of certain conditions preliminary to the formation of new Joint-Stock Banks. But I have thought it more prudent to deal, in the first instance, with the issue of promissory notes in England and Wales; to establish certain principles for the regulation of that portion of the circulation; and to leave Ireland and Scotland for future legislation, in respect to their paper currency. That currency stands on a different footing in each country, from that in which it stands in this part of the United Kingdom; and the single measure I have to propose is so extensive, and affects such numerous and powerful interests, that I have been unwilling to encumber it with enactments requiring separate consideration, or to cloud the prospects of success by having to encounter too powerful a combination of opponents. It will be remembered that to banks in Ireland and Scotland the law permits the issue of notes of a less value than five pounds, and that in Scotland there is no single bank partaking of the character of the Bank of England. In Ireland there is the Bank of Ireland, with privileges somewhat similar to the Bank of England; but, on the whole, the circumstances of the two countries are so far different, that I should be unwilling to propose any measure affecting the circulation either of Scotland or Ireland, without the opportunity of much more mature consideration than it has been in the power of the Government to give to this branch of the subject. Permit, me, before I conclude, briefly to recapitulate the outlines of the plan recommended by Her Majesty's servants. It is proposed that the Bank of England shall continue in possession of its present privileges—that it shall retain the exclusive right of issue, within a district of which sixty-five miles from London as a centre is the radius. The private banks within that district, which now actually issue notes, will of course be permitted to continue their issues to the amount of the average of the last two years. Two Departments of the Bank will be constituted: one for the issue of notes, the other for the transaction of the ordinary business of banking. The bullion now in the possession of the Bank will be transferred to the Issue Department. The issue of notes will be restricted to an issue of 14,-000l. upon securities—the remainder being issued upon bullion—and governed in amount by the fluctuations in the stock of bullion. If there be, under certain defined circumstances, an increase of the issues of securities, it can only take place with the knowledge and consent of the Government; and the profit derivable from such issue will belong to the public, Bankers now actually enjoying the privilege of issue, will be allowed to continue their issues, provided the maximum in the case of each bank does not exceed the average of a certain prescribed period. A weekly publication of issues will be required from every Bank of Issue. The names of shareholders and partners in all banks will be registered and published. No new Bank of Issue can be hereafter formed, and no Joint-Stock Company for banking purposes can be established, except after application to the Government and compliance with various regulations which will be hereafter submitted to the consideration of Parliament. I have now concluded the duty which I have to perform, and trust I have clearly explained to the House the principle and details of the plan which the Government proposes for the future regulation of the currency, and the grounds upon which it is founded. I ask for no vote to-night on the resolutions which I shall propose, *pro forma,* and, if I might give advice on such a subject, would recommend the postponement of discussion to a future day. To-morrow the correspondence which has taken place with the Bank, explaining more in detail our communications with the Bank, and the nature of the pecuniary arrangements between the Bank and the Government, will be laid upon the Table. The knowledge of that correspondence is important as a preliminary to full and satisfactory discussion on the merits of our proposal. Considering the part which I took in the year 1819 in terminating the system of inconvertible paper currency, and in re-establishing the ancient standard of value, it will no doubt be a source of great personal satisfaction to me, if I shall now succeed, after the lapse of a quarter of a century since those measures were adopted, in obtaining the assent of the House to proposals which are, in fact, the complement of them, and which are calculated to guarantee their permanence, and to facilitate their practical operation. But my gratification will be of a higher and purer nature than any connected with the satisfaction of personal feelings, if I may look forward to the mitigation or termination of evils, such as those which have at various times afflicted the country in consequence of rapid fluctuation in the amount and value of the medium of exchange. When I call to mind the danger to which the Bank of England has been exposed, the various effects of a sudden change from an overabundant to a contracted circulation, the reckless speculation of some of the Joint-Stock Banks, the losses entailed on their shareholders, the insolvency of so many private banks, the miserable amount of the dividends which have in many cases been paid, the ruin inflicted on innocent creditors, the shock to public and private credit, then indeed I rejoice on public grounds in the hope, that the wisdom of Parliament will at length devise measures which shall inspire just confidence in the medium of exchange, shall put a check on improvident speculations, and shall ensure, so far as legislation can ensure, the just reward of industry, and the legitimate profit of commercial enterprise conducted with integrity and controlled by provident calculation.

   The right hon. Baronet concluded by moving—

"That it is expedient to continue to the Bank of England, for a time to be limited, certain of the privileges now by law vested in that Corporation, subject to such conditions as may be provided by any Act to be passed for that purpose."

Richard Cobden

Richard Cobden

[*Born* JUNE 13, 1804—*Died* APRIL 2, 1865]

He had a curiously flat bridge to his nose, which was rather soft; his whole face was soft in appearance, with very straight eyes; and face of a farmer who has lived indoors for some years; with fine broad hands like a farmer's.—IAN BOWEN

•W•

ith increased democratization
resulting from the Reform Act of 1832, a larger number of men
sympathetic to the needs of the working class were elected to the
House of Commons. Foremost among them was Richard Cobden,
elected in 1841 for Stockport, and imbued with "a spirit and an influence which have changed the whole temper of English public
life." [1] From the very beginning of the Anti-Corn Law League in
1838 to Corn Law repeal in 1846, Richard Cobden was the architect
and statesman for "the most important legislative event in British
history during the nineteenth century." [2]

Although repeal of the Corn Laws was his greatest contribution
during his twenty-five-year tenure in Commons, Lord Hobart ranks
as a second triumph Cobden's participation in the formulation of
the Commercial Treaty with France in 1859–60.[3] J. A. Hobson,
among others, calls this Treaty "the first valid act" in bringing about
permanent improvement in British relations with France.[4] Cobden,
by no means confining his speaking to these two questions, however,
spoke often on matters affecting International Sea Law, the danger
of British intervention in Continental affairs, arbitration, expenditures on armaments, and the wrongfulness of war.[5]

Cobden was truly an international man, having traveled more
extensively than any other British statesman of his time,[6] and his
speeches contain an international flavor. Cobden was convinced that
the key to world peace and to the prosperity of the working man
was to abolish the greatest tie to nationalism—tariff restrictions.
Were this to be accomplished, all the nations of the world could
better understand one another by engaging in customs-free commerce, securing world peace for all time.

Cobden's efforts toward repeal of the Corn Laws took two forms.

---

1 J. R. Thursfield, *Peel* (London: Macmillan Co., Ltd., 1904), p. 223.
2 E. A. Johnson, *An Economic History of Modern England* (New York: Thomas
Nelson and Sons, 1939), p. 89.
3 Lord Hobart, The *"Mission of Richard Cobden"* (London: Cassell, Petter, and
Galpin), p. 3.
4 J. A. Hobson, *Richard Cobden: The International Man* (New York: Henry Holt
and Company, 1919), p. 13.
5 William Harbutt Dawson, *Richard Cobden and Foreign Policy* (London: George
Allen and Unwin Ltd., 1926), p. 29.
6 Hobson, *op. cit.*, p. 10.

As an organizer of the Anti-Corn Law League, he helped to establish a machine which profoundly changed the British political party system.[7] Contrary to the unsystematic and vague party ties of the British politician who accepted a party label as a creed, the League operated from a central office, smoothly coordinating the campaign of "education" to win advocates for Repeal. Up to 1843, about 2,000 lectures had been delivered by eloquent spokesmen, including Cobden, John Bright, and W. J. Fox.[8] The League was also active in pamphleteering. Nine million Tracts weighing close to one hundred tons and 20,000 copies weekly of the League's newspaper plus other publications had been issued from the office.[9]

It was in Parliament, however, that Cobden's influence was determinant.[10] From 1841 to Robert Peel's conversion to Repeal in 1846, with no intervening General Election, Cobden transformed a dream considered "impossible, impracticable, the wild dream of irresponsible theorists and enthusiasts," [11] and produced a change of opinion which Richard Gowing extravagantly suggests was "perhaps wholly unexampled in the history of Parliament." [12]

In his speeches, Cobden seldom spoke unless he was sure of his ground. His extensive travels and studies abroad coupled with "unusually acute powers of observation" [13] equipped him to understand better than most the subject matter of his own "controversial province." [14] His speeches bristled with categorical statements and challenges, for he knew that his opponents were probably less sure of their positions.[15]

John Morley, in his definitive biography of Cobden, calls his speaking manner "thoroughly businesslike," but never dull:

They were delighted by mingled vivacity and ease, by directness, by spontaneousness and reality, by the charm so effective and so uncommon between a speaker and his audience, of personal friendliness and undisguised cordiality.[16]

---

7 Ian Bowen, *Cobden* (London: Duckworth, 1935), p. 41.

8 Henry Ashworth, *Recollections of Richard Cobden, M.P. and the Anti-Corn Law League* (London: Cassell, Petter and Galpin), p. 121.

9 Richard Gowing, *Richard Cobden* (London: Cassell and Co., Ltd., 1885), p. 84.

10 *Ibid.*, p. 99.

11 *Ibid.*, p. 84.

12 Dawson, *op. cit.*, p. 68.

13 *Ibid.*

14 *Ibid.*, p. 69.

15 John Morley, *The Life of Richard Cobden*, I (London: T. Fisher Unwin, 1896), p. 196.

16 *Ibid.*, p. 318.

Although Morley considers much of Cobden's speaking to be "loose in its form and slipshod in arrangement," [17] two notable exceptions were those delivered on March 12, 1844, and March 13, 1845. These speeches are considered models of the way a great case should be presented to the House of Commons:

[They are] admirable examples of effective selection, luminous arrangement, and honest cogency of reasoning in intricate and difficult matters. Besides all this, they show how completely Cobden had worked out the whole conception of economic policy and the whole scheme of statesmanship, of which the repeal of the Corn Law was only a detail and a condition precedent.[18]

His speech delivered on March 13, 1845 is probably the more significant of the two. Before entering the chamber, a friend found Cobden to be "pale, nervous, and confident that he should break down in the middle of his speech." [19] Immediately following the address, which members from both sides of the House declared to be his best, the highest tribute was paid Cobden by Sir Robert Peel who "crumpled up the notes which he had been taking, and was heard by an onlooker, who was close by, to say to Mr. Sidney Herbert . . . '*You* must answer this, for *I* cannot.' "

---

17 *Ibid.*, p. 319.
18 *Ibid.*, p. 317.
19 *Ibid.*, p. 318.

Effects of Corn Laws
on Agriculturists[1]

•

*M*r. *Cobden having presented a petition in favour of his Motion for a Committee of Inquiry, addressed the House as follows:—* Sir, I am relieved upon the present occasion from any necessity for apologizing to the other side of the House for the Motion which I am about to submit. It will be in the recollection of hon. Members, that a fortnight before putting this Notice upon the Book, I expressed a hope that the matter would be taken up by some hon. Member opposite. I do not think, therefore, that in reply to any observations that I may have to make upon the question, I shall hear, as I did last year, an observation that the quarter from which this Motion came was suspicious. I may also add, Sir, that I have so framed my Motion as to include in it the objects embraced in both the Amendments which are made to it; I therefore conclude, that having included the hon. Gentlemen's Amendments (Mr. Stafford O'Brien and Mr. Wodehouse), they will not now feel it necessary to press them. Sir, the object of this Motion is to appoint a Select Committee to inquire into the present condition of the agricultural interests; and, at the same time, to ascertain how the laws regulating the importation of agricultural produce have affected the agriculturists of this country. As regards the distress among farmers, I presume we cannot go to a higher authority than those hon. Gentlemen who profess to be the farmers' friends and protectors. I find it stated by those hon. Gentlemen who recently paid their respects to the Prime Minister, that the agriculturists are in a state of great embarrassment and distress. I find that one gentleman from Norfolk (Mr. Hudson) stated that the farmers in the county are

---

paying their rents, but paying them out of capital, and not profits. I find Mr. Turner, of Upton, in Devonshire, stating that one-half of the smaller farmers in that county are insolvent, and that the others are rapidly falling into the same condition; that the farmers with larger holdings are quitting their farms with a view of saving the rest of their property: and that, unless some remedial measures be adopted by this House, they will be utterly ruined. The accounts which I have given you of those districts are such as I have had from many other sources. I put it to hon. Gentlemen opposite, whether the condition of the farmers in Suffolk, Wiltshire, and Hampshire, is better than that which I have described in Norfolk and Devonshire? I put it to county Members, whether—taking the whole of the south of England, from the confines of Nottinghamshire to the Land's End—whether, as a rule, the farmers are not now in a state of the greatest embarrassment? There may be exceptions; but I put it to them whether, as a rule, that is not their condition in all parts? Then, Sir, according to every precedent in this House, this is a fit and proper time to bring forward the Motion of which I have given notice. I venture to state, that had his Grace of Buckingham possessed a seat in this House, he would have done now what he did when he was Lord Chandos—have moved this Resolution which I am now about to move. The distress of the farmer being admitted, the next question which arises is, what is its cause? I feel a greater necessity to bring forward this Motion for a Committee of Inquiry, because I find great discrepancies of opinion among hon. Gentlemen opposite as to what is the cause of the distress among the farmers. In the first place, there is a discrepancy as to the generality or locality of the existing distress. I find the right hon. Baronet at the head of the Government saying that the distress is local; and he moreover says it does not arise from the legislation of this House. The hon. Member of Dorsetshire declares, on the other hand, that the distress is general, and that it does not arise from legislation. I am at a loss to understand what this protection to agriculture means, because I find such contradictory accounts given in this House by the promoters of that system. For instance, nine months ago, when my hon. Friend the Member of Wolverhampton brought forward his Motion for the Abolition of the Corn Laws, the right hon. Gentleman then the President of the Board of Trade, in replying to him, said that the present Corn Law had been most successful in its operations. He took great credit to the Government for the steadiness of price that was obtained under that law. I will read you the quotation, because we find these statements so often controverted. He said,—

Was there any man who had supported the law in the year 1842 who could honestly say that he had been disappointed in its workings? Could any one point out a promise or a prediction hazarded in the course of the protracted debates upon the measure, which promise or prediction has been subsequently falsified?

Now, recollect that the right hon. Gentleman was speaking when wheat was 56s. per quarter, and that wheat is now 45s. The right hon. Baronet at the head of the Government now says, "My legislation has had nothing to do with wheat being at 45s. a quarter;" but how are we to get over the difficulty that the responsible Member of Government at the head of the Board of Trade, only nine months ago, claimed merit for the Government having kept up the price of wheat at 56s.? These discrepancies themselves between the Government and its supporters, render it more and more necessary that this question of protection should be inquired into. I ask, what does it mean? The price of wheat is 45s. this day. I have been speaking to the highest authority in England upon this point—one who is often quoted by this House—within the last week, and he tells me, that with another favourable harvest, he thinks it very likely that wheat will be 35s. a quarter. What does this legislation mean, or what does it purport to be, if you are to have prices fluctuating from 56s. down to 35s. a quarter, and probably lower? Can you prevent it by the legislation of this House? That is the question. There is a great delusion spread abroad amongst the farmers; and it is the duty of this House to have that delusion dissipated by inquiring into the matter. Now, there are these very different opinions on the other side of the House; but there are Members upon this side representing very important interests, who think that farmers are suffering because they have this legislative protection. There is all this difference of opinion. Now, is not that a fit and proper subject for your inquiry? I am prepared to go into a Select Committee, and to bring forward evidence to show that the farmers are labouring under great evils—evils that I would connect with the legislation of this House, though they are evils which appear to be altogether dissociated from it. The first great evil under which the farmer labours is the want of capital. No one can deny that. I do not mean at all to disparage the farmers. The farmers of this country are just the same race as the rest of us; and, if they were placed in a similar position, theirs would be as good a trade—I mean that they would be as successful men of business as others—but it is notorious as a rule that the farmers of this country are deficient in capital; and I ask, how can any business be carried on successfully where there is a deficiency of capital? I take it that hon. Gentlemen opposite, acquainted with farming, would admit that 10l. an acre, on an arable farm, would be a sufficient amount of capital for carrying on the business of farming successfully. I will take it, then, that 10l. an acre would be a fair capital for an arable farm. I have made many inquiries upon this subject in all parts of the kingdom, and I give it to you as my decided conviction, that at this

present moment farmers do not average 5*l.* an acre capital on their farms.
I speak of England, and I take England south of the Trent, though, of
course, there are exceptions in every county; there are men of large capital in all parts—men farming their own land; but, taking it as a rule, I
hesitate not to give my opinion—and I am prepared to back that opinion
by witnesses before your Committee—that, as a rule, farmers have not,
upon an average, more than 5*l.* an acre capital for their arable land. I
have given you a tract of country to which I may add all Wales; probably
20,000,000 of acres of cultivable land. I have no doubt whatever, that
there are 100,000,000*l.* of capital wanting upon that land. What is the
meaning of farming capital? There are strange notions about the word
"capital." It means more manure, a greater amount of labour, a greater
number of cattle, and larger crops. Picture a country in which you can say
there is a deficiency of one-half of all those blessings which ought to, and
might, exist there, and then judge what the condition of labourers wanting employment and food is. But you will say, capital would be invested if
it could be done with profit. I admit it; that is the question I want you to
inquire into. How is it that in a country where there is a plethora of
capital, where every other business and pursuit is overflowing with
money, where you have men going to France for railways and to Pennsylvania for bonds, embarking in schemes for connecting the Atlantic with
the Pacific by canals, railways in the valley of the Mississippi, and sending
their money to the bottom of the Mexican mines—while you have a country rich and overflowing, ready to take investments in every corner of the
globe—how is it, I say, that this capital does not find its employment in
the most attractive of all forms—upon the soil of this country? The cause
is notorious—it is admitted by your highest authorities: the reason is,
there is not security for capital in land. Capital shrinks instinctively from
insecurity of tenure; and you have not in England that security which
would warrant men of capital investing their money in the soil. Now, is it
not a matter worthy of consideration, how far this insecurity of tenure
is bound up with that protective system of which you are so enamoured?
Suppose it can be shown that there is a vicious circle; that you have made
politics of Corn Laws, and that you want voters to maintain them; that
you very erroneously think that the Corn Laws are your great mine of
wealth, and therefore, you must have a dependent tenantry, that you may
have their votes at elections to maintain this law in Parliament. Well, if
you will have dependent voters, you cannot have men of spirit and capital. Then your policy reacts upon you. If you have not men of skill and
capital, you cannot have improvements and employment for your labourers. Then comes round that vicious termination of the circle—you have
pauperism, poor-rates, county-rates, and all the other evils of which you
are now speaking and complaining. Now, Sir, I like to quote from the

highest authority upon that side of the House. I will just state to you
what is the opinion of the hon. Member for Berkshire (Mr. Pusey) upon
this subject. When speaking at a meeting of the Agricultural Society, he
says,—

He knew this country well, and he knew that there was not a place from
Plymouth to Berwick in which the landlords might not make improvements; but
when the tenant was short of money, the landlord generally would be short of
money too. But he would tell them how to find funds. There were many districts
where there was a great superfluity not only of useless but of mischievous
timber, and if they would cut that down which excluded the sun and air and
fed on the soil, and sell it, they would benefit the farmer by cutting it down,
and they would benefit the farmer, and the labourer too, by laying out the
proceeds in under-draining the soil. There was another mode in which they
might find money. He knew that on some properties a large sum was spent in
the preservation of game. It was not at all unusual for the game to cost 500*l.*
or 600*l.* a year; and if this were given up the money would employ one hundred able-bodied labourers during the winter in improving the property. This
was another fund for the landlords of England to benefit the labourers and the
farmers at the same time.

Now, there is another authority—a very important member of your Pro-
tection-Society—Mr. Fisher Hobbes, who thus speaks at a meeting of the
Colchester Agricultural Association,—

He was aware that a spirit of improvement was abroad. Much was said about
the tenant-farmers doing more. He agreed they might do more; the soil of the
country was capable of greater production; if he said one fourth more he should
be within compass. But that could not be done by the tenant-farmer alone; they
must have confidence; it must be done by leases; by draining; by extending the
length of fields; by knocking down hedgerows and clearing away trees which
now shielded the corn.

I will quote a still higher authority. Lord Stanley, at a late meeting at
Liverpool, said,—

I say, and as one connected with the land I feel myself bound to say it, that
a landlord has no right to expect any great and permanent improvement of his
land by the tenant, unless that tenant be secured the repayment of his outlay,
not by the personal character or honour of his landlord, but by a security which
no casualties can interfere with—the security granted him by the terms of a
lease for years.

Now, Sir, not only does the want of security prevent capital flowing into
the farming business, but it actually deters from the improvement of the
land those who are already in the occupation of it. There are many men,

tenants of your land, who could improve their farms if they had a sufficient security, and they have either capital themselves or their friends
could supply it; but with the absence of leases, and the want of security,
you are actually deterring them from laying out their money upon your
land. They keep everything the same from year to year. You know that it
is impossible to farm your estates properly unless a tenant has an investment for more than one year. A man ought to be able to begin a farm
with at least eight years before him, before he expects to see a return for
the whole of the outlay of his money. You are, therefore, keeping your
tenants-at-will at a yearly kind of cultivation, and you are preventing
them carrying on their businesses in a proper way. Not only do you prevent the laying out of capital upon your land, and disable the farmers
from cultivating it, but your policy tends to make them servile and dependent; so that they are actually disinclined to improvement, afraid to
let you see that they can improve, because they are apprehensive that you
will pounce upon them for an increase of rent. I see the hon. Member for
Lincolnshire opposite, and he rather smiled at the expression when I said
that the state of dependence of the farmers was such that they were actually afraid to appear to be improving their land. Now, that hon. Gentleman the Member for Lincolnshire (Mr. Christopher), upon the Motion
made last year for agricultural statistics, by my hon. Friend the Member
for Manchester, (Mr. Milner Gibson), made the following statement,—

It is most desirable for the farmer to know the actual quantity of corn grown
in this country, as such knowledge would insure steadiness of prices, which was
infinitely more valuable to the agriculturist than fluctuating prices. But to ascertain this there was extreme difficulty. They could not leave it to the farmer
to make a return of the quantity which he produced, for it was not for his interest to do so. If in any one or two years he produced four quarters per acre on
land which had previously grown but three, he might fear that his landlord
would say, 'Your land is more productive than I imagined, and I must therefore
raise your rent.' The interest of the farmers, therefore, would be to under-rate,
and to furnish low returns.

And here is further evidence of the same kind, which I find at a meeting
of the South Devonshire Agricultural Association. The Rev. C. Johnson
said,—

He knew it had been thought that landlords were ready to avail themselves
of such association, on account of the opportunity it afforded them for diving
into their tenants' affairs, and opening their eyes. An instance of this occurred
to him at a recent ploughing match, where he met a respectable agriculturist
whom he well knew, and asked him if he was going to it. He said, 'No.' 'Why?'
Because he did not approve of such things. This 'why' produced another 'why,'

and the man gave a reason why. Suppose he sent a plough and man with two superior horses, the landlord at once would say, 'This man is doing too well on my estate,' and increase the rent.

Now, I ask hon. Gentlemen here, the landed gentry of England, what a state of things is that when, upon their own testimony respecting the farming capitalists in this country, they dare not appear to have a good horse—they dare not appear to be growing more than four quarters instead of three? (*Mr. Christopher: Hear.*) The hon. Member cheers, but I am quoting from his own authority. I say, this condition of things, indicated by those two quotations, brings the tenant-farmers—if they are such as these Gentlemen describe them to be—it brings them down to a very low point of servility. In Egypt, Mehemet Ali takes the utmost grain of corn from his people, who bury it beneath their hearth-stones in their cottages, and will suffer the bastinado rather than tell how much corn they grow. Our tenants are not afraid of the bastinado, but they are terrified at the rise of rent. This is the state of things amongst the tenant-farmers, farming without leases. In England leases are the exception, and not the rule. But even when you have leases in England—where you have leases or agreements—I doubt whether they are not in many cases worse tenures than where there is no lease at all; the clauses being of such an obsolete and preposterous character as to defy any man to carry on the business of farming under them profitably. I do not know whether the hon. Member of Cheshire is here, but if so I will read him a passage from an actual Cheshire lease, showing what kind of covenants farmers are called on to perform:—

To pay the landlord 20*l.* for every statute acre of ground, and so in proportion for a less quantity, that shall be converted into tillage, or used contrary to the appointment before made; and 5*l.* for every cwt. of hay, thrave of straw, load of potatoes, or cartload of manure, that shall be sold or taken from the premises during the term; and 10*l.* for every tree fallen, cut down, or destroyed, cropped, lopped, or stopped, or willingly suffered so to be; and 20*l.* for any servant or other person so hired or admitted as to gain a settlement in the township; and 10*l.* per statute acre, and so in proportion for a less quantity, of the said land, which the tenant shall let off or underlet. Such sums to be paid on demand after every breach, and in default of payment to be considered as reserved rent, and levied by distress and sale as rent in arrear may be levied and raised. And to do six days' boon team work whenever called upon; and to keep for the landlord one dog, and one cock or hen; and to make no marlpit without the landlord's consent being first obtained in writing, after which the same is to be properly filled in; nor to allow any inmate to remain on the premises after six days' notice; nor to keep or feed any sheep except such as are used for the consumption of the family.

Now, what is such an instrument but a trap for the unwary man? It is a barrier against men of intelligence and capital, and it is a fetter to the mind of any free man. No man could farm under such a lease as that, or under such clauses as it contains. (*Sir C. Burrell: Hear, hear.*) I perceive that the hon. Member for Shoreham (Sir Charles Burrell) is cheering. I will by and by allude to one of the hon. Member's own leases. You will find in your own leases, though there be not stipulations for cocks and hens, and dogs, and probably team-work, yet there are almost as great absurdities in every lease and agreement you have. What are those leases? Why, they are generally some old musty instruments which a lawyer's clerk takes out of a pigeon-hole, and writes out for every fresh incoming tenant; —a thing which seems to have been in existence for 100 years. You tie them down by the most absurd restrictions; you do not give men credit for being able to discover any improvement next year and the year after; but you go upon the assumption that men are not able to improve, and you do your best to prevent them from doing so. Now, I do not know why we should not in this country have leases for land upon similar terms to the leases of manufactories, or any "plant" or premises. I do not think that farming will ever be carried on as it ought to be until you have leases drawn up in the same way as a man takes a manufactory, and pays perhaps 1,000*l.* a year for it. I know people who pay 4,000*l.* a year for manufactories to carry on their business, and at fair rents. There is an hon. Gentleman near me who pays more than 4,000*l.* a year for the rent of his manufactory. What covenants do you think he has in his lease? What would he think if it stated how many revolutions there should be in a minute of the spindles, or if they prescribed the construction of the straps or the gearing of the machinery? Why, he takes his manufactory with a schedule of its present state—bricks, mortar, and machinery—and when the lease is over, he must leave it in the same state, or else pay a compensation for the dilapidation. (*The Chancellor of the Exchequer: Hear, hear.*) The right hon. Gentleman the Chancellor of the Exchequer cheers that statement. I want to ask his opinion respecting a similar lease for a farm. I am rather disposed to think that the Anti-Corn-Law Leaguers will very likely form a joint-stock association, having none but free traders in the body, that we may purchase an estate and have a model farm; taking care that it shall be in one of the rural counties, one of the most purely agricultural parts of the country, where we think there is the greatest need of improvement—perhaps in Buckinghamshire—and there shall be a model farm, homestead, and cottages; and I may tell the noble Lord the Member for Newark, that we shall have a model garden, and we will not make any boast about it. But the great object will be to have a model lease. We will have as the farmer a man of intelligence and capital. I am not so unreasonable as to tell you that you ought to let your land to men who have not a competent capital, or are not sufficiently intelligent; but I say, select such a man as that, let him know his business and have a sufficient capital, and you cannot give him too wide a scope. We will find such a man, and will let him our farm; there shall be a lease precisely such as that upon which my hon. Friend takes his factory. There shall be no clause inserted in it to dictate to him how he shall cultivate his farm; he shall do what he likes with the old pasture. If he can make more by ploughing it up he shall do so; if he can grow white crops every year— which I know there are people doing at this moment in more places than one in this country, or if he can make any other improvement or discovery, he shall be free to do so. We will let him the land, with a schedule of the state of tillage and the condition of the homestead, and all we will bind him to will be this:—"You shall leave the land as good as when you entered upon it. If it be in an inferior state it shall be valued again, and you shall compensate us; but if it be in an improved state it shall be valued, and we, the landlords, will compensate you." We will give possession of everything upon the land, whether it be wild or tame animals; he shall have the absolute control. Take as stringent precautions as you please to compel the punctual payment of the rent; take the right of re-entry as summarily as you like if the rent be not duly paid; but let the payment of rent duly be the sole test as to the well-doing of the tenant; and so long as he can pay the rent, and do it promptly, that is the only criterion you need have that the farmer is doing well; and if he is a man of capital, you have the strongest possible security that he will not waste your property while he has possession of it. I have sometimes heard hon. Gentlemen opposite say, "It is all very well for you to preach up leases, but there are many farmers who do not want them. We have asked them, and they will not take them." *("Hear, hear.")* The hon. Gentleman cheers that remark. But what does it argue? That by that process which the Member for Lincolnshire has described—that degrading process—you have rendered those tenants servile, hopeless, and dejected, so that they have not the spirit of men when they are carrying on their business. Now, hear what Professor Low states, he being, as you are aware, a professor of agriculture,—

The argument has again and again been used against an extension of leases, that the tenants themselves set no value upon them; but to how different a conclusion ought the existence of such a feeling amongst the tenantry of a country to conduct us! The fact itself shows that the absence of leases may render a tenantry ignorant of the means of employing their own capital with advantage, indisposed to the exertions which improvements demand, and better contented with an easy rent and dependent condition than with the prospect of an independence to be earned by increased exertion.

Whilst you have a tenantry in the state pictured by the hon. Member for Lincolnshire, what must be the state of the peasantry? Your labourers can never be prosperous when the tenants are depressed. Go through the length and breadth of the land, and you will find that where capital is in the greatest abundance, and capitalists are most intelligent, there you will invariably find the working classes most prosperous and happy; and, on the other hand, show me an impoverished and enfeebled tenantry—go to the north of Devonshire, for instance, and show me a tenantry like that— and there you will find a peasantry sunk into the most hopeless and degraded condition. Now, Sir, I have mentioned a deficiency of capital as being the primary want amongst farmers. I have stated the want of security in leases as the cause of the want of capital; but you may still say, "You have not connected this with the Corn Laws and the protective system." I will read the opinion of an hon. Gentleman who sits upon this side of the House; it is in a published letter of Mr. Hayter, who, I know, is himself an ardent supporter of agriculture. He says,—

The more I see of and practise agriculture, the more firmly am I convinced that the whole unemployed labour of the country could, under a better system of husbandry, be advantageously put into operation; and moreover, that the Corn Laws have been one of the principal causes of the present system of bad farming, and consequent pauperism. Nothing short of their entire removal will ever induce the average farmer to rely upon anything else than the Legislature for the payment of his rent; his belief being that all rent is paid by corn, and nothing else than corn; and that the Legislature can, by enacting Corn Laws, create a price which will make his rent easy. The day of their (the Corn Laws) entire abolition ought to be a day of jubilee and rejoicing to every man interested in land.

Now, Sir, I do not stop to connect the cause and effect in this matter, and inquire whether your Corn Laws or your protective system have caused the want of leases and capital. I do not stop to make good my proof, and for this reason, that you have adopted a system of legislation in this House by which you profess to make the farming trade prosperous. I show you, after thirty years' trial, what is the depressed condition of the agriculturists; I prove to you what is the impoverished state of farmers, and also of the labourers, and you will not contest any one of those propositions. I say it is enough, having had thirty years' trial of your specific with no better results than these, for me to ask you to go into Committee to see if something better cannot be devised. I am going to contend, that free trade in grain would be more advantageous to farmers—and with them I include labourers—than restriction; to oblige the hon. Member for Norfolk, I will take with them also the landlords; and I contend that free trade in corn and grain of every kind would be more beneficial to them than to any other class of the community. I should have contended the same before the passing of the late Tariff, but now I am prepared to do so with tenfold more force. What has the right hon. Baronet (Sir R. Peel) done? He has passed a law to admit fat cattle at a nominal duty. Some foreign fat cattle were selling in Smithfield the other day at about 15*l.* or 16*l.* per head, paying only about 7½ per cent. duty; but he has not admitted the raw material out of which these fat cattle are made. Mr. Huskisson did not act in this manner when he commenced his plan of free trade. He began by admitting the raw material of manufactures before he admitted the manufactured article; but in your case you have commenced at precisely the opposite end, and have allowed free trade in cattle instead of that upon which they are fattened. I say, give free trade in that grain which goes to make the cattle. I contend, that by this protective system the farmers throughout the country are more injured than any other class in the community. I would take, for instance, the article of cloverseed. The hon. Member for North Northamptonshire put a question the other night to the right hon. Baronet at the head of the Government. He looked so exceedingly alarmed, that I wondered what the subject was which created the apprehension. He asked the right hon. Baronet whether he was going to admit cloverseed into this country? I believe cloverseed is to be excluded from the Schedule of free importation. Now, I ask for whose benefit is this exception made? I ask the hon. Gentleman the Member of North Northamptonshire, whether those whom he represents, the farmers of that district of the county, are, in a large majority of instances, sellers of cloverseed? I will undertake to say they are not. How many counties in England are there which are benefited by the protection of cloverseed? I will take the whole of Scotland. If there be any Scotch Members present, I ask them whether they do not in their country import the cloverseed from England? They do not grow it. I undertake to say that there are not ten counties in the United Kingdom which are interested in the exportation of cloverseed out of their own borders. Neither have they any of this article in Ireland. But yet we have cloverseed excluded from the farmers, although they are not interested as a body in its protection at all. Again, take the article of beans. There are lands in Essex where they can grow them alternate years with wheat. I find that beans come from that district to Mark-lane; and I believe also that in some parts of Lincolnshire and Cambridgeshire they do the same; but how is it with the poor lands of Surrey or the poor downland of Wiltshire? Take the whole of the counties. How many of them are there which are exporters of beans, or send them to market? You are taxing the whole of the farmers who do not sell their beans, for the pretended benefit of a few counties or districts of counties where they do. Mark you, where they can grow beans on the stronger and better soils, it is not in one case out of ten that they grow them for the market. They may grow them for their own use; but where they do not cultivate beans, send them to market, and turn them into money, those farmers can have no interest whatever in keeping up the money price of that which they never sell. Take the article of oats. How many farmers are there who ever have oats down on the credit side of their books, as an item upon which they rely for the payment of their rents? The farmers may, and do generally, grow oats for feeding their own horses; but it is an exception to the rule—and a rare exception too— where the farmer depends upon the sale of his oats to meet his expenses. Take the article of hops. You have a protection upon them for the benefit of the growers in Kent, Sussex, and Surrey, but yet the cultivators of hops are taxed for the protection of others in articles which they do not them- selves produce. Take the article of cheese. Not one farmer in ten in the country makes his own cheese, and yet they and their servants are large consumers of it. But what are the counties which have the protection on this article? Cheshire, Gloucestershire, Wiltshire, part of Derbyshire, and Leicestershire. Here are some four or five dairy counties having an inter- est in the protection of cheese: but recollect that those counties are pecul- iarly hardly taxed in beans and oats, because in those counties where they are chiefly dairy farms, they are most in want of artificial food for their cattle. There are the whole of the hilly districts; and I hope my friend the Member for Nottingham (Mr. Gisborne) is here, because he has a special grievance in this matter; he lives in Derbyshire, and very commendably employs himself in rearing good cattle upon the hills: but he is taxed for your protection for his beans, peas, oats, Indian corn, and everything which he wants for feeding them. He told me, only the other day, that he should like nothing better than to give up the little remnant of protection on cattle, if you would only let him buy a thousand quarters of black oats for the consumption of his stock. Take the whole of the hilly districts, and the down county of Wiltshire; the whole of that expanse of downs in the South of England; take the Cheviots, where the flockmasters reside; the Grampians in Scotland; and take the whole of Wales, they are not bene- fited in the slightest degree by the protection on these articles; but, on the contrary, you are taxing the very things they want. They require proven- der as abundantly and cheaply as they can get it. Allowing a free importa- tion of food for cattle is the only way in which those counties can improve the breed of their lean stocks, and the only manner in which they can ever bring their land up to anything like a proper state of fertility. I will go farther and say, that farms with thin soil, I mean the stock farmers, which you will find in Hertfordshire and Surrey, farmers with large capitals, arable farmers, I say those men are deeply interested in having a free importation of food for their cattle, because they have thin poor land. This land of its ownself does not contain the means of its increased fertility; and the only way is the bringing in of an additional quantity of food from elsewhere, that they can bring up their farms to a proper state of cultivation. I have been favoured with an estimate made by a very experienced clever farmer in Wiltshire—probably hon. Gentlemen will bear me out, when I say a man of great intelligence and skill, and entitled to every consideration in this House. I refer to Mr. Nathaniel Atherton, Kington, Wilts. That gentleman estimates that upon 400 acres of land he could increase his profits to the amount of 280*l*., paying the same rent as at present, provided there was a free importation of foreign grain of all kinds. He would buy 500 quarters of oats at 15 s., or the same amount in beans or peas at 14 s. or 15 s. a sack, to be fed on the land or in the yard; by which he would grow additional 160 quarters of wheat, and 230 quarters of barley, and gain an increased profit of 300*l*. upon his sheep and cattle. His plan embraces the employment of an additional capital of 1,000*l*.; and he would pay 150*l*. a year more for labour. I had an opportunity, the other day, of speaking to a very intelligent farmer in Hertfordshire, Mr. Lattimore, of Wheathampstead. Very likely there are hon. Members here to whom he is known. I do not know whether the noble Lord the Member for Hertfordshire is present; if so, he will, no doubt, know that Mr. Lattimore stands as high in Hertford market as a skillful farmer and a man of abundant capital as any in the county. He is a gentlemen of most unquestionable intelligence; and what does he say? He told me that last year he paid 230*l*. enhanced price on his beans and other provender which he bought for his cattle:—230*l*. enhanced price in consequence of that restriction upon the trade in foreign grain, amounting to 14 s. a quarter on all the wheat he sold off his farm. Now, I undertake to say, in the names of Mr. Atherton, of Wiltshire, and Mr. Lattimore, of Hertfordshire, that they are as decided advocates for free trade in grain of every kind as I am. I am not now quoting merely solitary cases. I told hon. Gentlemen once before that I have probably as large an acquaintance among farmers as any one in the House. I think I could give you from every county the names of some of the first-rate farmers who are as ardent free-traders as I am. I requested the Secretary of this much dreaded Anti-Corn Law League to make me out a list of the farmers who are subscribers to that Association, and I find there are upwards of 100 in England and Scotland who subscribe to the League Fund, comprising, I hesitate not to say, the most intelligent men to be found in the kingdom. I went into the Lothians, at the invitation of twenty-two farmers there, several of whom were paying upwards of 1,000*l*. a year rent. I spent two or three days among them, and I never found a body of more intelligent, liberal-minded men in my life. Those are men who do not want restrictions upon the importation of grain. They desire nothing but fair play. They say, "Let us have our Indian corn, Egyptian beans, and Polish oats as freely as we have our linseed cake, and we can bear competition with any corn-growers in the world." But by excluding the provender for cattle, and at the same time admitting the cattle almost duty free, I think you are giving an example of one of the greatest absurdities and perversions of nature and common sense which ever was seen. We have heard of great absurdities in legislation in commercial matters of late. We know that there has been such a case as sending coffee from Cuba to the Cape of Good Hope, in order to bring it back to England under the law; but I venture to say, that in less than ten years from this time people will look back with more amazement in their minds at the fact that, while you are sending ships to Ichaboe to bring back the guano, you are passing a law to exclude Indian corn, beans, oats, peas, and everything else that give nourishment to your cattle, which would give you a thousand times more productive manure than all the guano of Ichaboe. Upon the last occasion when I spoke upon this subject, I was answered by the right hon. Gentleman the President of the Board of Trade. He talked about throwing poor lands out of cultivation, and converting arable lands into pasture. I hope that we men of the Anti-Corn Law League may not be reproached again with seeking to cause any such disasters. My belief is—and the conviction is founded upon a most extensive inquiry amongst the most intelligent farmers, without stint of trouble and pains—that the course you are pursuing tends every hour to throw land out of cultivation, and make poor lands unproductive. Do not let us be told again that we desire to draw the labourers from the land, in order that we may reduce the wages of the work-people employed in factories. I tell you that, if you bestow capital on the soil, and cultivate it with the same skill as manufacturers bestow upon their business, you have not population enough in the rural districts for the purpose. I yesterday received a letter from Lord Ducie, in which he gives precisely the same opinion. He says, "If we had the land properly cultivated, there are not sufficient labourers to till it." You are chasing your labourers from village to village, passing laws to compel people to support paupers, devising every means to smuggle them abroad—to the antipodes, if you can get them there; why, you would have to run after them, and bring them back again, if you had your land properly cultivated. I tell you honestly my conviction, that it is by these means, and these only, that you can avert very great and serious troubles and disasters in your agricultural districts. Sir, I remember, on the last occasion when this subject was discussed, there was a great deal said about disturbing an interest. It was said this inquiry could not be gone into, because we were disturbing and unsettling a great interest. I have no desire to undervalue the agricultural interest. I have heard it said that they are the greatest consumers of manufactured goods in this country; that they are such large consumers of our goods that we had better look after the home trade, and not think of destroying it. But what sort of consumers of manufactures think you the labourers can be, with the wages they are now getting in agricultural districts? Understand me: I am arguing for a principle that I solemnly believe would raise the wages of the labourers in the agricultural districts. I believe you would have no men starving upon 7s. a week, if you had abundant capital and competent skill employed upon the soil; but I ask what is this consumption of manufactured goods that we have heard so much about? I have taken some pains, and made large inquiries as to the amount laid out in the average of cases by agricultural labourers and their families for clothing; I probably may startle you by telling you that we have exported in one year more of our manufactures to Brazil than have been consumed in a similar period by the whole of your agricultural peasantry and their families. You have 960,000 agricultural labourers in England and Wales, according to the last census; I undertake to say they do not expend on an average 30s. a year on their families, supposing every one of them to be in employ. I speak of manufactured goods excluding shoes. I assert that the whole of the agricultural peasantry and their families in England and Wales do not spend a million and a half per annum for manufactured goods, in clothing and bedding. And, with regard to your exciseable and duty-paying articles, what can the poor wretch lay out upon them, who out of 8s. or 9s. a week has a wife and family to support? I undertake to prove to your satisfaction—and you may do it yourselves if you will but dare to look the figures in the face—I will undertake to prove to you that they do not pay, upon an average, each family, 15s. per annum; that the whole of their contributions to the Revenue do not amount to 700,000*l.* Now, is not this a mighty interest to be disturbed? I would keep that interest as justly as though it were one of the most important; but I say, when you have by your present system brought down your agricultural peasantry to that state, have you anything to offer for bettering their condition, or at all events to justify resisting an inquiry? On the last occasion when I addressed the House upon this subject, I recollect stating some facts to show that you had no reasonable ground to fear foreign competition; those facts I do not intend to reiterate, because they have never been contradicted. But there are still attempts made to frighten people by telling them, "If you open the ports to foreign corn, you will have corn let in here for nothing." One of the favourite fallacies which are now put forth is this: "Look at the price of corn in England, and see what it is abroad; you have prices low here, and yet you have corn coming in from abroad and paying the maximum duty. Now, if you had not 20s. duty to pay, what a quantity of corn you would have brought in, and how low the price would be!" This statement arises from a fallacy—I hope not dishonestly put forth—in not understanding the difference between the real and the nominal price of corn. The price of corn at Dantzic now, when there is no regular sale, is nominal; the price of corn when it is coming in regularly is the real price. Now, go back to 1838: in January of that year the price of wheat at Dantzic was nominal; there was no demand for England; there were no purchasers except for speculation, with the chance, probably, of having to throw the wheat into the sea; but in the months of July and August of that year, when apprehensions arose of a failure of our harvest, then the price of corn in Dantzic rose instantly, sympathising with the markets in England; and at the end of the year, in December, the price of wheat at Dantzic had doubled the amount at which it had been in January; and during the three following years, when you had a regular importation of corn, during all that time, by the averages laid upon the Table of this House, wheat at Dantzic averaged 40s. Wheat at Dantzic was at that price during the three years 1839, 1840, and 1841. Now, I mention this just to show the fact to hon. Gentlemen, and to entreat them that they will not go and alarm their tenantry by this outcry of the danger of foreign competition. You ought to be pursuing a directly opposite course—you ought to be trying to stimulate them in every possible way—by showing that they can compete with foreigners; that what others can do in Poland, they can do in England. I have an illustration of this subject in the case of a Society of which the hon. Member for Suffolk is Chairman. We have lately seen a new light spreading amongst agricultural gentlemen. We are told the salvation of this country is to arise from the cultivation of flax. There is a National Flax Society, of which Lord Rendlesham is the President. This Flax Society state in their prospectus, a copy of which I have here, purporting to be the First Annual Report of the National Flax Agricultural Improvement Association—after talking of the Ministers holding out no hope from legislation, the Report goes on to state that upon these grounds the National Flax Society call upon the nation for its support, on the ground that they are going to remedy the distresses of the country. The founder of this Society is Mr. Warnes of Norfolk. I observe Mr. Warnes paid a visit to Sussex, and he attended an agricultural meeting at which the hon. Baronet the Member for Shoreham (Sir Charles Burrell) presided. After the usual loyal toasts, the hon. Baronet proposed the toast of the evening, "Mr. Warnes and the cultivation of flax." The hon. Baronet was not aware, I dare say, that he was then furnishing a most deadly weapon to the lecturers of the Anti-Corn Law League. We are told you cannot compete with foreigners unless you have a high protective duty. You have a high protective duty on wheat, amounting at this moment to 20 s. a quarter. A quarter of wheat at the present time is just worth the same as one cwt. of flax. On a quarter of wheat you have a protective duty against the Pole and Russian of 20 s.; upon the one cwt. of flax you have a protective duty of 1 d. And I did not hear a murmur from hon. Gentlemen opposite when the Prime Minister proposed to take off that protective duty of 1 d., totally and immediately. But we are told that English agriculturists cannot compete with foreigners, and especially with that serf labour that is to be found somewhere up the Baltic. Well, but flax comes from the Baltic, and there is no protective duty. Hon. Gentlemen say we have no objection to raw materials where there is no labour connected with them; but we cannot contend against foreigners in wheat, because there is such an amount of labour in it. Why, there is twice as much labour in flax as there is in wheat; but the Member for Shoreham favours the growth of flax in order to restore the country, which is sinking into abject and hopeless state for want of agricultural protections. But the hon. Baronet will forgive me—I am sure he will, he looks as if he would—if I allude a little to the subject of leases. The hon. Gentleman on that occasion, I believe, complained that it was a great pity that farmers did not grow more flax. I do not know whether it was true or not, that the same hon. Baronet's leases to his own tenants forbade them to grow that article. Now, it is quite as possible that the right hon. Baronet does not exactly know what covenants or clauses there are in his leases. But I know that it is a very common case to preclude the growth of flax; and it just shows the kind of management by which the landed proprietors have carried on their affairs, that actually, I believe, the original source of the error that flax was very pernicious to the ground was derived from Virgil; I believe there is a passage in the Georgics to that effect. From that classic authority, no doubt, some learned lawyer put this clause into the lease, and there it has remained ever since. Now, I have alluded to the condition of the labourers at the present time; but I am bound to say, that while the farmers at the present moment are in a worse condition than they have been for the last ten years, I believe the agricultural labourers have passed over the winter with less suffering and distress, although it has been a five months' winter, and a severer one, too, than they endured in the previous year. ("Hear.") I am glad to find that corroborated by hon. Gentlemen opposite, because it bears out, in a remarkable degree, the opinion that we who are in connexion with the free-trade question entertain. We maintain that a low price of food is beneficial to the labouring classes. We assert, and we can prove it, at least in the manufacturing districts, that whenever provisions are dear wages are low, and whenever food is cheap wages invariably rise. We have had a strike in almost every business in Lancashire since the price of wheat has been down to something like 50 s.; and I am glad to be corroborated when I state that the agricultural labourers have been in a better condition during the last winter than they were in the previous one. But does not that show that, even in your case, though your labourers have in a general way only just as much as will find them a subsistence, they are benefited by a great abundance of the first necessaries of life? Although their wages may rise and fall with the price of food,—although they may go up with the advance in the price of corn, and fall when it is lowered,—still, I maintain that it does not rise in the same proportion as the price of food rises, nor fall to the extent to which food falls. Therefore, in all cases the agricultural labourers are in a better state when food is low than when it is high. I have a very curious proof that high-priced food leads to pauperism in the agricultural districts, which I will read to you. It is a labourer's certificate seen at Stowupland, in Suffolk, in July, 1844, which was placed upon the mantel-piece of a peasant's cottage there:—

West Suffolk Agricultural Association, established in 1833, for the advancement of agriculture and the encouragement of industry and skill, and good conduct, among labourers and servants in husbandry, President—the Duke of Grafton, Lord Lieutenant of the county: This is to certify that a prize of 2*l.* was awarded to William Burch, aged 82, labourer of the parish of Stowupland, in West Suffolk, September 25, 1840, for having brought up nine children without relief, except when flour was very dear; and for having worked on the same farm twenty-eight years.

(Signed) Rt. Rushbrooke, Chairman.

Now I need not press that point. It is admitted by hon. Gentlemen opposite—and I am glad it is so—that after a very severe winter, in the midst of great distress among farmers, when there have been a great many able-bodied men wanting employment, still there have been fewer in the streets and workhouses than there had been in the previous year; and I hope we shall not again be told by hon. Gentlemen opposite that cheap bread is injurious to the labourers. But the condition of the agricultural labourer is a bad case at the very best. You can look before you, and you have to foresee the means of giving employment to those men. I need not tell you that the late census shows that you cannot employ your own increasing population in the agricultural districts. But you say the farmers should employ them. Now, I am bound to say, that, whatever may be the condition of the agricultural labourer, I hold that the farmer is not responsible for that condition while he is placed in the situation in which he now is by the present system. I have seen during the last autumn and winter a great many exhortations made to the farmers, that they should employ more labourers. I think that is very unfair towards the farmer; I believe he is the man who is suffering most; he stands between you and your impoverished, suffering peasantry; and it is rather too bad to point to the farmer as the man who should relieve them. I have an extract from Lord Hardwick's address to the labourers of Haddenham. He says,—

Conciliate your employers, and if they do not perform their duty to you and themselves, address yourselves to the landlords; and I assure you that you will find us ready to urge our own tenants to the proper cultivation of their farms, and consequently, to the just employment of the labourer.

Now, I hold that this duty begin nearer home, and that the landed proprietors are the parties who are responsible if the labourers have not employment. You have absolute power; there is no doubt about that. You can, if you please, legislate for the labourers, or yourselves. Whatever you may have done besides, your legislation has been adverse to the labourer, and you have no right to call upon the farmers to remedy the evils which you have caused. Will not this evil—if evil you call it—press on you more and more every year? What can you do to remedy the mischief? I only appear here now because you have proposed nothing. We all know your system of allotments, and we are all aware of its failure. What other remedy have you? for mark you, that is worse than a plaything, if you were allowed to carry out your own views. (*"Hear."*) Ay, it is well enough for some of you that there are wiser heads than your own to lead you, or you would be conducting yourselves into precisely the same condition in which they are in Ireland, but with this difference—this increased difficulty—that there they do manage to maintain the rights of property by the aid of the English Exchequer and 20,000 bayonets; but divide your own country into small allotments, and where would be your rights of property? What do you propose to do now? That is the question. Nothing has been brought forward this year, which I have heard, having for its object to benefit the great mass of the English population; nothing I have heard suggested which has at all tended to alleviate their condition. You admit that the farmer's capital is sinking from under him, and that he is in a worse state than ever. Have you distinctly provided some plan to give confidence to the farmer, to cause an influx of capital to be expended upon his land, and so bring increased employment to the labourer? How is this to be met? I cannot believe that you are going to make this a political game. You must set up some specific object to benefit the agricultural interest. It is well said, that the last election was an agricultural triumph. There are 200 county Members sitting behind the Prime Minister who prove that it was so. What, then, is your plan for this distressing state of things? That is what I want to ask you. Do not, as you have done before, quarrel with me because I have imperfectly stated my case; I have done my best; and I again ask you what you have to propose? I tell you that this "Protection," as it has been called, is a failure. It was so when you had the prohibition up to 80s. You know the state of your farming tenantry in 1821. It was a failure when you had a protection price of 60s.; for you know what was the condition of your farm tenantry in 1835. It is a failure now with your last amendment, for you have admitted and proclaimed it to us; and what is the condition of your agricultural population at this time. I ask, what is your plan? I hope it is not a pretence; a mere political game that has been played throughout the last election, and that you have not all come up here as mere politicians. There are politicians in the House; men who look with an ambition—probably a justifiable one—to the honours of office. There may be men who—with thirty years of continuous service, having been pressed into a groove from which they can neither escape nor retreat—may be holding office, and high office, maintained there, probably at the expense of their present convictions, which do not harmonize very well with their early opinions. I make allowances for them; but the great body of the hon. Gentlemen opposite came up to this House, not as politicians, but as the farmers' friends, and protectors of the agricultural interests. Well, what do you propose to do? You have heard the Prime Minister declare that, if he could restore all the protection which you have had, that protection would not benefit agriculturists. Is that your belief? If so, why not proclaim it; and if it is not your conviction, you will have falsified your mission in this House, by following the right hon. Baronet out into the lobby, and opposing inquiry into the condition of the very men who sent you here. With mere politicians I have no right to expect to succeed in this Motion. But I have no hesitation in telling you, that, if you give me a Committee of this House, I will explode the delusion of agricultural protection! I will bring forward such a mass of evidence, and give you such a preponderance of talent and of authority, that when the Blue Book is published and sent forth to the world, as we can now send it, by our vehicles of information, your system of protection shall not live in the public opinion for two years afterwards. Politicians do not want that. This cry of protection has been a very convenient handle for politicians. The cry of protection carried the counties at the last election, and politicians gained honours, emoluments, and place by it. But is that old tattered flag of protection, tarnished and torn as it is already, to be kept hoisted still in the counties for the benefit of politicians; or will you come forward honestly and fairly to inquire into this question? Why, I cannot believe that the gentry of England will be made mere drumheads to be sounded upon by a Prime Minister to give forth unmeaning and empty sounds, and to have no articulate voice of their own. No! You are the gentry of England who represent the counties. You are the aristocracy of England. Your fathers led our fathers: you may lead us if you will go the right way. But, although you have retained your influence with this country longer than any other aristocracy, it has not been by opposing popular opinion, or by setting yourselves against the spirit of the age. In other days, when the battle and the hunting-fields were the tests of manly vigour, why, your fathers were first and foremost there. The aristocracy of England were not like the noblesse of France, the mere minions of a court; nor were they like the hidalgos of Madrid, who dwindled into pigmies. You have been Englishmen. You have not shown a want of courage and firmness when any call has been made upon you. This is a new era. It is the age of improvement, it is the age of social advancement, not the age for war or for feudal sports. You live in a mercantile age, when the whole wealth of the world is poured into your lap. You cannot have the advantages of commercial rents and feudal privileges; but you may be what you always have been, if you will identify yourselves with the spirit of the age. The English people look to the gentry and aristocracy of their country as their leaders. I who am not one of you, have no hesitation in telling you, that there is a deep-rooted, an hereditary prejudice, if I may so call it, in your favour in this country. But you never got it, and you will not keep it, by obstructing the spirit of the age. If you are indifferent to enlightened means of finding employment to your own peasantry; if you are found obstructing that advance which is calculated to knit nations more together in the bonds of peace by means of commercial intercourse; if you are found fighting against the discoveries which have almost given breath and life to material nature, and setting up yourselves as obstructives of that which destiny has decreed shall go on,—why, then, you will be the gentry of England no longer, and others will be found to take your place. And I have no hesitation in saying that you stand just now in a very critical position. There is a wide-spread suspicion that you have been tampering with the best feelings and with the honest confidence of your constituents in this cause. Everywhere you are doubted and suspected. Read your own organs, and you will see that this is the case. Well, then, this is the time to show that you are not the mere party politicians which you are said to be. I have said that we shall be opposed in this measure by politicians; they do not want inquiry. But I ask you to go into this Committee with me. I will give you a majority of county Members. You shall have a majority of the Central Society in that Committee: I ask you only to go into a fair inquiry as to the causes of the distress of your own population. I only ask that this matter may be fairly examined. Whether you establish my principle or yours, good will come out of the inquiry; and I do, therefore, beg and entreat the honourable independent country Gentlemen of this House that they will not refuse, on this occasion, to go into a fair, a full, and an impartial inquiry.

John Bright

John Bright

[*Born* NOVEMBER 16, 1811—*Died* MARCH 27, 1889]

The broad shoulders, the bulk of the figure, the solid massiveness of his masterful individuality, the immovable grasp of his feet upon the firm earth, his uprightness of bearing, the body knit to the head as clearly as capitol to column—all together made the least careful observer feel that here was one in whose armour the flaws were few.—GEORGE W. SMALLEY

F

ew men in British history, writes George Trevelyan, have exerted so much influence on the "thoughts and hearts of his fellow countrymen" as has John Bright,[1] and Asa Briggs considers him to be the "most important figure in the history of mid-Victorian radicalism." [2] Bright's political contributions occurred during the thirty years commencing with his first association with the Anti-Corn Law League and extending to passage of the Reform Bill of 1867.[3] Most notable among the events of his political career was his participation in the American and franchise questions.[4] Bright's influence in the "Trent Affair" in 1861 is considered by J. Travis Mills to have been the most singular force which prevented war between Great Britain and the United States.[5] On the franchise question, although ultimate credit for passage of the Reform Bill of 1867 must go to Disraeli, Bright's "single-handed agitation" at half a dozen vast gatherings probably accounted for the change of mood in the Conservative party.[6]

Trevelyan calls Bright's speeches "his one form of perfect achievement . . . his one great political weapon." [7] Rosebery refers to them as "masterpieces of sustained and restrained oratory." [8] In presentation, he used few gestures except to raise his hand occasionally to the level of his breast, but his great asset was his voice, described by Trevelyan as a "gift of heaven:"

. . . he had never to shout in order that it might thrill with its music the farthest corner of the largest hall.[9]

In composition, Bright was sensitive to the artistic effect of the proper words spoken in the proper context. Although he wrote *verbatim*

---

1 George Macaulay Trevelyan, *The Life of John Bright* (London: Constable and Co., Ltd., 1913), p. 3.

2 Asa Briggs, *Victorian People* (Chicago: U. of Chicago Press, 1955), p. 197.

3 Trevelyan, *op. cit.*

4 *Ibid.*

5 J. Travis Mills, *John Bright and the Quakers,* II (London: Methuen and Co. Ltd., 1935), p. 231.

6 Trevelyan, *op. cit.,* p. 359. See also p. 362: "Half a dozen great outdoor demonstrations at the principal centres of population, and a dozen speeches in great halls by Bright, sufficed to awe the Conservative party into submission."

7 *Ibid.*, p. 4.

8 Lord Rosebery, *Lord Randolph Churchill* (New York: Harper and Brothers, 1906), p. 117.

9 Trevelyan, *op. cit.,* p. 384.

only the peroration, he took great pains to select words which could excite imagery in the minds of his listeners. These expressions often took the form of homely, common-life allusions.[10] One of Bright's speeches which serves well to illustrate his speaking style was presented to the House of Commons, March 19, 1869, on the Second Reading of the Irish Church Bill.[11] Mills says of this speech, "In artistic arrangement, in felicitous phrasing, in style, in splendour of imagery, it is worthy alike of the man and of his theme." [12]

The speech included in this volume is on the "Trent Affair," and was delivered in Rochdale on December 4, 1861. This was the second of Bright's fourteen important speeches on the American question. It took place just one week after news had arrived in England of the forceable removal from the British sloop *Trent* of two Confederate envoys, James Mason and John S. Slidell, by Captain Charles Wilkes of the United States Navy. The purpose of this and other speeches on the American question was to instruct the public in Britain on the merits of the Union cause in the Civil War struggle. R. A. J. Walling calls the Rochdale speech "the first clear call to sanity amid the thunders of *The Times* (London) and the ravings of politicians of the baser sort." [13]

While Bright sought popular support with the hope of thwarting precipitate military action by the Palmerston government, he urged Lincoln and Seward to release the two envoys. This was done on January 9, and the clouds of war lifted. Although his private business suffered severely from the cotton shortage induced by the Union blockade of Southern ports, Bright never wavered in his sympathies for the United States in its struggle against the Confederacy.[14]

---

10 *Ibid.*, p. 385.

11 Mills, *op. cit.*, p. 138. See 194 H.C. Deb. 3 s., 1876–1894.

12 *Ibid.*

13 R. A. J. Walling, *The Diaries of John Bright* (New York: William Morrow and Co., 1931), p. 254.

14 Margaret E. Hirst, *John Bright* (London: Headley Bros., 1945), p. 74.

The "Trent" Affair [1]

•

When the gentlemen who invited me to this dinner called upon me I felt their kindness very sensibly, and now I am deeply grateful to my friends around me and to you all for the abundant manifestations of it with which I have been received to-night. I am, as you all know, at this moment surrounded by my neighbours and friends (*hear, hear*), and I may say with the utmost truth that I value the good opinion of those who now hear my voice far beyond the opinion of any equal number of the inhabitants of this country selected from any portion of it. You have by this great kindness that you have shown me given a proof that in the main you do not disapprove of my public labours (*cheers*), that at least you are willing to express an opinion that the motives by which I have been actuated have been honest and honourable to myself, and that that course has not been entirely without service to my country. (*Cheers.*) Coming to this meeting, or to any similar meeting, I always find that the subjects for discussion appear to be infinite, and far more than it is possible to treat. In these times in which we live, by the inventions of the telegraph and the steamboat, and the railroad, and the multiplication of newspapers, we seem continually to stand as on the top of an exceeding high mountain, from which we behold all the kingdoms of the earth and all the glory of them, and, unhappily, not only their glory, but their crimes, and their follies, and their calamities. (*Hear, hear.*) Seven years ago our eyes were turned with anxious expectation to a remote corner of Europe where five nations were contending in bloody strife for an object which, possibly, hardly one of them comprehended,

1 *The Times* (London), December 6, 1861, pp. 5, 6.

and, if they did comprehend it, which all sensible men among them must have known to be absolutely impracticable. Four years ago we were looking still further to the East, and we saw there a gigantic revolt in a great dependency of the British Crown, arising mainly from gross neglect, and from the incapacity of England, up to that moment, to govern a country which it had known how to conquer. Two years ago we looked south to the plains of Lombardy. We saw a strife there, in which every man in England took a strange interest (*hear, hear*); and we have welcomed, as the result of that strife, the addition of a new and great kingdom to the list of European States. (*Cheers.*) Well, now our eyes are turned in a contrary direction; we look to the west, and there we see a struggle in progress of the very highest interest to England and to humanity at large. We see there a nation, which I shall call the transatlantic English nation (*hear, hear*), the inheritor and partaker of the historic glories of this country. (*Hear.*) We see it torn with intestine broils, and suffering from calamities from which for more than a century past,—in fact, for nearly two centuries past, this country has been exempt. That struggle is of especial interest to us. We remember a description which one of our great poets gives of Rome in its condition of decay. He describes it as—

"Lone mother of dead empires."

But England is the living mother of great nations on the American and on the Australian continents, and she promises to belt the whole world with her knowledge, her civilisation, and even something more than the freedom that she herself enjoys. (*Cheers.*) Eighty-five years ago, about the time when some of our oldest townsmen were very little children, there were on the North American continent colonies, mainly of Englishmen, containing about 3,000,000 souls. These colonies we have seen a year ago constituting the United States of North America, and comprising a population of not less than 30,000,000 of souls. We know that in agriculture and manufacture, with the exception of this kingdom, there is no country in the world which as to these arts may be placed in advance of the United States. (*Applause.*) With regard to inventions, I believe, within the last 30 years, we have received more useful inventions from the United States than we have received from all the countries of Europe. (*Hear, hear.*) In that country there are probably ten times as many miles of telegraph as there are in this country, and there are at least five or six times as many miles of railways. The tonnage of its shipping is at least equal to ours, if it does not exceed ours. The prisons of that country—for even in countries the most favoured, so far, prisons are needful—have been models for the other nations of the earth; and many European Governments have sent commissions beyond the Atlantic to inquire into the admirable system of education established universally in their free schools throughout the Free and Northern States. (*Cheers.*) If I were to speak of them in a religious aspect, I should say that within that period of time to which their short history goes back there is nothing on the face of the earth, and never has been besides, to equal the magnificent arrangement of churches and ministers, and of all the appliances which are thought necessary for a nation to teach morality and Christianity to the people. Besides all this, when I state that for many years past the annual public expenditure of the Government of that country has been somewhere between ten and fifteen millions, I need not perhaps say further, that there has existed in that country, among all the people, an amount of comfort and prosperity, of abounding plenty, such as I believe no other country in the world, in any age, has displayed. This is a very fine, but still a very true, picture (*hear, hear*); but it has another side, to which I must advert. There has been one great feature in that country—one great contrast, which has been pointed to by all men who have commented upon the United States as a feature of danger and a contrast calculated to give pain. You have had in that country the utmost liberty to the white man, but bondage and degradation to the black man. Now, rely upon it that wherever Christianity lives and flourishes there must grow up from it necessarily a conscience which is hostile to any oppression and to any wrong; and therefore from the hour when the United States' Constitution was formed, so long as it left there this great evil, then comparatively small, but now become so great, it left there the seeds of that which an American statesman has so happily described of that "irrepressible conflict" of which now the whole world is witness. (*Cheers.*) It has been a common thing for men disposed to carp at the United States to point at this blot upon their fair fame, and to compare it with the boasted declaration of equality in their deed and Declaration of Independence. But we must recollect who sowed this seed of trouble and how and by whom it has been cherished. Without dwelling upon this for more than a moment, I should like to read to you a paragraph from "Instructions proposed to be given to the Virginian Delegates to Congress," in the month of August, 1774, and from the pen of Mr. Jefferson, perhaps the ablest man produced in the United States at that time, and actively engaged in its affairs, and who was afterwards, I think, for two periods President of the Republic. He writes this from a Slave State—from the State of Virginia:—

For the most trifling reasons, and sometimes for no conceivable reason at all, His Majesty the King of England has rejected laws of the most salutary tendency. The abolition of domestic slavery is the great object of desire in those colonies, where it was unhappily introduced in their infant State. But, previous to the enfranchisement of the slaves we have, it is necessary to exclude all further importations from Africa. Yet our repeated attempts to effect this, by prohibitions and by imposing duties which might amount to prohibition, have been hitherto defeated by His Majesty's negative, thus preferring the immediate advantage of a few British corsairs to the lasting interests of the American States, and to the rights of human nature deeply wounded by this infamous practice.

(*Loud cheers.*) I read that merely to show that two years before the Declaration of Independence was signed Mr. Jefferson, acting on behalf of those whom he represented in Virginia, wrote that protest against the course of the British Government which prevented the colonists abolishing the slave trade, preparatory to the abolition of slavery itself. The United States' Constitution left the slave question for every State to manage for itself. It was a question then too difficult to settle, apparently; but every man had the hope and belief that in a few years slavery would of itself become extinct. Then there happened that great event in the annals of manufactures and commerce; it was discovered that in those States that article which we in this country so much depend upon could be produced of the best quality needful for manufacturing, and at a moderate price; and from that day to this growth of cotton has increased there, its consumption has increased here, and a value which no man dreamt of when Jefferson wrote that paper has been given to slaves and slave industry, and thus it has grown up to that gigantic institution which now threatens either its own overthrow or the overthrow of that which is a million times more valued—the great republic of the United States. (*Loud cheers.*) The crisis at which we have arrived now—I say "we," for, after all, we are as much interested in the crisis nearly as if I were making this speech in the city of Boston or New York—the crisis which has now arrived was inevitable. I say that the conscience of the North, never satisfied with the institution, was constantly pricking some man forward to take a more extreme view of the question, and there grew up naturally a section—it may be not a very numerous one—in favour of abolition. And a great and powerful party resolved at least upon the restraint and control of slavery, so that it should not extend beyond the States and the area which it now occupies. But now, if we look at the Government of the United States, almost ever since the Union, we shall find that the Southern power has been mostly dominant there. If you take six-and-thirty years after the formation of the present constitution, I think about 1787, you will find that for 32 of those years every President was a Southern man; and if you take the period from 1828 until 1860 you will find that on every election for President the South voted in the majority. Well, we know what an election is in the United States for President of the Republic. There is a most extended suffrage, and there is a ballot-box. The President and the House of Representatives are elected by the same electors, and generally they are elected at the same time; and it follows, therefore, almost inevitably, that the House of Representatives is in complete accord in public policy with the President for the time being. Every four years there springs from the vote created by the whole people a President over that great nation. I think the world affords no finer spectacle than this; I think it affords no higher dignity,—that there is no greater object of ambition on the political stage on which men are permitted to move. You may point, if you like, to hereditary Royalty, to crowns coming down through successive generations in the same families, to thrones based on prescription or on conquest, to sceptres wielded over veteran legion, or subject realms, but to my mind there is nothing more worthy of reverence or obedience, nothing more sacred, than the authority of the freely chosen magistrate of a great and free people. (*Loud cheers.*) And, if there be on earth and among men any right divine to govern, surely it rests with a ruler so chosen and so appointed. (*Cheers.*) This process of a great election was gone through a year ago, and the South, that had so long been successful, found itself defeated. That defeat was followed instantly by secession, insurrection, and war. In the multitude of articles which have been brought before us in the newspapers within the last few months I have no doubt you have seen, as I have seen it stated, that this question was very much like that upon which the colonies originally revolted against the Crown of England. It is amazing either how little many newspaper writers know, or how little they think that you know. (*Laughter.*) When the War of Independence commenced in America, 90 years ago or more, there was no representation there at all. The question was whether a Ministry in Downing Street, and a corrupt and boroughmongering Parliament at Westminster, should impose taxes upon three millions of English subjects who had left their native country and established themselves in North America. But now the question is not of under-representation or of no representation, because, as is perfectly notorious, the representation of the South is not only complete, but in excess, for in distributing the number of representatives to the number of people—which is done every 10 years in the United States—three out of every five slaves are counted for the South as if they were white men and free men, and the number of members given to them is so much greater than it would be if the really free men and white men only were counted, and it has followed from that that the South has had in the House of Representatives about 20 members more than it had any right to, upon the principle upon which members were apportioned to the Northern and the Free States. Therefore you will see at once that there is no kind of comparison between the state of things when the colonies revolted and the state of things now, when this fearful and wicked insurrection has broken out. But there is another cause which is sometimes in England assigned for this great misfortune, which is the protective theories in operation in the Union, and the maintenance of a high tariff. It happens in regard to this that no American, certainly no one I ever met with, attributes the disaster of the Union to that cause. It is an argument made use of by ignorant Englishmen, but never by informed Americans. Have not I already shown you that the South, during almost the whole existence of the Union, has been dominant at Washington, and during that period the tariff has existed? There has been dissatisfaction occasionally with it, there can be no doubt; and at times the tariff has been higher than was thought just or reasonable, or necessary, by some of the States of the South. But the very first Act of the United States which levies duties on imports, passed immediately after the Union was formed, recites that "It is necessary for the encouragement and protection of manufactures to levy the duties which follow;" and during the war with England, from 1812 to 1815, the people of the United States had to pay for all the articles they brought from Europe many times over the natural cost of those articles, on account of the interruption of the traffic by the English navy, and when the war was over it was felt by everybody desirable that they should encourage manufactures in their own country; and seeing that England was at that precise moment passing a law to prevent any wheat coming from America until wheat in England had risen to the price of 84s. per quarter, we may feel quite satisfied that the doctrines of protection originally entertained did not find less favour at the close of the war in 1815. Now, there is one remarkable point with regard to this matter which should not be forgotten. Twelve months ago, at the meeting of the Congress of the United States, which takes place on the first Monday in December, there were various proposals of compromise, and committee meetings of various kinds held, to try and devise some mode of settling the question between the North and South, so that the disunion might not go on; but, though I read carefully everything that was published in the English newspapers from the United States on that subject, I do not recollect that in any single instance the question of the tariff was referred to, or that any change was proposed or suggested in that matter as likely to have any effect whatever upon the question of secession. (Hear.) Now, there is another point, too,—that whatever be the influence of tariffs upon the United States, it is as pernicious to the West as to the South; and further, Louisiana, which is a Southern State and a seceded State, has always voted along with Pennsylvania, until last year, in favour of protection for its sugar; while Pennsylvania wished protection for its coal and iron. But if the tariff was onerous and grievous, was that a reason for this great insurrection? Has ever a country had a tariff—especially in the article of food—more onerous and more cruel than that which we had in this country twenty years ago? (Cheers.) We did not secede. We did not rebel. What we did was to raise money for the purpose of distributing over all the country perfect information upon that question; and many men, as you know, devoted all their labours for several years to teach the great and wise doctrines of free trade to the people of England. Why, the price of a single gunboat, the keep of a single regiment, the garrison of a single fort, the cessation of their trade for a single day, costs more than it would have cost them to spread all over the intelligent people of the United States the most complete statement of the whole question; and West and South, having no interest in protection, could, united, have easily revised, or, if need had been, could have repealed the tariff altogether. No, the question is a very different and far more grave question. It is the question of slavery. (*Hear, hear.*) For 30 years it has been constantly coming to the surface, disturbing social life, and overthrowing almost all political harmony in the working of the United States. In the North there is no secession, there is no collision. These disturbances and this insurrection are found wholly in the South and in the slave States, and therefore I think the man who says otherwise, and who contends that it is the tariff or anything whatsoever other than slavery, is either himself deceived or he endeavours to deceive others. The object of the South is this—to escape from the majority which wishes to limit the area of slavery. (*Hear.*) They wish to found a slave State freed from the influences and the opinion of freedom. The free States in the North, then, now stand before the world the advocates and defenders of freedom and civilisation. The slave States of the South offer themselves for the recognition of Christian nations based upon the foundation, the unchangeable foundation in their eyes, of slavery and barbarism. (*Hear, hear.*) I will not discuss the guilt of men who, Ministers of a great nation, only last year conspired to overthrow it. I will not point out or recapitulate the statements of the fraudulent manner in which they disposed of the funds in the national exchequer. I will not point out by name any of the men in this conspiracy, whom history will designate by titles that they would not like to hear. But I say that slavery has sought to break up the most free government in the world, and to found a new State in this nineteenth century, whose corner stone is the perpetual bondage of millions of men. (*Hear, hear.*) Having thus described what appears to me briefly the truth of this matter, what is the course that England would be expected to pursue? We should be neutral so far as regards mingling in the strife. We were neutral in the strife in Italy, but we were not neutral in opinion or in sympathy. (*Hear, hear.*) You know perfectly well that throughout the whole of Italy, at this moment, there is a feeling that, though no shot was fired from an English ship, though no English soldier trod their soil, still the opinion of England was potent in Europe, and did much for the creation of the Italian kingdom. (*Hear.*) Well, with regard to the United States, you know how much we hate slavery—that is, awhile ago you thought you knew that we had given 20,000,000*l.*, that is 1,000,000*l.* a year nearly in taxes, to free

800,000 slaves in the English colonies. You knew, or you thought you knew, how much you were in love with free government everywhere, although it might not take precisely the form of our government—free government in Italy, free government in Switzerland, free government, under republican forms, in the United States of America, and with all this every man would have said that England would wish the American Union to be prosperous and eternal. Now, suppose we turn our eyes to the East, to the empire of Russia, for a moment. In Russia, as you know, there has been one of the most important and magnificent changes of policy ever seen in any country within the last year or two. The present Emperor of Russia, following the wishes of his father, has insisted upon the abolition of serfdom in that empire (*hear, hear*), and 23,000,000 human beings, lately serfs, little better than real slaves, have been put in a path of elevation to the ranks of freedom. (*Cheers.*) Now, suppose that the millions of serfs of Russia had been chiefly in the south of Russia. We hear that the nobles of Russia, to whom these serfs belong in a great measure, have been very hostile to this change, and that there has even been some danger that the peace of that empire might be disturbed during this change. Suppose these nobles, for the purpose of maintaining in perpetuity the serfdom of Russia, and barring out 23 millions of your fellow-creatures from the rights of freedom, had established a great and secret conspiracy, and had risen in a great and dangerous insurrection against the Russian Government, I say that the people of England, although but seven years ago they were in mortal combat with Russia, in the south of Europe, I believe that at this moment they would have prayed Heaven in all sincerity and fervour to give strength to the arm and success to the great wishes of the Emperor, and that that vile and pernicious insurrection might be suppressed. (*Great cheering.*) Now, let us look a little at what has been said and done in this country since the period when Parliament rose in the beginning of August. There have been two speeches to which I wish to refer, and in terms of approbation. The Duke of Argyll, a member of the present Government—and though I have not the smallest personal acquaintance with him, I am free to say that I believe him to be one of the most intelligent and liberal of his order (*hear, hear*)—the Duke of Argyll delivered a speech which was fair and friendly to the Government of the United States. Lord Stanley (*hear, hear*) only a fortnight ago made a speech which it is impossible to read without remarking the thought, the liberality, and the wisdom by which it is distinguished. He doubted, it is true, whether the Union could be restored—but a man need not be hostile, and must not necessarily be friendly, to doubt that or the contrary—but he spoke with fairness and friendliness of the Government of the United States, and he said they were right and justifiable in the course they took (*hear*); and he gave a piece of advice, now more important than it was even at the moment when he gave it, that in the various incidents and accidents of a struggle of this nature, it became a people like this to be very moderate and very calm, and to avoid getting into that feeling of irritation which sometimes arises, and sometimes leads to danger. (*Hear, hear.*) I mention these two speeches as from noblemen of great distinction in this country—speeches which I believe would have a beneficial effect on the other side of the Atlantic. Lord John Russell, in the House of Commons during the last Session, made a speech, too, in which he re-buked the impertinence of a young member of the House who spoke about the "bursting of the bubble Republic." (*"Hear, hear," and cheers.*) It was a speech worthy of the best days of Lord John Russell. (*Cheers.*) But at a later period he spoke at Newcastle, on an occasion something like this, when the inhabitants, or some portion of the inhabitants of that town, invited him to a public dinner. He described the contest in words something like these (I speak only from memory),—"That the North is contending for empire, and the South for independence." Did he mean that the North was contending for empire, as England, when making some fresh conquest in India? If he meant that, what he said was not true. But I recollect Lord John Russell, in the House of Commons some years ago, on an occasion when I had made some observations as to the unrea-sonable expenditure of the colonies, and complained that the people of England should be taxed to defray the expenses which the colonies them-selves should be well able to bear, turned to me with a sharpness which was not necessary, and said, "The hon. Member has no objection to make a great empire into a small one, but I have." (*Loud cheers and laughter.*) Perhaps if he lived in the United States, if he were a member of the Sen-ate or House of Representatives there, he would doubt whether it was his duty to consent at once to the destruction of a great country; to its separa-tion, it may be, into two hostile camps; or whether he would not try all means open to him, and open to the Government, to avert so un-looked-for and so dire a calamity. There are other speeches that have been made. I will not refer to them by any quotation. I will not out of pity to some of the men who have uttered them (*laughter and cheers*); I will not bring their names even before you, to give to them an endurance which I hope they will not have (*hear, hear*); but I will leave them in the obscurity which they so richly merit. (*Cheers.*) But now you know as well as I do that of all the speeches made since the end of the Session of Parliament by public men and politicians, the majority of them displayed either strange ignorance of American affairs, or a strange absence of that cordiality and friendship which, I maintain, our American kinsmen had a right to look for at our hands. (*Hear, hear.*) And if we part from the speakers and turn to the writers, what do we find there? We find that which is reputed abroad, and has hitherto been reputed at home as the most powerful representative of English opinion—at least of the richer classes—we find that in that particular newspaper there has not been, since Mr. Lincoln took office in March last as President of the United States, one fair, and honourable, and friendly article on American affairs. (*Hear, hear.*) Some of you, I dare say, read it, but fortunately now every district is so admirably supplied with local newspapers, that I trust in all time to come the people of England will drink of "purer streams nearer home" (*cheers and laughter*), and not from those streams which are muddied by party feeling and political intrigues, and by many motives that tend to anything rather than the enlightenment and advantage of the people. Now, it has been said, and by that very paper, over and over again, "Why this war? Why not separate peaceably? Why this fratricidal strife?" I hope they will all be against "fratricidal strife" in other respects, for, if it is true that God has made of one blood all the families of man to dwell on the face of all the earth, it must be a fratricidal strife, whether we are slaughtering Russians in the Crimea or bombarding the towns on the seacoast of the United States. (*Cheers.*) Now, no none will expect that I should stand forward as the advocate of war, or the defender of that great sum of all crime which is involved in war; but when you are discussing a question of this nature it is only fair you should discuss it upon principles which are acknowledged not only in the country where the strife is being carried on, but all but universally acknowledged in this country. When I discussed the question of the Russian war seven or eight years ago I always discussed it on the principles which were avowed by the Government and the people of England, and I took my facts from the blue books which were presented to Parliament. I take the liberty of doing that now in this case. I say that, looking at the principles avowed in England, and at all its policy, there is no man that is not absolutely a non-resistant in every sense who can fairly challenge the conduct of the American Government in this war. It is a curious thing to find that the party in this country which on every public question is in favour of war at any cost, when it comes to speak of the duty of the Government of the United States, is in favour of "peace at any price." (*Hear, hear.*) I want to know whether it has ever been admitted by politicians and statesmen or by any people that great nations can be broken up at any time by the will of any particular section of those nations? It has been tried occasionally in Ireland (*laughter*), and, if it had succeeded, history would have said, with very good cause. (*Hear, hear.*) But if anybody tries now to get up a secession or insurrection in Ireland— which would be infinitely less disturbing to everything than secession in the United States, because there is a boundary which nobody can dispute —I am quite sure *The Times* newspaper would have special correspondents, and would describe with all the glowing exultation in the world the manner in which the Irish insurrectionists were cut down and made an end of. Let any man try in England to restore the Heptarchy. Do you think that any politician in this country would think it a thing to be tolerated for a moment? But if you will look at the map of the United States, you will see that there is no country in the world, probably, at this moment, where any plan of separation between North and South, as far as the question of boundary is concerned, is so surrounded with insurmountable difficulties. For example,—Maryland is a slave State, but Maryland has by a very large majority voted for the Union. Would Maryland go South or North? Kentucky is a slave State, and one of the finest in the Union, containing a fine people. Kentucky has voted for the Union, but has been invaded from the South. Missouri is a slave State; Missouri has not seceded, but has been invaded from the South, and there is a Secession party in that State. There are parts of Virginia which have formed themselves into a new State, resolving to adhere to the North, and there is no doubt a considerable Northern and Union feeling in the State of Tennessee; and I have no doubt that there is in every other State. Indeed, I am not sure that there is not now within the sound of my voice a citizen of the United States (*hear*), a citizen of the State of Alabama, who can tell you that there the question of secession has never been put to the vote, and that there are great numbers of most reasonable, thoughtful, and just men in the State who entirely deplore the condition of things there existing. Well, then, what would you do with all these States, and with what may be called the loyal portion of the population of these states? Would you allow them to be dragooned into this insurrection, and into becoming parts of a new State, to which they themselves are hostile? But what would you do with the city of Washington? Washington is in a slave State. Would anybody have advised President Lincoln and his Cabinet, and all the members of Congress (House of Representatives and Senate) from the North, with their wives and children, and everybody else who was not positively in favour of the South, to set off on their melancholy pilgrimage northwards, leaving that capital—hallowed to them by such associations, having its name even from the father of their country—leaving Washington to the South, because Washington is situated in a slave State? Again, what do you say to the Mississippi river, as you see it upon the map, the "father of waters" rolling that gigantic stream to the ocean? Do you think that the 50 millions which one day will occupy the banks of that river northward, will ever consent that that great stream should roll through a foreign and, it may be, a hostile State? And more, there are four millions of negroes in subjection. For them the American Union is directly responsible. They are not Secessionists; they are now, as they always were, not citizens nor subjects, but legally under the care and power of the Government of the United States. Would you consent that these should be delivered up to the tender mercies of their taskmasters, the defenders of slavery as an everlasting institution? (*Cheers.*) Well, if all had been surrendered without a struggle, what then? What would the writers in this newspaper and other newspapers have said? If a bare rock in your empire, that would not keep a goat, a single goat, alive, be touched by any foreign Power, why, the whole empire is roused to resistance. And if there be, from accident or from passion, the smallest insult to your flag, what do your newspaper writers say upon that subject, and what is said in all your towns and upon all your exchanges? I will tell you what they would have said if the Government of the United States and the North had taken their insidious and dishonest advice. They would have said the great Republic is a failure, and Democracy has murdered patriotism, that history affords no example of such meanness, and of such cowardice, and they would have heaped unmeasured obloquy and contempt upon the people and Government who had taken that course. (*Loud cheering.*) Well, they tell you, these candid friends of the United States, they tell you that all freedom is gone; that the Habeas Corpus Act, if they ever had one, is known no longer; and that any man may be arrested at the *dictum* of the President or of the Secretary of State. Well, but in 1848, you recollect, many of you, that there was a small insurrection in Ireland. It was an absurd thing altogether; but what was done then? I saw, in one night, in the House of Commons, a Bill for the suspension of the Habeas Corpus Act passed through all its stages. What more did I see? I saw a Bill brought in by the Whig Government of that day, Lord John Russell being the Premier, which made speaking against the Government and against the Crown, which up to that time had been sedition, which proposed to make it felony, and it was only by the greatest exertions of a few of the members that that act, in that particular, was limited to a period of two years. In the same Session a Bill was brought in called an Alien Bill, which enabled the Home Secretary to take any foreigner whatsoever, not being a naturalized Englishman, and in 24 hours to send him out of the country. Although a man might have committed no crime, this might be done to him, apparently only on suspicion. But suppose that an insurgent army had been so near to London that you could see its outposts from every suburb of London—what then do you think would have been the regard of the Government of Great Britain for personal liberty, if it interfered with the necessity, and as they might think with the salvation of the State? I recollect in 1848, when the Habeas Corpus Act was suspended, that a number of persons in Liverpool, men there of position and of wealth, presented a petition to the House of Commons, praying—what? That the Habeas Corpus Act should not be suspended? No, but because they were not content with its suspension in Ireland, praying the House of Commons to extend that suspension to Liverpool. (*Laughter.*) I recollect that at that time—and I am sure my friend Mr. Wilson will bear me out in what I say—the Mayor of Liverpool telegraphed to the Mayor of Manchester, and messages were sent on to London nearly every hour, and the Mayor of Manchester heard from the Mayor of Liverpool that certain Irishmen in Liverpool, conspirators, or fellow-conspirators, with those in Ireland, were going to burn the cotton warehouses of Liverpool and the cotton mills of Lancashire. (*Laughter.*) And I read that petition, I took it from the table of the House of Commons and read it, and I handed it over to a statesman of great eminence, who has been but just removed from us—a man not second to any in the House of Commons for his knowledge of affairs and for his great capacity—I refer to Sir James Graham (*hear, hear*)—I handed to him this petition. He read it; and after he had read it, he rose from his seat, and laid it upon the table with a gesture of abhorrence and disgust. (*Loud cheers.*) Now, that was a petition from the town of Liverpool, in which some persons have lately been making themselves very ridiculous by their conduct in this matter. (*Hear, hear.*) There is one more point. It has been said, "How much better it would be"—not for the United States, but "for us that these States should be divided." I recollect meeting a gentleman in Bond street one day before the Session was over— a rich man, and one whose voice is very much heard in the House of Commons; but his voice is not heard there when he is on his legs, but when he is cheering other speakers (*laughter*); and he said to me, "After all, this is a sad business about the United States; but still I think it is very much better that they should be split up. In 20 years" (or in 50 years, I forget which it was) "they will be so powerful that they will bully all Europe." (*Laughter.*) And a distinguished member of the House of Commons—distinguished there by his eloquence, distinguished more by his many writings—I mean Sir Edward Bulwer Lytton—he did not exactly express a hope, but he ventured on something like a prediction, that the time would come when there would be, I don't know how many but as many Republics or States in America as you can count upon your fingers. There cannot be a meaner motive than this that I am speaking of, in forming a judgment on this question—that it is "better for us;" for whom? the people of England, or the Government of England?—that the United States should be severed, and that the continent should be as the continent of Europe is, in many States, and subject to all the contentions and disasters which have accompanied the history of the States of Europe. (*Applause.*) I should say that if a man had a great heart within him he would rather look forward to the day when, from that point of land which is habitable nearest to the Pole to the shores of the Great Gulf, the whole of that vast continent might become one great federation of States—that without a great army and without a great navy, not mixing itself up with the entanglements of European politics—without a Custom-house inside through the whole length and breadth of its territory, but with freedom everywhere, equality everywhere, law everywhere, peace everywhere—would afford at last some hope that man is not forsaken of Heaven, and that the future of our race might be better than the past. (*Prolonged cheering.*) It is a common observation that our friends in America are very irritable. Well, I think it is very likely, of a considerable number of them, to be quite true. Our friends in America are involved in a great struggle. There is nothing like it before in their history. No country in the world was ever more entitled, in my opinion, to the sympathy and the forbearance of all friendly nations than are the United States at this moment. (*Hear, hear.*) They have there newspapers that are no wiser than ours. (*Laughter.*) They have there some papers, one at least, which up to the election of Mr. Lincoln, were his bitterest and unrelenting foes, but when the war broke out, and it was not safe to take the line of Southern support, were obliged to turn round and to support the prevalent opinion of the country. But they undertook to serve the South in another way, and that was by exaggerating every difficulty and mis-stating every fact, if so doing could serve their object of creating distrust between the people of the Northern States and the people of this United Kingdom. (*Hear, hear.*) If *The Times* in this country has done all that it could to poison the minds of the people of England, and to irritate the minds of the people of America, the *New York Herald,* I am sorry to say, has done, I think, all that it could, or that it dared, to provoke mischief between the Government in Washington and the Government in London. (*Hear, hear.*) Now there is one thing which I must state, that I think they have a solid reason to complain of; and I am very sorry to have to mention it, because it blames our present Foreign Minister, against whom I am not anxious to say a word, and, recollecting his speech in the House of Commons, I should be slow to conclude that he had any feeling hostile to the United States' Government. You recollect that during the Session—it was on the 14th of May—a proclamation came out which acknowledged the South as a belligerent Power, and proclaimed the neutrality of England. A little time before that—I forget how many days—Mr. Dallas, the late Minister from the United States, had left London for Liverpool and for America. He did not wish to undertake any affairs for this Government, by which he was not appointed—I mean that of President Lincoln—and he left what had to be done to his successor, who was on his way, and whose arrival was daily expected. Mr. Adams, the present Minister from the United States, is a man who, if he lived in England, you would say was of one of the noblest families of the country. I think his father and his grandfather were Presidents of the United States. His grandfather was one of the great men who achieved the independence of the United States. There is no family in that country having more claims upon what I should call the veneration and the affection of the people than the family of Mr. Adams. Mr. Adams came to this country. He arrived in London on the night of the 13th of May. On the 14th that proclamation was issued. It was known that he was coming; but he was not consulted; the proclamation was not delayed for a day, although nothing pressed that he might be notified about it. If communications of a friendly nature had taken place with him and with the American Government, they could have found no fault with this step, because it was almost inevitable, before the struggle had proceeded far, that this proclamation would be issued. But I have the best reasons for knowing that there is no single thing that has happened during the course of these events which has created more surprise, more irritation, and more distrust in the United States with respect to this country than the fact that that proclamation did not wait one single day, until the Minister from America could come here, and until it could be done with his consent or concurrence, and in that friendly manner that would have avoided all the unpleasantness which has occurred. (*Hear, hear.*) Now, I am obliged to say—and I say it with the utmost pain—that without this country doing things that were hostile to the North, and without men expressing affection for slavery, and, outwardly and openly hatred for the Union—I say that there has not been here that friendly and cordial neutrality which, if I had been a citizen of the United States, I should have expected; and I say further, that if there has existed considerable irritation at that, it must be taken as a measure of the high appreciation which the people of those States place upon the opinion of the people of England. (*Hear, hear.*) If I had been addressing this audience ten days ago, so far as I know, I should have said just what I have said now; and, although by an untoward event circumstances are somewhat, even considerably altered, yet I have thought it desirable to make this statement, with a view, so far as I am able to do it, to improve the opinion in England, and to assuage, if there be any, the feelings of irritation in America, so that no further difficulties may arise in the progress of this unhappy strife. (*Hear, hear.*) But there has occurred an event which was announced to us only a week ago, which is one of great importance, and it may be one of some peril. (*Hear, hear.*) It is asserted that what is called "International Law" has been broken by the seizure of the Southern Commissioners on board an English trading steamer by a steamer of war of the United States. Now, what is maritime law? You have heard that the opinions of the law officers of the Crown are in favour of this view of the case—that the law has been broken. I am not at all going to say that it has not. It would be imprudent in me to set my opinion on a legal question which I have only partially examined against their opinion on the same question, which I presume they have carefully examined. But this I say, that maritime law is not to be found in an Act of Parliament; it is not in so many clauses. You know that it is difficult to find the law. I can ask the mayor, or any magistrate around me, whether it is not very difficult to find the law, even when you have found the Act of Parliament and found the clause. (*Laughter.*) But when you have no Act of Parliament and no clause you may imagine that the case is still more difficult. (*Hear, hear.*) Maritime law, or international law, consists of opinions and precedents for the most part, and it is very unsettled. The opinions are the opinions of men of different countries, given at different times, and the precedents are not always like each other. The law is very unsettled, and, for the most part, I believe it to be exceedingly bad. In past times, as you know from the histories you read, this country has been a fighting country; we have been belligerents, and, as belligerents, we have carried maritime law, by our own powerful hand, to a pitch that has been very oppressive to foreign, and peculiarly to neutral, nations. Now, almost for the first time, unhappily, in our history for the last 200 years, we are not belligerents, but neutrals; and we are disposed to take, perhaps, rather a different view of maritime and international law. The act which has been committed by the American steamer, in my opinion, whether it was illegal or not, was both impolitic and bad. That is my opinion. I think it may turn out, and is almost certain, that, so far as the taking those men from that ship was concerned, it was wholly unknown to and unauthorized by the American Government. And if the American Government believe, on the opinion of their law officers, that the act is illegal, I have no doubt they will make fitting reparation; for there is no Government in the world that has so strenuously insisted upon modifications of international law, and been so anxious to be guided always by the most moderate and merciful interpretation of that law. Our great advisers of *The Times* newspaper have been persuading people that this is merely one of a series of acts which denote the determination of the Washington Government to pick a quarrel with the people of England. But did you ever know anybody, who was not very near dead drunk, who, having as much upon his hands as he could manage, would offer to fight everybody about him? (*Prolonged laughter and cheering.*) Do you believe that the United States Government, presided over by President Lincoln, so constitutional in all his acts, so moderate as he has been, representing, at this moment, that great party in the United States, happily now in the ascendancy, which has always been specially in favour of peace, and specially in favour of England—do you believe that that Government, having upon its hands now an insurrection of the most formidable character in the South, would invite the armies and the fleets of England to combine with that insurrection, and it might be—though it did exasperate the struggle—render it impossible that the Union should ever again be restored? (*Loud cheers.*) I say that single statement, whether it came from a public writer or a public speaker, is enough to stamp him for ever with the character of being an insidious enemy of both countries. (*Cheers.*) Well, what have we seen during the last week? People have not been, I am told—I have not seen much of it—quite so calm as sensible men should be. Here is a question of law. I will undertake to say that when you have from the United States Government—if they think the act legal—a statement of their view of the case, they will show you that 50 or 60 years ago, during the wars of that time, there were scores of cases that were at least as bad as this, and some infinitely worse. And, if it were not so late to-night, and I am not anxious now to go into this question further, I could easily place before you cases of wonderful outrage, committed by us when we were at war, and for many of which, I am afraid, little or no reparation was offered. But let us bear this in mind, that during this struggle "incidents and accidents" will happen. Bear in mind the advice of Lord Stanley, so opportune and so judicious. Don't let your newspapers or your public speakers, or any man, take you off your guard, and bring you into that frame of mind under which your Government, if it desires war, can have it with the public assent, or, if it does not desire war, may be driven to engage in it; for one may be as evil and as fatal as the other. What can be now more monstrous than that we, as we call ourselves, to some extent, an educated, a moral, and a Christian nation—at a moment when an accident of this kind occurs, before we have made a representation to the American Government, before we have heard a word from them in reply—should be all up in arms, every sword leaping from its scabbard, and every man looking about for his pistols and his blunderbusses? (*Cheers.*) Why, I think the conduct pursued—and I have no doubt it is pursued by a certain class in America just the same—is much more the conduct of savages than of Christian and civilised men. No, let us be calm. (*Hear, hear.*) You recollect how we were dragged into the Russian war—"drifted" into it. (*Cheers.*) You know that I, at least, have not upon my head any of the guilt of that fearful war. (*Hear, hear.*) You know that it cost one hundred millions of money to this country; that it cost, at least, the lives of 40,000 Englishmen; that it disturbed your trade; that it nearly doubled the armies of Europe; that it placed the relations of Europe on a much less peaceful footing than before; and that it did not effect one single thing of all those that it was promised to effect. (*Cheers.*) I recollect speaking on this subject within the last two years to a man whose name I have already mentioned—Sir J. Graham—in the House of Commons. He was a Minister at the time of that war. He was reminding me of a severe onslaught which I had made upon him and Lord Palmerston for attending a dinner on the Reform Club, when Sir C. Napier was appointed to the command of the Baltic fleet, and he remarked, "What a severe thrashing"—(*laughter*)—I had given them in the House of Commons. I said, "Sir James, tell me candidly, did you not deserve it?" He said, "Well, you were entirely right about that war; we were entirely wrong, and we never should have gone into it." (*Loud cheers.*) And this is exactly what everybody will say, if you go into a war about this business, when it is over. When your sailors and your soldiers, so many of them as may be slaughtered, are gone to their last account; when your taxes are increased, your business permanently, it may be, injured; and when embittered feelings for generations have been created between America and England, then your statesmen will tell you that "we ought not to have gone into the war." (*Cheers.*) But they will very likely say, as many of them tell me, "What could we do in the frenzy of the public mind?" Let them not add to the frenzy (*hear, hear*), and let us be careful that nobody drives us into that frenzy. Remembering the past, remembering at this moment the perils of a friendly people, and seeing the difficulties by which they are surrounded, let us, I entreat of you, see if there be any real moderation in the people of England, and if magnanimity, so often to be found among individuals, is not absolutely wanting in a great nation. (*Great cheering.*) Government may discuss this matter—they may arrange it—they may arbitrate it. I have received here, since I came into the room, a despatch from a friend of mine in London referring to this question. I believe some portion of it is in the papers this evening, but I have not seen them. But he states that General Scott, whom you know by name, who has come over from America to France, being in a bad state of health, the General, lately, of the American army, and a man of a reputation in that country not second hardly to that which the Duke of Wellington held during his lifetime in this country, General Scott has written a letter on the American difficulty. He denies that the Cabinet of Washington had ordered the seizure of the Southern Commissioners, even if under a neutral flag. The question of legal right involved in the seizure the General thinks a very narrow ground on which to force a quarrel with the United States. As to Messrs Slidell and Mason being or not being contraband the General answers for it that, if Mr. Seward cannot convince Earl Russell that they bore that character, Earl Russell will be able to convince Mr. Seward that they did not. He pledges himself that if this Government cordially agree with that of the United States in establishing the immunity of neutrals from the oppressive right of search and seizure on suspicion the Cabinet of Washington will not hesitate to purchase so great a boon to peaceful trading vessels. (*Great cheering.*) Before I sit down, let me ask what is this people, about which so many men in England at this moment are writing, and speaking, and thinking, with harshness, with injustice, if not with great bitterness? Two centuries ago multitudes of the people of this country found a refuge on the North American continent, escaping from the tyranny of the Stuarts, and from the bigotry of Laud. Many noble spirits from our country endeavoured to establish great experiments in favour of human freedom on that continent. Bancroft, the greatest historian of his own country, has said, in his own graphic and emphatic language, "The history of the colonization of America is the history of the crimes of Europe." (*Hear, hear.*) From that time down to our own period, America has admitted the wanderers from every clime. Since 1815, a time which many here remember, and which is within my lifetime, more than three millions of persons have emigrated from the United Kingdom to the United States. During the 15 years from 1845 or 1846 to 1859 or 1860, a time so recent that we all remember the events, even the most trivial circumstances that have happened in that time—during those fifteen years more than 2,320,000 persons left the shores of the United Kingdom as emigrants for the States of North America. At this very moment, then, there are millions in the United States who personally, or whose immediate parents, have at one time been citizens of this country, and perhaps known to some of the oldest of those whom I am now addressing. They found a home in the far west; they subdued the wilderness; they met with plenty there, which was not afforded them in their native country; and they are become a great people. There may be those persons in England who are jealous of the States. There may be men who dislike democracy, and who hate a Republic; there may be even those whose sympathies warm towards the slave oligarchy of the South. But of this I am certain, that only misrepresentation the most gross, or calumny the most wicked, can sever the tie which unites the great mass of the people of this country with their friends and brethren beyond the Atlantic. (*Loud cheers.*) Whether the Union will be restored or not, or the South will achieve an unhonoured independence or not, I know not, and I predict not. But this I think I know—that in a few years, a very few years, the 20 millions of free men in the North will be 30 millions or even 50 millions—a population equal to or exceeding that of this kingdom. (*Hear, hear.*) When that time comes I pray that it may not be said among them that in the darkest hour of their country's trials England, the land of their fathers, looked on with icy coldness, and saw unmoved the perils and the calamities of her children. (*Cheers.*) As for me, I have but this to say,—I am one in this audience and but one in the citizenship of this country: but if all other tongues are silent, mine shall speak for that policy which gives hope to the bondsmen of the South, and tends to generous thoughts, and generous words, and generous deeds, between the two great nations that speak the English language, and from their origin are alike entitled to the English name. (*Great cheering.*)

Benjamin Disraeli

THE EARL OF BEACONSFIELD

Benjamin Disraeli, the Earl of Beaconsfield
[*Born* DECEMBER 21, 1804—*Died* APRIL 19, 1881]

He . . . always appeared calm, dignified, mysterious, solemn, only his dark flashing eyes giving life to his face, his talk being measured, grave, epigrammatic, and delivered in a deep equable tone.—HESKETH PEARSON

·**D**·

israeli," writes Hearnshaw, "as no Prime Minister before or since has ever done, excited the interest of the nation, quickened their imagination, fired their ambition, and inspired their affection." [1] Having entered British politics in 1832 as a "romantic dandy, flirting with radicalism," [2] Disraeli became one of the real leaders of the Tory Party in 1846, helping reshape it after its ranks were split by Sir Robert Peel's conversion to Corn Law Repeal. Viewed with Gladstone as a "creator" of the nineteenth century rather than a product of the eighteenth,[3] he was instrumental in the passage of the Parliamentary Reform Act of 1867 and the Treaty of Berlin in 1878.

Hearnshaw describes Disraeli's parliamentary speaking as outstanding. He had few equals in debate with his "quickness in seeing his opponent's point . . . [and] in effectiveness in parrying and turning it." [4] T. E. Kebbel believes that in his time Disraeli had no equal endowed with that special combination of humor and sarcasm "by which he originally gained the ear of the House of Commons, and which served him more effectively than the most impassioned declamation . . . ." [5] Hesketh Pearson declares that Disraeli was gifted with a "rich melodious voice" enhanced by careful modulation, and a "sphinx-like immobility of countenance." [6] Such a description perhaps explains why reporters in the gallery found his speeches easy to report,[7] and better to read than to hear.[8] The preponderance of Disraeli's speeches were delivered in the House of Commons before he was given an earldom in 1876, and are viewed by Kebbel to be the most interesting "because . . . the most original side of his mind is turned toward us." [9]

---

1 F. J. C. Hearnshaw (ed.), *Prime Ministers of the Nineteenth Century* (London: Macmillan and Co., 1936), p. 210.

2 Asa Briggs, *Victorian People* (Chicago: U. of Chicago Press, 1955), p. 265.

3 Joseph Hendershot Park, *British Prime Ministers of the Nineteenth Century* (New York: New York University Press, 1950), p. 191.

4 Hearnshaw, *op. cit.*, p. 227.

5 Earl of Beaconsfield, *Selected Speeches* with Intro. by T. E. Kebbel, I (London: Longmans, Green, and Co., 1882), p. xi.

6 Hesketh Pearson, *Dizzy* (New York: Harper and Brothers, 1951), p. 78.

7 Kebbel, *op. cit.*, p. xii.

8 Lord Rosebery, *Lord Randolph Churchill* (London: Harper and Brothers, 1906), p. 110.

9 Kebbel, *op. cit.*

Three speeches characterize Disraeli's political stature; two were delivered while he was a member of the House of Commons, and the third as a member of the House of Lords. The first is Disraeli's Speech on the Address in the House of Commons on January 22, 1846.[10] Justin McCarthy calls this speech the first really successful one he delivered in the House of Commons,[11] and Sir Edward Clarke calls it one which "deserves and rewards careful study . . . [as] perhaps the finest example of the skill of a great master of debate," [12] and which caused a "reeling and staggering" conservative party to rally behind Disraeli as the real inspiration and guide of the party.[13]

Sir Robert Peel had devoted two hours to a very detailed speech filled with statistics and quotations used to explain his conversion to Corn Law Repeal. McCarthy calls it an *"apologia pro vita sua*—an account of the speaker's own conversion." [14] Disraeli then aroused the House from a condition of "puzzled exhaustion" to "excitement and enthusiasm." [15] As a consequence, with his "unrivalled skill in sarcasm and invective," he further weakened Peel's prestige while enhancing his own.[16]

The second speech dealt with the Reform Bill of 1867. Although Clarke believes Disraeli's address, closing debate on the Second Reading in the House of Commons on March 26, 1867, is one of the finest speeches he ever delivered,[17] his address at Edinburgh on October 29 is included in this volume as a clearer explanation of Disraeli's position. He went to Edinburgh disabled by illness, according to Clarke, but reacted to the occasion with courage:

'Luckily, my attack is as regular as the trade winds and occurs at a time when it little signifies, and can be kept secret. Unfortunately, this year I have something to do—the Edinburgh banquet. How I am to get there I know not, but I feel I shall. I think of troops that have marched thirty miles, and then, on empty stomachs too, have to fight. They do fight, and often conquer.' [He went to Edinburgh, and did unquestionably conquer.] [18]

---

10 See, *Selected Speeches,* I, pp. 98–110.
11 Justin McCarthy, *Sir Robert Peel* (New York: Harper and Brothers, 1891), p. 154.
12 Sir Edward Clarke, *Benjamin Disraeli* (New York: The Macmillan Co., 1926), p. 92.
13 McCarthy, *op. cit.*
14 *Ibid.,* p. 153.
15 Clarke, *op. cit.*
16 *Ibid.,* p. 77.
17 *Ibid.,* p. 164. This speech may be found in 186 H.C. Deb. 3 S., Cols. 642–663.
18 *Ibid.,* p. 165.

Asa Briggs calls passage of the Reform Bill the "great landmark in the making of modern democracy," and a "dazzling personal triumph" for Disraeli.[19]

The third speech by Disraeli was delivered to the House of Lords on July 18, 1878,[20] announcing the Berlin Treaty which Clarke describes as "the most important political action of his career." [21] Almost single-handedly Disraeli dominated the diplomats at the Congress of Berlin, including the great Bismarck. By urging settlement of a boundary dispute between Bulgaria and Turkey, he precluded the possibility of war between Great Britain and Russia. Upon returning from Berlin on July 16, he proclaimed "Peace with Honour." Two days later, he delivered a two and one-half hour speech urging acceptance of the terms of the Treaty, and it was approved without division. Disraeli had reached the pinnacle of a long political career. Soon his ministry was to be successfully challenged by Gladstone.

---

19 Briggs, *op. cit.*, p. 266.
20 See *Selected Speeches*, II, pp. 179–202.
21 Clarke, *op. cit.*, p. 265.

Reform Bill of 1867[1]

•

EDINBURGH   *October 29, 1867*

MR. Chairman, my Lords and Gentlemen:—I know nothing more gratifying in the life of a public man—nothing in its toils and in its asperities more satisfactory and soothing, than an expression of sympathy from a body of his countrymen—nor is that gratification diminished if the sympathy comes from those who are not connected with him by any local sentiment. However much we may value the kind feeling of our neighbours, we are conscious that their estimate of our conduct may not be free from partiality.

In thanking you, Mr. Chairman, for the too kind manner in which you have introduced my name to this assembly, I cannot for a moment forget—for you have yourself expressed it with frankness—that it is chiefly to be attributed to the passing of a memorable measure which has distinguished the present session of Parliament, and with which I have in some degree been connected. I had heard that her Majesty's Ministers had carried a measure for which they were entitled to no distinction, since they had only carried a measure for which for more than seventy years the Whig party had toiled in vain—since the period when, in the year 1793, Lord Grey had been defeated by the machinations of Mr. Pitt.

Now, my lords and gentlemen, I should not take an occasion like the present to treat of the pedigree of parties, though I think myself, and have ever thought, it a subject not to be despised, and full of very serious considerations and consequences—but when a statement like this is made, and upon it is founded a series of arguments which, if left untouched and unnoticed, appear to me to have the tendency of depreciating and misrepresenting the character and conduct of public men, I cannot allow it to pass for a moment utterly uncontradicted. It is important, because it is

---

1 Earl of Beaconsfield, *Selected Speeches*, II (London: Longmans, Green, and Co., 1882), pp. 470–489.

in another form a revival and repetition of the old party dogma, that upon the most important of political subjects—namely, the question how power should be distributed in the State—one of the great historical parties of England is to be forbidden ever to touch it. My lords and gentlemen, on principle—on abstract principle—I shall protest against such a dogma; but when it is introduced to us with historical illustrations, and recommended to our notice by an appeal to the annals of our country, and to the deeds of our statesmen, I cannot help pointing out to you and to the country the entire error of the statement. Why, the question of Parliamentary reform, if we are to go to the origin of that question since the constitution of this country was settled upon its present basis, was purely and entirely a Tory question. The question of Parliamentary reform was first introduced to public notice by the great statesman [sic] who flourished at the beginning of the eighteenth century. What their motives might have been—what were the merits of their measures—it is quite unnecessary for us now to consider or to touch upon, but the fact, and the historical fact remains. The great Tory leaders of that day, no doubt, were in a great minority in the House of Commons; and they believed, as has since been established as a fact, that they were in a great majority in the nation, and therefore they were anxious to alter the principles upon which the representation of the country should take place. Why, you had then motions for shorter Parliaments—motions for extending the suffrage far beyond the settlement of this year. You had motions brought forward even for secret voting, and that by men who, from their birth, their rank, their possessions, and their eloquence, are second to few of the great statesmen that ever flourished in this country. And when we are told that it was by the machinations of Mr. Pitt, who defeated Lord Grey in 1793, that the Whigs had been baffled in their perpetual efforts to carry household suffrage for seventy years—and now have been deprived of their rightful heritage by the manoeuvres of the Government of Lord Derby—allow me to say that the great leaders at the commencement of the eighteenth century who brought forward these measures for Parliamentary reform, and for a number of years with signal eloquence vindicated and recommended these measures, were defeated by a powerful and no doubt a very intelligent oligarchy, through whose paramount influence for a great number of years these opinions were in abeyance.

But reaction is the law of life. A time came when, at a period of public calamity, the country began to doubt whether it was wise to entrust to an oligarchy the most considerable portion of the power of the State, and began to believe that they ought to trust more to the power of the Sovereign and the independence of the nation; and when these opinions became prevalent shortly after the American war, and when the man, as always happens, appeared to advocate these opinions, who was that man?

Why, it was a youth who had formed his mind by studying the conduct of the great statesmen of the commencement of the century. It is upon record that he gave up his days and nights to the study of their eloquence. His principles of finance and commerce he found in that treaty of Utrecht which was baffled by faction, and which would have given us the advantages of that free trade, now so much vaunted, a century before or more. There, too, he found those principles of religious toleration which now have been adopted; and among other matters, Parliamentary reform; and he advocated it as the means by which alone he could control the oligarchy then predominant. And who was that youthful statesman? It was the son of Chatham—that very Mr. Pitt who we are now told by his machinations prevented Lord Grey, and has for seventy years prevented the Whig party, from conferring upon the English people the boon of household suffrage.

My lords and gentlemen, no doubt in 1832 Lord Grey was perfectly entitled to take the line which he did—Lord Grey fairly earned the leadership upon that question of Parliamentary Reform; but when Lord Grey made his Government he never pretended that in the policy which he recommended he was recommending a policy peculiar to the Whig party. On the contrary, he said from the first that it was impossible for him to form a Government except it was upon a broad basis. He appealed, and successfully appealed, to the followers of Mr. Canning—brilliant men, experienced in administration; but that was not enough, though it gave him experienced colleagues. He felt that he could not succeed in forming a Government without a considerable support from the Tory party, and he appealed to the Duke of Richmond, the father of one of my colleagues. Therefore I say that nothing can be more idle than this statement recently brought forward, that we have invaded a land upon which we had no right to enter—that they, our political opponents, had a vested interest in this question of the representation of the people; that for seventy years they have been toiling in order to confer the boon of household suffrage upon the people of England, and that we have come forward in a manner most unauthorised, at the last moment, and are claiming a reputation for a result to which we are not entitled. I readily admit that after the Reform Bill of 1832 was passed, Sir Robert Peel, by that important political paper, the Tamworth Manifesto, and by his speeches in the House of Commons, pledged the Tory party not to disturb that settlement. Whether it was a wise step on the part of Sir Robert Peel or not, no one will deny that that compact was religiously observed by the Conservative party. Every man who ever acted with them most scrupulously assisted Sir Robert Peel in carrying that compact into fulfilment; and I never heard it for a moment whispered that we ever departed from that public engagement. Well, but of course when the very minister who brought forward in the House of Commons the Bill of 1832—Lord Grey's Bill—announced only twenty years after it was passed, in the year 1852, himself then in the high capacity of Prime Minister of England, that that law was no longer adequate to the circumstances, and that he should himself introduce a measure which would supersede it,—the Tory party were immediately freed from the engagement into which they had entered, and it was for them to consider the course that they ought to pursue. I touch upon this point because it is a matter which now has, for a very long time, circulated with impunity, but with mischievous impunity, in the country. I want to show to you that our title was clear, even historically, to deal with the greatest and most important of political questions—namely, the distribution of power in the State. After Lord John Russell had announced that he had retreated from his doctrine of finality, and that he should take an opportunity of introducing a new Reform Bill, there was a meeting of the most considerable men at that time connected with the Tory party. Sir Robert Peel had then unfortunately quitted this scene; but there were such men as Lord Derby himself—others, some of whom are now in his cabinet—there were men who have left us like Sir Robert Peel—there was Lord George Bentinck, and others—men associated in the public mind with the maintenance of what are called high Tory opinions, many of them—they met, they considered the circumstances of the case, and arrived at a definite and determined conclusion, that under no circumstances whatever was the Tory party ever to be induced to oppose a new Reform Bill—that they would always assist its introduction, and then attempt to mould it into that form which they believed would be most advantageous to the country. To that resolution, passed nearly twenty years ago, they have invariably and religiously adhered; and I can only say for myself, that from the time I ever presumed at the request of my friends to take any lead in public affairs, I have never omitted any opportunity of claiming, whenever this question was brought forward, the right of the Tory party to deal with it.

Well, if the question is one which we had a right to deal with, the next question—and it is a much more important one—is this:—Having a right to deal with it, ought we to have dealt with it? Well, now it does appear to me that any man of sound mind—any man accustomed to consider political affairs—must have felt it was absolutely necessary for Lord Derby, in 1866, to deal with this question. Why, what are the facts of the case? They are these. For fifteen years—from 1852 till the end of 1866—the Government of the Queen, not merely the House of Commons, had been dealing with the question of Parliamentary Reform. It is a totally different thing for the Government of the Queen to deal with a question, and a mere Parliamentary party, who may endeavour to obtain the public confidence and public applause by supporting a particular line of policy.

A question may be a Parliamentary question, and it may be right that it should not be precipitated in its solution, and should be matured by frequent and continuous discussions—not merely of years, but if necessary in some questions of generations; but the moment the Queen's Government comes forward and says that a question ought to be settled, the country has a right to suppose that the wisest men have given their consideration to it, and that State necessity requires that some settlement should be arrived at. You might say that it was merely the Whig party who were of this opinion. But is that the case? Every Prime Minister during these fifteen years, and every party that has been in power during these fifteen years, had announced from the Throne that the question of Parliamentary reform, which is the question of distribution of power in the State, was one which demanded consideration and settlement. Lord John Russell had dealt with the question, and had failed. Lord Aberdeen had dealt with the question, and had failed. Lord Palmerston had dealt with the question, and had failed. Lord Derby had dealt with the question, and had failed; and afterwards Lord John Russell had dealt with the question again, and had failed. You talk about agitation in the country; but what a premium do you give for agitation when, year after year, the ministry of the Queen announce that the most important political question, the one that concerns the rights of every individual in the country, requires settlement; and year after year the attempt is made and no settlement arrived at! Why, what is the practical conclusion, under such circumstances at which every man would arrive? Why, the practical conclusion must be this, and everybody feels it, and everybody felt it, in England, that the Government of the country was not adequate to the occasion, that it could not meet the difficulty. Well, if the Government of the country is not adequate to that which the Government of the country says is necessary to be accomplished, why, what is that but a premium on revolution?

Now, I say that no man can form a fair and accurate opinion upon that momentous question unless he clearly ascertains, in the first place, what were the relations of Lord Derby and his party to this question of Parliamentary Reform. Lord Derby acceded to office as Prime Minister for the first time in 1852, Lord John Russell having then just failed on the question of Parliamentary Reform. It was not necessary for Lord Derby in 1852 to deal with the question; and everybody felt that, however wise it might be to consider it with regard to ultimate settlement, there was no pressure for immediate solution. The measure of Lord John Russell of 1852 was generally considered even by his friends—though I think there was much to vindicate his course, to which I may afterwards advert—an immature movement. We came into office in 1852. We had not been in office ten days before notice of motions on Parliamentary Reform—some complete and comprehensive schemes, some of an isolated character—

were showered upon the table like a snowstorm. Mr. Hume gave notice of a motion which he had annually made for three or four years, and the pressure of which motion had forced Lord John Russell to introduce a Bill—of making the same motion about a month after we acceded to office. The Government of Lord Derby had therefore to consider the course they would take, and the general policy they would announce. It fell to my lot in the year 1852, as leader of the House of Commons, to express the policy of Lord Derby on the subject. It is upon record. It is upon the authentic annals of what is done in the great assembly at Westminster. We were not prepared, we told the House of Commons, in answer to the motion of Mr. Hume and those made by Mr. Locke King and others—we said we were not prepared to deal with the question of Parliamentary Reform; but we claimed our right even then if we thought it necessary to deal with it. But we said, if it be necessary on any future occasion to deal with the representation of the people, it is our opinion that a very great mistake was made on that subject in the year 1832. It was the manner in which Parliament abolished the relations between the labouring classes and the constitution of this country; and I said then, on the part of Lord Derby, that if ever we felt it to be our duty to deal with the question, we should endeavour to remedy that great deficiency. There was another great feature of policy with regard to that question to which I also on that occasion in that year called the attention of the House of Commons. I said if there is ever to be another Reform Bill, we can consent to no new measure unless adequate justice is done to that majority of the population who live in the counties. Now, those were the two great points on the part of Lord Derby—the two great conditions which we publicly announced as a party we should insist upon if ever we had to deal with the question of Reform. Well, in 1852, after the retirement of Lord Derby, Lord Aberdeen introduced a very considerable measure of reform, and failed. Then came the Government of Lord Palmerston. The Government of Lord Palmerston was much employed with the Crimean war, and that was supposed to be an excuse, and was a fair excuse, for his not continuing to legislate on the subject of reform; but mark this important fact: when allusions are made to Lord Palmerston's feeling on the subject of reform, and after his successfully carrying to a conclusion the Crimean war, he appealed to the country in a most triumphant manner. What did he do? The moment that Parliament met he advised Her Majesty to recommend that legislation on the subject of Parliamentary Reform should be introduced. In the following year Lord Derby again found himself Prime Minister, when Lord Palmerston informed him that he considered it of the greatest importance that the question should be settled. The subject embarrassed the Crown, it embarrassed Parliament, it might be a source of disorder to the State, and if a temperate and well-considered measure were introduced he would give it a fair and candid consideration.

Lord Derby did make an effort in 1859. This is the next connection of Lord Derby and his party with the question of reform. He had to deal with that question. It was his opinion, after the most deliberate thought, and after the most painful investigation on the subject, that with regard to the borough franchise, any degradation of the borough franchise from 10 *l.* to 8 *l.,* or 7 *l.,* or 6 *l.,* or so on, would be utterly unsatisfactory, that it would lead to no settlement, and that you could arrive at no settlement unless you came to some household suffrage without the condition of rental value. He was not prepared to recommend that; he did not believe the country would have supported him in such a course, and therefore he endeavoured to carry out the policy which he recommended as to facilitating the admission of the working classes into the constitution by a variety of franchises. I shall not go into them, now. The lodger franchise was one of them; then treated, of course, with contempt, but now, I understand, without doubt the palladium of our liberties. Well, now, these are the relations of Lord Derby to Reform. He had from the beginning laid it down as his view of the case that no Bill which did not revive the relation of the working classes with the Constitution of the country, and at the same time did not do justice to the population in the counties that were so feebly represented, would be satisfactory. In 1859 you know what occurred. We were expelled from power by a resolution of Lord John Russell that no settlement of the question of Parliamentary Reform would be satisfactory which did not involve the lowering of the borough franchise. We resisted that. We believed that it was a policy which ought not to be sanctioned by the House of Commons unless it was definitely brought forward; and feeling confident that there was no mere degradation of the borough franchise that could bring any satisfactory settlement, we recommended Her Majesty to dissolve Parliament. Upon that issue we appealed to the country. The country did not give us a majority; and therefore both Parliament and the country were henceforth pledged to a lowering of the franchise in boroughs.

Well, now, what happened in the memorable seven years which elapsed from 1859 to 1866, when Lord Derby was again called to power, and when he did me the honour again to ask me to attempt to lead the House of Commons? Now, observe what has occurred in Parliament on the subject of reform in these seven years. They commenced with the measure of Lord Palmerston in 1860. That failed. They concluded with the measure of Lord John Russell in 1866, which also failed; and in the interval there were all these separate motions of Mr. Locke King and of Mr. Baines of which we have heard. Therefore, during these years—from

1860 to 1866—the question of Parliamentary Reform was constantly before the public mind and the examination of Parliament.

During that period of seven years, with the advice, I may say under the instructions of my colleagues, I expressed the principles upon which any measure of Parliamentary Reform ought to be established. Now, mark this, because there are things which you may not have heard in any speech which has been made in the city of Edinburgh. I had to prepare the mind of the country, and to educate—if it be not arrogant to use such a phrase—to educate our party. It is a large party, and requires its attention to be called to questions of this kind with some pressure. I had to prepare the mind of Parliament and the country on this question of Reform. This was not only with the concurrence of Lord Derby, but of my colleagues. The first great point which it was my duty always to impress upon Parliament was, that we should listen to nothing that was not a complete and comprehensive measure, that all the points of the subject of Parliamentary Reform should be treated together, because we knew that upon our so treating them depended the political equilibrium which has hitherto prevailed in this country. That is the first question. What is the second? During these seven years I had to vindicate the principles on which disfranchisement and enfranchisement should take place. I said, 'We cannot listen a moment to the reasons assigned for grouping boroughs. We cannot say the representation of any place should be entirely abrogated." We insisted in our Bill, that no centre of representation should be abolished, and we said, 'For the increased representation you want in England, you must look to a certain class of boroughs, no doubt, to give up a portion of their claim.' And what was the third question? It was whether any Parliamentary Reform could be made satisfactory, unless you had a real and *bona fide* boundary commission. What was the fourth point? That justice should be done to the representation of the majority of the English nation who live in counties, and that it should be done, not merely by giving representation to the great towns which have sprung into importance since Lord Grey's Act of 1832, but by adding a considerable number directly to their representatives. What was the fifth point? We insisted upon, and supported by our vote, that the borough franchise should be established on the principle of rating. These are the five points which, for seven weary and toilsome years, I have, with the entire concurrence and at the instigation of those who share your confidence, endeavoured in the House of Commons to impress upon the conscience and conviction of Parliament.

In 1866 Lord Derby came into power. Lord Derby had to consider the state of the country, and he resolved that in his opinion it was necessary to bring in a Reform Bill. We brought in a Reform Bill; we passed a Reform

Bill. Our Reform Bill was a complete and comprehensive measure. We did vindicate the principles upon which enfranchisement and disfranchisement should take place; we did not abolish entirely the representation of any borough; we did successfully appeal to a certain class of boroughs to spare their surplusage of representation to supply the wants of the Constitution. We did do justice to the counties, by adding greatly to their direct representation and enfranchising the towns that had grown into importance since 1832. We did issue a Boundary Commission, that has been and is now examining the Parliamentary boundaries in every part of the kingdom. And, fifth and lastly, we did establish a suffrage for the boroughs founded on the principle of rating; and then I am told, when measures recommended to the country during seven years have been so triumphantly carried into effect, that we have done nothing, that it is our opponents who have suggested the Bill.

It may be said, you have established a democratic government in England, because you have established household suffrage, and you have gone much further than the measures which you previously opposed. Well, now let us see if there is anything in that. Now, I am not at all prepared to admit that household suffrage, with the constitutional conditions upon which we have established it—namely, residence and rating—has established a democratic government. But it is unnecessary to enter into that consideration, because we have not established household suffrage in England. There are, I think I may say, probably four million houses in England. Under our ancient laws, and under the Act of Lord Grey, about a million of those householders possess the franchise. Under the new Act of 1867, something more than 500,000 will be added to that million. Well, then, I want to know if there are four million householders, and a million and a half in round numbers have the suffrage, how can household suffrage be said to be established in England?

I say Lord Derby could not have fixed upon any other solution of the question of the franchise than the one that he did. Remember that every degradation of the franchise—I used the term first—I don't shrink from it: it is correct language[1]—I say that whatever degradation of value you make, whether it be 8*l.*, or 7*l.*, or 6*l.*, or 5*l.*, you are equally far from a principle and a settlement. Why, what was the reason all these Reform Bills failed? How is it—a thing utterly unknown in the history of this country—how is it that five Prime Ministers consecutively failed upon a question? Look to the history of the country. Those who live rapidly, in a rapid age, don't stop to think. But think of five Prime Ministers—the wisest men in the country—the prime and chief men in the country, representing all the great parties, failing consecutively in settling a question.

---

1 The word of course means 'lowering by one or more steps.'

There must be some cause why they failed. The cause was this. Every independent man in the House of Commons, Tory and Radical alike, felt there was no permanent settlement in any of these schemes because there was no principle in them. When you try to settle any great question, there are two considerations which statesmen ought not to forget. And, first of all, let your plan be founded upon some principle. But that is not enough. Let it also be a principle that is in harmony with the manners and customs of the people you are attempting to legislate for. Now, I say, when you come to this question of the suffrage for boroughs, there is a principle in saying a man shall have a vote who has, by his residence and his contribution to local taxation, proved that he is interested in the welfare of his community. That man is a man whom you may trust in preference to a migratory pauper. That is a principle; and then, if you can apply that principle in harmony with the manners and customs of your country, then I say that you have a chance of a solution—a happy solution—of a great question. When you find it was an old custom of the country that the householder should possess this suffrage—that the man who, by his residence and his rate, proved he was one who on an average might fairly be looked upon as a responsible and trustworthy individual, you had your principle, and you had your traditionary practice to consecrate your principle. A rating and residential borough franchise was not new even in modern times. It had been tried in the Municipal Act, and for many years with great success. Men were not elected under it hostile to the institutions of the country; excellent measures of public improvement were passed. True it is, after many years' trial, the elections under the Municipal Act have become in many instances corrupt and unsatisfactory. But the Committee of the House of Lords that has investigated the subject, in their Report drawn up by Lord Grey, attribute all these evil consequences to an alternation in the law, which allows men now to vote without the condition of personal payment of rates. Well, then, I say that in these circumstances the measure which we have carried was the only measure which could have been passed. And that seems now to be universally acknowledged, even by those who complain that we have been successful.

There is one other point which I must notice. I speak of an animal not known in Scotland, and, thank God, no longer known in England—the compound householder. The compound householder is a being who wants a vote without paying rates. Well, that we opposed. Nothing in the world would induce us to consent to any man having a vote who did not personally pay his rates, and I believe that is a sound principle. If we had attempted to do away with the compound householder when Parliament first met, we should have had all the vestries of London agitating the country; and Mr. Gladstone himself, quite contemplating our difficulties,

had announced that the laws under which compound householding existed were the result of the civilisation of the age. But as the thing went
on, we got a little stronger, and matters were more understood; and
months afterwards the Liberal party themselves proposed to do away with
the great result of civilisation. What was our obvious course? We had
insisted that no man should vote who did not pay rates. We had sympa-
thised with the compound householder by having prepared clauses by
which his vote might be facilitated, and if he chose to come forward, and
commit suicide, and say, 'I will no longer be a compound householder,
but I will give up these privileges and pay rates,' what was our duty? It
would have been most inconsistent in us to resist such a proposal. I say
that the compound householder bowing down, and giving up his peculiar
position, and saying, "In order to exercise the suffrage I will pay the
rate," was the very triumph of the principle of our Bill. So there was an
end of the compound householder, but the benefit did not rest there.
That decision will restore the municipal elections to their primitive order
and purity, for it was the admission of the compound householder to the
suffrage which disordered and degraded our corporation elections.

And now, my lords and gentlemen, you have, by what I have told you,
some notion of what a speech in detail is in the House of Commons.
There must be considerable zeal for party to induce you to listen with so
much attention to a narrative of this description; and yet is it not expedient that statements of this kind should be made by those who, however
unworthily, occupy great positions upon these questions; especially when,
week after week, and month after month, the enormous nonsense that you
have listened to has been circulated through the country? and therefore I
think that, as you have been so kind to me as to ask me to be your guest
and offer me your congratulations, and your encouragement for the work
that I have done, my observations are not altogether out of place. I think
I have shown to you, if you will allow me briefly to summarise what I
have said, that we were perfectly justified as a party in dealing with this
question, that it ought to be dealt with, and that we have dealt with it in
a proper manner. I think I have shown to you that the story that we have
democratised the country by establishing household suffrage is a fable. I
think I have shown to you that the assertion that we have misled and
betrayed our friends by giving up all securities that were talked of, is
unfounded; and that we have carried on our Bill on the principle upon
which we always insisted. But if I am right in this assertion, pardon some
feeling on my part when I remember that it is in consequence of my
conduct—in consequence of our unprincipled withdrawal of those securities, and the betrayal of our friends, who insisted upon being betrayed—
that I miss to-day the presence of one of my oldest and most valued

friends.[1] I should like to have been welcomed by his cordial heart, and by that ripe scholarship which no one appreciates more than myself. He has commemorated the withdrawal of his confidence in a letter which, strange to say, has not a quotation. I picture him to myself at this moment in the castellated shades of Thurso, with the 'Edinburgh Review' on one side, and on the other the Conservative surrender. He who has written the summary of the session in the 'Edinburgh,' is not mounted on the fiery barb of Francis Jeffrey; he is rather placed upon a prancing hearse horse, with which he consummates the entombment of Whig principles. The Conservative surrender—to borrow an expression from the pleasing volume of art of my friend the chairman[2]—is what one would call a *replica*. You have had the subject treated in speeches, in articles, in reviews, and sometimes in manifestoes. The colouring is not without charm, but the drawing is inaccurate, the perspective is false, the subject is monotonous. Far be it from me to discover a man from his style. The wittiest of poets has commemorated for ever the character who knows you under these circumstances.[3] If, therefore, I make an observation on the 'Conservative Surrender,' it is founded entirely on abstract principles. I should say that article was written by a very clever man who has made a very great mistake. The leaders of the Conservative party are traitors; the Conservative party are false. They do not know that they have been abused; they have not recognised that their confidence has been betrayed and outraged.

I see many gentlemen here who have been, no doubt, inspectors like myself, as magistrates, of peculiar asylums, who meet there some cases which I have always thought at the same time the most absurd and the most distressing—it is when the lunatic believes all the world is mad, and that he himself is sane. But to pass from such gloomy imagery, really these 'Edinburgh' and 'Quarterly Reviews,' no man admires them more than myself. But I admire them as I do first-rate, first-class post-houses, which in old days, for half a century or so—to use a Manchester phrase—carried on a roaring trade. Then there comes some revolution or progress which no person can ever have contemplated. They find things are altered. They do not understand them, and instead of that intense competition and mutual vindictiveness which before distinguished them, they suddenly quite agree. The 'boots' of the 'Blue Boar' and the chambermaid of the 'Red Lion' embrace, and are quite in accord in this—in denouncing the infamy of railroads.

---

1 Mr. Tollemache Sinclair, now Sir J. Tollemache Sinclair, of Thurso Castle.
2 Sir William Stirling Maxwell.
3 Poor guiltless I, and can I choose but smile
    When every coxcomb knows me by my style?
        Pope, Prologue to the *Satires*, 281—.

With regard to the question of education—ever since I have been in public life I have done everything I possibly could to promote the cause of the education of the people generally. I have done so because I have always felt that with the limited population of this United Kingdom, compared with the great imperial position which it occupies with reference to other nations, it is not only our duty, but it is an absolute necessity, that we should study to make every man the most effective being that education can possibly constitute him. In the old wars there used to be a story that one Englishman could beat three members of some other nation: but I think if we want to maintain our power we ought to make one Englishman equal really in the business of life to three other men that any other nation can furnish. I do not see how otherwise, with our limited population, we can fulfil the great destiny that I believe waits us, and the great position we occupy. Therefore, so far as I am concerned, whether it be a far greater advanced system of primary education—whether it be that system of competitive examination which I have ever supported, though I am not unconscious of some pedantry with which it is accompanied, or whatever may be the circumstances, I shall ever be its supporter.

May I be allowed to say, in reference to the subject of education generally, that the issue that has been raised is in a certain sense a false issue; but as it touches very great principles and affects the character of the nation, I would say myself I do not believe that in this United Kingdom any monotonous form of education, founded on a compulsory principle of forcing every part of the country to adopt the same system, will be successful. I am not prepared at this moment to agree that the same system ought to be extended to every part of Her Majesty's dominions, and to admit that the British nation generally is an uneducated one. So far as our primary education is concerned, there is no doubt that the multiplicity of our occupations and the value of labour has prevented that complete education in a primary sense which is to be desired. But if you look even to our primary education as compared with the primary education of other countries for the last thirty years, though it may not reach in some respects the alleged points which other nations have accomplished, still, on the whole, during these thirty years the advance of England has been greatest. But I deny that the education of the people of England entirely depends—I am talking now of the general population—on our system of primary education. I say that the technical education of the English artisan—especially since what we may describe as the Albertine movement took place—since Prince Albert first laid down those principles and doctrines which have been carried into felicitous effect—the technical education of the English artisan has been immensely improved. But if you come to mere secular education, there is an influence prevalent in England which exists in no other country, and which forms in a very great degree the character and conduct of the English people, and that is the influence of a free press. That influence is never considered. The press of this country, conducted by whatever party, but, on the whole, conducted with great knowledge, with great intelligence, and with a high moral feeling, imparts a secular education to the people of this country which none of the boasted countries which are brought forward as models, and which we are called upon to make great efforts to equal, can for a moment compete with.

Gentlemen, I cannot deny that the great measure which has been passed this year will give in some degree a new character to the Constitution, and introduce some new powers and influences into its play and action. Indeed, to accomplish these ends was the object of those who brought it forward. I am told, at least I hear every day, that in consequence of the change which has been effected one must expect great questions to arise. Well, great questions no doubt will arise, and I shall be very sorry if great questions should not arise. Great questions are a proof that a country is progressing. In a progressive country change is constant; and the great question is, not whether you should resist change which is inevitable, but whether that change should be carried out in deference to the manners, the customs, the laws, and the traditions of a people, or whether it should be carried out in deference to abstract principles and arbitrary and general doctrines. The one is a national system; the other, to give it an epithet, a noble epithet—which, perhaps, it may deserve—is a philosophic system. Both have great advantages: the national party is supported by the fervour of patriotism; the philosophical party has a singular exemption from the force of prejudice.

Now, my lords and gentlemen, I have always considered that the Tory party was the national party of England. It is not formed of a combination of oligarchs and philosophers who practise on the sectarian prejudices of a portion of the people. It is formed of all classes, from the highest to the most homely, and it upholds a series of institutions that are in theory, and ought to be in practice, in embodiment of the national requirements and the security of the national rights. Whenever the Tory party degenerates into an oligarchy, it becomes unpopular; whenever the national institutions do not fulfil their original intention, the Tory party becomes odious; but when the people are led by their natural leaders, and when, by their united influence, the national institutions fulfil their original intention, the Tory party is triumphant, and then, under Providence, will secure the prosperity and the power of the country.

My lords and gentlemen, the times in which we happen to meet are no doubt serious. At this moment events may be occurring which may influence the destiny of Europe, and affect the position of this country. But, no doubt, whatever ministry may have to regulate the fortunes of this country, whatever may be their abilities, whatever may be the favouring circumstances they can command, they are nothing without the confidence of the great body of the nation. I am the last man who would for a moment affect to depreciate the difficulties which a British minister has now to meet, or would attempt for a moment to exaggerate the qualities which I, or even my colleagues better than myself, possess to encounter them. Indeed, when I remember the elements and interests of these British Isles, so vast, so various, and so complicated; when I even call to recollection the difference of race which, however blended, leaves significant characteristics; when I recollect that the great majority of the population of the United Kingdom rise every day and depend for their subsistence—their daily subsistence—on their daily labour; when I recollect the delicate marvel of our credit—more wonderful, in my opinion, than our accumulated capital—the constant collision between those ancient institutions that give permanence to the State, and the requirements of the new populations that arise, and which they do not completely or adequately meet—when I remember that it is upon the common sense, the prudence, and the courage of the community thus circumstanced that depends the fate of uncounted millions in Asian provinces, and that around the globe there is a circle of domestic settlements that watch us for example and inspiration—when I know that not a sun rises upon a British minister that does not bring him care, and often inexpressible anxiety—some unexpected war, a disturbed or discontented colony, a pestilence, a famine, a mutiny, a collapse of credit, a declining trade, a decaying revenue, perhaps some insensate and fantastic conspiracy, I declare I often wonder where is the strength of thought and the fund of feeling that are adequate to cope with such colossal circumstances. But when I withdraw from the pressure of individual interests, and take a larger and deeper view of human affairs, I recognise that in this country, whatever may have been the tumult and the turmoil of now many generations, there have ever been three master influences that have at all times guided and controlled all other powers and passions. And these are Industry, Liberty, and Religion. So long as this sacred combination influences the destiny of this country it will not die. History will recognise its life, not record its decline and fall. It will say—This is a great and understanding people, and it is from such materials we make the magnificence of nations and establish the splendour of terrestrial thrones.

William Ewart Gladstone

.

William Ewart Gladstone

[BORN DECEMBER 29, 1809—*Died* MAY 19, 1898]

Gladstone was a tall, handsome man with a strong profile, firm mouth, thin lips and prominent chin.—HON. CLIVE BIGHAM

illiam Ewart Gladstone entered public life in 1852 as a member of the House of Commons at the age of twenty-three, and was in the forefront of British politics until 1894. On four occasions Gladstone was Prime Minister, "the most eminent man in his own party," [1] and throughout Europe was recognized as "almost the personification of the Liberal idea. . . ." [2] As party leader, A. F. Thompson pictures him as always playing a "grand part, possessing the ability to conceive and execute policy as well as to denounce that of his opponents." [3]

As for specific acts of statesmanship there is no single feat which stands out above others. Thompson believes the most enduring monument of his tenure in office was his setting forth the pattern for the relationship between sovereign and Prime Minister—the beginning, as it were, of constitutional monarchy.[4]

Gladstone is probably the most prolific speaker Britain has ever known. Aside from his numerous speeches delivered before popular audiences, Arthur Tilney Bassett reports that his parliamentary utterances are "scattered through no less than 366 volumes of Hansard's . . . and fill some 15,000 columns of print. . . ." [5]

Like so many other British statesmen, Gladstone was a man of letters, but unlike most when he addressed an audience he was "everything at once—actor, missionary, debater, exponent of legislative detail," [6] who could "sway masses of opinion as no one before or since." [7] Prime examples of his persuasive ability are his speeches delivered to the electorate in the county of Midlothian, Scotland, which stand out as the only successful instance up to that time "of leading a party to victory by an appeal to nothing but moral standards." [8] D. C. Somervell calls these speeches "a new conception . . .

1 *Gladstone's Speeches* ed. by Arthur Tilney Bassett with Preface by Viscount Bryce (London: Methuen and Co., 1916), p. v.

2 Francis Birrell, *Gladstone* (New York: Macmillan Co., 1933), p. 30.

3 A. F. Thompson, "Gladstone," in *British Prime Ministers*, ed. by Duff Cooper (New York: Roy Publishers, no publication date), p. 124.

4 *Ibid.*, p. 133.

5 Bassett, *op. cit.*, p. 5.

6 George Trevelyan, *The Life of John Bright* (London: Constable and Co., Ltd., 1913), p. 384.

7 Birrell, *op. cit.*, p. 30.

8 *Ibid.*, p. 98.

appealing over the head of Parliament directly to the people," [9] and through victory at the ballot box, smashing the Conservative majority in Parliament led by Lord Beaconsfield.

Erich Eyck calls the Midlothian campaign "an epoch in English history," conducted in "flat contradiction of all the aristocratic traditions which had hitherto governed English political life."[10] John Morley reports that the speeches contained 85,840 words constructed as "rallying battle-cries" containing "political facts of a political indictment, not an aerial fabric of moral abstractions." [11]

Gladstone's oratory is best characterized by his attention to detail accompanied by a dynamic presentation. Morley describes the content in this manner:

. . . the only flattery in the Midlothian speeches was the manly flattery contained in the fact that he took care to address all these multitudes of weavers, farmers, villagers, artisans, just as he would have addressed the House of Commons,—with the same breadth and accuracy of knowledge, the same sincerity of interest, the same scruple in right reasoning, and the same appeal to the gravity and responsibility of public life.[12]

In presentation Trevelyan pictures Gladstone as always a debater "meeting his opponent's every argument, instructing his audience, often exciting them over the details of some financial or legislative measure," [13] and Morley cites his "overflowing vivacity, the fine voice and flashing eye and a whole frame in free, ceaseless, natural and spontaneous motion." [14]

Eyck recommends the speech delivered at West Calder on November 27, 1879, as one deserving special attention because "contrary of his usual custom—he attempted . . . to declare its leading aspects in a few programmatic statements." [15] This speech was the third of a series extending from November 24 to December 9. An-

---

9 D. C. Somervell, *Disraeli and Gladstone* (New York: Garden City Publishing Co., Inc., 1926), p. 220.

10 Erich Eyck, *Gladstone* (London: George Allen and Unwin Ltd., 1938), p. 272.

See also Somervell, *op. cit.*, p. 220. It was not only unusual to carry political and moral issues to the people in the hustings, but a contributing cause for the Conservative defeat is attributed to the debarring of peers from taking part in a general election campaign since they had no constituents. The three "weightiest" men, Beaconsfield, Salisbury, and Cairns were unable to campaign against Gladstone.

11 John Morley, *The Life of William Ewart Gladstone*, II (New York: Macmillan Co., 1903), p. 592.

12 *Ibid.*, p. 589.

13 Trevelyan, *op. cit.*, p. 383.

14 Morley, *op. cit.*, p. 593. For a concise, well-documented description of Gladstone as a speaker see Albert A. Austin, "The British Orators, IV, Gladstone's Characteristics as a Speaker," *Quarterly Journal of Speech*, XLIV (1958), 244–254.

15 Eyck, *op. cit.*, p. 276.

ticipating Gladstone's arrival in West Calder, the residents prepared a warm reception:

. . . triumphal arches had been erected all the way along the route from Dalmeny, and the popular excitement was intense. The town itself was decorated with arches and the streets were illuminated with multitudes of fairy lanterns at night.[16]

After the election the following year, it was determined that ninety percent of the electorate of Midlothian had cast ballots— 1,579 for Gladstone and 1,368 for Dalkeith who was thought to have a substantial majority of the populace on his side. A clear majority of 211 votes elected Gladstone to the House of Commons and established him, once again, as the leader of a new ministry. Upon announcing the results of the election, *The Times* of London reported "the streets thronged by excited crowds, whose feelings again find vent in loud cheers for Gladstone." [17]

---

[16] Philip Magnus, *Gladstone: A Biography* (New York: E. P. Dutton and Co., Inc., 1954), p. 262.

[17] *The Times*, April 5, 1880.

On Domestic and Foreign Affairs [1]

•

WEST CALDER *November 27, 1879*

M R. CHAIRMAN AND GENTLEMEN: In addressing you today, as in addressing like audiences assembled for a like purpose in other places of the county, I am warmed by the enthusiastic welcome which you have been pleased in every quarter and in every form to accord to me. I am, on the other hand, daunted when I recollect, first of all, what large demands I have to make on your patience; and secondly, how inadequate are my powers and how inadequate almost any amount of time you can grant me, to set forth worthily the whole of the case which ought to be laid before you in connection with the coming election.

To-day, gentlemen, as I know that many among you are interested in the land, and as I feel that what is termed "agricultural distress" is at the present moment a topic too serious to be omitted from our consideration, I shall say some words upon the subject of that agricultural distress, and particularly, because in connection with it there have arisen in some quarters of the country proposals, which have received a countenance far beyond their deserts, to reverse or to compromise the work which it took us one whole generation to achieve, and to revert to the mischievous, obstructive, and impoverishing system of protection. Gentlemen, I speak of agricultural distress as a matter now undoubtedly serious. Let none of us withhold our sympathy from the farmer, the cultivator of the soil, in the struggle he has to undergo. His struggle is a struggle of competition with the United States. But I do not fully explain the case when I say the United States. It is not with the entire United States, it is with the western portion of these States—that portion remote from the sea-board; and I wish in the first place, gentlemen, to state to you all a fact of very great interest and importance, as it seems to me, relating to and defining the

---

1 *Orations of British Orators,* II, from The World's Great Classics (New York: The Colonial Press, 1900), pp. 253–282.

point at which the competition of the western States of America is most severely felt. I have in my hand a letter received recently from one well known, and honourably known, in Scotland—Mr. Lyon Playfair, who has recently been a traveller in the United States, and who, as you well know, is as well qualified as any man upon earth for accurate and careful investigation. The point, gentlemen, at which the competition of the western States of America is most severely felt is in the eastern States of America. Whatever be agricultural distress in Scotland, whatever it be, where undoubtedly it is more felt, in England, it is greater by much in the eastern States of America. In the States of New England the soil has been to some extent exhausted by careless methods of agriculture, and these, gentlemen, are the greatest of all the enemies with which the farmer has to contend.

But the foundation of the statement I make, that the eastern States of America are those that most feel the competition of the West, is to be found in facts—in this fact above all, that not only they are not in America, as we are here, talking about the shortness of the annual returns, and in some places having much said on the subject of rents, and of temporary remission or of permanent reduction. That is not the state of things; they have actually got to this point, that the capital values of land, as tested by sales in the market, have undergone an enormous diminution. Now I will tell you something that actually happened, on the authority of my friend Mr. Playfair. I will tell you something that has happened in one of the New England States—not, recollect, in a desert or a remote country—in an old cultivated country, and near one of the towns of these States, a town that has the honourable name of Wellesley.

Mr. Playfair tells me this: Three weeks ago—that is to say, about the first of this month, so you will see my information is tolerably recent—three weeks ago a friend of Mr. Playfair bought a farm near Wellesley for $33 an acre, for £6 12s. an acre—agricultural land, remember, in an old settled country. That is the present condition of agricultural property in the old States of New England. I think by the simple recital of that fact I have tolerably well established my case, for you have not come in England, and you have not come in Scotland, to the point at which agricultural land is to be had—not wild land, but improved and old cultivated land—is to be had for the price of £6 12s. an acre. He mentions that this is by no means a strange case, an isolated case, that it fairly represented the average transactions that have been going on; and he says that in that region the ordinary price of agricultural land at the present time is from $20 to $50 an acre, or from £4 to £10. In New York the soil is better, and the population is greater; but even in the State of New York land ranges for agricultural purposes from $50 to $100, that is to say, from £10 to £20 an acre.

I think those of you, gentlemen, who are farmers will perhaps derive some comfort from perceiving that if the pressure here is heavy the pressure elsewhere and the pressure nearer to the seat of this very abundant production is greater and far greater still.

It is most interesting to consider, however, what this pressure is. There has been developed in the astonishing progressive power of the United States—there has been developed a faculty of producing corn for the subsistence of man, with a rapidity and to an extent unknown in the experience of mankind. There is nothing like it in history. Do not let us conceal, gentlemen, from ourselves the fact; I shall not stand the worse with any of you who are farmers if I at once avow that this greater and comparatively immense abundance of the prime article of subsistence for mankind is a great blessing vouchsafed by Providence to mankind. In part I believe that the cheapness has been increased by special causes. The lands from which the great abundance of American wheat comes are very thinly peopled as yet. They will become more thickly peopled, and as they become more thickly peopled a larger proportion of their produce will be wanted for home consumption and less of it will come to you, and at a higher price. Again, if we are rightly informed, the price of American wheat has been unnaturally reduced by the extraordinary depression, in recent time, of trade in America, and especially of the mineral trades, upon which many railroads are dependent in America, and with which these railroads are connected in America in a degree and manner that in this country we know but little of. With a revival of trade in America it is to be expected that the freights of corn will increase, and all other freights, because the employment of the railroads will be a great deal more abundant, and they will not be content to carry corn at nominal rates. In some respects, therefore, you may expect a mitigation of the pressure, but in other respects it is likely to continue.

Nay, the Prime Minister is reported as having not long ago said—and he ought to have the best information on this subject, nor am I going to impeach in the main what he stated—he gave it to be understood that there was about to be a development of corn production in Canada which would entirely throw into the shade this corn production in the United States. Well, that certainly was very cold comfort, as far as the British agriculturist is concerned, because he did not say—he could not say—that the corn production of the United States was to fall off, but there was to be added an enormous corn production from Manitoba, the great province which forms now a part of the Canada Dominion. There is no doubt, I believe, that it is a correct expectation that vast or very large quantities of corn will proceed from that province, and therefore we have to look forward to a state of things in which, for a considerable time to come, large quantities of wheat will be forthcoming from America, probably larger quantities, and perhaps frequently at lower prices than those at which the corn-producing and corn-exporting districts of Europe have commonly been able to supply us. Now that I believe to be, gentlemen, upon the whole, not an unfair representation of the state of things.

How are you to meet that state of things? What are your fair claims? I will tell you. In my opinion your fair claims are, in the main, two. One is to be allowed to purchase every article that you require in the cheapest market, and have no needless burden laid upon anything that comes to you and can assist you in the cultivation of your land. But that claim has been conceded and fulfilled.

I do not know whether there is an object, an instrument, a tool of any kind, an auxiliary of any kind, that you want for the business of the farmer, which you do not buy at this moment in the cheapest market. But beyond that, you want to be relieved from every unjust and unnecessary legislative restraint. I say every unnecessary legislative restraint, because taxation, gentlemen, is unfortunately a restraint upon us all, but we cannot say that it is always unnecessary, and we cannot say that it is always unjust. Yesterday I ventured to state—and I will therefore not now return to the subject—a number of matters connected with the state legislation in which it appears to me to be of vital importance, both to the agricultural interest and to the entire community, that the occupiers and cultivators of the land of this country should be relieved from restraints under the operation of which they now suffer considerably. Beyond those two great heads, gentlemen, what you have to look to, I believe, is your own energy, your own energy of thought and action, and your care not to undertake to pay rents greater than, in reasonable calculation, you think you can afford. I am by no means sure, though I speak subject to the correction of higher authority—I am by no means sure that in Scotland within the last fifteen or twenty years something of a speculative character has not entered into rents, and particularly, perhaps, into the rents of hill farms. I remember hearing of the augmentations which were taking place, I believe, all over Scotland—I verified the fact in a number of counties— about twelve or fourteen years ago, in the rents of hill farms, which I confess impressed me with the idea that the high prices that were then ruling, and ruling increasingly from year to year, for meat and wool, were perhaps for once leading the wary and shrewd Scottish agriculturist a little beyond the mark in the rents he undertook to pay. But it is not this only which may press. It is, more broadly, in a serious and manful struggle that you are engaged, in which you will have to exert yourselves to the uttermost, in which you will have a right to claim everything that the legislature can do for you; and I hope it may perhaps possibly be my privilege and honour to assist in procuring for you some of those provisions of necessary liberation from restraint; but beyond that, it is your own energies, of thought and action, to which you will have to trust.

Now, gentlemen, having said thus much, my next duty is to warn you against quack remedies, against delusive remedies, against the quack remedies that there are plenty of people found to propose, not so much in Scotland as in England; for, gentlemen, from Mid-Lothian at present we are speaking to England as well as to Scotland. Let me give a friendly warning from this northern quarter to the agriculturist of England not to be deluded by those who call themselves his friends in a degree of special and superior excellence, and who have been too much given to delude him in other times; not to be deluded into hoping relief from sources from which it can never come. Now, gentlemen, there are three of these remedies. The first of them, gentlemen, I will not call a quack remedy at all, but I will speak of it notwithstanding in the tone of rational and dispassionate discussion. I am not now so much upon the controversial portion of the land question—a field which, Heaven knows, is wide enough—as I am upon matters of deep and universal interest to us in our economic and social condition. There are some gentlemen, and there are persons for whom I for one have very great respect, who think that the difficulties of our agriculture may be got over by a fundamental change in the land-holding system of this country.

I do not mean, now pray observe, a change as to the law of entail and settlement, and all those restraints which, I hope, were tolerably well disposed of yesterday at Dalkeith; but I mean those who think that if you can cut up the land, or a large part of it, into a multitude of small properties, that of itself will solve the difficulty, and start everybody on a career of prosperity.

Now, gentlemen, to a proposal of that kind, I, for one, am not going to object upon the ground that it would be inconsistent with the privileges of landed proprietors. In my opinion, if it is known to be for the welfare of the community at large, the legislature is perfectly entitled to buy out the landed proprietors. It is not intended probably to confiscate the property of a landed proprietor more than the property of any other man; but the state is perfectly entitled, if it please, to buy out the landed proprietors as it may think fit, for the purpose of dividing the property into small lots. I don't wish to recommend it, because I will show you the doubts that to my mind hang about that proposal; but I admit that in principle no objection can be taken. Those persons who possess large portions of the spaces of the earth are not altogether in the same position as the possessors of mere personalty; that personalty does not impose the same limitations upon the action and industry of man, and upon the well-being of the community, as does the possession of land; and, therefore, I freely own that compulsory expropriation is a thing which for an adequate public object is in itself admissable and so far sound in principle.

Now, gentlemen, this idea about small proprietors, however, is one which very large bodies and parties in this country treat with the utmost contempt; and they are accustomed to point to France, and say: "Look at France." In France you have got 5,000,000—I am not quite sure whether it is 5,000,000 or even more; I do not wish to be beyond the mark in anything—you have 5,000,000 of small proprietors, and you do not produce in France as many bushels of wheat per acre as you do in England. Well, now I am going to point out to you a very remarkable fact with regard to the condition of France. I will not say that France produces— for I believe it does not produce—as many bushels of wheat per acre as England does, but I should like to know whether the wheat of France is produced mainly upon the small properties of France. I believe that the wheat of France is produced mainly upon the large properties of France, and I have not any doubt that the large properties of England are, upon the whole, better cultivated, and more capital is put into the land than in the large properties of France. But it is fair that justice should be done to what is called the peasant proprietary. Peasant proprietary is an excellent thing, if it can be had, in many points of view. It interests an enormous number of the people in the soil of the country, and in the stability of its institutions and its laws. But now look at the effect that it has upon the progressive value of the land—and I am going to give you a very few figures which I will endeavour to relieve from all complication, lest I should unnecessarily weary you. But what will you think when I tell you that the agricultural value of France—the taxable income derived from the land, and therefore the income of the proprietors of that land—has advanced during our lifetime far more rapidly than that of England? When I say England I believe the same thing is applicable to Scotland, certainly to Ireland; and I shall take England for my test, because the difference between England and Scotland, though great, does not touch the principle; and, because it so happens that we have some means of illustration from former times for England, which are not equally applicable for all the three kingdoms.

Here is the state of the case. I will not go back any further than 1851. I might go back much further: it would only strengthen my case. But for 1851 I have a statement made by French official authority of the agricultural income of France, as well as the income of other real property, viz., houses. In 1851 the agricultural income of France was £76,000,000. It was greater in 1851 than the whole income from land and houses together had been in 1821. This is a tolerable evidence of progress; but I will not enter into the detail of it, because I have no means of dividing the two—the house income and the land income—for the earlier year, namely, 1821. In

1851 it was £76,000,000—the agricultural income; and in 1864 it had risen from £76,000,000 to £106,000,000. That is to say, in the space of thirteen years the increase of agricultural values in France—annual values—was no less than forty per cent., or three per cent. per annum. Now, I go to England. Wishing to be quite accurate, I shall limit myself to that with respect to which we have positive figures. In England the agricultural income in 1813–14 was £37,000,000; in 1842 it was £42,000,000, and that year is the one I will take as my starting-point. I have given you the years 1851 to 1864 in France. I could only give you those thirteen years with a certainty that I was not misleading you, and I believe I have kept within the mark. I believe I might have put my case more strongly for France.

In 1842, then, the agricultural income of England was £42,000,000; in 1876 it was £52,000,000—that is to say, while the agricultural income of France increased forty per cent. in thirteen years, the agricultural income of England increased twenty per cent. per annum; the increase in England was about one-half or three-fifths per cent. per annum. Now, gentlemen, I wish this justice to be done to a system where peasant proprietary prevails. It is of great importance. And will you allow me, you who are Scotch agriculturists, to assure you that I speak to you not only with the respect which is due from a candidate to a constituency, but with the deference which is due from a man knowing very little of agricultural matters to those who know a great deal? And there is one point at which the considerations that I have been opening up, and this rapid increase of the value of the soil in France, bear upon our discussions. Let me try to explain it. I believe myself that the operation of economic laws is what in the main dictates the distribution of landed property in this country. I doubt if those economic laws will allow it to remain cut up into a multitude of small properties like the small properties of France. As to small holdings, I am one of those who attach the utmost value to them. I say that in the Lothians—I say that in the portion of the country where almost beyond any other large holdings prevail—in some parts of which large holdings exclusively are to be found—I attach the utmost value to them. But it is not on that point I am going to dwell, for we have no time for what is unnecessary. What I do wish very respectfully to submit to you, gentlemen, is this. When you see this vast increase of the agricultural value of France, you know at once it is perfectly certain that it has not been upon the large properties of France, which, if anything, are inferior in cultivation to the large properties of England. It has been upon those very peasant-properties which some people are so ready to decry. What do the peasant-properties mean? They mean what, in France, is called the small cultivation—that is to say, cultivation of superior articles, pursued upon a small scale—cultivation of flowers, cultivation of trees and shrubs, cultivation of fruits of every kind, and all that, in fact, which rises above the ordinary character of farming produce, and rather approaches the produce of the gardener.

Gentlemen, I cannot help having this belief, that, among other means of meeting the difficulties in which we may be placed, our destiny is that a great deal more attention will have to be given than heretofore by the agriculturalists of England, and perhaps even by the agriculturalists of Scotland, to the production of fruits, of vegetables, of flowers, of all that variety of objects which are sure to find a market in a rich and wealthy country like this, but which have hitherto been consigned almost exclusively to garden production. You know that in Scotland, in Aberdeenshire —and I am told also in Perthshire—a great example of this kind has been set in the cultivation of strawberries—the cultivation of strawberries is carried on over hundreds of acres at once. I am ashamed, gentlemen, to go further into this matter, as if I was attempting to instruct you. I am sure you will take my hint as a respectful hint—I am sure you will take it as a friendly hint. I do not believe that the large properties of this country, generally or universally, can or will be broken up into small ones. I do not believe that the land of this country will be owned, as a general rule, by those who cultivate it. I believe we shall continue to have, as we have had, a class of landlords and a class of cultivators, but I most earnestly desire to see—not only to see the relations of those classes to one another harmonious and sound, their interests never brought into conflict; but I desire to see both flourishing and prospering, and the soil of my country producing, as far as may be, under the influence of capital and skill, every variety of product which may give an abundant livelihood to those who live upon it. I say, therefore, gentlemen, and I say it with all respect, I hope for a good deal from the small culture, the culture in use among the small proprietors of France; but I do not look to a fundamental change in the distribution of landed property in this country as a remedy for agricultural distress.

But I go on to another remedy which is proposed, and I do it with a great deal less of respect; nay, I now come to the region of what I have presumed to call quack remedies. There is a quack remedy which is called reciprocity, and this quack remedy is under the special protection of quack doctors, and among the quack doctors, I am sorry to say, there appear to be some in very high station indeed; and if I am rightly informed, no less a person than Her Majesty's Secretary of State for Foreign Affairs has been moving about the country, and indicating a very considerable expectation that possibly by reciprocity agricultural distress will be relieved. Let me test, gentlemen, the efficacy of this quack remedy for your, in some places, agricultural pressure, and generally distress—the pressure that has been upon you, the struggle in which you are engaged. Pray watch its operation; pray note what is said by the advocates of reciprocity. They always say, We are the soundest and best free-traders. We recommend reciprocity because it is the truly effectual method of bringing about free trade. At present America imposes enormous duties upon our cotton goods and upon our iron goods. Put reciprocity into play and America will become a free-trading country. Very well, gentlemen, how would that operate upon you agriculturists in particular? Why, it would operate thus: If your condition is to be regretted in certain particulars, and capable of amendment, I beg you to cast an eye of sympathy upon the condition of the American agriculturist. It has been very well said, and very truly said—though it is a smart antithesis—the American agriculturist has got to buy everything that he wants at prices which are fixed in Washington by the legislation of America, but he has got to sell everything that he produces at prices which are fixed in Liverpool—fixed by the free competition of the world. How would you like that, gentlemen— to have protective prices to pay for everything that you use—for your manures, for your animals, for your implements, for all your farming stock, and at the same time to have to sell what you produce in the free and open market of the world? But bring reciprocity into play, and then, if reciprocity doctors are right, the Americans will remove all their protective duties, and the American farmer, instead of producing, as he does now, under the disadvantage, and the heavy disadvantage, of having to pay protective prices for everything that constitutes his farming stock, will have all his tools, and implements, and manures, and everything else purchased in the free, open market of the world at free-trade prices. So he will be able to produce his corn to compete with you even cheaper than he does now. So much for reciprocity considered as a cure for distress. I am not going to consider it now in any other point of view.

But, gentlemen, there are another set of men who are bolder still, and who are not for reciprocity; who are not content with that milder form of quackery; but who recommend a reversion, pure and simple, to what I may fairly call, I think, the exploded doctrine of protection. And upon this, gentlemen, I think it necessary, if you will allow me, to say to you a few words, because it is a very serious matter, and it is all the more serious because Her Majesty's Government—I do not scruple to say—are coquetting with this subject in a way which is not right. They are tampering with it; they are playing with it. A protective speech was made in the House of Commons in a debate last year by Mr. Chaplin, on the part of what is called "the agricultural interest." Mr. Chaplin did not use the word protection, but what he did say was this: He said he demanded that the malt tax should be abolished, and the revenue supplied by a tax upon foreign barley or some other foreign commodity. Well, if he has a measure of that kind in his pocket I don't ask him to affix the word protection to it. I can do that for myself. Not a word of rebuke, gentlemen, was uttered to the doctrines of Mr. Chaplin. He was complimented upon the ability of his speech and the well-chosen terms of his motion. Some of the members of Her Majesty's Government—the minor members of Her Majesty's Government—the humbler luminaries of that great constellation—have been going about the country and telling their farming constituents that they think the time has come when a return to protection might very wisely be tried. But, gentlemen, what delusions have been practised upon the unfortunate British farmer! When we go back for twenty years, what is now called the Tory party was never heard of as the Tory party. It was always heard of as the party of protection. As long as the chiefs of the protective party were not in office, as long as they were irresponsible, they recommended themselves to the good-will of the farmer as protectionists, and said they would set him up and put his interests on a firm foundation through protection. We brought them into office in the year 1852. I gave with pleasure a vote that assisted to bring them into office. I thought bringing them into office was the only way of putting their professions to the test. They came into office, and before they had been six months in office they had thrown protection to the winds. And that is the way in which the British farmer's expectations are treated by those who claim for themselves in the special sense the designation of his friends.

It is exactly the same with the malt tax. Gentlemen, what is done with the malt tax? The malt tax is held by them to be a great grievance on the British farmer. Whenever a Liberal government is in office, from time to time they have a great muster from all parts of the country to vote for the abolition of the malt tax. But when a Tory government comes into office, the abolition of the malt tax is totally forgotten; and we have now had six years of a Tory government without a word said, as far as I can recollect—and my friend in the chair could correct me if I were wrong—without a motion made, or a vote taken, on the subject of the malt tax. The malt tax, great and important as it is, is small in reference to protection. Gentlemen, it is a very serious matter indeed if we ought to go back to protection, because how did we come out of protection to free trade? We came out of it by a struggle which in its crisis threatened to convulse the country, which occupied Parliaments, upon which elections turned, which took up twenty years of our legislative life, which broke up parties. In a word, it effected a change so serious that if, after the manner in which we effected that change, it be right that we should go back upon our steps, then all I can say is, that we must lose that which has ever been one of the most honourable distinctions of British legislation in the general estimation of the world—that British legislation, if it moves slowly, always moves in one direction—that we never go back upon our steps.

But are we such children that, after spending twenty years—as I may say from 1840 to 1860—in breaking down the huge fabric of protection, in

1879 we are seriously to set about building it up again? If that be right, gentlemen, let it be done, but it will involve on our part a most humiliating confession. In my opinion it is not right. Protection, however, let me point out, now is asked for in two forms, and I am next going to quote Lord Beaconsfield for the purpose of expressing my concurrence with him.

Mostly, I am bound to say, as far as my knowledge goes, protection has not been asked for by the agricultural interest, certainly not by the farmers of Scotland.

It has been asked for by certain injudicious cliques and classes of persons connected with other industries—connected with some manufacturing industries. They want to have duties laid upon manufacturers.

But here Lord Beaconsfield said—and I cordially agree with him—that he would be no party to the institution of a system in which protection was to be given to manufactures, and to be refused to agriculture.

That one-sided protection I deem to be totally intolerable, and I reject it even at the threshold as unworthy of a word of examination or discussion.

But let us go on to two-sided protection, and see whether that is any better—that is to say, protection in the shape of duties on manufactures, and protection in the shape of duties upon corn, duties upon meat, duties upon butter and cheese and eggs, and everything that can be produced from the land. Now, gentlemen, in order to see whether we can here find a remedy for our difficulties, I prefer to speculation and mere abstract argument the method of reverting to experience. Experience will give us very distinct lessons upon this matter. We have the power, gentlemen, of going back to the time when protection was in full and unchecked force, and of examining the effect which it produced upon the wealth of the country. How, will you say, do I mean to test that wealth? I mean to test that wealth by the exports of the country, and I will tell you why, because your prosperity depends upon the wealth of your customers—that is to say, upon their capacity to buy what you produce. And who are your customers? Your customers are the industrial population of the country, who produce what we export and send all over the world. Consequently, when exports increase, your customers are doing a large business, are growing wealthy, are putting money in their pockets, and are able to take that money out of their pockets in order to fill their stomachs with what you produce. When, on the contrary, exports do not increase, your customers are poor, your prices go down, as you have felt within the last few years, in the price of meat, for example, and in other things, and your condition is proportionally depressed. Now, gentlemen, down to the year 1842 no profane hand had been laid upon the august fabric of protection. For recollect that the farmers' friends always told us that it was a very august fabric, and that if you pulled it down it would involve the ruin of the country. That, you remember, was the commonplace of every Tory speech delivered from a country hustings to a farming constituency. But before 1842 another agency had come into force, which gave new life in a very considerable degree to the industry of the country, and that was the agency of railways, of improved communication, which shortened distance and cheapened transit, and effected in that way an enormous economical gain and addition to the wealth of the country. Therefore, in order to see what we owe to our friend protection, I won't allow that friend to take credit for what was done by railways in improving the wealth of the country. I will go to the time when I may say there were virtually no railways—that is the time before 1830. Now, gentlemen, here are the official facts which I shall lay before you in the simplest form, and, remember, using round numbers. I do that because, although round numbers cannot be absolutely accurate, they are easy for the memory to take in, and they involve no material error, no falsification of the case. In the year 1800, gentlemen, the exports of British produce were thirty-nine and a half millions sterling in value. The population at that time—no, I won't speak of the exact figure of the population, because I have not got it for the three kingdoms. In the years 1826 to 1830—that is, after a medium period of eight-and-twenty years—the average of our exports for those five years, which had been thirty-nine and a half millions in 1800, was thirty-seven millions. It is fair to admit that in 1800 the currency was somewhat less sound, and therefore I am quite willing to admit that the thirty-seven millions probably meant as much in value as the thirty-nine and a half millions; but substantially, gentlemen, the trade of the country was stationary, practically stationary, under protection. The condition of the people grew, if possible, rather worse than better. The wealth of the country was nearly stationary. But now I show you what protection produced; that it made no addition, it gave no onward movement to the profits of those who are your customers. But on these profits you depend; because, under all circumstances, gentlemen, this, I think, nobody will dispute—a considerable portion of what the Englishman or the Scotchman produces will, some way or other, find its way down his throat.

What has been the case, gentlemen, since we cast off the superstition of protection, since we discarded the imposture of protection? I will tell you what happened between 1830, when there were no railways, and 1842, when no change, no important change, had been made as to protection, but when the railway system was in operation, hardly in Scotland, but in England to a very great extent, to a very considerable extent upon the main lines of communication. The exports which in 1830 had been somewhere about £37,000,000, between 1840 and 1842 showed an average amount of £50,000,000. That seems due, gentlemen, to the agency of railways; and I wish you to bear in mind the increasing benefit now derived from that agency, in order that I may not claim any undue credit for freedom of trade. From 1842, gentlemen, onward, the successive stages of free trade began; in 1842, in 1845, in 1846, in 1853, and again in 1860, the large measures were carried which have completely reformed your customs tariff, and reduced it from a taxation of twelve hundred articles to a taxation of, I think, less than twelve.

Now, under the system of protection, the export trade of the country, the wealth and the power of the manufacturing and producing classes to purchase your agricultural products, did not increase at all. In the time when railways began to be in operation, but before free trade, the exports of the country increased, as I have shown you, by £13,000,000 in somewhere about thirteen years—that is to say, taking it roughly, at the rate of £1,000,000 a year.

But since 1842, and down to the present time, we have had, along with railways, always increasing their benefits—we have had the successive adoption of free-trade measures; and what has been the state of the export business of the country? It has risen in this degree, that that which from 1840 to 1842 averaged £50,000,000, from 1873 to 1878 averaged £218,000,000. Instead of increasing, as it had done between 1830 and 1842, when railways only were at work, at the rate of £1,000,000 a year—instead of remaining stagnant as it did when the country was under protection pure and simple, with no augmentation of the export trade to enlarge the means of those who buy your products, the total growth in a period of thirty-five years was no less than £168,000,000, or, taking it roughly, a growth in the export trade of the country to the extent of between £4,000,000 and £5,000,000 a year. But, gentlemen, you know the fact. You know very well, that while restriction was in force, you did not get the prices that you have been getting for the last twenty years. The price of wheat has been much the same as it had been before. The price of oats is a better price than was to be had on the average of protective times. But the price, with the exception of wheat, of almost every agricultural commodity, the price of wool, the price of meat, the price of cheese, the price of everything that the soil produces, has been largely increased in a market free and open to the world; because, while the artificial advantage which you got through protection, as it was supposed to be an advantage, was removed, you were brought into that free and open market, and the energy of free trade so enlarged the buying capacity of your customers that they were willing and able to give you, and did give you, a great deal more for your meat, your wool, and your products in general, than you would ever have got under the system of protection. Gentlemen, if that be true—and it cannot, I believe, be impeached or impugned—if that be true, I don't think I need further discuss the matter, especially when so many other matters have to be discussed.

I will therefore ask you again to cross the seas with me. I see that the time is flying onward, and, gentlemen, it is very hard upon you to be so much vexed upon the subject of policy abroad. You think generally, and I think, that your domestic affairs are quite enough to call for all your attention. There was a saying of an ancient Greek orator, who, unfortunately, very much undervalued what we generally call the better portion of the community—namely, women; he made a very disrespectful observation, which I am going to quote, not for the purpose of concurring with it, but for the purpose of an illustration.

Pericles, the great Athenian statesman, said with regard to women, their greatest merit was to be never heard of.

Now, what Pericles untruly said of women, I am very much disposed to say of foreign affairs— their great merit would be to be never heard of. Unfortunately, instead of being never heard of, they are always heard of, and you hear almost of nothing else; and I can't promise you, gentlemen, that you will be relieved from this everlasting din, because the consequences of an unwise meddling with foreign affairs are consequences that will for some time necessarily continue to trouble you, and that will find their way to your pockets in the shape of increased taxation.

Gentlemen, with that apology I ask you again to go with me beyond the seas. And as I wish to do full justice, I will tell you what I think to be the right principles of foreign policy; and then, as far as your patience and my strength will permit, I will, at any rate for a short time, illustrate those right principles by some of the departures from them that have taken place of late years. I first give you, gentlemen, what I think the right principles of foreign policy.

The first thing is to foster the strength of the empire by just legislation and economy at home, thereby producing two of the great elements of national power—namely, wealth, which is a physical element, and union and contentment, which are moral elements—and to reserve the strength of the empire, to reserve the expenditure of that strength for great and worthy occasions abroad. Here is my first principle of foreign policy: good government at home.

My second principle of foreign policy is this, that its aim ought to be to preserve to the nations of the world—and especially, were it but for shame, when we recollect the sacred name we bear as Christians, especially to the Christian nations of the world—the blessings of peace. That is my second principle.

My third principle is this: Even, gentlemen, when you do a good thing you may do it in so bad a way that you may entirely spoil the beneficial effect; and if we were to make ourselves the apostles of peace in the sense of conveying to the minds of other nations that we thought ourselves more entitled to an opinion on that subject than they are, or to deny their rights—well, very likely we should destroy the whole value of our doctrines. In my opinion the third sound principle is this: to strive to cultivate and maintain, aye, to the very uttermost, what is called the concert of Europe; to keep the powers of Europe in union together. And why? Because by keeping all in union together you neutralize, and fetter, and bind up the selfish aims of each. I am not here to flatter either England or any of them. They have selfish aims, as, unfortunately, we in late years have too sadly shown that we too have had selfish aims; but their common action is fatal to selfish aims. Common action means common objects; and the only objects for which you can unite together the powers of Europe are objects connected with the common good of them all. That, gentlemen, is my third principle of foreign policy.

My fourth principle is: That you should avoid needless and entangling engagements. You may boast about them, you may brag about them, you may say you are procuring consideration for the country. You may say that an Englishman can now hold up his head among the nations. You may say that he is now not in the hands of a Liberal ministry, who thought of nothing but pounds, shillings, and pence. But what does all this come to, gentlemen? It comes to this, that you are increasing your engagements without increasing your strength; and if you increase engagements without increasing strength, you diminish strength, you abolish strength; you really reduce the empire and do not increase it. You render it less capable of performing its duties; you render it an inheritance less precious to hand on to future generations.

My fifth principle is this, gentlemen: To acknowledge the equal rights of all nations. You may sympathize with one nation more than another. Nay, you must sympathize in certain circumstances with one nation more than another. You sympathize most with those nations, as a rule, with which you have the closest connection in language, in blood, and in religion, or whose circumstances at the time seem to give the strongest claim to sympathy. But in point of right all are equal, and you have no right to set up a system under which one of them is to be placed under moral suspicion or espionage, or to be made the constant subject of invective. If you do that, but especially if you claim for yourself a superiority, a pharisaical superiority over the whole of them, then I say you may talk about your patriotism if you please, but you are a misjudging friend of your country, and in undermining the basis of the esteem and respect of other people for your country you are in reality inflicting the severest injury upon it. I have now given you, gentlemen, five principles of foreign policy. Let me give you a sixth, and then I have done.

And that sixth is: That in my opinion foreign policy, subject to all the limitations that I have described, the foreign policy of England should always be inspired by the love of freedom. There should be a sympathy with freedom, a desire to give it scope, founded not upon visionary ideas, but upon the long experience of many generations within the shores of this happy isle, that in freedom you lay the firmest foundations both of loyalty and order; the firmest foundations for the development of individual character, and the best provision for the happiness of the nation at large. In the foreign policy of this country the name of Canning ever will be honoured. The name of Russell ever will be honoured. The name of Palmerston ever will be honoured by those who recollect the erection of the kingdom of Belgium, and the union of the disjoined provinces of Italy. It is that sympathy, not a sympathy with disorder, but, on the contrary, founded upon the deepest and most profound love of order—it is that sympathy which in my opinion ought to be the very atmosphere in which a foreign secretary of England ought to live and to move.

Gentlemen, it is impossible for me to do more to-day than to attempt very slight illustrations of those principles. But in uttering those principles I have put myself in a position in which no one is entitled to tell me—you will hear me out in what I say—that I simply object to the acts of others, and lay down no rules of action myself. I am not only prepared to show what are the rules of action which in my judgment are the right rules, but I am prepared to apply them, nor will I shrink from their application. I will take, gentlemen, the name which, most of all others, is associated with suspicion, and with alarm, and with hatred in the minds of many Englishmen. I will take the name of Russia, and at once I will tell you what I think about Russia, and how I am prepared as a member of Parliament to proceed in anything that respects Russia. You have heard me, gentlemen, denounced sometimes, I believe, as a Russian spy, sometimes as a Russian agent, sometimes as perhaps a Russian fool, which is not so bad, but still not very desirable. But, gentlemen, when you come to evidence, the worst thing that I have ever seen quoted out of any speech or writing of mine about Russia is that I did one day say, or I believe I wrote these terrible words: I recommended Englishmen to imitate Russia in her good deeds. Was not that a terrible proposition? I cannot recede from it. I think we ought to imitate Russia in her good deeds, and if the good deeds be few I am sorry for it, but I am not the less disposed on that account to imitate them when they come. I will now tell you what I think just about Russia.

I make it one of my charges against the foreign policy of Her Majesty's Government that, while they have completely estranged from this country —let us not conceal the fact—the feelings of a nation of eighty millions, for that is the number of the subjects of the Russian Empire—while they have contrived completely to estrange the feelings of that nation, they have aggrandized the power of Russia. They have aggrandised the power of Russia in two ways, which I will state with perfect distinctness. They

have augmented her territory. Before the European powers met at Berlin,
Lord Salisbury met with Count Schouvaloff, and Lord Salisbury agreed
that, unless he could convince Russia by his arguments in the open Congress of Berlin, he would support the restoration to the despotic power
of Russia of that country north of the Danube which at the moment constituted a portion of the free state of Roumania. Why, gentlemen, what
had been done by the Liberal government, which, forsooth, attended to
nothing but pounds, shillings and pence? The Liberal government had
driven Russia back from the Danube. Russia, which was a Danubian
power before the Crimean War, lost this position on the Danube by the
Crimean War; and the Tory government, which has been incensing and
inflaming you against Russia, yet, nevertheless, by binding itself beforehand to support, when the judgment was taken, the restoration of that
country to Russia, has aggrandised the power of Russia.

It further aggrandised the power of Russia in Armenia; but I would
not dwell upon that matter if it were not for a very strange circumstance.
You know that an Armenian province was given to Russia after the war,
but about that I own to you I have very much less feeling of objection. I
have objected from the first, vehemently, and in every form, to the granting of territory on the Danube to Russia, and carrying back the population of a certain country from a free state to a despotic state; but with
regard to the transfer of a certain portion of the Armenian people from
the government of Turkey to the government of Russia I must own that I
contemplate that transfer with much greater equanimity. I have no fear
myself of the territorial extensions of Russia, in Asia, no fear of them
whatever. I think the fears are no better than old women's fears. And I
don't wish to encourage her aggressive tendencies in Asia, or anywhere
else. But I admit it may be, and probably is, the case that there is some
benefit attending upon the transfer of a portion of Armenia from Turkey
to Russia.

But here is a very strange fact. You know that that portion of Armenia
includes the port of Batoum. Lord Salisbury has lately stated to the country that, by the Treaty of Berlin, the port of Batoum is to be only a
commercial port. If the Treaty of Berlin stated that it was to be only a
commercial port, which, of course, could not be made an arsenal, that fact
would be very important. But, happily, gentlemen, although treaties are
concealed from us nowadays as long and as often as is possible, the Treaty
of Berlin is an open instrument. We can consult it for ourselves; and
when we consult the Treaty of Berlin we find it states that Batoum shall
be essentially a commercial port, but not that it shall be only a commercial port. Why, gentlemen, Leith is essentially a commercial port, but
there is nothing to prevent the people of this country, if in their wisdom
or their folly they should think fit, from constituting Leith as a great

naval arsenal or fortification; and there is nothing to prevent the Emperor of Russia, while leaving to Batoum a character that shall be essentially commercial, from joining with that another character that is not in the slightest degree excluded by the treaty, and making it as much as he pleases a port of military defence. Therefore, I challenge the assertion of Lord Salisbury; and as Lord Salisbury is fond of writing letters to the "Times" to bring the Duke of Argyll to book, he perhaps will be kind enough to write another letter to the "Times" and tell in what clause of the Treaty of Berlin he finds it written that the port of Batoum shall be only a commercial port. For the present, I simply leave it on record that he has misrepresented the Treaty of Berlin.

With respect to Russia, I take two views of the position of Russia. The position of Russia in Central Asia I believe to be one that has, in the main, been forced upon her against her will. She has been compelled— and this is the impartial opinion of the world—she has been compelled to extend her frontier southward in Central Asia by causes in some degree analogous to, but certainly more stringent and imperative than, the causes which have commonly led us to extend, in a far more important manner, our frontier in India; and I think it, gentlemen, much to the credit of the late Government, much to the honour of Lord Clarendon and Lord Granville that, when we were in office, we made a covenant with Russia, in which Russia bound herself to exercise no influence or interference whatever in Afghanistan, we, on the other hand, making known our desire that Afghanistan should continue free and independent. Both the powers acted with uniform strictness and fidelity upon this engagement until the day when we were removed from office. But Russia, gentlemen, has another position—her position in respect to Turkey; and here it is that I have complained of the Government for aggrandising the power of Russia; it is on this point that I most complain.

The policy of Her Majesty's Government was a policy of repelling and repudiating the Slavonic populations of Turkey in Europe, and of declining to make England the advocate for their interests. Nay, more, she became in their view the advocate of the interests opposed to theirs. Indeed, she was rather the decided advocate of Turkey; and now Turkey is full of loud complaints—and complaints, I must say, not unjust—that we allured her on to her ruin; that we gave the Turks a right to believe that we should support them; that our ambassadors, Sir Henry Elliot and Sir Austin Layard, both of them said we had most vital interests in maintaining Turkey as it was, and consequently the Turks thought if we had vital interests we should certainly defend them; and they were thereby lured on into the ruinous, cruel and destructive war with Russia. But by our conduct to the Slavonic populations we alienated those populations from us. We made our name odious among them. They had every disposition to sympathize with us, every disposition to confide in us. They are, as a people, desirous of freedom, desirous of self-government, with no aggressive views, but hating the idea of being absorbed in a huge despotic empire like Russia. But when they found that we, and the other powers of Europe, under our unfortunate guidance, declined to become in any manner their champions in defence of the rights of life, of property, and of female honour—when they found that there was no call which could find its way to the heart of England through its government, or to the hearts of other powers, and that Russia alone was disposed to fight for them, why naturally they said, Russia is our friend. We have done everything, gentlemen, in our power to drive these populations into the arms of Russia. If Russia has aggressive dispositions in the direction of Turkey—and I think it probable that she may have them—it is we who laid the ground upon which Russia may make her march to the south—we who have taught the Bulgarians, the Servians, the Roumanians, the Montenegrins, that there is one power in Europe, and only one, which is ready to support in act and by the sword her professions of sympathy with the oppressed populations of Turkey. That power is Russia, and how can you blame these people if, in such circumstances, they are disposed to say, Russia is our friend? But why did we make them say it? Simply because of the policy of the Government, not because of the wishes of the people of this country. Gentlemen, this is the most dangerous form of aggrandizing Russia. If Russia is aggressive anywhere, if Russia is formidable anywhere, it is by movements toward the south, it is by schemes for acquiring command of the straits or of Constantinople; and there is no way by which you can possibly so much assist her in giving reality to these designs as by inducing and disposing the populations of these provinces, who are now in virtual possession of them, to look upon Russia as their champion and their friend, to look upon England as their disguised, perhaps, but yet real and effective enemy.

Why, now, gentlemen, I have said that I think it not unreasonable either to believe, or at any rate to admit it to be possible, that Russia has aggressive designs in the east of Europe. I do not mean immediate aggressive designs. I do not believe that the Emperor of Russia is a man of aggressive schemes or policy. It is that, looking to that question in the long run, looking at what has happened, and what may happen in ten or twenty years, in one generation, in two generations, it is highly probable that in some circumstances Russia may develop aggressive tendencies towards the south.

Perhaps you will say I am here guilty of the same injustice to Russia that I have been deprecating, because I say that we ought not to adopt the method of condemning anybody without cause, and setting up exceptional principles in proscription of a particular nation. Gentlemen, I will explain to you in a moment the principle upon which I act, and the grounds upon which I form my judgment. They are simply these grounds; I look at the position of Russia, the geographical position of Russia relatively to Turkey. I look at the comparative strength of the two empires; I look at the importance of the Dardanelles and the Bosphorus as an exit and a channel for the military and commercial marine of Russia to the Mediterranean; and what I say to myself is this: If the United Kingdom were in the same position relatively to Turkey which Russia holds upon the map of the globe, I feel quite sure that we should be very apt indeed both to entertain and to execute aggressive designs upon Turkey. Gentlemen, I will go further, and will frankly own to you that I believe if we, instead of happily inhabiting this island, had been in the possession of the Russian territory, and in the circumstances of the Russian people, we should most likely have eaten up Turkey long ago. And consequently, in saying that Russia ought to be vigilantly watched in that quarter, I am only applying to her the rule which in parallel circumstances I feel convinced ought to be applied, and would be justly applied, to judgments upon our own country.

Gentlemen, there is only one other point on which I must still say a few words to you, although there are a great many upon which I have a great many words yet to say somewhere or other.

Of all the principles, gentlemen, of foreign policy which I have enumerated, that to which I attach the greatest value is the principle of the equality of nations; because, without recognizing that principle, there is no such thing as public right, and without public international right there is no instrument available for settling the transactions of mankind except material force. Consequently the principle of equality among nations lies, in my opinion, at the very basis and root of a Christian civilisation, and when that principle is compromised or abandoned, with it must depart our hopes of tranquillity and of progress for mankind.

I am sorry to say, gentlemen, that I feel it my absolute duty to make this charge against the foreign policy under which we have lived for the last two years, since the resignation of Lord Derby. It has been a foreign policy, in my opinion, wholly, or to a perilous extent, unregardful of public right, and it has been founded upon the basis of a false, I think an arrogant and a dangerous, assumption, although I do not question its being made conscientiously and for what was believed the advantage of the country—an untrue, arrogant, and dangerous assumption that we are entitled to assume for ourselves some dignity, which we should also be entitled to withhold from others, and to claim on our own part authority to do things which we would not permit to be done by others. For example, when Russia was going to the Congress at Berlin, we said: "Your Treaty of San Stefano is of no value. It is an act between you and Turkey;

but the concerns of Turkey by the Treaty of Paris are the concerns of Europe at large. We insist upon it that the whole of your treaty of San Stefano shall be submitted to the Congress at Berlin, that they may judge how far to open it in each and every one of its points, because the concerns of Turkey are the common concerns of the powers of Europe acting in concert."

Having asserted that principle to the world, what did we do? These two things, gentlemen: Secretly, without the knowledge of Parliament, without even the forms of official procedure, Lord Salisbury met Count Schouvaloff in London, and agreed with him upon the terms on which the two powers together should be bound in honour to one another to act upon all the most important points when they came before the Congress at Berlin. Having alleged against Russia that she should not be allowed to settle Turkish affairs with Turkey, because they were but two powers, and these affairs were the common affairs of Europe, and of European interest, we then got Count Schouvaloff into a private room, and on the part of England and Russia, they being but two powers, we settled a large number of the most important of these affairs in utter contempt and derogation of the very principle for which the Government had been contending for months before, for which they had asked Parliament to grant a sum of £6,000,000, for which they had spent that £6,000,000 in needless and mischievous armaments. That which we would not allow Russia to do with Turkey, because we pleaded the rights of Europe, we ourselves did with Russia, in contempt of the rights of Europe. Nor was that all, gentlemen. That act was done, I think, on one of the last days of May, in the year 1878, and the document was published, made known to the world, made known to the Congress at Berlin, to its infinite astonishment, unless I am very greatly misinformed.

But that was not all. Nearly at the same time we performed the same operation in another quarter. We objected to a treaty between Russia and Turkey as having no authority, though that treaty was made in the light of day—namely, to the Treaty of San Stefano; and what did we do? We went not in the light of day, but in the darkness of the night—not in the knowledge and cognizance of other powers, all of whom would have had the faculty and means of watching all along, and of preparing and taking their own objections and shaping their own policy—not in the light of day, but in the darkness of the night, we sent the ambassador of England in Constantinople to the minister of Turkey, and there he framed, even while the Congress of Berlin was sitting to determine these matters of common interest, he framed that which is too famous, shall I say, or rather too notorious, as the Anglo-Turkish Convention.

Gentlemen, it is said, and said truly, that truth beats fiction; that what happens in fact from time to time is of a character so daring, so strange, that if the novelist were to imagine it and put it upon his pages, the whole world would reject it from its improbability. And that is the case of the Anglo-Turkish Convention. For who would have believed it possible that we should assert before the world the principle that Europe only could deal with the affairs of the Turkish empire, and should ask Parliament for six millions to support us in asserting that principle, should send ministers to Berlin who declared that unless that principle was acted upon they would go to war with the material that Parliament had placed in their hands, and should at the same time be concluding a separate agreement with Turkey, under which those matters of European jurisdiction were coolly transferred to English jurisdiction; and the whole matter was sealed with the worthless bribe of the possession and administration of the island of Cyprus! I said, gentlemen, the worthless bribe of the island of Cyprus and that is the truth. It is worthless for our purposes—not worthless in itself; an island of resources, an island of natural capabilities, provided they are allowed to develop themselves in the course of circumstances, without violent and unprincipled methods of action. But Cyprus was not thought to be worthless by those who accepted it as a bribe. On the contrary, you were told that it was to secure the road to India; you were told that it was to be the site of an arsenal very cheaply made, and more valuable than Malta; you were told that it was to revive trade. And a multitude of companies were formed, and sent agents and capital to Cyprus, and some of them, I fear, grievously burned their fingers there. I am not going to dwell upon that now. What I have in view is not the particular merits of Cyprus, but the illustration that I have given you in the case of the agreement of Lord Salisbury with Count Schouvaloff, and in the case of the Anglo-Turkish Convention, of the manner in which we have asserted for ourselves a principle that we had denied to others—namely, the principle of overriding the European authority of the Treaty of Paris, and taking the matters which that treaty gave to Europe into our own separate jurisdiction.

Now, gentlemen, I am sorry to find that that which I call the pharisaical assertion of our own superiority has found its way alike into the practice, and seemingly into the theories of the government. I am not going to assert anything which is not known, but the Prime Minister has said that there is one day in the year—namely, the ninth of November, Lord Mayor's Day—on which the language of sense and truth is to be heard amidst the surrounding din of idle rumors generated and fledged in the brains of irresponsible scribes. I do not agree, gentlemen, in that panegyric upon the ninth of November. I am much more apt to compare the ninth of November—certainly a well-known day in the year—but as to some of the speeches that have lately been made upon it, I am very much disposed to compare it with another day in the year, well known to British tradition, and that other day in the year is the first of April. But, gentlemen, on that day the Prime Minister, speaking out—I do not question for a moment his own sincere opinion—made what I think one of the most unhappy and ominous allusions ever made by a minister of this country. He quoted certain words, easily rendered, as "empire" and "liberty"—words (he said) of the Roman statesman, words descriptive of the state of Rome —and he quoted them as words which were capable of legitimate application to the position and circumstances of England. I join issue with the

Prime Minister upon that subject, and I affirm that nothing can be more fundamentally unsound, more practically ruinous, than the establishment of Roman analogies for the guidance of British policy. What, gentlemen, was Rome? Rome was indeed an imperial state, you may tell me—I know not, I cannot read the counsels of Providence—a State having a mission to subdue the world, but a State whose very basis it was to deny the equal rights, to proscribe the independent existence of other nations. That, gentlemen, was the Roman idea. It has been partially and not ill described in three lines of a translation from Vergil by our great poet Dryden, which run as follows:

> "O Rome! 'tis thine alone with awful sway
> To rule mankind, and make the world obey,
> Disposing peace and war thine own majestic way."

We are told to fall back upon this example. No doubt the word "empire" was qualified with the word "liberty." But what did the two words "liberty" and "empire" mean in a Roman mouth? They meant simply this: "Liberty for ourselves, empire over the rest of mankind."

I do not think, gentlemen, that this ministry, or any other ministry, is going to place us in the position of Rome. What I object to is the revival of the idea. I care not how feebly, I care not even how, from a philosophic or historical point of view, how ridiculous the attempt at this revival may be. I say it indicates an intention—I say it indicates a frame of mind, and the frame of mind, unfortunately, I find, has been consistent with the policy of which I have given you some illustrations—the policy of denying to others the rights that we claim ourselves. No doubt, gentlemen, Rome may have had its work to do, and Rome did its work. But modern times have brought a different state of things. Modern times have established a sisterhood of nations, equal, independent, each of them built up under that legitimate defence which public law affords to every nation, living within its own borders, and seeking to perform its own affairs; but if one thing more than another has been detestable to Europe, it has been the appearance upon the stage from time to time of men who, even in the times of the Christian civilisation, have been thought to aim at universal dominion. It was this aggressive disposition on the part of Louis XIV, King of France, that led your forefathers, gentlemen, freely to spend their blood and treasure in a cause not immediately their own, and to struggle against the method of policy which, having Paris for its centre, seemed to aim at an universal monarchy.

It was the very same thing, a century and a half later, which was the charge launched, and justly launched, against Napoleon, that under his dominion France was not content even with her extended limits, but Germany, and Italy, and Spain, apparently without any limit to this pestilent and pernicious process, were to be brought under the dominion or influence of France, and national equality was to be trampled under foot, and national rights denied. For that reason England in the struggle almost exhausted herself, greatly impoverished her people, brought upon herself, and Scotland, too, the consequences of a debt that nearly crushed their energies, and poured forth their best blood without limit, in order to resist and put down these intolerable pretensions.

Gentlemen, it is but in a pale and weak and almost despicable miniature that such ideas are now set up, but you will observe that the poison lies—that the poison and the mischief lie—in the principle and not the scale.

It is the opposite principle which, I say, has been compromised by the action of the ministry, and which I call upon you, and upon any who choose to hear my views, to vindicate when the day of our election comes; I mean the sound and the sacred principle that Christendom is formed of a band of nations who are united to one another in the bonds of right; that they are without distinction of great and small; there is an absolute equality between them—the same sacredness defends the narrow limits of Belgium as attaches to the extended frontiers of Russia, or Germany, or France. I hold that he who by act or word brings that principle into peril or disparagement, however honest his intentions may be, places himself in the position of one inflicting—I won't say intending to inflict—I ascribe nothing of the sort—but inflicting injury upon his own country, and endangering the peace and all the most fundamental interests of Christian society.

Charles Stewart Parnell

.

Charles Stewart Parnell

[*Born* JUNE 27, 1846—*Died* OCTOBER 6, 1891]

Parnell, tall and of stately bearing, was always fastidiously dressed, and often wore a flower . . . Parnell's eye had the fascination of the mesmerist's; and, when he was roused, the yellow glints that glanced again and again across them seemed like the emission of sparks.—SIR ALFRED ROBBINS

$\mathbb{C}$harles Stewart Parnell is "the first Irishman who played the game of high politics on something like equal terms with the best exponents England could produce."[1] By his effective use of obstruction in Parliament and persuasion before the masses of Irishmen, Parnell expedited the opening of an Irish Parliament beyond all possible expectations by accomplishing more in fifteen years than others had in the previous seventy-five.[2]

Although Morley refers to Parnell as "one of the two noblest English orators of our day,"[3] he was also an effective parliamentarian. So successful was his campaign of obstruction as an irritant, which he began in the Spring of 1877, the leaders of both the Liberal and Tory parties sought to negotiate a settlement with Parnell, as leader of the Home Rulers, in order to pass needed legislation affecting matters of the realm.

As a debater, his speaking lacked ornateness, but it possessed quality in its "clearness, its directness and terseness."[4] He avoided the dramatic by speaking without advertisement when his hearers were few; yet, he always commanded the utmost attention from the leading political figures of his day.[5]

As a popular speaker, he was capable of exerting a profound influence on his fellow Irishmen. Those speeches best remembered were delivered during the recess of 1880. Speaking at Ennis, New Ross, Kilkenny, Cork (his constituency), Langford, Galway, Tipperary, Limerick, Athlone, Dublin, and elsewhere, he shaped an epoch as no public utterances had before by dictating policy to the Irish people who avidly put it into practice.[6]

The most remarkable of these speeches occurred at Ennis on September 19, 1880. According to Claude G. Bowers, "few [speeches] have been so historic or effective, for this speech at Ennis brought

---

1 M. M. O'Hara, *Chief and Tribune: Parnell and Davitt* (Dublin: Maunsel and Co., Ltd., 1919), p. 329.
2 *Ibid.*
3 Viscount John Morley, *Recollections,* I (New York: The Macmillan Co., 1917), p. 242.
4 Claude G. Bowers, *The Irish Orators* (Indianapolis: The Bobbs-Merrill Co., 1916), p. 503.
5 William O'Brien, *The Parnell of Real Life* (London: T. Fisher Unwin Ltd., 1926), p. 79.
6 O'Hara, *op. cit.,* p. 143.

the boycott into action for the first time." [7] R. Barry O'Brien, in his well-documented biography of Parnell, refers to this speech as one which "rang throughout the land":

. . . he struck the keynote of the agitation; he laid down the lines on which the [Land] League should work. Slowly, calmly, deliberately, without a quiver of passion, a note of *rhetoric* [italics mine], or an exclamation of anger, but in a tone that penetrated his audience like the touch of cold steel, he proclaimed war against all who should resist the mandates of the League. [8]

A second notable address was delivered in the House of Commons on June 7, 1886, closing the Home Rule debate. [9] O'Hara calls it "one of his finest performances—finished and adequate in diction; carefully reasoned, confident in its tone, rich and varied in its matter." [10] Unlike most of Parnell's speeches in which he seldom used a written note, [11] this speech had been carefully prepared. [12] It was listened to with "rapt attention" by friend and foe alike, and although the Bill was defeated by a vote of 313 to 343, the principle of Irish Home Rule became indelibly stamped on the minds of all legislators until it became a reality following World War I.

Parnell's campaign for Irish rights were not confined to the British Isles. In his attempt to win sympathetic support in America, Bowers believes Parnell gave more attention to the speeches delivered on his American tour than to all others. [13] The speech especially to be remembered was delivered to the United States' House of Representatives. Bowers describes it as the most complete exposition of the Irish cause and the one most conscientiously prepared. [14]

---

[7] Bowers, *op. cit.*, p. 459.

[8] R. Barry O'Brien, *The Life of Charles Stewart Parnell* (New York: Harper and Brothers, 1898), p. 236. Incidents leading up to Parnell's boycott declaration are explained by O'Hara, *op. cit.*, p. 141. "At the root of the anarchy was the tyranny of the landlord class. During 1879, 6,239 tenants were evicted, and there were 863 agrarian outrages committed. In 1880, 10,457 people were thrown upon the roadside, and there were 2,590 agrarian outrages. Crime increased almost in exact ratio with the growth of evictions." The effects of the policy of social ostracism are explained by J. L. Hammond, *Gladstone and the Irish Nation* (London: Longmans, Green and Co., 1938), p. 193: "The general result of boycott and outrage combined was to put such terror into the landlords that evictions were checked. Out of 2,110 evictions in 1880, only 198 occurred in the last quarter."

[9] See 306 H.C. Deb. 3 s., Cols. 1168–1184.

[10] O'Hara, *op. cit.*, p. 279.

[11] *Ibid.*, p. 79.

[12] Katharine O'Shea, *Charles Stewart Parnell*, II (London: Cassell and Co., 1914), p. 39.

[13] Bowers, *op. cit.*, p. 504.

[14] *Ibid.*, p. 505.

For a man who began his career in Parliament as a "halting speaker," [15] great tribute to Parnell's speaking was contributed by Gladstone, who once said to Morley, " 'he has got the very rarest of all qualities in a speaker—*measure*. He always says exactly as much as, and not any more nor less than, he means to say'." [16]

It is now generally agreed that public disclosure of his illicit romance with Mrs. Katherine O'Shea, whom he later married, was an act of political vengeance which failed in the long run to discredit Parnell's achievements. Its immediate effect was to break his spirit— death followed soon after.

---

[15] *Ibid.*, p. 503.
[16] Morley, *op. cit.*, p. 241.

The Irish Land Question[1]

•

ENNIS, IRELAND *September 19, 1880*

M r. Parnell, who was received with loud cheering, then came forward and said:
In acknowledging my gratification at this splendid reception which you have given us and at this magnificent meeting, I wish to say that it gives me additional pleasure to have the opportunity of addressing for the first time after the session of Parliament a meeting in Ennis, which was the first constituency in Ireland to send me help in the last Parliament. (*Cheers.*) I may perhaps also be permitted to point out to you a noteworthy feature connected with this meeting, especially as I think it is a sign of the times and a sign of the progress of our movement. When first I addressed you last July twelve months this square was glittering with the bayonets of police—(*cheers*),—and I promised you then, pointing to the force, that if we could build up a determined and united Irish party that in a very few years this military force would be abolished altogether. (*Cheers.*) To-day there is not a single constable present at this meeting (*cheers*),—and it is the first of Irish land meetings which have not been attended by scores—some of them by several scores—of constables. Let us look upon this as a happy omen of the future, as the first recognition in our history by the Government of England of the ability of our people to maintain order for themselves (*cheers*), and, consequently, to govern themselves (*cheers*), and let me ask in return so to bear yourselves during this meeting and after this meeting as to show that you are worthy of the practical power of self-government. (*Cheers.*) The resolution[2] which has

---

1 *The Manchester Guardian*, September 20, 1880, p. 8.
2 "That we cordially endorse the action of the Irish party under the guidance of Mr. Parnell during the last session of Parliament, but we view with regret the secession of one section of the party, that which followed the Whigs across the floor of the House and we trust that next session the Irish members will sit in a body in Parliament in op-

346

been proposed and seconded is one inculcating the necessity of union, and independence of every English Ministry, whether it be Tory or Radical. (*Hear.*) I have always believed in the necessity of this, but my convictions have been tenfold strengthened by the experience of the past session. I have seen that the more independence the Irish party showed the more respect it gained for itself and for Ireland. (*Hear.*) I don't complain of our party. Our party on the whole has been a good and a worthy one. It is true that a very small section followed the Government across the House of Commons, and refused to sit with the great majority of their colleagues, and the spectacle was presented of an apparently divided Irish party, perhaps 40 on one side and some 20 on the other. I regret this appearance of division and dissension, but I trust that those members, recognising that the overwhelming opinion of their constituents is in favour of union and unity, will retrace their steps and will join the great body of their colleagues in presenting a solid front to every Government. For ourselves, in the last Parliament, when we had a Tory Government to face, I never at the time hid my convictions that with a Liberal Government in power it would be necessary for us somewhat to change or modify our action. Nothing was to be gained from the Tories, and it was therefore necessary for the Irish party to punish them without sparing them. (*Cheers.*) This present Liberal Government has made great promises. Up to the present it has absolutely given us not one single performance, but through the mouth of a Chief Secretary of Ireland it was entreated that it be given one year's time in order to see whether it cannot benefit Ireland, and we have been willing to give it the time and trial. But I stand here today to express my conviction that whenever it is necessary for us to resume our ancient policy, such as we practised against the Tories, whenever we find that this Liberal Government falls short of either its professions or its performances, on that day it will be the duty of the present strong Irish party to show that it can punish the Liberal Government as well as the Tory. (*Cheers.*) Now, we have had issued a Land Commission, and there has been some difference of opinion as to whether the tenant farmers ought to give evidence before the Committee or not. I have not yet had an opportunity of saying anything in public against this matter, but I may say that in the main my opinions coincide with those of Mr. John Dillon with reference to this Committee. (*Hear, hear.*) At the same time—I only wish to express my opinion; and I don't wish to coerce the Irish tenant farmer with reference to this matter one way or the other—I am bound to tell you honestly that I believe this Committee was appointed in order to try and whittle down the demands of the Irish Secretary, to find out for the English Government what was the very least measure of reform that

position to every English minister until the right of Ireland to self-government has been restored."

had a chance of being accepted in Ireland, and to a great extent to divert
the minds of tenant farmers from agitating and organising to the useless
work of going before this Committee and giving evidence. I cannot possibly see what useful effect evidence before this Committee can have. We
know that the report, if there is any report, must be of a one-sided character and against the interests of the people of this country. The composition of the Committee is a guarantee of that. What will be said if the
tenant farmers come before this Committee in large numbers? It will be
said that you have accepted the Commission. It will be said that you will
be bound by its report, and if there is very much evidence given it will
form a very good excuse for the Government and for the English Tory
party to put off legislation on the land question until they have time to
read the evidence and consider its bearing and effect. My opinion, then,
decidedly is this—whatever harm you do to your cause by going before
the Committee, you certainly will be able to do no good. Depend upon it
that the measure of the Land Bill of next session will be the measure of
your activity and energy this winter. (*Cheers.*) It will be the measure of
your determination not to pay unjust rents. It will be the measure of your
determination to keep a firm grip of your homesteads. (*Cheers.*) It will be
the measure of your determination not to bid for farms from which others
have been evicted, and to use the strong force of public opinion to deter
the unjust men amongst yourselves—and there are many such—from bidding for such farms. (*Hear, hear.*) If you refuse to pay unjust rents, if you
refuse to take farms from which others have been evicted, the land question must be settled, and settled in a way that will be satisfactory to you.
It depends, therefore, upon yourselves, and not upon any Commission or
any governments when you have made this question ripe for settlement.
Then, and not till then, will it be settled. (*Cheers.*) It is very nearly ripe
already in many parts of Ireland. It is ripe in Mayo, Galway, Roscommon,
Sligo, and portions of the county Clare; but I regret to say that the tenant
farmers of the county Clare have been backward in organisation up to the
present time. You must take and band yourselves together in Land
Leagues. Every town and village must have its own branch. You must
know the circumstances of the holdings and of the tenures of the district
over which the League has jurisdiction. You must see that the principles
of the Land League are inculcated, and when you have done this in Clare,
then Clare will take her rank with the other active counties, and you will
be included in the next Land Bill brought forward by the Government.
(*Cheers.*) Now what are you to do to a tenant who bids for a farm from
which another tenant has been evicted? (*Several voices:* "Shoot him.") I
think I heard somebody say shoot him. I wish to point out to you a very
much better way, a more Christian and charitable way, which will give
the lost sinner an opportunity of repenting. (*Laughter and hear.*) When a

man takes a farm from which another has been evicted you must shun him on the roadside when you meet him. You must shun him in the streets of the town; you must shun him in the shop; you must shun him in the fair and in the market place; and even in the place of worship by leaving him severely alone, by isolating him from the rest of his country-men as if he were the leper of old. You must show him your detestation of the crime he has committed. If you do this you may depend on it that there will be no man so lost to shame as to dare the public opinion of all the right thinking men in the country and transgress your unwritten code of laws. (*Loud cheers.*) People are very much engaged at present in dis-cussing the way in which the land question is to be settled, just the same as when a few years since Irishmen were at each other's throats as to the sort of Parliament we would have if we got one. I am always thinking it is better first to catch your hare before you decide how you are going to cook him. I would strongly recommend public men not to waste their breath too much in discussing how the land question is to be settled, but rather to help and encourage the people in making it, as I said just now, ripe for settlement. (*Applause.*) When it is ripe for settlement you will probably have your choice as to how it shall be settled, and I said a year ago that the land question would never be settled until the Irish landlords were just as anxious to have it settled as the Irish tenants. (*Cheers.*) (*A Voice:* "They soon will be.") There are, indeed, so many ways in which it may be settled that it is almost superfluous to discuss them, but I stand here today to express my opinion that no settlement can be satisfactory or permanent which does not ensure the uprooting of that system of landlordism, which has brought the country three times in a century to famine. (*Cheers.*) The feudal system of land tenure has been tried in almost every European country, and it has been found wanting everywhere, but nowhere has it wrought more evil, produced more suffering, crime, and destitution than in Ireland. (*Cheers.*) It was abolished in Prussia by transferring the lands from the landlords to the occupying tenants. The landlords were given Government paper as compensation. Let the English Government give the landlords their paper tomorrow as compensation. (*Laughter.*) We want no money. Not a single penny of the money would be necessary. Why, if they give the Irish landlords—the bad section of them—the four or five millions a year that they spend on the police and military (*groans*) in helping them to collect their rents that would be a solution of it (*cheers*), and a very cheap solution of it. But perhaps, as with other reforms, they will try a little patch work and tinkering for a while until they learn better. (*Hear, hear.*) Well, let them patch and tinker if they wish. In my opinion the longer the landlords wait the worse the settlement they will get. (*Cheers.*) Now is the time for them to settle before the people learn the power of combination. We have been accused of preaching communistic doctrine when we told the people not to pay an unjust rent, and the following out of this advice in a few of the Irish counties had shown the English Government the necessity for a radical alteration to the land laws; but how would they like it if we told the people some day or other not to pay any rent until this question is settled? (*Cheers.*) We have not told them that yet, and I hope it may never be necessary for us to speak in that way. (*Hear, hear.*) I hope the question will be settled peaceably and justly to all parties. (*Hear.*) If it should not be settled, we cannot continue to allow this mill-stone to hang round the neck of our country, throttling its industry and preventing progress. (*Cheers.*) It will be for the consideration of wiser heads than mine whether if the landlords continue obdurate and refuse all just concessions we shall not be obliged to tell the people of Ireland to strike against rent until the question has been settled (*Cheers*), and if the 500,000 tenant farmers of Ireland struck against 10,000 landlords, I should like to see where they would get police and soldiers enough to make them pay. (*Loud cheers.*)

A resolution was then passed pledging them not to take a farm from which a tenant had been evicted for the non-payment of any unjust rent.

Mr. T. D. SULLIVAN, M.P., supported the resolution and said that amongst the Irish party there was not a more courageous or more resolute man than the member for the borough of Ennis, who, he believed, if ordered by Mr. Parnell, would lay hold of the mace that lay in front of the Speaker in the House of Commons and throw it out of the window.— (*Cheers.*)

A vote of thanks to the Chairman terminated the proceedings.

Lord Randolph
Churchill

.

Lord Randolph Churchill

[*Born* FEBRUARY 13, 1849—*Died* JANUARY 24, 1895]

His slim and boyish figure, his mustache which had an emotion of its own, his round protruding eye, gave a compound interest to his speeches and his conversation.—LORD ROSEBERY

$\mathbf{T}$he parliamentary career of Lord Randolph Churchill, states Rosebery, is "one of the most singular and interesting of that century, only less dramatic than that of Disraeli." [1] To study Lord Randolph is to observe a man who indeed represents "the fruit and blossom" of the parliamentary system.[2] He attacked administrative proposals when out of office, and he defended them well when in office.

Lord Randolph's name cannot be associated with the passage of any one significant piece of legislation, for he represents a movement which was to have significance on virtually all legislation. This movement is called Tory Democracy, an influence which liberalized Tory influence toward the masses. His oratory was a great contributing factor to his success. According to his son, "By the end of 1882 he was already unquestionably the most popular speaker in the Conservative party. In 1884 and 1885 he equalled, if he did not surpass, Mr. Gladstone himself in the interest and enthusiasm which his personality aroused." [3] In the Spring of 1881, for example, the speeches of Lord Randolph were being carried *verbatim* by the *Morning Post* and *The Times*, papers read by "the worthy, pious, and substantial citizen who . . . ate it up line by line with snorts of indignation or gurglings of mirth." [4]

Rosebery describes Lord Randolph's speechmaking as "almost unbroken triumph" from 1880 to 1886.[5] After his resignation from the Ministry of Lord Salisbury, he began losing his confidence when he was not asked to return, and his effectiveness as a speaker declined accordingly.

At his height as an orator, Lord Randolph is said to have possessed "fascination, audacity, tact, great and solid ability welded with the priceless gift of concentration; marvellous readiness in debate, and an almost unrivalled skill and attraction on the platform." [6]

Peter DeMendelssohn describes his speeches as "models of con-

---

1 Lord Rosebery, *Lord Randolph Churchill* (London: Harper and Brothers, 1906), p. 81.

2 *Ibid.*, p. 181.

3 Winston Spencer Churchill, *Lord Randolph Churchill*, II (London: Macmillan and Co., Ltd., 1906), p. 274.

4 *Ibid.*, I, p. 277.

5 Rosebery, *op. cit.*, p. 196.

6 *Ibid.*, p. 82.

struction." [7] Before delivering a major address, Lord Randolph would shut himself up absolutely for about two days, write a manuscript, have it virtually memorized upon completion, arm himself with copious notes, and emerge to speak with freshness and spontaneity. Mindful of the influence of the press, he would have delivered to them copies of the speech,[8] "quite without alteration" from what he actually said on the platform.[9]

Of Lord Randolph's many eloquent addresses, Rosebery believes the speech delivered at Blackpool on January 24, 1884, to be "the most brilliant of his platform speeches. . . ." [10] Robert Rhodes James said of that particular speech, "if I had to choose any single speech which characterized all his qualities as a public speaker I should select this." [11]

---

7 Peter DeMendelssohn, *The Age of Churchill* (London: Thames and Hudson, 1961), p. 52.

8 Robert Rhodes James, *Lord Randolph Churchill* (London: Weidenfeld and Nicholson, 1959).

9 Churchill, *op. cit.*, I, p. 276.

10 Rosebery, op. cit., p. 95.

11 James, op. cit., p. 135.

Financial Reform:
The Administration of "Chips"[1]

•

Two years have elapsed since I had the honour of addressing a Lancashire audience. At that time I endeavoured to describe to the electors of Manchester the true state of Ireland, and the probable effect upon that country and upon our own of the mixture of treachery and incapacity which poisoned the councils of Mr. Gladstone's administration. The truth of the remarks which I then made was very soon afterwards signally illustrated by the release from prison of the leaders of the revolutionary party in Ireland, the bargain struck between Mr. Gladstone and Mr. Parnell for mutual political support (more popularly known as the Kilmainham Treaty), and the assassination of Lord Frederick Cavendish and Mr. Burke by the 'Invincible' emissaries of the Irish party.

This crowning atrocity gave a slight shock to the political association between Mr. Gladstone and Mr. Parnell. It even produced a temporary estrangement during the passing of the Coercion Bill. But this unpleasantness soon wore off. The parties led by these two great men have too much in common to be alienated from each other for long. General destruction and all-round plunder are alike their duty, their pleasure, and their pride. Mr. Gladstone has a weakness for effecting his objects by Act of Parliament; the Irish a slight preference for more rapid and violent action. A little difference as to method, you see, but a precisely similar result. These two parties are now at this moment preparing to meet Parliament with a demand for a repeal of the Union. Mr. Parnell, with his customary candour, will use the word 'Repeal'; Mr. Gladstone, with his customary ambiguity, will describe the policy as an assimilation of Irish

---

1 *Speeches of the Right Honourable Lord Randolph Churchill, 1880–1888*, I (London: Longmans, Green, and Co., 1889), pp. 97–117.

and English political rights, and as placing in the hands of the people the local government of the country. It is a monstrous and dangerous coalition we have to face; it strikes at the vitals of the empire. The union of England, Scotland, and Ireland is the nerve-centre of the wide-spread dominions of the Queen. If you sever it, the empire is dead; if you injure it, the empire is paralysed. It is to Lancashire that the eyes of the Tory party are hopefully turned. Lancashire, we confidently anticipate, will lead the van of the army of resistance. We remember that Lancashire, first of all English counties, discerned the germs of this movement in 1868, when Mr. Gladstone, flying with impetuous haste from one corner of the country to another, was hurled down by your Southern Division. Down through electoral space he fell, nor was his fall arrested till he reached the distant borough of Greenwich. Down, too, at that time fell Lord Hartington, his colleague, whom an obscure group of villages in Wales received and nourished. We remember that but for Lancashire in 1868 the Tory party was almost gone, and by those memories we call upon you now to rouse yourselves to the fight, and to rally the British counties against the Prime Minister and his Irish allies. Soon, very soon, this Parliament—'the best of all modern Parliaments'—will be scattered to the winds, its members scurrying helter-skelter about the country; soon the destinies of this Parliament will be in the hands of the leaders of the Opposition, and if, for once, they can nerve themselves to a struggle, and wisely use the golden moments, Mr. Gladstone's days as a Minister of the Crown are numbered.

It is not only in Ireland that your Imperial interests are imperilled. In Egypt a tremendous storm is gathering. I cannot believe that the anarchy and the misery and the insecurity which now distract that country and threaten the entire civilisation of the East with ruin will be tolerated much longer by the Powers of Europe. The original object of our expedition to Egypt was distinctly immoral and base. It has tainted and corrupted all our efforts to restore order, and still remains a withering blight and curse. I said at Edinburgh, what I have said all along, that the Khedive Tewfik was a person unfit from his character and by his actions to be supported by Great Britain. This position has never been seriously contested either by the Government or by the leaders of the Opposition, but within the last few days has received a most remarkable confirmation. The name of 'Gordon' is a household word, not only in Egypt, but here at home, for courage, honesty, and truth. A statement from General Gordon appeared in all the papers the other day on the crisis in the Soudan. That high-souled officer recommended that Nubar Pasha should be placed at the head of the Egyptian Government. And what was the great danger he saw to Nubar Pasha's influence for good? One danger, and one alone—the intrigues of the Khedive Tewfik, the false and treacherous character of the Khedive Tewfik. That was the danger against which he warned his countrymen. General Gordon had just left this country for the Soudan with dictatorial authority conferred upon him by the English Government. What was the one condition which he made, the *sine qua non* on which he insisted, before undertaking his Herculean task? One condition, and one only—that he should be entirely independent of the Khedive Tewfik, should receive no orders from him, should be brought into no connection with him, but that all his instructions and all his authority should emanate from Downing Street, and not from the Palace of Cairo. Could I, I ask you—could I have obtained a more tremendous corroboration of my charges against the Khedive Tewfik than this irrefutable testimony of General Gordon? I said at Edinburgh, what I have said all along, that the Egyptian war was a bondholders' war, and I say now that our occupation of Egypt is a bondholders' occupation. Is there any one so simple as to suppose that we should have interfered with the movements of Arabi had there been no such things as Egyptian bonds? There are those who tell you that the protection of the Suez Canal was the object of our expedition to Egypt. A more erroneous statement was never made. The Suez Canal was at no time in the smallest danger. The Suez Canal will always take care of itself. The whole world, the East and the West, are equally and mutually interested in the freedom of the Suez Canal. Surely, you will not be misled by such an obvious and transparent fiction. It was bonds and bondholders and no other power which diverted Mr. Gladstone, greatly hesitating, from his path, and which drew the British fleet to Alexandria. It was bonds and bondholders only which commanded the British troops. I pray you mark this. England has never before interfered with the internal affairs of other nations on account of bonds or debts which might be owing to her people. We have always looked upon these matters as altogether outside the range of active Government interference. The Southern States of America took a lot of money from us which they never paid. Did we go to war with the United States? The Republics of Honduras, Costa Rica, and Venezuela ruined an immense number of British subjects. Did we occupy those countries with our forces? I am afraid to say how many people in this country lost their all when Turkey repudiated her debts. The Government of England took no action. It has been left for Mr. Gladstone's Government to depart from this wise and time-honoured tradition—for this Government, whose cardinal principle of foreign policy was non-intervention; it has been left for them to intervene, and intervene actively and violently, and on the side of oppression as against the cause of freedom, in the one particular sphere in which till now non-intervention had been acquiesced in by both parties in the State. But I do not ask you to take my assertion as sufficient proof of this accusation. I refer you to Lord Granville's despatch in 1882.

Then, in answer to Sir E. Malet's inquiry as to whether the Egyptian Government might be allowed to superintend the expenditure of those taxes which had not been assigned to the bondholders, Lord Granville refuses his consent, 'regard being had,' he says, 'to those pecuniary interests on whose behalf her Majesty's Government are acting;' and from the moment of that despatch the troubles in Egypt grew. This despatch is the proof of my indictment against Mr. Gladstone, that he has used the resources, dishonoured the name, and imperilled the position of this country in the East, on account of and in the interests of a gang of speculators and stock-jobbers who hold Egyptian bonds.

I am not raking up the past for the mere purpose of raking up the past, nor for the mere purpose of attacking Her Majesty's Government. I am raking up the past, and will continue to rake it up till voice and breath shall fail me, because I want the people to look into this question of our business in Egypt; because I know that until the people do look into it, and settle and solve it for themselves, no good will be done. These speculators and stock-jobbers who have dragged this country into war, and have saddled this overburdened Empire of ours with the occupation of Egypt, are comparatively few in number, but are very powerful. They have their creatures in the Government offices, they have their organs and writers in the London Press, they have their emissaries and agents hard at work in London society. The pressure they can bring to bear is tremendous, and I am convinced that until the masses of the people smash up and scatter this ring, our operations in Egypt will continue to be attended with failure, disgrace, and disaster. I know this, if I know anything at all, that if once the people of this country as a whole can be induced to interest themselves in any matter, to take it up, to make it their own, to settle it one way or another, the people will not go wrong. Governments will go wrong, Parliaments will go wrong, classes will go wrong, London society and the Pall-Mall clubs always go wrong; but the people do not go wrong. You must take up this Egyptian question and examine it for yourselves. I use the expression 'you must' advisedly, because if you would for one moment grasp the tremendous responsibilities towards Egypt, towards Europe, towards civilisation, which we have already incurred, the unknown and infinite liabilities we are drifting into, the terrible and crushing dangers which may at any moment burst upon us, you would not lose a day, or even an hour, before speaking out your mind.

I said that the occupation of Egypt was a bondholders' occupation. The policy of Her Majesty's Government in this Soudan question is proof enough of that, if proof were wanted. Had we been in Egypt for the interests of Egypt, or of Europe, or of civilisation and freedom generally should we have abandoned the entire territory of the Soudan, with all its government, garrisons, European and Egyptian subjects, to be massacred by a cruel and fanatical barbarian? Every honest man will answer no. But it is because we are not in Egypt for the benefit of Egypt, or of Europe, or of civilisation and freedom, and because an effort to hold the Soudan would have depreciated Egyptian bonds, would have led very probably to their ultimate repudiation and made the speculators and stock-jobbers howl—it is because of all this that we have abandoned the Soudan, and with it all our honour and all our prestige in the East. I know well what the people of England would say if they examined for themselves this Egyptian affair. They would say that the original expedition to Egypt was unnecessary and iniquitous; that Mr. Gladstone allowed a revolutionary movement to proceed far enough to destroy and shatter a corrupt and filthy dynasty; but that just when the revolutionary movement, which had at its back the entire Egyptian nation, was about to construct on the ruins of the former Government an administration of its own, that at that critical moment Mr. Gladstone intervened and shattered the revolutionary movement; that from that disastrous day till now he has wandered amid the ruins, purposeless and bewildered, has made no effort to reconstruct Egyptian society, no effort to relieve from their burdens Egyptian people; but that, haunted and distracted by the guiltiness of his intervention, he has added misery to misery, and woe to woe, till he has transformed the fair land of Egypt into a perfect hell upon earth. The people of England would say that such a state of things must cease; that a Government must be established which must possess the confidence of the Egyptian people; that a dynasty which is repudiated by a nation of six millions shall not be forced upon that nation by the armies and the navies of the liberty-loving and liberty-spreading Anglo-Saxon race; that the financial resources of Egypt shall be assigned to the full and entire satisfaction of the demands of Egyptian government; and if there is any surplus, that and that only, shall go to the Egyptian bonds, thus reversing the process which is going on now under our auspices of assigning all the financial resources of Egypt to Egyptian bonds, and leaving any niggardly surplus which may remain for Egyptian government, for the maintenance of society, law, and order in that country, and for the development of the resources of that impoverished and plundered land. They would say that, as our Government has rashly but irrevocably committed England to the resettlement of Egypt, those purposes, and those purposes alone, shall be the object of the employment of British troops; that until those purposes are accomplished British troops shall remain in Egypt, flinching from no obstacles, no difficulties, no dangers, and that when those purposes have been accomplished, that on that glad day, and not before, the British troops shall evacuate Egypt with genuine glory, added honours, and increased renown. This is what the people of England would say; this is how the British race would fulfil its great mission upon earth; and it is because

I know that it is only the mass of the people as a whole which will give this brave and noble answer, that I implore the people to turn their eyes steadily to the East.

Let us now look for a few moments at our own domestic affairs. A stupendous programme of legislation is prepared by the Ministers for a jaded and worn-out Parliament in the coming session. The extension of the franchise, county government for the three kingdoms, local taxation, the municipal administration of the metropolis, University education for Scotland, intermediate education for Wales—these are but the leading items of a long list which the Government, apparently in all seriousness, profess to expect to deal with in a thoroughly comprehensive fashion before New Year's day shall again come round. And if they fail to deal with any of these subjects, as fail they will and must, the ready excuse will burst from their lips that the cause of their failure is the villainy of the Tory party, and the atrocious baseness of the House of Lords; whereas, if for a passing moment, by the exertion of some supernatural power, they could be clothed in the garb of truth, they would be the first to acknowledge that their own prodigious imbecility was alone to blame for the catastrophe. I will not conceal my opinion, that should one and all of the great questions which I have enumerated remain *in statu quo* for another five or ten years, no one of the Queen's subjects would be a penny the worse. A starving population is not to be fed by votes; a ruined commerce and agriculture are not to be resuscitated by the abolition of quarter sessions; and a tottering empire will not be maintained by the creation of a new Lord Mayor. I would recommend the people of England to leave legislation alone for a while, and to insist upon the House of Commons devoting itself to a little practical business. At any rate, this course would have all the charm of novelty. I will explain what I mean. The first and most vital interest of a nation is finance. Upon finance everything connected with government hinges. Good finance insures good government and national prosperity; bad finance is the cause of inefficient government and national depression. Great and endless controversies have been carried on for some years between rival Chancellors of the Exchequer, as to whether Liberals are more extravagant than Conservatives, or *vice versa*. Do not trouble yourselves about these quarrels—they are perfectly idle, fruitless, and beside the real question; figures and statistics are jumbled up, added to, subtracted from, multiplied, and divided by the frantic combatants, until a perfectly insoluble Chinese puzzle has been created, in which every one is hopelessly lost. The truth is—and I speak with the advantages of a looker-on, who, as you know, generally sees most of the game—that both parties are extravagant, and that all Governments are lavish. The only difference between the Liberals and the Conservatives on this most vital question is, that Conservative extravagance is honest and above board; Liberal extravagance is dishonest and surreptitious. The great fact which I am anxious to impress upon you is, that in twenty-five years your expenditure has increased five and twenty millions. The gross revenue now collected by the Chancellor of the Exchequer amounts to nearly ninety millions. The sum is so enormous that you will be inclined to agree that the most ordinary prudence compels rigid inquiry. It may be all right, perfectly natural, and quite satisfactory; but let us make certain of this. When you are spending such colossal sums as ninety millions a year, do not let any doubt remain in your minds for a moment as to how the money goes. You can easily do this if you like. Year by year the control of the House of Commons over the expenditure is getting more slender and more feeble. To such an extent is this deterioration going on that, last session, under the financial guidance of Mr. Gladstone, the sublime spectacle was witnessed of thirty millions of taxation being voted by the House of Commons in about thirty minutes of time.

For many years there has been no overhauling by Parliament of the spending departments. It is a great mistake to suppose that Ministers preside over their departments. They do nothing of the kind. They merely appear for them in Parliament. The public departments are despotically presided over by permanent officials, perfectly irresponsible, caring nothing for the House of Commons, which has for years left them to themselves, and always putting back in his place, with the greatest success and rapidity, any Minister who should be such an egregious fool as to imagine he was really a Minister. Under this kind of *régime* you are spending ninety millions of money on your Government, and this kind of *régime* has grown up on account of the House of Commons of late years being entirely given over to legislation. No time is ever left for what I call business, and year after year public accounts are left to look after themselves. Now, in all seriousness, this is an ominous change. It was not so, it was not on such principles that our financial character and credit were built up. We are come now upon bad times; if ever national thrift was necessary, it is necessary now. I should like to see the House of Commons devote one or even two entire sessions to finance, and nothing but finance. I should like to turn the House of Commons loose into our public departments on a voyage of discovery. I should like to see every one of our public departments rigorously inquired into by small committees of about seven experienced and practical members of Parliament, each. Depend upon it, we should discover some arrangements of extraordinary interest and curiosity. The inquiry should include the amount of work which any department is expected or supposed to transact, the amount of work which it actually does transact, the number of hands employed in transacting that work, the hours of labour of each clerk or *employé,* the salaries received by each, and then let all these be carefully compared, under the same headings, with the arrangements in some of our great commercial establishments. Such an inquiry could not but be most useful, and such an inquiry is compulsorily and peremptorily dictated to 'you when you consider the vast scale of your expenditure and the present bad times. My firm belief is, that such an inquiry would demonstrate that those useful arrangements of economy of time, economy of labour, and economy of money are absolutely unknown in our public departments.

I believe that such an inquiry would lead to the decrease of our Foreign Office establishments at home and abroad by at least one-third. I do not imagine that the public has the smallest idea of the utter uselessness of a great portion of that department. I allude especially to the large staff of secretaries and *attachés* which is kept up abroad for purely ornamental purposes. The Foreign Office would have a very bad time before a Committee of the House of Commons which was firmly intent on effecting a great economy. Take the War Office again. We should find, in all probability, that nearly all the mechanical work of that department could be discharged by intelligent and meritorious non-commissioned officers at about one-half of the salaries now paid to the War Office clerks. We should find that we spend annually from fifteen to sixteen millions on our army. Germany, Austria, and France do not spend much more; but we should find that while these Powers have great armies, we have no army at all. We have regiments of various sorts; but if by an army you mean a perfect fighting machine fully equipped in all its parts, composed of seasoned soldiers, and ready to take the field at the shortest notice, then we have not got an army or anything approaching it; and yet we spend over fifteen millions on it annually. You would have to consider whether it is worth while going on spending such an enormous sum of money for a thing which you do not possess. Look at the navy. We spend ten or eleven millions annually upon our navy. The highest naval authorities will tell you that our navy against a coalition of France and Russia, or France and Italy, would be absolutely impotent to protect our coasts, our commerce, and our colonies. Some day when we have a great war—and with Egypt on our hands such a war may come at any moment—we shall discover all these trifles; but do not you think that there would be no harm in spending a little time now, while you are at peace, in looking into all this, in making certain about it, and of not placing such implicit confidence in the optimist statements of either one Minister or another? Do not you think that the time would be as well spent, and even better spent, by the House of Commons than in wrangling over the order and course of legislation, whether reform or redistribution should come first, whether they should be dealt with together or singly, whether Ireland should be included or excluded, whether the 40s. freeholder should be abolished or preserved? All these questions are infinitely little and unimportant when compared with the real practical business matters which I have suggested, and if to the line of business which I am most anxious to see adopted you add the prospect and the chance—and the very good chance—of saving some millions of money at present absolutely wasted, I think you will agree that the suggestions I have made are neither foolish, unattractive, nor unworthy of your serious attention. The Radicals are always denouncing financial extravagance. They profess on this point great independence of party, but just test the sincerity of their denunciations by some such proposals as I have made to you, that all legislation should be put off for a year, and that we should apply the whole of our abilities and time to saving public money. You would have such a howl of fury from them as never was heard. Rather than lose their chance of subverting the Constitution of this country, they would allow you to spend 200 millions a year. I believe that the English people would rather have an economical and thrifty Government than a republican Government, and yet of this I am certain, that you will never have an economical and thrifty Government until you positively direct and order the House of Commons to adopt some such course as I have proposed.

There is another inquiry which might be carried on simultaneously with those which I have mentioned, of the most vital importance to the working classes of this country, and that is an inquiry into the present condition of British industry, and as to how that industry is affected by our present methods of raising revenue for the service of the State. I think that such an inquiry is needed even if it was only to compose the public mind. What is the state of things in the world of British industry? We are suffering from a depression of trade extending as far back as 1874, ten years of trade depression, and the most hopeful either among our capitalists or our artisans can discover no signs of a revival. Your iron industry is dead, dead as mutton; your coal industries, which depend greatly on the iron industries, are languishing. Your silk industry is dead, assassinated by the foreigner. Your woollen industry is *in articulo mortis,* gasping, struggling. Your cotton industry is seriously sick. The shipbuilding industry, which held out longest of all, is come to a standstill. Turn your eyes where you will, survey any branch of British industry you like, you will find signs of mortal disease. The self-satisfied Radical philosophers will tell you it is nothing; they point to the great volume of British trade. Yes, the volume of British trade is still large, but it is a volume which is no longer profitable; it is working and struggling. So do the muscles and nerves of the body of a man who has been hanged twitch and work violently for a short time after the operation. But death is there all the same, life has utterly departed, and suddenly comes the *rigor mortis.* Well, but with this state of British industry what do you find going on? You find foreign iron, foreign wool, foreign silk and cotton pouring into the country, flooding you, drowning you, sinking you, swamping you; your labour market is congested, wages have sunk below the level of life, the misery in our large towns is too frightful to contemplate, and emigration or starvation is the remedy which the Radicals offer you with the most undisturbed complacency. But what produced this state of things? Free imports? I am not sure; I should like an inquiry; but I suspect free imports of the murder of our industries much in the same way as if I found a man standing over a corpse and plunging his knife into it I should suspect that man of homicide, and I should recommend a coroner's inquest and a trial by jury. Of this you may be certain—that an impartial inquiry into this great question will put more hope into your hearts than any Reform Bill. Do you know what free trade means in the mouth of the latter-day Radicals? It means that articles of food, necessaries of life coming from abroad, which cannot be produced at home, shall be taxed heavily, and that articles of manufacture, luxuries coming from abroad, and which might be produced at home, shall be admitted duty free. Do you know that your cocoa is taxed at 13 per cent., your coffee at 18 per cent., your dried fruits, currants, &c., 26 per cent., your tea 47 per cent., tobacco 504 per cent., rum 504 per cent., brandy 114 per cent.? Observe this curiosity—that rum, which comes from a British colony, is taxed five times as heavily as brandy, which comes from France; and with all this, silk, leather, wool, and iron are all coming into the country duty free, and hopelessly underselling your own products and driving your industrial population to America, to the colonies, to the workhouse or to the prison. Do you understand the reason of all this? I frankly confess I do not. Do you think the House of Commons would be wasting its time if it looked into all these matters carefully? Suppose a merchant were to find his expenditure greatly increased, his revenue greatly diminished, and his resources greatly failing, and under these circumstances were to occupy the whole of his time with the differential calculus, or with inquiries into interplanetary space. You would think him very foolish, not to say mad, and you would anticipate his speedy ruin. Well, the English people will be exactly like that merchant if at such a moment as the present they occupy the whole of their time with wild schemes of legislation, and leave the real, hard, practical business of life to take care of itself. Yet that is the course recommended to you by the Radical party.

Now, if there is one thing more than another of which the Radical party is proud it is their land legislation, and their policy with respect to land tenure. Yet I think I can show you that this boasted legislation and policy have grievously affected the labour markets in the towns. What is the great cry of the moment? Is it not the congested state of our great towns and the overcrowding of our urban population? And what has produced that congestion and overcrowding? Principally the migration into our towns of an immense population which used to subsist on agriculture. That migration has not only overcrowded your towns, but has increased the competition in the labour market up to starvation level, and has lowered the wages of the artisan classes. Well, in my judgment, the land legislation and avowed land policy of the Radical party are the chief causes of that migration. The Radical party have destroyed nearly all the privileges, all the pleasures, all the amenities which used to attach to the tenure of land, by their recent legislation, and announce that as speedily as possible they intend to destroy those which may remain, and they threaten the very title itself of individual landed possessions. What is the effect of all this? In former times, and not so very long ago, the moment that a man had made a fortune in trade he invested that money in a landed estate; the possession of a landed estate gave him social status, political influence, sporting rights, and possessed many other amenities and attractions. The investment of capital by a capitalist in landed estates meant the employment of capital in the development of that estate, in drainage, in extensive building operations, in road making, and every other kind of improvement; in a word, it meant active employment for the agricultural labourer. Investment in land was never a highly remunerative investment, but there was a bloom on it which other investments did not possess, and it was regarded as perfectly safe. But now all that is gone; the investment is no longer safe, and the bloom has been altogether rubbed off the peach. There is no political influence, there are no sporting rights, and few amenities. Formerly you had a constant and regular migration of capitalists from our large centres of industrial activity into the country, and a healthy circulation of capital among the country population. But now, in consequence of the Radical land policy, that migration has almost entirely ceased. Auctioneers will tell you that it is no use trying to sell large landed estates. The capitalist is not such a fool as to invest his hard-earned fortune in a security which has been deprived of all its great attractions; he invests his money now in colonial securities, or in landed property abroad. Instead of a migration of wealthy and enterprising capitalists from the town into the country, you have a migration of ruined and starving agricultural labourers into your towns, lowering your wages and increasing your rates; and this disastrous process may be directly traced to the doctrines on the tenure of land which have been put in practice or are about to be put in practice by the Radical party. Never did the land require capital so much as it does now, never was land so easily and cheaply in the grasp of the capitalist as it is now, if he chose to put out his hand; and yet there is not a capitalist in his senses who would touch it. I commend this subject to your most careful consideration. These Radical nostrums are like certain drugs which seem to be pleasant to take at the moment, and which seem to produce a good result at the moment, but which in a very short time are found to be destructive to health and fatal to life. I am certain of this, that the more the English people examine into the Radical policy, the more the Radical party develops itself and comes closer to the eye, the more clearly you will perceive what transparent humbug the Radical policy is, and what transcendent impostors the Radical party is composed of.

'Vanity of vanities,' says the preacher, 'all is vanity.' 'Humbug of humbugs,' says the Radical, 'all is humbug.' Gentlemen, we live in an age of advertisement, the age of Holloway's pills, of Colman's mustard, and of Horniman's pure tea; and the policy of lavish advertisement has been so successful in commerce that the Liberal party, with its usual enterprise, has adapted it to politics. The Prime Minister is the greatest living master of the art of personal political advertisement. Holloway, Colman, and Horniman are nothing compared with him. Every act of his, whether it be for the purposes of health, or of recreation, or of religious devotion, is spread before the eyes of every man, woman, and child in the United Kingdom on large and glaring placards. For the purposes of an autumn holiday a large transatlantic steamer is specially engaged, the Poet Laureate adorns the suite, and receives a peerage as his reward, and the incidents of the voyage are luncheon with the Emperor of Russia and tea with the Queen of Denmark. For the purposes of recreation he has selected the felling of trees, and we may usefully remark that his amusements, like his politics, are essentially destructive. Every afternoon the whole world is invited to assist at the crashing fall of some beech or elm or oak. The forest laments in order that Mr. Gladstone may perspire, and full accounts of these proceedings are forwarded by special correspondents to every daily paper every recurring morning. For the purposes of religious devotion the advertisements grow larger. The parish church at Hawarden is insufficient to contain the thronging multitudes of flycatchers who flock to hear Mr. Gladstone read the lessons for the day, and the humble parishioners are banished to hospitable Non-conformist tabernacles in order that mankind may be present at the Prime Minister's rendering of Isaiah, or Jeremiah, or the Book of Job. This, gentlemen, all this, is the great art of advertisement, and there can be no doubt that it pays when undertaken on the grandiose scale adopted by Mr. Gladstone. I am not sure whether in our calmer and more reflective moments we should not prefer a little more real simplicity in our public men, whether their private lives should not be more genuinely private, and whether their special family interests and family events would not be more natural if they were confined to the family circle. People used to say that Lord Beaconsfield was theatrical; but Lord Beaconsfield was a perfect child in this matter; he had not even mastered the rudiments of the art, and he never dreamt of such grand and theatrical representations as those with which Mr. Gladstone and his starring company astonish the British public week by week.

However, these remarks of mine are merely preliminary to a couple of concluding political observations to which I am led by two of the Gladstonian advertisements which appeared in the papers the other day. The first described the journey of a deputation of working-men from the pure and immaculate borough of Chester to Hawarden Castle. It has always appeared to me somewhat incongruous and inappropriate that the great chief of the Radical party should reside in a castle. But to proceed. One would have thought that the deputation would have been received in the house, in the study, in the drawing-room, or even in the dining-room. Not at all. That would have been out of harmony with the advertisement 'boom.' Another scene had been arranged. The working-men were guided through the ornamental grounds, into the wide-spreading park, strewn with the wreckage and the ruins of the Prime Minister's sport. All around them, we may suppose, lay the rotting trunks of once umbrageous trees: all around them, tossed by the winds, were boughs and bark and withered shoots. They come suddenly on the Prime Minister and Master Herbert, in scanty attire and profuse perspiration, engaged in the destruction of a gigantic oak, just giving its last dying groan. They are permitted to gaze and to worship and adore, and, having conducted themselves with exemplary propriety, are each of them presented with a few chips as a memorial of that memorable scene.

Is not this, I thought to myself as I read the narrative, a perfect type and emblem of Mr. Gladstone's government of the Empire? The working classes of this country in 1880 sought Mr. Gladstone. He told them that he would give them and all other subjects of the Queen much legislation, great prosperity, and universal peace, and he has given them nothing but chips. Chips to the faithful allies in Afghanistan, chips to the trusting native races of South Africa, chips to the Egyptian fellah, chips to the British farmer, chips to the manufacturer and the artisan, chips to the agricultural labourer, chips to the House of Commons itself. I ask you who have followed with care the events of this Parliament, to carry your minds back to the beginning of 1880, to the demonstration of Dulcigno, to the slaughter of Maiwand, to the loss of Candahar, to the rebellion in the Transvaal, to the Irish Land League with all its attendant horrors, to the scenes in the House of Commons, to the loss of freedom and dignity sustained by that assembly, to the abortive sessions, to the Egyptian muddle, with its sham military glories, to the resignation of Cabinet Ministers, to the spectacle recently afforded of two Ministerial colleagues openly defying each other, to the illusory programme spread before you for the coming year, to the immense dangers and difficulties which surround you on every side—turn over all these matters in your minds, search your memories, look at them as you will; I ask you again, is there in any quarter of the globe, where the influence of Mr. Gladstone's Government has been felt, is there one single item, act, expression, or development on which you can dwell with any pride, or even satisfaction? Is there one single solid, real, substantial construction or improvement which can benefit permanently, or even momentarily, either directly or indirectly, your own countrymen at home, your own countrymen abroad, or any worthy portion of the human race? Chips you will find, nothing but chips—hard, dry, unnourishing, indigestible chips. To all those who leaned upon Mr. Gladstone, who trusted in him, and who hoped for something from him, chips, nothing but chips; to those who defied him, trampled upon his power, insulted and reviled his representatives and his policy, to the barbarous Boer and the rebel Irish, to them, and to them alone, booty and great gain.

The other startling advertisement I wish to allude to was as follows:—'Hawarden Castle.—The Prime Minister attended Divine service this morning. He was guarded as usual.' 'Guarded as usual!' 'As usual!' Gracious heavens! What a commentary on Liberal government in those two words 'as usual'! Do you know that from the day when first there was what is called a Prime Minister, to the present, there has been no Prime Minister about whom such a statement could be made? Many Prime Ministers have come and gone, good, bad, and indifferent; but the best and the worst have never been guarded by aught else save the English people. And has it come to this? Are the times so terrible, are bad passions so rife and unrestrained, after four years of Liberal rule, that the apostle of freedom, the benefactor of his country, the man for whom no flattery is too fulsome, no homage too servile, cannot attend Divine service in his parish church without being 'guarded as usual'? Surely a world of serious reflection is opened up; surely the art of government must have sunk to a very low ebb when the first servant of the Crown has to be watched night and day by alguazils armed to the teeth. I hope and pray that they will guard him well, for it would be an indelibe stain on our name and our fame if a man who has spent fifty years of his life in the service of the State were to be the victim of an infamous assassin. But I ask myself, are we to blame humanity for this state of things? Is our civilisation all in vain? Is Christianity but a phantom and a fiction? Is human nature the awful and incurable cause? Surely not. It is more natural to blame the policy of the statesmen who, to possess themselves of power, to overthrow a hated rival, set class against class and race against race; who use their eloquence for no nobler purpose than to lash into frenzy the needy and the discontented; who for party purposes are ready to deride morality and paralyse law; who, to gain a few votes either in Parliament or in a borough, ally themselves equally with the atheist or with the rebel, and who lightly arouse and lightly spring from one delirium of the multitude to another in order to maintain themselves at a giddy and a perilous height. This is the true explanation, the deep-seated reason of the words 'guarded as usual.' Mr. Gladstone and his colleagues, to destroy Lord Beaconsfield, did not scruple to appeal to the most desperate instincts of the human race; and now, to control and crush down this legion of foul friends, the resources of civilisation are almost exhausted.

The Tory party calls upon the country with a sonorous and warning cry to turn away from guides so dangerous, to repudiate betimes a policy so vile, and, by giving over the Government to other men, and, above all, to other principles, to restore to the Empire that great calm which in 1880 you were falsely promised, which in 1884 you so dearly need. The Tory party sets out no long programme, it commits itself to no irredeemable pledges; it does not ask you to embark on any wild and unknown enterprises; it promises you one thing, and one thing only—one thing which is worth everything else, which will bring with it inevitably prosperity and peace—it promises you government, government which for four years you have not had, government for which you vainly pay heavy taxes, government which alone you lack, government which the Tories alone can give —for they are united, homogeneous, patriotic, and true. Can you look for government, can you expect anything but anarchy from an administration which contains Lord Hartington and Mr. Chamberlain, from a party which comprises Mr. Samuel Morley and Mr. Bradlaugh, from a heterogeneous agglomeration of Whigs and Radicals, in which 'pull devil, pull baker,' is the order of the day? Surely these last four years—four years of base compromise and sickening indecision—must have proved to the most infatuated that the Liberal party of the present day has not one single common principle of policy, either in home or foreign affairs, on which for purposes of efficient government it can unite even for a day. For the Whigs are a class with all the selfish prejudices and all the vices of a class; the Radicals are a sect with all the grinding tyranny and all the debasing fanaticism of a sect. The Whig class and the Radical sect have succeeded, by an amount of political cunning rarely equalled in the history of States, in acquiring a power which their monstrous union is impotent to wield; but their unnatural connection cannot last. It has arisen from the marvellous talents, stupefying eloquence, and illimitable ambition of one man, and with him it will pass away. The well-known proverb, 'Vox populi, vox Dei,' is to the Whigs as sounding brass and tinkling cymbals, for they have always existed by corrupting and deceiving the people. To the Radicals it is a fetish of the lowest order, for they exist by driving and tyrannising over the people. But to the Tories 'Vox populi, vox Dei' is an ever-springing faith, a vivifying principle, an undying truth, without which their politics would be as nought, without a future and without a hope. The Whigs tell you that the institutions of this kingdom, as illustrated by the balance of Queen, Lords and Commons, and the Established Church, are but conveniences and useful commodities, which may be safely altered, modified, or even abolished, so long as the alteration, modification, or abolition is left to the Whigs to carry out. The Radicals tell you that these institutions are hideous, poisonous, and degrading, and that the divine caucus is the only machine which can turn out, as if it was a patent medicine, the happiness of humanity. But the Tories, who are of the people, know and exclaim that these institutions, which are not so much the work of the genius of man, but rather the inspired offspring of Time, are the tried guarantees of individual liberty, popular government, and Christian morality; that they are the only institutions which possess the virtue of stability, of stability even through all ages; that the harmonious fusion of classes and interests which they represent corresponds with and satisfies the highest aspirations either of peoples or of men; that by them has our empire been founded and extended in the past; and that by them alone can it prosper or be maintained in the future. Such is the Tory party and such are its principles, by which it can give to England the government she requires—democratic, aristocratic, parliamentary, monarchical, uniting in an indissoluble embrace religious liberty and social order. And this party—this Tory party of to-day—exists by the favour of no caucus, nor for the selfish interests of any class. Its motto is—of the people, for the people, by the people; unity and freedom are the beacons which shed their light around its future path, and amid all political conflict this shall be its only aim—to increase and to secure within imperishable walls the historic happiness of English homes.

Robert Cecil

·

THE MARQUIS OF SALISBURY

Robert Cecil, the Marquis of Salisbury

[*Born* FEBRUARY 3, 1830—*Died* AUGUST 22, 1903]

Everyone knew the tall, broad, stooping figure with the thick head of hair, the bent brows, and the careless, shabby costume.—JUSTIN MC CARTHY

Britain's ever-changing national character requires men of different personalities to lead it through various historical eras. Lord Salisbury was such a man when called to national leadership as Prime Minister in the 'eighties and 'nineties, years of relative peace. A. L. Kennedy writes that to the outside world Salisbury was England.[1] Lord Rosebery considers him during this period to have exercised a "singular and prolonged influence over her destinies."[2] His attention to foreign affairs resulted in the addition of six million square miles to the British Empire. This was an accomplishment "no one could approach except the elder Pitt."[3]

Lord Salisbury's success as Prime Minister is said to have been due to "an unconscious participation in the mentality, the sympathies, the points of view . . . of men whom he was addressing."[4] His biographers generally agree that he never attained flights of "exalted eloquence," but in a rather plain style, with clarity and simplicity, he was, according to Clive Bigham, "extremely effective on his fellow-peers in the House of Lords."[5] This success, however, was but a continuation of the effectiveness he displayed as a young man in the House of Commons where many of his phrases found acceptance in the spectrum of political and social life.

Impressed by Gladstone's remarkable success at Midlothian, Lord Salisbury often departed from Westminster to speak to popular audiences. Joseph Hendershot Park indicates that between 1880 and 1886 Salisbury spoke on more than seventy public platforms to audiences that often could be counted by thousands.[6] Lady Gwendolen Cecil attributes his popularity outside of Parliament to his personal qualities attractive to "unsophisticated audiences":

The crispness of his style, his gift for lucid statement, served to gain and hold the attention of minds unexercised in elaborate vocabularies; his

---

1 A. L. Kennedy, *Salisbury, 1802–1903* (London: John Murray, 1953), p. 347.

2 Lord Rosebery, *Miscellanies: Literary and Historical*, II (London: Hodder and Stoughton, 1921), p. 274.

3 Kennedy, *op. cit.*, p. 341.

4 Lady Gwendolen Cecil, *Life of Robert, Marquis of Salisbury*, III (London: Hodder and Stoughton, 1931), p. 64.

5 Clive Bigham, *The Prime Ministers of Britain, 1721–1921* (London: John Murray, 1922), p. 307.

6 Joseph Hendershot Park, *British Prime Ministers of the Nineteenth Century* (New York: New York University Press, 1950), p. 318.

claim to come to close quarters with facts; the impression of solidity induced by his independence of other men's opinions,—were all qualities
to attract unsophisticated audiences.[7]

Kennedy describes Lord Salisbury's speaking outside of Parliament as
"homely, disjointed . . . and . . . inclined to be repetitive." [8] Yet
in many of his speeches are found "profound" political maxims or a
"terse and characteristic reflection of his own philosophy." [9]

His speeches were the result of careful preparation. He made no
notes, but would arrange a sequence of ideas in his mind, and re-
hearse repeatedly, focusing on key words.

The speech presented here was delivered on May 7, 1902. Kennedy believes it should be examined in detail even with all of its
strengths and weaknesses as the "last utterance of a politician, a sage
and a seer." [10]

---

7 Lady Gwendolen Cecil, op. cit., p. 64.
8 Kennedy, op. cit., p. 245.
9 Ibid., p. 142.
10 Ibid., p. 340.

Speech to the Primrose League

•

LONDON   *May 7, 1902*[1]

L ord Salisbury was the principal speaker at the annual demonstration
of the Primrose League, which was held yesterday afternoon at the
Albert-hall. The hall, which was filled with an enthusiastic audience, was decorated with the banners of the local habitations, and at the
back of the platform were displayed in large characters the words "Impe-
rium et Libertas." . . .

*LORD SALISBURY, who was received with loud cheers, proceeded to
deliver his address as Grand Master. He said:—*

My Lords, Ladies, and Gentlemen,—I have first to congratulate you
upon the constant, the increasing, the steady prosperity of the splendid
organization to which you belong. There is no question that the statistics
which have been laid before you show that it does not relent or slacken in
its power of attracting the attention and the allegiance of the British race
amongst whom it exercises so potent an influence. And, in doing so, allow
me as a matter of pious reflection to express the undying debt which this
organization owes to those from whom, in beginnings then very small, it
originally sprang. (*Hear, hear.*) We cannot forget the names of the late
Lord Randolph Churchill (*cheers*), of Lord Glenesk (*cheers*) and of Sir
Henry Wolff (*cheers*), who are still with us. The organization owes to
them an enormous debt from the judgment and the vigour with which it
was started on its course. We might then have prophesied, as we can now
realise, the enormous skill with which that commencement was originally
planned. We have to thank them for much that has since occurred, and
we have to recognise that it is not merely in words or in protestations that
their power and their zeal have been expended. During the last 17 years
we have passed through a troublous time of political experience. We have

---

[1] *THE TIMES* (London), May 8, 1902, p. 8.

had to meet great dangers, to solve difficult and subtle questions, and through them the League has held its banner high and has procured the acceptance of its principles by vast numbers of its countrymen. (*Cheers.*) Undoubtedly the experience that we have had is not of a kind which we can attribute to the merit or the effort of any one organization.

Egypt and Ireland

We cannot tell how much of the success of the last 17 years has been due to the principles of the Primrose League and the energy with which they have been preached. But we can note this remarkable coincidence— that in 1884 or 1885 we were confronted with the problems of Egypt and of Ireland, not to mention any others; that we now look back on them and are able to assure ourselves that in Egypt at present we are supreme, and that in Ireland we at all events have no longer to fear the support given by any statesman to the insane and suicidal projects of Imperial disruption. (*Cheers.*) The mission of the Primrose League is to operate on British opinion, and if it has succeeded up to the point that I have named, surely that is an enormous gain. We must not expect that the ashes of past conflicts shall be extinguished at once; we must not imagine that the necessity for our exertions will be so soon dispensed with; but we must see that in these 17 years we have had a tremendous recognition of the effect of patriotic combination, of which this Primrose League is the highest instance, and that by its force we have, if not absolutely dissipated, to a large extent conjured the most formidable dangers that threatened us 17 years ago. This is the reward the Primrose League has a right to look to. When we met in those times we looked with consternation to the growth of a separatist power sustained by the highest statesman of our time, we looked to misfortune and disaster succeeding each other in the valley of the Nile, we reflected on the disgrace which the death of Gordon had inflicted upon us (*cheers*), we saw that our voice and our power in the council of nations had fallen in consequence of the disastrous events which we had had to face. We did not at all give way or quail before the dangerous indications of that time. We fought resolutely for the Empire and liberty, whether it was in Egypt or in Ireland or in other parts of the Empire. And, as time went on, strengthened by the stanchness of the members of this League, encouraged by the vigour which the organisation showed in all its parts, we held on tightly to our duty in sustaining the power of the Empire, and we were rewarded by a success which I am sure in 1885 we should never have dared to anticipate. (*Cheers.*) But of course we must recognise that those most satisfactory events are not the only lines which have marked the portraiture of recent years.

The War

We have had towards the end of that time a great and serious war. All wars are horrible. It is frightful to reflect upon the human misery which they involve and the sorrow and privation which they bring with them to multitudes of our fellow-subjects. But when we have allowed for all that feeling, a most just and necessary feeling—when we have allowed for it—we still recognise that there are other considerations to be brought into view, and that it is not only the sorrowful part of the picture on which we have to gaze. We can recognise that, deep as our sacrifices have been, and are still, much as we have had to give up, terrible as the loss of those whom we have loved has been, we yet can recognise that the power, the prestige, the influence, aye, and the magic effect of our great Empire is more potent, more efficient, more admirable than it was when that period began. (*Cheers.*) We have suffered, but we have greatly won. And it is impossible not to feel that the efforts of the people of this country, that the efforts of those through whom and with whom we have worked, have in some cases not been worthily recognised by those for whom they have sacrificed so much. I had hoped that this matter of the South African war might have been kept largely out of the bounds of party conflict (*hear, hear*), and that with the highest interests of their nation in issue men would have forborne to use the passing events of the day for the somewhat squalid purpose of injuring their opponents. (*Cheers.*) Though I frankly recognise that among many of our opponents a feeling of that kind has shown itself, and that we have to thank them for recognising that there is a duty superior to party in such crises as that through which we have passed, yet it is impossible not to feel that we have not entirely enjoyed a judicial treatment in reference to this war or in reference to the duties that have been imposed upon us. Men will not recognise what they would have recognised in any other conflict—that, in defence of the interests of the Empire, it is necessary for us to overlook and override all minor considerations. (*Cheers.*) I have noted some words spoken by one of the men who is most admired, most justly admired, upon the side of the Opposition, words which seem to me to be a grave departure from that judicial assignment of merit and of claim which in such a crisis we have a right to expect. I find the other day Mr. Morley, speaking to a sympathetic audience (*laughter*), said:—"Suppose that some preternatural power had, by virtue of some magic crystal, led the Cabinet in 1899 to see the results of the policy on which they were then launching their country, do you believe there was one of them who would not then have checked the diplomacy which was leading pretty straight to these deplorable results?" Well, as one of the Cabinet who was concerned in those times, I wish to meet with the most indignant denial this statement. (*Hear, hear.*) Then, or at any other time, if I am informed that a neighbouring Power or tribe has attacked the dominions of my Sovereign and has boldly assumed that they have gained a dominion and power over them, I would say without any hesitation whatever, or without inquiring into any previous negotiations, that that attack by the neighbouring Power was a gross and flagrant outrage, and that it was an outrage which only could have been met as we have met it (*cheers*), by fighting in their own homes those who have despised the rights and the sovereignty of our Sovereign and those who attempted to convert his subjects into the subjects of a foreign Power. (*Cheers.*) There is a kind of maudlin sentiment which induces people to pass over the conduct of our assailants and to treat it as though it were a matter open to controversy, and that we might admit that they were in the right. I energetically entreat all who have to deal with that subject to repudiate any such method of treating it. The Boers chose without any right, without any ground for complaint of any violation of international law, to invade our territory and to seize the lands that belonged to our Sovereign; they chose to convert the rights of our fellow-subjects into that of persons forced to submit to their domination; they chose to dispute our rights without a vestige of a ground for doing so. And I entirely resist the idea that we can treat that as a matter of no importance or that we can for a moment admit that there is any doubt in the right of our Sovereign and our Government to resist any invasion of our territory to the utmost possible extent. (*Hear, hear.*) Well, this brings us to matters that are of deep interest at the present moment.

The Settlement

Even if I knew more than I do I should feel that I was not at liberty while negotiations are actually going on to speak to you with respect to the various chances which those negotiations may have, or the various questions on which their issue may depend. That is obviously what you cannot do while negotiations are going on. I only wish to guard against misapprehension which I think I have seen, to the effect that the willingness we have shown to listen to all that may be said to us is a proof that we have retreated or receded from our former position and are willing to recognise that the rights we claimed are no longer valid. There is no ground for such assertion. (*Hear, hear.*) In the rights we claim, in the policy we intend to carry out, we are exactly where we were. (*Cheers.*) We cannot afford after such terrible sacrifices, not only of treasure but of men, after the exertions, unexampled in our history, that we have made—we cannot afford to submit to the idea that we are to allow things to slide back into a position where it will be in the power of our enemy again, when the opportunity suits him and the chance is favourable to him, to renew again the issue that we have fought for this last three years. (*Cheers.*) There are many things on which discussion may arise, many points upon which men may reasonably hold different opinions, but of this, at all events, there can be no doubt—that our hold, the hold of His Majesty's Government, over the country is to be such that there shall be no possibility of renewing the struggle from which we are now slowly issuing. It is important that this should be made clear, for there are men who think that on this question, so vital to the Empire, it is possible that we may be tired out. (*Laughter.*) I regret that any such feeling should have arisen. I do not wish in expressing it to convey any note of bitterness to those who were or who are our foes. There is nothing which we wish more earnestly than that they would join with us in setting up and in entering into a political structure which shall enable them to enjoy to the full all the order and all the strength which is conferred upon our brother nations by our colonial system, which has lasted and which has endured so long. We see that in the world the system of our colonial government has procured peace, acquiescence, and in the long run a deep affection between the mother and the daughter countries. We believe that that process cannot be multiplied too much for the advantage of the Empire or the benefit of the world. We earnestly hope that those who were and who are now our foes will see with us all the merit which those traditional arrangements can claim, and all that we can do to mould them into a portion of that Empire which has conferred so many blessings on the human race we certainly shall do. But what we shall not do is to place it in the power of any man of ill-will to renew the conflict of the past time or to challenge the complete supremacy of our Sovereign. (*Cheers.*) We cannot look upon the past, as we have looked, without casting an eye upon the future. The Primrose League has played a great part; it has fulfilled a great mission. Is its mission over and its part closed? I do not think so. (*Hear, hear.*) I think there are dangers quite as serious that concern us in the future as those with which in the past we have successfully dealt. There is no doubt that this conflict which has taken place has left the world changed in some respects. There are colonies which existed before, but as this struggle has gone on they are colonies which have warmed more and more in their affection to the mother country, which have shown a zeal for the progress of the Empire and an appreciation of its benefits which I think some five years ago very few men would have guessed was possible. That is a phenomenon which has come so suddenly, which has come in so vast a volume, that I cannot believe it is transitory or precarious in its results. I believe that it indicated a vast amount of feeling which we did not here entirely realise and which, under the stress of circumstances, under the impulse of a strong sympathy, has made itself felt throughout the Empire. And we feel, perhaps without much merit of our own, but, at all events, we feel, that throughout the Empire a strong feeling has developed itself which has added enormously to the stability of its structure and to the strength of its rulers in the world. (*Cheers.*) We cannot doubt that we are much stronger for the feeling in our behalf that has been evidenced by so many of our daughter countries at a time of our greatest difficulty and stress. And there has been a converse feeling, of which I wish to speak with all restraint, but which I cannot entirely ignore, and that is the sudden hatred on the part of our rivals which the present circumstances and the vicissitudes of the present struggle have exhibited. Both are matters of the very highest importance; both are matters which will affect the future which stands before us; both are matters which all statesmen must take into account. But, though I believe it is true that we are at the commencement of a movement of causes, of opinions, and of feelings which will end in changes largely modifying the present distribution of power and the present distribution, I may say, of allegiance—though I believe this is true, I do not, therefore, on that account advocate any impatient handling of the phenomena which we have to deal with.

Imperial Federation

There are very important men, men of great intellect and authority, who think that the moment has come for some legislative action on our part which should federate the colonies. I exhort them before they do so carefully to consider what steps they are going to take and what results they expect to come from them. We have no power by legislation to affect the flow of opinion and of affection which has arisen so largely between the mother country and her daughter States. They will go on in their own power, in their own irresistible power, and I have no doubt they will leave combinations behind them which will cast into the shade all the glories that the British Empire has hitherto displayed. But we cannot safely interfere by legislative action with the natural development of our relations with our daughter countries. All kinds of difficulties are there before us— difficulties as to the burden of finance, difficulties as to the duty of defence, difficulties as to the rights of decision which the mother country should retain, and, unless feeling is running very strong and we have a great force behind us, I look with some apprehension upon any attempt to anticipate events or to foreclose the results, the precious results, which, if we are only patient and careful, the future has in store for the Empire.

(*Cheers.*) The tendency of human beings, and of statesmen—who are human beings (*laughter*)—is to anticipate all such matters and to think that, because their own wretched lives are confined to some 60 or 70 years, therefore it is open to them to force an anticipation of the results which the natural play of forces and of affections and the alteration of the judgments and the mutual feelings of various people in the world will bring before us. There is nothing more dangerous than to force a decision before a decision is ready, and, therefore, to produce feelings of discontent, feelings of difficulty, which if we will only avoid, if we will only wait, will of themselves bring about the results that we desire. There is no danger that appears to me more serious for the time that lies before us than an attempt to force the various parts of the Empire into a mutual arrangement and subordination for which they are not ready and which may only produce a reaction in favour of the old state of things. (*Hear, hear.*) This is a matter upon which it is very difficult to speak with freedom, but which I commend to your own consideration. If we will be patient and careful, there is a tremendous destiny before us; if we are hasty, there may be the reverse of such a destiny; there may be the breaking apart of those forces which are necessary to construct the majestic fabric of a future Empire. What we have to remember is that matters have changed, are changing, that there are forces in the world much more powerful than used to work, and that we must watch them with care in order to avoid that their energy should be directed against the great interests which it is our business to preserve.

New Political Conditions

Remember that out of the confusion that recent events have caused, that out of the terrible difficulties that have arisen, there is arising a state of things perfectly new to the world, a condition in which an Empire depending not on any territorial contiguity, but merely upon the action of its naval defences—that such an Empire is slowly arising out of the sea, that it has behind it the feelings and the affections of some of the most vehement races upon the face of the world, that the future destinies of the Empire depend upon the prudence and judgment with which those forces are guided, that the guidance of those forces must be in such a country as ours largely affected by the trend of popular opinion. And popular opinion in this country is largely affected, is largely modified, by those organisations which command popular opinion; and most of all among all the organisations that have that power there is assigned to the Primrose League an influence on the present condition of political society which they will be both unwise and criminal to neglect. It is with them that the power will rest of determining whether the movement of these great forces that have been unchanged shall be for evil or for good. If they act up to the call of their high destiny, their mission will be remembered as the greatest blessing which the Empire of England has been able to obtain. (*Loud cheers.*)

Joseph
Chamberlain

·

Joseph Chamberlain
[*Born* JULY 8, 1836—*Died* JULY 2, 1914]

. . . a pale, slender, delicate looking, and closely shaven personage, very neatly dressed, with short and carefully brushed hair, and wearing a dainty eyeglass constantly fixed in his eye.—JUSTIN MC CARTHY

• J •

Joseph Chamberlain is described by Peter Fraser as the first middle-class politician to reach the highest rank, and in a sense "the first 'professional' politician." [1] With the cooperation of Lord Salisbury, Chamberlain provided an impetus for social and political reform which, according to Sir Charles Petrie, "it has never since lost, but which it would otherwise have hardly acquired." [2]

John Morley calls Chamberlain's ideas neither new nor unique, but characterized his personality as a force perhaps as powerful in the world as projects and ideas. [3] His advocacy of tariff and imperial unity, during the last decade and a half of his political career, are probably best remembered. Early in his parliamentary service, however, he consistently championed the cause of "Radical reform," advocating various programs for the social welfare of the people from better educational facilities to a more equitable relation between capital and labor. [4]

Chamberlain was a superb tactician who lived both publicly and privately in the political element. [5] Alexander Mackintosh writes that for a quarter of a century the most passionate hours in the House of Commons occurred when Chamberlain dominated the scene:

Cool as a cucumber himself, he excites turmoil in others, the upright figure, the aggressive face, the mocking lips, the keen challenging eyes, the defiant nose, the eyeglass coolly placed in position, the clear-cut phrases, the many toned voice, have been conspicuous in numberless debates when passion ran high at St. Stephan's. [6]

Chamberlain, in fact, introduced a new style of debate, characterized by directness, audacity, intense practicality, vigor and plainness. [7] With equal effectiveness he could deliver an impromptu speech or

---

1 Peter Fraser, *Joseph Chamberlain* (New York: A. S. Barnes and Co., 1967), p. xii.

2 Sir Charles Petrie, *Joseph Chamberlain* (London: Duckworth, 1940), p. 137.

3 John Morley, *Recollections*, I (New York: The Macmillan Co., 1917), p. 147.

4 Elsie E. Gulley, *Joseph Chamberlain and English Social Politics* (New York: Elsie E. Gulley, 1926), p. 326.

5 Fraser, *op. cit.* See Chapter V, "Chamberlain and Beatrice Webb."

6 Alexander Mackintosh, *Joseph Chamberlain* (London: Hodder and Stoughton, 1906), p. 393.

7 *Ibid.*, p. 395.

one from only brief notes.[8] Justin McCarthy considers Chamberlain to have "proved himself to be one of the ablest debaters" in the House of Commons with his "keen eye for all the weak points of an opponent's case and a flow of clear and easy language."[9] Of his early parliamentary speaking, Peel considered him " 'the best debater without exception.' "[10] Morley describes Chamberlain's speaking as original, impressing his character upon the country:

. . . a character of vivid and resolute energy, fearless tenacity of will, vehement confidence both in the merits and the triumph of any cause with which he was induced to concern himself.[11]

Sparing of gesture, he possessed a "clear and musical voice" which carried well and was never monotonous.[12]

The speech included here was delivered in Birmingham on May 15, 1903, on the first political visit to Birmingham since his return from South Africa. He was given a tumultuous welcome by citizens who jammed into Town Hall, leaving thousands on the street cheering his arrival. Because few people expected him to renounce Free Trade, the speech produced an enormous sensation. Mackintosh calls his announcement a *"coup de théâtre,"*[13] and Wallace Notestein claims that few announcements, unless that of Peel's conversion to the repeal of the corn laws, have proved so great a political sensation, and "none has cut a deeper furrow across the political levels of the time."[14]

---

8 *Ibid.*, p. 396. "He does not write his speeches; he prepares only brief notes; but with his clear, cool, narrow mind, with his direct intellect and his literary instinct, he frames his sentences in so orderly a manner that they may be reproduced without sub-editing."

9 Justin McCarthy, *British Political Portraits* (New York: The Outlook Co., 1903), p. 81.

10 Petrie, *op. cit.*

11 Morley, *op. cit.*

12 Petrie, *op. cit.*, p. 141.

13 Mackintosh, *op. cit.*, p. 300.

14 Wallace Notestein, "Joseph Chamberlain and Tariff Reform," *Sewanee Review*, XXV (January 1917), p. 40.

Imperial Union and Tariff Reform [1]

•

MR. CHAMBERLAIN was most cordially received on rising to address the meeting, the audience rising and singing "For he's a jolly good fellow." He said:—

Mr. Chairman, Ladies, and Gentlemen,—I thank you from the bottom of my heart for the warmth of your welcome, for the assurance, which is always delightful to me, of your continued confidence and support. Mr. Jephcott is quite right when he says that I am proud of being the representative of West Birmingham, of an essentially working-class constituency. I have ventured before now in the House of Commons to claim that I represented more labour than any other Labour representative (*"Hear, hear," and cheers*); and I do not think the less of that position, because I believe that I represent labour in no narrow and selfish sense. I represent labour as it constitutes the majority of the people of this country, and as it is characterized by the virtues and the qualities that have made this country what it is—by labour, that is, which thinks not of itself as a class opposed to any other class in the community, but as responsible for the obligations of the country and the Empire to which it belongs, and as participators in all that concerns the prosperity and the welfare of the whole. (*Hear, hear.*) Mr. Payton, it is now two months since I returned home from a voyage which will always be one of the most memorable incidents of my life (*hear, hear*); but I have not forgotten—I shall never forget—that my constituents and fellow-citizens sent me forth to make a great experiment encouraged by their good wishes and by the most splendid and inspiriting demonstration that was ever accorded to any public man. (*Cheers.*) It was to me also a matter of greatest gratification that when I returned the first to greet me on these shores was a deputation

---

1 *The Times* (London), May 16, 1903, p. 8.

from you, my friends and constituents, assuring me of your welcome home and of your congratulations; and during the interval between those two events I was constantly reminded of you. I could come to no great city in South Africa, hardly to any village, but always it seemed to me I was cheered by the presence and the enthusiasm of Birmingham men (*cheers*), proud to recall their connexion with our city and anxious to prove that neither time nor distance had lessened their affection for their old home. (*Cheers.*) I go back often to my old associations; I think of the time when I entered upon public life, thanks to the support of those who in St. Paul's Ward sent me to the Town Council of Birmingham; and amongst all my recollections there is none of which I am prouder than of the fact that I was permitted at that time to co-operate with men, our then leaders, most of whom have passed away, but who have left behind them an imperishable legacy, who have impressed upon us and instilled into our lives that intense feeling of local patriotism which makes it the duty of every Birmingham man at home and abroad to maintain and to raise the reputation of the city from which he came.

The South African Problem

On my return, as is right and proper, I am called upon to make my first political speech to my constituents. (*Cheers.*) You will excuse me if I am a little out of touch. (*Laughter.*) It is true that in South Africa I did a deal of talking; but I am bound to say that my party weapons are a little rusty. When I was in South Africa it was not of our controversial politics that I was speaking; and for a considerable period my whole mind was turned towards the problems connected with the birth of a new nation in South Africa, and, above all, to the question of how it was possible to reconcile the two strong races who were bound to live together there as neighbours, and who, I hope, will live together as friends. (*Cheers.*) In connexion with that I had to think also of how this new nation would stand, how these races would be concerned in the future of the empire which belongs to both of them, Dutch and English—great people with many virtues in common, but still with great differences. Who would wish that the traditions of either should be forgotten, that their peculiarities should disappear? And yet we have to make of them a united nation. Here in the United Kingdom we have different races but one people. It would be rather difficult, I imagine, that an Englishman should feel exactly the same in regard to, let us say, Bannockburn as a Scotsman would do (*a laugh*); yet both Scotch and English may equally be proud of having had their full part in Waterloo or Trafalgar. Why should it not be the same, I ask, of the Dutchman that he should not forget any of the traditions of which he may justly be proud, that he should not abandon any of the peculiarities or prejudices of his race any more than I would ask it of any Briton? But my confident hope and belief is that in the future both these representatives of different races will be able to co-operate and to create for themselves a common existence in which they may have a common pride. It is, therefore, to the empire with all that that means that I look to produce that union in South Africa which we all desire to achieve. (*Cheers.*) But you will understand that in the absorbing preoccupation of these thoughts in a work which strained every nerve, and which filled every waking moment, I had no time to keep myself abreast of purely party politics in this country. I am still under the glamour of this new experience. (*Laughter.*) My ideas even now run more on these questions, which are connected with the future of the Empire, than they do upon the smaller controversies, upon which depend the fate of by-elections (*laughter*), and sometimes even the fate of Governments. When you are 6,000 miles away from the House of Commons, it is perfectly extraordinary how events and discussions and conflicts of opinion present themselves in different—I think I may even say in truer—proportion. You are excited at home about an Education Bill (*laughter*), about temperance reforms (*loud laughter*), about local finance. Yes, I should be if I had remained at home. But these things matter no more to South Africa, to Canada, to Australia than their local affairs matter to you; and, on the other hand, everything that touches Imperial policy, everything which affects their interests as well as yours, has for them, as it ought to have for us, a supreme importance. Our Imperial policy is vital to them and vital to us. Upon that Imperial policy and what you do in the next few years depends that enormous issue whether this great Empire of ours is to stand together, one free nation, if necessary, against all the world (*hear, hear*), or whether it is to fall apart into separate States, each selfishly seeking its own interest alone, losing sight of the commonweal, and losing also all the advantages which union alone can give.

The Recent By-Elections

I came here, as I have said, after an experience which seems to me now almost a dream, and I find that here it has not been Imperial but local questions which were filling the minds of the people of this country. The political meteorologist had been at work (*laughter*), and had been predicting in the course of a few short months an entire change in the situation, had been predicting disaster and confusion to the Unionist party. Meanwhile, there seemed to me to be on the part of the Opposition an unseemly exultation. They were occupied greedily apportioning out the spoils of the victory which they anticipated (*laughter*), just as the Boers before the war were casting lots for the farms which they expected to wrest from their British possessors. When I inquired what had happened to suggest the depression on the one side and the elation on the other, I was told that a reaction was in progress (*laughter*); that the Education Bill had caused many persons to leave the Unionist party; that caves were being formed; that younger members of the party, tired of the monotony of a loyal support, had sought a freer and more strenuous life as troglodytes, political troglodytes, in the caves of their selection. Yet we found, however, even at the commencement that very few occupied the same cave. I was told that the by-elections were going against the Government; I was told that the constituencies were prepared to forgive the pro-Boers their want of patriotism and the Little Englanders their want of courage, and that they were now ready to give to Home Rule and the Newcastle programme a new chance. (*Laughter.*) Well, it may be that I am less sensible to sudden emotion since I returned from my travels in South Africa. The calm which is induced by the solitude of the illimitable veld may have affected my constitution. (*Laughter.*) At any rate, I was not moved by those depressing statements. I was not brought to think that my countrymen were so inclined to rapid change. I was not induced to believe the by-elections were of this excessive importance; and when I came to examine the particular elections from which so much was anticipated, when I found that in one of them the Liberal party, so-called (*laughter*), had gained a supporter in a gentleman who proposed to hand back the Transvaal to the Boers (*laughter*), and, at the same time, had gained another supporter in a gentleman who professed himself to be a sincere Imperialist thoroughly convinced of the justice of the war—when I found that Sir Wilfrid Lawson declared that he came to Parliament in order to confiscate the property of every publican, and that Dr. Hutchinson came to Parliament determined to give compensation to every publican (*laughter*)—and that all of these were going to join the Liberal party (*laughter and cheers*), it seemed to me that the combination was not so terrible. And while I was prepared to congratulate Sir Henry Campbell-Bannerman on the flexibility of adaptation which his followers displayed; while I was disposed to say, as of Cleopatra, "age cannot wither nor custom stale her infinite variety" (*laughter*), I was not prepared unduly to excite myself as to the prospect of the Government and its supporters. There must be ups and downs in politics. I have had now a long experience, and I will safely predict of any Government that if it endeavours honestly to grapple with the great problems of its time it will lose a certain amount of support. You cannot deal with any domestic question and find an absolutely united party to support it; and the more bold your policy, the more drastic the changes which you propose to bring about, the more certain it is that you will pay the price, for the time at any rate, in the votes of a certain number of those whose support you greatly value.

Well, but that is the business of the Government. Under ordinary circumstances the business of the Government is to spend itself doing what it thinks to be right. And, let me say, in all seriousness, that if I were assured that the main lines of our Imperial and national policy, those things which touch our existence, were assured, if I could tell that there was that continuity in foreign and Colonial policy which I have known to exist in past times, I for one should be very willing indeed to allow to my political opponents their chance in their turn to try their hands at the difficult domestic problems with which we have to deal. After eight years of such strenuous work as seldom falls to the lot of a politician, I can say for myself, and I believe I can say for all my colleagues, that I would rejoice if I could be relieved, at all events for a time, and if I could occupy instead of the post of a prominent actor the much more easy and less responsible post of universal critic.

The Opposition: The Empire

But what do I want in order to face the future not only without regret, but with absolute relief and rejoicing? I want to know that the party which would take our place has frankly abandoned that disastrous policy of Home Rule (*hear, hear*), which would begin by the disruption of the United Kingdom and which would end in the disruption of the Empire (*hear, hear*); for, believe me, it is borne in upon me now more than ever, you cannot weaken the centre without destroying all that depends upon the centre. If you want an Empire you must be strong and united at home. (*Hear, hear.*) If separation begins here, take my word for it, it will not stop here. The Empire itself will be dissolved into its component atoms. If I could believe, however, that our opponents had frankly abandoned Home Rule—if Sir Henry Campbell-Bannerman, as the leader of the party, should divest himself of that curious antagonism to everything British ("*Hear, hear,*" *and laughter*) which makes him the friend of every country but his own—if I thought that his followers were animated by that broader patriotism by which alone our Empire can be held together, then, indeed, I would be the first to sing *nunc dimittis*. (*Hear, hear.*) But this assurance is wanting. (*Hear, hear.*) I have read with care and interest all the speeches that have been made by the leaders of the Liberal party; and in none of them do I find a frank acceptance of that national and Imperial policy which I believe at the present time is the first necessity of a united kingdom. As long as that is the case, however anxious I may be personally for rest, I confess I cannot look forward without dread of handing over the security and existence of this great Empire to the hands of those who have made common cause with its enemies (*hear, hear*), who have charged their own countrymen with methods of barbarism (*hear,*

hear), and who apparently have been untouched by that pervading senti-ment which I found everywhere where the British flag floats and which has done so much in recent years to draw us together. I should not re-quire to go to South Africa in order to be convinced that this feeling has obtained deep hold on the minds and hearts of our children beyond the seas. It has had a hard life of it. This feeling of Imperial patriotism was checked for a generation by the apathy and the indifference which were the characteristics of our former relations with our colonies. It was dis-couraged by our apparent acceptance of the doctrines of the Little Eng-landers, of the provincial spirit which taught us to consider ourselves alone and to regard with indifference all that concerned those, however loyal they might be, who left these shores in order to go to our colonies abroad. But it was never extinguished. The embers were still alight. And when in the late war this old country of ours showed that it was still possessed by the spirit of our ancestors, showed that it was still prepared to count no sacrifice that was necessary in order to maintain the honour and the interests of the Empire that was committed to its charge, then you found a response from your brethren, your children across the seas, a re-sponse such as has not been known before, that astonished the world by a proof, an undeniable proof, of affection and regard. (*Cheers.*) I have said that that was a new chapter, the beginning of a new era. Is it to end there? ("*No.*") Is it to end with the end of the war, with the termination of the crisis that brought it forth? Are we to sink that with the old policy of selfish isolation, which went very far to dry and even to sap the loyalty of our Colonial brethren? I do not think so. I think these larger issues touch the people of this country. I think they have awakened to the enor-mous importance of a creative time like the present, taking advantage of the opportunities that are offered in order to make permanent what has begun so well. Remember, we are a kingdom, an old country. We proceed here upon settled lines. We have our quarrels and our disputes and we pass legislation which may be good or bad, but which, at any rate, can be altered; but we go towards an object which is sufficiently defined. We know that whatever changes there may be, whatever meandering of the current, at all events the main stream ultimately reaches its appointed destination. That is the result of centuries of constitutional progress and freedom, but the Empire is not old. The Empire is new, the Empire is in its infancy. Now is the time when we can mould that Empire and when we and those who live with us can decide its future destinies.

The Growth of the Empire

Just let us consider what that Empire is. I am not going to-night to speak of those millions, hundreds of millions, of our Indian and native fellow-subjects for whom we have become responsible. It is upon us that the obligation lies to give them good government and in every way to promote their development and prosperity; and some day it might be worth my while, and it might be possible for me to discuss with you, to confer with you upon all the important questions which such an enormous obligation imposes. But to-night I put that aside, and I consider only our relations to our own kinsfolk, to that white British population that constitutes the majority in the great self-governing colonies of the Empire. What is our position in regard to them? Here in the United Kingdom there are some 40 millions of us; outside there are ten millions of men either directly descended from ancestors who left this country or more probably men who themselves in their youth left this country in order to find their fortunes in our possessions abroad. Now how long do you suppose that this proportion of population is going to endure? How long are we going to be four times as many as our kinsfolk abroad? The development of those colonies has been delayed by many reasons—partly, as I think, by our inaction, partly by the provincial spirit which we have not done enough to discourage, that spirit which attaches undue importance to the local incidents and legislation of each separate State and gives insufficient regard to the interests of the whole—but mainly probably by a more material reason, by the fact that the United States of America has offered a greater attraction to British emigration. But that has changed. The United States of America with all their vast territory are filling up; and even now we hear of thousands and tens of thousands of emigrants leaving the United States of America in order to take up the fresh and rich lands of our colony of Canada. And it seems to me to be not at all an impossible assumption that before the end of this present century we may find that our population, our fellow-subjects beyond the seas, may be as numerous as we are at home. I want you to look forward. I want you to consider the infinite importance of this not only to yourselves but to your descendants. Now is the time when you can exert influence. Do you wish that if these ten millions become 40 millions they shall still be closely, intimately, affectionately united to you (*cheers*)? or do you contemplate the possibility of their being separated, going off each in his own direction under a separate flag? Think what it means to your power and influence as a country; think what it means to your position among the nations of the world; think what it means to your trade and commerce. I put that last. The influence of the Empire is the thing I think most about; and that influence I believe will always be used for the peace and civilisation of the world. (*Hear, hear.*) But the question of trade and commerce is one of the greatest importance. Unless that is satisfactorily settled, I for one do not believe in a continued union of the Empire. I am told—I hear it stated again and again by what I believe to be the representatives of a small minority of the people of this country, those whom I describe, because I know no other words for them, as "Little Englanders" —I hear it stated by them, what is a fact, that our trade with those countries is much less than our trade in foreign countries; and therefore it appears to be their opinion that we should do everything in our power to cultivate that trade with foreigners, and that we can safely disregard the trade with our children. Now, Sir, that is not my conclusion. (*Cheers.*) My conclusion is exactly the opposite. (*Renewed cheers.*)

Union or Separation?

Look into the future. I say it is the business of British statesmen to do everything they can, even at some present sacrifice, to keep the trade of the colonies with Great Britain (*cheers*), to increase that trade, to promote it, even if in doing so we lessen somewhat the trade with our foreign competitors. (*"Hear, hear," and cheers.*) Are we doing everything at the present time to direct the patriotic movement which I see not only here, but through all the colonies, in the right channel? are we, in fact, by our legislation, by our action—are we making for union or are we drifting to separation? That is a critical issue. In my opinion the germs of a federal union that will make the British Empire powerful and influential for good beyond the dreams of any one now living—the germs of that union are in the soil; but it is a tender and delicate plant and requires careful handling. (*Hear, hear.*) I wish you would look back to our history. Consider what might have been, in order that you may be influenced now to do what is right. Supposing, when self-government was first conceded to these colonies, the statesmen who gave it had had any idea of the possibilities of the future. Do you not see that they might have laid broad and firm the foundations of an Imperial edifice of which every part would have contributed something to the strength of the whole? But in those days the one idea of statesmen was to get rid of the whole business. They believed that separation must come. What they wanted to do was to make it smooth and easy; and none of these ideas which subsequent experience has put into our minds appears ever to have been suggested to them. By their mistakes and their neglect our task has been made more difficult— more difficult, but not impossible. (*Hear, hear.*) There is still time to consolidate the Empire. We also have our chance, and it depends upon what we do now whether this great idea is to find fruition or whether we will for ever and ever dismiss it from our consideration and accept our fate as one of the dying Empires of the world.

The Burden of the Colonies

Now, what is the meaning of an Empire? What does it mean to us? We have had a little experience. We have had a war—a war in which the majority of our children abroad had no apparent direct interest. We had no hold over them, no agreement with them of any kind; and yet at one time during this war, by the voluntary decision of these people, at least 50,000 Colonial soldiers were standing shoulder to shoulder with British troops, displaying a gallantry equal to their own and the keenest intelligence. (*Loud cheers.*) It is something for a beginning; and if this country were in danger—I mean if we were, as our forefathers were, face to face some day, Heaven forfend, with some great coalition of hostile nations— then, when we had with our backs to the wall to struggle for our very lives, it is my firm conviction that there is nothing within the power of these self-governing colonies they would not do to come to our aid. I believe their whole resources in men and in money would be at the disposal of the mother country in such an event. Well, as I say, that is something— that is something which it is wonderful to have achieved, which it is worth almost any sacrifice to maintain. So far as personal sacrifices are involved, risking your life and encountering every hardship, the colonies did their duty in the late war. If it came to another question, the question of the share they bore in the pecuniary burden which the war involved, well I think they might have done more. (*Hear, hear.*) I did not hesitate to tell my fellow-subjects in the colonies of South Africa, whether in the new colonies or in the old ones, that, though they had done much, they had not done enough, they had left substantially the whole burden on the shoulders of the mother country; and that in the future, if they valued empire and its privileges, they must be prepared to take a greater share of the obligations. (*Hear, hear.*) If I had been speaking in Australia or in Canada I would have said the same thing (*hear, hear*), and perhaps I should have been inclined to say it even in stronger terms; and, if I may judge by the reception of my utterances in South Africa, I should give no offence by this frank speaking. (*Hear, hear.*) There is something, however, to be remembered on behalf of our colonies, and that is that this idea of a common responsibility is altogether a new one, and we have done nothing to encourage it. It is presented to them in the light of a new tax, and people have an extraordinary way of regarding a new tax with a suspicion (*laughter*), and even with dislike. (*Hear, hear.*) But what happened? I spoke in Natal, and the people of Natal responded by taking upon their shoulders a burden which for a small colony was considerable, and which they had thought of placing upon ourselves. I spoke in the

Transvaal; and the representatives of every class in the Transvaal, and none more enthusiastically than the working people, took upon themselves a burden of £80 per head of the white population, a burden which, indeed, the riches of the country justified, but which was something altogether in excess of any similar obligation placed upon any other country in the world. (*Hear, hear.*) I spoke in Cape Colony, and only in Cape Colony, owing to the division of opinion which has prevailed there, I neither expected nor asked for a contribution towards the war. I do expect—I do not know whether I shall be disappointed—but I do expect in the time to come Dutch and English will both feel, as the Empire belongs to them as well as to us, bound towards the future expenditure of the country to contribute more liberally than they have done in the past. Well, all have done something; and, to my mind, it is a great thing to get the principle accepted; and I think it depends upon us whether in future the application of this principle should be made with greater liberality or whether, as I have said, we are all to fall back each to care for himself and "The devil take the hindmost." (*Laughter.*) Sir, my idea of British policy, I mean the policy of the United Kingdom, is that here, at the beginning of things, at the beginning of this new chapter, we should show our appreciation, our cordial appreciation, of the first step to be taken by our colonies to show their solidarity with us. Every advance which they make should be reciprocated. We should set ourselves a great example of community of interest, and, above all, that community of sacrifice on which alone the Empire can permanently rest. I have admitted that the colonies have hitherto been backward in their contributions towards Imperial defence. They are following their own lines. I hope they will do better. But in the meantime they are doing a great deal, and they are trying to promote this union which I regard as of so much importance in their own way and by their own means.

Preferential Tariffs

And first among those means is the offer of preferential tariffs. (*Cheers.*) Now, that is a matter which at the present moment is of the greatest possible importance to every one of you. It depends upon how we treat this policy for the colonies—not a policy inaugurated by us, but it is a policy which comes to us from our children abroad—it depends upon how we treat it, whether it is developed in the future or whether it is withdrawn as being non-acceptable to those whom it is sought to benefit. The other day, immediately after I left South Africa, a great conference was held for the first time of all the colonies in South Africa, the new colonies as well as the old. Boers and the Dutch were represented as well as the British. And this conference recommended the other Legislatures of the different colonies to give to us, the mother country, preference upon all dutiable goods of 25 per cent. (*Cheers.*) Last year at the Conference of Premiers the representatives of Australia and New Zealand accepted the same principle. They said in their different colonies there might be some difference of treatment; but so far as the principle was concerned they pledged themselves to recommend to their constituents a substantial preference in favour of goods produced in the mother country. Now, that again is a new chapter in our Imperial history; and again I ask is it to end there? In my opinion, these recommendations and these pledges will bear fruit just in proportion as you show your appreciation of them; and they will depend largely upon the experience of Canada, which has been their precursor in a similar movement. Canada is the greatest, the most prosperous of our self-governing colonies. At the present time it is in the full swing of an extraordinary prosperity, which, I hope, I believe, will lead to a great increase in its population, its strength, its importance in the constellation of free nations which constitutes the British Empire. Canada is of all our colonies the most backward in contributing to common defence; but Canada has been the most forward in endeavouring to unite the Empire by the other means of strengthening our commercial relations and by giving to us special favour and preference. If we appreciate this action properly it seems to me that not only is it certain that every other colony of the Empire will necessarily and in due time follow this example, but Canada herself and the other colonies also, as the bonds are drawn closer, as we become more and more one people united by interest as well as by sentiment, will be more and more ready to take its fair share in these burdens of defence to which I have referred.

The Example of Canada

Now, what has Canada done for us? Let me say, however, before I come to that that my policy which I wish to make clear to you is not to force our colonies—that is hopeless; they are as independent as we are—but to meet everything they do. If they see a way of drawing the Empire together, let us help them in that, even if they may not be prepared to join us in some other way from which we think the same result would be achieved. But let us be prepared to accept every indication on their part of this desire. Let us show we appreciate it, and believe me it will not be long before all will come into line; and the results which follow will be greater than perhaps it would be prudent now to anticipate. Well, I say, what has Canada done for us? Canada in 1898 freely, voluntarily of her own accord, as a recognition of her obligations to the mother country, as a recognition especially of the fact that we were the greatest of the free markets open to Canadian produce, gave us a preference on all dutiable goods of 25 per cent. In 1900 she increased that preference, also freely of her own accord, to 33⅓ per cent. (*Cheers.*) I have had occasion to point out that the results of this great concession have been to a certain extent in some respects disappointing. The increase in our trade with Canada has been very great, but it has not increased largely out of proportion to the increase of the trade between Canada and other countries; but this remains true that, whereas before these concessions the trade of this country with Canada was constantly reducing, getting less and less, that reduction has been stayed and the trade has continually increased (*hear, hear*), and, to put it in a word, the trade between our colony of Canada and the mother country, which was 6½ millions in 1897–1898, is now carried on at a rate of probably a good deal more; but at all events I will say, to be safe, of 11 millions sterling in the present year (*cheers*), and the increase is chiefly in textile goods, cotton, woollen, and goods of that kind, and in manufactures of hardware and iron and steel. At the same time, whereas the percentage of the total trade had fallen from 40 per cent., I think, or at all events from a large percentage, to 23½ per cent. in these last two years, it has been gradually climbing up again, and it has now reached for the present year 26½ per cent. Well, that is an important result; but the Ministers of Canada when they were over here last year made me a further definite offer. They said:—"We have done for you as much as we can do voluntarily and freely and without return. If you are willing to reciprocate in any way we are prepared to reconsider our tariff with a view of seeing whether we cannot give you further reductions, especially in regard to those goods in which you come into competition with foreigners, and we will do this if you will meet us by giving us a drawback on the small tax of ls. which you have put upon corn." That was an offer which we had to refuse. I must say that, if I could treat matters of this kind solely in regard to my position as Secretary of State for the Colonies, I should have said, "That is a fair offer; that is a generous offer from your point of view, and it is an offer which we might ask our people to accept." But, speaking for the Government as a whole, not in the interests of the colonies, I am obliged to say that it is contrary to the established fiscal policy of this country, and that we hold ourselves bound to keep an open market for all the world even if they close their markets to us (*laughter*), and that, therefore, so long as that is the mandate of the British public we are not in a position to offer any preference or favour whatever even to our own children. We cannot make any difference between those who treat us well and those who treat us badly. (*Cries of "Shame,"*) Yes; but that is the doctrine which I am told is the accepted doctrine of the free-trader; and we are all free-traders. (*Cries of "No, no," and laughter.*) Well, I am. (*Loud laughter.*) I have considerable doubt whether the interpretation of free trade which is current amongst a certain limited section is the true interpretation. (*Hear, hear.*) But I am perfectly certain that I am not a protectionist. But I want to point out that if the interpretation is that our only duty is to buy in the cheapest market without regard to whether we can sell, if that is the theory of free trade which finds acceptance here and elsewhere, then in pursuance of that policy you will have to forgo the advantage of a reduction, a further reduction, in duty which your great colony of Canada offers to you manufacturers of this country; and you may lose a great deal more, because in the speech which the Chancellor of the Exchequer, the Minister of Finance as he is called in Canada, made to the Canadian Parliament the other day, which he has just sent me, I find he says that if we are told definitely Great Britain, the mother country, can do nothing for us in the way of reciprocity we must reconsider our position and reconsider the preference that we have already given.

German Retaliation on Canada

Well, these are big questions, and this particular question is complicated in a rather unexpected manner. The policy which prevents us from offering an advantage to our colonies prevents us from defending them if they are attacked. Now I suppose you and I are agreed that the British Empire is one and indivisible. (*Cheers.*) You and I are agreed that we absolutely refuse to look upon any of the States that form the British Empire as in any way excluded from any advantage or privilege to which the British Empire is entitled. We may well, therefore, have supposed an agreement of this kind by which Canada does a kindness to us a matter of family agreement concerning nobody else; but unfortunately Germany thinks otherwise. There is a German Empire. The German Empire is divided into states—Bavaria and, let us say, Hanover, Saxony, and Wurtemberg. They may deal between themselves in any way they please. As a matter of fact, they have entire free trade among themselves. We do not consider them separate entitites; we treat the German Empire as a whole. We do not complain because one State gives an advantage to another State in that Empire and does not give it to all the rest of the world. But in this case of Canada Germany insists upon treating Canada as though it were a separate country, refuses to recognize it as a part of one Empire, entitled to claim, as I have said, the privileges of that Empire, regards this agreement as being something more than a domestic agreement; and it has penalized Canada by placing upon Canadian goods an additional duty. Well now the reason for that is clear. The German newspapers very frankly explain that this is a policy of reprisal, and that it is intended to deter other colonies from giving to us the same advantage. Therefore it is not merely punishment inflicted by Germany upon Canada but it is a threat to South Africa, to Australia, and to New Zealand; and this policy, as a policy of dictation and interference, is justified by the belief that we are so wedded to our fiscal system that we cannot interfere, that we cannot defend our colonies, and that in fact any one of them which attempts to establish any kind of special relations with us does so at her own risk and must be left to bear the brunt of foreign hostility. In my mind that is putting us in a rather humiliating position. (*Hear, hear.*) I do not like it at all. I know what will follow if we allow it to prevail. It is easy to predict the consequences. How do you think that under such circumstances we can approach our colonies with appeals to aid us in promoting the union of the Empire, or ask them to bear a share of the common burden? Are we to say to them, "This is your Empire, take pride in it, share its privileges?" They say:—"What are its privileges? The privileges appear to be if we treat you as relations and friends; if we show you kindness, we give you preference, you who benefit by our action can only leave us alone to fight our own battles against those who are offended by our action." Now is that free trade? (*Cries of "Go on."*) My object is to put the position before you; and above all, as I have just come home from great colonies, I want you to see these matters as they appear to our colonial fellow-subjects. There is no doubt what they think, and there is no doubt of what great issues hang upon their decision.

The Alternatives

I said just now is this free trade? No, it is absolutely a new situation. (*Cheers.*) There has been nothing like it in our history. It was a situation that was never contemplated by any of those whom we regard as the authors of free trade. What would Mr. Bright, what would Mr. Cobden, have said to this state of things? I do not know. It would be presumptuous to imagine; but this I can say. Mr. Cobden did not hesitate to make a treaty of preference and reciprocity with France (*hear, hear*), and Mr. Bright did not hesitate to approve his action; and I cannot believe if they had been present among us now and known what this new situation was, I cannot believe that they would have hesitated to make a treaty of preference and reciprocity with our own children. (*Loud and prolonged cheers.*) Well, you see the point. You want an Empire. (*Hear, hear.*) Do you think it better to cultivate the trade with your own people or to let that go in order that you may keep the trade of those who, rightly enough, are your competitors and rivals? I say it is a new position. I say the people of this Empire have got to consider it. I do not want to hasten their decision. They have two alternatives before them. They may maintain if they like in all its severity the interpretation, in my mind an entirely artificial and wrong interpretation, which has been placed upon the doctrines of free trade by a small remnant of Little Englanders of the Manchester school who now profess to be the sole repositories of the doctrines of Mr. Cobden and Mr. Bright. They may maintain that policy in all its severity, although it is repudiated by every other nation and by all your own colonies. In that case they will be absolutely precluded either from giving any kind of preference or favour to any of their colonies abroad or even protecting their colonies abroad when they offer to favour us. That is the first alternative. The second alternative is that we should insist that we will not be bound by any purely technical definition of free trade, that, while we seek as one chief object free interchange of trade and commerce between ourselves and all the nations of the world, we will nevertherless recover our freedom, resume that power of negotiation, and, if necessary, retaliation (*loud cheers*), whenever our own interests or our relations between our colonies and ourselves are threatened by other people. (*Cheers.*) I leave the matter in your hands. I desire that a discussion on this subject should be opened. The time has not yet come to settle it; but it seems to me that for good or for evil this is an issue much greater in its consequences than any of our local disputes. (*Hear, hear.*) Make a mistake in legislation, yet it can be corrected; make a mistake in your Imperial policy, it is irretrievable. You have an opportunity; you will never have it again.

The Issue of the Next Election

I do not think myself that a general election is very near (*Laughter*); but, whether it is near or distant, I think our opponents may perhaps find that the issues which they propose to raise are not the issues on which we shall take the opinion of the country. (*Cheers.*) If we raise an issue of this kind, the answer will depend not upon petty personal considerations, not upon temporary interests, but upon whether the people of this country really have it in their hearts to do all that is necessary, even if it occasionally goes against their own prejudices, to consolidate an Empire which can only be maintained by relations of interest as well as by relations of sentiment. For my own part I believe in a British Empire, in an Empire which, although it should be its first duty to cultivate friendship with all the nations of the world, should yet, even if alone, be self-sustaining and self-sufficient, able to maintain itself against the competition of all its rivals; and I do not believe in a Little England which shall be separated from all those to whom it would in the natural course look for support and affection, a Little England which would then be dependent absolutely on the mercy of those who envy its present prosperity, and who have shown they are ready to do all in their power to prevent its future union with the British races throughout the world. (*Loud and continued cheers.*)

MR. CHAMBERLAIN, rising again, said:—Ladies and Gentlemen, —Before we separate there is a duty which we are none of us unwilling to perform. It is usual on these occasions. I have been asked to commend to you a vote of thanks to Mr. Henry Payton for his able conduct of the business of this meeting. Before I say a word on the subject of the resolution I would like to say something upon another matter of purely local interest and importance, but which I think concerns the honour of Birmingham. In the war which is now happily over I do not think there was any community which contributed more largely in proportion to its numbers than the city of Birmingham. Although we are an inland town, although we see very little of military pomp and display, yet we contribute no inconsiderable proportion to the military defence of the Empire. Many of our citizens went from here to take their part in the danger and in the hardship of the war. Many of them have come back, as I hope, to be honoured and respected for their patriotism; many of them died in South Africa, died of wounds received in battle, or died by the still more deadly diseases which accompany an army in the field. We have to mourn more than 500 of our citizens. They have set an example to posterity. Let us honour them for their patriotism; let us hold them up a model to those who come after. A subscription list was opened in this town in order to provide a suitable memorial for these our fellow-citizens; but in the pressure of other things insufficient funds have up to the present time been provided. Now I think that this is not creditable to us, and I make an appeal here, and I myself, I need scarcely say, will gladly head the appeal. I make an appeal here to all in Birmingham that they will not allow it to be said hereafter that we sent these men out to the war and forgot their services or failed to hold them up to recollection and to gratitude. I appeal to you all in your several capacities and with your several opportunities to contribute to the fund which was being established by the *Daily Mail* in Birmingham in order to erect a suitable memorial to those of our fellow-citizens who fell in the late war. (*Cheers.*) It might seem a formal matter to propose a vote of thanks to our chairman. It is hardly that to me. This is the first time, I think, that I have to welcome him as the chairman of our local organization; but he and I go back, I am afraid to say how many years, but, at all events, in my very first connexion with public life in Birmingham I find Mr. Henry Payton as one of my most active co-operators. Since then we have continued on the same lines, I am happy to say, never separated; and now it is a great pleasure to me to commend him to your applause, not only for what he has done in controlling the meeting, for that, indeed, has been very little, but for all his services, not only to the city, but to the party he represents. (*Cheers.*)

David Lloyd George

.

David Lloyd George

[*Born* JANUARY 17, 1863—*Died* MARCH 26, 1945]

Full of audacity and daring, a great showman, confident of his own judgment . . . able to sway the crowd even in the teeth of the most bitter opposition, keen student of 'mob psychology'.—A. J. SYLVESTER

A

torch-bearer of revolution"[1] is David Lloyd George who, as E. T. Raymond suggests, "may fairly claim admission to the small company of great, and even very great, British statesmen."[2] In 1890 Lloyd George was elected to the House of Commons as a Liberal candidate, and retained his seat for fifty-five years. During this long tenure in politics, he dominated the British political scene for sixteen of those years—from 1906 when he was appointed President of the Board of Trade to 1922 when he resigned as Prime Minister.

His claims to greatness lay in his introduction of the "People's Budget" in 1909 as Chancellor of the Exchequer in the Asquith cabinet, and as the architect of victory in the First World War.[3] The famed budget of 1909 contained, among other provisions, Insurance Acts which Thomas Jones contends were the "greatest measures of social reform ever placed upon the statute book and made smooth the transition to the Welfare State."[4]

The eloquence of Lloyd George is unquestioned, He has been variously described as the "orator of the new Social Order,"[5] to an "impassioned Celt" who could add to the "note of political passion" the "fervor of the prophet."[6] He was at his best before popular audiences where he spoke to their "primitive emotions . . . drawing his images from the elemental forces of nature and the incidents of common life."[7]

His speaking was seldom witty, but as an alternative Raymond considers Lloyd George unequalled in the use as a weapon of a certain "verbal gaiety:"

He blows bubbles, so to speak, that seem to be the mere emanation of high spirits, but they give off, in bursting, a gas of deadly corrosive power.[8]

---

[1] R. H. Kiernan, *Lloyd George* (London: George G. Harrap & Co., Ltd., 1940), p. 85.

[2] E. T. Raymond, *Mr. Lloyd George* (New York: George H. Doran Co., 1922), p. 351.

[3] Thomas Jones, *Lloyd George* (Cambridge, Mass.: Harvard University Press, 1951), p. 290.   [4] *Ibid.*

[5] Beriah Evans, *The Life Romance of Lloyd George,* Intro. by Charles Sarolea (Birmingham: C. Combridge, no date), p. xii.

[6] Lewis Broad, *Winston Churchill: The Years of Preparation* (New York: Hawthorn Books, Inc., 1958), p. 33.

[7] Thomas Jones, *op. cit.,* p. 265.

[8] E. T. Raymond, *op. cit.,* p. 345.

Although adroit at presenting effective debate speeches in the House of Commons when the occasion demanded it, Lloyd George chose to prepare carefully all important addresses. His usual procedure was to dictate to a typist when time permitted, and would then seek to summarize important passages with the aid of key words. Upon delivering the prepared speech he would openly and deliberately refer to the manuscript, precisely adapted to the circumstances.

The speech included in this volume was delivered in the great hall of "The Edinburgh Castle" in the east end of London, commonly known as the Limehouse section. Herbert DuParcq claims this speech "must stand high among the great popular orations of history," [9] and Frank Owen calls it the speech that "rang around the world." [10] Political opponents of the day, Tories and Whigs alike, labelled the speech "Slimehouse" because of its attack on the landed aristocracy.

This speech was one of a series of vituperative speeches delivered in 1909 and 1910 in defense of his budget. But this address, delivered on July 30, 1909, carried the greatest impact with partisans and foes, alike. Delivered on the hottest summer of the new century before a "densely-packed, rowdy Cockney audience of 4,000 people, who interrupted almost every sentence with their cheers and laughter," [11] Lloyd George had his audience completely under his spell.[12] He attacked the privileged class largely through examples and with "restraint of manner and tone," [13] by insisting they assume a greater burden of taxation to meet increased defense needs and to provide comfort to the poor.

As an epilogue to the campaign of Lloyd George, the budget was finally passed by the House of Lords, the remaining aristocratic stronghold, on August 10, 1911, by a vote of 131 to 114. Passage resulted only after King Edward VII threatened to create 300 new peerages from those in sympathy with the budget, that Lords capitulated and forever lost its power of permanent veto.

It is perhaps exaggeration, but perhaps not, when Thomas Jones remarks that the "People's Budget . . . anticipated and prevented revolution" by softening the asperities of the postwar world for the rank and file.[14]

---

9 Herbert DuParcq, *Life of David Lloyd George*, III (London: Caxton Publishing Co., Ltd., 1912), p. 539.
10 Frank Owen, *Tempestuous Journey: Lloyd George, His Life and Times* (London: Hutchinson, 1954), p. 177.
11 *Ibid.*
12 Herbert DuParcq, *op. cit.*, p. 539.
13 *Ibid.*, p. 538.
14 Thomas Jones, *op. cit.*, p. 290.

The Budget[1]

•

A few months ago a meeting was held not far from this hall, in the heart of the City of London, demanding that the Government should launch out and run into enormous expenditure on the Navy. That meeting ended up with a resolution promising that those who passed that resolution would give financial support to the Government in their undertaking. There have been two or three meetings held in the City of London since (*laughter and cheers*), attended by the same class of people, but not ending up with a resolution promising to pay. (*Laughter.*) On the contrary, we are spending the money, but they won't pay. (*Laughter.*) What has happened since to alter their tone? Simply that we have sent in the bill. (*Laughter and cheers.*) We started our four Dreadnoughts. They cost eight millions of money. We promised them four more; they cost another eight millions. Somebody has got to pay, and these gentlemen say, "Perfectly true; somebody has got to pay, but we would rather that somebody were somebody else." (*Laughter.*) We started building; we wanted money to pay for the building; so we sent the hat round. (*Laughter.*) We sent it round amongst the workmen (*hear, hear*), and the miners of Derbyshire (*loud cheers*) and Yorkshire, the weavers of High Peak (*cheers*), and the Scotchmen of Dumfries (*cheers*), who, like all their countrymen, know the value of money. (*Laughter.*) They all brought in their coppers. We went round Belgravia, but there has been such a howl ever since that it has completely deafened us.

Old-Age Pensions

But they say "It is not so much the Dreadnoughts we object to, it is the pensions." (*Hear, hear.*) If they object to pensions, why did they promise

---

1 *The Times* (London), July 31, 1909, p. 9.

them? (*Cheers.*) They won elections on the strength of their promises. It is true they never carried them out. (*Laughter.*) Deception is always a pretty contemptible vice, but to deceive the poor is the meanest of all crimes. (*Cheers.*) But they say, "When we promised pensions we meant pensions at the expense of the people for whom they were provided. We simply meant to bring in a Bill to compel workmen to contribute to their own pensions." (*Laughter.*) If that is what they meant, why did they not say so? (*Cheers.*) The Budget, as your chairman has already so well reminded you, is introduced not merely for the purpose of raising barren taxes, but taxes that are fertile taxes, taxes that will bring forth fruit—the security of the country which is paramount in the minds of all. The provision for the aged and deserving poor—it was time it was done. (*Cheers.*) It is rather a shame for a rich country like ours—probably the richest country in the world, if not the richest the world has ever seen—that it should allow those who have toiled all their days to end in penury and possibly starvation. (*Hear, hear.*) It is rather hard that an old workman should have to find his way to the gates of the tomb, bleeding and footsore, through the brambles and thorns of poverty. (*Cheers.*) We cut a new path through it (*cheers*), an easier one, a pleasanter one, through fields of waving corn. We are raising money to pay for the new road (*cheers*), aye, and to widen it so that 200,000 paupers shall be able to join in the march. (*Cheers.*) There are many in the country blessed by Providence with great wealth, and if there are amongst them men who grudge out of their riches a fair contribution towards the less fortunate of their fellow-countrymen they are shabby rich men. (*Cheers.*) We propose to do more by means of the Budget. We are raising money to provide against the evils and the sufferings that follow from unemployment. (*Cheers.*) We are raising money for the purpose of assisting our great friendly societies to provide for the sick and the widows and orphans. We are providing money to enable us to develop the resources of our own land. (*Cheers.*) I do not believe any fair-minded man would challenge the justice and the fairness of the objects which we have in view in raising this money.

The Land Taxes

But there are some of them who say that the taxes themselves are unjust, unfair, unequal, oppressive—notably so the land taxes. (*Laughter.*) They are engaged, not merely in the House of Commons, but outside the House of Commons, in assailing these taxes with a concentrated and a sustained ferocity which will not allow even a comma to escape with its life. (*"Good," and laughter.*) How are they really so wicked? Let us examine them, because it is perfectly clear that the one part of the Budget that attracts all this hostility and animosity is that part which deals with the taxation of land. Well, now let us examine it. I do not want you to consider merely abstract principles. I want to invite your attention to a number of concrete cases and fair samples to show you how these concrete illustrations—how our Budget proposals work. Now let us take them. Let us take first of all the tax on undeveloped land and on increment.

Unearned Increment at the Docks

Not far from here not so many years ago, between the Lea and the Thames, you had hundreds of acres of land which was not very useful even for agricultural purposes. In the main it was a sodden marsh. The commerce and the trade of London increased under free trade (*loud cheers*), the tonnage of your shipping went up by hundreds of thousands of tons and by millions, labour was attracted from all parts of the country to help with all this trade and business done here. What happened? There was no housing accommodation. This part of London became overcrowded and the population overflowed. That was the opportunity of the owners of the marsh. All that land became valuable building land, and land which used to be rented at £2 or £3 an acre has been selling within the last few years at £2,000 an acre, £3,000 an acre, £6,000 an acre, £8,000 an acre. Who created that increment? (*Cheers.*) Who made that golden swamp? (*More cheers.*) Was it the landlord? (*Cries of "No."*) Was it his energy? Was it his brains (*laughter and cheers*), his forethought? It was purely the combined efforts of all the people engaged in the trade and commerce of that part of London—the trader, the merchant, the shipowner, the dock labourer, the workman—everybody except the landlord. (*Cheers.*) Now you follow that transaction. The land worth £2 or £3 an acre ran up to thousands. During the time it was ripening the landlord was paying his rates and his taxes not on £2 or £3 an acre. It was agricultural land, and because it was agricultural land a munificent Tory Government (*laughter*) voted a sum of two millions to pay half the rates of those poor distressed landlords. (*Laughter, and cries of "Shame."*) You and I had to pay taxes in order to enable those landlords to pay half their rates on agricultural land, while it was going up every year by hundreds of pounds from your efforts and the efforts of your neighbours. Well, now that is coming to an end. (*Loud and long-continued cheering.*) On the walls of Mr. Balfour's meeting last Friday were the words, "We protest against fraud and folly." (*Laughter.*) So do I. (*Great cheering.*) These things I am going to tell you of have only been possible up to the present through the fraud of the few and the folly of the million. (*Cheers.*) In future those landlords will have to contribute to the taxation of the country on the basis of the real value (*more cheers*) only one-halfpenny in the pound! (*Laughter.*) And that is what all the howling is about. But there is another little tax called the increment tax. For the future what will happen? We mean to value all the land in the kingdom. (*Cheers.*) And here you can draw no distinction between agricultural land and other land, for the simple reason that East and West Ham was agricultural land a few years ago. And if land goes up in the future by hundreds and thousands an acre through the efforts of the community the community will get 20 per cent. of that increment. (*Cheers.*) What a misfortune it is that there was not a Chancellor of the Exchequer who did this 30 years ago. (*Cheers and cries of "Better late than never."*) Only 30 years ago and we should now have an abundant revenue from this source. (*Cheers.*)

More Examples

Now I have given you West Ham. Let me give you a few more cases. Take a case like Golder's-green and other cases of a similar kind where the value of land has gone up in the course, perhaps, of a couple of years through a new tramway or a new railway being opened. Golder's-green is a case in point. A few years ago there was a plot of land there which was sold at £160. Last year I went and opened a tube railway there. What was the result? That very piece of land has been sold at £2,100 ("*Shame*"); £160 before the railway was opened—before I went there (*laughter*); £2,100 now. So I am entitled to 20 per cent. on that. (*Laughter.*) Now there are many cases where landlords take advantage of the exigencies of commerce and of industry—take advantage of the needs of municipalities and even of national needs and of the monopoly which they have got in land in a particular neighbourhood in order to demand extortionate prices. Take the very well-known case of the Duke of Northumberland (*hear, hear*), when a county council wanted to buy a small plot of land as a site for a school to train the children who in due course would become the men labouring on his property. The rent was quite an insignificant thing; his contribution to the rates—I forget—I think on the basis of 30s. an acre. What did he demand for it for a school? £900 an acre. ("*Hear, hear,*" and "*Shame.*") Well all we say is this, Mr. Buxton and I say—if it is worth £900, let him pay taxes on £900. (*Cheers.*)

The Case of Bootle

Now there are several of these cases that I want to give to you. Take the town of Bootle, a town created very much in the same way as these towns in the east of London—purely by the commerce of Bootle. In 1879 the rates of Bootle were £9,000 a year—the ground-rents were £10,000—so that the landlord was receiving more from the industry of the community than all the rates derived by the municipality for the benefit of the town.

In 1900 the rates were £94,000 a year—for improving the place, construct-ing roads, laying out parks, and extending lighting and so on. But the ground landlord was receiving in ground-rents £100,000. It is time that he should pay for all this value. (*Cheers.*) A case was given me from Rich-mond which is very interesting. The Town Council of Richmond recently built some workmen's cottages under a housing scheme. The land ap-peared on the rate-book as of the value of £4, and being agricultural (*laughter*) the landlord only paid half the rates, and you and I paid the rest for him. (*Laughter.*) It is situated on the extreme edge of the bor-ough, therefore it is not very accessible, and the town council thought they would get it cheap. (*Laughter.*) But they did not know their land-lord. They had to pay £2,000 an acre for it. ("*Shame.*") The result is that instead of having a good housing scheme with plenty of gardens, of open space, plenty of breathing space, plenty of room for the workmen at the end of their days, 40 cottages had to be crowded on the two acres. Now if the land had been valued at its true value that landlord would have been at any rate contributing his fair share of the public revenue, and it is just conceivable that he might have been driven to sell at a more reasonable price.

An Illustration from Wales

Now, I do not want to weary you with these cases. (*Cries of "Go on!"*) I could give you many. I am a member of a Welsh county council, and landlords even in Wales are not more reasonable. (*Laughter.*) The police committee the other day wanted a site for a police station. Well, you might have imagined that if a landlord sold land cheaply for anything it would have been for a police station. (*Laughter.*) The housing of the working classes—that is a different matter. (*Laughter.*) But a police sta-tion means security to property. (*Laughter and cheers.*) Not at all. The total population of Carnarvonshire is not as much—I am not sure it is as much—as the population of Limehouse alone. It is a scattered area, with no great crowded population. And yet they demanded for a piece of land which was contributing 2s. a year to the rates £2,500 an acre! All we say is, "If the land is as valuable as all that, let it have the same value on the assessment book (*cheers*) as it seems to possess in the auction room." (*Cheers.*) There are no end of these cases. There was a case at Greenock the other day. The Admiralty wanted a torpedo range. Here was an op-portunity for patriotism! (*Laughter.*) These are the men who want an efficient navy to protect our shores, and the Admiralty state that one ele-ment in efficiency is straight shooting, and say "We want a range for prac-tice for torpedoes on the west of Scotland." There was a piece of land there. It was rated at something like £11 2s. a year. They went to the

landlord, and it was sold to the nation for £27,225. And these are the
gentlemen who accuse us of robbery and spoliation! (*Cheers.*) Now, all we
say is this—"In future you must pay one-halfpenny in the pound on the
real value of your land. In addition to that if the value goes up, not owing
to your efforts—though if you spend money on improving it we will give
you credit for it—but if it goes up owing to the industry and the energy of
the people living in that locality one-fifth of that increment shall in future be taken as a toll by the State." (*Cheers.*) They say "Why should you
tax this increment on landlords and not on other classes of the community?" They say, "You are taxing the landlord because the value of his
property is going up through the growth of population with the increased
prosperity of the community. Does not the value of a doctor's business go
up in the same way?" Ha! fancy comparing themselves for a moment.
What is the landlord's increment? Who is the landlord? The landlord is a
gentleman—I have not a word to say about him in his personal capacity—
who does not earn his wealth. He does not even take the trouble to receive
his wealth. (*Laughter.*) He has a host of agents and clerks that receive for
him. He does not even take the trouble to spend his wealth. He has a host
of people around him to do the actual spending for him. He never sees it
until he comes to enjoy it. His sole function, his chief pride is stately
consumption of wealth produced by others. (*Cheers.*) What about the
doctor's income? How does the doctor earn his income? The doctor is a
man who visits our homes when they are darkened with the shadow of
death; his skill, his trained courage, his genius bring hope out of the grip
of despair, win life out of the fangs of the Great Destroyer. (*Cheers.*) All
blessings upon him and his divine art of healing that mends bruised
bodies and anxious hearts. (*Cheers.*) To compare the reward which he
gets for that labour with the wealth which pours into the pockets of the
landlord purely owing to the possession of his monopoly is a piece of
insolence which no intelligent community will tolerate. (*Cheers.*) So
much for the halfpenny tax and the unearned increment.

The Reversion Tax

Now I come to the reversion tax. What is the reversion tax? You have
got a system in this country which is not tolerated in any other country in
the world, except, I believe, Turkey (*laughter*)—the system whereby
landlords take advantage of the fact that they have got complete control
over the land, to let it for a term of years, spend money upon it in building, in developing. You improve the building and year by year the value
passes into the pockets of the landlord, and at the end of 60, 70, 80, or 90
years the whole of it passes away to the pockets of that man, who never
spent a penny upon it. In Scotland they have a system of 999 years' lease.

The Scotsmen have a very shrewd idea that at the end of 999 years there will probably be a better land system in existence (*laughter and cheers*), and they are prepared to take their chance of the millennium coming round by that time. But in this country we have 60 years' leases. I know districts in Wales where a little bit of barren rock where you could not feed a goat, where the landlord could not get a shilling an acre of agricultural rent, is let to quarrymen for the purposes of building houses, where 30s. or £2 a house is charged for ground-rent. The quarryman builds his house. He goes to a building society to borrow money. He pays out of his hard-earned weekly wage to the building society for 10, 20, or 30 years. By the time he becomes an old man he has cleared off the mortgage, and more than half the value of the house has passed into the pockets of the landlord. You have got cases in London here. (*A voice.—"Not hal."* and *laughter.*) There is the famous Gorringe case. In that case advantage was taken of the fact that a man has built up a great business, and they say, "Here you are, you have built up a great business here; you cannot take it away; you cannot move to other premises because your trade and goodwill are here; your lease is coming to an end, and we decline to renew it except on the most oppressive terms." The Gorringe case is a very familiar case. It was the case of the Duke of Westminster. (*"Oh, oh," laughter, and hisses.*) Oh! these dukes (*loud laughter*), how they harass us. (*More laughter.*) Mr. Gorringe had got a lease of the premises at a few hundred pounds a year ground-rent. He built up a great business there. He was a very able business man, and when the end of the lease came he went to the Duke of Westminster, and he said, "Will you renew my lease? I want to carry on my business here." He said, "Oh, yes, I will, but I will do it on condition that the few hundreds a year you pay for ground-rent shall in the future be £4,000 a year." (*Groans.*) In addition to that he had to pay a fine—a fine, mind you!—of £50,000, and he had to build up huge premises at enormous expense according to plans submitted to the Duke of Westminster. (*"Oh, oh."*) All I can say is this—if it is confiscation and robbery for us to say to that duke that, being in need of money for public purposes, we will take 10 per cent. after all you have got for that purpose, what would you call his taking nine-tenths? (*Cheers.*) These are the cases we have got to deal with. Look at all this leasehold system. A case like that is not business; it is blackmail. (*Loud cheers.*) No doubt some of you have taken the trouble to peruse some of those leases. They are all really worth reading, and I will guarantee that if you circulate copies of some of these building and mining leases at tariff reform meetings (*hisses*), and if you can get the workmen at these meetings and the business men to read them they will come away sadder and wiser men. (*Cheers.*) What are they? Ground-rent is a part of it—fines, fees; you are to make no alteration without somebody's consent. Who is that somebody? It is the agent of the landlord. A fee to whom? You must submit the plans to the landlord's architect and get his consent. There is a fee to him. There is a fee to the surveyor, and then, of course, you cannot keep the lawyer out. (*Laughter.*) (Set a lawyer to catch a lawyer, *Mr. Lloyd-George continued, pointing to one of his audience amidst laughter*.) And a fee to him. Well that is the system, and the landlords come to us in the House of Commons and they say:—"If you go on taxing reversions we will grant no more leases." Is not that horrible? (*Loud laughter.*) No more leases, no more kindly landlords. (*Laughter.*) With all their rich and good fare, with all their retinue of good fairies ready always to receive (*laughter*)—ground-rents, fees, premiums, fines, reversions—no more, never again. (*Laughter.*) They will not do it. You cannot persuade them. (*Laughter.*) They won't have it. (*Renewed laughter.*) The landlord has threatened us that if we proceed with the Budget he will take his sack (*loud laughter*) clean away from the cupboard and the grain which we all are grinding to our best to fill his sack will go into our own. Oh! I cannot believe it. There is a limit even to the wrath of an outraged landlord. We must really appease them; we must offer some sacrifice to them. Supposing we offer the House of Lords to them. (*Loud and prolonged cheers.*) Well now you seem rather to agree with that. I will make the suggestion.

The Tax on Royalties

Now unless I am wearying you (*loud cries of "No, no"*), I have got just one other land tax, and that is a tax on royalties. The landlords are receiving eight millions a year by way of royalties. What for? They never deposited the coal there. (*Laughter.*) It was not they who planted these great granite rocks in Wales, who laid the foundations of the mountains. Was it the landlord? (*Laughter.*) And yet he, by some Divine right, demands—for merely the right for men to risk their lives in hewing these rocks—eight millions a year! Take any coalfield. I went down to a coalfield the other day (*cheers*), and they pointed out to me many collieries there. They said:—"You see that colliery there. The first man who went there spent a quarter of a million in sinking shafts, in driving mains and levels. He never got coal. The second man who came spent £100,000—and he failed. The third man came along and he got the coal." But what was the landlord doing in the meantime? The first man failed; but the landlord got his royalties, the landlord got his dead-rents. The second man failed, but the landlord got his royalties. These capitalists put their money in. When the scheme failed, what did the landlord put in? He simply put in the bailiffs. (*Loud laughter.*) The capitalist risks at any rate the whole of his money; the engineer puts his brains in, the miner risks his life. (*Hear, hear.*) Have you been down a coal mine? (*Cries of "Yes."*)

Then you know. I was telling you I went down the other day. We sank down into a pit half a mile deep. We then walked underneath the mountain and we did about three-quarters of a mile with rock and shale above us. The earth seemed to be straining—around us and above us—to crush us in. You could see the pit-props bent and twisted and sundered until you saw their fibres split. Sometimes they give way, and then there is mutilation and death. Often a spark ignites, the whole pit is deluged in fire, and the breath of life is scorched out of hundreds of breasts by the consuming fire. In the very next colliery to the one I descended, just three years ago 300 people lost their lives in that way; and yet when the Prime Minister and I knock at the door of these great landlords and say to them: —"Here, you know these poor fellows who have been digging up royalties at the risk of their lives, some of them are old, they have survived the perils of their trade, they are broken, they can earn no more. Won't you give something towards keeping them out of the workhouse?" they scowl at you and we say, "Only a ha'penny, just a copper." They say, "You thieves." And they turn their dogs on to us, and every day you can hear their bark. (*Loud laughter and cheers.*) If this is an indication of the view taken by these great landlords of their responsibility to the people who, at the risk of their life, create their wealth, then I say their day of reckoning is at hand. (*Loud cheers.*)

Traditional Duties of Ownership

The other day, at the great Tory meeting held at the Cannon-street Hotel, they had blazoned on the walls, "We protest against the Budget in the name of democracy—(*loud laughter*)—liberty, and justice." Where does the democracy come in in this landed system? Where is the justice in all these transactions? We claim that the tax we impose on land is fair, just, and moderate. (*Cheers.*) They go on threatening that if we proceed they will cut down their benefactions and discharge labour. What kind of labour? (*A voice, "Hard labour," and laughter.*) What is the labour they are going to choose for dismissal? Are they going to threaten to devastate rural England, while feeding themselves, and dressing themselves? Are they going to reduce their gamekeepers? That would be sad! (*Laughter.*) The agricultural labourer and the farmer might then have some part of the game which they fatten with their labour. But what would happen to you in the season? No week-end shooting with the Duke of Norfolk for any of us! (*Laughter.*) But that is not the kind of labour that they are going to cut down. They are going to cut down productive labour— builders and gardeners—and they are going to ruin their property so that it shall not be taxed. All I can say is this—the ownership of land is not merely an enjoyment, it is a stewardship. (*Cheers.*) It has been reckoned as such in the past, and if they cease to discharge their functions, the security and defence of the country, looking after the broken in their villages and neighbourhoods—then those functions which are part of the traditional duties attached to the ownership of land and which have given to it its title—if they cease to discharge those functions, the time will come to reconsider the conditions under which land is held in this country. (*Loud cheers.*) No country, however rich, can permanently afford to have quartered upon its revenue a class which declines to do the duty which it was called upon to perform. (*Hear, hear.*) And, therefore, it is one of the prime duties of statesmanship to investigate those conditions. But I do not believe it. They have threatened and menaced like that before. They have seen it is not to their interest to carry out these futile menaces. They are now protesting against paying their fair share of the taxation of the land, and they are doing so by saying:—"You are burdening the community; you are putting burdens upon the people which they cannot bear." Ah! they are not thinking of themselves. (*Laughter.*) Noble souls! (*Laughter.*) It is the market gardener (*laughter*), it is the builder, and it was, until recently, the small holder. (*Hear, hear.*) In every debate in the House of Commons they said:—"We are not worrying for ourselves. We can afford it with our broad acres; but just think of the little man who has only got a few acres"; and we were so very impressed with this tearful appeal that at last we said, "We will leave him out." (*Cheers.*) And I almost expected to see Mr. Pretyman jump over the table and say—"Fall on my neck and embrace me." (*Loud laughter.*) Instead of that, he stiffened up, his face wreathed with anger, and he said, "The Budget is more unjust than ever." (*Laughter and cheers.*) Oh! no. We are placing the burdens on the broad shoulders. (*Cheers.*) Why should I put burdens on the people? I am one of the children of the people. (*Loud and prolonged cheering, and a voice,* "Bravo, David: stand by the people and they will stand by you.") I was brought up amongst them. I know their trials; and God forbid that I should add one grain of trouble to the anxiety which they bear with such patience and fortitude. (*Cheers.*) When the Prime Minister did me the honour of inviting me to take charge of the National Exchequer (*A voice,* "He knew what he was about," *and laughter*) at a time of great difficulty, I made up my mind, in framing the Budget which was in front of me, that at any rate no cupboard should be bared (*loud cheers*), no lot would be harder to bear. (*Cheers.*) By that test, I challenge them to judge the Budget. (*Loud and long-continued cheers, during which the right hon. gentleman resumed his seat.*)

Afterwards the audience rose and sang, "For he's a jolly good fellow."

A resolution was carried in favour of the Budget.

Overflow Meeting

Mr. Lloyd George afterwards addressed an overflow meeting in an adjacent hall.

After recapitulating some points of his former speech Mr. Lloyd George said.—It is the beginning of new things if you only come along with us. We have, I will not say lions, but jackals in the path, but there are a good many jackals which will run away if you stand up to them. But you have got to do it, and if they know you are going to do it they won't be there when the Budget passes. But if they have any doubt about it, if they think you are faltering or faint they will murder it on the road, it will never get alive out of that big house across the corridor of the House of Commons—the great slaughterhouse of good Bills. Lord Curzon, Mr. Lloyd George proceeded, had threatened to amputate the Budget. Well, he did not mind Lord Curzon as long as he kept to those bombastic commonplaces which had been his stock-in-trade through life; but if he were going to try here that arrogance which was too much even for the gentle Hindu, they would just tell him they would have none of his Oriental manners. Mr. Lloyd George reminded "those of them who were looking out for the super-tax" that they would not begin paying it until they had £5,000 a year. The action of the brewers in raising prices of beer and spirits before the increased duties had come into force was denounced as "theft by false pretences." When the Government were going to give a million a year towards ensuring against unemployment and two or three hundred thousand pounds towards labour exchanges he thought it was not too much to ask workmen to contribute on their tobacco towards funds of that kind. (*Cheers.*) "Finally," concluded the Chancellor, "I say to you, without you we can do nothing, with your help we can brush the Lords like chaff before us." (*Cheers.*)

Ernest Bevin

Ernest Bevin

[*Born* MARCH 7, 1881—*Died* APRIL 14, 1951]

He has a powerful thick-set figure which gives the impression of great physical strength, and he speaks with such emphasis, and in such direct terms, that he always seems to be laying down the law rather than putting forward a case.—PATRICIA STRAUSS s a national statesman in the Labour government of Clement Atlee, Ernest Bevin was instrumental in assisting European reconstruction following World War II. Perhaps his greatest achievement while Foreign Secretary was assisting in the establishment of the North Atlantic Treaty Organization. Mr. Atlee calls him "one of the outstanding men of his generation." [1] Bevin's accomplishments in the forties served to climax a brilliant thirty-year career, transcended only by his fervent dedication to trade unionism. According to Trevor Evans, Bevin has perhaps done more than any other man to bring the unions to their present accepted position.[2] Francis Williams believes Bevin to be "universally accepted as one of the great architects of modern trade unionism," [3] having assumed a position of power in the "great revolution" of the early twentieth century.

As a speaker, Bevin sought to be emphatic since his main concern was "putting over his ideas so . . . they can be grasped quickly by his hearers." [4] Patricia Strauss claims that he spoke with such emphasis that he always seemed to be "laying down the law rather than putting forward a case." [5] Although lacking the sophisticated style of the classical orators of the nineteenth century, he, nevertheless, possessed power to influence great audiences.[6] While his persuasiveness is unquestioned, Francis Williams does not consider Bevin a "tidy or a logical speaker":

He tangles himself up in sentences that often have no true beginning or middle or end. Often he leaves some of the thought he utters hanging in mid-air. He abandons the high road of exposition to follow the gleam of inspiration down a side road and returns to the main track upon which

---

1 Francis Williams, *Ernest Bevin* with Foreword by Rt. Hon. Clement Atlee (London: Hutchinson and Co., Ltd., 1952), p. 7.

2 Trevor Evans, *Bevin of Britain* (New York: W. W. Norton and Company, Inc., 1946), p. 18.

3 Williams, *op. cit.*, p. 173.

4 Evans, *op. cit.*, p. 22.

5 Patricia Strauss, *Bevin and Co. The Leaders of British Labour* (New York: G. P. Putnam's Sons, 1941), p. 212.

6 Williams, *op. cit.*, p. 179. "He was not by any classical standard a fine orator, but by the test of his power to influence great audiences he may perhaps be regarded as such."

he originally set out only after the most prolonged and often baffling digressions. He is profuse and ungrammatical.[7]

Historians appear to agree unanimously that on February 3, 1920, a milestone was reached both for himself and for the unions. After an eleven-hour speech which "occupied practically two whole Court days," [8] Bevin became famous almost overnight, helping the trades unions win a national minimum wage. Events leading up to the speech begin actually in Manchester in 1868 with the founding of the Trades Union Congress (T.U.C.). Gradually it added workers to its ranks until by 1920 there were over 4,360,000 members.[9] They became increasingly discontent over long working hours and short pay. In 1919 there were nearly 35,000,000 days of strike action, and such action was carried into 1920. On behalf of the Transport Workers Federation, Bevin agreed that the workers' grievances should go before arbitration, and the Court of Inquiry was set up by the Ministers of Labour. Meetings were held in the London Law Courts with three representatives from the unions, three from the employers, and one from the Ministry of Labour, with Lord Shaw presiding. The court was open to the public and was "full to overflowing" on each day of the proceedings.[10] As Bevin rose to open the case for the "dockers," he was "very self-conscious and very much aware of the unusual environment, but he soon adapted himself." [11] The transport workers had asked mainly for a standard minimum wage of 16s. a day, and the Court saw fit to award it to them along with other items. A precedent had been set for the Trades Union Movement, and Bevin "stepped at once into its front ranks." [12]

[7] Francis Williams, *The Triple Challenge* (Melbourne: William Heinemann Ltd., 1948), p. 77.

[8] *The Times* (London), February 7, 1920, p. 5.

[9] J. T. Murphy, *Labour's Big Three* (London: The Bodley Head, 1948), p. 71.

[10] *Ibid.*

[11] *Ibid.*

[12] *Ibid.*

Testimony at
the "Docker's Inquiry"[1]

•

LONDON   *February 3, 5, 6, 1920*

M r. *Bevin:* My Lord and Gentlemen, I think you will appreciate that this is rather an unusual environment for me to be in, and also these proceedings are very novel for the whole of the Labour movement in this country. We have agreed as the Transport Workers' Federation to submit this claim to the gauntlet of a public inquiry because we are convinced of the justice of the claim which is made, and secondly we have no objection to the whole question of the standard of life being open for public inquiry, which in the end we hope will serve not only to obtain what our men desire, but, at any rate, to influence public opinion to a higher conception of what that standard of life ought to be.

The claim which has led to the inquiry was submitted to the Employers' Associations of the country in October last. Our usual practice had been to meet and negotiate, to argue the case in all its details, clause by clause, with the employers with the view of trying ultimately to arrive at an agreement. In this case, however, rather a different method was adopted. On November 27, we were invited to a meeting with the Employers' Association and asked to present our case, to explain exactly what the claim amounted to, and what its likely effect would be, and what would be our attitude towards the various ports which had differential rates in existence. The employers at the end of that conference said: "We

1 *Minutes of Evidence of the Court of Inquiry concerning Transport Workers' Wages and Conditions of Employment of Dock Labour.* The minutes occupy about 500 foolscap pages in double column, and that portion involving Mr. Bevin's testimony with interpolations consists of 108 columns. Consequently, only the Introduction and Conclusion are included in this volume. *The Times* (London) of February 4, 5, 6, and 7 summarizes the proceedings, but does not present a verbatim account.

have heard what you have had to say. We have really no power to act; we must consult our constituents." Copies of the note, I understand, were printed and sent to the whole of the ports. We met again on December 18 to hear the employers' reply, and at that meeting they suggested this Court of Inquiry. We submitted that to our governing body of the Federation on December 30. I call your attention to these periods because I want the Court to appreciate the very great patience which the men have exhibited in the adoption of this new machinery of investigation. I think this is about the first time that a powerful body like that which I represent has been content, especially when the conditions were so depressing as they are at the present moment, to take the advice offered and to wait for all this machinery to be established and to be brought into operation. At a later date when we met to set up this Court we were asked for still further time for the employers to prepare their case. This was rather significant, because at the previous meeting we were told that they had considered the case in all its bearings, and they had found the claims so tremendous, and they had found that the public would have added to them such an enormous cost on their foodstuffs and their materials that it could not be borne; but, after all this investigation between November 27 and December 18, in the second week in January they asked for further time before the Court sat to prepare their case, when they had already decided that it could not be granted. Since that time, from the evidence which I have seen, very large staffs have been engaged all over the country in trying to find evidence of every little kind of delinquency, or every little kind of obstinacy in which the workers may have indulged in order to try and bring a case to present to your Court, when they had made up their minds three months ago that our application could not be granted. However, I understand that I am called upon to show the justification of the amount claimed as a minimum basis for a minimum standard of life. In the second place, I think the public are looking for some evidence or some suggestion as to ways and means of increasing the standard of life—because I am absolutely convinced that the British public are anxious to see a much higher standard of life than ever existed hitherto—without automatically increasing prices to the public. That, I think, is what the public are looking for, and while I should not admit that on the present wages which the men receive, even if it had to increase the cost to the community, our men would not be entitled to it, I think before the end of this case we shall be able to show a new method of breaking what has been described as the vicious circle. In the past we have been told by press and politician alike that if you advance wages, then, automatically, you must increase prices. I think the figures which will be submitted to this Court during these proceedings will show that you must begin the inverse way;

you must reduce profits and increase wages to break the vicious circle. Therefore I propose to deal with the case in the following order: I shall submit first, the ground of the claim; secondly, the effect of the claim, and try to explain the method of application of the claim to all the ports of the country; I shall then, thirdly, endeavour to show the justification for the claim. . . .

. . . I have one other request to make before I conclude, and it is this: When we commenced this demand for wages we commenced it in the ordinary trade union way; we arrived at what we thought would be a reasonable figure to ask for, and we submitted it, and we have been forced to this Inquiry, which was not our request. This Inquiry has revealed to the Transport Workers' Federation a condition of affairs in this country which is menacing the whole country, in our judgment. This consolidated capital as exhibited on the Charts which I handed in yesterday is a very serious matter, one which, probably rightly, you have said is a matter that your Court cannot pronounce a judgment upon as to whether it is moral or wise, or anything else, but I do urge the Court in the public interest to request that a Royal Commission be set up to investigate the whole of these exactions on capital in all these different forms, so that we may out of this Inquiry, get back those exactions if the State will not pay labour its proper wages. You indicated yesterday that it was a matter for the Chancellor of the Exchequer. I doubt whether the ordinary Chancellor of the Exchequer, passing through those offices, has given serious consideration to the problem that has been revealed by these investigations. I have here before me now over 150 balance-sheets which I did not submit to the Court because I thought it would take up too much time, but all of them reveal that we are being asked as a community to contribute too much; and if the Exchange of the world is against us it is not by keeping down the standard of living that it will be balanced, but by an investigation to show what part is being played by those who, I suggest, have a heavy responsibility upon them by their exactions out of the people who are suffering as the result of the late war. I therefore would urge that a Royal Commission, public, I hope, as this Inquiry is, will be set up, because if there is a disease in the State (and that consolidated capital is a disease in the community) it should be rooted out. There are only two ways of doing it, one by turning the light of day upon it and public opinion altering it through its constitutional methods, and the other the people coming up against its force and a clash which leads to revolution. Those are the only two ways, and I see the tremendous power of control over the people's lives that these consolidated shipowners and general capitalists have as revealed by these investigations. I make an urgent appeal to your Lordship to make a recommendation that there shall be still further investigation, not in the interests of the docker, but in the interests of the public as a whole.

I want now to make my concluding remarks. The claim which has been submitted covers practically all phases of dock work. . . . It will apply directly to the general cargo workers, to the piece workers whose wages have been regulated and influenced by them, to lightermen, to barge workers, and in many cases it will influence the wages of maintenance staffs and others whose wages have previously followed or been influenced by the national awards and war wages. We have submitted that claim to a public inquiry, and I think to a greater public as well, and I think you will realise, my Lord, that this Federation undertook a grave responsibility when, on its own, without consulting the whole of the movement, it made this departure in dealing with wage questions. That, on the other hand, I think increases the responsibilities of the Court itself. It is a novel method, as I said in opening. I would that the employers were willing before they added a charge upon the public to come to a public tribunal and justify the putting on of that charge, as we have tried to justify our increase of wages at this moment. If it is right for labour to have a Court of Inquiry, I claim that they cannot charge the community in return until they prove before a similar Court that they have a right to charge that on in a like manner. That is a challenge which I throw out to them, and if they refuse it they have no right to say: "We claim by resolution or by the power that the control of our capital gives us to increase the profit to ourselves, to benefit as members of the community ourselves while we use that same power to compel you to go to a Court of Inquiry." I suggest that your Court cannot refuse our claim either on grounds of equity or of reason. I challenge counsel when he speaks presently to show that a family can maintain themselves on less than I have indicated so as to keep them in physical efficiency. If he cannot do that I say he has no case for refusing. On the other hand, if the captains of industry who have claimed monopoly control for themselves, who have argued in effect that we are not capable of taking part in control, say through him that they are unable so to organise their concern as to give us work for a decent standard of life, then I say that they ought to lose their place as captains of industry in this civilisation. They stand condemned if their control of the means which have been placed into their hands either by fortune or by luck or whatever it is is inefficient. Whatever the reason may be for those means getting into their hands, it cannot be by thrift, because no one could save their millions in any one man's lifetime. But by whatever means they have got control that carries with it responsibility, and if they cannot improve the organisation of industry then I say they ought to make way.

If your Court refuse our claim, I suggest you must adopt an alternative. I have shown, or tried to show, that labour has growing aspirations. I have tried to show that cultural development is as much to us as it is to the middle or to the upper classes. They are building us houses containing one living room, which I consider is an insult to us, an insult to our people. The old parlour may have been disused, but it will be the workman's library of the future. The houses that will be built now must stand for years; and imagine the conception of the architect, the conception of the sociologist, who thinks that a workman can develop his brain, his education, his knowledge, his social life, in a room with all the children around him and the domestic difficulties and all the rest of it. They will not even build a house to give him a decent place for a study and culture. What would our captains of industry think if with their families they had to sit in one room and do all their business, read all their books, and study all their music or their other arts? They want culture, they want leisure, they want their home, and we want the same; and we claim it, and if our people have not been educated up to the appreciation of these arts, yet the day is coming when they will be; and I want them to have a chance for their proper development. But if you, my Lord, say in spite of all this that we have not established our claim, you have one alternative: you must go to the Prime Minister, you must go to the Minister of Education, and tell him to close our schools, tell him that industry can only be run by artisan labour on the pure fodder or animal basis, teach us nothing, let us learn nothing, because to create aspirations in our minds, to create the love of the beautiful, and then at the same time to deny us the wherewithal to obtain it, is a false policy and a wrong method to adopt. Better keep us in dark ignorance, never to know anything, if you are going to refuse us the wherewithal to give expression to those aspirations which have thus been created.

I do not believe that it can be shown that this industry in which we are engaged cannot pay: I have proved that they have the ability to pay, and on grounds of citizenship I submit that the men have established their claim, and I do not believe, with all that civilisation offers, that your Court can possibly refuse the demand we have submitted.

Stanley Baldwin

Stanley Baldwin

[*Born* AUGUST 2, 1867—*Died* DECEMBER 14, 1947]

. . . Baldwin was a sturdy countryman of medium height, broad-shouldered, with mobile countenance, sandy, shaggy eyebrows, and sandy hair parted in the middle and well smoothed down . . . He had a shrewd, quizzical expression and a musical voice which carried well.—THOMAS JONES

·G· reat Britain in the twenties was in a period of transition. The restlessness of the worker caused the Labour party to solidify and the Liberal party to melt. Trade unionism was on the rise, and its demands for better wages, better hours, and improved working conditions created a new internal peril for the nation threatened by an impending split between unionism and the reactionary forces resistant to change.[1] Such was the temper of the times when Stanley Baldwin smothered the class war without bloodshed by exerting a "tranquillizing influence" over the elements of unrest.[2] Baldwin possessed a "mysterious alchemy of character and good humour," [3] which he put to effective use to unify the English people "in a changing and difficult world." [4]

Although Baldwin removed the wedge which might have permanently split the classes in Britain, the ultimate effect, according to Lewis Broad, was to give "a tone to public life" that was to be the source of national strength when World War II eventually came.[5]

As a speaker, when the occasion arose, Baldwin was capable of captivating the minds of his listeners in the House of Commons with his "grace, ease, charm: alluring listeners to agree with him if they could, and, if they could not, at least to listen." [6] Young refers to him as the "unequalled master . . . of a new eloquence: direct, conversational, mono-syllabic: rising and falling without strain or effort, between the homeliest humour and the most moving appeal." [7] So elegant was Baldwin's speech style that Wickham Steed comments, "the hold he retains upon public goodwill . . . [is] largely an orator's hold." [8]

Two of Baldwin's speeches stand out above all others. The first was delivered in the House of Commons on March 6, 1925. D. C. Somervell states that as a result of this speech, Baldwin truly established

---

[1] Lewis Broad, *Winston Churchill: The Years of Preparation* (New York: Hawthorn Books, Inc., 1958), p. 345.

[2] *Ibid.*

[3] Arthur Bryant, *Stanley Baldwin* (New York: Coward-McCann, Inc., 1937), p. 141.

[4] G. M. Young, *Stanley Baldwin* (London: Rupert-Hart-Davis, 1952), p. 144.

[5] Broad, *op. cit.*, p. 403.

[6] Young, *op. cit.*, p. 144.

[7] *Ibid.*, p. 40.

[8] Wickham Steed, *The Real Stanley Baldwin* (London: Nisbet and Co., Ltd., 1930), p. 147.

himself as a party leader.[9] Alarmed by the news that Trades Unions were considering direct action as a means of imposing their will, a back-bench Conservative introduced a private member's Bill to alter the legal arrangements affecting trade unionists who did not wish to subscribe to the party-political funds of their unions. Although the Conservatives had a huge majority in Commons, Baldwin pleaded with his own party to reject the bill in the name of British unity. The bill was defeated by 325 to 153. The parliamentary correspondent for *The Times* of London stated that few parliamentary speeches "of recent times have created a deeper impression among members of the House of Commons. . . ." [10]

While the vote did not avert the General Strike of 1926, Baldwin's calm but firm counter-measures quickly forced the unions back to work. The end of the General Strike "saw the Prime Minister's repution standing higher than that of any Englishman since the death of Gladstone," writes Arthur Bryant.[11]

The second speech by Baldwin was delivered on October 31, 1935, to the Peace Society on the subject of world peace.[12] Young considers this speech to rank probably as the masterpiece in the vein of high, impersonal persuasion:

He asked for no votes; he announced no policy. Rather, one may say, it is perhaps the essential achievement of the orator, he created a mood.[13]

The Times called this speech "profoundly characteristic of the Prime Minister." [14]

9 D. C. Somervell, "Stanley Baldwin," in *British Prime Ministers*, Ed. by Duff Cooper (New York: Roy Publishers), p. 159.
10 *The Times* (London), March 7, 1925, p. 14.
11 Bryant, *op. cit.*, p. 141.
12 See *The Times* (London), November 1, 1935, p. 21.
13 Young, *op. cit.*, p. 215.
14 *The Times* (London), *op. cit.*, p. 16.

Industrial Peace[1]

•

HOUSE OF COMMONS *March 6, 1925*

T*he Prime-Minister (Mr. Baldwin):* I beg to move, to leave out from the word "That" to the end of the Question, and to add instead thereof the words

this House, while approving the principle of political liberty embodied in the Trade Union (Political Fund) Bill, is of opinion that a measure of such far-reaching importance should not be introduced as a Private Member's Bill.

I very much regret the tendency in this Parliament for Friday to become the principal debating day of the week. Old Members of the House have long looked forward to Friday as a day of comparative leisure. When Bills of great importance are brought in on that day, it is perfectly impossible to provide adequate time in which to discuss them. I apologise to my hon. and learned Friend the Member for Argyllshire (Mr. Macquisten) for being unable to be in the House at the beginning of his speech. I got here as soon as I could after my engagements elsewhere, and I had the pleasure of hearing quite half his speech and the whole of the speech of my hon. and learned Friend the Member for Norwood (Mr. Greaves-Lord). I think those speeches themselves clinch the point I made about the absence of time for discussion of matters of such importance, because it was perfectly obvious from the interruptions which punctuated them, particularly the speech of the Seconder, that there will be a great deal to be said controverting the statements which have been made; and there can be no doubt, in the case of a subject of this importance, that before the House can come to a decision, there ought to be far more time for debate than possibly can be found between 11 and 4 o'clock.

In my own view, the equity of the case made by my hon. and learned

[1] 181 H. C. Deb. 5 s., Cols. 833–841.

433

Friend is one of great strength. It will probably be supported in various quarters of the House, and indeed as violently opposed. And I suggest that very much of what I said with reference to the Reform Bill a fortnight ago is equally true of a Bill of this magnitude being brought in by private Members on a Friday. But as I do not wish to detain the House longer than I can, I will do my best now to get away from the direct treatment of the points that have been raised, in order to give the House the reasons that have induced me to put down the Amendment which stands in my name. In some ways this is a very difficult speech for me to make. The matter of the Bill itself digs right into one of the most difficult and fundamental questions in the country to-day, and touches at various points, questions which have interested me during the whole of my working life. I have thought so much about them, and I feel that I have so much to say about them, that my difficulty will be in choosing the little that I can possibly say to-day and finding words to express clearly to the House what is in my mind.

I often wonder if all the people in this country realise the inevitable changes that are coming over the industrial system in England. People are apt either to get their knowledge of the industrial system from textbooks, which must inevitably be half a generation behind, or from some circumstances familiar to them at a fixed and static point in their lives, whereas, as a matter of fact, ever since the industrial system began in this country, it has been not only in a state of evolution, but in a state of evolution which, I think, historians in the centuries to come, when they write its history, will acknowledge to be an evolution that has developed at a far more rapid rate than was visible to the people who lived in these times.

I hope the House will bear with me, and forgive me, if I draw for a few minutes on my own experience, because it so happens that, owing to the peculiar circumstances of my own life, I have seen a great deal of this evolution taking place before my own eyes. I worked for many years in an industrial business, and had under me a large number, or what was then a large number, of men. And it so happened, owing to the circumstances of this being an old family business, with an old and, I venture to say, a very good tradition, that when I was first in business, I was probably working under a system that was already passing. I doubt if its like could have been found in any of the big modern industrial towns of this country, even at that time. It was a place where I knew, and had known from childhood, every man on the ground, a place where I was able to talk with the men not only about the troubles in the works, but troubles at home where strikes and lock-outs were unknown. It was a place where the fathers and grandfathers of the men then working there had worked, and where their sons went automatically into the business. It was also a place where nobody ever "got the sack," and where we had a natural sympathy for those who were less concerned in efficiency than is this generation, and where a number of old gentlemen used to spend their days sitting on the handle of a wheelbarrow, smoking their pipes. Oddly enough, it was not an inefficient community. It was the last survivor of that type of works, and ultimately became swallowed up in one of those great combinations towards which the industries of to-day are tending.

I remember very well the impact of the outside world that came on us which showed how industry was changing in this country. Nothing had interrupted the even tenor of our ways for many years, until one day there came a great strike in the coalfields. It was one of the earlier strikes, and it became a national strike. We tried to carry on as long as we could, but of course it became more and more difficult to carry on, and gradually furnace after furnace was damped down; the chimneys ceased to smoke, and about 1,000 men who had no interest in the dispute that was going on were thrown out of work through no fault of their own, at a time when there was no unemployment benefit. I confess that that event set me thinking very hard. It seemed to me at that time a monstrous injustice to these men, because I looked upon them as my own family, and it hit me very hard—I would not have mentioned this only it got into the Press two or three years ago—and I made an allowance to them, not a large one, but something, for six weeks to carry them along, because I felt that they were being so unfairly treated.

But there was more in it really than that. There was no conscious unfair treatment of these men by the miners. It simply was that we were gradually passing into a new state of industry, when the small firms and the small industries were being squeezed out. Business was all tending towards great amalgamations on the one side of employers and on the other side of the men, and when we came in any form between these two forces, God help those who stood outside! That has been the tendency of industry. There is nothing that could change it, because it comes largely, if not principally, from that driving force of necessity in the world which makes people combine together for competition, and for the protection they need against that competition.

Those two forces with which we have to reckon are enormously strong, and they are the two forces in this country to which now, to a great extent, and it will be a greater extent in the future, we are committed. We have to see what wise statesmanship can do to steer the country through this time of evolution, until we can get to the next stage of our industrial civilisation. It is obvious from what I have said that the organisations of both masters and men—or, if you like the more modern phrase invented by economists, who always invent beastly words, "employers and employés"—these organisations throw an immense responsibility on the representatives themselves and on those who elect them. And, although big men have been thrown up on both sides, there are a great many on both sides who have not got the requisite qualities of head and heart for business. There are many men with good heads and no hearts, and many men with good hearts and no heads.

What the country wants to-day from the men who sit on this side of the House and on that is to exercise the same care as the men who have to conduct those great organisations from inside. I should like to try to clear our minds of cant on this subject, and recognise that the growth of these associations is not necessarily a bad thing in itself, but that, whatever associations may call themselves, it is the same human nature in both, and exactly the same problems have to be met, although we hear a good deal more of some of those problems than of others. Now, if you look at an employers' organisation for a moment—and we will assume that it has come into being to protect the industry in the world market—we cannot lose sight of the fact that in that organisation, just as much as in the men's organisation, the mere fact of organising involves a certain amount of sacrifice of personal liberty. That cannot be helped. Everybody knows that perfectly well, both employers and employés.

To a certain extent both these organisations must on one side be un-economic. A trade union is uneconomic in one sense of the word when it restricts output, and when it levels down the work to a lower level. It is an association for the protection of the weaker men, which has often proved uneconomic. Exactly the same thing happens in the employers' organisa-tion. Primarily, it is protective, but in effect it is very often uneconomic, because it keeps in existence works which, if left to the process of competi-tion, would be squeezed out, and whose prolonged existence is really only a weakness to the country. It has also another very curious effect, not at all dissimilar from that of the trade union reaction, which shows that both those organisations are instinct with English traditions. The workmen's organisation is formed to see that under the conditions a workman cannot get his living in a particular trade unless he belong to that union. An employers' organisation is formed in that particular trade for the protec-tion of the trade, and it has the result of effectively preventing any new man starting in that trade.

In this great problem which is facing the country in years to come, it may be from one side or the other that disaster may come, but surely it shows that the only progress that can be obtained in this country is by those two bodies of men—so similar in their strength and so similar in their weaknesses—learning to understand each other, and not to fight each other. It is perfectly true—every point raised by my hon. and learned Friends is true—that trade unionism has its weak spots. We are primarily discussing trade unions, and that is why I shall content myself to speak about trade unions only. It is perfectly true that my hon. and learned

Friends have laid their finger on three points which trade unionists themselves know are their weak spots. That can be seen by the interruptions that came from the Labour benches. Those three points are, the question whether in all cases the subject of the levy is treated fairly, the question of the ballot, and the question of book-keeping. To my mind, it is impossible to dissociate one of these questions from the other, and they really all hang together. The whole tradition of our country has been to let Englishmen develop their own associations in their own way, and with that I agree. But there are limits to that.

I spoke some time ago—and I spoke with a purpose—about the recognition of the change in the industrial situation in those works with which I was connected, when for the first time what was done in the way of organising the coal strike suddenly came and hit thousands of men who had nothing to do with it, and had no direct interest in it. As these associations come along and become more powerful, on whichever side they are, there may come a time when not only they may injure their own members —about which probably there would be a good deal of argument—but when they may directly injure the State. It is at that moment any Government should say that, whatever freedom and latitude in that field may be left to any kind of association in this free country, nothing shall be done which shall injure the State, which is the concern of all of us and far greater than all of us or of our interests.

I have not very much more to say. I have just tried to put as clearly as I can in a few words, my conviction that we are moving forward rapidly from an old state of industry into a newer, and the question is: What is that newer going to be? No man, of course, can say what form evolution is taking. Of this, however, I am quite sure, that whatever form we may see, possibly within this generation, or, at any rate, in the time of the next generation, it has got to be a form of pretty close partnership, however that is going to be arrived at. And it will not be a partnership the terms of which will be laid down, at any rate not yet, in Acts of Parliament, or from this party or that. It has got to be a partnership of men who understand their own work, and it is little help that they can get really either from politicians or from intellectuals. There are few men fitted to judge, to settle and to arrange the problem that distracts the country to-day between employers and employed. There are few men qualified to intervene who have not themselves been right through the mill. I always want to see, at the head of these organisations on both sides, men who have been right through the mill, who themselves know exactly the points where the shoe pinches, who know exactly what can be conceded and what cannot, who can make their reasons plain; and I hope that we shall always find such men trying to steer their respective ships side by side, instead of making for head-on collisions.

Having said what I have said about that, what am I to say about the attitude of the party of which I have the honour to be the head? I do not know whether the House will forgive me if I speak for a minute or two on a rather personal note. For two years past in the face of great difficulties, perhaps greater than many were aware of, I have striven to consolidate, and to breathe a living force into, my great party. Friends of mine who have done me the honour to read my speeches during that time have seen pretty clearly, however ill they may have been expressed, the ideals at which I have been aiming. I spoke on that subject again last night at Birmingham, and I shall continue to speak on it as long as I am where I am. We find ourselves, after these two years in power, in possession of perhaps the greatest majority our party has ever had, and with the general assent of the country. Now how did we get there? It was not by promising to bring this Bill in; it was because, rightly or wrongly, we succeeded in creating an impression throughout the country that we stood for stable Government and for peace in the country between all classes of the community.

Those were the principles for which we fought; those were the principles on which we won; and our victory was not won entirely by the votes of our own party, splendidly as they fought. I should think that the number of Liberals who voted for us at the last Election ran into six figures, and I should think that we probably polled more Labour votes than were polled on the other side. That being so, what should our course be at the beginning of a new Parliament? I have not myself the slightest doubt. Last year the Leader of the Labour party, when he was Prime Minister, suspended what had been settled by the previous Government, and that was further progress for the time being on the scheme of Singapore. He did it on the ground that it was a gesture for peace, and he hoped that it would be taken as such by all the countries in the world. He hoped that a gesture of that kind might play its part in leading to what we all wish to see, that is, a reduction in the world's armaments.

I want my party to-day to make a gesture to the country of a similar nature, and to say to them: "We have our majority; we believe in the justice of this Bill which has been brought in to-day, but we are going to withdraw our hand, and we are not going to push our political advantage home at a moment like this. Suspicion which has prevented stability in Europe is the one poison that is preventing stability at home, and we offer the country to-day this: We, at any rate, are not going to fire the first shot. We stand for peace. We stand for the removal of suspicion in the country. We want to create an atmosphere, a new atmosphere in a new Parliament for a new age, in which the people can come together. We abandon what we have laid our hands to. We know we may be called cowards for doing it. We know we may be told that we have gone back on our principles.

But we believe we know what at this moment the country wants, and we believe it is for us in our strength to do what no other party can do at this moment, and to say that we at any rate stand for peace."

I know—I am as confident as I can be of anything—that that will be the feeling of all those who sit behind me, and that they will accept the Amendment which I have put down in the spirit in which I have moved it. And I have equal confidence in my fellow-countrymen throughout the whole of Great Britain. Although I know that there are those who work for different ends from most of us in this House, yet there are many in all ranks and all parties who will re-echo my prayer:

"Give peace in our time, O Lord."

Aneurin Bevan
·

Aneurin Bevan

[Born NOVEMBER 15, 1897—*Died* JULY 6, 1960]

Sometimes in repose Bevan's face . . . wore a brooding look. The lines from nose to chin had deepened, the brow furrowed, the hair admitted patches of silver, but he was still likely to release a gale of laughter into any argument, as a devilishly eloquent boy.—VINCENT BROME

• I •

In contemporary British political circles, there is probably no figure in history who has created more controversy than has Aneurin Bevan. His association with Sir Stafford Cripps' British united front movement led to his expulsion from the Labour Party in 1939. Later that year, Bevan was readmitted, and became an outspoken critic of the Churchill ministry throughout World War II. After serving in the postwar cabinet of Clement Atlee, Bevan resigned in 1951 to lead a faction within the Labour Party critical of its policies. "He breathes freest," writes Francis Williams, "when the air is heavy with the dust of political controversy." [1]

"Nye" Bevan's place in British political history is summarized by Vincent Brome, who believes "no one in British politics over the last fifty years had excited quite such forthright attacks, no one except Churchill coined phrases whose echo still hung on the air, no one had so overwhelmingly won the support of the Labour Party's rank and file at its great annual conferences." [2] Bevan's great political achievement was his establishment of National Health Service. Its birth constituted a radically new philosophy of government—that all citizens are deserving of adequate health care from the cradle to the grave. Although vexed with problems in its earlier years, its severest critics have been unable to suspend its operation, and its principles have been embraced by the Conservatives as well as the Labour Party.

Bevan ranks with Churchill as among the most eloquent spokesman of our time.[3] Michael Foot calls him the "prince of parliamentary debaters." [4] Mark Krug indicates that Bevan was generally regarded as the best speaker and debater in the House of Commons, with the exception of Winston Churchill.[5] With his political principles well formulated, he was a ready speaker prepared to articulate them at a moment's notice. According to Williams, Bevan takes an artist's pleasure in words: "To suppress a vivid phrase when it springs to his

---

1 Francis Williams, "Aneurin Bevan," *Spectator*, September 24, 1948, p. 390.

2 Vincent Brome, *Aneurin Bevan* (London: Longmans, Green and Co., 1953), p. 4.

3 *Ibid.*, p. 140. "Churchill and Bevan represent opposite poles of the British political scene but there are threads running through their careers, and qualities of personality which reveal curious identities."

4 Michael Foot, *Aneurin Bevan*, I (New York: Atheneum, 1963), p. 259.

5 Mark M. Krug, *Aneurin Bevan: Cautious Rebel* (New York: Thomas Yoseloff, 1961), p. 41.

lips is a physical impossibility. . . ." [6] Whether he was a purveyor
of invective, such as in his Manchester speech of July 4, 1948, or of
conciliation, Bevan possessed "immense vitality" and "great personal
charm." [7] Vincent Brome captures Bevan's style graphically on one
such occasion when he speaks of his antagonist, Sir Winston Churchill:

. . . his magnetic personality always held members as he swung into
his stride, eyes flashing, finger pointing, a man uncompromisingly alive
with the fascination of the spell-binder. This rugged, piratical Bevan continued to shock the House of Commons and the country with his attacks,
continued to challenge his own party's policy, flourishing in opposition.
He had not so much mastered as brought to life within his personality
every skill known to oratory. He knew every graduation of pause and
just how long it could be sustained, his gestures were infinite, his sudden
use of an exotic word . . . exciting, and he enjoyed a big word along
with the scholars. His immense range of inflexion rose and fell like a
coloured fountain. His stutter added the exhilaration of danger, the hope
that perhaps this time he might at last break down. Even the Tories
dropped the banter and laughter which preceded a speech in the House
with the idea of disconcerting the speaker, to watch the spectacle of
Bevan soaring higher and higher with verbal felicities, building up what
appeared to be a eulogy of Churchill.[8]

The speech included in this volume was delivered on April 29,
1946, moving the Second Reading of the National Health Service
Bill. Although the Bill did not become law until July 5, 1948, its
evolution is a testament to the skill of Bevan in his negotiations with
the British Medical Association. He was severely criticized by members of his own party for his generosity in allowing doctors to practice
in and out of the service. As a result of this concession, however, by
1949 ninety-five percent of all British doctors had voluntarily joined
the plan.[9]

6 Williams, op. cit., p. 391
7 Ibid.
8 Brome, op. cit., p. 10.
9 Krug, op. cit., p. 90.

National Health Service Bill[1]

•

HOUSE OF COMMONS *April 30, 1946*

O*rder for Second Reading read.*
  3:47 p.m.
    The Minister of Health (Mr. Aneurin Bevan): I beg to move,
That the Bill be now read a Second time.

  In the last two years there has been such a clamour from sectional
interests in the field of national health that we are in danger of forgetting
why these proposals are brought forward at all. It is, therefore, very welcome to me—and I am quite certain to hon. Members in all parts of the
House—that consideration should now be given, not to this or that sectional interest, but to the requirements of the British people as a whole.
The scheme which anyone must draw up dealing with national health
must necessarily be conditioned and limited by the evils it is intended to
remove. Many of those who have drawn up paper plans for the health
services appear to have followed the dictates of abstract principles, and
not the concrete requirements of the actual situation as it exists. They
drew up all sorts of tidy schemes on paper, which would be quite inoper-
able in practice.

  The first reason why a health scheme of this sort is necessary at all is
because it has been the firm conclusion of all parties that money ought
not to be permitted to stand in the way of obtaining an efficient health
service. Although it is true that the national health insurance system provides a general practitioner service and caters for something like 21 million of the population, the rest of the population have to pay whenever
they desire the services of a doctor. It is cardinal to a proper health organisation that a person ought not to be financially deterred from seeking
medical assistance at the earliest possible stage. It is one of the evils of

---

[1] 422 H.C. Deb. 5 s., cols. 43–63. The same text, with the inclusion of main headings,
appears in *British Speeches of the Day*, Vol. IV (May 1946), pp. 286–308.

having to buy medical advice that, in addition to the natural anxiety that
may arise because people do not like to hear unpleasant things about
themselves, and therefore tend to postpone consultation as long as possible, there is the financial anxiety caused by having to pay doctors' bills.
Therefore, the first evil that we must deal with is that which exists as a
consequence of the fact that the whole thing is the wrong way round. A
person ought to be able to receive medical and hospital help without
being involved in financial anxiety.

In the second place, the national health insurance scheme does not provide for the self-employed, nor, of course, for the families of dependants.
It depends on insurance qualification, and no matter how ill you are, if
you cease to be insured you cease to have free doctoring. Furthermore, it
gives no backing to the doctor in the form of specialist services. The doctor has to provide himself, he has to use his own discretion and his own
personal connections, in order to obtain hospital treatment for his patients and in order to get them specialists, and in very many cases, of
course—in an overwhelming number of cases—the services of a specialist
are not available to poor people.

Not only is this the case, but our hospital organisation has grown up
with no plan, with no system; it is unevenly distributed over the country
and indeed it is one of the tragedies of the situation, that very often the
best hospital facilities are available where they are least needed. In the
older industrial districts of Great Britain hospital facilities are inadequate. Many of the hospitals are too small—very much too small. About
70 per cent. have less than 100 beds, and over 30 per cent. have less than
30. No one can possibly pretend that hospitals so small can provide general hospital treatment. There is a tendency in some quarters to defend
the very small hospital on the ground of its localism and intimacy, and for
other rather imponderable reasons of that sort, but everybody knows to-
day that if a hospital is to be efficient it must provide a number of specialised services. Although I am not myself a devotee of bigness for bigness'
sake, I would rather be kept alive in the efficient if cold altruism of a large
hospital than expire in a gush of warm sympathy in a small one.

In addition to these defects, the health of the people of Britain is not
properly looked after in one or two other respects. The condition of the
teeth of the people of Britain is a national reproach. As a consequence of
dental treatment having to be bought, it has not been demanded on a
scale to stimulate the creation of sufficient dentists, and in consequence
there is a woeful shortage of dentists at the present time. Furthermore,
about 25 per cent. of the people of Great Britain can obtain their spectacles and get their eyes tested and seen to by means of the assistance
given by the approved societies, but the general mass of the people have
not such facilities. Another of the evils from which this country suffers is

the fact that sufficient attention has not been given to deafness and hardly any attention has been given so far to the provision of cheap hearing aids and their proper maintenance. I hope to be able to make very shortly a welcome announcement on this question.

One added disability from which our health system suffers is the isolation of mental health from the rest of the health services. Although the present Bill does not rewrite the Lunacy Acts—we shall have to come to that later on—nevertheless, it does, for the first time, bring mental health into the general system of health services. It ought to be possible, and this should be one of the objectives of any civilised health service, for a person who feels mental distress, or who fears that he is liable to become unbalanced in any way to go to a general hospital to get advice and assistance, so that the condition may not develop into a more serious stage. All these disabilities our health system suffers from at the present time, and one of the first merits of this Bill is that it provides a universal health service without any insurance qualifications of any sort. It is available to the whole population, and not only is it available to the whole population freely, but it is intended, through the health service, to generalise the best health advice and treatment. It is intended that there shall be no limitation on the kind of assistance given—the general practitioner service, the specialist, the hospitals, eye treatment, spectacles, dental treatment, hearing facilities, all these are to be made available free.

There will be some limitations for a while, because we are short of many things. We have not enough dentists and it will therefore be necessary for us, in the meantime, to give priority treatment to certain classes— expectant and nursing mothers, children, school children in particular and later on we hope adolescents. Finally we trust that we shall be able to build up a dental service for the whole population. We are short of nurses and we are short, of course, of hospital accommodation, and so it will be some time before the Bill can fructify fully in effective universal service. Nevertheless, it is the object of the Bill, and of the scheme, to provide this as soon as possible, and to provide it universally.

Specialists will be available not only at institutions but for domiciliary visits when needed. Hon. Members in all parts of the House know from their own experience that very many people have suffered unnecessarily because the family has not had the financial resources to call in skilled people. The specialist services, therefore, will not only be available at the hospitals, but will be at the back of the general practitioner should he need them. The practical difficulties of carrying out all these principles and services are very great. When I approached this problem, I made up my mind that I was not going to permit any sectional or vested interests to stand in the way of providing this very valuable service for the British people.

There are, of course, three main instruments through which it is intended that the Health Bill should be worked. There are the hospitals; there are the general practitioners; and there are the health centres. The hospitals are in many ways the vertebrae of the health system, and I first examined what to do with the hospitals. The voluntary hospitals of Great Britain have done invaluable work. When hospitals could not be provided by any other means, they came along. The voluntary hospital system of this country has a long history of devotion and sacrifice behind it, and it would be a most frivolously minded man who would denigrate in any way the immense services the voluntary hospitals have rendered to this country. But they have been established often by the caprice of private charity. They bear no relationship to each other. Two hospitals close together often try to provide the same specialist services unnecessarily, while other areas have not that kind of specialist service at all. They are, as I said earlier, badly distributed throughout the country. It is unfortunate that often endowments are left to finance hospitals in those parts of the country where the well-to-do live while, in very many other of our industrial and rural districts there is inadequate hospital accommodation. These voluntary hospitals are, very many of them, far too small and, therefore, to leave them as independent units is quite impracticable.

Furthermore—I want to be quite frank with the House—I believe it is repugnant to a civilised community for hospitals to have to rely upon private charity. I believe we ought to have left hospital flag days behind. I have always felt a shudder of repulsion when I have seen nurses and sisters who ought to be at their work, and students who ought to be at their work, going about the streets collecting money for the hospitals. I do not believe there is an hon. Member of this House who approves that system. It is repugnant, and we must leave it behind—entirely. But the implications of doing this are very considerable.

I have been forming some estimates of what might happen to voluntary hospital finance when the all-in insurance contributions fall to be paid by the people of Great Britain, when the Bill is passed and becomes an Act, and they are entitled to free hospital services. The estimates I have go to show that between 80 per cent. and 90 per cent. of the revenues of the voluntary hospitals in these circumstances will be provided by public funds, by national or rate funds. (*An hon. Member:* "By workers' contributions.") And, of course, as the hon. Member reminds me, in very many parts of the country it is a travesty to call them voluntary hospitals. In the mining districts, in the textile districts, in the districts where there are heavy industries it is the industrial population who pay the weekly contributions for the maintenance of the hospitals. When I was a miner I used to find that situation, when I was on the hospital committee. We had an annual meeting and a cordial vote of thanks was moved and passed with great enthusiasm to the managing director of the colliery company for his generosity towards the hospital; and when I looked at the balance sheet, I saw that 97½ per cent. of the revenues were provided by the miners' own contributions; but nobody passed a vote of thanks to the miners.

Major Guy Lloyd (Renfrew, Eastern): What was the right hon. Gentleman doing?

Mr. Bevan: I can assure the hon. and gallant Member that I was no more silent then than I am now. But, of course, it is a misuse of language to call these "voluntary hospitals." They are not maintained by legally enforced contributions; but, mainly, the workers pay for them because they know they will need the hospitals, and they are afraid of what they would have to pay if they did not provide them. So it is, I say, an impossible situation for the State to find something like 90 per cent. of the revenues of these hospitals and still to call them "voluntary." So I decided, for this and other reasons, that the voluntary hospitals must be taken over.

I knew very well when I decided this that it would give rise to very considerable resentment in many quarters, but, quite frankly, I am not concerned about the voluntary hospitals' authorities: I am concerned with the people whom the hospitals are supposed to serve. Every investigation which has been made into this problem has established that the proper hospital unit has to comprise about 1,000 beds—not in the same building but, nevertheless, the general and specialist hospital services can be provided only in a group of that size. This means that a number of hospitals have to be pooled, linked together, in order to provide a unit of that sort. This cannot be done effectively if each hospital is a separate, autonomous body. It is proposed that each of these groups should have a large general hospital, providing general hospital facilities and services, and that there should be a group round it of small feeder hospitals. Many of the cottage hospitals strive to give services that they are not able to give. It very often happens that a cottage hospital harbours ambitions to the hurt of the patients, because they strive to reach a status that they never can reach. In these circumstances, the welfare of the patients is sacrificed to the vaulting ambitions of those in charge of the hospital. If, therefore, these voluntary hospitals are to be grouped in this way, it is necessary that they should submit themselves to proper organisation, and that submission, in our experience, is impracticable if the hospitals, all of them, remain under separate management.

Now, this decision to take over the voluntary hospitals meant, that I then had to decide to whom to give them. Who was to be the receiver? So I turned to an examination of the local government hospital system. Many of the local authorities in Great Britain have never been able to exercise their hospital powers. They are too poor. They are too small. Furthermore, the local authorities of Great Britain inherited their hospitals from the Poor Law, and some of them are monstrous buildings, a cross between a workhouse and a barracks (*An hon. Member:* "And a prison.")—or a prison. The local authorities are helpless in these matters. They have not been able to afford much money. Some local authorities are first-class. Some of the best hospitals in this country are local government hospitals. But, when I considered what to do with the voluntary hospitals when they had been taken over, and who was to receive them I had to reject the local government unit, because the local authority area is no more an effective gathering ground for the patients of the hospitals than the voluntary hospitals themselves. My hon. Friend said that some of them are too small, and some of them too large. London is an example of being too small and too large at the same time.

It is quite impossible, therefore, to hand over the voluntary hospitals to the local authorities. Furthermore—and this is an argument of the utmost importance—if it be our contract with the British people, if it be our intention that we should universalise the best, that we shall promise every citizen in this country the same standard of service, how can that be articulated through a rate-borne institution which means that the poor authority will not be able to carry out the same thing at all? It means that once more we shall be faced with all kinds of anomalies, just in those areas where hospital facilities are most needed, and in those very conditions where the mass of the poor people will be unable to find the finance to supply the hospitals. Therefore, for reasons which must be obvious—because the local authorities are too small, because their financial capacities are unevenly distributed—I decided that local authorities could not be effective hospital administration units. There are, of course, a large number of hospitals in addition to the general hospitals which the local authorities possess. Tuberculosis sanatoria, isolation hospitals, infirmaries of various kinds, rehabilitation, and all kinds of other hospitals are all necessary in a general hospital service. So I decided that the only thing to do was to create an entirely new hospital service, to take over the voluntary hospitals, and to take over the local government hospitals and to organise them as a single hospital service. If we are to carry out our obligation and to provide the people of Great Britain, no matter where they may be, with the same level of service, then the nation itself will have to carry the expenditure, and cannot put it upon the shoulders of any other authority.

A number of investigations have been made into this subject from time to time, and the conclusion has always been reached that the effective hospital unit should be associated with the medical school. If you grouped the hospitals in about 16 to 20 regions around the medical schools, you would then have within those regions the wide range of disease and disability which would provide the basis for your specialised hospital service. Furthermore, by grouping hospitals around the medical schools, we should be providing what is very badly wanted, and that is a means by which the general practitioners are kept in more intimate association with new medical thought and training. One of the disabilities, one of the shortcomings of our existing medical service, is the intellectual isolation of the general practitioners in many parts of the country. The general practitioner, quite often, practises in loneliness and does not come into sufficiently intimate association with his fellow craftsmen and has not the stimulus of that association, and in consequence of that the general practitioners have not got access to new medical knowledge in a proper fashion. By this association of the general practitioner with the medical schools through the regional hospital organisation, it will be possible to refresh and replenish the fund of knowledge at the disposal of the general practitioner.

This has always been advised as the best solution of the difficulty. It has this great advantage to which I call the close attention of hon. Members. It means that the bodies carrying out the hospital services of the country are, at the same time, the planners of the hospital service. One of the defects of the other scheme is that the planning authority and executive authority are different. The result is that you get paper planning or bad execution. By making the regional board and regional organisation responsible both for the planning and the administration of the plans, we get a better result, and we get from time to time, adaptation of the plans by the persons accumulating the experience in the course of their administration. The other solutions to this problem which I have looked at all mean that you have an advisory body of planners in the background who are not able themselves to accumulate the experience necessary to make good planners. The regional hospital organisation is the authority with which the specialised services are to be associated, because, as I have explained, this specialised service can be made available for an area of that size, and cannot be made available over a small area.

When we come to an examination of this in Committee, I daresay there will be different points of view about the constitution of the regional boards. It is not intended that the regional boards should be conferences of persons representing different interests and different organisations. If we do that, the regional boards will not be able to achieve reasonable and efficient homogeneity. It is intended that they should be drawn from members of the profession, from the health authorities in the area, from the medical schools and from those who have long experience in voluntary hospital administration. While leaving ourselves open to take the best sort of individuals on these hospital boards which we can find, we hope before very long to build up a high tradition of hospital administration in the boards themselves. Any system which made the boards conferences, any proposal which made the members delegates, would at once throw the hospital administration into chaos. Although I am perfectly prepared and shall be happy to cooperate with hon. Members in all parts of the House in discussing how the boards should be constituted, I hope I shall not be pressed to make these regional boards merely representative of different interests and different areas. The general hospital administration, therefore, centres in that way.

When we come to the general practitioners we are, of course, in an entirely different field. The proposal which I have made is that the general practitioner shall not be in direct contract with the Ministry of Health, but in contract with new bodies. There exists in the medical profession a great resistance to coming under the authority of local government—a great resistance, with which I, to some extent, sympathise. There is a feeling in the medical profession that the general practitioner would be liable to come too much under the medical officer of health, who is the administrative doctor. This proposal does not put the doctor under the local authority; it puts the doctor in contract with an entirely new body—the local executive council, coterminous with the local health area, county or county borough. On that executive council, the dentists, doctors and chemists will have half the representation. In fact, the whole scheme provides a greater degree of professional representation for the medical profession than any other scheme I have seen.

I have been criticised in some quarters for doing that. I will give the answer now: I have never believed that the demands of a democracy are necessarily satisfied merely by the opportunity of putting a cross against someone's name every four or five years. I believe that democracy exists in the active participation in administration and policy. Therefore, I believe that it is a wise thing to give the doctors full participation in the administration of their own profession. They must, of course, necessarily be subordinated to lay control—we do not want the opposite danger of syndicalism. Therefore, the communal interests must always be safeguarded in this administration. The doctors will be in contract with an executive body of this sort. One of the advantages of that proposal is that the doctors do not become—as some of them have so wildly stated—civil servants. Indeed, one of the advantages of the scheme is that it does not create an additional civil servant.

It imposes no constitutional disability upon any person whatsoever. Indeed, by taking the hospitals from the local authorities and putting them under the regional boards, large numbers of people will be enfranchised who are now disfranchised from participation in local government. So far from this being a huge bureaucracy with all the doctors little civil servants—the slaves of the Minister of Health, as I have seen it described—instead of that, the doctors are under contract with bodies which are not under the local authority, and which are at the same time, ever open to their own influence and control.

One of the chief problems that I was up against in considering this scheme was the distribution of the general practitioner service throughout the country. The distribution, at the moment, is most uneven. In South Shields before the war there were 4,100 persons per doctor; in Bath 1,590; in Dartford nearly 3,000 and in Bromley 1,620; in Swindon 3,100; in Hastings under 1,200. That distribution of general practitioners throughout the country is most hurtful to the health of our people. It is entirely unfair, and, therefore, if the health services are to be carried out, there must be brought about a re-distribution of the general practitioners throughout the country.

Captain Crowder (Finchley): Does that mean the number on the panel or the population?

Mr. Bevan: The population. Indeed, I could amplify those figures a good deal, but I do not want to weary the House, as I have a great deal to say. It was, therefore, decided that there must be redistribution. One of the first consequences of that decision was the abolition of the sale and purchase of practices. If we are to get the doctors where we need them, we cannot possibly allow a new doctor to go in because he has bought somebody's practice. Proper distribution kills by itself the sale and purchase of practices. I know that there is some opposition to this, and I will deal with that opposition. I have always regarded the sale and purchase of medical practices as an evil in itself. It is tantamount to the sale and purchase of patients. Indeed, every argument advanced about the value of the practice is itself an argument against freedom of choice, because the assumption underlying the high value of a practice is that the patient passes from the old doctor to the new. If they did not pass there would be no value in it. I would like, therefore, to point out to the medical profession that every time they argue for high compensation for the loss of the value of their practices, it is an argument against the free choice which they claim. However, the decision to bring about the proper distribution of general practitioners throughout the country meant that the value of the practices were destroyed. We had, therefore, to consider compensation.

I have never admitted the legal claim, but I admit at once that very great hardship would be inflicted upon doctors if there were no compensation. Many of these doctors looked forward to the value of their practices for their retirement. Many of them have had to borrow money to buy practices and, therefore, it would, I think, be inhuman, and certainly most unjust, if no compensation were paid for the value of the practices destroyed. The sum of £66,000,000 is very large. In fact, I think that every one will admit that the doctors are being treated very generously. However, it is not all loss, because if we had, in providing super-annuation, given credit for back service, as we should have had to do, it would have cost £35 million. Furthermore, the compensation will fall to be paid to the dependants when the doctor dies, or when he retires, and so it is spread over a considerable number of years. This global sum has been arrived at by the actuaries, and over the figure, I am afraid, we have not had very much control, because the actuaries have agreed it. But the profession itself will be asked to advise as to its distribution among the claimants, because we are interested in the global sum, and the profession, of course, is interested in the equitable distribution of the fund to the claimants.

The doctors claim that the proposals of the Bill amount to direction— not all the doctors say this but some of them do. There is no direction involved at all. When the Measure starts to operate, the doctors in a particular area will be able to enter the public service in that area. A doctor newly coming along would apply to the local executive council for permission to practise in a particular area. His application would then be re-referred to the Medical Practices Committee. The Medical Practices Committee, which is mainly a professional body, would have before it the question of whether there were sufficient general practitioners in that area. If there were enough, the committee would refuse to permit the appointment. No one can really argue that that is direction, because no profession should be allowed to enter the public service in a place where it is not needed. By that method of negative control over a number of years, we hope to bring about over the country a positive redistribution of the general practitioner service. It will not affect the existing situation, because doctors will be able to practise under the new service in the areas to which they belong, but a new doctor, as he comes on, will have to find his practice in a place inadequately served.

I cannot, at the moment, explain to the House what are going to be the rates of remuneration of doctors. The Spens Committee report is not fully available. I hope it will be out next week. I had hoped that it would be ready for this Debate, because this is an extremely important part of the subject, but I have not been able to get the full report. Therefore, it is not possible to deal with remuneration. However, it is possible to deal with some of the principles underlying the remuneration of general practitioners. Some of my hon. Friends on this side of the House are in favour of a full salaried service. I am not. I do not believe that the medical profession is ripe for it, and I cannot dispense with the principle that the payment of a doctor must in some degree be a reward for zeal, and there must be some degree of punishment for lack of it. Therefore, it is proposed that capitation should remain the main source from which a doctor will obtain his remuneration. But it is proposed that there shall be a basic salary and that for a number of very cogent reasons. One is that a young doctor entering practice for the first time needs to be kept alive while he is building up his lists. The present system by which a young man gets a load of debt around his neck in order to practise is an altogether evil one. The basic salary will take care of that.

Furthermore, the basic salary has the additional advantage of being something to which I can attach an increased amount to get doctors to go into unattractive areas. It may also—and here our position is not quite so definite—be the means of attacking additional remuneration for special courses and special acquirements. The basic salary, however, must not be too large otherwise it is a disguised form of capitation. Therefore, the main source at the moment through which a general practitioner will obtain his remuneration will be capitation. I have also made—and I quite frankly admit it to the House—a further concession which I know will be repugnant in some quarters. The doctor, the general practitioner and the specialist, will be able to obtain fees, but not from anyone who is on any of their own lists, nor will a doctor be able to obtain fees from persons on the lists of his partner, nor from those he has worked with in group practice, but I think it is impracticable to prevent him having any fees at all. To do so would be to create a black market. There ought to be nothing to prevent anyone having advice from another doctor other than his own. Hon. Members know what happens in this field sometimes. An individual hears that a particular doctor in some place is good at this, that or the other thing, and wants to go along for a consultation. He gets a consultation and pays a fee for it. If the other doctor is better than his own all he will need to do is to transfer to him and he gets him free. It would be unreasonable to keep the patient paying fees to a doctor whose services can be got free. So the amount of fee payment on the part of the general population will be quite small. Indeed, I confess at once if the amount of fee paying is great, the system will break down, because the whole purpose of this scheme is to provide free treatment with no fee paying at all. The same principle applies to the hospitals.

Mr. Sydney Silverman (Nelson and Colne): Before we leave that point, I should like to ask whether we are to gather from the right hon. Gentleman that a doctor will be entitled to receive a fee for consultation from a patient who is on some other doctor's list?

Mr. Bevan: Yes.

Mr. Silverman: I always understood it was improper for a doctor to see a patient who was being treated by another doctor.

Mr. Bevan: He would not be treated by another doctor, but would be on the panel of the other doctor. We are hoping when our scheme gets going properly that everybody will be on somebody's panel, and unless an individual on someone else's panel is able to pay a fee no one will be able to pay a fee.

Mr. Logan (Liverpool, Scotland Division): If a patient can get specialist advice under the scheme what necessity will there be for him to pay for a consultant?

Mr. Bevan: I hope there will be very little necessity. Nevertheless, this is a field in which idiosyncrasies are prevalent. If an individual wishes to consult, there is no reason why he should be stopped. As I have said, the fact that a person can transfer from one doctor to another ought to keep fee paying within reasonable proportions.

The same principle applies to the hospitals. Specialists in hospitals will be allowed to have fee-paying patients. I know this is criticised and I sympathise with some of the reasons for the criticism, but we are driven inevitably to this fact, that unless we permit some fee-paying patients in the public hospitals, there will be a rash of nursing homes all over the country. If people wish to pay for additional amenities, or something to which they attach value, like privacy in a single ward, we ought to aim at providing such facilities for everyone who wants them. But while we have inadequate hospital facilities, and while rebuilding is postponed it inevitably happens that some people will want to buy something more than the general health service is providing. If we do not permit fees in hospitals, we will lose many specialists from the public hospitals for they will go to nursing homes. I believe that nursing homes ought to be discouraged. They cannot provide general hospital facilities, and we want to keep our specialists attached to our hospitals and not send them into nursing homes. Behind this there is a principle of some importance. If the State owned a theatre it would not charge the same prices for the different seats. (*Interruption*) It is not entirely analogous, but it is an illustration. For example, in the dental service the same principle will prevail. The State will provide a certain standard of dentistry free, but if a person wants to have his teeth filled with gold, the State will not provide that.

The third instrument to which the health services are to be articulated is the health centre, to which we attach very great importance indeed. It has been described in some places as an experimental idea, but we want it to be more than that, because to the extent that general practitioners can operate through health centres in their own practice, to that extent will be raised the general standard of the medical profession as a whole. Furthermore, the general practitioner cannot afford the apparatus necessary for a proper diagnosis in his own surgery. This will be available at the health centre. The health centre may well be the maternity and child welfare clinic of the local authority also. The provision of the health centre is, therefore, imposed as a duty on the local authority. There has been criticism that this creates a trichotomy in the services. It is not a trichotomy at all. If you have complete unification it would bring you back to paper planning. You cannot get all services through the regional authority, because there are many immediate and personal services which the local authority can carry out better than anybody else. So, it is proposed to leave those personal services to the local authority, and some will be carried out at the health centre. The centres will vary; there will be large centers at which there will be dental clinics, maternity and child welfare services, and general practitioners' consultative facilities, and there will also be smaller centres—surgeries where practitioners can see their patients.

Mr. Sidney Marshall (Sutton and Cheam): Will the executive councils have anything to do with the public health centres, or will the latter be managed entirely by the public health authorities?

Mr. Bevan: By the health authorities. The health centre itself will be provided by the local health authority, and facilities will be made available there to the general practitioner. The small ones are necessary, because some centres may be considerable distance from people's homes. So it will be necessary to have simpler ones, nearer their homes, fixed in a constellation with the larger ones.

Mr. Marshall: Will the executive councils have anything to do with it? That is the question I asked.

Mr. Bevan: The representatives on the local executives will be able to coordinate what is happening at the health centres. As I say, we regard these health centres as extremely valuable, and their creation will be encouraged in every possible way. Doctors will be encouraged to practise there, where they will have great facilities. It will, of course, be some time before these centres can be established everywhere, because of the absence of these facilities.

There you have the three main instruments through which it is proposed that the health services of the future should be articulated. There has been some criticism. Some have said that the preventive services should be under the same authority as the curative services. I wonder whether Members who advance that criticism really envisage the situation which will arise. What are the preventive services? Housing, water, sewerage, river pollution prevention, food inspection—are all these to be under a regional board? If so, a regional board of that sort would want the Albert Hall in which to meet. This, again, is paper planning. It is unification for unification's sake. There must be a frontier at which the local joins the national health service. You can fix it here or there, but it must be fixed somewhere. It is said that there is some contradiction in the health scheme because some services are left to the local authority and the rest to the national scheme. Well, day is joined to night by twilight, but nobody has suggested that it is a contradiction in nature. The argument that this is a contradiction in health services is purely pedantic, and has no relation to the facts.

It is also suggested that because maternity and child welfare services come under the local authority, and gynaecological services come under the regional board, that will make for confusion. Why should it? Continuity between one and the other is maintained by the user. The hospital is there to be used. If there are difficulties in connection with birth, the gynaecologist at the hospital centre can look after them. All that happens is that the midwife will be in charge—the mother will be examined properly, as she ought to be examined—then, if difficulties are anticipated, she can have her child in hospital, where she can be properly looked after by the gynaecologist. When she recovers, and is a perfectly normal person, she can go to the maternity and child welfare centre for post-natal treatment. There is no confusion there. The confusion is in the minds of those who are criticising the proposal on the ground that there is a trichotomy in the services, between the local authority, the regional board and the health centre.

I apologise for detaining the House so long, but there are other matters to which I must make some reference. The two Amendments on the Order Paper rather astonish me. The hon. Member for Denbigh (Sir H. Morris-Jones) informs me, in the Amendment, that I have not sufficiently consulted the medical profession . . .

Sir Henry Morris-Jones (Denbigh): That is not the wording on the Order Paper. I said there were no consultations.

Mr. Bevan: I intend to read the Amendment to show how extravagant the hon. Member has been. He says that he and his friends are

. . . unable to agree to a measure containing such far-reaching proposals involving the entire population without any consultations having taken place between the Minister and the organisations and bodies representing those who will be responsible for carrying out its provisions . . .

I have had prepared a list of conferences I have attended. I have met the medical profession, the dental profession, the pharmacists, nurses and midwives, voluntary hospitals, local authorities, eye services, medical aid services, herbalists, insurance committees, and various other organisations. I have had 20 conferences. The consultations have been very wide. In addition, my officials have had 13 conferences, so that altogether there have been 33 conferences with the different branches of the profession about the proposals. Can anybody argue that that is not adequate consultation? Of course, the real criticism is that I have not conducted negotiations. I am astonished that such a charge should lie in the mouth of any Member of the House. If there is one thing that will spell the death of the House of Commons it is for a Minister to negotiate Bills before they are presented to the House. I had no negotiations, because once you negotiate with outside bodies two things happen. They are made aware of the nature of the proposals before the House of Commons itself; and furthermore, the Minister puts himself into an impossible position, because, if he has agreed things with somebody outside he is bound to resist Amendments from Members in the House. Otherwise he does not play fair with them. I protested against this myself when I was a Private Member. I protested bitterly, and I am not prepared, strange though it may seem, to do something as a Minister which as a Private Member I thought was wrong. So there has no been negotiation, and there will not be negotiation, in this matter. The House of Commons is supreme, and the House of Commons must assert its supremacy, and not allow itself to be dictated to by any body, no matter how powerful and how strong he may be.

Sir H. Morris-Jones: Would the right hon. Gentleman apply that doctrine to the Miners' Federation?

Mr. Bevan: Certainly. That is exactly what I did. The hon. Member was a Member of the House at the time, and he should remember it. These consultations have taken place over a very wide field, and, as a matter of fact, have produced quite a considerable amount of agreement. The opposition to the Bill is not as strong as it was thought it would be. On the contrary, there is very considerable support for this Measure among the doctors themselves. I myself have been rather aggrieved by some of the statements which have been made. They have misrepresented the proposals to a very large extent, but as these proposals become known to the medical profession, they will appreciate them, because nothing should please a good doctor more than to realise that, in future, neither he nor his patient will have any financial anxiety arising out of illness.

The leaders of the Opposition have on the Order Paper an Amendment which expresses indignation at the extent to which we are interfering with charitable foundations. The Amendment states that the Bill

> gravely menaces all charitable foundations by diverting to purposes other than those intended by the donors the trust funds of the voluntary hospitals.

I must say that when I read that Amendment I was amused. I have been looking up some precedents. I would like to say, in passing, that a great many of these endowments and foundations have been diversions from the Chancellor of the Exchequer. The main contributor was the Chancellor of the Exchequer. But I seem to remember that, in 1941, hon. Members opposite were very much vexed by what might happen to the public schools, and they came to the House and asked for the permission of the House to lay sacrilegious hands upon educational endowments centuries old. I remember protesting against it at the time—not, however, on the grounds of sacrilege. These endowments had been left to the public schools, many of them for the maintenance of the buildings, but hon. Members opposite, being concerned lest the war might affect their favourite schools, came to the House and allowed the diversion of money from that purpose to the payment of the salaries of the teachers and the masters. There have been other interferences with endowments. Wales has been one of the criminals. Disestablishment interfered with an enormous number of endowments. Scotland also is involved. Scotland has been behaving in a most sacrilegious manner; a whole lot of endowments have been waived by Scottish Acts. I could read out a large number of them, but I shall not do so.

Do hon. Members opposite suggest that the intelligent planning of the modern world must be prevented by the endowments of the dead? Are we to consider the dead more than the living? Are the patients of our hospitals to be sacrificed to a consideration of that sort?

Major Lloyd: Henry VIII did it.

Mr. Bevan: He was a good king, too; he had many good points. We are not, in fact, diverting these endowments from charitable purposes. It would have been perfectly proper for the Chancellor of the Exchequer to have taken over these funds, because they were willed for hospital purposes, and he could use them for hospital purposes; but we are doing no such thing. The teaching hospitals will be left with all their liquid endowments and more power. We are not interfering with the teaching hospitals' endowments. Academic medical education will be more free in the future than it has been in the past. Furthermore, something like £32 million belonging to the voluntary hospitals as a whole is not going to be taken from them. On the contrary, we are going to use it, and a very valuable thing it will be; we are going to use it as a shock absorber between the Treasury, the central Government, and the hospital administration. They will be given it as free money which they can spend over and above the funds provided by the State.

I welcome the opportunity of doing that, because I appreciate, as much as hon. Members in any part of the House, the absolute necessity for having an elastic, resilient service, subject to local influence as well as to central influence; and that can be accomplished by leaving this money in their hands. I shall be prepared to consider when the Bill comes to be examined in more detail, whether any other relaxations are possible, but certainly, by leaving this money in the hands of the regional board, by allowing the regional board an annual budget and giving them freedom of movement inside that budget, by giving power to the regional board to distribute this money to the local management committees of the hospitals, by various devices of that sort, the hospitals will be responsive to local pressure and subject to local influence as well as to central direction.

I think that on those grounds the proposals can be defended. They cover a very wide field indeed, to a great deal of which I have not been able to make reference; but I should have thought it ought to have been a pride to hon. Members in all parts of the House that Great Britain is able to embark upon an ambitious scheme of this proportion. When it is carried out, it will place this country in the forefront of all countries of the world in medical services. I myself, if I may say a personal word, take very great pride and great pleasure in being able to introduce a Bill of this comprehensiveness and value. I believe it will lift the shadow from millions of homes. It will keep very many people alive who might otherwise be dead. It will relieve suffering. It will produce higher standards for the medical profession. It will be a great contribution towards the wellbeing of the common people of Great Britain. For that reason, and for the other reasons I have mentioned, I hope hon. Members will give the Bill a Second Reading.

Sir Winston Leonard Spencer Churchill

.

Winston Leonard Spencer Churchill

[*Born* NOVEMBER 30, 1874—*Died* JANUARY 24, 1965]

The oldest among us can recall nothing to compare with him, and the younger ones among us, however long we live, will never see the like again. —HAROLD MACMILLAN

·W·

inston Churchill is without doubt the Man of the Century in British political history. A. L. Rowse believes he sums up "the whole first half of our century as no other statesman does." [1] Churchill was a member of Parliament for 63 years, beginning with the "khaki election" of 1900 until he relinquished his seat in October of 1964. He held cabinet positions in both Liberal and Conservative governments, serving four Prime Ministers before he himself was appointed to head the government in its hour of peril. [2] It was the Churchillian determination to subdue the forces of Nazi Germany and Fascist Italy when Great Britain seemed all but obliterated which will best be remembered. According to Henry Grunwald, "a matchless leader who might have built and administered new worlds," Churchill could only rescue the old:

But in that role he won a victory more famous than any that can be claimed by the great warrior-statesmen from Alexander to his own ancestor, John Churchill. [3]

Rowse calls him "the greatest leader in war this country has ever had." [4] At one time or another he served as head of all the fighting services, and was more keenly aware of the state of Britain's military preparedness than even the military chiefs.

For a man who, like his father, had little faith in spontaneous expression, he was an excellent debater. [5] The prose of his speech is

---

[1] A. L. Rowse, "Churchill's Place in History," in *Churchill by His Contemporaries,* ed. by Charles Eade (London: Hutchinson, 1953), p. 507.

[2] In the ministry of H. H. Asquith, Churchill was appointed to the Board of Trade as president in 1908, Home Secretary in 1910, and the Admiralty in 1911. In the coalition government of David Lloyd George, Churchill became Minister of Munitions in 1917, Secretary of War in 1919, and Colonial Secretary in 1921. Under Stanley Baldwin, he was Exchequer in 1924. In 1939, Neville Chamberlain appointed Churchill to the Admiralty.

[3] Henry Anatole Grunwald, "Man of the Century," in *Churchill: The Life Triumphant* (American Heritage Publishing Co., Inc., 1965), p. 8.

[4] Rowse, *op. cit.,* p. 501.

[5] Violet Bonham Carter, *Winston Churchill: An Intimate Portrait* (New York: Harcourt, Brace and World, Inc., 1965), p. 61. "It was largely to this gift of inspired and accurate prevision [preparing rebuttals in advance] that he owed his mastery of debate. For in spite of his command of words, unequaled in its power, originality and range, he never was a ready speaker. The artist in him forbade slipshod spontaneity. He was too verbally fastidious to leave his words to chance. To him a speech must be, in substance and in form, a work of art."

remarkably similar to that of his writing, probably because he relied heavily on dictation in composing his many books. In both instances of composition, his prose possesses "a rhythm and cadence which . . . are consistently notable. You get the same kind of arrangement of words, so that they flow instead of staggering." [6]

His war speeches are well-remembered and widely quoted. To many historians and biographers, they epitomize his finest hours. Anthologies abound with these speeches along with scores of his postwar speeches. Not since Edmund Burke have an individual's thoughts been so ardently transcribed and circulated. Less attention, however, has been focused upon Churchill's speeches delivered before World War II, although some observers believe a number of those speeches are deserving of immortality. Colin Coote indicates that he "shall always think that this period in his career was in many respects his 'finest hour.' " [7]

Certainly, one speech deserving of immortality was delivered on October 5, 1938, containing Churchill's denunciation of the Munich Agreement, proclaimed by Neville Chamberlain as assurance of "Peace with Honour." At that moment in history, Churchill's fortunes were at their "nadir." [8] For some six years, he had been subjected to an "all-pervasive hostility":[9]

Discredited by his opponents for his brilliance, his judgment suspect, it seemed that his fate would be that of the politician who has outlived his day. He was over sixty and they began to speak of him as the Elder Statesman.[10]

During those days, Churchill's seat in Commons was located below the gangway, the "retreat of members out of step with their party." [11] As he rose to speak on October 5, he was greeted by the "howls and catcalls that had become the normal accompaniment of his remarks." [12] He faced an audience which seemed truly to believe with "hysterical relief" that war had been averted. As he concluded, it was obvious that he converted no one, but it is possible some were led to think that the agreement might have been a false assurance.

---

6 *Maxims and Reflections,* with Introduction by Colin Coote (Boston: Houghton-Mifflin Co., 1947), p. 16.

7 *Ibid.,* p. 21.

8 Lewis Broad, *Winston Churchill: The Years of Preparation* (New York: Hawthorn Books, Inc., 1958), p. 401.

9 Coote, *op. cit.,* p. 22.

10 Broad, *op. cit.*

11 *Ibid.*

12 Geoffrey Bocca, *The Adventurous Life of Winston Churchill* (New York: Julian Messner, Inc., 1958), p. 156.

As one who never trusted Hitler, this speech was a further step in assuring his later appointment as First Lord of the Admiralty.

In addition to his public war speeches, Churchill delivered a number of speeches of major importance in secret sessions of the House of Commons.[13] One of them, delivered on September 17, 1940, is included in this volume because it reveals Churchill's profound regard for constitutional government in a time of crisis when it might have been recessed with justifiable cause. It was never within Churchill's character to suggest that the institution for which he had spent more than half a century to strengthen and preserve should ever be suspended.

Words coupled to prophesy were forces which, even out of power, made Churchill the "real leader of Western opinion" in the postwar years of 1945–1951.[14] His "iron-curtain" speech at Fulton, Missouri, on March 5, 1946, though not included in this volume, stands as one of the finest examples of his influence in both literary and political circles.

---

[13] See *Secret Session Speeches*, compiled by Charles Eade (London: Cassell and Company, Ltd., 1946), p. v.

[14] Rowse, *op. cit.*, p. 505.

Government Policy [1]

•

HOUSE OF COMMONS   *October 5, 1938*

r. Churchill: If I do not begin this afternoon by paying the usual, and indeed almost invariable, tributes to the Prime Minister for handling of this crisis, it is certainly not from any lack of personal regard. We have always, over a great many years, had very pleasant relations, and I have deeply understood from personal experiences of my own in a similar crisis the stress and strain he has had to bear; but I am sure it is much better to say exactly what we think about public affairs, and this is certainly not the time when it is worth anyone's while to court political popularity. We had a shining example of firmness of character from the late First Lord of the Admiralty two days ago. He showed that firmness of character which is utterly unmoved by currents of opinion, however swift and violent they may be. My hon. Friend the Member for South-West Hull (Mr. Law), to whose compulsive speech the House listened on Monday—which I had not the good fortune to hear, but which I read, and which I am assured by all who heard it revived the memory of his famous father, so cherished in this House, and made us feel that his gifts did not die with him—was quite right in reminding us that the Prime Minister has himself throughout his conduct of these matters shown a robust indifference to cheers or boos and to the alternations of criticism and applause. If that be so, such qualities and elevation of mind should make it possible for the most severe expressions of honest opinion to be interchanged in this House without rupturing personal relations, and for all points of view to receive the fullest possible expression.

Having thus fortified myself by the example of others, I will proceed to emulate them. I will, therefore, begin by saying the most unpopular and most unwelcome thing. I will begin by saying what everybody would

---

1 339 H. C. Deb. 5s., Cols. 359–373.

like to ignore or forget but which must nevertheless be stated, namely, that we have sustained a total and unmitigated defeat, and that France has suffered even more than we have.

Viscountess Astor: Nonsense.

Mr. Churchill: When the Noble Lady cries "Nonsense," she could not have heard the Chancellor of the Exchequer admit in his illuminating and comprehensive speech just now that Herr Hitler had gained in this particular leap forward in substance all he set out to gain. The utmost my right hon. Friend the Prime Minister has been able to secure by all his immense exertions, by all the great efforts and mobilisation which took place in this country, and by all the anguish and strain through which we have passed in this country, the utmost he has been able to gain—[*Hon. Members:* "Is peace."] I thought I might be allowed to make that point in its due place, and I propose to deal with it. The utmost he has been able to gain for Czechoslovakia and in the matters which were in dispute has been that the German dictator, instead of snatching his victuals from the table, has been content to have them served to him course by course.

The Chancellor of the Exchequer said it was the first time Herr Hitler had been made to retract—I think that was the word—in any degree. We really must not waste time, after all this long Debate, upon the difference between the positions reached at Berchtesgaden, at Godesberg and at Munich. They can be very simply epitomised, if the House will permit me to vary the metaphor. £1 was demanded at the pistol's point. When it was given, £2 were demanded at the pistol's point. Finally, the dictator consented to take £1 17s. 6d. and the rest in promises of good will for the future.

Now I come to the point, which was mentioned to me just now from some quarters of the House, about the saving of peace. No one has been a more resolute and uncompromising struggler for peace than the Prime Minister. Everyone knows that. Never has there been such intense and undaunted determination to maintain and to secure peace. That is quite true. Nevertheless, I am not quite clear why there was so much danger of Great Britain or France being involved in a war with Germany at this juncture if, in fact, they were ready all along to sacrifice Czechoslovakia. The terms which the Prime Minister brought back with him—I quite agree at the last moment; everything had got off the rails and nothing but his intervention could have saved the peace, but I am talking of the events of the summer—could easily have been agreed, I believe, through the ordinary diplomatic channels at any time during the summer. And I will say this, that I believe the Czechs, left to themselves and told they were going to get no help from the Western Powers, would have been able to make better terms than they have got—they could hardly have worse—after all this tremendous perturbation.

There never can be any absolute certainty that there will be a fight if one side is determined that it will give way completely. When one reads the Munich terms, when one sees what is happening in Czechoslovakia from hour to hour, when one is sure, I will not say of Parliamentary approval but of Parliamentary acquiescence, when the Chancellor of the Exchequer makes a speech which at any rate tries to put in a very powerful and persuasive manner the fact that, after all, it was inevitable and indeed righteous—right—when we saw all this, and everyone on this side of the House, including many Members of the Conservative Party who are supposed to be vigilant and careful guardians of the national interest, it is quite clear that nothing vitally affecting us was at stake, it seems to me that one must ask, What was all the trouble and fuss about?

The resolve was taken by the British and the French Governments. Let me say that it is very important to realise that it is by no means a question which the British Government only have had to decide. I very much admire the manner in which, in the House, all references of a recriminatory nature have been repressed, but it must be realised that this resolve did not emanate particularly from one or other of the Governments but was a resolve for which both must share in common the responsibility. When this resolve was taken and the course was followed—you may say it was wise or unwise, prudent or short-sighted—once it had been decided not to make the defence of Czechoslovakia a matter of war, then there was really no reason, if the matter had been handled during the summer in the ordinary way, to call into being all this formidable apparatus of crisis. I think that point should be considered.

We are asked to vote for this Motion which has been put upon the Paper, and it is certainly a Motion couched in very uncontroversial terms, as, indeed, is the Amendment moved from the Opposition side. I cannot myself express my agreement with the steps which have been taken, and as the Chancellor of the Exchequer has put his side of the case with so much ability I will attempt, if I may be permitted, to put the case from a different angle. I have always held the view that the maintenance of peace depends upon the accumulation of deterrents against the aggressor, coupled with a sincere effort to redress grievances. Herr Hitler's victory, like so many of the famous struggles that have governed the fate of the world, was won upon the narrowest of margins. After the seizure of Austria in March we faced this problem in our Debates. I ventured to appeal to the Government to go a little further than the Prime Minister went, and to give a pledge that in conjunction with France and other Powers they would guarantee the security of Czechoslovakia while the Sudeten-Deutsch question was being examined either by a League of Nations Commission or some other impartial body, and I still believe that if that course had been followed events would not have fallen into this disastrous state. I agree very much with my right hon. Friend the Member for Sparkbrook (Mr. Amery) when he said on that occasion—I cannot remember his actual words—"Do one thing or the other; either say you will disinterest yourself in the matter altogether or take the step of giving a guarantee which will have the greatest chance of securing protection for that country."

France and Great Britain together, especially if they had maintained a close contact with Russia, which certainly was not done, would have been able in those days in the summer, when they had the prestige, to influence many of the smaller States of Europe, and I believe they could have determined the attitude of Poland. Such a combination, prepared at a time when the German dictator was not deeply and irrevocably committed to his new adventure, would, I believe, have given strength to all those forces in Germany which resisted this departure, this new design. They were varying forces, those of a military character which declared that Germany was not ready to undertake a world war, and all that mass of moderate opinion and popular opinion which dreaded war, and some elements of which still have some influence upon the German Government. Such action would have given strength to all that intense desire for peace which the helpless German masses share with their British and French fellow men, and which, as we have been reminded, found a passionate and rarely permitted vent in the joyous manifestations with which the Prime Minister was acclaimed in Munich.

All these forces, added to the other deterrents which combinations of Powers, great and small, ready to stand firm upon the front of law and for the ordered remedy of grievances, would have formed, might well have been effective. Of course you cannot say for certain that they would. [*Interruption.*] I try to argue fairly with the House. At the same time I do not think it is fair to charge those who wished to see this course followed and followed consistently and resolutely, with having wished for an immediate war. Between submission and immediate war there was this third alternative, which gave a hope not only of peace but of justice. It is quite true that such a policy in order to succeed demanded that Britain should declare straight out and a long time beforehand that she would, with others, join to defend Czechoslovakia against an unprovoked aggression. His Majesty's Government refused to give that guarantee when it would have saved the situation, yet in the end they gave it when it was too late, and now, for the future, they renew it when they have not the slightest power to make it good.

All is over. Silent, mournful, abandoned, broken, Czechoslovakia recedes into the darkness. She has suffered in every respect by her association with the Western democracies and with the League of Nations, of which she has always been an obedient servant. She has suffered in particular from her association with France, under whose guidance and policy she has been actuated for so long. The very measures taken by His Majesty's Government in the Anglo-French Agreement to give her the best chance possible, namely, the 50 per cent. clean cut in certain districts instead of a plebiscite, have turned to her detriment, because there is to be a plebiscite too in wide areas, and those other Powers who had claims have also come down upon the helpless victim. Those municipal elections upon whose voting the basis is taken for the 50 per cent. cut were held on issues which had nothing to do with joining Germany. When I saw Herr Henlein over here he assured me that was not the desire of his people. Positive statements were made that it was only a question of home rule, of having a position of their own in the Czechoslovakian State. No one has a right to say that the plebiscite which is to be taken in areas under Saar conditions, and the clean-cut of the 40 per cent. areas—that those two operations together amount in the slightest degree to a verdict of self-determination. It is a fraud and a farce to invoke that name.

We in this country, as in other Liberal and democratic countries, have a perfect right to exalt the principle of self-determination, but it comes ill out of the mouths of those in totalitarian States who deny even the smallest element of toleration to every section and creed within their bounds. But, however you put it, this particular block of land, this mass of human beings to be handed over, has never expressed the desire to go into the Nazi rule. I do not believe that even now—if their opinion could be asked, they would exercise such an option.

What is the remaining position of Czechoslovakia? Not only are they politically mutilated, but, economically and financially, they are in complete confusion. Their banking, their railway arrangements, are severed and broken, their industries are curtailed, and the movement of their population is most cruel. The Sudeten miners, who are all Czechs and whose families have lived in that area for centuries, must now flee into an area where there are hardly any mines left for them to work. It is a tragedy which has occurred. I did not like to hear the Minister of Transport yesterday talking about Humpty Dumpty. It was the Minister of Transport who was saying that it was a case of Humpty Dumpty that could never be put together again. There must always be the most profound regret and a sense of vexation in British hearts at the treatment and the misfortunes which have overcome the Czechoslovakian Republic. They have not ended here. At any moment there may be a hitch in the programme. At any moment there may be an order for Herr Goebbels to start again his propaganda of calumny and lies; at any moment an incident may be provoked, and now that the fortress line is given away what is there to stop the will of the conqueror? [*Interruption.*] It is too serious a subject to treat lightly. Obviously, we are not in a position to give them the slightest help at the present time, except what everyone is glad to know has been done, the financial aid which the Government have promptly produced.

I venture to think that in future the Czechoslovak State cannot be maintained as an independent entity. You will find that in a period of time which may be measured by years, but may be measured only by months, Czechoslovakia will be engulfed in the Nazi régime. Perhaps they may join it in despair or in revenge. At any rate, that story is over and told. But we cannot consider the abandonment and ruin of Czechoslovakia in the light only of what happened only last month. It is the most grievous consequence which we have yet experienced of what we have done and of what we have left undone in the last five years—five years of futile good intention, five years of eager search for the line of least resistance, five years of uninterrupted retreat of British power, five years of neglect of our air defences. Those are the features which I stand here to declare and which marked an improvident stewardship for which Great Britain and France have dearly to pay. We have been reduced in those five years from a position of security so overwhelming and so unchallengeable that we never cared to think about it. We have been reduced from a position where the very word "war" was considered one which would be used only by persons qualifying for a lunatic asylum. We have been reduced from a position of safety and power—power to do good, power to be generous to a beaten foe, power to make terms with Germany, power to give her proper redress for her grievances, power to stop her arming if we chose, power to take any step in strength or mercy or justice which we thought right—reduced in five years from a position safe and unchallenged to where we stand now.

When I think of the fair hopes of a long peace which still lay before Europe at the beginning of 1933 when Herr Hitler first obtained power, and of all the opportunities of arresting the growth of the Nazi power which have been thrown away, when I think of the immense combinations and resources which have been neglected or squandered, I cannot believe that a parallel exists in the whole course of history. So far as this country is concerned the responsibility must rest with those who have the undisputed control of our political affairs. They neither prevented Germany from rearming, nor did they rearm ourselves in time. They quarrelled with Italy without saving Ethiopia. They exploited and discredited the vast institution of the League of Nations and they neglected to make alliances and combinations which might have repaired previous errors, and thus they left us in the hour of trial without adequate national defence or effective international security.

In my holiday I thought it was a chance to study the reign of King Ethelred the Unready. The House will remember that that was a period of great misfortune, in which, from the strong position which we had gained under the descendants of King Alfred, we fell very swiftly into chaos. It was the period of Danegeld and of foreign pressure. I must say that the rugged words of the Anglo-Saxon Chronicle, written 1,000 years ago, seem to me apposite, at least as apposite as those quotations from Shakespeare with which we have been regaled by the last speaker from the Opposition Bench. Here is what the Anglo-Saxon Chronicle said, and I think the words apply very much to our treatment of Germany and our relations with her:

> All these calamities fell upon us because of evil counsel, because tribute was not offered to them at the right time nor yet were they resisted; but when they had done the most evil, then was peace made with them.

That is the wisdom of the past, for all wisdom is not new wisdom.

I have ventured to express those views in justifying myself for not being able to support the Motion which is moved to-night, but I recognise that this great matter of Czechoslovakia, and of British and French duty there, has passed into history. New developments may come along, but we are not here to decide whether any of those steps should be taken or not. They have been taken. They have been taken by those who had a right to take them because they bore the highest executive responsibility under the Crown. Whatever we may think of it, we must regard those steps as belonging to the category of affairs which are settled beyond recall. The past is no more, and one can only draw comfort if one feels that one has done one's best to advise rightly and wisely and in good time. I, therefore, turn to the future, and to our situation as it is to-day. Here, again, I am sure I shall have to say something which will not be at all welcome.

We are in the presence of a disaster of the first magnitude which has befallen Great Britain and France. Do not let us blind ourselves to that. It must now be accepted that all the countries of Central and Eastern Europe will make the best terms they can with the triumphant Nazi Power. The system of alliances in Central Europe upon which France has relied for her safety has been swept away, and I can see no means by which it can be reconstituted. The road down the Danube Valley to the Black Sea, the resources of corn and oil, the road which leads as far as Turkey, has been opened. In fact, if not in form, it seems to me that all those countries of Middle Europe, all those Danubian countries, will, one after another, be drawn into this fast system of power politics—not only power military politics but power economic politics—radiating from Berlin, and I believe this can be achieved quite smoothly and swiftly and will not necessarily entail the firing of a single shot. If you wish to survey the havoc of the foreign policy of Britain and France, look at what is happening and is recorded each day in the columns of the "Times." Why, I read this morning about Yugoslavia—and I know something about the details of that country—

The effects of the crisis for Yugoslavia can immediately be traced. Since the elections of 1935, which followed soon after the murder of King Alexander, the Serb and Croat Opposition to the Government of Dr. Stoyadinovitch have been conducting their entire campaign for the next elections under the slogan: 'Back to France, England, and the Little Entente; back to democracy.' The events of the past fortnight have so triumphantly vindicated Dr. Stoyadinovitch's policy . . .

—his is a policy of close association with Germany—

that the Opposition has collapsed practically overnight; the new elections, the date of which was in doubt, are now likely to be held very soon and can result only in an over-whelming victory for Dr. Stoyadinovitch's Government.

Here was a country which, three months ago, would have stood in the line with other countries to arrest what has occurred.

Again, what happened in Warsaw? The British and French Ambassadors visited Colonel Beck, or sought to visit him, the Foreign Minister, in order to ask for some mitigation in the harsh measures being pursued against Czechoslovakia about Teschen. The door was shut in their faces. The French Ambassador was not even granted an audience and the British Ambassador was given a most curt reply by a political director. The whole matter is described in the Polish Press as a political indiscretion committed by those two Powers, and we are to-day reading of the success of Colonel Beck's blow. I am not forgetting, I must say, that it is less than 20 years ago since British and French bayonets rescued Poland from the bondage of a century and a half. I think it is indeed a sorry episode in the history of that country, for whose freedom and rights so many of us have had warm and long sympathy.

Those illustrations are typical. You will see, day after day, week after week, entire alienation of those regions. Many of those countries, in fear of the rise of the Nazi Power, have already got politicians, Ministers, Governments, who were pro-German, but there was always an enormous popular movement in Poland, Rumania, Bulgaria and Yugoslavia which looked to the Western democracies and loathed the idea of having this arbitrary rule of the totalitarian system thrust upon them, and hoped that a stand would be made. All that has gone by the board. We are talking about countries which are a long way off and of which, as the Prime Minister might say, we know nothing. [*Interruption.*] The noble Lady says that that very harmless allusion is—

Viscountess Astor: Rude.

Mr. Churchill: She must very recently have been receiving her finishing course in manners. What will be the position, I want to know, of France and England this year and the year afterwards? What will be the position of that Western front of which we are in full authority the guarantors? The German army at the present time is more numerous than that of France, though not nearly so matured or perfected. Next year it will grow much larger, and its maturity will be more complete. Relieved from all anxiety in the East, and having secured resources which will greatly diminish, if not entirely remove, the deterrent of a naval blockade, the rulers of Nazi Germany will have a free choice open to them in what direction they will turn their eyes. If the Nazi dictator should choose to look westward, as he may, bitterly will France and England regret the loss of that fine army of ancient Bohemia which was estimated last week to require not fewer than 30 German divisions for its destruction.

Can we blind ourselves to the great change which has taken place in the military situation, and to the dangers we have to meet? We are in process, I believe, of adding, in four years, four battalions to the British Army. No fewer than two have already been completed. Here at least 30 divisions which must now be taken into consideration upon the French front, besides the 12 that were captured when Austria was engulfed. Many people, no doubt, honestly believe that they are only giving away the interests of Czechoslovakia, whereas I fear we shall find that we have deeply compromised, and perhaps fatally endangered, the safety and even the independence of Great Britain and France. This is not merely a question of giving up the German colonies, as I am sure we shall be asked to do. Nor is it a question only of losing influence in Europe. It goes far deeper than that. You have to consider the character of the Nazi movement and the rule which it implies. The Prime Minister desires to see cordial relations between this country and Germany. There is no difficulty at all in having cordial relations with the German people. Our hearts go out to them. But they have no power. You must have diplomatic and correct relations, but there can never be friendship between the British democracy and the Nazi Power, that Power which spurns Christian ethics, which cheers its onward course by a barbarous paganism, which vaunts the spirit of aggression and conquest, which derives strength and perverted pleasure from persecution, and uses, as we have seen, with pitiless brutality the threat of murderous force. That Power cannot ever be the trusted friend of the British democracy.

What I find unendurable is the sense of our country falling into the power, into the orbit and influence of Nazi Germany, and of our existence becoming dependent upon their good will or pleasure. It is to prevent that that I have tried my best to urge the maintenance of every bulwark of defence—first the timely creation of an Air Force superior to anything within striking distance of our shores; secondly, the gathering together of the collective strength of many nations; and thirdly, the making of alliances and military conventions, all within the Covenant, in order to gather together forces at any rate to restrain the onward movement of this Power. It has all been in vain. Every position has been successively undermined and abandoned on specious and plausible excuses. We do not want to be led upon the high road to becoming a satellite of the German Nazi system of European domination. In a very few years, perhaps in a very few months, we shall be confronted with demands with which we shall no doubt be invited to comply. Those demands may affect the surrender of territory or the surrender of liberty. I foresee and foretell that the policy of submission will carry with it restrictions upon the freedom of speech and debate in Parliament, on public platforms, and discussions in the Press, for it will be said—indeed, I hear it said sometimes now—that we cannot allow the Nazi system of dictatorship to be criticised by ordinary, common English politicians. Then, with a Press under control, in part direct but more potently indirect, with every organ of public opinion doped and chloroformed into acquiescence, we shall be conducted along further stages of our journey.

It is a small matter to introduce into such a Debate as this, but during the week I heard something of the talk of Tadpole and Taper. They were very keen upon having a general election, a sort of, if I may say so, inverted khaki election. I wish the Prime Minister had heard the speech of my hon. and gallant Friend the Member for the Abbey Division of Westminster (Sir S. Herbert) last night. I know that no one is more patient and regular in his attendance than the Prime Minister, and it is marvellous how he is able to sit through so much of our Debates, but it happened that by bad luck he was not here at that moment. I am sure, however, that if he had heard my hon. and gallant Friend's speech he would have felt very much annoyed that such a rumour could even have been circulated. I cannot believe that the Prime Minister, or any Prime Minister possessed of a large working majority, would be capable of such an act of historic, constitutional indecency. I think too highly of him. Of course, if I have misjudged him on the right side, and there is a dissolution on the Munich Agreement, on Anglo-Nazi friendship, on the state of our defences and so forth, everyone will have to fight according to his convictions, and only a prophet could forecast the ultimate result; but, whatever the result, few things could be more fatal to our remaining chances of survival as a great Power than that this country should be torn in twain upon this deadly issue of foreign policy at a moment when, whoever the Ministers may be, united effort can alone make us safe.

I have been casting about to see how measures can be taken to protect us from this advance of the Nazi Power, and to secure those forms of life which are so dear to us. What is the sole method that is open? The sole method that is open is for us to regain our old island independence by acquiring that supremacy in the air which we were promised, that security in our air defences which we were assured we had, and thus to make ourselves an island once again. That, in all this grim outlook, shines out as the overwhelming fact. An effort at rearmament the like of which has not been seen ought to be made forthwith, and all the resources of this country and all its united strength should be bent to that task. I was very glad to see that Lord Baldwin yesterday in the House of Lords said that he would mobilise industry to-morrow. But I think it would have been much better if Lord Baldwin had said that $2\frac{1}{2}$ years ago, when everyone demanded a Ministry of Supply. I will venture to say to hon. Gentlemen sitting here behind the Government Bench, hon. Friends of mine, whom I thank for the patience with which they have listened to what I have to say, that they have some responsibility for all this too, because, if they had given one tithe of the cheers they have lavished upon this transaction of Czechoslovakia to the small band of Members who were endeavouring to get timely rearmament set in motion, we should not now be in the position in which we are. Hon. Gentlemen opposite, and hon. Members on the Liberal benches, are not entitled to throw these stones. I remember for two years having to face, not only the Government's deprecation, but their stern disapproval. Lord Baldwin has now given the signal, tardy though it may be; let us at least obey it.

After all, there are no secrets now about what happened in the air and in the mobilisation of our anti-aircraft defences. These matters have been, as my hon. and gallant Friend the Member for the Abbey Division said, seen by thousands of people. They can form their own opinions of the character of the statements which have been persistently made to us by Ministers on this subject. Who pretends now that there is air parity with Germany? Who pretends now that our anti-aircraft defences were adequately manned or armed? We know that the German General Staff are well informed upon these subjects, but the House of Commons has hitherto not taken seriously its duty of requiring to assure itself of these matters. The Home Secretary said the other night that he would welcome investigation. Many things have been done which reflect the greatest credit upon the administration. But the vital matters are what we want to know about. I have asked again and again during these three years for a secret Session where these matters could be thrashed out, or for an investigation by a Select Committee of the House, or for some other method. I ask now that, when we meet again in the autumn, that should be a matter on which the Government should take the House into its confidence, because we have a right to know where we stand and what measures are being taken to secure our position.

I do not grudge our loyal, brave people, who were ready to do their duty no matter what the cost, who never flinched under the strain of last week—I do not grudge them the natural, spontaneous outburst of joy and relief when they learned that the hard ordeal would no longer be required of them at the moment; but they should know the truth. They should know that there has been gross neglect and deficiency in our defences; they should know that we have sustained a defeat without a war, the consequences of which will travel far with us along our road; they should know that we have passed an awful milestone in our history, when the whole equilibrium of Europe has been deranged, and that the terrible words have for the time being been pronounced against the Western democracies:

Thou art weighed in the balance and found wanting.

And do not suppose that this is the end. This is only the beginning of the reckoning. This is only the first sip, the first foretaste of a bitter cup which will be proffered to us year by year unless by a supreme recovery of moral health and martial vigour, we arise again and take our stand for freedom as in the olden time.

At last he moved, and in the dim light I could see that tears were running unchecked down his cheeks. Turning abruptly to an official, he controlled his voice with an effort and said quietly: 'This Chamber must be rebuilt—just as it was! Meanwhile, we shall not miss a single day's debate through this!'—GUY EDEN

Parliament in the Air Raids[1]

·

On Tuesday, September 17, 1940, while German bombers raided London unceasingly throughout the night, the House of Commons went into Secret Session to hear from Mr. Winston Churchill how Parliament would carry on with its duties during the Battle of Britain and in face of the heavy bombardment from the air which was going to be inflicted on the capital during the months ahead.

The notes used by Mr. Churchill on that occasion were, fortunately, so full as to form an almost exact record of what he said. After explaining why the dates of sittings would be kept secret and the hours altered, Mr. Churchill warned the House of the ever-growing dangers of an invasion attempt. He revealed that upwards of 1,700 self-propelled barges and more than 200 sea-going ships were already gathered at ports in German occupation. He rejected any thought that these preparations might be only pretence and said that some of these vessels, when bombed by the R.A.F., had blown up with tremendous explosions, showing that they were fully loaded with all the munitions needed for the invading armies.

Despite all these threats and perils, the Prime Minister ended by assuring his listeners that he was "as sure as the sun will rise to-morrow" that Britain would be victorious.

The reason why I asked the House to go into Secret Session was not because I had anything particularly secret or momentous to say. It was only because there are some things which it is better for us to talk over among ourselves than when we are overheard by the Germans. I wish to speak about the Sittings of the House and how we are to discharge our Parliamentary duties.

[1] *Secret Session Speeches,* compiled by Charles Eade. (New York: Simon and Schuster, Inc., 1946), pp. 15–22. Mr. Eade writes in the Introduction that these speeches were carefully prepared in advance and submitted to other interested Ministries to assure accuracy and to avoid breaches of security. While it is impossible to guarantee complete accuracy of the text, it is unlikely that Churchill varied from it to any great extent. p. vii.

A few days ago I had a notification from the Chiefs of the Staff. They considered that the date and time of this meeting of ours to-day had been so widely advertised that to hold it would be to incur an undue risk, and that it should be put off to some date and hour which had not been publicly announced. I felt, however, that Members would be offended if any course was taken which suggested for a moment that we should shirk our duty out of considerations of personal safety. And then there is all that argument which occurs to everyone of our setting an example, and of the incongruity of our ordering Government Departments, and urging factory workers to remain at work, while we ourselves did not assemble on particular occasions as we had resolved to do. Moreover, the rules of the House are such that we could only have avoided meeting at this hour by an earlier meeting on Monday, which would alter the hour, and a Monday meeting would have caused much inconvenience under the present conditions of travel.

I, therefore, took the responsibility of disregarding the very well-meant warning which we had received from those charged with the technical burden of national defence.

Nevertheless, this is a matter on which there should be clear thinking. We should fail in our duty if we went to the other extreme, and in a spirit of mettlesome bravado made it unduly easy for the enemy to inflict loss and inconvenience upon the public service. We ought not to flatter ourselves by imagining that we are irreplaceable, but at the same time it cannot be denied that two or three hundred by-elections would be a quite needless complication of our affairs at this particular juncture. Moreover, I suppose that if Hitler made a clean sweep of the Houses of Parliament it would give wide-spread and unwholesome satisfaction throughout Germany, and be vaunted as another triumph for the Nazi system of Government. We must exercise reasonable prudence and a certain amount of guile in combating the malice of the enemy. It is no part of good sense to proclaim the hour and dates of our meetings long beforehand.

There are two kinds of air risks, the general and the particular. The general risk in air raids is largely negligible. It is at least a thousand to one. But the risk of staying in a particular building which the enemy undoubtedly regard as a military objective, is of a different order. Here we are sitting on the target. This group of well-known, prominent buildings and towers between three major railway stations, with the river as a perfect guide by night and day, is the easiest of all targets, and I have very little doubt that they will need extensive repairs before very long. We have seen how unscrupulous and spiteful the enemy is by his daylight attacks on Buckingham Palace. And anyone has only to walk to Smith Square or St. Thomas's Hospital to see the kind of damage that a single

aeroplane can do. We have not got to think only of ourselves in considering the matter. There is a large number of officials and staff attached to
the House who have to be in attendance upon us when we are sitting.
This building itself is not well constructed to withstand aerial bombardment. There is an immense amount of glass about the place, and the
passages are long and narrow before the blast and splinter-proof shelters
can be reached. There is no certain defence against the attacks which
might so easily be made. There is no guarantee that the warning will be
given in time. Even our watcher up aloft would very likely give his signal
only at the moment when the bombs were already released. The firing of
the artillery is no useful warning because it fires so often, and we should
be hindered in our business if we attended to that.

If we are to do our duty properly we ought to adapt our arrangements
to the peculiar conditions under which we live. Therefore, I am going to
propose to the House three measures which they will find fully consonant
with their dignity and with their duty, and with your permission, Mr.
Speaker, I now propose to outline their character.

The first is that the hours and dates of our sittings shall not be made
public in the Press or announced beforehand, and that they shall be
lapped in uncertainty. This is a very considerable protection, because it
removes a large part of the incentive to the enemy. If we are not known to
be gathered here, a large part of the attractiveness of the Palace of Westminster as a target will be gone, and we may have the use of the building
and its conveniences for a longer period than is otherwise possible. Therefore I propose to move that when we adjourn to-day it will be to an hour
and a date which will as far as possible be kept secret. The date should
evidently be to-morrow, because it is inconvenient for Members to come
from all over the country under present conditions merely for a single
day's sitting.

But the Second Measure which I propose is that we should alter the
hour of our sittings. We must expect that at any time after dark the
nightly air raiding will begin. Our barrage will be firing, and, apart from
bombs, great numbers of shell splinters usually described most erroneously as shrapnel, will be falling in the streets. It is better for Members
and the officials and staff of the House to be in their homes or in their
shelters before this begins. I shall therefore propose that we meet at
eleven in the morning, and conclude our business at four in the afternoon, with half-an-hour for the Debate on the Adjournment.

This brings me to my third proposal. The fact that we meet in the
mornings will be a great convenience to Members, but it only throws a
heavier burden on Ministers and the Public Departments. Not only Cabi-
nets but many scores of important meetings take place every morning,

and the whole work of the Staffs and the Departments in the afternoon is affected by their decisions. If any large number of Ministers have to be in attendance upon the House, the whole progress of War Administration will be delayed or even deranged. Take the case of the Minister of Health, who is to-morrow to be in charge of a Debate upon the general health of the nation. That is a most interesting and important topic. But the Minister of Health is already working to the utmost limit of his strength on the many difficult situations created by the bombing of London; by its effects on drainage which is a serious problem, some of our great sewers having been broken; upon the rehousing of persons rendered homeless through their dwellings being destroyed or damaged, or because they have to be evacuated from districts on account of unexploded bombs or other special causes. He has also to deal with the dangers to national health arising out of people being crowded together in shelters, and contracting diseases which under these conditions, unless they are vigorously coped with, may foster epidemics of diphtheria, typhoid and influenza. In fact he is fighting the danger of pestilence.

Now I am first of all a Parliamentarian and House of Commons man. If I have any say in matters at the present time, it is due mainly to this House, and I therefore set Parliamentary duties above everything, subject, of course, to the leave of the House which I am sure would be generously given. My right hon. Friend will therefore carry out the programme as it has been arranged if the House so desires. But I must appeal to the House to show its consideration for Ministers, and for a Government in whom it has recorded its confidence almost unanimously. We are really doing our very best. There are no doubt many mistakes and shortcomings. A lot of things are done none too well. Some things that ought to be done have not yet been done. Some things have been done that had better have been left undone. But looking broadly at the whole picture as it is viewed by any impartial eye, the way in which our system of Government and society is standing up to its present ordeals, which will certainly increase in severity, constitutes a magnificent achievement, and has justly commanded the wonder and admiration of every friendly nation in the world. I ask therefore for the indulgence of the House, and for its support in not requiring too many sittings in the next month or two. I shall propose when we adjourn on Thursday that we adjourn until Tuesday, October 15. We shall, of course, meet a good deal earlier, but the House will be asked to leave the exact date unspecified and to be proposed by me as Leader of the House to Mr. Speaker, giving sufficient notice to Members for their convenience. Of course if anything happens which raises any novel or fundamental issue, for which the authority of Parliament is required, we shall immediately summon Parliament even if it were only a few days after we have separated, and we shall make it our business to keep in touch with all parties and groups, not only through what are called "the usual channels" but through any other channels which may be open.

Some ignorant people suppose that Members of Parliament are only doing their duty when they are sitting in this Chamber, either making or listening to speeches. But surely at this time of all others Members not otherwise occupied in national service may do invaluable work in their own constituencies. This is especially true of constituencies which have been knocked about by the enemy's fire, and where the people will have need of having their representative among them to share their dangers, resolve their perplexities, and if it were ever necessary, uphold their spirit.

These next few weeks are grave and anxious. I said just now in the Public Session that the deployment of the enemy's invasion preparations and the assembly of his ships and barges is steadily proceeding, and that at any moment a major assault may be launched upon this Island. I now say in secret that upwards of 1,700 self-propelled barges and more than 200 sea-going ships, some very large ships, are already gathered at the many invasion ports in German occupation. If this is all a pretence and strategem to pin us down here, it has been executed with surprising thoroughness and on a gigantic scale. Some of these ships and barges, when struck by our bombing counter-attack and preventive attack, have blown up with tremendous explosions, showing that they are fully loaded with all the munitions needed for the invading armies and to beat us down and subjugate us utterly. The shipping available and now assembled is sufficient to carry in one voyage nearly *half* a million men. We should, of course, expect to drown a great many on the way over, and to destroy a large proportion of their vessels. But when you reflect upon the many points from which they could start, and upon the fact that even the most likely sector of invasion, i.e., the sector in which enemy fighter support is available for their bombers and dive-bombers, extending from the Wash to the Isle of Wight, is nearly as long as the whole front in France from the Alps to the sea, and also upon the dangers of fog or artificial fog, one must expect many lodgments or attempted lodgments to be made on our Island simultaneously. These we shall hope to deal with as they occur, and also to cut off the supply across the sea by which the enemy will seek to nourish his lodgments.

The difficulties of the invader are not ended when he sets foot on shore. A new chapter of perils opens upon him. I am confident that we shall succeed in defeating and largely destroying this most tremendous onslaught by which we are now threatened, and anyhow, whatever happens, we will all go down fighting to the end. I feel as sure as the sun will rise to-morrow that we shall be victorious. But I ask the House to assist us in solving these problems, worse than any that have ever threatened a civilised community before, by meeting the wishes of the Government in the arrangement of Parliamentary business and in lightening the burden which rests upon the men in charge.

Formal Resolutions in accordance with what I have said will be proposed to the House for their approval this afternoon while the House is still in Secret Session.

Bibliography

•

Ashworth, Henry. *Recollections of Richard Cobden, M. P. and the Anti-Corn Law League* (London: Cassell, Petter and Galpin, n.d.).

Aspinall, Arthur. *Lord Brougham and the Whig Party* (Manchester: At the University Press, 1927).

Austin, Albert A. "The British Orators, IV, Gladstone's Characteristics as a Speaker," *Quarterly Journal of Speech*, XLIV (1958), pp. 244–254.

Ausubel, Herman. *John Bright: Victorian Reformer* (New York: John Wiley and Sons, Inc., n.d.).

Barrington, Mrs. Russell (ed.). *Works and Life of Walter Bagehot*. Vol. IV (London: Longmans, Green and Co., 1915).

Bassett, Arthur Tilney (ed.). *Gladstone's Speeches*, with a Preface by Viscount Bryce (London: Methuen and Co., 1916).

Beaconsfield, Earl of. *Selected Speeches*, with Introduction by T. E. Kebbel. Vol. I (London: Longmans, Green and Co., 1882).

Bennet, William Heath. *Select Biographical Sketches from the Note-Books of a Law Reporter* (London: George Routledge and Sons, 1867).

Bigham, Clive. *The Prime Ministers of Britain, 1791–1921* (London: John Murray, 1922).

Birrell, Francis. *Gladstone* (New York: The Macmillan Co., 1933).

Bleackley, Horace. *Life of John Wilkes* (London: The Bodley Head, 1917).

Bocca, Geoffrey. *The Adventurous Life of Winston Churchill* (New York: Julian Messner, 1958).

Bowen, Ian. *Cobden* (London: Duckworth, 1935).

Bowen, Marjorie. *Peter Porcupine* (London: Longmans, Green and Co., 1935).

Bowers, Claude G. *The Irish Orators* (Indianapolis: The Bobbs-Merrill Co., 1916).

Briggs, Asa. *The Making of Modern England, 1783–1867* (New York: Harper & Row, 1959).

———. *Victorian People* (Chicago: University of Chicago Press, 1955).

Broad, Lewis. *Winston Churchill: The Years of Preparation* (New York: Hawthorn Books, 1958).

Brome, Vincent. *Aneurin Bevan* (London: Longmans, Green and Co., 1953).

Brougham, Henry Lord. *Historical Sketches of Statesmen Who Flourished in the Time of George III.* Vol. I. 2nd ed. (London: Charles Knight and Co., 1839).

Bryant, Arthur. *Stanley Baldwin* (New York: Coward-McCann, 1937).

Carter, Violet Bonham. *Winston Churchill: An Intimate Portrait* (New York: Harcourt, Brace and World, 1965).

Cecil, Lady Gwendolen. *Life of Robert, Marquis of Salisbury.* Vol. III (London: Hodder and Stoughton, 1931).

Chatterton, E. Keble. *England's Greatest Statesman: A Life of William Pitt* (Indianapolis: The Bobbs-Merrill Co., 1930).

Churchill: The Life Triumphant. Compiled by American Heritage Magazine and United Press International (New York: American Heritage Publishing Co., 1965).

Churchill, Winston Spencer. *Lord Randolph Churchill.* Vol. II (London: Macmillan and Co., 1906).

Clark, George Kitson. *Peel and the Conservative Party* (London: Frank Cass and Co., 1964).

Clarke, Sir Edward. *Benjamin Disraeli* (New York: The Macmillan Co., 1926).

Cole, G. D. H. *The Life of William Cobbett* (New York: Harcourt, Brace and Co., 1924).

Dawson, William Harbutt. *Richard Cobden and Foreign Policy* (London: George Allen and Unwin, 1926).

DeMendelssohn, Peter. *The Age of Churchill* (London: Thames and Hudson, 1961).

Derry, John W. *William Pitt* (New York: Arco Publishing Co., 1963).

Drinkwater, John. *Charles James Fox* (New York: Cosmopolitan Book Corp., 1928).

DuParcq, Herbert. *Life of David Lloyd George.* Vol. III (London: Caxton Publishing Co., 1912).

Edwards, J. Hugh. *The Life of David Lloyd George,* Vol. I (London: The Waverly Book Co., 1913).

Evans, Beriah. *The Life Romance of Lloyd George,* with an Introduction by Charles Sarolea (Birmingham: C. Combridge, n.d.).

Evans, Trevor. *Bevin of Britain* (New York: W. W. Norton, 1946).

Eyck, Erich. *Gladstone* (London: George Allen and Unwin, 1938).

Fitzgerald, Percy. *The Life and Times of John Wilkes.* Vol. II (London: Ward and Downey, 1888).

Foot, Michael. *Aneurin Bevan.* Vol. I (New York: Atheneum, 1963).

Fortescue, Sir John. *Wellington* (London: Williams and Norgate, 1927).

Garratt, G. T. *Lord Brougham* (London: Macmillan and Co., 1935).

Gash, Norman. *Mr. Secretary Peel* (Cambridge, Mass.: Harvard University Press, 1961).

Gleig, G. R. *History of the Life of Arthur, Duke of Wellington.* Vol. IV (London: Longman, Green, Longman, and Roberts, 1860).

Gowing, Richard. *Richard Cobden* (London: Cassell and Co., 1885).

Green, Walford Davis. *William Pitt: Earl of Chatham* (New York: G. P. Putnam's Sons, 1906).

Grunwald, Henry Anatole. "Man of the Century," *Churchill: The Life Triumphant* (American Heritage Publishing Co., 1965).

Gulley, Elsie E., *Joseph Chamberlain and English Social Politics* (New York: Elsie E. Gulley, 1926).

Gwynn, Denis. *Daniel O'Connell* (Oxford: Cork University Press, 1947).

Hammond, J. L. *Gladstone and the Irish Nation* (London: Longmans, Green and Co., 1938).

Hammond, J. L. and Barbara. *Lord Shaftesbury* (London: Constable and Co., 1925).

Harrison, Frederic. *Chatham* (New York: The Macmillan Co., 1905).

Hawes, Frances. *Henry Brougham* (London: Jonathan Cape, 1957).

Hawkins, Gary J., "The Speech Education of Sir Samuel Romilly," Unpublished M.A. Thesis, Ohio University, 1960.

Hazlitt, William. *The Spirit of the Age.* Fourth ed. (London: George Bell and Sons, 1906).

Hearnshaw, F. J. C., (Ed.). *Prime Ministers of the Nineteenth Century* (London: Macmillan and Co., 1936).

Hirst, Margaret E. *John Bright* (London: Headley Bros., 1945).

Hobart, Lord. *The Mission of Richard Cobden* (London: Cassell, Petter, and Galpin).

Hobson, J. A. *Richard Cobden: The International Man* (New York: Henry Holt and Co., 1919).

Irish Orators and Oratory, with an Introduction by T. M. Kettle (Dublin: The Talbot Press, n.d.).

James, Robert Rhodes. *Lord Randolph Churchill* (London: Weidenfeld and Nicholson, 1959).

Johnson, E. A. *An Economic History of Modern England* (New York: Thomas Nelson and Sons, 1939).

Jones, Thomas. *Lloyd George* (Cambridge, Mass.: Harvard University Press, 1951).

Kennedy, A. L. *Salisbury, 1830–1903* (London: John Murray, 1953).

Kiernan, R. H. *Lloyd George* (London: George G. Harrap and Co., 1940).

Krug, Mark M., *Aneurin Bevan: Cautious Rebel* (New York: Thomas Yoseloff, 1961).

Lascelles, Edward. *The Life of Charles James Fox* (London: Oxford University Press, 1936).

Lee, Sidney. *Dictionary of National Biography* (New York: The Macmillan Co., 1896; plus Supplements).

Lever, Tresham. *The Life and Times of Sir Robert Peel* (London: George Allen and Unwin, 1942).

Macaulay, Thomas Babington. *Macaulay's Second Essay on the Earl of Chatham* (Boston: Leach, Shewell, and Sanborn, 1891).

MacDonagh, Michael. *The Reporter's Gallery* (London: Hodder and Stoughton, 1921).

MacKay, Charles. *Life and Times of Sir Robert Peel.* Vol. IV (London: Peter Jackson, Late Fisher, and Son, and Co., n.d.).

Macknight, Thomas. *History of the Life and Times of Edmund Burke*. Vol. I (London: Chapman and Hall, 1858).

Magnus, Philip. *Gladstone: A Biography* (New York: E. P. Dutton and Co., 1954).

———. *Edmund Burke* (London: John Murray, 1939).

Maxims and Reflections, with an Introduction by Colin Coote (Boston: Houghton-Mifflin Co., 1947).

Maxwell, Herbert. *The Life of Wellington* (London: Sampson Law, Marston and Co., 1907).

McCarthy, Justin. *British Political Portraits* (New York: The Outlook Co., 1903).

———. *Sir Robert Peel* (New York: Harper and Brothers, 1891).

Mills, J. Travis. *John Bright and the Quakers*. Vol. II (London: Methuen and Co., 1935).

Morley, John. *Burke* (London: Macmillan and Co., 1888).

———. *The Life of Richard Cobden*. Vol. I (London: T. Fisher Unwin, 1896).

———. *The Life of William Ewart Gladstone*. Vol. II (New York: The Macmillan Co., 1903).

Morley, Viscount John. *Recollections*. Vol. I (New York: The Macmillan Co., 1917).

Murphy, J. T. *Labour's Big Three* (London: The Bodley Head, 1948).

Murray, Robert H. *Edmund Burke* (Oxford: Oxford University Press, 1931).

New, Chester W. *The Life of Henry Brougham to 1830* (Oxford: Clarendon Press, 1961).

Newman, Bertram. *Edmund Burke* (London: G. Bell and Sons, 1927).

Notestein, Wallace. "Joseph Chamberlain and Tariff Reform," *Sewanee Review*, XXV (January 1917), pp. 40–56.

Oakes, C. G. *Sir Samuel Romilly* (London: George Allen and Unwin, 1935).

O'Brien, R. Barry. *The Life of Charles Stewart Parnell* (New York: Harper and Brothers, 1898).

O'Brien, William. *The Parnell of Real Life* (London: T. Fisher Unwin Ltd., 1926).

O'Faoláin, Seán. *King of the Beggars* (New York: The Viking Press, 1938).

O'Hara, M. M. *Chief and Tribune: Parnell and Davitt* (Dublin: Maunsel and Co., 1919).

Oliver, Robert T. *Four Who Spoke Out* (Syracuse: Syracuse University Press, 1946).

Osborne, John W. *William Cobbett: His Thought and His Times* (New Brunswick, N.J.: Rutgers University Press, 1966).

O'Shea, Katharine. *Charles Stewart Parnell*. Vol. II (London: Cassell and Co., 1914).

Owen, Frank. *Tempestuous Journey: Lloyd George, His Life and Times* (London: Hutchinson, 1954).

Park, Joseph Hendershot. *British Prime Ministers of the Nineteenth Century* (New York: New York University Press, 1950).

Pearl, M. L. *William Cobbett*, with a Foreword by G. D. H. Cole (London: Oxford University Press, 1953).

Pearson, Hesketh. *Dizzy* (New York: Harper and Brothers, 1951).

Petrie, Sir Charles. *Joseph Chamberlain* (London: Duckworth, 1940).

———. *Wellington* (London: James Barrie, 1956).

Phillipson, Coleman. *Three Criminal Law Reformers: Beccaria, Bentham, Romilly* (London: J. M. Dent and Sons, 1923).

Plucknett, Theodore F. T. *Taswell-Langmead's English Constitutional History* (Boston: Houghton Mifflin Co., 1960).

Plumb, J. H. *Chatham* (London: Collins, 1953).

Postgate, R. W. *That Devil Wilkes* (New York: The Vanguard Press, 1929).

Prior, Sir James. *A Life of Edmund Burke* (London: George Bell and Sons, 1891).

Raymond, E. T. *Mr. Lloyd George* (New York: George H. Doran Co., 1922).

Romilly, Sir Samuel. *Memoirs.* Vol. II (London: John Murray, 1842).

Rose, J. Holland. *William Pitt and National Revival* (London: G. Bell and Sons, 1911).

Rosebery, Lord. *Lord Randolph Churchill* (London: Harper and Brothers, 1906).

———. *Miscellanies: Literary and Historical.* Two volumes (London: Hodder and Stoughton, 1921).

———. *Pitt* (London: Macmillan and Co., 1904).

Rowse, A. L. "Churchill's Place in History," in *Churchill by His Contemporaries,* edited by Charles Eade (London: Hutchinson, 1953), pp. 491–507.

Secret Session Speeches, compiled by Charles Eade (London: Cassell and Co., 1946).

Sherrard, O. A. *Lord Chatham: A War Minister in the Making* (London: The Bodley Head, 1952).

Somervell, D. C. *Disraeli and Gladstone* (New York: Garden City Publishing Co., 1926).

———. "Stanley Baldwin," in *British Prime Ministers,* Edited by Duff Cooper (New York: Roy Publishers, n.d.), pp. 154–167.

Stanhope, Earl. *Life of the Right Honourable William Pitt.* Four volumes (London: John Murray, 1862).

Steed, Wickham. *The Real Stanley Baldwin* (London: Nisbet and Co., 1930).

Stewart, Charles. "The Duke of Wellington," in *British Prime Ministers* (New York: Roy Publishers, n.d.), pp. 68–79.

Strauss, Patricia. *Bevin and Co. The Leaders of British Labour* (New York: G. P. Putnam's Sons, 1941).

Taylor, W. Cooke. *Life and Times of Sir Robert Peel.* Vol. I (London: Peter Jackson, Late Fisher, Son, and Co., n.d.).

Thompson, A. F. "Gladstone," in *British Prime Ministers,* pp. 123–133.

Thomson, David. *England in the Nineteenth Century* (Baltimore: Penguin Books, 1962).

Thursfield, J. R. *Peel* (London: Macmillan Co., 1904).

Tierney, Michael. *Daniel O'Connell* (Dublin: Browne and Nolan, 1949).

Treloar, William Purdie. *Wilkes and the City* (London: John Murray, 1917).

Trench, Charles Chenevix. *Portrait of a Patriot* (Edinburgh: William Blackwood and Sons, 1962).

Trevelyan, George Macaulay. *The Life of John Bright* (London: Constable and Co., 1913).

Trevelyan, George Otto. *The Early History of Charles James Fox* (New York: Harper and Brothers, 1904).

Walling, R. A. J. *The Diaries of John Bright* (New York: William Morrow and Co., 1931).

Walpole, B. C. *Charles James Fox* (London: The Grolier Society, *c.* 1806).

Williams, Basil. *The Life of William Pitt: Earl of Chatham.* Vol. II (London: Longmans, Green, and Co., 1913).

Williams, Francis. "Aneurin Bevan," *Spectator,* 181 (September 24, 1948), pp. 390–391.

———. *Ernest Bevin,* with Foreword by Rt. Hon. Clement Atlee (London: Hutchinson and Co., 1952).

———. *The Triple Challenge* (Melbourne: William Heinemann, 1948).

Wilson, P. W. *William Pitt, the Younger* (Garden City: Doubleday, Doran and Co., 1930).

Wraxall, Sir Nathaniel William. *Memoirs.* Vol. II (London: Bickers and Son, 1884).

Young, G. M. *Stanley Baldwin* (London: Rupert Hart-Davis, 1952).

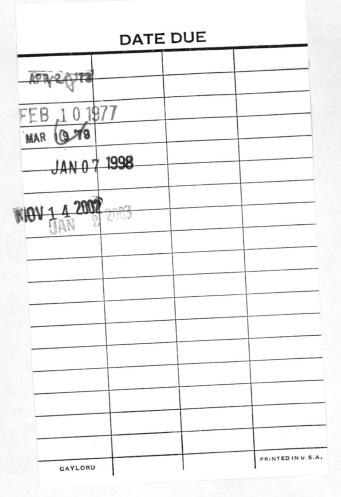

DATE DUE

APR 2 1973			
FEB 1 0 1977			
MAR 1 0 78			
JAN 0 7 1998			
NOV 1 4 2002			
JAN 2 2003			
GAYLORD			PRINTED IN U.S.A.